Fodor's

W9-AXE-809

CHILE

3rd Edition

Where to Stay and Eat for All Budgets

Must-See Sights and Local Secrets

Ratings You Can Trust

Fodor's Travel Publications   New York, Toronto, London, Sydney, Auckland
www.fodors.com

FODOR'S CHILE
Editor: Sarah Gold

Editorial Production: Tom Holton
Editorial Contributors: Felice Aarons, Robin Goldstein, Brian Kluepfel, Mark Sullivan, Jeffrey Van Fleet
Maps: David Lindroth, Inc., and Eureka Cartography, *cartographers;* Rebecca Baer and Bob Blake, *map editors*
Design: Fabrizio La Rocca, *creative director;* Guido Caroti, *art director;* Moon Sun Kim, *cover design;* Melanie Marin, *senior picture editor*
Production/Manufacturing: Angela L. McLean
Cover Photo (Torres del Paine National Park): Art Wolfe

COPYRIGHT

Third Edition

ISBN: 1–4000–1646–0

ISBN-13: 978–1–4000–1646–4

ISSN: 1535–5055

SPECIAL SALES

Fodor's Travel Publications are available at special discounts for bulk purchases for sales promotions or premiums. Special editions, including personalized covers, excerpts of existing guides, and corporate imprints, can be created in large quantities for special needs. For more information, contact your local bookseller or write to Special Markets/Premium Sales, 1745 Broadway, MD 6-2, New York, NY 10019, or e-mail specialmarkets@randomhouse.com.

IMPORTANT TIP & AN INVITATION

Although all prices, opening times, and other details in this book are based on information supplied to us at press time, changes occur all the time in the travel world, and Fodor's cannot accept responsibility for facts that become outdated or for inadvertent errors or omissions. So **always confirm information when it matters,** especially if you're making a detour to visit a specific place. Your experiences—positive and negative—matter to us. If we have missed or misstated something, **please write to us.** We follow up on all suggestions. Contact the Chile editors at editors@fodors.com or c/o Fodor's at 1745 Broadway, New York, New York 10019.

PRINTED IN THE UNITED STATES OF AMERICA

10 9 8 7 6 5 4 3 2 1

Be a Fodor's Correspondent

Your opinion matters. It matters to us. It matters to your fellow Fodor's travelers, too. And we'd like to hear it. In fact, we *need* to hear it.

When you share your experiences and opinions, you become an active member of the Fodor's community. That means we'll not only use your feedback to make our books better, but we'll publish your names and comments whenever possible. Throughout our guides, look for "Word of Mouth," excerpts of your unvarnished feedback.

Here's how you can help improve Fodor's for all of us.

Tell us when we're right. We rely on local writers to give you an insider's perspective. But our writers and staff editors—who are the best in the business—depend on you. Your positive feedback is a vote to renew our recommendations for the next edition.

Tell us when we're wrong. We're proud that we update most of our guides every year. But we're not perfect. Things change. Hotels cut services. Museums change hours. Charming cafés lose charm. If our writer didn't quite capture the essence of a place, tell us how you'd do it differently. If any of our descriptions are inaccurate or inadequate, we'll incorporate your changes in the next edition and will correct factual errors at fodors.com *immediately.*

Tell us what to include. You probably have had fantastic travel experiences that aren't yet in Fodor's. Why not share them with a community of like-minded travelers? Maybe you chanced upon a beach or bistro or B&B that you don't want to keep to yourself. Tell us why we should include it. And share your discoveries and experiences with everyone directly at fodors.com. Your input may lead us to add a new listing or highlight a place we cover with a "Highly Recommended" star or with our highest rating, "Fodor's Choice."

Give us your opinion instantly at our feedback center at www.fodors.com/feedback. You may also e-mail editors@fodors.com with the subject line "Chile Editor." Or send your nominations, comments, and complaints by mail to Chile Editor, Fodor's, 1745 Broadway, New York, NY 10019.

You and travelers like you are the heart of the Fodor's community. Make our community richer by sharing your experiences. Be a Fodor's correspondent.

¡Feliz viaje!

Tim Jarrell, Publisher

CONTENTS

About This Book F6
What's Where F7
If You Like F14
Quintessential Chile F16
Great Itineraries F18
When to Go F21
On the Calendar F22
Smart Travel Tips F25

CHILE

1 SANTIAGO 1
Exploring Santiago 2
Where to Eat 24
Where to Stay 36
Nightlife & the Arts 43
Sports & the Outdoors 47
Shopping .48
Side Trips from Santiago 51
Santiago Essentials 61

2 THE CENTRAL COAST 68
Valparaíso & Viña del Mar 71
The Southern Beaches 91
The Northern Beaches 96
The Central Coast Essentials 104

3 EL NORTE CHICO 107
The Elqui Valley 110
The Huasco Valley 120
The Copiapó Valley 122
El Norte Chico Essentials 127

4 EL NORTE GRANDE 130
The Nitrate Pampa 133
San Pedro & the Atacama Desert 141
Iquique Area 146
Arica Area 155
El Norte Grande Essentials 161

5 THE CENTRAL VALLEY 164
The Wine Country 166
Río Bío Bío 179
The Central Valley Essentials 185

6 THE LAKE DISTRICT 188
La Araucanía 190
Los Lagos 210
The Lake District Essentials 230

7 CHILOÉ 236
Chiloé Essentials 253

8 THE SOUTHERN COAST 256
The Southern Coast Essentials 270

9 PATAGONIA & TIERRA
DEL FUEGO 274
Patagonia 279
Tierra del Fuego 302
Patagonia & Tierra del Fuego
Essentials 311

10 EASTER ISLAND 317
Exploring Easter Island 319
Where to Eat 329
Where to Stay 330
Nightlife & the Arts 333
Sports & the Outdoors 334
Shopping 335
Easter Island Essentials 335

11 ADVENTURE VACATIONS 338

UNDERSTANDING CHILE

Essay: Traveling in a Thin Country . . .356
Spanish Vocabulary 358
INDEX 365
ABOUT OUR WRITERS 382

CLOSEUPS

Wine Tours Around Santiago 60
Central Coast Festivals &
    Seasonal Events 70
Chilean Coastal Cuisine 80
Neruda's Inspiration 95
El Norte Chico Festivals &
    Seasonal Events 110
Chile's National Drink 117
El Norte Grande Festivals &
    Seasonal Events 132
Etched in Stone 153
Eiffel's Other Tower 156
Central Valley Festivals &
    Seasonal Events 166
Through the Grapevine 170
Lake District Festivals &
    Seasonal Events 192
The People of the Land 196
Outdoor Adventures 199
Hier Ist Alles so Deutsch 215
Chiloe Festivals & Seasonal
    Events 238
Witches and Ghost Ships 244
Chiloé's Chapels 246
Chile's Road to Riches 264
Patagonia's Penguins 283
El Parque Nacional
    Los Glaciares 299
Easter Island Festivals &
    Seasonal Events 320
Mysteries of the Moais 326

MAPS

Chile F11
South America F12–F13
Santiago 6–7
Santiago Centro & La Alameda 8
Parque Forestal 15
Bellavista & Parque Metropolitano ...19
Parque Quinta Normal 22
Where to Stay & Eat in Santiago
    Centro & Bellavista 26–27
Where to Stay & Eat in Providencia
    & Las Condes 30
Where to Stay & Eat in Vitacura 43
Santiago Side Trips 52
The Central Coast 72
Valparaíso 74–75
Viña de Mar 85
El Norte Chico 112
El Norte Grande 136
San Pedro de Atacama & Environs ...142
The Central Valley 168
The Lake District 194
Lago Villarrica 201
Pucón 203
Valdivia 213
Chiloé 240
The Southern Coast 262
Patagonia & Tierra del Fuego 278
Punta Arenas 281
Parque Nacional Torres del Paine ...294
Easter Island 322
Hanga Roa 324

ABOUT THIS BOOK

Our Ratings

Sometimes you find terrific travel experiences and sometimes they just find you. But usually the burden is on you to select the right combination of experiences. That's where our ratings come in.

As travelers we've all discovered a place so wonderful that its worthiness is obvious. And sometimes that place is so unique that superlatives don't do it justice: you just have to be there to know. These sights, properties, and experiences get our highest rating, Fodor's Choice, indicated by orange stars throughout this book.

Black stars highlight sights and properties we deem Highly Recommended, places that our writers, editors, and readers praise again and again for consistency and excellence.

By default, there's another category: any place we include in this book is by definition worth your time, unless we say otherwise. And we will.

Disagree with any of our choices? Care to nominate a place or suggest that we rate one more highly? Visit our feedback center at www. fodors.com/feedback.

Budget Well

Hotel and restaurant price categories from ¢ to $$$$ are defined in the opening pages of each chapter. For attractions, we always give standard adult admission fees; reductions are usually available for children, students, and senior citizens. Want to pay with plastic? AE, DC, MC, V following restaurant and hotel listings indicate whether American Express, Discover, Diner's Club, MasterCard, and Visa are accepted.

Restaurants

Unless we state otherwise, restaurants are open for lunch and dinner daily. We mention dress only when there's a specific requirement and reservations only when they're essential or not accepted—it's always best to book ahead.

Hotels

Hotels have private bath, phone, TV, and air-conditioning and operate on the European Plan (aka EP, meaning without meals), unless we specify that they use the Continental Plan (CP, with a Continental breakfast), Breakfast Plan (BP, with a full breakfast), or Modified American Plan (MAP, with breakfast and dinner) or are all-inclusive (AI, including all meals and most activities). We always list facilities but not whether you'll be charged an extra fee to use them, so when pricing accommodations, find out what's included.

Many Listings

- ★ Fodor's Choice
- ★ Highly recommended
- ⊠ Physical address
- ✛ Directions
- ⌂ Mailing address
- ☎ Telephone
- 🖷 Fax
- ⊕ On the Web
- ✍ E-mail
- 💷 Admission fee
- ☉ Open/closed times
- ▶ Start of walk/itinerary
- Ⓜ Metro stations
- ▭ Credit cards

Hotels & Restaurants

- 🏨 Hotel
- ⇱ Number of rooms
- ⚕ Facilities
- ⑩ Meal plans
- ✕ Restaurant
- 🖑 Reservations
- 🏛 Dress code
- ↘ Smoking
- 🍸 BYOB
- ✕🏨 Hotel with restaurant that warrants a visit

Outdoors

- 🏌 Golf
- ⛺ Camping

Other

- ⌚ Family-friendly
- ⓘ Contact information
- ⇨ See also
- ⊠ Branch address
- ☞ Take note

WHAT'S WHERE

SANTIAGO	Santiago doesn't get the same press as Rio or Buenos Aires, but this metropolis of 5 million people anchoring the Chilean axis is as cosmopolitan as its flashier South American neighbors, if in a bit more subdued way. Ancient and modern stand side by side in the heart of the city—the neoclassical cathedral reflected in the glass of a nearby office tower is the quintessential postcard view. Downtown you're never far from leafy Plaza de Armas or the paths that meander along the Río Mapocho. On a clear day you can see the Andes in the distance. But that air is none too clear in the winter when a dreary smog hangs over the city. And you may have the city to yourself in the heat of the summer when Santiaguinos flee for vacation. Spring and fall are the best times to visit.

THE CENTRAL COAST	One gritty, one glittery, Chile's odd couple anchors the coast from adjacent bays west of Santiago: port city Valparaíso wins rave reviews for the stunning views from the promenades atop its more than 40 hills; and Viña del Mar, home to Chile's beautiful people, has nonstop nightlife, streets lined with trendy boutiques, and the country's most popular stretch of shoreline. Head north to the rugged beaches to get close to penguins and sea lions. In the south, pay homage to the Nobel Prize–winning poet Pablo Neruda, whose hillside house faces the ocean at Isla Negra. Any time of year makes an ideal visit to this easy-to-reach region, but proximity to the capital and quick toll-highway access mean everybody else has the same idea in the summer.

EL NORTE CHICO	There's no reason for the so-called "little north" to live in the shadow of its vaster northern neighbor, El Norte Grande. El Norte Chico, a land of dusty brown hills, stretches for some 700 km (435 mi) from Río Aconcagua to Río Copiapó, north of Santiago. In the lush Elqui Valley, just about everyone you meet is involved in growing the grapes used to make *pisco,* the heady brew that has become Chile's national drink. Inland lies Parque Nacional Nevado Tres Cruces, where four species of flamingos fly across dazzling white salt flats. On the coast is Parque Nacional Pan de Azúcar, home to sea lions, sea otters, and stunning beaches. Astronomers flock to the region for the crisp, clear night skies; you never knew the heavens contained so many stars.

WHAT'S WHERE

EL NORTE GRANDE 	Stark doesn't begin to describe Chile's great north, a region bordering Peru to the north and Bolivia to the east. This is the driest place on Earth, site of the Atacama Desert, where no measurable precipitation has ever been recorded. The climate helped to preserve tantalizing clues of the indigenous peoples of the past, including the Chinchorro mummies near Arica. If you seek solitude, the inland desert is your place. But the coast is not the beastly hot Sahara, and Chileans flock to the region's beaches with their quite bearable temperatures each summer. As you ascend into the Andes, the air becomes dramatically cooler. In Parque Nacional Lauca the landscape is dotted with a brilliant emerald-green moss called *llareta,* and llamas and groups of galloping vicuñas and alpacas make their homes here.
THE CENTRAL VALLEY 	A jug of wine, a loaf of bread . . . in a different century, Omar Khayyam might easily have written about Chile's Central Valley, its breadbasket and source of world-renowned wines. Head south from Santiago to the Valle de Colchagua, where you can sample vintages at many wineries. Also in the area are the beautiful manor houses of the sprawling haciendas once run by Chile's most powerful families. The region's many rivers, such as the Río Bío Bío in the southern Central Valley, are great for white-water rafting and other water sports. A drive through the valley is beautiful any time of year, but makes an especially nice summer respite from the heat of the capital.
THE LAKE DISTRICT 	You half expect to see Julie Andrews twirling around, arms outstretched, as you make your way through the Lake District's hills; they really are alive with Central European history, evidenced by the alpine-style houses nestled among its forests, lakes, and mountains. But long before waves of German-speaking immigrants arrived, this was the homeland of the indigenous Mapuche people, still proud, though, today, displaced and disenfranchised. The austral summer doesn't get more glorious than it does in this compact 400-km (250-mi) stretch of land between Temuco and Puerto Montt. It has fast become Chile's vacation central, drawing people from around the country to resorts such as Pucón, Villarrica, and Puerto Varas. More than 50 snow-covered peaks, many of them still smoldering volcanoes, offer splendid hiking.

CHILOÉ	More than 40 islands sprinkled across the Golfo de Ancud make up the rainy archipelago of Chiloé, home to no-nonsense farmers who have tilled the land for centuries. The largest by far, and easiest to reach, is the appropriately named Isla Grande, a 30-minute ferry ride from the mainland south of Puerto Montt. Dense forests cover the western part of the island, and gently rolling farmland dominates its eastern half. Dozens of simple wooden churches, constructed by Jesuit missionaries during the colonial era, dot the landscape and are Chiloé's main draw. Summer is the best time to visit, and provides one of the few opportunities you'll have to see the sun here. Fog and rain blanket the islands the rest of the year.

THE SOUTHERN COAST	This stretch of coastline between the Lake District and Patagonia is one of the most remote regions on Earth. Anchoring the region's spine is the Carretera Austral, one of the world's amazing, hair-raising, "I survived" road trips. Flying is an easier option; a cruise south from Puerto Montt in the Lake District through the labyrinth of icy fjords, imminently more stylish. The only town of any size, Coyhaique, sits in the middle of everything and therefore makes a good base for exploring the area. To the north is the privately owned Parque Pumalín, one of the last-remaining temperate rain forests in the world. The most popular attraction, and the hardest to reach, is the spectacular glacier that forms the centerpiece of Parque Nacional Laguna San Rafael.

PATAGONIA & TIERRA DEL FUEGO	Look up "end of the world" in the dictionary and you might see a picture of Chile's southernmost region. Impenetrable forests and impassable mountains meant that Chilean Patagonia went largely unexplored until the beginning of the 20th century. It's still sparsely inhabited. The region's hub, the colorful provincial city of Punta Arenas, looks like it's about to be swept into the Strait of Magellan. Drive north to reach the snow-covered peaks of Parque Nacional Torres del Paine, the country's most magnificent natural wonder and iconic travel-brochure image. To the east is mythical Tierra del Fuego, the windswept island at the continent's southern tip. Considering the vast distance, flying is the quickest, and not a prohibitively expensive, option for getting here, but boats ply the coast and will take you south from Puerto Montt.

WHAT'S WHERE

EASTER ISLAND

Few places on Earth can match the mystique-per-square-kilometer quotient of Easter Island. At 3,700 km (2,295 mi) off the Chilean coast, it deserves its common description as "the loneliest place on Earth." (On the topic of names, you'll endear yourself to residents by referring to the island as they do: Rapa Nui.) Dutch explorer Jacob Roggeveen happened upon the island in 1722, at first thinking it was inhabited by giants, but he soon realized he was looking at hundreds of stone idols standing along the coast. You've seen dozens of photos of these eerie moais, but nothing beats seeing them in person. Getting here requires a spirit of adventure and a lot of pesos; Lan Airlines, the only game in town, rarely discounts the expensive airfare.

Chile (North)

PERU

Arica

Iquique

El Norte Grande

Pan American Hwy

BOLIVIA

Calama

San Pedro
de Atacama

Antofagasta

PACIFIC
OCEAN

*El Norte
Chico*

ARGENTINA

Copiapó

Vallenar

La Serena

Ovalle

Zapallar

Viña del Mar

Valparaíso

Santiago

← TO EASTER
ISLAND

Rancagua

Curicó

Pan American Hwy

Talca

Concepción

Chillán

Temuco

Valdivia

0		100 miles
0		150 km

Chile (South)

Valparaíso

Santiago

The Central Valley

Concepción

Temuco

Pucón

Villarrica

Valdivia

The Lake District

Osorno

Puerto Varas

Puerto Montt

Castro

Isla de Chiloé

ARGENTINA

The Southern Coast

Coihaique

Cochrane

PACIFIC
OCEAN

Torres del Paine National Park

Puerto Natales

Punta Arenas

Estrecho de Magallanes

Penguin Island

Tierra del Fuego

0		100 miles
0		150 km

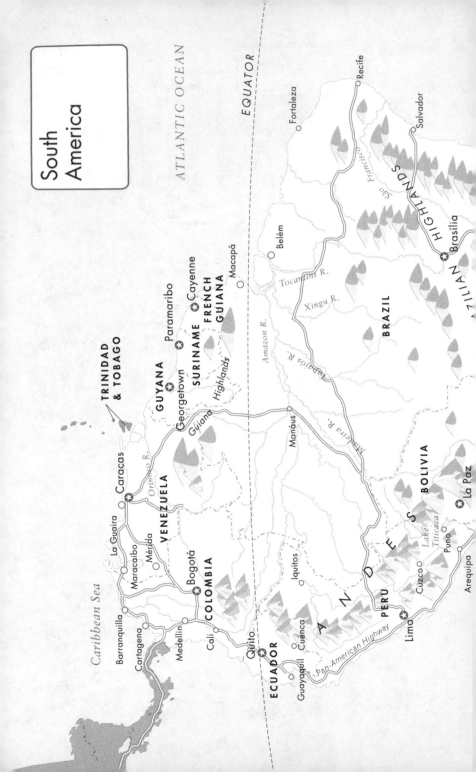

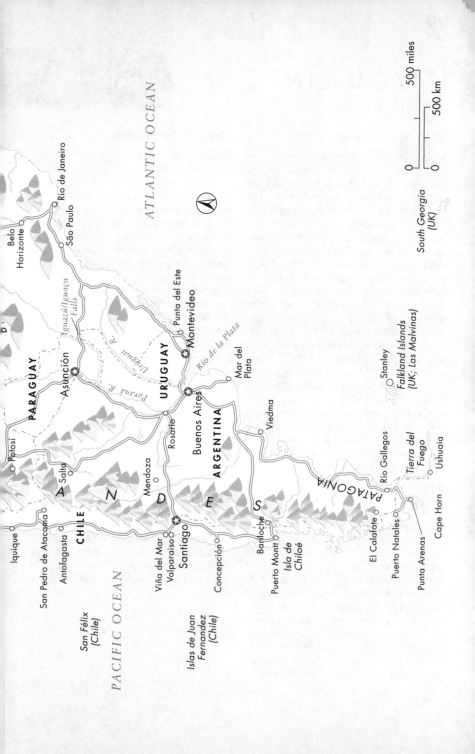

IF YOU LIKE . . .

Distinctive Cuisine

Mountains plummet to hills, tumble to plains, and fall to ocean quickly in the thin strip of land that is Chile, and the seascape–landscape variety provides the ingredients for a distinctive cuisine. From the ocean come delicacies such as conger eel, sea bass, king crab, and *locos* (abalone the size of fat clams). But the Pacific isn't Chile's only answer to fine dining—European immigrants brought with them a love for robust country cooking. Indeed, many simple country dishes are among the best offerings of Chilean cuisine, including *cazuela,* a superb stew made of meat, potatoes, and corn on the cob in a thick broth; *porotos granados,* a thick bean, corn, and squash stew; and *humitas,* ground corn seasoned and steamed in its own husk. At markets all over the country, vendors try to woo you with the ubiquitous and delicious *pastel de choclo,* a corn pie that usually contains ground beef, chicken, and seasonings. Empanadas, pastries stuffed with meat or cheese, are popular everywhere.

International cuisine has caught on here, too, especially in the cosmopolitan capital, where you can dine in every type of ethnic restaurant from Japanese to Jamaican. But be sure to sample those restaurants that capture the essence of local cuisine. There are several standouts: Santiago's **Aquí Está Coco** dishes up the capital's best fish and shellfish, but **Azul Profundo**'s unadorned seafood grilled to perfection gives it a run for its money; an elegant 19th-century mansion high above the Valparaíso is the setting for fine dining at **Café Turri**; way down south in Punta Arenas, waiters dressed as gauchos carve lamb off the spit at **Los Ganaderos.**

Sports & the Outdoors

The Lake District is Chile's outdoor-tourism center, with outfitters and guides ready to fix you up and take you out for any activity your adventurous heart desires. Fly-fishing, hiking, and rafting top the list there, but the entire country has begun to get the outdoor bug, and activities abound. Though far from complete, the ambitious **Sendero de Chile** project will eventually provide a continuous north–south hiking trail running the entire length of the country. And with the Andes forming Chile's eastern border, and also running the entire length of the country, serious mountaineers flock here from all over the world. If you're a trekking enthusiast, you likely already know about the challenging **Volcán Ojos del Salado** in El Norte Chico. The world's highest active volcano, it soars to 6,893 meters (22,609 feet). There are dozens of other challenging climbs all along the eastern border of the country.

Skiing deserves special mention. The runs at Vail and Grenoble are closed for the season? Never fear. Since Chile's seasons are the opposite of those of North America, you can ski or snowboard from June to September. Most of Chile's ski resorts, including **Portillo,** are in the Andes close to Santiago. With the top elevations at the majority of ski areas extending to 3,300 meters (10,825 feet), you can expect long runs and deep, dry snow.

Natural Wonders

Norway has fjords. Bavaria has forests. Nepal has mountains. Arizona has deserts. Chile offers all these—so it's understandable if you feel disoriented each time you step off a domestic flight that's whisked you from one region to another with a vastly different landscape.

Many of Chile's natural wonders can be described only with superlatives. El Norte Grande's **Atacama Desert** is the most arid spot on Earth; no measurable precipitation has ever been recorded there. The region's **Cerros Pintados** form the largest group of geoglyphs in the world. Perpetually smoldering **Volcán Villarrica** in the Lake District is one of the world's most active volcanoes—although you shouldn't let that fact stop you from hiking to the snow-covered summit. Yet even when Chile's natural wonders can't lay claim to adjectives like "biggest" or "most," they might find themselves at the top of your list of favorites. The 4-km (2½-mi) glacier at southern **Laguna San Rafael** is a doubly arresting attraction: a looming, fearsome, cobalt-blue mountain of ice, it gives off thunderous sounds as chunks of it break off and stir up the water as you pass by (safely on your ship, of course). **Parque Nacional Fray Jorge** is Chile's only cloud forest, and a great retreat from the relentless sun of El Norte Chico. The south's privately administered **Parque Pumalín** comprises 800,000 acres of one of the world's last remaining temperate rain forests. And no photo can ever do justice to the ash-gray, glacier-molded spires of Patagonia's **Torres del Paine**.

The Pleasures of the Vine

Back in the 1980s, when formerly inexpensive California wines started to jump in price, Chilean vintners saw an opening and began to introduce their product to the world. The rest, as they say, is history.

An oft-repeated fact about Chilean wine is that the best is reserved for the export market. Although this is true, there are still some high-quality wines to be found inside the country.

Chile's largest winery, **Concha y Toro,** has a number of different labels (some made exclusively for the Chilean market) that usually offer good value. At one end is the affordable and popular Casillero del Diablo label; at the other is the export-oriented Trio wines. Highly regarded **Cousiño-Macul,** the second big player in the market, gears itself to tourist visits, as does Concha y Toro, with organized tours. (Reservations are required for most winery visits in Chile.) Both wineries make easy day visits from Santiago. **Santa Rita** also lies a short distance from the capital. The long-established **Errázuriz** winery holds court in the warm Aconcagua Valley north of Santiago, where warm summers and mild winters translate into full-bodied merlots and cabernets. **Santa Carolina**'s new Santa Isabel estate, in the cool Casablanca Valley near Valparaíso, produces highly regarded white wines. It complements its older operations in the Maipo and Rapel valleys known for their deep-bodied reds. A smaller, newer venture, **Casa Lapostolle,** was founded in 1994 by France's Marnier-Lapostolle family (of Grand Marnier fame). Its reds are highly regarded—if not as widely available; its signature product is its Clos Apalta, a blend of merlot and carmenere, a grape imported from the Bordeaux region of France in the 1850s.

QUINTESSENTIAL CHILE

Rodeos

The country's national folkloric figure is the *huaso,* or Chilean cowboy. Think Old West, but deck him out in a flat-topped, wide-brimmed hat, short vested jacket, sash, and colorful blanket called a manta draped over his shoulders. Huasos are still seen in the countryside, especially in the Central Valley, mounted on their trusty horses to round up livestock.

Sometime in the 19th century, the process transformed itself into Chile's national sport, the rodeo. The season runs September–May, with national championships taking place in late March–early April in the Central Valley city of Rancagua, the community most associated with the sport. A huaso pair rounds up a steer in the town's *medialuna,* a half-moon-shape ring, and pins the animal to the corral's padded walls, a maneuver requiring the horse to gallop sideways. (No U.S.-style roping or

riding of the bull take place in Chile.) Although animal-rights activists would not appreciate a rodeo, huasos earn more *puntos buenos* (good points) with gentler treatment rounding up the steer.

Would a Chilean ever cry out: "Ride 'em, cowgirl!"? Perhaps in the future, but rodeos here remain a demonstration of horse-*man*ship and masculine pride. Women are expected to prepare the post-rodeo feast, and participate in the *cueca,* Chile's fast-paced national scarf dance, complete with guitars and hand clapping and symbolizing the courting ritual. No one claims these events aren't sexist.

Parrilladas

Chile and neighboring Argentina compare themselves almost endlessly, especially when it comes to *parrilladas,* a method of grilling meat over hot coals common to both

countries. In Chile, not just steak gets grilled: restaurants prepare chicken, fish, seafood, burgers, sausage—especially common in the German-influenced Lake District—potatoes, corn, and vegetables parrillada-style, too.

Típico eateries might have a big pit for grilling in the center of the floor. Upscale restaurants may prepare your food at your table on a mini-grill with all the flair of a Japanese *teppanyaki* chef. Either system, however, is guaranteed to elicit anticipatory "oohs" and "aahs" from you while you nurse a pre-meal pisco sour.

Fjord Cruises

Beyond Puerto Montt at the far southern end of the Lake District, Chile's coastline fracture into some 1,500 km (1,000 mi) of jagged inlets, mountains, glaciers, and islands. The terrain has meant an age-old headache

for national planning: How to provide access to such an isolated, forbidding region? The answer: by boat.

Transport along this sector of the southern coast ranges from the yummy to the utilitarian. At the top of the line are the luxury Cruseros Australis boats, with all the buffet tables and social activity any cruiseship passenger could desire. At the other end are serviceable, no-frills freighters and ferries, where your passengers will be locals, rather than tourists.

No matter which end of the travel spectrum you choose, though, all boats navigate the same stunning scenery. They also take you past fishing villages, forests, mountains, ice floes, glaciers, whales, and penguins.

GREAT ITINERARIES

SANTIAGO & NORTHERN CHILE

The number of wonderful natural and cultural attractions in Chile and the great distances between them mean that fitting all the highlights into one trip can be a challenge, especially with Santiago, the main point of entry by air into Chile, smack dab in the center of the country. It doesn't help that two of the country's most extraordinary natural attractions—the Atacama Desert in the north and Parque Nacional Torres del Paine in the south—are at extreme opposite ends of the country. Traveling by air is one way of moving around the country, and domestic air fares are not outrageously expensive. But if you don't have a lot of time to spend in Chile, consider breaking your trip into Santiago and northern Chile or Santiago and southern Chile.

10 DAYS
Days 1, 2 & 3: Arrival/Santiago

No matter where you fly from, you'll likely arrive in Chile's capital early in the morning after an all-night flight. Unless you're one of those rare people who can sleep the entire night on a plane and arrive refreshed at your destination, reward yourself with a couple of hours' shut-eye at your hotel before setting out to explore the city.

The neighborhoods, small and large, that make up Santiago warrant at least a day and a half of exploration. A trip up one of the nearby hills—opt for the funicular ride to the top of Cerro San Cristóbal in Parque Metropolitano—lets you survey the capital and its grid of streets. Any tour of any city begins with its historic center; the cathedral and commercial office tow-

ers on the Plaza de Armas reflect Santiago's old and new architecture. The nearby Bohemian quarter of Bellavista, with its bustling markets and colorful shops, was built for walking. But Santiago's zippy, efficient Metro can also whisk you to most places in the city, and lets you cover ground more quickly.

Alas, if you're here in the winter, a gloomy smog can hang over the city for days at a time. Your first instinct may be to flee, and one of the nearby wineries in the Valle de Maipo provides the perfect respite. (It's a fitting trip no matter what the season.) And if it's winter and you brought your skis, the Valle Nevado, Chile's largest downhill-resort area, lies a scant 16 km (10 mi) outside the city. ⇨ *Exploring Santiago and Side Trips from Santiago in Chapter 1.*

Days 4 & 5: Valparaíso & Viña del Mar

A 90-minute drive west from Santiago takes you to the Central Coast and confronts you with one of Chilean tourism's classic choices: Valparaíso or Viña del Mar? If you fancy yourself one of the glitterati, you'll go for Viña and its chic cafés and restaurants and miles of beach. But "Valpo" offers you the charm and allure of a port city, rolling hills, and cobblestone streets with better views of the sea. And nothing says you can't do both; a scant 10 km (6 mi) separate the two. Overnight in either city. ⇨ *Valparaíso & Viña del Mar in Chapter 2.*

Days 6 & 7: San Pedro de Atacama

You certainly *could* drive the nearly 1,500 km (900 mi) to Chile's vast El Norte

Grande, but a time-saving flight from Santiago to Calama puts you close to one of the country's top tourist draws, San Pedro de Atacama. That such a city with such a polished tourism infrastructure lies in the heart of one the world's loneliest regions comes as a surprise. This is one of the most-visited towns in Chile, for good reason: it sits right in the midst of the Atacama Desert, with striking sights all around. You'll need at least two days here to do justice to the alpine lakes, ancient fortresses, Chile's largest salt flat, and the surreal landscape of the Valle de la Luna. ⇨ *The Nitrate Pampa in Chapter 4.*

Day 8: Iquique

San Pedro to Iquique is a drivable 500-km (300-mi) journey, but a flight up from Calama saves you more hours of precious vacation time. There's not much of interest in Iquique itself, other than some nice white-sand beaches and the nearby ghost town of Humberstone, but the town makes a good base for visiting the hundreds of geoglyphs at the Cerros Pintados—it's the world's largest collection—in the Reserva Nacional Pampa del Tamarugal. The largest geoglyph on Earth, the Gigante de Atacama, lies nearby. ⇨ *Iquique Area in Chapter 4.*

Days 9 & 10: Arica/Departure

If you've come this far, head to Chile's northernmost city, with a temperate climate and a couple of creations by French architect Gustave Eiffel. The main attraction, however, is the nearby Museo Arqueológico de San Miguel de Azapa and its famed Chinchorro mummies. Their Egyptian cousins are mere youngsters by comparison. The Chinchorro specimens are the world's oldest, dating from 6000 BC. Arica's coastal location keeps temperatures bearable year-round and make it a favorite summer beach location.

A morning flight back on your last day gets you back to Santiago in plenty of time to connect with an overnight flight back to North America or Europe. ⇨ *Arica Area in Chapter 4.*

TRANSPORTATION: Although it's quite easy, and even preferable, to explore Santiago, Viña del Mar, and Valparaíso by using public transportation, a car makes it easier to visit the other sights and towns here, all of which are in El Norte Grande. That said, it is possible to get around using the bus, which connects most of the cities of El Norte Grande. There are also frequent flights from Santiago to Calama, and from Arica back to Santiago.

GREAT ITINERARIES

SANTIAGO & SOUTHERN CHILE

16 DAYS

Days 1 & 2: Santiago

Arrive in Santiago early the morning of your first day. After a brief rest, set out to explore the city's museums, shops, and green spaces using the power of your own two feet, and the capital's efficient Metro. (*See* the "Santiago & Northern Chile" itinerary above for details.) ⇨ *Exploring Santiago in Chapter 1.*

Days 3, 4, 5 & 6: The Lake District

Head south 675 km (405 mi) from Santiago, either by car or plane, to Temuco, the gateway to Chile's Lake District. The city and environs are one of the best places in the region to observe the indigenous Mapuche culture. About an hour south, and just 15 minutes apart on the shores of Lago Villarrica, lie the twin resort towns of flashy, glitzy Pucón and quiet, pleasant Villarrica. Both have access to the lake and surrounding national parks. Drive south through the region from the graceful old city of Valdivia to Puerto Montt, stopping at the various resort towns. Frutillar, Puerto Octay, and Puerto Varas still bear testament to the Lake District's German-Austrian-Swiss immigrant history. Be sure to make time to relax in one of the region's many hot springs. ⇨ *La Araucanía and Los Lagos in Chapter 6.*

Days 7, 8, 9, 10 & 11: Parque Nacional Laguna San Rafael

From Puerto Montt, take a five-day round-trip cruise through the maze of fjords down the coast to the unforgettable cobalt-blue glacier in Parque Nacional Laguna San Rafael. If you're lucky, you'll see the huge glacier calving off pieces of ice that cause noisy, violent waves in the brilliant blue water. Transport runs from the utilitarian passenger–auto type ships to luxury cruises. ⇨ *Parque Nacional Laguna San Rafael in Chapter 8.*

Days 12, 13, 14, 15 & 16: Parque Nacional Torres del Paine/Departure

When you return from your cruise back to Puerto Montt, take a spectacular morning flight over the Andes to the Patagonian city of Punta Arenas. On the next day drive north to Puerto Natales, gateway to the Parque Nacional Torres del Paine. You'll need at least two days to wander through the wonders of the park's granite spires. On your final day head back to Punta Arenas, stopping en route at one of the penguin sanctuaries, and catch an afternoon flight back to Santiago, in time to connect with a night flight home to North America or Europe. ⇨ *Parque Nacional Torres del Paine in Chapter 9.*

TRANSPORTATION: A combination of flights, rental car, and boat works best for seeing the sights in this legion. From Santiago, drive south through the Lake District. Take the boat cruise down to Parque Nacional Laguna San Rafael—book far in advance for January or February—and on your return to Puerto Montt fly into the city of Punta Arenas. From there drive north to Puerto Natales and to Parque Nacional Torres del Paine. Buses can also be used to visit most of the towns. Car rental in the far south tends toward the expensive, and road conditions leave something to be desired. You may be just as happy to leave the driving to someone else.

WHEN TO GO

°F SANTIAGO   °C

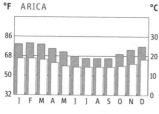

°F ARICA   °C

°F PUNTA ARENAS   °C

Climate

Chile's seasons are the reverse of the Northern Hemisphere's—that is, June–August is Chile's winter. Lift Chile out of its map and transfer it to corresponding latitudes in the Northern Hemisphere. You'd have a nation stretching from Cancún to Hudson Bay. (Or from a European perspective, make that from Scotland to the African Sahel.) Expect vast north–south climatic differences.

Tourism peaks during the hot summer months of January and February, except in Santiago, which tends to empty as most Santiaguinos take their summer holiday. Though prices are at their highest, it's worth braving the summer heat if you're interested in lying on the beach or enjoying the many concerts, folklore festivals, and outdoor theater performances offered during this period.

If you're heading to the Lake District or Patagonia and want good weather without the crowds, the shoulder seasons of December and March are the months to visit. The best time to see the Atacama Desert is late spring, preferably in November, when temperatures are bearable and air clarity is at its peak. In spring, Santiago blooms, and the fragrance of the flowers distracts even the most avid workaholic. A second tourist season occurs in the winter, as skiers flock to Chile's mountaintops for some of the world's best skiing, available at the height of northern summers. Winter smog is a good reason to stay away from Santiago during July and August, unless you're coming for a ski holiday and won't be spending much time in the city.

🖪 **Forecasts Weather Channel Connection** ☎ 900/932-8437 95¢ per min from a Touch-Tone phone ⊕ www.weather.com.

The following are the average daily maximum and minimum temperatures for Santiago, Arica, and Punta Arenas.

ON THE CALENDAR

	Note that Chile's seasons are the reverse of North America's and Europe's.
SUMMER December	**Navidad** (Christmas) is huge in Chile, as in any predominantly Christian nation, but December 25 has the added distinction of kicking off the summer tourist season. Cities begin to empty as residents flock to the beaches and mountains.
	The **Fiesta Grande de la Virgen** (Great Festival), honoring the patron saint of miners, culminates in frenzied festivities on December 26 in Andacolla, a small town in El Norte Chico. More than 100,000 pilgrims come to watch the masked dancers.
January	No place in Chile welcomes the **Año Nuevo** (New Year) with quite the bang as does Valparaíso and its mammoth fireworks display.
	The **Festival Foclórico** (Folklore Festival) is held in Santiago during the fourth week of January.
January– February	January and February see the two-month-long **Verano en Valdivia**, a favorite summer celebration in the Lake District honoring the founding of the city.
	In late January and early February, **Semanas Musicales** (Music Weeks) in the Lake District town of Frutillar bring virtuoso performances of classical music. The Lake District town of Villarrica hosts the **Muestra Cultural Mapuche** (Mapuche Cultural Show) from January 3 to February 28. Here you'll find examples of the indigenous people's art and music. Look for the reproduction of a *ruka*, the Mapuche traditional dwelling. The pastoral quiet of Isla Huapi is broken in late January or early February with **Lepún**, the annual Mapuche harvest festival, one of the Lake District's most interesting celebrations. The **Fiestas Costumbristas**, celebrating Chilote customs and folklore, take place over several weekends during January and February in the Chiloé towns of Ancud and Castro.
	The annual **Tapati Rapa Nui** festival, a two-week celebration of Easter Island's heritage, takes place every year in January and February. The normally laid-back village of Hanga Roa bursts to life in a colorful festival that includes much singing and dancing.
February	The **Fiesta de la Virgen de la Candelaria**, a three-day romp that begins on February 2, is held in the tiny antiplano village of Parinacota in El Norte Grande, and also in the town of Chonchi in Chiloe. It includes music and traditional dancing. The entire country remains glued to their television sets for a week in mid-February watching

		the annual **Festival Internacional de la Canción** (International Song Festival), a competition modeled on the Eurovision song contest. But if you can be there at contest central in Viña del Mar, so much the better.
AUTUMN	March	The four-day **Fiesta de la Vendimia**, the annual grape harvest festival, takes place in the Central Valley town of Curicó the first weekend in March. It includes grape-stomping contests and the selection of a queen, whose weight is measured out in grapes on a massive scale. A similar celebration is held in nearby Santa Cruz.
	March–April	**Semana Santa**, or Holy Week, is popular all over Chile. Different events are held each day between Palm Sunday and Easter Sunday. But don't expect to find much open from Thursday to Sunday.
	April	The Sunday after Easter is **Fiesta de Cuasimodo**, a celebration in which priests in decorated carriages ride through villages as parishioners cheer. The village of Colina, north of Santiago, has one of the largest gatherings.
	May	The **Fiesta de las Cruces** (Festival of the Crosses) takes place in the tiny city of Putre in El Norte Grande on May 3.
		Military pomp and circumstance in Iquique mark **Glorias Navales**, the anniversary of the 1879 naval Battle of Iquique with Peru and Bolivia.
WINTER	June	In Valparaíso, colorful processions mark the **Día de San Pedro** (St. Peter's Day) on June 29. A statue of the patron saint of fisherfolk is paraded through town.
	July	In honor of the **Virgen del Carmen**, the town of La Tirana in El Norte Grande hosts one of the country's most famous celebrations from July 12 to July 18. During this time some 80,000 dancing pilgrims converge on the central square.
		Residents of Punta Arenas come out of hibernation each July for their **Carnaval de Invierno**, a rollicking winter carnival in this southernmost region of Chile.
SPRING	September	The September 11 **anniversary of the 1973 coup** that deposed President Salvador Allende and brought General Augusto Pinochet to power is no longer a legal holiday, but sees political demonstrations in Santiago. It may be a good time to be elsewhere.
		On September 18 **Fiestas Patrias** (patriotic festivals) take place all over the country to mark National Independence Day. The most

ON THE CALENDAR

	fun is around Rancagua, in the Central Valley, where you'll find hard-fought rodeo competitions.
October	The **Fiesta Chica** (Little Festival), honoring the Virgen del Rosario, is held in Andacolla in El Norte Chico on the first Sunday of October. In the **Fiesta de San Francisco**, held October 4 in the Central Valley town of Huerta de Maule, more than 200 cowboys gather from all over the country for a day of riding and roping.
November	November 1 is **Todos los Santos** (All Saints Day), when Chileans traditionally tend to the graves of relatives. It's followed on November 2 by **Día de los Muertos** (All Souls Day). In late November, the Chilean wine industry shows off the fruits of its hard labor at the annual **Feria International de Vino del Hemisferio Sur** in Santiago.

SMART TRAVEL TIPS

The organizations in this section can provide information to supplement this guide; contact them for up-to-the-minute details, and consult the Essentials sections that end each chapter for facts on the various topics as they relate to Chile's many regions.

ADDRESSES

Numbering individual buildings isn't as popular in South America as it is elsewhere. In Chile, you'll find that even street names are sometimes abbreviated, both in conversation and on signage—Calle Bolívar, for instance, will simply be called Bolívar. In extreme cases, where neither address nor cross street is available, you may find the notation "s/n," meaning "no street number." In these cases the towns are usually so small that finding a particular building won't be a problem.

A bigger problem, especially away from the major cities, is that streets may not have names. Even if they do, they are often unmarked. In these places, locals are likely to give directions from major landmarks. In these cases, remember that a *cuadra* is a block.

The most common street terms in Spanish are *avenida* (avenue) and *calle* (street). The term *local,* which sometimes appears in an address, means the location is in a small room or office, quite often in an arcade or passageway.

AIR TRAVEL

Miami, New York, and Atlanta are the primary departure points for flights to Chile from the United States, though there are also frequent flights from Dallas and other cities. Other international flights often connect through other major South American cities like Buenos Aires and Lima.

Here's the bad news: arriving from abroad, American citizens must pay a "reciprocity" fee (to balance out fees Chileans pay upon entering the United States) of $100. Canadian and Australian citizens pay $55 and $30, respectively. The good news is that in addition to cash, credit cards are now also accepted. A departure tax of $18 is included in the cost of your ticket.

Addresses
Air Travel
Airports
Bike Travel
Boat & Ferry Travel
Bus Travel
Business Hours
Cameras & Photography
Car Rental
Car Travel
Children in Chile
Computers on the Road
Consumer Protection
Cruise Travel
Customs & Duties
Disabilities & Accessibility
Discounts & Deals
Eating & Drinking
Electricity
Embassies
Emergencies
English-Language Media
Gay & Lesbian Travel
Health
Holidays
Insurance
Internet Access
Language
Lodging
Mail & Shipping
Money Matters
Packing
Passports & Visas
Safety
Senior-Citizen Travel
Shopping
Students in Chile
Taxes
Telephones
Time
Tipping
Tours & Packages
Train Travel
Transportation Around Chile
Travel Agencies
Visitor Information
Web Sites

CARRIERS

The largest North American carrier is American Airlines, which has direct service from Dallas and Miami; Delta flies from Atlanta. Lan flies nonstop to Santiago from both Miami and Los Angeles and with a layover in Lima from New York. Air Canada flies nonstop from Toronto.

Air France flies nonstop from Paris, and Iberia has nonstop flights from Madrid. From Australia, Lan flies directly from Sydney to Santiago via Auckland, New Zealand.

Lan has daily flights from Santiago to most cities throughout Chile. Aerolineas del Sur and Sky also fly to most large cities within Chile.

🔃 International Airlines **Air Canada** ☎ 800/268-0024 in North America, 2/690-1115 in Chile. **Air France** ☎ 800/237-2747 in North America, 2/690-9696 in Chile. **American Airlines** ☎ 800/433-7300 in North America, 2/601-9272 in Chile. **Delta Airlines** ☎ 800/221-1212 in North America, 2/690-1555 in Chile. **Iberia** ☎ 800/504-8030 in North America, 2/870-1070 in Chile. **Lan** ☎ 800/735-5526 in North America, 2/565-2000 in Chile, 1300/361-400 in Australia, 09/309-8673 in New Zealand.

🔃 National Flights **Aerolineas del Sur** ☎ 2/690-1422. **Lan** ☎ 2/565-2000 in Chile. **Sky** ☎ 600/600-2828.

CUTTING COSTS

The least-expensive airfares to Chile are often priced for round-trip travel and must usually be purchased in advance. Airlines generally allow you to change your return date for a fee; most low-fare tickets, however, are nonrefundable. It's smart to call a number of airlines and check the Internet; when you are quoted a good price, book it on the spot—the same fare may not be available the next day, or even the next hour. Always check different routings and look into using alternate airports. Also, price off-peak flights and red-eye, which may be significantly less expensive than others.

Consolidators are another good source. They buy tickets for scheduled flights at reduced rates from the airlines, then sell them at prices that beat the best fare available directly from the airlines. (Many also offer reduced car-rental and hotel rates.) Sometimes you can even get your money back if you need to return the ticket. Carefully read the fine print detailing penalties for changes and cancellations, purchase the ticket with a credit card, and confirm your consolidator reservation with the airline.

Many airlines, singly or in collaboration, offer discount air passes that allow foreigners to travel economically in a particular country or region. These visitor passes usually must be reserved and purchased before you leave home. Information about passes often can be found on most airlines' international Web pages, which tend to be aimed at travelers from outside the carrier's home country. Also, try typing the name of the pass into a search engine, or search for "pass" within the carrier's Web site.

🔃 Consolidators **AirlineConsolidator.com** ☎ 888/468-5385 ⊕ www.airlineconsolidator.com; for international tickets. **Best Fares** ☎ 800/880-1234 ⊕ www.bestfares.com; $59.90 annual membership. **Cheap Tickets** ☎ 800/377-1000 or 800/652-4327 ⊕ www.cheaptickets.com. **Expedia** ☎ 800/397-3342 or 404/728-8787 ⊕ www.expedia.com. **Hotwire** ☎ 866/468-9473 or 920/330-9418 ⊕ www.hotwire.com. **Now Voyager Travel** ☎ 212/459-1616 ⊕ www.nowvoyagertravel.com. **Onetravel.com** ⊕ www.onetravel.com. **Orbitz** ☎ 888/656-4546 ⊕ www.orbitz.com. **Priceline.com** ⊕ www.priceline.com. **Travelocity** ☎ 888/709-5983, 877/282-2925 in Canada, 0870/111-7061 in U.K. ⊕ www.travelocity.com.

FLYING TIMES

Traveling between the Americas is usually less tiring than traveling to Europe or Asia because you cross fewer time zones. New York is 1 hour behind Santiago, and Los Angeles is 4 hours behind Santiago. London is 3 to 5 hours ahead of Santiago, depending on the time of year. New Zealand and Australia are 11 hours ahead.

The major North American departure points for Santiago are New York (11½ hours), Miami (9 hours), and Atlanta (9 hours). From London to Santiago takes about 17 hours, including a stopover in a European or South American city; it's an 18-hour flight from Sydney, including a stopover in Auckland. Note that flight times may vary according to the size of the plane.

HOW TO COMPLAIN

If your baggage goes astray or your flight goes awry, complain right away. Most carriers require that you **file a claim immediately.** The Aviation Consumer Protection Division of the Department of Transportation publishes *Fly-Rights,* which discusses airlines and consumer issues and is available online. You can also find articles and information on mytravelrights.com, the Web site of the nonprofit Consumer Travel Rights Center.

🚩 **Airline Complaints Aviation Consumer Protection Division** ⊠ U.S. Department of Transportation, Office of Aviation Enforcement and Proceedings, C-75, Room 4107, 400 7th St. SW, Washington, DC 20590 ☎ 202/366-2220 ⊕ airconsumer.ost.dot.gov. **Federal Aviation Administration Consumer Hotline** ⊠ For inquiries: FAA, 800 Independence Ave. SW, Washington, DC 20591 ☎ 800/322-7873 ⊕ www.faa.gov.

RECONFIRMING

Check the status of your flight before you leave for the airport. You can do this on your carrier's Web site, by linking to a flight-status checker (many Web booking services offer these), or by calling your carrier or travel agent. Always confirm international flights at least 72 hours ahead of the scheduled departure time. This is particularly true for travel within South America, where flights tend to operate at full capacity—often with passengers who have a great deal of baggage to process before departure.

AIRPORTS

Most international flights head to Santiago's Comodoro Arturo Merino Benítez International Airport (SCL), also known as Pudahuel, about 30 minutes west of the city. Domestic flights leave from the same terminal.

🚩 **Airport Information Comodoro Arturo Merino Benítez International Airport** ☎ 2/690-1900 ⊕ www.aeropuertosantiago.cl.

BIKE TRAVEL

Riding a bike will put you face to face with the people and landscapes of Chile.

However, the rugged terrain and varying road conditions pose considerable challenges. **Consider a mountain bike,** since basic touring bikes are too fragile for the potholes on the best roads. Many tour operators in Santiago and other places offer bike trips—sometimes including equipment rental—that range in length from a half day to several days. Always remember to **lock your bike when you make stops,** and **avoid riding in congested urban areas,** where it's difficult and dangerous.

BIKES IN FLIGHT

Most airlines accommodate bikes as luggage, provided they are dismantled and boxed; check with individual airlines about packing requirements. Some airlines sell bike boxes, which are often free at bike shops, for about $20 (bike bags can be considerably more expensive). International travelers often can substitute a bike for a piece of checked luggage at no charge; otherwise, the cost is about $100. Most U.S. and Canadian airlines charge $40–$80 each way.

BOAT & FERRY TRAVEL

Boats and ferries are the best way to reach many places in Chile, such as Chiloé and the Southern Coast. They are also a great alternative to flying when your destination is a southern port like Puerto Natales or Punta Arenas. Navimag and Transmarchilay are the two main companies operating routes in the south. Further details on boat travel are discussed in the various chapter Essentials sections throughout this guide.

Navimag and Transmarchilay both maintain excellent Web sites with complete schedule and pricing information. You can also buy tickets online, or book through a travel agent.

🚩 **Boat & Ferry Information Navimag** ⊠ Av. El Bosque Norte 0440, Piso 11, Las Condes, Santiago ☎ 2/442-3120 ⊠ Angelmó 2187, Puerto Montt ☎ 65/432-300 ⊕ www.navimag.cl. **Transmarchilay** ⊠ Av. Providencia 2653, Local 24, Providencia, Santiago ☎ 2/234-1464 ⊕ www.transmarchilay.cl ⊠ Angelmó 2187, Puerto Montt ☎ 65/270-430.

BUS TRAVEL

Long-distance buses are safe and affordable. Intercity bus service is a comfortable, safe, and reasonably priced alternative for getting around. Luxury bus travel between cities costs about one-third that of plane travel and is more comfortable, with wide reclining seats, movies, drinks, and snacks. The most expensive service offered by most bus companies is called *cama* or *semi-cama,* which indicate that the seats fold down into a bed. Service billed as *ejectivo* is nearly as luxurious.

Without doubt, the low cost of bus travel is its greatest advantage; its greatest drawback is the time you need to cover the distances involved. A trip from Santiago to San Pedro de Atacama, for example, takes between 23 and 24 hours.

When traveling by bus, **pack light** and **dress comfortably.** Be sure to get a receipt for any luggage you check beneath the bus and **keep a close watch on your belongings** that you take on the bus.

For more information on local bus service, see the Essentials sections at the end of each chapter.

FARES & SCHEDULES
Bus fares are substantially cheaper than in North America or Europe. In Chile you'll usually pay between $1 and $3 per hour of travel. Competing bus companies serve all major and many minor routes, so it can pay to **shop around.** Always speak to the counter clerk, as cutthroat competition may mean you can ride for less than the posted fare.

Tickets are sold at bus-company offices and at city bus terminals. Note that in larger cities there may be different terminals for buses to different destinations, and some small towns may not have a terminal at all. You'll be picked up and dropped off at the bus line's office, invariably in a central location. Expect to pay with cash, as only the large bus companies such as Pullman Bus and Tur-Bus accept credit cards.

Note that reservations for advance ticket purchases aren't necessary except for trips to resort areas in high season or during major holidays. You should **arrive at bus stations extra early for travel during peak seasons.** Companies are notoriously diffi-

cult to reach by phone, so it's often better to stop by the terminal to check on prices and schedules.

Pullman Bus and Tur-Bus are two of the best-known companies in Chile. They travel to much of the country.

Bus Information Pullman Bus ☎ 600/320-3200 ⊕ www.pullman.cl. **Tur-Bus** ☎ 600/660-6600 ⊕ www.turbus.com.

BUSINESS HOURS
Most retail businesses are open weekdays 10–7 and Saturday until 2; most are closed Sunday. Many businesses close for lunch between about 1 and 3 or 4, though this is becoming less common, especially in larger cities.

BANKS & OFFICES
Most banks are open weekdays 9–2, although some are open until 4. *Casas de cambio* are open weekdays 9–7 and weekends 9–3 for currency exchange.

GAS STATIONS
Gas stations in major cities and along the Pan-American Highway tend to stay open 24 hours. Others follow regular business hours.

MUSEUMS & SIGHTS
Most tourist attractions are open during normal business hours during the week and for at least the morning on Saturday and Sunday. Most museums are closed Monday.

SHOPS
Shops generally are open weekdays 9–8 and Saturday 9–2. Large malls often stay open daily 10–10. In small towns, shops often close for lunch between 1 and 3 or 4.

CAMERAS & PHOTOGRAPHY
Chile, with its majestic landscapes and varied cityscapes, is a photographer's dream. Chileans seem amenable to having picture-taking tourists in their midst, but you should always **ask permission before taking pictures of individuals.** Be aware that photos shouldn't be taken in or around government or military areas. Photography of Chilean warships docked in Valparaíso is not permitted.

To avoid the blurriness caused by shaking hands, **buy a mini tripod**—they're available in sizes as small as 6 inches. A small bean-bag can be used to support your camera on uneven surfaces. If you'll be visiting the Andes, **get a skylight (81B or 81C) or polarizing filter to minimize haze and light problems.** The higher the altitude, the greater the proportion of ultraviolet rays. Light meters don't read these rays and consequently, except for close-ups or full-frame portraits where the reading is taken directly off the subject, photos may be overexposed. These filters may also help with the glare caused by white adobe buildings, sandy beaches, and so on. You may want to invest in a telephoto lens to photograph wildlife: even standard zoom lenses of the 35–88 range won't capture a satisfying amount of detail. **Bring high-speed film to compensate for low light in the rain forest.** The thick tree canopy blocks out more light than you might expect. The *Kodak Guide to Shooting Great Travel Pictures* (available at bookstores everywhere) is loaded with tips.

EQUIPMENT PRECAUTIONS

Don't pack film or equipment in checked luggage, where it is much more susceptible to damage. X-ray machines used to view checked luggage are extremely powerful and therefore are likely to ruin your film. Try to ask for hand inspection of film, which becomes clouded after repeated exposure to airport X-ray machines, and keep videotapes and computer disks away from metal detectors. Always keep film, tape, and computer disks out of the sun. Carry an extra supply of batteries, and be prepared to turn on your camera, camcorder, or laptop to prove to airport security personnel that the device is real.

CAR RENTAL

On average it costs 25,000 pesos (about $47) a day to rent the cheapest type of car with unlimited mileage. To access some of Chile's more remote regions, it may be necessary to rent a four-wheel-drive vehicle, which can cost up to 48,000 pesos (about $90) a day. You can often get a discounted weekly rate. The rate you are quoted usually includes insurance, but make sure to ask whether there is a deductible you will have to pay in case of an accident. You can usually pay slightly more and have no deductible.

It is by far easier to rent a car in Santiago, where all the international agencies have branches at the airport and in town. You'll find mostly local rental agencies in the rest of the country.

Always **give the rental car a once-over** to make sure that the headlights, jack, and tires (including the spare) are in working condition. Be sure to **alert the agency about any scratches and dents** before you set off on your trip or you may be held liable for damages you didn't cause.

An annoying fact about Chilean rental companies is that they often deliver the car to you with the gas gauge empty. Make sure to **ask about the nearest gas station,** or your trip may be extremely short.

In order to drive to Punta Arenas in Patagonia you will need to cross into Argentina at Chile Chico or at one of the international border crossings beforehand. If you plan to do this you must tell your car-rental company, which will provide notarized authorization—otherwise you will be refused permission to cross.

🚗 **Major Agencies Alamo** ☎ 800/522-9696 in U.S., 2/225-3061 in Chile ⊕ www.alamo.com. **Avis** ☎ 800/331-1084 in U.S., 2/690-1382 in Chile, 800/879-2847 in Canada, 0870/606-0100 in U.K., 02/9353-9000 in Australia, 09/526-2847 in New Zealand ⊕ www.avis.com. **Budget** ☎ 800/472-3325 in U.S., 2/690-1386 in Chile, 800/268-8900 in Canada, 1300/794-344 in Australia, 0800/283-438 in New Zealand ⊕ www.budget.com. **Dollar** ☎ 800/800-6000 in U.S., 2/202-5510 in Chile, 0800/085-4578 in U.K. ⊕ www.dollar.com. **Hertz** ☎ 800/654-3001 in U.S., 2/496-1111 in Chile, 800/263-0600 in Canada, 0870/844-8844 in U.K., 02/9669-2444 in Australia, 09/256-8690 in New Zealand ⊕ www.hertz.com. **National Car Rental** ☎ 800/227-7368 in U.S., 2/223-4117 in Chile ⊕ www.nationalcar.com.

CUTTING COSTS

If you don't want to drive yourself, **consider hiring a car and driver** through your hotel concierge, or **make a deal with a taxi driver** for some extended sightseeing at a longer-term rate. Drivers charge an hourly rate regardless of the distance traveled.

You'll often spend less than you would for a rental car.

Local companies are sometimes a cheaper option. Rosselot is a reputable local company with offices in Santiago and many other cities.

⑦ Local Agency Rosselot ☎ 800/201-298.

INSURANCE

When driving a rented car you are generally responsible for any damage to or loss of the vehicle. You also may be liable for any property damage or personal injury that you may cause while driving. Before you rent, see what coverage you already have under the terms of your personal auto-insurance policy and credit cards.

REQUIREMENTS & RESTRICTIONS

Your own driver's license makes it legal for you to drive in Chile. The minimum age for driving is 18. To rent a car you usually have to be 25, but a few companies let you rent at 22.

CAR TRAVEL

Certain areas of Chile are most enjoyable when explored on your own in a car, such as beaches of the Central Coast, the wineries of the Central Valley, the ski areas east of Santiago, and the Lake District in the south. Some regions, such as parts of the Atacama Desert, are impossible to explore without your own wheels.

Drivers in Chile are not particularly aggressive, but neither are they particularly polite. Some commonsense rules of the road: before you set out, establish an itinerary. Be sure to **plan your daily driving distance conservatively,** as distances are always longer than they appear on maps. Obey posted speed limits and traffic regulations. And above all, **if you get a traffic ticket, don't argue**—and plan to spend longer than you want settling it.

International driving permits (IDPs) are available from the American and Canadian automobile associations and, in the United Kingdom, from the Automobile Association and Royal Automobile Club. These international permits, valid only in conjunction with your regular driver's license, are universally recognized; having

one may save you a problem with local authorities.

AUTO CLUBS

El Automóvil Club de Chile offers low-cost road service and towing in and around the main cities to members of the Automobile Association of America (AAA).

⑦ Auto Club Information El Automóvil Club de Chile ✉ Av. Andrés Bello 1863, Providencia, Santiago ☎ 2/431-1000 ⊕ www.automovilclub.cl.

GASOLINE

Most service stations are operated by an attendant and accept credit cards. They are open 24 hours a day along the Pan-American Highway and in most major cities, but not in small towns and villages. Attendants will often ask you to glance at the zero reading on the gas pump to show that you are not being cheated.

At this writing, a liter of gas cost about 600 pesos ($1.12). To make sure you don't run out of gas, always **ask about gas stations** en route.

PARKING

Depending on the area, you can park on the street, in parking lots, or in parking garages in Santiago and large cities in Chile. Expect to pay anywhere from 600 to 800 pesos. There are parking meters for street parking, but more often a parking attendant will be there to direct and charge you.

ROAD CONDITIONS

Between May and August, roads, underpasses, and parks can flood when it rains. It's very dangerous, especially for drivers who don't know their way around. Avoid driving if it has been raining for several hours.

The Pan-American Highway runs from Arica in the far north down to Puerto Montt, in the Lake District. Much of it is now double lane, or in the process of being widened, and bypasses most large cities. The Carretera Austral, an unpaved road that runs for more than 1,000 km (620 mi) as far as Villa O'Higgins in Patagonia, starts just south of Puerto Montt. A few stretches of the road are broken by water and are linked only by car ferries. Some parts of the Carretera can be washed away in heavy rain; it is wise to consult local police for details.

Many cyclists ride without lights in rural areas, so be careful when driving at night, particularly on roads without street lighting. This also applies to horse- and bull-drawn carts.

RULES OF THE ROAD

Keep in mind that the speed limit is 60 km/h (37 mph) in cities and 120 km/h (75 mph) on highways unless otherwise posted. The police regularly enforce the speed limit, handing out *partes* (tickets) to speeders.

Seat belts are mandatory in the front and back of the car, and police give on-the-spot fines for not wearing them. If the police find you with more than 0.5 milligrams of alcohol in your blood, you will be considered to be driving under the influence and arrested.

Plan to rent snow chains for driving on the road up to the ski resorts outside Santiago. Police will stop you and ask if you have them—if you don't, you will be forced to turn back.

CHILDREN IN CHILE

Children are welcome in most hotels and restaurants, especially on weekends, when families go out for lunch in droves. The *balnearios* (beach towns) along Chile's Central Coast expect you to bring the kids—the most common form of lodging is family-size bungalows. Children are also a common sight in the pine-covered mountains of the Lake District and the ski resorts of the Central Valley.

If you are renting a car, don't forget to arrange for a car seat when you reserve. For general advice about traveling with children, consult *Fodor's FYI: Travel with Your Baby* (available in bookstores everywhere).

FLYING

If your children are two or older, ask about children's airfares. As a general rule, infants under two not occupying a seat fly at greatly reduced fares or even for free. But if you want to guarantee a seat for an infant, you have to pay full fare. Consider flying during off-peak days and times; most airlines will grant an infant a seat without a ticket if there are available seats. When booking, confirm carry-on allowances if you're traveling with infants. In general, for babies charged 10% to 50% of the adult fare you are allowed one carry-on bag and a collapsible stroller; if the flight is full, the stroller may have to be checked or you may be limited to less.

Experts agree that it's a good idea to use safety seats aloft for children weighing less than 40 pounds. Airlines set their own policies: if you use a safety seat, U.S. carriers usually require that the child be ticketed, even if he or she is young enough to ride free, because the seats must be strapped into regular seats. And even if you pay the full adult fare for the seat, it may be worth it, especially on longer trips. Do **check your airline's policy about using safety seats during takeoff and landing.** Safety seats are not allowed everywhere in the plane, so get your seat assignments as early as possible.

When reserving, request children's meals or a freestanding bassinet (not available at all airlines) if you need them. But note that bulkhead seats, where you must sit to use the bassinet, may lack an overhead bin or storage space on the floor.

LODGING

Most hotels in Chile allow children under a certain age to stay in their parents' room at no extra charge, but others charge for them as extra adults; be sure to find out the cutoff age for children's discounts.

SIGHTS & ATTRACTIONS

There's plenty for kids to do in Chile. Santiago is filled with interesting museums that appeal to the entire family. Every town has public parks where parents can relax while their children romp. Kids are fascinated by the *ascensores* (funiculars) of Valparaíso. The ferries around Puerto Montt are a great way to see the coastline. And most children delight at the penguin colonies near Punta Arenas.

Places that are especially appealing to children are indicated by a rubber-duckie icon (☺) in the margin.

COMPUTERS ON THE ROAD

If you're planning to bring a laptop computer into the country, check the manual first to see if it requires a converter. Newer laptops will require only an adapter plug. Chile uses the same phone plugs as the United States, so plan accordingly if you'll be using a modem. Remember to ask about electrical surges before plugging in your computer. Note that South America's luxury hotels typically offer business centers with computers. Very few have wireless connections.

Carrying a laptop computer could make you a target for thieves; **conceal your laptop in a generic bag** and keep it close to you at all times.

CONSUMER PROTECTION

Whether you're shopping for gifts or purchasing travel services, **pay with a major credit card** whenever possible, so you can cancel payment or get reimbursed if there's a problem (and you can provide documentation). If you're doing business with a particular company for the first time, contact your local Better Business Bureau and the attorney general's offices in your state and (for U.S. businesses) the company's home state as well. Have any complaints been filed? Finally, if you're buying a package or tour, always consider travel insurance that includes default coverage (⇨ Insurance).

⁊ BBBs Council of Better Business Bureaus ✉ 4200 Wilson Blvd., Suite 800, Arlington, VA 22203 ☎ 703/276-0100 🖷 703/525-8277 ⊕ www.bbb.org.

CRUISE TRAVEL

Several international cruise lines, including Celebrity Cruises, Holland America, Norwegian Cruise Lines, Princess Cruises, Royal Olympic, and Silversea Cruises, call at Chile or offer cruises that start in Chile, typically in Valparaíso, following the coastline to the southern archipelago and its fjords. Some companies, such as Holland America and Orient Lines, have itineraries that include Antarctica. Victory Yacht Cruises and Adventure Associates operate in southern Chile and also have cruises to Antarctica.

You can spend a week aboard the luxury *Skorpios,* run by Cruceros Maritimos Skorpios, which leaves from Puerto Montt and sails through the archipelago to the San Rafael glacier. In the far south, you can board Navimag's *Terra Australis* and motor through the fjords to the Beagle Channel, stopping in Puerto Williams, Chile's most southerly settlement.

⁊ Cruise Lines Adventure Associates ☎ 2/9389-7466 in Australia. Celebrity Cruises ☎ 800/760-0654. Cruceros Maritimos Skorpios ☎ 2/477-1900. Holland America ☎ 877/724-5425. Navimag ☎ 2/442-3120. Norwegian Cruise Lines ☎ 800/327-7030. Orient Lines ☎ 800/333-7300. Princess Cruises ☎ 800/746-2377. Royal Olympic ☎ 800/872-6400, 020/7440-9090 in U.K. Silversea Cruises ☎ 866/721-3422, 0800/056-9885 in U.K. Victory Yacht Cruises ☎ 61/621-010 in Chile.

CUSTOMS & DUTIES

When shopping abroad, keep receipts for all purchases. Upon reentering the country, **be ready to show customs officials what you've bought.** Pack purchases together in an easily accessible place. If you think a duty is incorrect, appeal the assessment. If you object to the way your clearance was handled, note the inspector's badge number. In either case, first ask to see a supervisor. If the problem isn't resolved, write to the appropriate authorities, beginning with the port director at your point of entry.

IN AUSTRALIA

Australian residents who are 18 or older may bring home A$900 worth of souvenirs and gifts (including jewelry), 250 cigarettes or 250 grams of cigars or other tobacco products, and 2.25 liters of alcohol (including wine, beer, and spirits). Residents under 18 may bring back A$450 worth of goods. If any of these individual allowances are exceeded, you must pay duty for the entire amount (of the group of products in which the allowance was exceeded). Members of the same family traveling together may pool their allowances. Prohibited items include meat products. Seeds, plants, and fruits need to be declared upon arrival.

⁊ Australian Customs Service 🕀 Customs House, 10 Cooks River Dr., Sydney International Airport, Sydney, NSW 2020 ☎ 1300/363263 or 02/6275–6666, 1800/020–504 or 02/8334–7444 quarantine-inquiry line 🖷 02/8339–6714 ⊕ www.customs.gov.au.

IN CANADA
Canadian residents who have been out of Canada for at least seven days may bring in C$750 worth of goods duty-free. If you've been away fewer than seven days but more than 48 hours, the duty-free allowance drops to C$200. If your trip lasts 24 to 48 hours, the allowance is C$50; if the goods are worth more than C$50, you must pay full duty on all of the goods. You may not pool allowances with family members. Goods claimed under the C$750 exemption may follow you by mail; those claimed under the lesser exemptions must accompany you. Alcohol and tobacco products may be included in the seven-day and 48-hour exemptions but not in the 24-hour exemption. If you meet the age requirements of the province or territory through which you reenter Canada, you may bring in, duty-free, 1.5 liters of wine *or* 1.14 liters (40 imperial ounces) of liquor *or* 24 12-ounce cans or bottles of beer or ale. Also, if you meet the local age requirement for tobacco products, you may bring in, duty-free, 200 cigarettes, 50 cigars or cigarillos, and 200 grams of tobacco. You may have to pay a minimum duty on tobacco products, regardless of whether or not you exceed your personal exemption. Check ahead of time with the Canada Border Services Agency or the Department of Agriculture for policies regarding meat products, seeds, plants, and fruits.

You may send an unlimited number of gifts (only one gift per recipient, however) worth up to C$60 each duty-free to Canada. Label the package UNSOLICITED GIFT—VALUE UNDER $60. Alcohol and tobacco are excluded.

🚩 **Canada Border Services Agency** ✉ Customs Information Services, 191 Laurier Ave. W, 15th fl., Ottawa, Ontario K1A 0L5 ☎ 800/461–9999 in Canada, 204/983–3500, 506/636–5064 ⊕ www.cbsa.gc.ca.

IN CHILE
You may bring into Chile up to 400 cigarettes, 500 grams of tobacco, 50 cigars, two open bottles of perfume, 2.5 liters of alcoholic beverages, and gifts. Prohibited items include plants, fruit, seeds, meat, and honey. Spot checks take place at airports and border crossings.

Visitors, although seldom questioned, are prohibited from leaving with handicrafts and souvenirs worth more than $500. You are generally prohibited from taking antiques out of the country without special permission (⇨ Shopping).

🚩 **Chilean Embassy** ✉ 1732 Massachusetts Ave. NW, Washington, DC 20036 USA ☎ 202/785–1746 ⊕ www.chile-usa.org.

IN NEW ZEALAND
All homeward-bound residents may bring back NZ$700 worth of souvenirs and gifts; passengers may not pool their allowances, and children can claim only the concession on goods intended for their own use. For those 17 or older, the duty-free allowance also includes 4.5 liters of wine or beer; one 1,125-ml bottle of spirits; and either 200 cigarettes, 250 grams of tobacco, 50 cigars, *or* a combination of the three up to 250 grams. Meat products, seeds, plants, and fruits must be declared upon arrival to the Agricultural Services Department.

🚩 **New Zealand Customs** ✉ Head office: The Customhouse, 17–21 Whitmore St., Box 2218, Wellington ☎ 0800/428–786 or 09/300–5399 ⊕ www.customs.govt.nz.

IN THE U.K.
From countries outside the European Union, including Chile, you may bring home, duty-free, 200 cigarettes, 50 cigars, 100 cigarillos, or 250 grams of tobacco; 1 liter of spirits or 2 liters of fortified or sparkling wine or liqueurs; 2 liters of still table wine; 60 ml of perfume; 250 ml of toilet water; plus £145 worth of other goods, including gifts and souvenirs. Prohibited items include meat and dairy products, seeds, plants, and fruits.

🚩 **HM Customs and Excise** ✉ Portcullis House, 21 Cowbridge Rd. E, Cardiff CF11 9SS ☎ 0845/010–9000 or 0208/929–0152 advice service, 0208/929–6731 or 0208/910–3602 complaints ⊕ www.hmce.gov.uk.

IN THE U.S.

U.S. residents who have been out of the country for at least 48 hours may bring home, for personal use, $800 worth of foreign goods duty-free, as long as they haven't used the $800 allowance or any part of it in the past 30 days. This exemption may include 1 liter of alcohol (for travelers 21 and older), 200 cigarettes, and 100 non-Cuban cigars. Family members from the same household who are traveling together may pool their $800 personal exemptions. For fewer than 48 hours, the duty-free allowance drops to $200, which may include 50 cigarettes, 10 non-Cuban cigars, and 150 ml of alcohol (or 150 ml of perfume containing alcohol). The $200 allowance cannot be combined with other individuals' exemptions, and if you exceed it, the full value of all the goods will be taxed. Antiques, which U.S. Customs and Border Protection defines as objects more than 100 years old, enter duty-free, as do original works of art done entirely by hand, including paintings, drawings, and sculptures. This doesn't apply to folk art or handicrafts, which are in general dutiable.

You may also send packages home duty-free, with a limit of one parcel per addressee per day (except alcohol or tobacco products or perfume worth more than $5). You can mail up to $200 worth of goods for personal use; label the package PERSONAL USE and attach a list of its contents and their retail value. If the package contains your used personal belongings, mark it AMERICAN GOODS RETURNED to avoid paying duties. You may send up to $100 worth of goods as a gift; mark the package UNSOLICITED GIFT. Mailed items do not affect your duty-free allowance on your return.

To avoid paying duty on foreign-made high-ticket items you already own and will take on your trip, register them with a local customs office before you leave the country. Consider filing a Certificate of Registration for laptops, cameras, watches, and other digital devices identified with serial numbers or other permanent markings; you can keep the certificate for other trips. Otherwise, bring a sales receipt or insurance form to show that you owned the item before you left the United States.

For more about duties, restricted items, and other information about international travel, check out U.S. Customs and Border Protection's online brochure, *Know Before You Go*. You can also file complaints on the U.S. Customs and Border Protection Web site, listed below.

⑦ U.S. Customs and Border Protection ⊠ For inquiries and complaints: 1300 Pennsylvania Ave. NW, Washington, DC 20229 ⊕ www.cbp.gov ☎ 877/227-5551 or 202/354-1000.

DISABILITIES & ACCESSIBILITY

Tough new laws mean that Chile is much better equipped to handle travelers with disabilities. There are more curb cuts to make the streets more accessible, new buildings are being constructed with ramps, and older buildings are having them added. Many places, however, will still be a challenge. It takes effort and planning to negotiate cobbled city streets or explore the countryside. Some regions, such as the Atacama Desert and Parque Nacional Torres del Paine, are a challenge for those with mobility problems. Valparaíso, with its hillside topography and unending staircases, could be unmanageable.

LODGING

If you have mobility problems, ask for the lowest floor on which accessible services are offered. If you have a hearing impairment, check whether the hotel has devices to alert you visually to the ring of the telephone, a knock at the door, and a fire/emergency alarm. Some hotels provide these devices without charge. Discuss your needs with hotel personnel if this equipment isn't available, so that a staff member can personally alert you in the event of an emergency.

If you're bringing a guide dog, get authorization ahead of time and write down the name of the person with whom you spoke.

RESERVATIONS

When discussing accessibility with an operator or reservations agent, ask hard questions. Are there any stairs, inside *or* out? Are there grab bars next to the toilet *and* in the shower/tub? How wide is the doorway to the room? To the bathroom? For the most extensive facilities meeting the latest legal specifications, opt for newer accommodations. If you reserve through a toll-free number, consider also calling the hotel's local number to confirm the information from the central reservations office. Get confirmation in writing when you can.

SIGHTS & ATTRACTIONS

Few sights in Chile were designed with travelers who use wheelchairs in mind, but many have been renovated to meet their needs. Most museums in Santiago and other larger cities now have ramps and elevators. Call ahead or ask someone who has visited before.

TRANSPORTATION

The U.S. Department of Transportation Aviation Consumer Protection Division's online publication *New Horizons: Information for the Air Traveler with a Disability* offers advice for travelers with a disability, and outlines basic rights. Visit DisabilityInfo.gov for general information. **Information & Complaints Aviation Consumer Protection Division** (⇨ Air Travel) for airline-related problems; ⊕ airconsumer.ost.dot.gov/publications/horizons.htm for airline travel advice and rights. **Departmental Office of Civil Rights** ✉ For general inquiries: U.S. Department of Transportation, S-30, 400 7th St. SW, Room 10215, Washington, DC 20590 ☎ 202/366-4648, 202/366-8538 TTY ⊟ 202/366-9371 ⊕ www.dotcr.ost.dot.gov. **Disability Rights Section** ✉ NYAV, U.S. Department of Justice, Civil Rights Division, 950 Pennsylvania Ave. NW, Washington, DC 20530 ☎ 800/514-0301, 202/514-0301 ADA information line, 800/514-0383 or 202/514-0383 TTY ⊕ www.ada.gov. **U.S. Department of Transportation Hotline** ☎ For disability-related air-travel problems, 800/778-4838 or 800/455-9880 TTY.

TRAVEL AGENCIES

In the United States, the Americans with Disabilities Act requires that travel firms serve the needs of all travelers. Some agencies specialize in working with people with disabilities. **Travelers with Mobility Problems Access Adventures/B. Roberts Travel** ✉ 1876 East Ave., Rochester, NY 14610 ☎ 800/444-6540 ⊕ www.

brobertstravel.com, run by a former physical-rehabilitation counselor. **CareVacations** ✉ No. 5, 5110-50 Ave., Leduc, Alberta, Canada T9E 6V4 ☎ 877/478-7827 or 780/986-6404 ⊟ 780/986-8332 ⊕ www.carevacations.com, for group tours and cruise vacations. **Flying Wheels Travel** ✉ 143 W. Bridge St., Box 382, Owatonna, MN 55060 ☎ 507/451-5005 ⊟ 507/451-1685 ⊕ www.flyingwheelstravel.com.

DISCOUNTS & DEALS

Be a smart shopper and compare all your options before making decisions. A plane ticket bought with a promotional coupon from travel clubs, coupon books, and direct-mail offers or purchased on the Internet may not be cheaper than the least-expensive fare from a discount ticket agency. And always keep in mind that what you get is just as important as what you save.

DISCOUNT RESERVATIONS

To save money, look into discount reservations services with Web sites and toll-free numbers, which use their buying power to get a better price on hotels, airline tickets (⇨ Air Travel), even car rentals. When booking a room, always **call the hotel's local toll-free number** (if one is available) rather than the central reservations number—you'll often get a better price. Always ask about special packages or corporate rates.

When shopping for the best deal on hotels and car rentals, look for guaranteed exchange rates, which protect you against a falling dollar. With your rate locked in, you won't pay more, even if the price goes up in the local currency. **Hotel Rooms Hotels.com** ☎ 800/246-8357 ⊕ www.hotels.com. **Steigenberger Reservation Service** ☎ 800/223-5652 ⊕ www.srs-worldhotels.com. **Turbotrip.com** ☎ 800/473-7829 ⊕ w3.turbotrip.com.

PACKAGE DEALS

Don't confuse packages and guided tours. When you buy a package, you travel on your own, just as though you had planned the trip yourself. Fly/drive packages, which combine airfare and car rental, are often a good deal. In cities, ask the local visitor's bureau about hotel and local transportation packages that include tickets to major museum exhibits or other special events.

EATING & DRINKING

The restaurants (all of which are indicated by a ✕ symbol) that we list are the cream of the crop in each price category. Properties indicated by a ✕⌂ are lodging establishments whose restaurant warrants a special trip. It is customary to tip 10% in Chile; tipping above this amount is uncommon among locals.

MEALS & SPECIALTIES

Chile serves an incredible variety of foods. With such a long coastline, it's no surprise that you can get wonderful seafood. Salmon is caught off the Southern Coast and raised in farms in the Lake District. Other popular catches include sea bass and conger eel. Shellfish such as mussels and scallops are widely available, and *locos* (abalone) and *jaiba* (crab) are frequently prepared as *chupes* (stews) or *pasteles* (pies). Raw shellfish is best avoided, but cooked with cheese or white wine, lemon, and fresh coriander, it's an excellent introduction to Chilean cuisine. Awaken your palate with a seafood appetizer, such as *choritos al vapor* (mussels steamed in white wine), *machas a la parmesana* (similar to razor clams but unique to Chile, grilled with tomatoes and Parmesan cheese), or *chupe de centolla* (king crab). Simply seasoned grilled fish is a Chilean favorite, usually served with steamed potatoes or an *ensalada a la chilena* (sliced tomatoes and onions). Also worth tasting is the humble *merluza* (hake), which makes a delicious, cheap lunch.

But fish isn't all that's available. *Pastel de choclo* is a typical dish that you'll find just about everywhere in Chile. Served in a heavy clay bowl, it's a mixture of minced beef, chicken, olives, hard-boiled egg, and raisins, topped with a layer of creamy mashed corn. Then there are the tasty and filling *humitas,* mashed corn with chopped onion and basil served in the corn husk. Stews of vegetables with chicken, beef, or lamb are known as *cazuelas;* a hearty bean stew with chopped vegetables is known as *porotos granados.*

A *parrillada* is a platter of every cut of meat imaginable—often one order will serve many. Beefsteak *a la pobre* comes with a fried egg or two on top, plus onions and french fries. *Longanizas* are Spanish-style sausages.

For something lighter try an empanada, which you can order as a starter or a main course. These come most commonly stuffed with meat, olives, egg, and onions (*pino*), or with cheese (*queso*); occasionally they'll be stuffed with shellfish (*mariscos*). Toasted sandwiches are another option: a *barro luco* consists of slender steak topped with melted cheese, and a *barro jarpa* comes with ham and cheese.

Chileans know their sweets, with foamy meringues topping the list of indulgences, followed closely by *alfajor de manjar* (creamy, caramelized condensed milk smashed between wafers and bathed in chocolate). The German immigrants who came to the Lake District a century ago brought their tasty *küchen,* rich fruit-filled pastries. Spring and summer sunshine brings to life an unparalleled Chilean ice-cream culture; parlors line almost every pedestrian walkway, and vats filled with exotic fruit flavors tempt even the most dedicated of dieters.

MEALTIMES

Lunch, which usually begins at 1 or 2, is the most important meal of the day. It can take two hours or more. Some Chileans forgo dinner, making do with an *once,* a light evening meal similar in style to a high tea. Many restaurants have once meals, which include a sandwich (often ham and cheese), fresh juice, tea, and a dessert. Once is served from 5 to 8; dinner is eaten later than in North America, usually starting anywhere from 8 to 10. Unless otherwise noted, the restaurants listed in this guide are open daily for lunch and dinner.

PAYING

Credit cards are widely accepted at restaurants in Santiago and most other cities in Chile. In small villages restaurants may not accept credit cards, so it's advisable to carry cash.

RESERVATIONS & DRESS

Reservations are always a good idea; we mention them only when they're essential or not accepted. Book as far ahead as you can, and reconfirm as soon as you arrive. (Large parties should always call ahead to check the reservations policy.) For the most part, the dress code for restaurants is fairly casual in Chile. We mention dress only when men are required to wear a jacket or a jacket and tie.

WINE, BEER & SPIRITS

The national drink is *pisco,* a brandy distilled from small grapes. A pisco sour, a tangy cocktail, is made from pisco, fresh lemon juice, ice, and sugar. It is sometimes topped off with a thin layer of whisked egg white. Several Chilean wines, especially cabernet sauvignons, are on par with top European and American counterparts. They are also a terrific value. Local beer labels include Escudo, Royal, Becker, and Kunstmann, a tasty brew from Valdivia; Imperial, based in Punta Arenas, claims to be the world's most southerly brewery.

ELECTRICITY

Unlike the United States and Canada—which have a 110- to 120-volt standard—the current in Chile is 220 volts, 50 cycles alternating current (AC). The wall sockets accept plugs with two round prongs. To use electric-powered equipment purchased in the United States or Canada, **bring a converter and adapter.**

If your appliances are dual-voltage, as are most laptop computers, you'll need only an adapter. Don't use 110-volt outlets marked FOR SHAVERS ONLY for high-wattage appliances such as blow-dryers. Most laptops operate equally well on 110 and 220 volts and so require only an adapter.

EMBASSIES

🚩 Australia **Chile** ✉ 10 Culgoa Circuit O'Malley, Monaco Crescent, ACT 2606 Australia ☎ 262/862–2430.
🚩 Canada **Chile** ✉ 50 O'Conner St., Suite 1413, Ottawa, Ontario K1P 5A9 Canada ☎ 613/235–4402.
🚩 Chile **Australia** ✉ Isidora Goyenechea 3621, Piso 12–13, Las Condes, Santiago ☎ 2/550–3500. **Canada** ✉ Nueva Tajamar 481, Piso 12, Torre Norte, Las Condes, Santiago ☎ 2/362–9660. **New Zealand**

✉ El Golf 99, Oficina 703, Las Condes, Santiago ☎ 2/290–9800. **United Kingdom** ✉ Av. El Bosque Norte 0125, Piso 3, Las Condes, Santiago ☎ 2/231–3737. **United States** ✉ Av. Andrés Bello 2800, Las Condes, Santiago ☎ 2/232–2600.
🚩 New Zealand **Chile** ✉ 19 Bolton St., Wellington, New Zealand ☎ 4/471–6270.
🚩 United Kingdom **Chile** ✉ 12 Devonshire St., London W1G 7DS England ☎ 020/7580–6392.
🚩 United States **Chile** ✉ 1732 Massachusetts Ave. NW, Washington, DC 20036 USA ☎ 202/785–1746.

EMERGENCIES

The numbers to call in case of emergency are the same all over Chile.
🚩 Ambulance ☎ 131. Fire ☎ 132. Police ☎ 133.

ENGLISH-LANGUAGE MEDIA

The *Santiago Times* (www.tcgnews.com/santiagotimes) is an online newspaper that covers news and cultural events. For popular newspapers and magazines in English, check local newsstands and bookstores.

GAY & LESBIAN TRAVEL

Chile, as is the case with other South American countries, is more and more accepting of gay people. The government repealed its law banning gay sex in 1999 and since then has considered granting domestic partner benefits for gay couples.

There are gay bars and clubs in Santiago, where there is a small gay enclave in the Bellavista neighborhood, and a few other cities such as Iquique and Viña del Mar.

GAY & LESBIAN WEB SITES

For specific information about Chile's gay scene, try the online Gay Chile (www.gaychile.com). It lists all the local gay bars and clubs and gay-friendly businesses. Another good site is Santiago Gay (www.santiagogay.com). The best site online for general information about gay travel is Out and About (www.outandabout.com). Here you can scour through the back issues for information on gay-friendly destinations. You also can try PlanetOut (www.planetout.com/travel) and Gay.Com (www.gay.com), two general-interest gay sites.
🚩 Gay- & Lesbian-Friendly Travel Agencies **Different Roads Travel** ✉ 1017 N. LaCienega Blvd., Suite 308, West Hollywood, CA 90069 ☎ 800/429–8747 or 310/289–6000 [Ext. 14 for both] 🖷 310/855–

0323 ✎ lgernert@tzell.com. **Kennedy Travel**
✉ 130 W. 42nd St., Suite 401, New York, NY 10036
☎ 800/237-7433 or 212/840-8659 🖷 212/730-2269
⊕ www.kennedytravel.com. **Now, Voyager** ✉ 4406
18th St., San Francisco, CA 94114 ☎ 800/255-6951 or
415/626-1169 🖷 415/626-8626 ⊕ www.nowvoyager.
com. **Skylink Travel and Tour/Flying Dutchmen
Travel** ✉ 1455 N. Dutton Ave., Suite A, Santa Rosa,
CA 95401 ☎ 800/225-5759 or 707/546-9888
🖷 707/636-0951; serving lesbian travelers.

HEALTH
From a health standpoint, Chile is one of
the safer countries in which to travel. To
be on the safe side, **take the normal precautions** you would traveling anywhere in
South America.

In Santiago there are several large private
clinicas (clinics; ⇨ Santiago Essentials *in*
Chapter 1), and many doctors can speak
at least a bit of English. In most other
large cities there are one or two private
clinics where you can be seen quickly.
Generally, *hospitales* (hospitals) are for
those receiving free or heavily subsidized
treatment, and they are often crowded
with long lines of patients waiting to
be seen.

ALTITUDE SICKNESS
Altitude sickness—which causes shortness
of breath, nausea, and splitting
headaches—may be a problem when you
visit Andean countries. The best way to
prevent *soroche* is to **ascend slowly.** Spend
a few nights at 6,000–9,000 feet before
you head higher. If you must fly straight
in, plan on doing next to nothing for your
first few days. The traditional remedy is
herbal tea made from coca leaves. Over-
the-counter analgesics and napping also
help. If symptoms persist, return to lower
elevations. Note that if you have high
blood pressure and/or a history of heart
trouble, check with your doctor before
traveling to the mountains.

AIR POLLUTION
When it comes to air quality, Santiago
ranks as one of the most polluted cities in
the world. The reason is that the city is
surrounded by two mountain ranges that
keep the pollutants from cars and other
sources from dissipating. The pollution is
worse in winter, when wind and rainfall
levels are at their lowest.

What to do? First and foremost, avoid the
traffic-clogged streets when air pollution
levels are high. Santiago has a wonderful
subway that will whisk you to almost
anywhere you want to go. Spend your
days in museums and other indoor attractions. And take advantage of the city's
many parks.

DIVERS' ALERT
Scuba divers take note: **Do not fly within
24 hours of scuba diving.**

Neophyte divers should have a complete
physical exam before undertaking a dive.
If you have travel insurance, **make sure
your policy applies to scuba-related in-
juries,** as not all companies provide this
coverage.

FOOD & DRINK
Visitors seldom encounter problems with
drinking the water in Chile. Almost all
drinking water receives proper treatment
and is unlikely to produce health problems. If you have any doubts, stick to bottled water. Mineral water is good and
comes carbonated (*con gas*) and noncar-
bonated (*sin gas*).

Food preparation is strictly regulated by
the government, so outbreaks of food-
borne diseases are very rare. But it's still a
good idea to use the same commonsense
rules you would in any other part of South
America. Don't risk restaurants where the
hygiene is suspect or street vendors where
the food is allowed to sit around at room
temperature. To be on the safe side, **avoid
raw shellfish,** such as seviche. Remember
to **steer clear of raw fruits and vegetables**
unless you know they've been thoroughly
washed and disinfected.

MEDICAL PLANS
No one plans to get sick while traveling,
but it happens, so consider signing up with
a medical-assistance company. Members
get doctor referrals, emergency evacuation
or repatriation, hotlines for medical con-
sultation, cash for emergencies, and other
assistance.
🌏 **Medical-Assistance Companies International
SOS Assistance** ⊕ www.internationalsos.com

3600 Horizon Blvd., Suite 300, Trevose, PA 19053 ☎ 800/523-6586 or 215/942-8000 🖷 215/354-2338 ✉ Landmark House, Hammersmith Bridge Rd., 6th fl., London W6 9DP ☎ 20/8762-8008 🖷 20/8748-7744 ✉ 12 Chemin Riantbosson, 1217 Meyrin 1, Geneva, Switzerland ☎ 22/785-6464 🖷 22/785-6424 ✉ 331 N. Bridge Rd., 17-00, Odeon Towers, Singapore 188720 ☎ 6338-7800 🖷 6338-7611.

OVER-THE-COUNTER REMEDIES

Mild cases of diarrhea may respond to Imodium (known generically as loperamide), Pepto-Bismol (not as strong), and Lomotil. Drink plenty of purified water or tea—chamomile (*manzanilla* in Spanish) is a good folk remedy.

You will need to visit a *farmacia* (pharmacy) to purchase medications such as Tylenol and *aspirina* (aspirin), which are readily available. Pharmacists can often recommend a medicine for your condition, but they are not always certain of the dosage. Quite often the packaging comes with no instructions unless the drug is imported, in which case it will cost two or three times the price of a local product.

SHOTS & MEDICATIONS

All travelers to Chile should get up-to-date tetanus, diphtheria, and measles boosters, and a hepatitis A inoculation is recommended. Children traveling to Chile should have current inoculations against mumps, rubella, and polio. Always **check with your doctor** about which shots to get.

According to the Centers for Disease Control and Prevention, there's some risk of food-borne diseases such as hepatitis A and typhoid. There's no risk of contracting malaria, but a limited risk of several other insect-borne diseases, including dengue fever. They are usually restricted to jungle areas. The best way to avoid insect-borne diseases is to **prevent insect bites** by wearing long pants and long-sleeve shirts and by using insect repellents with DEET. If you plan to visit remote regions or stay for more than six weeks, **check with the CDC's International Travelers Hot Line.**

🚩 **Health Warnings National Centers for Disease Control and Prevention** (CDC) ✉ Office of Health Communication, National Center for Infectious Diseases, Division of Quarantine, Travelers' Health, 1600 Clifton Rd. NE, Atlanta, GA 30333 ☎ 877/394-8747 international travelers' health line, 800/311-3435 other inquiries, 404/498-1600 Division of Quarantine and international health information 🖷 888/232-3299 ⊕ www.cdc.gov/travel. **Travel Health Online** ⊕ tripprep.com. **World Health Organization** (WHO) ⊕ www.who.int.

HOLIDAYS

New Year's Day (January 1), Labor Day (May 1), Day of Naval Glories (May 21), Corpus Christi (in June), Feast of St. Peter and St. Paul (June 29), Independence Celebrations (September 18), Discovery of the Americas (October 12), Day of the Dead (November 1), Immaculate Conception (December 8), Christmas (December 25).

Many shops and services are open on most of these days, but transportation is always heavily booked up on and around the holidays. The two most important dates in the Chilean calendar are September 18 and New Year's Day. On these days shops close and public transportation is reduced to the bare minimum or is nonexistent. Trying to book a ticket around these dates will be impossible unless you do it well in advance.

INSURANCE

The most useful travel-insurance plan is a comprehensive policy that includes coverage for trip cancellation and interruption, default, trip delay, and medical expenses (with a waiver for preexisting conditions).

Without insurance you'll lose all or most of your money if you cancel your trip, regardless of the reason. Default insurance covers you if your tour operator, airline, or cruise line goes out of business—the chances of which have been increasing. Trip-delay covers expenses that arise because of bad weather or mechanical delays. Study the fine print when comparing policies.

If you're traveling internationally, a key component of travel insurance is coverage for medical bills incurred if you get sick on the road. Such expenses aren't generally covered by Medicare or private policies. U.K. residents can buy a travel-insurance policy valid for most vacations taken during the year in which it's purchased (but check preexisting-condition coverage). British and Australian citizens need extra medical coverage when traveling overseas.

Always **buy travel policies directly from the insurance company**; if you buy them from a cruise line, airline, or tour operator that goes out of business you probably won't be covered for the agency or operator's default, a major risk. Before making any purchase, review your existing health and home-owner's policies to find what they cover away from home.

Travel Insurers In the United States: **Access America** ✉ 2805 N. Parham Rd., Richmond, VA 23294 ☎ 800/284-8300 🖷 800/346-9265 or 804/673-1469 ⊕ www.accessamerica.com. **Travel Guard International** ✉ 1145 Clark St., Stevens Point, WI 54481 ☎ 800/826-1300 or 715/345-1041 🖷 800/955-8785 or 715/345-1990 ⊕ www.travelguard.com. **In the United Kingdom: Association of British Insurers** ✉ 51 Gresham St., London EC2V 7HQ ☎ 020/7600-3333 🖷 020/7696-8999 ⊕ www.abi.org.uk. In Canada: **RBC Insurance** ✉ 6880 Financial Dr., Mississauga, Ontario L5N 7Y5 ☎ 800/387-4357 or 905/816-2559 🖷 888/298-6458 ⊕ www.rbcinsurance.com. In Australia: **Insurance Council of Australia** ✉ Level 3, 56 Pitt St., Sydney, NSW 2000 ☎ 02/9253-5100 🖷 02/9253-5111 ⊕ www.ica.com.au. In New Zealand: **Insurance Council of New Zealand** ✉ Level 7, 111-115 Customhouse Quay, Box 474, Wellington ☎ 04/472-5230 🖷 04/473-3011 ⊕ www.icnz.org.nz.

INTERNET ACCESS

Chileans are generally savvy about the Internet, which is reflected by the number of Internet cafés around the country. Connection fees are generally no more than $1 for an hour. Very few hotels have wireless connections, but almost all have in-room data ports or a computer where you can get online.

LANGUAGE

Chile's official language is Spanish, so it's best to learn at least a few words and carry a good phrase book. Chilean Spanish is fast, clipped, and chock-full of colloquialisms. For example, the word for police officer isn't *policía*, but *carabinero*. Even foreigners with a good deal of experience in Spanish-speaking countries may feel like they are encountering a completely new

language. However, receptionists at most upscale hotels speak English.

When giving directions, Chileans seldom use left and right, indicating the way instead with a mixture of sign language and *para acá, para allá* (toward here, toward there) instructions.

LANGUAGES FOR TRAVELERS

A phrase book and language-tape set can help get you started. *Fodor's Spanish for Travelers* (available at bookstores everywhere) is excellent.

LODGING

Assume that hotels operate on the European Plan (EP, with no meals) unless we specify that they use the Continental Plan (CP, with a Continental breakfast), Breakfast Plan (BP, with a full breakfast), Modified American Plan (MAP, with breakfast and dinner), or the Full American Plan (FAP, with all meals).

The lodgings (all indicated with a 🏠 symbol) that we list are the cream of the crop in each price category. We always list the facilities that are available—but we don't specify whether they cost extra: when pricing accommodations, always ask what's included and what costs extra. All hotels listed have private bath unless otherwise noted. Properties indicated by ✕🏠 are lodging establishments whose restaurant warrants a special trip.

It's always good to **look at any room before accepting it.** Expense is no guarantee of charm or cleanliness, and accommodations can vary dramatically within one hotel. If you ask for a double room, you'll get a room for two people, but you're not guaranteed a double mattress. If you'd like to avoid twin beds, ask for a *cama de matrimonio.* Many older hotels in Chile have rooms with wrought-iron balconies or spacious terraces; ask if there's a room *con balcón* or *con terraza* when checking in.

Hotels in Chile do not charge taxes to foreign tourists. Knowing this in advance can save you some cash. When checking the price, make sure to ask for the *precio extranjero, sin impuestos* (foreign rate, without taxes).

Also, note that you can always ask for a *descuento* (discount) out of season or sometimes midweek during high season.

APARTMENT & VILLA [OR HOUSE] RENTALS

If you want a home base that's roomy enough for a family and comes with cooking facilities, consider a furnished rental. These can save you money, especially if you're traveling with a group. Home-exchange directories sometimes list rentals as well as exchanges.

International Agents Hideaways International ⊠ 767 Islington St., Portsmouth, NH 03801 ☎ 800/843-4433 or 603/430-4433 🖷 603/430-4444 ⊕ www.hideaways.com, annual membership $185.

HOME EXCHANGES

If you would like to exchange your home for someone else's, join a home-exchange organization, which will send you its updated listings of available exchanges for a year and will include your own listing in at least one of them. It's up to you to make specific arrangements.

Exchange Club HomeLink USA ⊠ 2937 N.W. 9th Terr., Wilton Manors, FL 33311 ☎ 800/638-3841 or 954/566-2687 🖷 954/566-2783 ⊕ www.homelink.org; $75 yearly for a listing and online access; $45 additional to receive directories.

HOSTELS

No matter what your age, you can save on lodging costs by staying at hostels. Youth hostels in Chile are not very popular, perhaps due to the prevalence of *residenciales* and other low-cost lodging. Still, Hostelling International (HI), the umbrella group for a number of national youth-hostel associations, offers single-sex, dorm-style beds and, at many hostels, rooms for couples and family accommodations. Membership in any HI national hostel association, open to travelers of all ages, allows you to stay in HI-affiliated hostels at member rates; one-year membership is about $28 for adults (C$35 for a two-year minimum membership in Canada, £15 in the United Kingdom, A$52 in Australia, and NZ$40 in New Zealand); hostels charge about $10–$30 per night. Members have priority if the hostel is full; they're also eligible for discounts around the

world, even on rail and bus travel in some countries.

Organizations Hostelling International-USA ⊠ 8401 Colesville Rd., Suite 600, Silver Spring, MD 20910 ☎ 301/495-1240 🖷 301/495-6697 ⊕ www.hiusa.org. **Hostelling International-Canada** ⊠ 205 Catherine St., Suite 400, Ottawa, Ontario K2P 1C3 ☎ 800/663-5777 or 613/237-7884 🖷 613/237-7868 ⊕ www.hihostels.ca. **YHA England and Wales** ⊠ Trevelyan House, Dimple Rd., Matlock, Derbyshire DE4 3YH U.K. ☎ 0870/870-8808, 0870/770-8868, 0162/959-2600 🖷 0870/770-6127 ⊕ www.yha.org.uk. **YHA Australia** ⊠ 422 Kent St., Sydney, NSW 2001 ☎ 02/9261-1111 🖷 02/9261-1969 ⊕ www.yha.com.au. **YHA New Zealand** ⊠ Level 1, Moorhouse City, 166 Moorhouse Ave., Box 436, Christchurch ☎ 0800/278-299 or 03/379-9970 🖷 03/365-4476 ⊕ www.yha.org.nz.

HOTELS

All hotels listed have private bath unless otherwise noted.

Chile's urban areas and resort areas have hotels that come with all of the amenities that are taken for granted in North America and Europe, such as room service, a restaurant, or a swimming pool. Elsewhere you may not have television or a phone in your room, although you will find them somewhere in the hotel. Rooms that have a private bath may have only a shower, and in some cases, there will be a shared bath in the hall. In all but the most upscale hotels, you may be asked to leave your key at the reception desk whenever you leave.

Chain Hotels Best Western ☎ 800/528-1234 ⊕ www.bestwestern.com. **Choice** ☎ 800/424-6423 ⊕ www.choicehotels.com. **Holiday Inn** ☎ 800/465-4329 ⊕ www.ichotelsgroup.com. **Hyatt Hotels & Resorts** ☎ 800/233-1234 ⊕ www.hyatt.com. **Inter-Continental** ☎ 800/327-0200 ⊕ www.ichotelsgroup.com. **Marriott** ☎ 800/228-9290 ⊕ www.marriott.com. **Quality Inn** ☎ 800/424-6423 ⊕ www.choicehotels.com. **Radisson** ☎ 800/333-3333 ⊕ www.radisson.com. **Ritz-Carlton** ☎ 800/241-3333 ⊕ www.ritzcarlton.com. **Sheraton** ☎ 800/325-3535 ⊕ www.starwood.com/sheraton.

RESIDENCIALES

Private homes that rent rooms, *residenciales,* are a unique way to get to know Chile, especially if you're on a budget. Sometimes residenciales are small, very basic accommodations and not necessarily private homes. *Hospedajes* are similar. Many rent rooms for less than $10. Some will be shabby, but others can be substantially better than hotel rooms. They also offer the added benefit of allowing you to interact with locals, though they are unlikely to speak English. Contact the local tourist office for details on residenciales and hospedajes.

MAIL & SHIPPING

The postal system is efficient, and, on average, letters take five–seven days to reach the United States, Europe, Australia, and New Zealand. They will arrive sooner if you send them *prioritaria* (priority) post, but the price will almost double. You can send them *certificado* (registered), in which case the recipient will need to sign for them. Vendors often sell stamps at the entrances to larger post offices, which can save you a potentially long wait in line—the stamps are valid, and selling them this way is legal.

OVERNIGHT SERVICES

Federal Express has offices in Santiago and operates an international overnight service. DHL, with offices in Santiago and most cities throughout Chile, provides overnight service. If you want to send a package to North America, Europe, Australia, or New Zealand, it will take one–four days, depending on where you're sending it from in Chile.

Chile's post office can ship overnight parcels of up to 33 kilograms (73 pounds) within Chile and internationally. ChileExpress and LanCourier also offer overnight services between most cities within Chile.
🔢 **Major Services ChileExpress** ☎ 800/200-102. **DHL** ☎ 800/800-345. **Federal Express** ☎ 800/ 363-030. **LanCourier** ☎ 800/800-400.

POSTAL RATES

Postage on regular letters and postcards to Canada and the United States costs 250 pesos and 230 pesos, respectively. The postage to Australia, the United Kingdom, and New Zealand is 290 pesos for letters and postcards.

RECEIVING MAIL

If you wish to receive a parcel in Chile and don't have a specific address to which it can be sent, then you can have it labeled *poste restante* and sent to the nearest post office.

SHIPPING PARCELS

A cheap, reliable method for sending parcels is to use the Chilean postal system, which although slow—up to 15 business days—is still reliable for sending packages weighing up to 33 kilograms (73 pounds). Shipping a small parcel of 2 kilograms (4 pounds) will cost 10,000 pesos to North America, 15,000 pesos to Europe, and 20,640 pesos to Australia and New Zealand. Express service is also available.

MONEY MATTERS

Credit cards and traveler's checks are accepted in most resorts and in many shops and restaurants in major cities, though you should **always carry some local currency** for minor expenses like taxis and tipping. Once you stray from the beaten path, you can often pay only with pesos.

Typically you will pay 500 pesos for a cup of coffee, 1,200 pesos for a glass of beer in a bar, 1,200 pesos for a ham sandwich, and 800 pesos for an average museum admission.

Prices throughout this guide are given for adults. Substantially reduced fees are almost always available for children, students, and senior citizens. For information on taxes, *see* Taxes.

ATMS

ATMs are widely available, and you can get cash with a Cirrus- or Plus-linked debit card or with a major credit card. Most ATMs in Chile have a special screen—accessed after entering your PIN code—for foreign-account withdrawals. In this case, you need to access your account first via the "foreign client" option. ATMs offer excellent exchange rates because they are based on wholesale rates offered only by major banks.
🔢 **ATM Locations MasterCard Cirrus** ☎ 800/424-7787 ⊕ www.mastercard.com. **Visa Plus** ☎ 800/ 843-7587 ⊕ www.visa.com.

CREDIT CARDS

Credit cards are widely accepted in hotels, restaurants, and shops in most cities and tourist destinations. Fewer establishments accept credit cards in rural areas. It may be easier to **use your credit card whenever possible.** The exchange rate varies by only a fraction of a cent, so you won't need to worry about whether your purchase is charged on the day of purchase or at some point in the future. Note, however, that you may get a slightly better deal if you pay with cash.

Throughout this guide, the following abbreviations are used: **AE,** American Express; **DC,** Diners Club; **MC,** MasterCard; and **V,** Visa.

Reporting Lost Cards American Express ☎ 801/964-6665 in U.S. **MasterCard** ☎ 1230/020-2012 in Chile (no carrier required). **Visa** ☎ 1230/020-2136 in Chile.

CURRENCY

The peso ($) is the unit of currency in Chile. Chilean bills are issued in 1,000, 2,000, 5,000, 10,000, and 20,000 pesos, and coins come in units of 1, 5, 10, 50, 100, and 500 pesos. Note that acquiring change for larger bills, especially from small shopkeepers, can be difficult. Make sure to **get smaller bills** when you exchange currency. Always **check exchange rates** in your local newspaper for the most current information; at press time, the exchange rate was approximately 378 pesos to the Australian dollar, 439 pesos to the Canadian dollar, 514 pesos to the U.S. dollar, 904 pesos to the British pound, and 351 pesos to the New Zealand dollar.

CURRENCY EXCHANGE

For the most favorable rates, **change money through banks.** Although ATM transaction fees may be higher abroad than at home, ATM rates are excellent because they're based on wholesale rates offered only by major banks. You won't do as well at exchange booths in airports or rail and bus stations, in hotels, in restaurants, or in stores. To avoid lines at airport exchange booths, get a bit of local currency before you leave home.

Exchange Services International Currency Express ✉ 427 N. Camden Dr., Suite F, Beverly Hills, CA 90210 ☎ 888/278-6628 orders 🖷 310/278-6410 ⊕ www.foreignmoney.com. **Travel Ex Currency Services** ☎ 800/287-7362 orders and retail locations ⊕ www.travelex.com.

TRAVELER'S CHECKS

Do you need traveler's checks? It depends on where you're headed. If you're going to rural areas and small towns, go with cash; traveler's checks are best used in cities. Lost or stolen checks can usually be replaced within 24 hours. To ensure a speedy refund, buy your own traveler's checks—don't let someone else pay for them: irregularities like this can cause delays. The person who bought the checks should make the call to request a refund.

PACKING

For a trip to Chile you'll need to **pack for all seasons**—no matter what time of year you're traveling. For sightseeing and leisure, casual clothing and good walking shoes are both desirable and appropriate. Travel in the forests requires long-sleeve shirts, long pants, socks, sneakers, a hat, a light waterproof jacket, a bathing suit, and insect repellent. Light colors are best, since mosquitoes avoid them. If you're visiting Patagonia or the Andes, bring a jacket and sweater or a fleece pullover. A high-factor sunscreen is essential at all times, especially in the far south where the ozone layer is much depleted.

Other useful items include a screw-top water bottle that you can fill with bottled water, a money pouch, a travel flashlight and extra batteries, a Swiss Army knife with a bottle opener, a medical kit, binoculars, and a pocket calculator to help with currency conversions. A sarong or light cotton blanket can have many uses: beach towel, picnic blanket, and cushion for hard seats, among other things. You can never have too many large resealable plastic bags, which are ideal for storing film, protecting things from rain and damp, and quarantining stinky socks.

To avoid customs and security delays, carry medications in their original packaging. **Never pack prescription drugs,**

valuables, or undeveloped film in luggage to be checked.

To avoid having your checked luggage chosen for hand inspection, don't cram bags full. The U.S. Transportation Security Administration suggests packing shoes on top and placing personal items you don't want touched in clear plastic bags.

CHECKING LUGGAGE

Baggage allowances vary by carrier, destination, and ticket class. On international flights, you're usually allowed to check two bags weighing up to 70 pounds (32 kilograms) each, although a few airlines allow checked bags of up to 88 pounds (40 kilograms) in first class. Some international carriers don't allow more than 66 pounds (30 kilograms) per bag in business class and 44 pounds (20 kilograms) in economy. If you're flying to or through the United Kingdom, your luggage cannot exceed 70 pounds (32 kilograms) per bag. On domestic flights, the limit is usually 50 to 70 pounds (23 to 32 kilograms) per bag. In general, carry-on bags shouldn't exceed 40 pounds (18 kilograms). Most airlines won't accept bags that weigh more than 100 pounds (45 kilograms) on domestic or international flights. Expect to pay a fee for baggage that exceeds weight limits. Check baggage restrictions with your carrier before you pack.

Airline liability for baggage is limited to $2,500 per person on flights within the United States. On international flights it amounts to $9.07 per pound or $20 per kilogram for checked baggage (roughly $640 per 70-pound bag), with a maximum of $634.90 per piece, and $400 per passenger for unchecked baggage. You can buy additional coverage at check-in for about $10 per $1,000 of coverage, but it often excludes a rather extensive list of items, shown on your airline ticket.

If your bag has been searched and contents are missing or damaged, file a claim with the U.S. Transportation Security Administration (TSA) Consumer Response Center as soon as possible. If your bags arrive damaged or fail to arrive at all, file a writ-ten report with the airline before leaving the airport.

⌗ Complaints U.S. Transportation Security Administration Contact Center ☎ 866/289-9673 ⊕ www.tsa.gov.

PASSPORTS & VISAS

When traveling internationally, carry your passport even if you don't need one. Not only is it the best form of ID, but it's also being required more and more. As of December 31, 2005, for instance, Americans need a passport to reenter the country from Bermuda, the Caribbean, and Panama. Such requirements also affect reentry from Canada and Mexico by air and sea (as of December 31, 2006) and land (as of December 31, 2007). **Make two photocopies of the data page** (one for someone at home and another for you, carried separately from your passport). If you lose your passport, promptly call the nearest embassy or consulate and the local police.

While traveling in Chile you might want to carry the copy of your passport and leave the original in your hotel safe. If you plan on paying by credit card you will often be asked to show identification or at least write down your passport number.

U.S. passport applications for children under age 14 require consent from both parents or legal guardians; both parents must appear together to sign the application. If only one parent appears, he or she must submit a written statement from the other parent authorizing passport issuance for the child. A parent with sole authority must present evidence of it when applying; acceptable documentation includes the child's certified birth certificate listing only the applying parent, a court order specifically permitting this parent's travel with the child, or a death certificate for the nonapplying parent. Application forms and instructions are available on the Web site of the U.S. State Department's Bureau of Consular Affairs (⊕ travel.state.gov).

ENTERING CHILE

American citizens must pay a "reciprocity" fee (to balance out fees Chileans pay upon entering the United States) of $100. Canadian and Australian citizens pay $55 and $30, respectively. The good news is that in addition to cash, credit cards are now also accepted. A departure tax of $18 is included in the cost of your ticket.

Citizens of the United States, Canada, Australia, New Zealand, and the United Kingdom need only a passport to enter Chile for up to three months.

Upon arrival in Chile, you will be given a flimsy piece of paper that is your three-month tourist visa. This has to be handed in when you leave; because getting a new one involves waiting in many lines and a lot of bureaucracy, put it somewhere safe.

PASSPORT OFFICES

The best time to apply for a passport or to renew is in fall and winter. Before any trip, check your passport's expiration date, and, if necessary, renew it as soon as possible.

Australian Citizens Passports Australia Australian Department of Foreign Affairs and Trade ☎ 131-232 ⊕ www.passports.gov.au.

Canadian Citizens Passport Office ✉ To mail in applications: 70 Cremazie St., Gatineau, Québec J8Y 3P2 ☎ 800/567-6868 or 819/994-3500 ⊕ www.ppt.gc.ca.

New Zealand Citizens New Zealand Passports Office ☎ 0800/22-5050 or 04/474-8100 ⊕ www.passports.govt.nz.

U.K. Citizens U.K. Passport Service ☎ 0870/521-0410 ⊕ www.passport.gov.uk.

U.S. Citizens National Passport Information Center ☎ 877/487-2778, 888/874-7793 TDD/TTY ⊕ travel.state.gov.

SAFETY

The vast majority of visitors to Chile never experience a problem with crime. Violent crime is a rarity; far more common is pickpocketing or thefts from purses, backpacks, or rental cars. Be on your guard in crowded places, especially markets and festivals.

Don't wear a money belt or a waist pack, both of which peg you as a tourist. Distribute your cash and any valuables (including your credit cards and passport) between a deep front pocket, an inside jacket or vest pocket, and a hidden money pouch. Do not reach for the money pouch once you're in public.

Wherever you go, **don't wear expensive clothing or flashy jewelry,** and **don't handle money in public. Keep cameras in a secure camera bag,** preferably one with a chain or wire embedded in the strap. Always **remain alert for pickpockets,** and **don't walk alone at night,** especially in the larger cities.

Volcano climbing is a popular pastime in Chile, with Volcán Villarrica, near Pucón, and Volcán Osorno the most popular. But some of these mountains are also among South America's most active volcanoes. CONAF, the agency in charge of national parks, cuts off access to any volcano at the slightest hint of out-of-normal activity. Check with CONAF before heading out on any hike in this region.

CONAF ☎ 45/298-221 in Temuco, 2/390-0125 in Santiago ⊕ www.conaf.cl

WOMEN IN CHILE

Many women travel alone or in groups in Chile with no problems. Chilean men are less aggressive in their machismo than men in other South American countries (they will seldom, for example, approach a woman they don't know), but it's still an aspect of the culture (they will make comments when a women walks by). It's a good idea for single women not to walk alone at night, especially in the larger cities.

SENIOR-CITIZEN TRAVEL

There's no reason that active, well-traveled senior citizens (*tercera edad*) shouldn't visit Chile, whether on an independent vacation, an escorted tour, or an adventure vacation. Before you leave home, however, determine what medical services your health insurance will cover outside the United States; note that Medicare doesn't provide for payment of hospital and medical services outside the United States. If you need additional travel insurance, buy it (⇨ Insurance).

Chile is full of good hotels and competent ground operators who will meet your flights and organize your sightseeing. Few museums and sights have discounts for senior citizens, but it's always worth asking. To qualify for age-related discounts, mention your senior-citizen status up front when booking hotel reservations (not when checking out) and before you're seated in restaurants (not when paying the bill). Be sure to have identification on hand. When renting a car, ask about promotional car-rental discounts, which can be cheaper than senior-citizen rates.

⚑ Educational Programs Elderhostel ✉ 11 Ave. de Lafayette, Boston, MA 02111 ☎ 877/426-8056, 978/323-4141 international callers, 877/426-2167 TTY ⎙ 877/426-2166 ⊕ www.elderhostel.org.

SHOPPING

Handicrafts and wine are probably the most popular purchases by visitors to Chile. Wine boutiques and supermarkets carry a tremendous selection of vintages. Handicrafts from across the country are available at crafts markets around Santiago. Generally, most large cities have a craft market selling products from that region, and in summer many host open-air markets in which vendors gather from across Chile.

It's fine to bargain. Normally you can ask a vendor in a market if he or she will accept 10% less than the listed price, or maybe a little more than 10% if the figure is being rounded down to the nearest 1,000 pesos, especially if you're paying cash. This is also acceptable in shops, which are not averse to giving small discounts for cash (al contado/efectivo) sales.

KEY DESTINATIONS

Temuco, in the Lake District, is known for its Mapuche rugs, ponchos, and jewelry. South of Temuco, in Villarica, you can buy salad bowls, spoons, and other products carved from raulí wood. If it's a warm woolen sweater you're after, head to the island of Chiloé.

Rustic clay pottery in all shapes and sizes is sold along the streets of the small village of Pomaire, 70 km (43 mi) west of Santiago. In the city of La Serena, in El Norte Chico, you can buy Diaguita-style ceramics (often with intricate geometric patterns) and trinkets made from combabalita, a local marble.

Santiago, however, sells the best selection of Diaguita-style ceramics as well as lapis lazuli products and Chilean copper bowls and pewter ware.

WATCH OUT

Any item more than 100 years old is categorized as an antique, and though enforcement is spotty you are generally required to obtain special permission to remove antiques from the country. If you have purchased or wish to purchase something and are unsure as to whether it, be it a book, painting, or other item, could be considered an antique, you will need to contact the Biblioteca National, Museo Nacional Bellas Artes, or Monumentos Nacionales, respectively. They will provide the necessary authorization in order for you to take your purchase out of the country.

⚑ Biblioteca National ☎ 2/360-5239. **Museo Nacional Bellas Artes** ☎ 2/633-0655. **Monumentos Nacionales** ☎ 2/420-2008.

STUDENTS IN CHILE

Although airfares to and within South America are high, you can take buses in Chile for mere dollars, and you can usually find safe, comfortable, affordable accommodations for a fraction of what it might cost back home. You can sometimes get student discounts at museums and sights, though you're usually required to show an ID. Many cities, especially Santiago and Valparaíso, have vibrant student populations.

⚑ IDs & Services STA Travel ✉ 10 Downing St., New York, NY 10014 ☎ 800/777-0112 24-hr service center, 212/627-3111 ⎙ 212/627-3387 ⊕ www.sta.com. **Travel Cuts** ✉ 187 College St., Toronto, Ontario M5T 1P7 Canada ☎ 800/592-2887 in U.S., 866/246-9762 or 416/979-2406 in Canada ⎙ 416/979-8167 ⊕ www.travelcuts.com.

TAXES

An 18% value-added tax (VAT, called IVA here) is added to the cost of most goods and services in Chile; often you won't notice because it's included in the price. When it's not, the seller gives you the price plus IVA. At many hotels you may receive an exemption from the IVA if you pay in American dollars or with a credit card.

TELEPHONES

AREA & COUNTRY CODES

The country code for Chile is 56. When dialing a Chilean number from abroad, drop the initial 0 from the local area code. The area code is 2 for Santiago, 58 for Arica, 55 for Antofagasta and San Pedro de Atacama, 42 for Chillán, 57 for Iquique, 56 for La Serena, 65 for Puerto Montt, 61 for Puerto Natales and Punta Arenas, 45 for Temuco, 63 for Valdivia, 32 for Valparaíso and Viña del Mar.

From Chile the country code is 01 for the United States and Canada, 61 for Australia, 64 for New Zealand, and 44 for the United Kingdom.

DIRECTORY & OPERATOR ASSISTANCE

You can reach directory assistance in Chile by calling 103. English-speaking operators are not available.

INTERNATIONAL CALLS

An international call at a public phone requires anywhere from a 400- or 500-peso deposit (depending on the phone box), which will give you anywhere between 47 and 66 seconds of talking time. You can call the United States for between 39 and 76 seconds (depending on the carrier you use) for 200 pesos.

LOCAL CALLS

A 100-peso piece is required to make a local call in a public phone booth, allowing 110 seconds of conversation between the hours of 9 AM and 8 PM, and 160 seconds of talk from 8 PM to 9 AM. Prefix codes are not needed for local dialing.

To call a cell phone within Chile you will need to insert 200 pesos in a phone box.

LONG-DISTANCE CALLS & SERVICES

AT&T, MCI, and Sprint access codes make calling long-distance relatively convenient, but you may find the local access number blocked in many hotel rooms. First ask the hotel operator to connect you. If the hotel operator balks, ask for an international operator, or dial the international operator yourself. One way to improve your odds of getting connected to your long-distance carrier is to travel with more than one company's calling card (a hotel may block Sprint, for example, but not MCI). If all else fails, call from a pay phone. If you are traveling for a longer period of time, consider renting a cell phone from a local company.

F Access Codes AT&T Direct ☎ 800/225-288. MCI Worldcom ☎ 800/444-4444. Sprint Express ☎ 800/793-1153.

PHONE CARDS

If you plan to call abroad while in Chile, it's in your best interest to buy a local phone card (sold in varying amounts at kiosks and calling centers) or use a calling center (*centro de llamadas*). For calls to the United States, EntelTicket phone cards, available in denominations of 1,000, 3,000, and 5,000 pesos, are a good deal. You can buy them in denominations ranging from 1,000 to 15,000 pesos.

PUBLIC PHONES

Having numerous telephone companies means that Chilean public phones all look different. Public phones use either coins (and require a 100-peso deposit) or phone cards. Telefónica and other companies sell telephone cards, but many locals continue to use coins. If you will be making only a few local calls, it's not necessary to purchase a phone card.

Most city areas have standing phone booths, but phones are also found at restaurants, calling centers, and even newsstands. You may have to wait several seconds after picking up the receiver before a steady humming sound signals that you may dial. After dialing, you'll hear a characteristic beep-beep as your call goes through; then there's a pause, followed by a long tone signaling that the other phone is ringing. A busy signal is similar but repeats itself with no pause in between. Some phones also include English-language instructions, accessed by pressing a button marked with a flag icon.

Instead of using a public phone, you can pay a little more and use a *centro de llamadas,* small phone shops divided into booths. Simply step into any available booth and dial the number. The charge will be displayed on a monitor near the phone.

TIME
Chile is one hour ahead of Eastern Standard Time and four hours ahead of Pacific Standard Time. Daylight saving time in Chile begins in October and ends in March.

TIPPING
The usual tip, or *propina,* in restaurants is 10%. Leave more if you really enjoyed the service. City taxi drivers don't usually expect a tip because most own their cabs. However, if you hire a taxi to take you around a city, you should consider giving a good tip. Hotel porters should be tipped at least 500 pesos per bag. Also give doormen and ushers about 500 pesos. Beauty- and barber-shop personnel generally get around 5%.

TOURS & PACKAGES
Because everything is prearranged on a prepackaged tour or independent vacation, you spend less time planning—and often get it all at a good price.

BOOKING WITH AN AGENT
Travel agents are excellent resources. But it's a good idea to collect brochures from several agencies, as some agents' suggestions may be influenced by relationships with tour and package firms that reward them for volume sales. If you have a special interest, find an agent with expertise in that area. The American Society of Travel Agents (ASTA) has a database of specialists worldwide; you can log on to the group's Web site to find one near you.

Make sure your travel agent knows the accommodations and other services of the place being recommended. Ask about the hotel's location, room size, beds, and whether it has a pool, room service, or programs for children, if you care about these. Has your agent been there in person or sent others whom you can contact?

Do some homework on your own, too: local tourism boards can provide information about lesser-known and small-niche operators, some of which may sell only direct.

BUYER BEWARE
Each year consumers are stranded or lose their money when tour operators—even large ones with excellent reputations—go out of business. So check out the operator. Ask several travel agents about its reputation, and try to **book with a company that has a consumer-protection program.** (Look for information in the company's brochure.) In the United States, members of the United States Tour Operators Association are required to set aside funds (up to $1 million) to help eligible customers cover payments and travel arrangements in the event that the company defaults. It's also a good idea to choose a company that participates in the American Society of Travel Agents' Tour Operator Program; ASTA will act as mediator in any disputes between you and your tour operator.

Remember that the more your package or tour includes, the better you can predict the ultimate cost of your vacation. Make sure you know exactly what is covered, and beware of hidden costs. Are taxes, tips, and transfers included? Entertainment and excursions? These can add up.

⁊ Tour-Operator Recommendations American Society of Travel Agents (⇨ Travel Agencies). **CrossSphere–The Global Association for Packaged Travel** ✉ 546 E. Main St., Lexington, KY 40508 ☎ 800/682-8886 or 859/226-4444 🖷 859/226-4414 ⊕ www.CrossSphere.com. **United States Tour Operators Association** (USTOA) ✉ 275 Madison Ave., Suite 2014, New York, NY 10016 ☎ 212/599-6599 🖷 212/599-6744 ⊕ www.ustoa.com.

TRAIN TRAVEL
Good train service is a thing of the past in Chile, though there is still limited service from Santiago to points south. Empresa de Los Ferrocarriles del Estado, better known as EFE, offers daily departures between Santiago and Temuco, but be prepared for a slow journey—if the train runs according to schedule it should take around nine hours. Reservations can be made in Santiago at the Estación Central or at the Estación Metro Universidad de Chile, online at the company's Web site (only in Spanish), or through a travel agent.

A journey between Santiago and Rancagua takes about an hour and costs between

4,500 and 10,000 pesos, depending on when you travel and the level of service you prefer. A trip between Santiago and Chillán takes 4¼ hours and costs 9,000 to 15,000 pesos. A sleeper between Santiago and Temuco takes 9 hours and costs 10,000 to 20,000 pesos.

⚑ Train Information EFE ☏ 2/585-5000 ⊕ www.efe.cl.

TRANSPORTATION AROUND CHILE

Distances are great in Chile, so if you're going to spend just one or two weeks here, it's best to fly to your destinations. If you have more time to spare, consider using buses, which are both cheap and dependable.

However, if you really want to get to know Chile well—aside from Santiago, where you can get around on foot, hop on the excellent Metro, or take any one of hundreds of taxis—then consider renting a car. If you plan to visit remote regions, such as the Carretera Austral, or a national park, then you'd be better off with a four-wheel-drive vehicle.

TRAVEL AGENCIES

A good travel agent puts your needs first. Look for an agency that has been in business at least five years, emphasizes customer service, and has someone on staff who specializes in your destination. In addition, **make sure the agency belongs to a professional trade organization.** The American Society of Travel Agents (ASTA) has more than 10,000 members in some 140 countries, enforces a strict code of ethics, and will step in to mediate agent-client disputes involving ASTA members. ASTA also maintains a directory of agents on its Web site; ASTA's TravelSense.org, a trip-planning and travel-advice site, can also help to locate a travel agent who caters to your needs. (If a travel agency is also acting as your tour operator, *see* Buyer Beware *in* Tours & Packages.)

⚑ Local Agent Referrals American Society of Travel Agents (ASTA) ✉ 1101 King St., Suite 200, Alexandria, VA 22314 ☏ 800/965-2782 or 703/739-2782 24-hr hotline 🖷 703/684-8319 ⊕ www.astanet.com and www.travelsense.org. **Association**

of British Travel Agents ✉ 68-71 Newman St., London W1T 3AH ☏ 020/7637-2444 🖷 020/7637-0713 ⊕ www.abta.com. **Association of Canadian Travel Agencies** ✉ 130 Albert St., Suite 1705, Ottawa, Ontario K1P 5G4 ☏ 613/237-3657 🖷 613/237-7052 ⊕ www.acta.ca. **Australian Federation of Travel Agents** ✉ Level 3, 309 Pitt St., Sydney, NSW 2000 ☏ 02/9264-3299 or 1300/363-416 🖷 02/9264-1085 ⊕ www.afta.com.au. **Travel Agents' Association of New Zealand** ✉ Level 5, Tourism and Travel House, 79 Boulcott St., Box 1888, Wellington 6001 ☏ 04/499-0104 🖷 04/499-0786 ⊕ www.taanz.org.nz.

VISITOR INFORMATION

The national tourist office Sernatur (Servicio Nacional de Turismo) has branches in Santiago and in major tourist destinations around the country. Sernatur offices, often the best source for general information about a region, are generally open daily from 9 to 6, with lunch generally from 2 to 3.

Municipal tourist offices, often located near a central square, usually have better information about their town's sights, restaurants, and lodging. Many have shorter hours or close altogether during low season, however.

Learn more about foreign destinations by checking government-issued travel advisories and country information. For a broader picture, consider information from more than one country.

⚑ Tourist Information Sernatur ✉ Providencia 1550, Providencia, Santiago ☏ 2/731-8336 or 2/731-8337 ⊕ www.sernatur.cl.

⚑ Government Advisories U.S. Department of State ✉ Bureau of Consular Affairs, Overseas Citizens Services Office, 2201 C St. NW, Washington, DC 20520 ☏ 202/647-5225, 888/407-4747 or 317/472-2328 for interactive hotline ⊕ www.travel.state.gov. **Consular Affairs Bureau of Canada** ☏ 800/267-6788 or 613/944-6788 ⊕ www.voyage.gc.ca. **U.K. Foreign and Commonwealth Office** ✉ Travel Advice Unit, Consular Directorate, Old Admiralty Bldg., London SW1A 2PA ☏ 0870/606-0290 or 020/7008-1500 ⊕ www.fco.gov.uk/travel. **Australian Department of Foreign Affairs and Trade** ☏ 300/139-281 travel advisories, 02/6261-1299 Consular Travel Advice ⊕ www.smartraveller.gov.au or www.dfat.gov.au. **New Zealand Ministry of Foreign Affairs and Trade** ☏ 04/439-8000 ⊕ www.mft.govt.nz.

WEB SITES

Do check out the World Wide Web when planning your trip. You'll find everything from weather forecasts to virtual tours of famous cities. Be sure to visit Fodors.com (⊕ www.fodors.com), a complete travel-planning site. You can research prices and book plane tickets, hotel rooms, rental cars, vacation packages, and more. In addition, you can post your pressing questions in the Travel Talk section. Other planning tools include a currency converter and weather reports, and there are loads of links to travel resources.

On Spanish-language sites, watch for the name of the country, region, state, or city in which you have an interest. The search terms for "look," "find," and "get" are *mirar* and *buscar* in Spanish. "Next" and "last" (as in "next/last 10") are *próximo* and *último/anterior* in Spanish. Keep an eye out for such words as *turismo* (tourism), *turístico* (tourist-related), *hoteles* (hotels), *hospedajes* (hotel-like accommodation), *residenciales* (guesthouses), *restaurantes* (restaurants), *gobierno* (government), *estado* (state), *región* (administrative region), *ciudad* (city), *carabinero* (police officer), and *municipalidad* (town hall).

The following sites are good places to start a search (unless otherwise noted, these sites have information in English): ⊕ www.gochile.cl and ⊕ www.visit-chile. org have travel information and online booking, ⊕ www.chilnet.cl has business listings, ⊕ www.santiagotimes.cl is an online English-language newspaper. In Spanish, ⊕ www.emol.com is the online edition of the top-notch national newspaper *El Mercurio*.

Santiago

WORD OF MOUTH

"My husband and I spent a few days in Santiago last February and found the city to be very inviting. The fine arts museum was in the process of renovation while we were there but, fortunately, part of it was open—the architecture is exquisite and I took some of my favorite 'architectural' photos inside. There is a definite Latin flavor to Santiago and it has charming neighborhoods to explore. But beware of the strength of the summer sun, even at 6:00 PM!"

—cordon

Updated by
Mark Sullivan

WHEN IT WAS FOUNDED by Spanish conquistador Pedro de Valdivia in 1541, Santiago was little more than the triangular patch of land embraced by two arms of the Río Mapocho. Today that area, known as Santiago Centro, is just one of 32 *comunas* that make up the city, each with its own distinct personality. You'd never mistake Patronato, a neighborhood north of downtown filled with Moorish-style mansions built by families who made their fortunes in textiles, with Providencia, where the modern skyscrapers built by international corporations crowd the avenues. The chic shopping centers of Las Condes have little in common with the outdoor markets in Bellavista.

Perhaps the neighborhoods have retained their individuality because many have histories as old as Santiago itself. Nuñoa, for example, was a hard-working farm town to the east. Farther away was El Arrayán, a sleepy village in the foothills of the Andes. As the capital grew, these and many other communities were drawn inside the city limits. If you ask Santiaguinos you meet today where they reside, they are just as likely to mention their neighborhood as their city.

Like many of the early Spanish settlements, Santiago suffered some severe setbacks. Six months after the town was founded, a group of the indigenous Picunche people attacked, burning every building to the ground. Undeterred, the Spanish rebuilt in the same spot. The narrow streets that radiated out then from the Plaza de Armas are the same ones that can be seen today.

The Spanish lost interest in Santiago after about a decade, moving south in search of gold. But fierce resistance from the Mapuche people in 1599 forced many settlers to retreat to Santiago. The population swelled, solidifying the city's claim as the region's colonial capital. Soon many of the city's landmarks, including the colorful Casa Colorada, were erected.

It wasn't until after Chile finally won its independence from Spain in 1818 that Santiago took the shape it has today. Broad avenues extended in every direction. Buildings befitting a national capital, such as the Congreso Nacional and the Teatro Municipal, won wide acclaim. Parque Quinta Normal and Parque O'Higgins preserved huge swaths of green for the people, and the poplar-lined Parque Forestal gave the increasingly proud populace a place to promenade.

Santiago today is home to more than 6 million people—nearly a third of the country's total population. It continues to spread outward to the so-called *barrios altos* (upper neighborhoods) east of the center. It's also growing upward, as new office towers transform the skyline. Yet in many ways, Santiago still feels like a small town, where residents are always likely to bump into an acquaintance along the city center's crowded streets and bustling plazas.

EXPLORING SANTIAGO

Pedro de Valdivia wasn't very creative when he mapped out the streets of Santiago. He stuck to the same simple grid pattern you'll find in almost all of the colonial towns along the coast. The city didn't grow much

1

Santiago is a compact city, small enough that you can visit all the must-see sights in a few days. Consider the weather when planning your itinerary—on the first clear day your destination should be **Parque Metropolitano**, where you'll be treated to exquisite views from **Cerro San Cristóbal.** After a morning gazing at the Andes, head back down the hill and spend the afternoon wandering the bohemian streets of **Bellavista,** with a visit to Nobel laureate Pablo Neruda's Santiago residence, **La Chascona.** Check out one of the neighborhood's colorful eateries.

The next day, head to **Parque Forestal,** a leafy park that runs along the Río Mapocho. Be sure to visit the lovely old train station, the **Estación Mapocho.** After lunch at the **Mercado Central,** uncover the city's colonial past in Santiago Centro. Requisite sights include the **Plaza de Armas,** around which you'll find the Casa Colorada and the Museo Chileno de Arte Precolombino. Stop for tea in the afternoon at a quaint café in **Plaza Mulato Gil de Castro.** On the third day explore the sights along the **Alameda,** especially the presidential palace of La Moneda and the landmark church, **Iglesia San Francisco.** For a last look at the city, climb **Cerro Santa Lucía.** That night put on your chicest outfit for dinner in the trendy neighborhood of **Providencia** or **Las Condes.**

---

larger before the meandering Río Mapocho impeded these plans. You may be surprised, however, at how orderly the city remains. It's difficult to get lost wandering around downtown.

Running through the center is the city's major thoroughfare, Avenida Libertador Bernardo O'Higgins, better known as the Alameda (the street is named for Chile's first president). East of Plaza Baquedano, the Alameda turns into Avenida Providencia, where you'll find an upscale shopping district. After this it becomes Avenida Apoquindo, full of high-rise apartment blocks, and farther along it turns into Avenida Las Condes.

Much of the city, especially communities such as Bellavista and Providencia, is best explored on foot. The subway is probably the quickest, cleanest, and most economical way to shuttle between neighborhoods. To travel to more distant neighborhoods, or to get anywhere in the evening after the subway closes, you'll probably want to hail a taxi.

About the Restaurants

Dining is one of Santiago's great pleasures, and one of its most affordable delectations. Everything from fine restaurants to informal *picadas,* restaurants that specialize in typical Chilean food, is spread across the city. Menus run the gamut of international cuisines, but don't miss the local bounty—seafood delivered directly from the Pacific Ocean. You can't beat a plate of fresh fish at Mercado Central, the city's bustling market.

Lunch and dinner are served later than in many places—beginning at 1 PM for lunch, 7 or 8 PM for dinner. People do dress smartly for dinner, but a coat and tie are rarely necessary.

About the Hotels

Santiago has more than a dozen five-star hotels, many of them in the burgeoning Las Condes and Vitacura neighborhoods. With the increased popularity of Chile as a travel destination, most major international chains are represented here. You won't find better service than at newer hotels such as the lavish Ritz-Carlton. But don't write off the old standbys such as Hotel Plaza San Francisco. Inexpensive small hotels, especially near the city center, are harder to find, but they do exist.

All the construction in the past decade means competition between hotels is heated. You can often find a room for considerably less than the advertised high-season rates. Ask about specials when you book.

When to Go

Santiaguinos tend to abandon their city every summer during the school holidays that run from the end of December to early March. February is a particularly popular vacation time, when nearly everybody who's anybody is out of town. If you're not averse to the heat this can be a good time for walking around the city; otherwise spring and fall are better choices, as the weather is more comfortable. Spring and fall are also good times to drive through the Cajón del Maipo, when the scenery is at its peak. Winters in the city aren't especially cold—temperatures rarely dip below freezing—but days are sometimes gray and gloomy. Ski season, depending on the resort, runs mid-June through mid-September. Good weather conditions, however, mean six-month-long seasons beginning in May and ending in October.

Santiago Centro

Shiny new skyscrapers may be sprouting up in neighborhoods to the east, but Santiago Centro is the place to start if you really want to take the pulse of the city. After all, this is the historic heart of Santiago. All the major traffic arteries cross here—creating the usual traffic headaches—and all the subway lines converge here before whisking riders out to the suburbs. In Santiago Centro you'll find interesting museums, imposing government buildings, and bustling commercial streets. But don't think you'll be lost in a sprawling area—it takes only about 10 minutes to walk from one edge of the neighborhood to the other.

Numbers in the text correspond to numbers in the margins and on the Santiago Centro & La Alameda map.

a good walk

To really know Santiago, get acquainted with the **Plaza de Armas** ❶ ▶. Across Calle Catedral is a block-long threesome of historic buildings, centered by the Palacio de la Real Audiencia, at one time the country's highest court and currently home to the **Museo Histórico Nacional** ❷. To the west of the museum is the whitewashed **Correo Central** ❸; to the east is the **Municipalidad de Santiago** ❹. The **Catedral** ❺, twice destroyed by earthquakes and once by fire before the current neoclassical structure was completed in the 18th century, looms over the western end of the plaza. A motley assortment of commercial arcades completes the fringes of the square, adding a touch of modernity to one of the city's most traditional neighborhoods.

Outdoor Adventures
Jagged mountain peaks ring the capital, a reminder of all the outdoor activities available just outside the city limits. In the Cajón del Maipú, a half-hour drive from the center of the city, you can leave behind the hustle and bustle of Santiago for horseback riding, hiking, and white-water rafting.

Great Crafts Markets
Fine woolen items, expertly carved figurines, lapis lazuli jewelry, and other handicrafts from across the country are bountiful in Santiago. Trendy boutiques line the streets of Providencia and Vitacura, and luxury department stores in modern shopping malls lure dedicated shoppers to Las Condes.

1

Spectacular Skiing
Between May and October, the slopes outside Santiago are covered with the finely packed powder that dedicated downhill skiers dream about. To top it off, some of the country's top resorts, such as La Parva, Valle Nevado, and Portillo, are all an easy drive from the capital. Many locals head out for a morning of skiing and are back in the city in plenty of time for dinner.

World-Class Wineries
Santiago nestles in the Maipo Valley, the country's oldest wine-growing district. Some of Chile's largest and best wineries—Concha y Toro, Undurraga, and Santa Rita—are within an hour's drive of the city. November to March is the best time to visit if you want to see the winemaking process. The *vendimia,* or annual harvest, takes place in late February and early March.

East of the Plaza de Armas along Calle Merced is a beautifully restored colonial mansion called the **Casa Colorada** ❻. The **Museo Chileno de Arte Precolombino** ❼ is two blocks west of Casa Colorada on the corner of Calle Compañía and Calle Bandera. Across the street stands Chile's lordly **Palacio de los Tribunales de Justicia** ❽. Encompassing an entire city block to the north is the **Ex Congreso Nacional** ❾ and its gated gardens, providing refuge from the hustle and bustle of Santiago Centro.

TIMING The walk itself should take less than an hour. If you explore a few museums, wander around the squares, and rest here and there, this itinerary could take a full morning or afternoon. Each of the small museums on this route should take about 45 minutes to see thoroughly.

What to See

❻ **Casa Colorada.** The appropriately named Red House is one of the best-preserved colonial structures in the city. Mateo de Toro y Zambrano, Santiago's most prosperous businessman of the 18th century, once made his home here. The building today houses the Museo de Santiago, a modest but informative museum that makes an excellent place to dive into the city's history. There are several dioramas, some of them life-size, depicting life in the colonial period. For an explanation of the exhibits,

Santiago

Dr. Ostornol

Av. Recoleta

Av. Arzobispo Valdivieso

RECOLETA

Union

Me

Cementerio General ◆

Av. Independencia

Cerro Blonco

A. Figueroa

Av. Recoleta

M **CERRO BLANCO**

Av. Santos Dumont

Olivos

Dominica

Manzano

PATRONATO

M **PATRONATO**

Sta. Filo

Patronato

Av. La Paz

Av. Independencia

Antonia Lopez De Bello

Artesanos

Av. Bellavi

Av. Santa María

Av. Cardenal Jos

Lastra

Ismael Valdes

B

Río Mapocho

M **CAL Y CANTO**

Bandera

Puente

San Antonio

Mac

San Pablo

Santo Domingo

M **PLAZA DE ARMAS** **i**

Av. San Martín

Compañía

PEDESTRIAN ONLY STREET

Montade

Av. Brazil

Almirante Barroso

SANTA ANA **M**

Av.

Agustinas

UNIVERIDAD DE CHILE

Catedral

Plaza Quinta Normal

Norte Sur

LA MONEDA **M**

KEY

M Metro stops

i Tourist information

Cable Car Line

Plaza Brazil

Huerfanos

LOS HÉROES **M**

Av. Idel Libertador

Gen. B. O'Higgins (Alame

TO E CEN

Parque O'Higg

Palacio Cousiño ◆

Erasmo Escala

San Ignacio

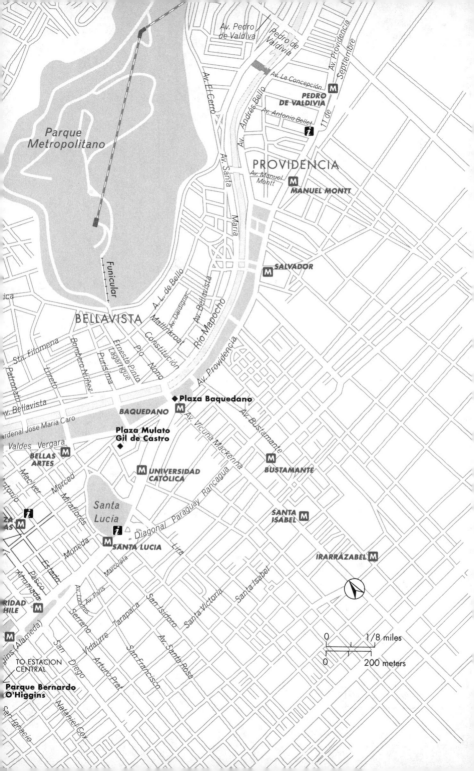

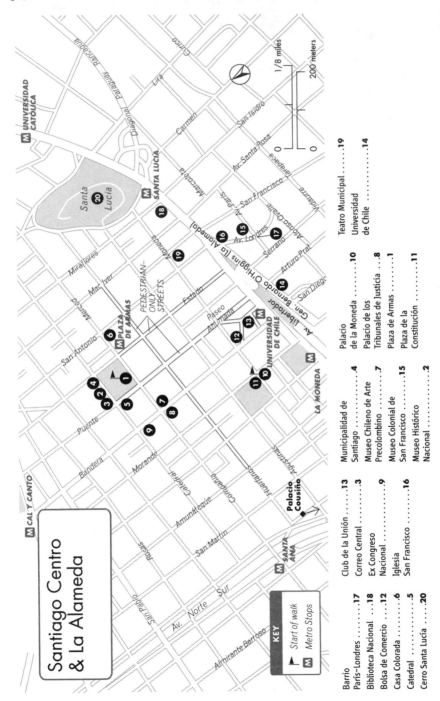

Santiago Centro & La Alameda

KEY
▲ Start of walk
Ⓜ Metro Stops

Barrio
París–Londres **17**
Biblioteca Nacional . . . **18**
Bolsa de Comercio **12**
Casa Colorada **6**
Catedral **5**
Cerro Santa Lucía **20**

Club de la Unión **13**
Correo Central **3**
Ex Congreso
Nacional **9**
Iglesia
San Francisco **16**

Municipalidad de
Santiago **4**
Museo Chileno de Arte
Precolombino **7**
Museo Colonial de
San Francisco **15**
Museo Histórico
Nacional **2**

Palacio
de la Moneda **10**
Palacio de los
Tribunales de Justicia . **8**
Plaza de Armas **1**
Plaza de la
Constitución **11**

Teatro Municipal **19**
Universidad
de Chile **14**

ask for an English guidebook. ⊠ *Merced 860, Santiago Centro* ☎ *2/ 633–0723* 🕮 *Tues.–Sat. 500 pesos, Sun. free* ⊙ *Tues.–Fri. 10–5:45, Sat. 10–4:45, Sun. 11–2* Ⓜ *Plaza de Armas.*

❺ Catedral. Conquistador Pedro de Valdivia declared in 1541 that a house of worship would be constructed at this site bordering the Plaza de Armas. The first adobe building burned to the ground, and the structures that replaced it were destroyed by the earthquakes of 1647 and 1730. The finishing touches of the neoclassical cathedral standing today were added in 1789 by Italian architect Joaquín Toesca. Be sure to see the stunning interior—a line of gilt arches topped by stained-glass windows parades down the long nave. ⊠ *Plaza de Armas, Santiago Centro* ☎ *2/ 696–2777* ⊙ *Daily 9–7* Ⓜ *Plaza de Armas.*

❸ Correo Central. Housed in what was once the ornate Palacio de los Gobernadores, this building dating from 1715 is one of the most beautiful post offices you are likely to see. It was reconstructed by Ricardo Brown in 1882 after being ravaged by fire and is a fine example of neoclassical architecture. The third story, which includes an attractive half dome, was added in the early 20th century. ⊠ *Catedral and Paseo Ahumada, Santiago Centro* ☎ *2/698–7274* ⊕ *www.correos.cl* ⊙ *Weekdays 8:30–7, Sat. 8:30–2* Ⓜ *Plaza de Armas.*

❾ Ex Congreso Nacional. Once the meeting place for the National Congress (the legislature moved to Valparaíso in 1990), this palatial neoclassical building now houses the offices of the Ministry of Foreign Affairs. The original structure on the site, the Iglesia de la Compañía de Jesús, was destroyed by a fire in 1863 in which 2,000 people perished. Inside the peaceful gated gardens is a monument commemorating the victims. ⊠ *Bandera 345, at Morandé, Santiago Centro* Ⓜ *Plaza de Armas.*

❹ Municipalidad de Santiago. Today's governmental center for Santiago can be found on the site of the colonial city hall and jail. The original structure, built in 1552, survived until a devastating earthquake in 1730. Joaquín Toesca, the architect who also designed the presidential palace and completed the cathedral, reconstructed the building in 1785, but it was destroyed by fire a century later. In 1891, Eugenio Joannon, who favored an Italian Renaissance style, erected the structure standing today. On the facade hangs an elaborate coat of arms presented by Spain. The interior is not open to the public. ⊠ *Plaza de Armas, Santiago Centro* Ⓜ *Plaza de Armas.*

need a break? You can shut out the hustle and bustle of the Plaza de Armas in the cool, dim, dark-wood-paneled room of the **Bar del City** (⊠ Compañía 1063, Santiago Centro ☎ 2/695–4526), the watering hole of the City Hotel. Order a coffee, cold beer, or sandwich and knock elbows with the dapper old Santiaguinos who enter through the wonderful wooden revolving doors.

❼ Museo Chileno de Arte Precolombino. If you plan to visit only one museum in Santiago, it should be the Museum of Pre-Columbian Art, a block from the Plaza de Armas. The well-endowed collection of artifacts of

Fodor'sChoice ★

the region's indigenous peoples, much of it donated by the family of collector Sergio García-Moreno, is displayed in the beautifully restored Royal Customs House that dates from 1807. The permanent collection, on the upper floor, showcases textiles and ceramics from Mexico to Patagonia. Unlike many of the city's museums, the displays here are well labeled in Spanish and English. One of the pair of gorgeous courtyards has a sunny café, making this a good place to recharge your batteries. ⊠ *Bandera 361, at Av. Compañía, Santiago Centro* ☎ *2/688–7348* ⊕ *www.museoprecolombino.cl* ✉ *Tues.–Sat. 2,000 pesos, Sun. free* ☉ *Tues.–Sun. 10–6* Ⓜ *Plaza de Armas.*

② Museo Histórico Nacional. The colonial-era Palacio de la Real Audiencia served as the meeting place of Chile's first Congress in September 1810. The building then functioned as a telegraph office before the museum moved here in 1911. It's worth the small admission charge to see the interior of the 200-year-old structure, where exhibits tracing Chile's history are arranged chronologically in rooms centered around a courtyard. Among the exhibits are large collections of coins, stamps, and traditional handicrafts, including more than 3,000 examples of native textiles. ⊠ *Plaza de Armas, Santiago Centro* ☎ *2/633–1815* ⊕ *www.museohistoriconacional.cl* ✉ *Tues.–Sat. 600 pesos, Sun. free* ☉ *Tues.–Sun. 10–5:30* Ⓜ *Plaza de Armas.*

❽ Palacio de los Tribunales de Justicia. During Augusto Pinochet's rule, countless human-rights demonstrations were held outside the Courts of Justice, which house the country's Supreme Court. Protests are still held near this stately neoclassical building a block from the Plaza de Armas, including some in support of the former dictator. In front of the building, perhaps ironically, is a monument celebrating justice and the promulgation of Chile's civil code. ⊠ *Bandera 344, Santiago Centro* Ⓜ *Plaza de Armas.*

off the beaten path

PARQUE BERNARDO O'HIGGINS – Named for Chile's first president and national hero, whose troops were victorious against the Spanish, this park has plenty of open space for everything from ball games to military parades. Street vendors sell *volantines* (kites) outside the park year-round; high winds make September and early October the prime kite-flying season. ⊠ *Av. Jorge Alessandri Rodríguez between Av. Blanca Encalada and Av. General Rondizzoni, Santiago Centro* ☎ *2/556–1927* ✉ *Free* ☉ *Daily 8–8* Ⓜ *Parque O'Higgins.*

★ ⚑ ❶ **Plaza de Armas.** This square has been the symbolic heart of Chile—as well as its political, social, religious, and commercial center—since Pedro de Valdivia established the city on this spot in 1541. The Palacio de los Gobernadores, the Palacio de la Real Audiencia, and the Municipalidad de Santiago front the square's northern edge. The dignified Catedral graces the western side of the square. Among the palm trees are distinctive fountains and gardens revealing the Chileans' pride about their history. Also here is a bronze well that once served as the city's main source of water. On any given day, the plaza teems with life—vendors selling religious icons, artists painting the activity around them, street performers juggling fire, and tourists clutching guidebooks. In the southern corner of the plaza you can watch people playing chess. ✉ *Compañía at Estado, Santiago Centro* Ⓜ *Plaza de Armas.*

La Alameda

Avenida Libertador Bernardo O'Higgins, more frequently called La Alameda, is the city's principal thoroughfare. Along with the Avenida Norte Sur and the Río Mapocho, it forms the wedge that defines the city's historic district. Many of Santiago's most important buildings, including landmarks such as the Iglesia San Francisco, stand along the avenue. Others, like Teatro Municipal, are just steps away.

a good walk

Unthinkable only a few years ago, today you can walk unescorted into the courtyard of the **Palacio de la Moneda** ⑩ ⌐, the nerve center of the Chilean government. Across Calle Moneda you'll find **Plaza de la Constitución** ⑪, a formal square where you can watch the changing of the guard. Walk a block east along Calle Moneda to the cobblestoned Calle La Bolsa. On this narrow diagonal street stands the ornate **Bolsa de Comercio** ⑫, the country's stock exchange. A block down, at a dainty fountain, the street turns into Calle Nueva York, where you'll find the **Club de la Unión** ⑬. Across the street is the main building, or *casa central,* of the **Universidad de Chile** ⑭. Reach it by crossing under the Universidad de Chile Metro stop, which contains monumental murals depicting Chilean history painted by Mario Toral, part of the fine MetroArte series in all subway stops. Two blocks east are the **Museo Colonial de San Francisco** ⑮ and the **Iglesia San Francisco** ⑯. Turn left after exiting Iglesia San Francisco onto Calle Londres and into the **Barrio París-Londres** ⑰. Enjoy a pleasant stroll through this charming area otherwise known as Little Europe. On returning to the Alameda, avoid the crazy drivers by crossing back to the other (north) side via the Santa Lucia Metro station. Directly ahead of you is the **Biblioteca Nacional** ⑱. After leaving the library make a left and then another left. Cross Calle Maciver and then turn right down pedestrian-only German Tenderini to the **Teatro Municipal** ⑲. Head east through Plaza Vicuña Mackenna to survey the entire city from **Cerro Santa Lucía** ⑳.

TIMING & PRECAUTIONS

The walk itself is fairly short, but it's full of beautiful old buildings where you'll likely want to linger. You could spend an hour alone at the Palacio de la Moneda—try to time your visit with the changing of the guard, which takes place every other day at 10 AM. Across the Alameda, take at least an hour and a half to explore Iglesia San Francisco, the adjacent museum, and the Barrio París-Londres. You could easily spend a bookish half hour perusing the stacks at the Biblioteca Nacional. Plan for an hour or more at Cerro Santa Lucía—don't get here too late, as the hilltop park isn't safe after dark.

What to See

⑰ **Barrio París-Londres.** Many architects contributed to what is frequently referred to as Santiago's Little Europe, among them Alamos, Larraín, and Mönckeberg. The string of small mansion houses lining the cobbled streets of Calles París and Londres sprang up in the mid-1920s on the vegetable patches and gardens that once belonged to the convent adjoining Iglesia San Francisco. The three- and four-story town houses are all unique; some have brick facades or terra-cotta-tile roofs, and others are done in Palladian style. ⊠ *Londres at París, La Alameda.*

⑱ Biblioteca Nacional. Near the foot of Cerro Santa Lucía is the block-long classical facade of the National Library. With more than 3 million titles, this is one of the largest libraries in South America. The vast interior includes arcane collections. The second-floor Sala José Toribio Medina, which holds the most important collection of prints by native peoples in Latin America, is well worth a look. The three levels of books, reached by curved-wood balconies, are lighted by massive chandeliers. ⊠ *La Alameda 651, La Alameda* ☏ *2/360–5200* ⊕ *www. dibam.cl* ⊠ *Free* ⊗ *Weekdays 9–6, Sat. 9–2* Ⓜ *Santa Lucía.*

⑫ Bolsa de Comercio. Chile's stock exchange is housed in a 1917 French neoclassical structure with an elegant clock tower surmounted by an arched slate cupola. Weekdays you can watch the shouting of traders in the three buying and selling circles called *redondeles.* ⊠ *La Bolsa 64, La Alameda* ☏ *2/399–3000* ⊕ *www.bolsadesantiago.com* ⊠ *Free* ⊗ *Weekdays noon–1:20 and 4–4:30* Ⓜ *Universidad de Chile.*

⑳ Cerro Santa Lucía. The mazelike park of St. Lucía is a hangout for souvenir vendors, park-bench smoochers, and photo-snapping tourists. Walking uphill along the labyrinth of interconnected paths and plazas takes about 30 minutes. An elevator two blocks north of the park's main entrance is a little faster, but its schedule is erratic. The crow's nest, reached via a series of steep and slippery stone steps, affords an excellent 360-degree view of the entire city. Be careful near dusk, as the park also attracts the occasional mugger. ⊠ *Santa Lucía and La Alameda, La Alameda* ☏ *No phone* ⊗ *Oct.–Mar., daily 9–6:30; Apr.–Sept., daily 7 AM–8 PM* Ⓜ *Santa Lucía.*

⑬ Club de la Unión. The facade of this neoclassical building, dating to 1925, is one of the city's finest. The interior of this private club, whose roster has included numerous Chilean presidents, is open only to members. ⊠ *La Alameda at Bandera, La Alameda* Ⓜ *Universidad de Chile.*

⑯ Iglesia San Francisco. Santiago's oldest structure, greatest symbol, and principal landmark, the Church of St. Francis is the last trace of 16th-century colonial architecture in the city. Construction began in 1586, and although the church survived successive earthquakes, early tremors took their toll and portions had to be rebuilt in 1698. Today's neoclassical tower, which forms the city's most recognizable silhouette, was added in 1857 by architect Fermín Vivaceta. Inside are rough stone-and-brick walls, marble columns, and ornate coffered wood ceilings. Visible on the main altar is the image of the Virgen del Socorro (Virgin of Assistance) that conquistador Pedro de Valdivia carried for protection and guidance. ⊠ *La Alameda 834, La Alameda* ☏ *2/638–3238* ⊗ *Daily 7 AM–8 PM* Ⓜ *Santa Lucía, Universidad de Chile.*

⑮ Museo Colonial de San Francisco. This gloomy former convent, adjacent to Iglesia San Francisco, houses the best collection of 17th-century colonial paintings on the continent. Inside the rooms wrapping around an overgrown courtyard are 54 large-scale canvases portraying the life of St. Francis (don't miss the huge painting of his religious order's "family tree"), as well as a plethora of religious iconography ranging from tiny paintings of the Virgin Mary to life-size carvings of Christ. Most pieces are labeled in Spanish and English. One gallery does double-duty as a gift shop, and it's difficult to tell exactly what is for sale. ⊠ *Londres 4, La Alameda* ☎ *2/639–8737* ✎ *1,000 pesos* ☉ *Tues.–Sat. 10–1:30 and 3–6, Sun. 10–2* Ⓜ *Santa Lucía, Universidad de Chile.*

off the beaten path

PALACIO COUSIÑO – Dating from 1871, this fabulous mansion was built by the wealthy Cousiño-Goyenechea family. All that mining money allowed them to build this palace with amenities such as one of the country's first elevators. The elegant furnishings were—of course—imported from France. ⊠ *Dieciocho 438, La Alameda* ☎ *2/ 698–5063* ✎ *1,500 pesos* ☉ *Tours Tues.–Fri. 9:30–12:30 and 2:30–4; weekends 9:30–12:30* Ⓜ *Toesca.*

🔟 **Palacio de la Moneda.** Originally the royal mint, this sober neoclassical edifice built by Joaquín Toesca in 1805 became the presidential palace in 1846 and served that purpose for more than a century. It was bombarded by the military in the 1973 coup, when Salvador Allende defended his presidency against the assault of General Augusto Pinochet. Allende's death is still shrouded in mystery—some say he went down fighting, others claim he took his own life before the future dictator entered the palace in triumph. The two central courtyards are open to the public, and tours of the interior can be arranged at the reception desk. ⊠ *Plaza de la Constitución, Moneda between Teatinos and Morandé, La Alameda* ☎ *2/690–4000* ☉ *Daily 10–6* Ⓜ *La Moneda.*

★ ⑪ **Plaza de la Constitución.** Palacio de la Moneda and other government buildings line Constitution Square, the country's most formal plaza. The changing of the guard takes place every other day at 10 AM within the triangle defined by 12 Chilean flags. Adorning the plaza are three monuments, each dedicated to a notable national figure: Diego Portales, founder of the Chilean republic; Jorge Alessandri, the country's leader from 1958 to 1964; and Don Eduardo Frei, president from 1964 to 1970. The plaza also serves as the roof of the underground bunker Pinochet had installed when he "redecorated" La Moneda. Pillars in each of the four corners of the square serve as ventilation ducts for the bunker, which is now a parking lot. Locals joke that these monoliths represent the four founding members of the military junta—they're made of stone, full of hot air, and no one knows their real function. One pillar has been converted into a memorial honoring President Salvador Allende. ⊠ *Moneda at Morande, La Alameda* Ⓜ *La Moneda.*

⑲ **Teatro Municipal.** The opulent Municipal Theater is the city's cultural center, with performances of opera, ballet, and classical music from April to November. Originally built in 1857, with major renovations in 1870 and 1906 following a fire and an earthquake, the Renaissance-style building is one of the city's most refined monuments. The lavish interior deserves a visit. Tours can be arranged with a week's notice. ⊠ *Plaza Alcade Mekis, Av. Agustinas 794, at Av. San Antonio, La Alameda* ☎ *2/463–8888* Ⓜ *Universidad de Chile, Santa Lucía.*

🄔 **Universidad de Chile.** The main branch of the University of Chile, the country's largest educational institution, is a symmetrical ocher edifice completed in 1872, when it was known as the University Palace. It's not officially open to the public, but you are free to stroll through the grounds. ⊠ *La Alameda, La Alameda* Ⓜ *Universidad de Chile.*

Parque Forestal

After building a canal in 1891 to tame the unpredictable Río Mapocho, Santiago found itself with a thin strip of land that it didn't quite know what to do with. The area quickly filled with the city's refuse. A decade later, under the watchful eye of Enrique Cousiño, it was transformed into the leafy Forest Park. It was and still is enormously popular with Santiaguinos. Parque Forestal is the perfect antidote to the spirited Plaza de Armas. The eastern tip, near Plaza Baquedano, is distinguished by the Wagnerian-scale Fuente Alemana (German Fountain), donated by the Germanic community of Santiago. The bronze-and-stone monolith commemorates the centennial of Chilean Independence.

Numbers in white bullets in the text correspond to numbers in black bullets in the margins and on the Parque Forestal map.

a good walk

Near the park's western edge you'll find the former train terminal, the **Estación Mapocho** 🄡. It now serves as the city's most prestigious cultural center. A block east along Ismael Valdés Vergara is the wrought-iron **Mercado Central** 🄢 ↳, the city's fish market. Cross over the Río Mapocho at San Antonio and take the second left, which is Antonia López de Bello. A block or so west is the bright blue entrance to the gritty **Vega Chica and Vega Central** 🄣 (Vega Central is a full block to the north of Vega Chica). Follow your nose another block west to the flower market **Pérgola de las Flores** 🄤.

Strolling east through the Parque Forestal will bring you to the jewel-like **Museo Nacional de Bellas Artes** 🄥 and the adjacent **Museo de Arte Contemporáneo** 🄦. Just south of the park, near where Calle Merced and Calle José Victorino Lastarria meet, is the Plaza Mulato Gil de Castro, a pleasant little nook with bookshops and cafés, as well as the **Museo Arqueológico de Santiago** 🄧 and the **Museo de Artes Visuales** 🄨.

TIMING & PRECAUTIONS You can have a pleasant, relaxing day strolling through the city's most popular park, losing yourself in the art museums, and exploring the Mercado Central. In Plaza Mulato Gil de Castro, allot at least 30 minutes for the Museo Arqueológico and the Museo de Artes Visuales. You can easily spend a few hours in the Museo Nacional de Bellas Artes and the Museo de Arte Contemporáneo. Vega Chica and Vega Central are usually crowded, so keep an eye on your personal belongings. When the markets are closing around sunset, it's best to return to safer neighborhoods south of the river.

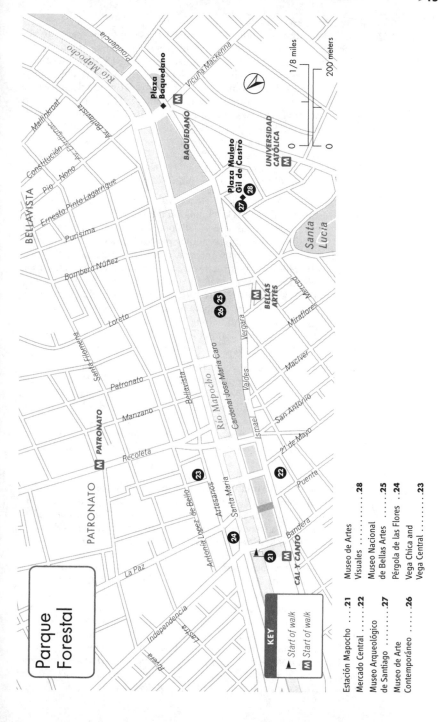

Parque Forestal

Estación Mapocho **21**
Mercado Central **22**
Museo Arqueológico
de Santiago **27**
Museo de Arte
Contemporáneo **26**

Museo de Artes
Visuales **28**
Museo Nacional
de Bellas Artes **25**
Pérgola de las Flores ..**24**
Vega Chica and
Vega Central **23**

KEY

▲ Start of walk

Ⓜ Start of walk

What to See

★ ▶ ㉑ **Estación Mapocho.** This mighty edifice, with its trio of two-story arches framed by intricate terra-cotta detailing, is as elegant as any train station in the world. The station was inaugurated in 1913 as a terminus for trains arriving from Valparaíso and points north, but steam engines no longer pull in here. A major conversion transformed the structure into one of the city's principal cultural centers. The Centro Cultural Estación Mapocho houses two restaurants, a fine bookstore and café, a large exhibition hall and arts space, and a handicrafts shop. The cavernous space that once sheltered steam engines now hosts musical performances and other events. ⊠ *Plaza de la Cultura, Independencia at Balmaceda, Parque Forestal* ☎ *2/361–1761* ⊕ *www.estacionmapocho. cl* ☉ *Daily 9–6* Ⓜ *Puente Cal y Canto.*

㉒ **Mercado Central.** At the Central Market you'll find a matchless selection of creatures from the sea. Depending on the season, you might see the delicate beaks of *picorocos,* the world's only edible barnacles; *erizos,* the prickly shelled sea urchins; or shadowy pails full of succulent bullfrogs. If the fish don't capture your interest, the architecture may: the lofty wrought-iron ceiling of the structure, reminiscent of a Victorian train station, was prefabricated in England and erected in Santiago between 1868 and 1872. Diners are regaled by musicians in the middle of the market, where two restaurants compete for customers. You can also find a cheap, filling meal at a stand along the market's southern edge. ⊠ *Ismael Valdés Vergara 900, Parque Forestal* ☎ *2/696–8327* ☉ *Mon.–Thurs. 5–5, Fri. 5–9, Sat. 5–7, Sun. 5–6* Ⓜ *Puente Cal y Canto.*

㉗ **Museo Arqueológico de Santiago.** This little archaeological museum is devoted specifically to the indigenous peoples of Chile. Some 3,000 artifacts bring the country's Mapuche, Aymara, Fueguino, Huilliche, and Pehuenche cultures vividly to life. It is located inside the Museo de Artes Visuales. ⊠ *José Victorino Lastarria 307, 2nd fl., Parque Forestal* ☎ *2/664–9337* ⊕ *www.mavi.cl* ▨ *1,000 pesos (includes Museo de Artes Visuales); Sun. free* ☉ *Tues.–Sun. 10:30–6:30* Ⓜ *Baquedano, Universidad Católica.*

┌─────────┐
│ need a │
│ break? │
└─────────┘

The pleasant Plaza Mulato Gil de Castro, a cobblestone square off the colorful Calle José Victorino Lastarria, is an unexpected treat. In the midst of it is **R** (⊠ Plaza Mulato Gil de Castro, Parque Forestal ☎ 2/664–9844), a cozy café serving English teas. Weary travelers relax beneath the kettles and cups hanging from the ceiling.

㉖ **Museo de Arte Contemporáneo.** After an ambitious restoration effort, the elegant Museum of Contemporary Art no longer has its rather dilapidated interior. On the opposite side of the building housing the Museo de Bellas Artes, the museum showcases a collection of modern Latin American paintings, photography, and sculpture. The museum is run by the art school of the Universidad de Chile, so it isn't afraid to take risks. Look for Fernando Botero's pudgy *Caballo* sculpture gracing the square out front. ⊠ *Bounded by Jose M. de la Barra and Ismael Valdés Vergara, Parque Forestal* ☎ *2/639–6488* ⊕ *www.mac.uchile.cl* ▨ *500 pesos* ☉ *Tues.–Sat. 11–7, Sun. 11–5* Ⓜ *Bellas Artes.*

★ ㉘ **Museo de Artes Visuales.** You'll never confuse this dazzling museum of contemporary art with the crumbling Museo de Arte Contemporáneo. Displaying the combined private holdings of Chilean construction moguls Manuel Santa Cruz and Hugo Yaconi, this gallery has one of the finest collections of contemporary Chilean art. The building itself is a masterpiece: six gallery levels float into each other in surprising ways. The wood floors and Plexiglas-sided stairways create an open and airy space for paintings and sculptures by Roberto Matta, Arturo Duclos, Roser Bru, José Balmes, and Eugenio Dittborn, among others. ⊠ *José Victorino Lastarria 307, Plaza Mulato Gil de Castro, Parque Forestal* ☎ *2/638–3502* ⊕ *www.mavi.cl* ✉ *1,000 pesos (includes Museo Arqueológico de Santiago), Sun. free* ☉ *Tues.–Sun. 10:30–6:30* Ⓜ *Bellas Artes.*

㉕ **Museo Nacional de Bellas Artes.** Paintings, drawings, and sculpture by 16th- to 20th-century Chilean and European artists fill the grand National Museum of Fine Arts. The elegant, neoclassical building, which was originally intended to house the city's school of fine arts, has an impressive glass-domed ceiling that illuminates the main hall. A theater on the second floor screens short films about the featured artists. ⊠ *Bounded by Jose M. de la Barra and Ismael Valdés Vergara, Parque Forestal* ☎ *2/633–0655* ⊕ *www.dibam.cl* ✉ *Tues.–Sat. 600 pesos, Sun. free* ☉ *Tues.–Sun. 10–7* Ⓜ *Bellas Artes.*

off the beaten path

PARQUE DE LAS ESCULTURAS – Providencia is mainly a business district, but it has one of the city's most captivating—and least publicized—public parks. Here, the gardens are filled with sculptures by Chile's top artists. Because of its pastoral atmosphere, the park is popular with joggers and cuddling couples. In the center is a wood pavilion that hosts sculpture exhibitions. To get here from the Pedro de Valdivia Metro stop, walk a block north to the Río Mapocho and cross the bridge to Avenida Santa María. The park is on your right.

㉔ **Pérgola de las Flores.** Santiaguinos come to the Trellis of Flowers to buy wreaths and flower arrangements to bring to the city's two cemeteries. *La Pérgola de las Flores*, a famous Chilean musical, is based on the conflict that arose in the 1930s when the mayor of Santiago wanted to shut down the market. Find a chatty florist at one of the two open-air markets—Pégola San Francisco and Pérgola Santa María—and you may learn all about it. ⊠ *Av. La Paz at Artesanos, Recoleta* ☎ *No phone* ☉ *Daily sunrise–sunset* Ⓜ *Puente Cal y Canto.*

㉓ **Vega Chica and Vega Central.** From fruit to furniture, meat to machinery, these lively markets stock just about anything you can name. Alongside the ordinary items you can find delicacies like *piñones*, giant pine nuts found on monkey puzzle trees. If you're undaunted by crowds, try a typical Chilean meal in a closet-size eatery or picada. Chow down with the locals on *pastel de choclo*, a pie filled with ground beef, chicken, olives, and boiled eggs and topped with mashed corn. ⊠ *Antonia López de Bello between Av. Salas and Av. Gandarillas, Recoleta* Ⓜ *Puente Cal y Canto.*

off the beaten path

VIÑA COUSIÑO-MACUL – There's no need to leave the city to visit a working winery: this 625-acre estate, where grapes have been grown since the mid-16th century, is in the suburb of Peñalolén. The Cousiño family home, set next to a beautiful 110-acre park, isn't open to the public, but you can visit the rest of the facilities. Especially interesting is the vaulted brick cellar, built in 1872, which can store more than 1 million bottles. It's a short taxi ride from Providencia or Los Condes. ⊠ *Av. Quilín 7100, Peñalolén* ☎ *2/351–4175* ⊕ *www.cousinomacul.cl* ⊠ *3,500 pesos* ☉ *Tours: Mon.–Sat. at 11 AM.*

Bellavista & Parque Metropolitano

If you happen to be in Santiago on one of the rare days when the smog dissipates, head straight for Parque Metropolitano. In the center is Cerro San Cristóbal, a hill reached via cable car or funicular. A journey to the top of the hill rewards you with spectacular views in all directions. In the shadow of Cerro San Cristóbal is Bellavista. The neighborhood has but one sight—the poet Pablo Neruda's hillside home of La Chascona—but it's perhaps the city's best place to wander. You're sure to discover interesting antiques shops, bustling outdoor markets, and adventurous and colorful eateries.

Numbers in the text correspond to numbers in the margins and on the Bellavista & Parque Metropolitano map.

a good walk

Starting from Plaza Baquedano, cross the bridge over the Río Mapocho to Bellavista. Acacia trees line the streets here, which are filled with boisterous cafés, trendy restaurants, and one-story homes painted in pinks, aquamarines, and blues. Walk three blocks north on Calle Pío Nono and turn right onto Calle Antonia López de Bello. Make a left onto Constitución and head north—you'll soon enter Santiago's most lively restaurant district. On Fernando Márquez de la Plata sits the house Pablo Neruda designed, **La Chascona** ㉙ ▶.

At the northern end of Calle Pío Nono is Plaza Caupolicán, the entrance to Parque Metropolitano. The funicular, housed in an old castlelike terminus, climbs up Santiago's highest hill, **Cerro San Cristóbal** ㉚. A quarter of the way up the hill, the funicular stops at the **Jardín Zoológico** ㉛, which you can also reach on foot by following the road. After reaching the summit, take in the expansive views, then follow the signs to the *teleférico* (cable car) and get out halfway at **Plaza Tupahue** ㉜. A short walk away is **Jardín Botánico Mapulemu** ㉝, an expansive botanical garden. A 15-minute walk east and slightly downhill will bring you to the authentic and well-kept **Jardín Japonés** ㉞.

TIMING & PRECAUTIONS   Plan on devoting an entire day to seeing Parque Metropolitano's major attractions. During the week the park is almost empty, and you can enjoy the views in relative solitude. Avoid walking down if you decide to watch the sunset from the lofty perch—the area is not well patrolled. Give yourself at least an hour to wander through Bellavista, and another hour for a tour of La Chascona.

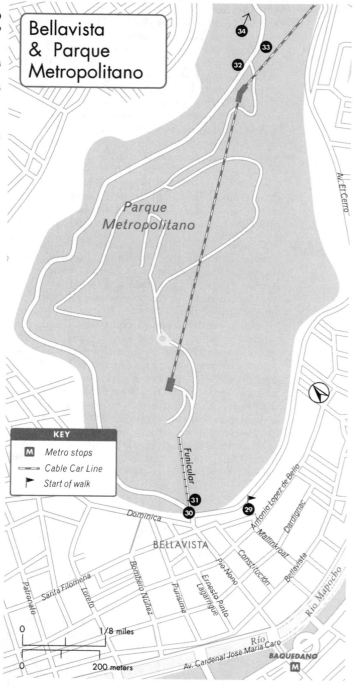

Cerro San
Cristóbal **30**

La Chascona . .**29**

Jardín
Botánico
Mapulemu . . .**33**

Jardín
Japonés **34**

Jardín
Zoológico **31**

Plaza
Tapahue **32**

Bellavista & Parque Metropolitano

Parque Metropolitano

KEY

Ⓜ *Metro stops*

▭▭▭ *Cable Car Line*

▶ *Start of walk*

Funicular

Av. El Cerro

Antonio Lopez de Bello

Dardignac

Mattinkroat

Constitución

Bellavista

Rio Mapocho

Dominica

BELLAVISTA

Patronato

Santa Filomena

Loreto

Bombero Nuñez

Purisima

Ernesto Pinto Lagarrigue

Pio Nono

0   1/8 miles

0   200 meters

Río

Av. Cardenal Jose María Caro

BAQUEDANO
Ⓜ

What to See

🖑 ㉚ **Cerro San Cristóbal.** St. Christopher's Hill, within Parque Metropolitano, is one of the most popular tourist attractions in Santiago. From the western entrance at Plaza Caupolicán you can walk—it's a steep but enjoyable one-hour climb—or take the funicular. Either route leads you to the summit, which is crowned by a gleaming white statue of the Virgen de la Inmaculada. If you are coming from the eastern entrance, you can ascend in the cable car that leaves seven blocks north of the Pedro de Valdivia Metro stop. The ride, which seats two in a colored-glass bubble, can be terrifying for acrophobics. Tree branches whack at your lift as you glide over the park. There is limited parking for 2,000 pesos at both the Pedro de Valdivia and Pío Nono entrances. ✉ *Cerro San Cristóbal, Bellavista* ☎ *2/730–1300* ⊕ *www.parquemet.cl* 🅿 *Park free; round-trip funicular 1,500 pesos; round-trip cable car 1,500 pesos* ⊙ *Park: Sun.–Thurs. 8 AM–10 PM, Fri. and Sat. 8 AM–midnight. Funicular: Mon. 1–8, Tues.–Fri. 10–8, weekends 10–8. Cable car: weekdays 2:30–6:30, weekends 10:30–7:30* Ⓜ *Baquedano, Pedro de Valdivia.*

★ ▐ ㉙ **La Chascona.** This house designed by the Nobel-winning poet Pablo Neruda was dubbed the "Woman with the Tousled Hair" after Matilde Urratia, the poet's third wife. The two met while strolling in nearby Parque Forestal, and for years the house served as a romantic hideaway before they married. The pair's passionate relationship was recounted in the 1995 Italian film *Il Postino.* Tours allow you to step into the extraordinary mind of the poet whose eclectic designs earned him the label "organic architect." Winding garden paths, stairs, and bridges lead to the house and its library stuffed with books, a bedroom in a tower, and a secret passageway. Scattered throughout are collections of butterflies, seashells, wineglasses, and other odd objects that inspired Neruda's tumultuous life and romantic poetry. Neruda, who died in 1973, had two other houses on the coast—one in Valparaíso, the other in Isla Negra. All three are open as museums. Though it's not as magical as Isla Negra, La Chascona can still set your imagination dancing. The house is on a little side street leading off Constitución. ✉ *Fernando Márquez de la Plata 0192, Bellavista* ☎🖨 *2/777–8741* ⊕ *www.neruda.cl* 🅿 *English tour: 3,100 pesos* ⊙ *Tues.–Sun. 10–6* Ⓜ *Baquedano.*

> **need a break?**
>
> A short walk from La Chascona is Calle Antonia López de Bello, a street overflowing with bars and restaurants. Here, the café **Off the Record** (✉ Antonia López de Bello 0155, Bellavista ☎ 2/777–7710) has a decidedly bohemian air. The wooden booths, for example, seem to have been designed with witty conversation and artistic bonhomie in mind. Black-and-white photographs recall visitors from Pablo Neruda to Uma Thurman.

㉝ **Jardín Botánico Mapulemu.** Gravel paths lead you to restful nooks among acres of well-labeled local flora at the Mapulemu Botanical Garden. Some 80 native-Chilean species grow here, including the araucaria, canelo, and macci trees. The botanical star is the squat *jubea chilena,* the ubiquitous Chilean palm. Every path and stairway seems to bring you to better views of Santiago and the Andes. Sunday mornings there are tai chi, yoga, and aerobics free of charge. ⊠ *Cerro San Cristóbal, Bellavista* ☎ *2/730–1300* 🔁 *Free* ⊙ *Daily 10–4* Ⓜ *Pedro de Valdivia, Baquedano.*

🐾 **Jardín Japonés.** The tranquil Japanese Garden affords a sumptuous view over the skyscrapers of Las Condes and Bellavista. Paths edged with bamboo and lighted by Japanese lanterns lead past lily ponds and a gazebo beside a trickling fountain. ⊠ *Cerro San Cristóbal, Bellavista* ☎ *2/730–1300* 🔁 *Free* ⊙ *Daily 10–6* Ⓜ *Pedro de Valdivia, Baquedano.*

🐾 ㉛ **Jardín Zoológico.** The Zoological Garden is a good place to see examples of many Chilean animals, some nearly extinct, that you might not otherwise encounter. As is often the case with many older zoos, the creatures aren't given a lot of room. A larger, modern zoo is being built outside the city near the Universidad de Chile. ⊠ *Cerro San Cristóbal, Bellavista* ☎ *No phone* 🔁 *2,000 pesos* ⊙ *Tues.–Sun. 10–6* Ⓜ *Baquedano.*

🐾 ㉜ **Plaza Tupahue.** The middle stop on the teleférico deposits you in the center of Parque Metropolitano. The main attraction here in summer is the delightful **Piscina Tupahue,** a 46-meter (150-foot) pool with a rocky crag running along one side. Beside the pool is the 1925 **Torreón Victoria,** a stone tower surrounded by a trellis of bougainvillea. If Piscina Tupahue is too crowded, try the nearby **Piscina Antilén.** From Plaza Tupahue you can follow a path below to **Plaza de Juegos Infantiles Gabriela Mistral,** a popular playground. ⊠ *Cerro San Cristóbal, Bellavista* ☎ *2/730–1300* 🔁 *Park free, Piscina Tupahue 4,500 pesos, Piscina Antilén 5,500 pesos* ⊙ *Nov.–Mar., Wed.–Mon. 10–7* Ⓜ *Pedro de Valdivia, Baquedano.*

Parque Quinta Normal Area

Just west of downtown is shady Parque Quinta Normal, a 75-acre park with three museums within its borders and another just across the street. This is an especially good place to take the kids, as all the museums were designed to stimulate eager young minds. The park was created in 1841 as a place to experiment with new agricultural techniques. On weekdays it is great for quiet strolls; on weekends you'll have to maneuver around noisy families. Pack a picnic or a soccer ball and you'll fit right in.

Numbers in the text correspond to numbers in the margins and on the Parque Quinta Normal map.

a good walk

Take a cab or the subway to the Estación Central stop. Outside the Metro is the **Estación Central** ㉟ ⌐, a graceful colossus that is the city's only functioning train station. Across the street is the **Planetario** ㊱, on the southeast corner of the Universidad de Santiago. Walk five blocks north on Avenida Matucana to Avenida Portales. Half a block west is the colorful **Museo Artequín** ㊲. Across the street is the main entrance to Parque Quinta Normal, where you'll find the **Museo Ferroviario** ㊳. Avenida Las Palmas, a wide pedestrian path, leads through the park to the **Museo Nacional de Historia Natural** ㊴ and the **Museo de Ciencia y Tecnología** ㊵.

TIMING You can visit the museums in and around the park, stroll along a wooded path, and even row a boat on a lake, all within a few hours. The hour-long presentation at the planetarium is shown only on weekends.

Estación
Central **35**

Museo
Artequín **37**

Museo de
Ciencia y
Tecnología ...**40**

Museo
Ferroviario ...**38**

Museo
Nacional
de Historia
Natural **39**

Planetario ...**36**

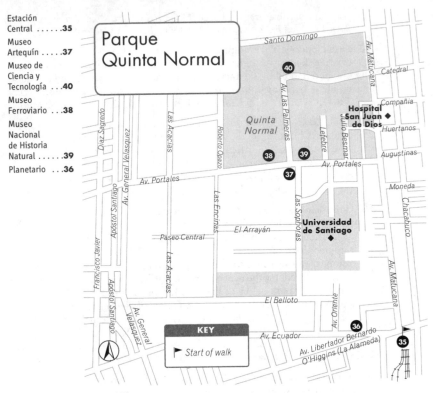

What to See

▶ **35** **Estación Central.** Inaugurated in 1897, Central Station is the city's last remaining train station, serving Concepción and points south. It's also the city's main bus station. The greenish iron canopy that once shielded the engines from the weather is flanked by two lovely beaux arts edifices. A lively market keeps this terminal buzzing with activity. ✉ *La Alameda 3170, Estación Central* ☎ *2/376–8500* 🎫 *Free* ⊙ *Daily 6 AM–midnight* Ⓜ *Estación Central.*

off the beaten path

CEMENTERIO GENERAL – It may be an unusual tourist attraction, but this cemetery in the northern part of the city reveals a lot about traditional Chilean society. After passing through the lofty stone arches of the main entrance you'll find well-tended paths lined with marble mausoleums, squat mansions belonging to Chile's wealthy families. The 8- or 10-story "niches" farther along—concrete shelves housing thousands of coffins—resemble middle-class apartment buildings. Their inhabitants lie here until the rent runs out and they're evicted. Look for former President Salvador Allende's final resting spot. A map at the main entrance to the cemetery can help you find it. This is an emotionally charged place around September 11, the anniversary of the 1973 military coup. ✉ *Av. Recoleta, Recoleta.*

★ ⏰ ㊲ **Museo Artequín.** The resplendent Pabellón París houses this interactive museum that teaches the fundamentals of art to children, but the pavilion itself is the real jewel. It was designed by French architect Henri Picq to house Chile's exhibition in the 1889 Paris International Exposition (where Gustave Eiffel's skyline-defining tower was unveiled). After the show the structure was shipped back to Santiago. Its glass domes, Pompeian-red walls, and blue-steel columns and supports make it a diaphanous box of exquisite beauty. Weekdays, school groups explore the two floors of reproductions of famous artworks, touch-screen computers, and didactic areas. On weekends there are more guides available to explain the pavilion's history. Call ahead to request an English-speaking tour. ✉ *Av. Portales 3530, Parque Quinta Normal* ☏ *2/682–5367* ⊕ *www.artequin.cl* 🎟 *500 pesos* ☺ *Tues.–Fri. 9–5, Sun. 11–6* Ⓜ *Estación Central.*

⏰ ㊵ **Museo de Ciencia y Tecnología.** This science-and-technology museum for children is rather unfocused but has a good collection of old phonographs and a dark and moody astronomy wing with exhibits that resemble overgrown science projects. It's worth a visit for its Internet room, which offers competitive connection rates. ✉ *Parque Quinta Normal* ☏ *2/681–6022 or 2/689–8026* ⊕ *www.corpdicyt.cl* 🎟 *800 pesos* ☺ *Tues.–Fri. 10–6, weekends 11–6* Ⓜ *Estación Central.*

⏰ ㊳ **Museo Ferroviario.** Chile's once-mighty railroads have been relegated to history, but this acre of Parque Quinta Normal keeps a bit of the romance alive. More than a dozen steam locomotives and three passenger coaches are set within quiet gardens with placards in Spanish and English. You can board two of the trains. Among the collection is the cross-Andes express, which operated between Chile and Argentina from 1911 until 1971. A re-creation of a typical station has photos and exhibits. ✉ *Av. Las Palmas, Parque Quinta Normal* ☏ *2/681–4627* ⊕ *www.corpdicyt.cl* 🎟 *750 pesos* ☺ *Tues.–Fri. 10–5:30, weekends 11–7* Ⓜ *Estación Central.*

⏰ ㊴ **Museo Nacional de Historia Natural.** The National Museum of Natural History is the centerpiece of Parque Quinta Normal. Paul Lathoud designed the building for Chile's first International Exposition, in 1875. After suffering damage from successive earthquakes, the neoclassical structure was rebuilt and enlarged. Though the exhibits are slightly outdated and there are no English texts to guide you, the large dioramas of stuffed animals against painted backdrops are still intriguing, as are the numerous stone heads from Easter Island. The skeleton of an enormous blue whale hangs in the central hall, delighting children of all ages. ✉ *Parque Quinta Normal s/n* ☏ *2/680–4615* ⊕ *www.mnhn.cl* 🎟 *Tues.–Sat. 600 pesos, Sun. free* ☺ *Tues.–Sat. 10–5:30, Sun. noon–5:30* Ⓜ *Estación Central.*

⏰ ㊱ **Planetario.** The Universidad de Chile's planetarium dome mimics a universe of stars with a weekend show open to the general public. During the week it buzzes with schoolchildren only. ✉ *La Alameda 3349, Estación Central* ☏ *2/681–2171* ⊕ *www.planetariochile.cl* 🎟 *2,000 pesos* ☺ *Weekend shows: noon, 3:30, and 5* Ⓜ *Estación Central.*

WHERE TO EAT

Santiago can be overwhelming when it comes to dining, as hundreds of restaurants are strewn about the city. No matter what strikes your fancy, there are likely to be half a dozen eateries within easy walking distance. Tempted to taste hearty Chilean fare? Pull up a stool at one of the counters at Vega Central and enjoy a traditional pastel de choclo. Craving seafood? Head to the Mercado Central, where you can choose from the fresh fish brought in that morning. Want a memorable meal? Trendy new restaurants are opening every day in neighborhoods like Bellavista, where hip Santiaguinos come to check out the latest hot spots.

In the neighborhood of Vitacura, a 15–20 minute taxi ride from the city center, a complex of restaurants called Borde Río attracts an upscale crowd. El Bosque, an area along Avenida El Bosque Norte and Avenida Isidora Goyenechea in Las Condes, has a cluster of restaurants and cafés. The emphasis is on creative cuisine, so you'll often be treated to familiar favorites with a Chilean twist. This is one of the few neighborhoods where you can stroll from restaurant to restaurant until you find exactly what you want.

One of the most pleasing aspects of the city's dining scene is the relatively low price of a fine meal. It's difficult to find an entrée in the city that tops $15. And many who assume that the best vintages have been exported are pleasantly surprised by extensive wine lists with good prices.

Remember that Santiaguinos dine a little later than the rest of us. Most fancier restaurants don't open for lunch until 1. (You may startle the cleaning staff if you rattle the doors at noon.) Dinner begins at 7:30 or 8, although most places don't get crowded until after 9. Many eateries close for a few hours before dinner.

WHAT IT COSTS In pesos (in thousands)				
$$$$	**$$$**	**$$**	**$**	**¢**
AT DINNER over 11	8–11	5–8	3–5	under 3

Prices are for a main course at dinner.

Bellavista

Chilean

$$–$$$$ ✕ **El Camino Real.** On a clear day, treat yourself to the stunning views of the city through the floor-to-ceiling windows at this restaurant atop Cerro San Cristóbal. The menu lists such dishes as pork tenderloin in mustard sauce with caramelized onions, and warm scallop salad with quail eggs and asparagus. Oenophiles appreciate the many Chilean vintages in the wine cellar. Neophytes can head across a central courtyard to Bar Dalí, where the servers can organize an impromptu *degustación* of a half dozen varietals. ⊠ *Parque Metropolitano, Bellavista* ☎ *2/232–3381 or 2/233–1238* ⌕ *Reservations essential* ▤ *AE, DC, MC, V* Ⓜ *Pedro de Valdivia, Baquedano.*

★ **$$–$$$$** ✕**Como Agua Para Chocolate.** Inspired by Laura Esquivel's romantic 1989 novel *Like Water for Chocolate*, this Bellavista standout is part restaurant, part theme park. It focuses on the aphrodisiacal qualities of food, so it shouldn't be surprising that one long table is actually an iron bed, with place settings arranged on a crisp white sheet. The food compares to the decor like the film version compares to the book: it's good, but not nearly as imaginative. *Ave de la pasión,* for instance, means Bird of Passion. It may be just chicken with mushrooms, but it's served on a copper plate. ⊠ *Constitución 88, Bellavista* ☎ *2/777–8740* ⊟ *AE, DC, MC, V* Ⓜ *Baquedano.*

$–$$ ✕**El Venezia.** Long before Bellavista became fashionable, this bare-bones picada was where movie stars and TV personalities rubbed elbows with the hoi polloi. Although gourmands now head a block or two in either direction to the latest hot spots, tacky El Venezia still fills to capacity each day at lunch. And what's not to like? The beer is icy, the waiters are efficient, and the food is abundant. The *congrio frito* (fried conger eel) is delicious, as are the *costillar de chancho* (pork ribs). As a nod to the name, there are also prodigious plates of pasta. ⊠ *Pío Nono 200, Bellavista* ☎ *2/737–0900* ⊟ *AE, DC, MC, V* Ⓜ *Baquedano.*

Seafood

$–$$ ✕**Azul Profundo.** Not so many years ago, this was the only restaurant
Fodor'sChoice you'd find on this street near Parque Metropolitano. Today it's one of
★ dozens of restaurants in trendy Bellavista, but its two-level dining room—with walls painted bright shades of blue and yellow, and racks of wine stretching to the ceiling—ensure that it stands out in the crowd. Choose your fish from the extensive menu—swordfish, sea bass, shark, flounder, salmon, trout, and haddock are among the choices—and enjoy it *a la plancha* (grilled) or *a la lata* (served on a sizzling plate with tomatoes and onions). ⊠ *Constitución 111, Bellavista* ☎ *2/738–0288* ⌂ *Reservations essential* ⊟ *AE, DC, MC, V* Ⓜ *Baquedano.*

¢**–$$** ✕**Eladio.** You can eat a succulent *bife de chorizo* (sirloin) or mouthwatering *costillas de cerdo* (pork ribs) or just about any other meat cooked as you like and enjoy it with a good bottle of Chilean wine—and your pockets wouldn't be much lighter. Finish with a slice of *amapola* (poppy-seed) sponge cake. Come to this second-floor dining room any night but Friday, as the place fills up fast with locals celebrating the arrival of the weekend. ⊠ *Pío Nono 251, Bellavista* ☎ *2/777–5083* ⊟ *AE, DC, MC, V* ☉ *Closed Sun.* Ⓜ *Baquedano.*

Spanish

★ **$–$$$** ✕**De Tapas y Copas.** Bucking the trend among this neighborhood's many restaurants, De Tapas y Copas isn't filled with antiques or wedged into a basement. The modern dining room is open and airy, with little to take the attention away from the food. Among the best dishes are *paella de mariscos* (seafood with rice) and tapas like *calamares fritos al alioli* (fried squid with garlic mayonnaise). And what about the copas? Glasses of many different Spanish wines are available at the curved wood bar. ⊠ *Dardignac 0192, at Mallinkrodt, Bellavista* ☎ *2/777–6477* ⊟ *AE, DC, MC, V* Ⓜ *Baquedano.*

Where to Stay & Eat in Santiago Centro & Bellavista

RECOLETA

Cementerio General

Cerro Blonco

Parque Metropolitano

BELLAVISTA

PATRONATO

24

Funicular

18
20
19
22 23
21

Plaza Ba
BAQUE

Plaza Mulato
Gil de Castro

BELLAS ARTES

16
15
17

UNIVERSIDAD CATÓLICA

Santa Lucia

Río Mapocho

CAL Y CANTO

12

13

14

10

11

PLAZA DE ARMAS

SANTA LUCIA

4

3

SANTA ANA

UNIVERIDAD DE CHILE

5
7
9
6
8

LA MONEDA

LOS HÉROES

Plaza Quinta Normal

Plaza Brazil

2

TO ESTACIÓN CENTRAL

1

Restaurants ▼

Atelier del Parque **14**

Azul Profundo **22**

Bristol **5**

Como Agua
Para Chocolate **21**

Confitería Torres **2**

De Tapas y Copas **23**

Donde Augusto **12**

Eladio **20**

El Camino Real **24**

El Venezia **19**

Gatopardo **17**

Govinda's **3**

La Bodeguilla **18**

Les Assassins **16**

Majestic **4**

Zully **1**

Hotels ▼

City Hotel **11**

El Marqués
del Forestal **13**

Foresta **15**

Hotel Fundador **6**

Hotel Majestic **4**

Hotel París **9**

Hotel Plaza
San Francisco **5**

Hotel Santa Lucia **10**

Hotel Vegas **7**

Residencial
Londres **8**

$–$$ ✕ **La Bodeguilla.** This authentic Spanish restaurant is a great place to stop for a glass of sangria after tackling Cerro San Cristóbal. After all, it's right at the foot of the funicular. The dozen or so tables are set among wine barrels and between hanging strings of garlic bulbs. Nibble on tasty tapas like *chorizo riojano* (a piquant sausage), *pulpo a la gallega* (octopus with peppers and potatoes), and *queso manchego* (a mild white cheese) while perusing the long wine list. Then consider ordering the house specialty—*cabrito al horno* (oven-roasted goat). ⊠ *Av. Dominica 5, Bellavista* ☎ *2/732–5215* ⊟ *No credit cards* ☉ *Closed Sun.* Ⓜ *Baquedano.*

Centro

Chilean

$$–$$$$ ✕ **Bristol.** The indefatigable Guillermo Rodríguez, who has commandeered
Fodor'sChoice the kitchen here for more than a decade, has won just about all the coun-
★ try's culinary competitions. No wonder he also serves as a private chef to Chilean president Ricardo Lagos. You won't find dishes like marinated scallops over octopus carpaccio or king crab tartar on any other menu in town. The expertise offered by the city's most prized sommelier, Alejandro Farias, is reason enough to visit. The only disappointment is the uninspired dining room, which pales next to the city's other top-notch eateries. ⊠ *Hotel Plaza San Francisco, La Alameda 816, Santiago Centro* ☎ *2/639–3832* ⊟ *AE, DC, MC, V* Ⓜ *Universidad de Chile.*

$$–$$$ ✕ **Zully.** In a massive stone house that once belonged to poet Vincente
Fodor'sChoice Huidobro, this is the destination for Santiago's see-and-be-seen crowd.
★ Each dining room is different: one is filled with sage-color chaise longues, another has white leather stools surrounding a raised glass table. The food is Chilean, but there are also hints of other cuisines. The risotto with shrimp, leeks, and truffle oil is a standout, as is the tuna with rice noodles and a black sesame sauce. After dinner, take a stroll through the quaint Concha y Toro neighborhood, a few blocks west of downtown. ⊠ *Concha y Toro 34, Concha y Toro* ☎ *2/696–3990* ⚔ *Reservations essential* ⊟ *AE, DC, MC, V* ☉ *No lunch weekends* Ⓜ *Republica.*

★ **$$** ✕ **Confitería Torres.** José Domingo Torres created such delicious dishes that other aristocrats "borrowed" him for their banquets. In 1879, he set up shop in this storefront on the Alameda. It remains of the city's best dining rooms, with red leather banquettes, mint-green tile floors, and huge chandeliers with tulip-shape globes. The food, such as *lomo al ajo arriego* (sirloin sautéed with peppers and garlic) comes from recipes by the mother of owner Claudio Soto Barría. He and his parents will likely greet you from their little table near the front door. ⊠ *Alameda 1570, Santiago Centro* ☎ *2/688–0751* ⊟ *AE, DC, MC, V* Ⓜ *Universidad de Chile.*

$–$$ ✕ **Atelier del Parque.** Alluding to its artistic leanings, this restaurant's menus come on palettes with their own paintbrushes. On offer are creations named for artists, such as the Da Vinci (inky black fettuccine tossed with squid) and the Neruda (risotto in a seafood sauce). Although it gets crowded, you can usually find an isolated table in the many little dining rooms, including one reached by a wrought-iron spiral staircase. A connected gallery showcases temporary exhibits of art and sculpture.

✉ *Santo Domingo 528, Parque Forestal* ☎ *2/639–5843* ▭ *AE, DC, MC, V* Ⓜ *Bellas Artes.*

French

$–$$ ✕ **Gatopardo.** It's a bit of a stretch to call this a French restaurant, but you can order delicious fare like the perfectly grilled entrecôte. For something a bit different, opt for the *chuletas de cordero al romero* (lamb chops with rosemary). The glass-roofed dining room is especially inviting on sunny afternoons. The bright orange building sits among a cluster of eateries south of Plaza Mulato Gil de Castro. ✉ *José Victorino Lastarria 192, Santiago Centro* ☎ *2/633–6420* ▭ *AE, DC, MC, V* Ⓜ *Universidad Católica.*

$–$$ ✕ **Les Assassins.** Although this appears at first glance to be a rather somber bistro, nothing could be further from the truth. The service is friendly, and the Provence-influenced food is first-rate. The steak au poivre and beef bourguignonne would make a Frenchman's eyes water. And where else in Santiago could you find crêpe suzettes? If you want to practice your Spanish, you're in luck: there's always a line of talkative locals in the cozy ground-floor bar. ✉ *Merced 297, Santiago Centro* ☎ *2/638–4280* ▭ *AE, DC, MC, V* ✆ *Closed Sun.* Ⓜ *Universidad Católica.*

Indian

★ **¢–$$** ✕ **Majestic.** Chef Haridas Chauhan, originally of the Sheraton in New Delhi, has turned a restaurant in a small hotel into a dining destination. Start with the mild samosas (vegetable turnovers), then turn up the heat with such deliciously spicy dishes as *rogan josh* (hot lamb curry) and *murgh makhanwala* (chicken in a tangy butter sauce). The *kulfi de almendras,* made from evaporated milk, ice cream, walnuts, and almonds, is a sweet finish to a meal. The smaller dining room used for lunch is a bit cramped, but the larger one opened for dinner is open and airy. ✉ *Santo Domingo 1526, Santiago Centro* ☎ *2/695–8366* ⌂ *Reservations essential* ▭ *AE, DC, MC, V* Ⓜ *Santa Ana.*

Seafood

★ **¢–$$$$** ✕ **Donde Augusto.** What was once a simple seafood stand has taken over almost all the interior of Mercado Central. If you don't mind the unhurried service and the odd tear in the tablecloth, you may have the time of your life dining on everything from sea urchins to baby eel. Placido Domingo eats here on every visit to Chile, attended to by the white-bearded Segovian Augusto Vasquez, who has run Donde Augusto for more than four decades. Go for simple dishes like the *corvina plancha* (grilled sea bass), which is mouthwateringly good. Get here early, as it closes at 6 PM. ✉ *Mercado Central, Santiago Centro* ☎ *2/672–2829* ⌂ *Reservations not accepted* ▭ *AE, DC, MC, V* ✆ *No dinner* Ⓜ *Puente Cal y Canto.*

Vegetarian

¢ ✕ **Govinda's.** Cheap but hearty vegetarian lunches are prepared here by Hari Krishnas. Small wooden tables and chairs are the extent of the decor, but the tofu and vegetable dishes and homemade bread are delicious. Try the yogurt with mixed fruit and honey for dessert. ✉ *Av. Compañía 1489, Santiago Centro* ☎ *2/673–0892* ▭ *No credit cards* ✆ *Closed weekends. No dinner* Ⓜ *Santa Ana.*

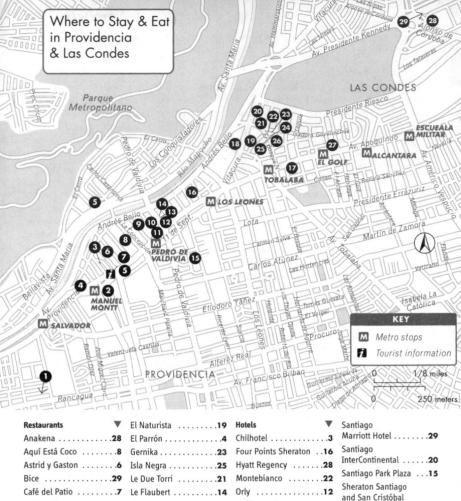

Where to Stay & Eat in Providencia & Las Condes

Restaurants ▼

Anakena **28**
Aquí Está Coco **8**
Astrid y Gaston **6**
Bice **29**
Café del Patio **7**
Café Melba **26**
Coco Loco **24**
De Cangrejo a Conejo . . .**1**
El Cid **5**
El Huerto **13**

El Naturista **19**
El Parrón **4**
Gernika **23**
Isla Negra **25**
Le Due Torri **21**
Le Flaubert **14**
Liguria **2, 10**
Lomit's **11**
Mare Nostum **9**
Matsuri **38**

Hotels ▼

Chilhotel **3**
Four Points Sheraton . .**16**
Hyatt Regency **28**
Montebianco **22**
Orly **12**
Radisson Plaza **18**
Ritz-Carlton **27**

Santiago
Marriott Hotel **29**
Santiago
InterContinental **20**
Santiago Park Plaza . . .**15**
Sheraton Santiago
and San Cristóbal
Tower **5**
Tarapacá **17**

Las Condes

Cafés

¢–$ ✕ **Café Melba.** Almost unheard of in Santiago, this storefront restaurant serves breakfast all day. If you're particularly hungry, order "The Works"— baked beans, mushrooms, sausage, and bacon. Drink it down with a caffe latte, served in a large white bowl. The interior is open and airy, with wooden tables scattered about the wood-floored dining room. In warm weather, grab a seat on the covered patio in front. Get here early, as it closes around 6. ⊠ *Don Carlos 2898, off Av. El Bosque Norte, Las Condes* ☎ *2/232–4546* ⊟ *AE, DC, MC, V* ⊘ *No dinner* Ⓜ *Tobalaba.*

Italian

★ $$–$$$$ ✕ **Bice.** Bice has revolutionized Santiago's notion of elegant dining. The small, two-tiered dining room has soaring ceilings that lend a dramatic flair, and gleaming floors of alternating stripes of dark and light wood add a touch of contemporary glamour. The service is a breed apart— white-jacketed waiters zip around, attending to your every need. The menu leans toward imaginatively prepared pastas, such as linguine with scallops, razor clams, shrimp, and mussels. Be sure to leave room for desserts such as the *cioccolatíssimo,* a hot, chocolate soufflé with melted chocolate inside, served with an exquisite *dulce de leche* ice cream. ⊠ *Hotel Inter-Continental, Av. Luz 2920, Las Condes* ☎ *2/381–5500* ⌦ *Reservations essential* ⊟ *AE, DC, MC, V* Ⓜ *Tobalaba.*

$$–$$$$ ✕ **Le Due Torri.** For excellent homemade pastas, head to this longtime favorite. If you think the *agnolotti,* stuffed with ricotta cheese and spinach, resembles a feathered hat, you're right. The affable owner, who lived in Italy during World War II, intentionally shaped it like a nurse's cap. The rear of the dining room, with its small cypress trees and a corner pergola, is traditional; seating in the front is more contemporary. The name of the restaurant, by the way, refers to the two towers erected by the dueling Garisenda and Asinelli families in the owner's native Bologna. ⊠ *Av. Isidora Goyenechea 2908, Las Condes* ☎ *2/231–3427* ⌦ *Reservations essential* ⊟ *AE, DC, MC, V* Ⓜ *Tobalaba.*

Japanese

$–$$ ✕ **Matsuri.** With a sleek design that calls to mind Los Angeles as much as Tokyo, this restaurant in the Hyatt Regency is one of Santiago's most stylish eateries. After passing through a foyer painted vivid red, you enter the calm dining area with its sliding screens and view of a waterfall. Downstairs are a sushi bar and two tatami rooms (no shoes allowed, but slippers are provided) with sliding screens for privacy, and upstairs are two grill tables. The menu is constantly changing, but look for the smoked duck with eggplant puree or the grilled tuna served with a seaweed salad. There is also a long list of sushi and sashimi available. ⊠ *Hyatt Regency Santiago, Av. Kennedy 4601, Las Condes* ☎ *2/363–3051* ⊟ *AE, DC, MC, V* Ⓜ *Escuela Militar.*

Seafood

$$–$$$$ ✕ **Coco Loco.** What's "loco" here is the price people plunk down for the lobsters. They're rare in these waters, but does that justify a price tag of nearly $50? The other items on the menu, including the king crab au

gratin and the squid-ink risotto with asparagus, are much better values. The dining room, with impressionistic murals of waves (they might remind you of Vincent van Gogh's *Starry Night*), is full of whimsy. Two lucky people get to dine in a brightly painted rowboat. ⊠ *Av. El Bosque Norte 0215, Las Condes* ☎ *2/233–8930* ⌦ *Reservations essential* ▤ *AE, DC, MC, V* Ⓜ *Tobalaba.*

$$ ✕ **Isla Negra.** The sails flying from the roof let you know that Isla Negra means business when it comes to seafood. The restaurant takes its name from a coastal town south of Santiago that was Nobel laureate Pablo Neruda's last home. The poet's favorite dish was conger eel soup, and you'll find it served here as a starter. Don't miss the empanadas stuffed with everything from cheese to razor clams. The *chupe de marisco*, a delicious seafood chowder, comes in a quaint earthenware bowl. ⊠ *Av. El Bosque Norte 0325, Las Condes* ☎ *2/231–3118* ▤▤ *2/233–0339* ⌦ *Reservations essential* ▤ *AE, DC, MC, V* Ⓜ *Tobalaba.*

Spanish

$–$$ ✕ **Gernika.** The Basque owners of this wood-and-stone restaurant have created a little slice of their homeland with graceful stone arches, tapestries bearing ancient coats of arms, and even jai alai equipment. Head upstairs to the more intimate upper level, which has three well-decorated private dining salons. Chilean seafood is cooked with Spanish flair, as in the *congrio donostiarra* (conger eel coated in chili sauce and fried in olive oil). Delicious *centolla* (king crab) is brought in from the chilly waters of Tierra del Fuego. Several hearty selections from Spain's Rioja region appear on the wine list. ⊠ *Av. El Bosque Norte 0227, Las Condes* ☎ *2/232–9954* ⌦ *Reservations essential* ▤ *AE, DC, MC, V* ⊘ *No lunch Sat.* Ⓜ *Tobalaba.*

Thai

★ $$–$$$ ✕ **Anakena.** Designed to resemble an outdoor market, this elegant eatery emphasizes fresh ingredients. You can order Thai favorites like pad thai (rice noodles, peanuts, egg, sprouts, and shrimp), but the best items on the menu are those that combine the cooking style of Asia with those of Europe and South America. That's how you can get unusual starters like fried oysters with bacon and spring rolls stuffed with lobster, goat cheese, and artichokes. If it's on the menu, don't pass up the grilled swordfish in a basil beurre blanc. There's a separate entrance for the restaurant, so you don't have to enter through the lobby of the Hyatt Regency. ⊠ *Hyatt Regency Santiago, Av. Kennedy 4601, Las Condes* ☎ *2/363–3177* ▤ *AE, DC, MC, V* Ⓜ *Escuela Militar.*

Vegetarian

¢–$ ✕ **El Naturista.** If you're used to vegetarian restaurants that look like they forgot to decorate, then this elegant eatery with its green-and-white-checkered floor will be a nice surprise. The kitchen here has sidled away from run-of-the-mill vegetarian fare. It conjures up such dishes as *fricasé de cochayuyo* (seaweed stew)—a distinctly slimy but good dish that's typically Chilean in that seaweed is widely eaten throughout the country. The scrumptious lasagna is made from homegrown eggplants. ⊠ *Av. Vitacura 2751, Las Condes* ☎ *2/236–5140* ▤ *AE, DC, MC, V* ⊘ *Closed Sun.* Ⓜ *Tobalaba.*

Providencia

Chilean

$$–$$$$
Fodor'sChoice
★
✕ **Astrid y Gaston.** The kitchen is the real star here—every seat in the pumpkin-color dining room has a great view of the chefs at work. You couldn't do better than start with the agnolottis, little pockets of squid-ink pasta stuffed with king crab and cherry tomatoes. After that, try one of the one-of-a-kind entrées, such as the lamb shank drenched in *pisco* (a brandy distilled from small grapes) and served with three kinds of yucca or the parrot fish with tamarind and ginger. Make sure to peruse the wine list, one of the best in town. Save room for one of Astrid's desserts, such as the creamy confection called *suspiro limeña*, "sigh of a lady from Lima": a meringue-topped dish of dulce de leche. ☒ *Antonio Bellet 201, Providencia* ☏ *2/650–9125* ⌕ *Reservations essential* ▤ *AE, DC, MC, V* Ⓜ *Pedro de Valdivia.*

$$–$$$$
Fodor'sChoice
★
✕ **El Cid.** Considered by critics to be one of the city's top restaurants, El Cid is the culinary centerpiece of the classic Sheraton Santiago. The dining room, which overlooks the pool, has crisp linens and simple place settings. All the excitement here is provided by the food, which is served with a flourish. Don't miss the famous grilled seafood—king crab, prawns, squid, and scallops with a sweet, spicy sauce. If you're new to Chilean cuisine, you can't go wrong with the excellent lunch buffet, which includes unlimited wine. ☒ *Av. Santa María 1742, Providencia* ☏ *2/233–5000* ▤ *AE, DC, MC, V* Ⓜ *Pedro de Valdivia.*

$–$$
✕ **El Parrón.** One of the city's oldest restaurants, dating from 1936, specializes in grilled meats. You can watch the action in the kitchen through enormous windows. The dining areas are large and slightly impersonal, but the extensive wine list and menu make up for them. The congenial, wood-paneled bar is the perfect place to sample the refreshing national aperitif—the pisco sour. For dessert try a popular Chilean street-trolley offering, *mote con huesillos* (peeled wheat kernels and dried peaches). ☒ *Av. Providencia 1184, Providencia* ☏ *2/251–8911* ▤ *AE, DC, MC, V* ⊘ *No dinner Sun.* Ⓜ *Manuel Montt.*

★ **¢–$$**
✕ **Lomit's.** There's nothing particularly smart about Lomit's, a traditional Chilean restaurant, but it unfailingly serves up some of the city's best *barros lucos,* steak sandwiches overflowing with melted cheese. You can eat at the long wooden bar and watch the sandwich maker at work, or find a small table to the side (prices are a bit less at the *mesón* than at the *mesas*). Black-trimmed red jackets are the everyday attire of the stern-faced waiters, who brighten up when a regular walks through the door. This is an institution, and shouldn't be missed. ☒ *Av. Providencia 1980, Providencia* ☏ *2/233–1897* ▤ *AE, DC, MC, V* Ⓜ *Pedro de Valdivia.*

¢–$
✕ **Liguria.** This extremely popular picada is always packed, so you might have to wait to be seated in the chandelier-lighted dining room or at one of the tables that spill out onto the sidewalk. A large selection of Chilean wine accompanies such favorites as *jardín de mariscos* (shellfish stew) and the filling *cazuela* (a stew of beef or chicken and potatoes). There are several branches in the neighborhood, but each has its own personality. Afternoons find locals bellying up to the bar. ☒ *Av. Providencia 1373, Providencia* ☏ *2/235–7914* Ⓜ *Manuel Montt*

✉ *Pedro de Valdivia 047, Providencia* ☎ *2/334–4346* Ⓜ *Pedro de Valdivia* 🖃 *No credit cards* ⊘ *Closed Sun.*

French

$$–$$$$ ✕ **Le Flaubert.** With table lamps casting a warm glow, racks full of magazines, and walls covered with black-and-white photographs, this little eatery could be in any small town in France. The menu of the day, written on a blackboard, might tempt you with such dishes as a traditional coq au vin—cooked to perfection. Homesick Brits come here to reminisce over freshly baked scones and refreshing cups of tea. There's a large, shady patio garden where the staff doesn't mind if you linger over a cup of coffee. ✉ *Orrego Luco 125, Providencia* ☎ *2/231–9424* 🖃 *AE, DC, MC, V* Ⓜ *Pedro de Valdivia.*

Mediterranean

$–$$ ✕ **De Cangrejo a Conejo.** Heavy wooden double doors bring you into a large, high-ceilinged interior of this hip eatery. Tables and chairs of pale wood and steel have been thoughtfully arranged around a long curving bar, and flourishing greenery extends out into the patio garden. The menu reflects its name, serving everything from *cangrejo* (crab) to *conejo* (rabbit). Try the crab pie or the lamb shanks on a bed of creamy mashed potatoes, or the sole with sautéed vegetables. ✉ *Av. Italia 805, Providencia* ☎ *2/634–4041 or 2/634–4064* 🖃 *No credit cards* ⊘ *Closed Sun.*

Seafood

$$–$$$$ ✕ **Aquí Está Coco.** The best seafood in Santiago is served in a dining room **Fodor**⌗**Choice** where the walls are covered with flotsam and jetsam found on Chilean ★ beaches. Ask your waiter—or friendly owner "Coco" Pacheco—which fish was caught that day. This is a good place to try Chile's famous *machas* (clams), served with tomatoes and Parmesan cheese, or *corvina* (sea bass) grilled with plenty of butter. Don't miss the cellar, where you can sample wines from the extensive collection of Chilean vintages. ✉ *La Concepción 236, Providencia* ☎ *2/235–8649* ⌒ *Reservations essential* 🖃 *AE, DC, MC, V* ⊘ *Closed Sun.* Ⓜ *Pedro de Valdivia.*

$$–$$$$ ✕ **Mare Nostum.** One of Santiago's most elegant dining rooms, Mare Nostrum doesn't look like a seafood restaurant. In fact, the only clue that it specializes in fish is the subtle ship's-wheel pattern in the deep blue carpeting. All the effort here is on the food, which leans toward Peruvian specialties like seviche (raw fish marinated in citrus) and *tiradito* (similar, but covered in a pepper sauce). A standout is the *ambrosia de pulpo*, a spicy grilled octopus. The friendly staff is happy to help you negotiate the menu or pick just the right wine. ✉ *La Concepción 281, Providencia* ☎ *2/251–5691* ⌒ *Reservations essential* 🖃 *AE, DC, MC, V* Ⓜ *Pedro de Valdivia.*

Vegetarian

$ ✕ **El Huerto.** In the heart of Providencia, this vegetarian eatery is a hangout for hip young Santiaguinos. Even the wood paneling and high windows here feel healthful. Simple dishes like spinach quiche and pancakes stuffed with asparagus and mushrooms are full of flavor, but it's the hearty soups and freshly squeezed juices that register the highest praise. Try the tasty *jugo de zanahoria* (carrot juice). A little shop sells all the ingredients you need to make these dishes at home. ⊠ *Orrego Luco 054, Providencia* ☎ *2/233–2690* ⊟ *AE, DC, MC, V* ⊘ *No lunch Sun.* Ⓜ *Pedro de Valdivia.*

¢–$ ✕ **Café del Patio.** The chef uses all organic produce, half of which is grown in the owner's garden, at this vegetarian eatery hidden in the back of quaint Galería del Patio. The chef's salad—with lettuce, tomato, hearts of palm, and Gruyère cheese—is exquisite, as is the vegetarian ravioli. The menu also includes expertly rolled sushi. At night, Café del Patio turns into a bar. ⊠ *Av. Providencia 1670, Providencia* ☎ *2/236–1251* ⊟ *AE, DC, MC, V* ⊘ *Closed Sun. No lunch Sat.* Ⓜ *Pedro de Valdivia.*

Vitacura

Chilean

$$$–$$$$ ✕ **Agua.** Talk about minimalist—this gleaming glass box of a dining room is almost devoid of ornamentation. But that's because the food here gets all the attention. Start with tuna tartar with mango and avocado, then move on to leg of lamb with plum puree or squid-ink ravioli with a scallop-and-shrimp brochette. The bar, with a slightly warmer tone than the rest of the restaurant, is the perfect place for early-evening drinks. If you get here before your reservations, stroll around the tony shops on the nearby streets. ⊠ *Av. Nueva Constanera 3467, Vitacura* ☎ *2/374–1540* ⌂ *Reservations essential* ⊟ *AE, DC, MC, V.*

French

¢–$ ✕ **Le Fournil.** Rumor has it that the French owners import even their flour from France at this authentic boulangerie. The *plato del dia* (dish of the day) is always a tasty concoction, but equally good bets are the mixed green salad with grilled goat's cheese and the succulent carpaccio of salmon. But the tarte tatin steals the show—large, thick chunks of perfectly baked apple atop a thin layer of pastry, served with a scoop of creamy vanilla ice cream. The shady terrace is lovely, but the upstairs dining room is the place for a romantic meal. If you like the baguettes, a little shop lets you take them home. ⊠ *Av. Vitacura 3841, Vitacura* ☎ *2/228–0219* ⊟ *AE, DC, MC, V.*

Middle Eastern

$$–$$$ ✕ **Zanzíbar.** Although you can order a tabouleh salad or lamb stew, this ostensibly Middle Eastern restaurant is more about conjuring up an exotic atmosphere than re-creating the cuisine of the region. (The first clue would be that Zanzibar isn't in the Middle East.) The food is tasty, but the real reason to come is to glide across the multicolor mosaic floors and settle into a chair placed beneath dozens of silver lanterns. Tables are just as fanciful, with designs made from pistachio nuts, red peppers, and beans. It's all a bit over-the-top, but fun nonetheless. ⊠ *Borde Río, Av. Monseñor Escrivá de Balaguer 6400, Vitacura* ☎ *2/218–0119* ⌂ *Reservations essential* ⊟ *AE, DC, MC, V.*

Seafood

$$–$$$ ✕ **Ibis de Puerto Varas.** Nattily nautical sails stretch taut across the ceiling, pierced here and there by mastlike wood columns, and the walls are a splashy blue at this seafood restaurant. Choose from appetizers

such as baby eels with hot pepper and garlic or shrimp and squid with an orange sauce. *Panqueque Ibis* is a pancake stuffed with shrimp, calamari, and scallops; the whole thing is sautéed in butter, flambéed in cognac, and served with a spinach-and-cream sauce. ⊠ *Borde Río, Av. Monseñor Escrivá de Balaguer 6400, Vitacura* ☏ 2/218–0111 ♠ *Reservations essential* ⊟ *AE, DC, MC, V.*

$$ ✕ **Europeo.** Whether you dine on the crisp white-linen tablecloths in the elegant dining room or under an umbrella in the open-air brasserie, you're in for a fine meal at this trendy yet relaxed eatery on Santiago's most prestigious shopping avenue. The menu leans toward fish: try the succulent grilled seafood with scallops, squid, salmon, and crispy fried noodles or the lightly grilled smoked salmon steak on a bed of watercress. This is one of the few places in town that serves wild game, such as venison ragout with creamy polenta. Save room for a dessert of crème brûlée *de lucuma* (lucuma is a fruit native to Peru) or chocolate mousse with almonds. ⊠ *Av. Alonso de Córdova 2417, Vitacura* ☏ 2/208–3603 ♠ *Reservations essential* ⊟ *AE, DC, MC, V.*

WHERE TO STAY

Santiago's accommodations range from luxurious *hoteles* to comfortable *residenciales*, which can be homey bed-and-breakfasts or simple hotel-style accommodations. The city also has more than a dozen five-star properties. Most newer hotels are in Providencia and Las Condes, a short taxi ride from Santiago Centro.

Although the official room rates are pricey, you'll undoubtedly find discounts. Call several hotels and ask for the best possible rate. It's a good idea to reserve in advance during the peak seasons (January, February, July, and August).

Note that the 18% hotel tax is removed from your bill if you pay in U.S. dollars or with a credit card.

WHAT IT COSTS In pesos (in thousands)				
$$$$	**$$$**	**$$**	**$**	**¢**
FOR 2 PEOPLE over 105	75–105	45–75	15–45	under 15

Prices are for a double room in high season, excluding tax

Centro

$$$ ▣ **Hotel Fundador.** On the edge of the quaint Barrio París-Londres, the Hotel Fundador captures the neighborhood's old-fashioned feeling while staying completely up to date. This hotel has business on its mind, so there are plenty of meeting rooms with high-tech equipment. But it also caters to travelers, so there are amenities like the small indoor pool illuminated by a skylight. Rooms are elegant, with rich fabrics and beautifully polished wood. Make sure to take a stroll across the iron bridge across Calle Londres that links the hotel's two halves. ⊠ *Passeo Serrano 34 , Santiago Centro* ☏ 2/387–1200 ☐ 2/387–1300 ⊕ *www.*

hotelfundador.cl ⇗ *123 rooms, 27 suites* ⚏ *2 restaurants, room service, in-room data ports, in-room safes, minibars, cable TV, indoor pool, exercise equipment, hair salon, hot tub, sauna, spa, bar, lobby bar, shops, laundry service, business services, convention center, meeting rooms, free parking, no-smoking floors* ▭ *AE, DC, MC, V* ⦿ *BP* Ⓜ *Universidad de Chile.*

$$ ⊞ **Hotel Plaza San Francisco.** Across from Iglesia San Francisco, this
Fodor'sChoice business hotel has everything traveling executives need, from secretar-
★ ial services to a slew of meeting rooms. Between meetings there's plenty to do—take a dip in the sparkling indoor pool, work out in the health club, stroll through the art gallery, or select a bottle from the well-stocked wineshop. Large beds, lovely antique furniture, and marble-trim baths fill the hotel's cozy rooms. And although all these amenities are tremendous draws, one of the best reasons to choose this hotel is for its helpful, professional staff. ⊠ *La Alameda 816, Santiago Centro* ☎ *2/639–3832, 800/223–5652 toll-free in U.S.* 🖷 *2/639–7826* ⊕ *www. plazasanfrancisco.cl* ⇗ *155 rooms, 8 suites* ⚏ *Restaurant, room service, in-room data ports, in-room safes, minibars, cable TV, in-room VCRs, Wi-Fi, indoor pool, health club, hair salon, hot tub, massage, sauna, bar, lobby lounge, piano bar, laundry service, business services, convention center, meeting rooms, free parking* ▭ *AE, DC, MC, V* ⦿ *BP* Ⓜ *Universidad de Chile.*

★ **$** ⊞ **City Hotel.** Suitably bedecked porters open the heavy front doors of this 70-year-old establishment, an art deco landmark. This grande dame is showing her age, but still has some old-fashioned charm. Don't miss the wrought-iron canopy that links the hotel's two wings. The slightly dated rooms are spacious with parquet floors and high ceilings, and bathrooms still have the original large white tubs. Request one of the quieter rooms not facing the street. It's in the heart of downtown, less than a minute from the Plaza de Armas. ⊠ *Compañía 1063, Santiago Centro* ☎☎ *2/695–4526* ⊕ *www.hotelcity.cl* ⇗ *72 rooms* ⚏ *Restaurant, room service, in-room safes, minibars, cable TV, bar, laundry service, meeting room, free parking; no a/c* ▭ *AE, DC, MC, V* ⦿ *CP* Ⓜ *Plaza de Armas.*

$ ⊞ **Foresta.** Staying in this seven-story hotel across the street from Cerro Santa Lucía is like visiting an elegant old home. Cheery floral wallpaper, lovely antique furnishings, and bronze-and-marble accents decorate the guest rooms. The best ones are those on the upper floors overlooking the hill. A rooftop restaurant-bar is a great place to enjoy the view. The quaint cafés and shops of Plaza Mulato Gil de Castro are just around the corner. ⊠ *Victoria Subercaseaux 353, Santiago Centro* ☎☎ *2/639–6261* ⇗ *35 rooms, 8 suites* ⚏ *Restaurant, room service, minibars, cable TV, bar, piano bar, laundry service, Internet, meeting room, free parking; no a/c* ▭ *AE, DC, MC, V* Ⓜ *Bellas Artes.*

$ ⊞ **Hotel Majestic.** Towering white pillars, peaked archways, and glittery brass ornaments in the lobby welcome you to this Indian-style hotel. A welcoming staff and a location several blocks from the Plaza de Armas make this a good choice. Even though the bright, airy rooms have "soundproof" windows, ask for one facing away from the street.

⊠ *Santo Domingo 1526, Santiago Centro* ☎ *2/695–8366* 🖷 *2/697–4051* ⊕ *www.hotelmajestic.cl* ⤳ *50 rooms* ⚭ *Restaurant, café, fans, in-room safes, minibars, cable TV, pool, bar, laundry service, travel services, meeting room, free parking, no-smoking rooms* ▭ *AE, DC, MC, V* ⦿⧟⦿ *BP* Ⓜ *Santa Ana.*

$ 🖭 **Hotel Santa Lucia.** The rooms at this centrally located hotel are on the small side and are a little tired looking—after all, it's been around for more than 40 years. But they're spotlessly clean and avoid most traffic noise because of their lofty position on the fourth floor of an office building. The lobby is bright, airy, and spacious. The large terrace restaurant, unusually quiet given its location, serves nothing but typical Chilean fare. ⊠ *San Antonio 327, Paseo Huérfanos 779, Santiago Centro* ☎ *2/639–8201* 🖷 *2/633–1844* ⤳ *70 rooms* ⚭ *Fans, in-room safes, minibars, cable TV, laundry service, Internet, meeting rooms, parking (fee); no a/c* ▭ *AE, DC, MC, V* ⦿⧟⦿ *CP* Ⓜ *Plaza de Armas.*

$ 🖭 **Hotel Vegas.** This colonial-style building, adorned with a bullet-shape turret on the corner, sits in the heart of the charming Barrio París-Londres. Rooms here are spacious and filled with comfortable modern furnishings. All have plenty of windows—ask for one with a sitting room inside the turret so you'll have a view of gently curving Calle Londres. ⊠ *Londres 49, Santiago Centro* ☎ *2/632–2498 or 2/632–2514* 🖷 *2/632–5084* ⊕ *www.hotelvegas.net* ⤳ *20 rooms* ⚭ *Café, room service, in-room safes, cable TV, bar, laundry service, Internet, free parking, no-smoking rooms; no a/c in some rooms* ▭ *AE, DC, MC, V* Ⓜ *Universidad de Chile.*

$ 🖭 **El Marqués del Forestal.** A good budget choice for families, this small hotel has spacious rooms that comfortably sleep up to four people. The bonus is that they also have tiny kitchenettes that are perfect for whipping up a quick breakfast or lunch. The bathrooms are sparkling, but have fixtures in colors not seen for a few decades. The orange building, not far from Mercado Central, overlooks a pretty section of Parque Forestal. The staff is friendly and eager to please. ⊠ *Ismael Valdés Vergara 740, Santiago Centro* ☎ *2/633–3462* 🖷 *2/639–4157* ⤳ *15 apartments* ⚭ *Kitchenettes, bar, laundry service, free parking; no a/c* ▭ *AE, DC, MC, V* ⦿⧟⦿ *CP* Ⓜ *Puente Cal y Canto, Plaza de Armas.*

★ $ 🖭 **Residencial Londres.** This 1920s-era hotel in the picturesque Barrio París-Londres is just a stone's throw from most of the city's major sights. Rooms are spacious, with high ceilings ringed by detailed moldings and expansive wood floors. The best rooms have stone balconies overlooking this charmingly atypical neighborhood. The staff is friendly and helpful. ⊠ *Londres 54, Santiago Centro* ☎🖷 *2/638–2215* ⤳ *27 rooms* ⚭ *Laundry service; no a/c, no room phones, no room TVs* ▭ *No credit cards* Ⓜ *Universidad de Chile.*

¢–$ 🖭 **Hotel París.** In the heart of Barrio París-Londres stands this mansion-turned-hotel. (Despite the name, the grand facade looks more Venetian than Parisian.) Pass through the large lobby and you'll find a quaint courtyard garden. Rooms are old-fashioned and have just the basic furnishings. Those in the more comfortable half, which you reach by a winding, marble staircase, are more spacious, come with cable TV, and are just a few thousand pesos extra. ⊠ *París 813, La Alameda*

☎ 2/664–0921 📠 2/639–4037 🛏 40 rooms 🍴 Café, bar, cable TV *in some rooms; no a/c* ▤ AE, DC, MC, V Ⓜ *Universidad de Chile, Santa Lucía.*

Las Condes

$$$$ ▦ **Ritz-Carlton.** The rather bland brick exterior of this 15-story hotel, the first Ritz-Carlton in South America, belies the luxurious appointments within. Mahogany-panel walls, cream marble floors, and enormous windows characterize the splendid two-story lobby, which faces a small leafy plaza just off busy Avenida Apoquindo. Elegant furnishings upholstered in brocade, and silk floral fabrics dominate the large guest rooms. Under a magnificent glass dome on the top floor you can swim or work out while pondering the panorama, smog permitting, of the Andes and the Santiago skyline. ✉ *El Alcade 15, Las Condes* ☎ *2/473–7500* 📠 *2/473–7505* ⊕ *www.ritzcarlton.com* 🛏 *189 rooms, 16 suites* 🍴 *Restaurant, room service, in-room data ports, in-room safes, minibars, cable TV, golf privileges, indoor pool, gym, hot tub, sauna, Turkish bath, 2 bars, lobby lounge, babysitting, laundry service, concierge, business services, convention center, meeting rooms, airport shuttle, car rental, travel services, free parking, no-smoking rooms* ▤ *AE, DC, MC, V* Ⓜ *El Golf.*

$$$$ ▦ **Santiago Marriott Hotel.** The first 25 floors of this gleaming copper tower—at 40 stories, it's the tallest building in Santiago—house the Marriott. An impressive two-story, cream-marble lobby has full-grown palm trees in and around comfortable seating areas. The hotel caters to those on business trips, and if you opt for an executive room you can breakfast in a private lounge while you scan the newspaper and marvel at the snowcapped Andes. You needn't venture out for entertainment either: there are tango evenings in the Latin Grill restaurant along with weekly wine-tasting sessions. One caveat: located in a suburban neighborhood, it's a bit removed from the action. ✉ *Av. Kennedy 5741, Las Condes* ☎ *2/426–2000, 800/228–9290 toll-free in U.S. and Canada* 📠 *2/426–2001* ⊕ *www.santiagomarriott.com* 🛏 *280 rooms, 60 suites* 🍴 *2 restaurants, in-room data ports, minibars, cable TV, indoor pool, health club, hot tub, sauna, bar, lobby lounge, shops, babysitting, laundry service, concierge, Internet, business services, convention center, meeting rooms, airport shuttle, travel services, free parking, no-smoking floor* ▤ *AE, DC, MC, V.*

★ $$$–$$$$ ▦ **Hyatt Regency Santiago.** The soaring spire of the Hyatt Regency resembles a rocket (and you might feel like an astronaut when you're shooting up a glass elevator through a 24-story atrium). The rooms wrap around the cylindrical lobby, providing a panoramic view of the Andes. Bright-color fabrics and sprays of flowers make the rooms a cut above the rest. As you might guess from the pair of golden lions flanking the entrance, the theme is vaguely Asian, which is why two of the three award-winning restaurants are Thai and Japanese. (Senso, which is Tuscan, is also well worth a visit.) Duke's, the spitting image of an English pub, fills to standing capacity each day after work hours. ✉ *Av. Kennedy 4601, Las Condes* ☎ *2/218–1234* 📠 *2/218–3155* ⊕ *www.santiago.hyatt.com*

⚡ *287 rooms, 23 suites ⚹ 3 restaurants, tea shop, room service, in-room data ports, some in-room faxes, in-room safes, minibars, cable TV, in-room VCRs, golf privileges, 2 tennis courts, pool, fitness classes, health club, hair salon, massage, sauna, bar, lobby lounge, shops, babysitting, laundry service, concierge, Internet, business services, convention center, meeting rooms, airport shuttle, free parking, no-smoking floor* ⊟ *AE, DC, MC, V.*

$$$–$$$$ 🏨 **Santiago InterContinental.** Attendants wearing top hats usher you into the two-story marble lobby of one of the city's top hotels. Beyond the reception desk there is a string of comfortable lounge areas, including one next to an indoor waterfall. In the rear is Bice, one of the city's most memorable restaurants. The rooms are sumptuous, with doors made from handsome panels of the native blond wood called *mañio* and a menu card listing five types of pillows, from "very soft" to "stiff." Five executive floors have express check-in, a sleek private dining area with open bar, and an elegant meeting room. ⊠ *Av. Vitacura 2885, Las Condes* ☎ *2/394–2000* 🖷 *2/394–2075* ⊕ *www.interconti.com/santiago* ⚡ *297 rooms, 9 suites ⚹ 2 restaurants, room service, in-room data ports, in-room safes, minibars, cable TV with movies and video games, indoor pool, gym, massage, sauna, 2 bars, lobby lounge, shops, babysitting, laundry service, concierge, Internet, business services, convention center, meeting rooms, travel services, free parking, no-smoking floors* ⊟ *AE, DC, MC, V* ⧖ *BP* Ⓜ *Tobalaba.*

$$$ 🏨 **Radisson Plaza Santiago.** Santiago's most dynamic office building, the World Trade Center, is also home to the Radisson, a combination that will make sense to many corporate travelers. The windows here are huge, with three wide glass panels for triptych perspectives of the city and the Andes beyond. The upholstered leather chairs and wood paneling in meeting rooms make it clear the hotel is serious in its attitude toward luxury. Even standard rooms have nice touches like wooden writing desks and small sitting areas with plush sofas. ⊠ *Av. Vitacura 2610, Las Condes* ☎ *2/203–6000, 800/333–3333 toll-free in U.S.* 🖷 *2/203–6001* ⊕ *www.radisson.com/santiagocl* ⚡ *159 rooms, 26 suites ⚹ Restaurant, room service, in-room data ports, in-room safes, minibars, cable TV, indoor pool, gym, bar, lounge, library, babysitting, laundry service, concierge, Internet, business services, meeting rooms, helipad, free parking, no-smoking floors* ⊟ *AE, DC, MC, V* Ⓜ *Tobalaba.*

$$ 🏨 **Montebianco.** The Montebianco—in a charming four-story building dwarfed by the towers surrounding it—has an informal setting and a friendly, helpful staff. The rooms, which wind around a central staircase, are on the small side; the king-size beds take up most of the space. Make sure to ask for a room with more space to spread out. The hotel is right on a popular dining thoroughfare. ⊠ *Av. Isidora Goyenechea 2911, Las Condes* ☎ *2/232–5034* 🖷 *2/233–0420* ⊕ *www.hotelmontebianco.cl* ⚡ *33 rooms ⚹ Cafeteria, dining room, in-room safes, some minibars, cable TV, bar, laundry service, Internet, business services, airport shuttle, travel services* ⊟ *AE, DC, MC, V* ⧖ *BP* Ⓜ *El Golf, Tobalaba.*

$ 🏨 **Tarapacá.** This smaller hotel may have a smudge here and there, but its location on the edge of fashionable Las Condes makes up for it. Rooms facing the commercial hub of Avenida Apoquindo are susceptible to traffic noise, so ask for one in the back. Better yet, pay a few extra dollars for one of two spacious suites on the 11th floor. The dormer windows add a bit of charm that rooms on the lower floors lack. ⊠ *Vecinal 40, at Av. Apoquindo, Las Condes* ☎ *2/233–2747* 🖷 *2/233–7072* ⊕ *www. hotelneruda.cl* ⟿ *52 rooms, 2 suites* ⚏ *Restaurant, room service, in-room safes, minibars, cable TV, sauna, bar, laundry service, Internet, business services, meeting rooms, free parking* ⊟ *AE, DC, MC, V* ⏐◉⏐ *BP* Ⓜ *El Golf, Tobalaba.*

Providencia

$$$$ 🏨 **Santiago Park Plaza.** It bills itself as a "classic European-style" hotel, and the receptionists that greet you from behind individual mahogany desks certainly call to mind the Continent. The refined decor, with rich burgundy and cream accents, extends to the adjoining Park Lane restaurant, whose chef masterfully combines international and Chilean cuisine. Although the glass-covered pool on the top floor is tiny, it has a great view. ⊠ *Av. Ricardo Lyon 207, Providencia* ☎ *2/233–6363* 🖷 *2/ 233–6668* ⊕ *www.parkplaza.cl* ⟿ *104 rooms, 6 suites* ⚏ *Restaurant, in-room data ports, in-room safes, minibars, cable TV, golf privileges, indoor pool, gym, health club, massage, sauna, bar, lobby lounge, shop, babysitting, laundry service, Internet, business services, convention center, meeting rooms, airport shuttle, travel services, free parking, no-smoking floor* ⊟ *AE, DC, MC, V* ⏐◉⏐ *BP* Ⓜ *Los Leones.*

★ **$$$** 🏨 **Sheraton Santiago and San Cristóbal Tower.** Two distinct hotels stand side by side at this unrivaled resort. The Sheraton Santiago is certainly a luxury hotel, but the adjoining San Cristóbal Tower is in a class by itself, popular with business executives and foreign dignitaries who value its efficiency, elegance, and impeccable service. A lavish, labyrinthine marble lobby links the two hotels, three fine restaurants, and the city's largest hotel convention center. Pampering is not all that goes on at the San Cristóbal Tower—attentive staff members at the business center can provide you with everything from secretarial services to Internet access. The modern rooms have elegant linens and are decorated with rich fabrics. ⊠ *Av. Santa María 1742, Providencia* ☎ *2/233–5000* 🖷 *2/234–1732* ⊕ *www.sheraton.cl* ⟿ *Sheraton Santiago: 379 rooms, 14 suites. San Cristóbal Tower: 139 rooms, 3 suites* ⚏ *3 restaurants, picnic area, in-room data ports, in-room faxes, in-room safes, minibars, tennis court, 2 pools, gym, hair salon, sauna, 2 bars, lobby lounge, shops, babysitting, laundry service, concierge, Internet, business services, convention center, meeting rooms, airport shuttle, car rental, helipad, travel services, no-smoking floors* ⊟ *AE, DC, MC, V* Ⓜ *Pedro de Valdivia.*

$$ 🏨 **Four Points Sheraton.** The heart of Providencia's shopping district is just steps away from this small, perfectly adequate hotel. The cool rooftop terrace is a real pleasure in summer, when you can relax with a pisco sour and take in the city views. If you prefer a more active nightlife scene, you're in luck. The hotel is adjacent to one of the city's main party thoroughfares: Suecia, lined with pubs, restaurants, and discos. Rooms facing these streets can be noisy, even through double-paned windows. ⊠ *Av. Santa Magdalena 111, Providencia* ☎ *2/750–0300* 🖷 *2/750–0350* ⊕ *www.fourpoints.com* ⤳ *112 rooms, 16 suites* ⚭ *Restaurant, room service, in-room data ports, in-room safes, mini-bars, cable TV, golf privileges, pool, gym, sauna, bar, laundry service, Internet, business services, convention center, meeting rooms, airport shuttle, travel services, free parking, no-smoking rooms* ⊟ *AE, DC, MC, V* Ⓜ *Los Leones.*

★ **$$** ⊞ **Hotel Orly.** Finding a treasure like this in the middle of Providencia is nothing short of a miracle. The shiny wood floors, country-manor furnishings, and glass-domed breakfast room make this hotel as sweet as it is economical. Rooms come in all shapes and sizes, so ask to see a few before you decide. Cafetto, the downstairs café, serves some of the finest coffee drinks in town. ⊠ *Av. Pedro de Valdivia 027, Providencia* ☎ *2/231–8947* 🖷 *2/252–0051* ⊕ *www.orlyhotel.com* ⤳ *25 rooms, 3 suites* ⚭ *Restaurant, café, room service, in-room data ports, in-room safes, minibars, cable TV, bicycles, laundry service, Internet, free parking* ⊟ *AE, DC, MC, V* ⦿ *BP* Ⓜ *Pedro de Valdivia.*

$ ⊞ **Chilhotel.** You won't empty your wallet at this small hotel, one of the few bargains in pricey Providencia. For about what you'd pay for a dinner for two you get a room that's clean and comfortable. Those overlooking the palm-shaded courtyard in back are especially lovely. It's in a funky old house, so no two rooms are alike. See a few before you decide. And talk about location—you're on a quiet side street, yet dozens of restaurants and bars are steps away. ⊠ *Cirujano Guzmán 103, Providencia* ☎ *2/264–0643* 🖷 *2/264–1323* ⊕ *www.chilhotel.cl* ⤳ *25 rooms, 2 suites* ⚭ *Dining room, in-room safes, minibars, cable TV, Internet, laundry service* ⊟ *AE, DC, MC, V* ⦿ *BP* Ⓜ *Manuel Montt.*

Vitacura

$$ ⊞ **Acacias de Vitacura.** The extraordinary location of this hotel—in the midst of towering eucalyptus and acacia trees thought to be more than a century old—is unforgettable. It's a pleasure to drink your morning coffee in the lush garden under one of the oversize umbrellas. The rooms here are simple but bright, decorated with pale creams and tans. The owner's collection of old carriages gives the hotel a quirky personality. ⊠ *El Manantial 1781, Vitacura* ☎ *2/211–8601* 🖷 *2/212–7858* ⊕ *www.hotelacacias.cl* ⤳ *33 rooms, 2 suites* ⚭ *Restaurant, dining room, minibars, cable TV, pool, gym, babysitting, Internet, meeting room, travel services, free parking* ⊟ *AE, DC, MC, V* ⦿ *BP.*

$$ ⊞ **Hotel Kennedy.** This glass tower may seem impersonal, but the small details—such as beautiful vases of flowers atop the wardrobes—show the staff cares about keeping guests happy. Bilingual secretarial services and an elegant boardroom are among the pluses for visiting executives. The Aquarium restaurant serves international cuisine and has a cellar full of excellent Chilean wines. ⊠ *Av. Kennedy 4570, Vitacura* ☎ *2/290–8100* 🖷 *2/219–3272* ⊕ *www.hotelkennedy.cl* ⤳ *123 rooms, 10 suites* ⚭ *Restaurant, room service, in-room data ports, minibars, cable TV, pool, gym, hair salon, massage, sauna, bar, laundry service, Internet, business services, meeting rooms, travel services, free parking, no-smoking floor* ⊟ *AE, DC, MC, V* ⦿ *BP.*

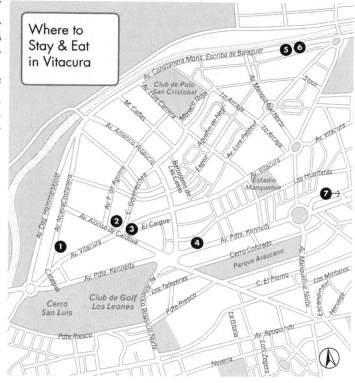

Hotels ▼

Acacias de
Vitacura **7**

Kennedy **4**

Restaurants ▼

Agua **1**

Europeo **2**

Ibis de Puerto
Varas **5**

Le Fournil **3**

Zanzíbar **6**

Where to
Stay & Eat
in Vitacura

NIGHTLIFE & THE ARTS

Although it can't rival Buenos Aires or Rio de Janeiro, Santiago buzzes with increasingly sophisticated bars and clubs. Santiaguinos often meet for drinks during the week, usually after work when most bars have happy hour. Then they call it a night, as most people don't really cut loose until Friday and Saturday. Weekends commence with dinner beginning at 9 or 10 and then a drink at a pub. (This doesn't refer to an English beer hall; a pub here is a bar with loud music and a lot of seating.) No one thinks of heading to the dance clubs until 1 AM, and they stay until 4 or 5 AM.

The Arts

With dozens of museums scattered around the city, it's clear Santiaguinos also have a strong love of culture. Music, theater, and other artistic endeavors supplement weekends spent dancing the night away.

Dance

The venerable **Ballet Nacional Chileno** (⊠ Av. Providencia 043, Providencia ☎ 2/634–4746), founded in 1945, performs from its repertoire of more than 150 pieces at the Teatro Universidad de Chile near Plaza Baquedano.

Film

Santiago's dozens of cinemas screen movies in English with Spanish subtitles. Movie listings are posted in *El Mercurio* and other dailies. Admission is generally 3,000 pesos; matinees often cost only 2,000 pesos. The newest multiplexes—with mammoth screens, plush seating, and fresh popcorn—are in the city's malls. Most of the city's art cinemas tend to screen international favorites. The old standby is **El Biógrafo** (⊠ José Victorino Lastarria 181, Santiago Centro ☎ 2/633–4435), which shows foreign films on its single screen. It's on a colorful street lined with cafés. Affiliated with one of the city's universities, the **Centro de Extensión Universidad Católica** (⊠ La Alameda 390, Santiago Centro ☎ 2/686–6516) screens only the classics. **Cine Arte Normandie** (⊠ Av. Tarapacá 1181, Santiago Centro ☎ 2/697–2979) is a popular theater south of Iglesia San Francisco. **Cine Hoyts Huérfanos** (⊠ Paseo Huérfanos 735, Santiago Centro ☎ 600/500–0400) has six screens.

Among the best theaters in town is the **Cinemark 12** (⊠ Av. Kennedy 9001, Las Condes ☎ 600/600–2463), in the Alto Las Condes mall. Its dozen screens show the latest releases. In the Parque Arauco mall, **Showcase Cinemas Parque Arauco** (⊠ Av. Kennedy 5413, Las Condes ☎ 2/224–7707) has the city's most modern facility. **Tobalaba** (⊠ Av. Providencia 2563, Las Condes ☎ 2/231–6630) shows arty and foreign films.

Music

Parque de las Esculturas (⊠ Av. Santa María between Av. Pedro de Valdivia Norte and Padre Letelier, Providencia ☎ No phone) hosts numerous open-air concerts in the early evenings in summer. The **Teatro Municipal** (⊠ Plaza Alcade Mekis, Av. Agustinas at Av. San Antonio, Santiago Centro ☎ 2/463–8888 ⊕ www.municipal.cl), Santiago's 19th-century theater, presents excellent classical concerts, opera, and ballet by internationally recognized artists from March to December. **Teatro Oriente** (⊠ Av. Pedro de Valdivia, between Costanera and Av. Providencia, Providencia ☎ 2/335–0023) is a popular venue for classical concerts, including many performances of Beethoven's works. The Coro Sinfónico and the Orquesta Sinfónica, the city's highly regarded chorus and orchestra, perform near Plaza Baquedano at the **Teatro Universidad de Chile** (⊠ Av. Providencia 043, Providencia ☎ 2/634–5295).

Theater

Provided that you understand at least a little Spanish, you may want to take in a bit of Chilean theater. It's widely regarded to be among the best in Latin America. Performances take place all year, mainly from Thursday to Sunday around 8 PM. In January, the year's best plays are performed at the Estación Mapocho and other venues in a program called the **Festival Internacional Teatro A Mil** (☎ 2/735–6167 ⊕ www.festivalteatroamil.cl). The name refers to the admission price of 1,000 pesos (less than $2).

The following theaters produce a mix of Latin American comedies and dramas. **El Conventillo** (⊠ Bellavista 173, Bellavista ☎ 2/777–4164). **Teatro Bellavista** (⊠ Dardignac 0110, Bellavista ☎ 2/735–2395). **Teatro Lo Castillo** (⊠ Candelaria Goyenechea 3820, Vitacura ☎ 2/244–5856). **Teatro San Ginés** (⊠ Mallinkrodt 76, Bellavista ☎ 2/738–2159).

The well-respected ICTUS theater company performs in the **Teatro la Comedia** (⊠ Merced 349, Santiago Centro ☎ 2/639–1523).

Nightlife

Bars and clubs are scattered all over Santiago, but a handful of streets have such a concentration of establishments that they resemble block parties on Friday and Saturday nights. Try pub-crawling along Avenida Pío Nono in Bellavista. The crowd here is young, as the drinking age is 18. To the east in Las Condes, Paseo San Damián is an outdoor complex of bars and clubs. It's a fashionable nighttime destination.

What you should wear depends on your destination. Bellavista has a mix of styles ranging from blue jeans to basic black. Paseo San Damián maintains a stricter dress code.

Note that establishments referred to as "nightclubs" are almost always female strip shows. The cheesy signs in the windows usually make it quite clear what goes on inside.

Bars & Clubs

BELLAVISTA The latest hot spot is **El Toro** (⊠ Loreto 33, Bellavista ☎ 2/737–5937), which is packed every night of the week except Sunday, when the staff gets a break. The tables are spaced close enough that you can eavesdrop on the conversations of the models and other celebrities who frequent the place. **La Casa en el Aire** (⊠ Antonia López de Bello 1025, Bellavista ☎2/735–6680) is a great place to listen to live bands. Much of what's on the bill at the House in the Air is traditional folk music. The **Libro Café** (⊠ Purísima 165, Bellavista ☎ 2/735–1542) is a late-night haunt for starving artists and those who wish they were. If you're hungry, head here for a tortilla *malageña* and a carafe of the house red. The sleek and stylish **Tantra** (⊠ Ernesto Pinto Lagarrigue 154, Bellavista ☎2/732–3268) is where a hip crowd heads well after midnight. The beat goes on until 6 AM, unless one of the frequent after-hours parties keeps it open even later. Upstairs are king-size beds used as tables—reserve one for a memorable evening.

CENTRO Near Cerro Santa Lucía, **Bar Berri** (⊠ Rosal 321, Santiago Centro ☎ 2/638–4734) is an old-fashioned place where the waiter may just place a bottle of pisco on the table in front of you. Identifiable by the leering devil on the sign, **El Diablito** (⊠Merced 536, Santiago Centro ☎No phone) is a charming hole-in-the-wall. The dimly lighted space is popular with the after-work crowd. A secret meeting place during the Pinochet regime, **El Rincón de las Canallas** (⊠ San Diego 379, Santiago Centro ☎ 2/699–1309) still requires a password to get in (*Chile libre*, meaning "free Chile"). The walls are painted with political statements such as *Somos todos inocentes* ("We are all innocent").

LAS CONDES **Flannery's** (⊠ Encomenderos 83, Las Condes ☎ 2/233–6675), close to the main drag of Av. El Bosque Norte, is an honest-to-goodness pub serving Irish food, beer, and occasionally Guinness on tap. **Pub Licity** (⊠ Av. El Bosque Norte 0155, Las Condes ☎ 2/333–1214) is a large, popular, glass-fronted building permanently teeming with people in their twenties and early thirties.

From the doorway, **Casa de Cena** (⊠ Almirante Simpson 20, Providencia ☎ 2/635–4418) looks like your average hole-in-the-wall, but it's actually a gem. Most nights a band wanders through the maze of wood-paneled rooms singing folk songs while the bartender listens to endless stories from inebriated regulars.

Many of the neighborhood's nightspots are found along the pedestrian street of Avenida Suecia. One of the most popular is **Mister Ed** (⊠ Av. Suecia 0152, Providencia ☎ 2/231–2624), the best place to hear up-and-coming local bands. **Boomerang** (⊠ General Holley 2285, Providencia ☎ 2/334–5081) is a raucous pub with a few pool tables. The **Phone Box** (⊠ Galería del Patio, Av. Providencia 1652, Providencia ☎ 2/235–9972) is a fairly convincing re-creation of a British pub that serves steak-and-kidney pie to homesick Brits. You'll easily spot the entrance—it's through a red phone booth.

Gay & Lesbian Clubs

Once mostly underground, Santiago's gay scene is bursting at the seams. Although some bars are so discreet they don't have a sign, others are known by just about everyone. Clubs like Bunker, for example, are so popular that they attract a fair number of nongays. There's a cluster of gay restaurants and bars on the streets parallel to Avenida Pío Nono in Bellavista. There's not as much for lesbians in Santiago, however, although some women can be found at most establishments catering to men.

On Bellavista's main drag, **Bokhara** (⊠ Pío Nono 430, Bellavista ☎ 2/732–1050 or 2/735–1271) is one of the city's largest and most popular gay discos. It has two dance floors playing house and techno. **Bunker** (⊠ Bombero Nuñez 159, Bellavista ☎ 2/737–1716 or 2/777–3760), a mainstay of the gay scene, is in a cavernous space with numerous platforms overlooking the dance floor. Don't get here too early—people don't arrive until well after midnight. Note that it's open only Friday and Saturday. The venerable **Fausto** (⊠ Av. Santa María 0832, Providencia ☎ 2/777–1041), in business for more than 20 years, has polished wood paneling that calls to mind a gentlemen's club. The disco pumps until the wee hours. **Femme** (⊠ Bombero Nuñez 169, Bellavista ☎ 2/738–2301) is a dance club for lesbians that opens late on Friday and Saturday nights.

If you're looking for a place to kick back with a beer, try **Friends** (⊠ Bombero Nuñez 365, Bellavista ☎ 2/777–3979). Live music performances and karaoke take place on Thursday, Friday, and Saturday. **Vox Populi** (⊠ Ernesto Pinto Lagarrigue 364, Bellavista ☎ 2/671–1267) is a longtime favorite in Bellavista.

Salsa Clubs

Arriba de la Bola (⊠ General Holley 171, Providencia ☎ 2/232–7965) shakes things up with a live Cuban band. It gets packed, so reservations are necessary. **Habana Salsa** (⊠ Dominíca 142, Bellavista ☎ 2/737–1737) thumps to the beat of salsa, merengue, and milonga from Thursday to Saturday night. At **Ilé Habana** (⊠ Bucarest 95, Providencia ☎ 2/231–5711), you can boogie to the beat of a live band. There are free salsa lessons Tuesday–Saturday at 9:30 PM.

SPORTS & THE OUTDOORS

Athletic Clubs & Spas

All of Santiago's larger hotels have health clubs on the premises, usually with personal trainers on hand to assist you with your workout. Even if you aren't staying at a particular hotel, you can usually pay to use the facilities for the day. **Balthus** (⌷ Av. Monseñor Escrivá de Balaguer 5970, Vitacura ☎ 2/218–1831) is the city's top health club. This high-tech marvel has all the latest equipment. You feel healthier just by walking into the complex, a sleek series of riverside structures in concrete and glass designed by Santiago's ArchiPlan. There are eight tennis courts, spas, pools, and numerous fitness programs.

Agua y Bién (⌷ Americo Vespucio Norte 1440, Vitacura ☎ 2/371–6554), a small club, offers massage, hydrotherapy, and other spa treatments. The modern **Spa Mund** (⌷ Cardenal Belarmino 1075, Vitacura ☎ 2/211–2717) is a sprawling aquatic spa where you can relax in saunas and hot tubs. Better yet, pamper yourself with a facial.

Bicycling

Santiago has no shortage of public parks, and they provide good opportunities to see the city. If you're ambitious you can even pedal up Cerro San Cristóbal, the city's largest hill. You can rent mountain bikes for 6,500 pesos from **Lys** (⌷ Av. Miraflores 537, Santiago Centro ☎ 2/633–7600).

Horse Racing

Betting on horses is popular in Santiago, which is the reason the city has two large racetracks. Races take place Monday and alternating Thursdays at **Club Hípico** (⌷ Blanco Encalada 2540, Santiago Centro ☎ 2/693–9600), south of downtown. El Ensayo, an annual race that's a century-old tradition, is held here in early November. **Hipódromo Chile** (⌷ Hipódromo Chile 1715, Independencia ☎ 2/270–9237) is the home of the prestigious Gran Premio Internacional, which draws competitors from around South America. Regular races are held Saturday and alternating Thursdays.

Skiing

If you're planning on hitting the slopes, **KL Ski Rental** (⌷ Augusto Mira Fernandez 14248, Las Condes ☎ 2/217–9101 ⌾ www.kladventure.com) not only rents skis and snowboards, but also arranges transportation to and from the nearby ski areas.

Soccer

Chile's most popular spectator sport is soccer, but a close second is watching the endless bickering among owners, trainers, and players whenever a match isn't going well. First-division *fútbol* matches, featuring the city's handful of local teams, are held in the **Estadio Nacional** (⌷ Av. Grecia 2001, Nuñoa ☎ 2/238–8102), southeast of the city center. Soccer is played year-round, with most matches taking place on weekends. It was here in the Estadio that Pinochet's henchmen killed thousands of political opponents in 1973, including Chilean folk singer Victor Jara. To assure that he would never again provoke Chileans to action with his music, Jara's hands were mutilated before he was put to death.

SHOPPING

Vitacura is, without a doubt, the destination for upscale shopping. Lined with designer boutiques where you'll find SUVs double parked out front, Avenida Alonso de Córdova is Santiago's equivalent of 5th Avenue in New York or Rodeo Drive in Los Angeles. "Drive" is the important word here, as nobody strolls from place to place. Although buzzing with activity, the streets are strangely empty. Other shops are found on nearby Avenida Vitacura and Avenida Nueva Costanera.

Providencia, another of the city's most popular shopping districts, has rows of boutiques. Avenida Providencia slices through the neighborhood, branching off for several blocks into the parallel Avenida 11 de Septiembre. The shops continue east to Avenida El Bosque Norte, after which Avenida Providencia changes its name to Avenida Apoquindo and the neighborhood becomes Las Condes. In this chic district you'll find modern shopping malls filled with hundreds of specialty shops and international brands such as Tommy Hilfiger and Gucci. A stroll down the wide tree-lined Avenida Alonso de Córdova and La Nueva Costanera in Vitacura will take you past lots of exclusive shops.

Bohemian Bellavista attracts those in search of the perfect woolen sweater or the right piece of lapis lazuli jewelry. Santiago Centro is much more down-to-earth. The Mercado Central is where anything fishy is sold, and nearby markets like Vega Chica and Vega Central sell just about every item imaginable. Stores downtown usually face the street, which makes window-shopping more entertaining. Pedestrian streets around the Plaza de Armas are crowded with children licking ice-cream cones, older women strolling arm in arm, and business executives sitting under wide umbrellas having their shoes shined.

Shops in Santiago are generally open weekdays 10–7 and Saturday 10–2. Malls are usually open daily 10–10.

Markets

Aldea de Vitacura (⊠ Av. Vitacura 6838, Vitacura ☎ 2/219–3161) is a pleasant outdoor market where you can browse among the various stands selling local and national craftwork. It's open Tuesday–Sunday 11–9.

Centro Artesanal Santa Lucía, an art fair at the base of Cerro Santa Lucía, is an excellent place to find Aymara and Mapuche crafts. It's open daily 10–7.

Bellavista's colorful **Feria Artesanal Pío Nono,** held in the park along Avenida Pío Nono, comes alive every night of the week. It's even busier on weekends, when more vendors gather in Parque Domingo Gómez to display their handicrafts.

Pueblito Los Dominicos (⊠ Av. Apoquindo 9085, Las Condes ☎ 2/248–2295) is a "village" of more than 200 shops where you can find everything from fine leather to semiprecious stones and antiques. There's also a wonderful display of cockatoos and other live birds. It's a nice place to visit, especially on weekends when traveling musicians entertain the crowds. It's open Tuesday–Saturday 10:30–9:30 and Sunday 10:30–8. Next door is an attractive whitewashed church dating from the late 18th century. It's rather far from the main drag, so take a taxi.

Shopping Malls

In Santiago, the shopping malls are so enormous that they have become attractions in their own right. Some even provide free transportation from the major hotels.

Alto Las Condes (⊠ Av. Kennedy 9001, Las Condes ☎ 2/299–6999) has 245 shops, three department stores, a multiplex, and a seemingly endless food court. Also here is a supermarket, appropriately named Jumbo, where the staff members wear roller skates while restocking the shelves. It carries excellent Chilean wines.

Parque Arauco (⊠ Av. Kennedy 5413, Las Condes ☎ 2/299–0500) is a North American–style shopping center with an eclectic mix of designer boutiques, including clothing outlets like Benetton, Ralph Lauren, and Laura Ashley. Chile's three largest department stores—Falabella, Ripley, and Almacenes París—sell everything from perfume to plates.

The **Mall del Centro** (⊠ Puente 689, Santiago Centro ☎ 2/361–0011) is a smaller version of Parque Arauco, with fewer international brands but a more central location.

Specialty Shops

Antiques

West of Estación Mapocho is **Antiguedades Balmaceda** (⊠ Av. Brasil at Balmaceda, Santiago Centro ☎ No phone ☉ Daily 10:30–7), a warehouse filled with antiques dealers. On display is everything from furniture to books to jewelry.

There is a group of antiques shops in Providencia. **Antiguedades Fernando Infante Diaz** (⊠ Av. Providencia 2348, Providencia ☎ 2/335–2375) is filled with beautiful antique light fixtures. Sharing the same space is **Landman Anticuario** (⊠ Av. Providencia 2348, Providencia ☎ 2/232–6829), where you'll find gilded mirrors, massive oil portraits, and painted screens.

Books

A cluster of bookstores can be found along Avenida Providencia in what is known as the Galería El Patio. The most interesting is **Libreria Australis** (⊠ Av. Providencia 1670 Providencia ☎ 2/236–8054), which stocks nothing but travel-related items. You can find travel guides in English as well as Spanish, language dictionaries, and beautiful photography books highlighting the region's natural wonders. Also in Galería El Patio, **Librería Books** (⊠ Av. Providencia 1652, Providencia ☎ 2/235–1205) stocks secondhand editions.

Clothing

If you've ever wondered where the men of Santiago buy their proper toppers, head to **Donde Golpea El Monita** (⊠ 21 de Mayo 707, Centro ☎ 2/638–4907). At this downtown shop, in business for nearly a century, the friendly staff will teach you the difference between a *texano* (cowboy hat) and a *paño* (a more formal hat).

In Providencia, a group of local designers banded together to form **GAM** (⊠ Calle Román Díaz 170, Providencia ☎ 2/474–5109). The name, which stands for Grupo Anti-Mall, sums up their countercultural stance. The second-story showroom has avant-garde fashions.

In Vitacura, you can wrap yourself in style on and near Avenida Alonso de Córdova. Make sure to ring the bell at these shops, as they usually keep their doors locked. (They don't let just anybody in.) Looking a bit like a fortress, **Hermés** (⊠ Av. Alonso de Córdova 2526, Vitacura ☎ 2/374–1576) occupies some prime real estate on the main drag. Chilean women spend hours selecting just the right scarf. Yards and yards of cashmere fill the window of **Matilde Medina** (⊠ Av. Vitacura 3660, Vitacura ☎ 2/206–6153). She imports her beautiful scarves and sweaters from England.

Ralph Lauren (⊠ Av. Vitacura 3634, Vitacura ☎ 2/228–3011) has a relaxed atmosphere and a friendly staff. At **Wool** (⊠ Av. Nueva Costanera 4010, Vitacura ☎ 2/208–8767), you can find a wide variety of items fashioned from its eponymous fiber.

Galleries

Galleries are scattered around the city, and admission is usually free. The newspaper *El Mercurio* lists current exhibitions in its Saturday supplement *Vivienda Decoración*. True to its name, **Casa Naranja** (⊠ Casa Naranja, Santo Domingo 528, Parque Forestal ☎ 2/639–5843) is a house painted a particularly vivid shade of orange. Inside, past the restaurant, is a gallery filled with pieces by local artists. **Galería del Cerro** (⊠ Antonía López de Bello 0135, Bellavista ☎ 2/737–3500 ⊕ www.delcerro.cl) features works by prominent local artists. At the foot of Cerro San Cristóbal, the bright and airy gallery is a short walk from Pablo Neruda's home of La Chascona.

Vitacura is the heart of a thriving gallery scene. See works by local artists at **Galería Animal** (⊠ Av. Alonso de Córdova 3105, Vitacura ☎ 2/377–9090). The large-scale pieces include sculpture and other types of installations. There's an outdoor café if all this art makes you peckish. **Galería Isabel Aninat** (⊠ Av. Alonso de Córdova 3053, Vitacura ☎ 2/263–2729) hosts exhibitions of international artists. A space that was an important gallery in the 1970s is now called **Trece** (⊠ Av. Nueva Costanera 3980, Vitacura ☎ 2/378–1981). The warehouse-like space is perfect for massive works.

Handicrafts

For everything from masks to mosaics, head to **Manos de Alma** (⊠ General Salvo 114, Providencia ☎ 2/235–3518). The staff at **Pura** (⊠ Av. Isidora Goyenechea 3226, Las Condes ☎ 2/333–3144) has picked out

Fodor'sChoice
★

the finest handicrafts from around the region. Here you can find expertly woven blankets and throws, colorful pottery, and fine leather goods. Shops of all sorts, selling crafts from all around the country, line the winding passageways of the **Centro de Artesanía Manquehue** (⊠ Av. Manquehue Sur at Av. Apoquindo, Las Condes ☎ No phone), alongside the Apumanque Mall. **Cooperativa Almacén Campesino** (⊠ Torreón Victoria, Bellavista ☎ 2/335–4443), in the middle of Parque Metropolitano, is a cooperative of artisans from various indigenous cultures. This shop sells the best handicrafts from all over Chile.

Jewelry

Chile is one of the few places in the world where lapis lazuli, a brilliant blue mineral, is found in abundance. In Bellavista, a cluster of shops deals solely in lapis lazuli, selling a range of products made from this semiprecious stone: paperweights, jewelry, and chess sets. Several larger shops selling lapis lazuli are dotted around the rest of the city.

In Plaza Mulato Gil de Castro, **Blue Andes** (⊠ José Victorino Lastarria 307, Santiago Centro ☎ 9/555–6281) has a small but intriguing collection of modern pieces. **Blue Stone** (⊠ Av. Costanera Norte 3863, Vitacura ☎ 2/207–4180) has lovely original designs. Near Plaza Mulato Gil de Castro is **Rocco** (⊠ José Victorino Lastarria 53, Santiago Centro ☎ 2/633–4036), one of the best destinations in Santiago Centro.

Wine

Chileans have discovered just how good their vintages are, and wineshops are popping up everywhere. **El Mundo del Vino** (⊠ Av. Isidora Goyenechea 2931, Las Condes ☎ 2/244–8888) is a world-class store with an international selection, in-store tastings, wine classes, and books for oenophiles. The store also provides sturdy boxes to protect your purchases on the flight home. **La Vinoteca** (⊠ Av. Isidora Goyenechea 2966, Las Condes ☎ 2/371–5942) proudly proclaims that it was Santiago's first fine wineshop. It offers personalized service and an excellent selection. **Vinopolis** (⊠ Av. El Bosque Norte 038, Las Condes ☎ 2/232–3814) stocks a top-notch selection and also has a shop at the airport for last-minute purchases.

SIDE TRIPS FROM SANTIAGO

For more than a few travelers, Santiago's main attraction is its proximity to the continent's best skiing. Three world-class ski resorts lie just outside the city, and another is only a little farther away. Others are curious to see the region where their favorite wines are produced. The wineries around Santiago provide the majority of the country's excellent exports. The Cajón del Maipo, deep in the Andes, is irresistible for those who want to soak in a natural hot spring, stroll through picturesque mountain villages where low adobe houses line the roads, or just take in the stark but majestic landscape.

It's also possible to take day trips to Pomaire, a crafts village some 70 km (43 mi) west of Santiago, or to go farther afield to Valparaíso, Viña del Mar, or Isla Negra (⇨ Chapter 2).

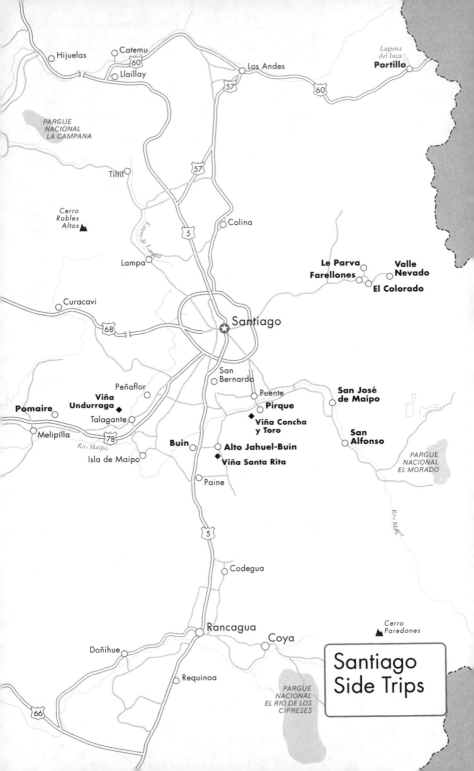

Santiago
Side Trips

Cajón del Maipo

The Cajón del Maipo, a stunning river valley southeast of Santiago, is so expansive that you can easily spend several days exploring the area. A narrow road runs parallel to the Río Maipo, the river that supplies Santiago with most of its drinking water, as it snakes up into the Andes. As you ascend, you'll see massive mountains of sedimentary rock, heaved up and thrown sideways millions of years ago when the Andes were formed. On a sunny day, the colors here are subtle but glowing, ranging from oranges and reds to ochers, buffs, beiges, browns, and even elusive greens. Locals in roadside stands sell homemade *chicha* (cider) and *miel* (honey). At the far end of the valley, you'll find an austere landscape where hot springs spill from the earth and the mountains display vibrant shades of blue and violet.

Whatever you do, don't hurry through the Cajón del Maipo. Any of the villages you pass is worth a visit. As the valley is a popular weekend getaway for Santiaguinos, most villages have small cafés providing basic meals and simple lodgings. There are also plenty of mercados where you can pick up supplies for a picnic. The canyon's main town, San José de Maipo, is a great place to get acquainted with small-town life in the Andes. Note that the going gets tougher shortly after you pass El Volcán, as the road is no longer paved. Make sure you have a four-wheel-drive vehicle if you want to venture farther, especially if there's rain in the forecast.

San José de Maipo

In the heart of the Cajón del Maipo is the old colonial town of San José de Maipo, founded in the late 18th century when silver was discovered nearby. Rows of quaint, single-story adobe dwellings with thatched roofs line the streets. In the center of town is a large shady plaza where you'll find the church with a mismatched steeple.

Although most of the best views are deeper in the canyon, you'll probably want to stop in San José de Maipo. The only automatic teller machine is here on the main square, as is the visitor center.

WHERE TO
STAY & EAT
$$–$$$

✕ **Casa Bosque.** If hobbits roamed the earth, this is where they'd stop for lunch. This eatery is a little J. R. R. Tolkien, a little Brothers Grimm. There are animals carved into the woodwork and staircases that swirl up to the second floor. There are a couple of enormous dining rooms with the sunlight filtering through fanciful stained-glass windows, but the best tables are outside on the sunny terrace. The menu includes steaks sized for big appetites as well as some wonderful concoctions with sole and sea bass. ⊠ *Camino El Volcán 16829, Guayacán* ☎ *2/871–1570* ▤ *AE, MC, V.*

$$

✕ **Calypso.** The fresh homemade pasta couldn't be better in this small Italian-owned restaurant close to the Río Maipo. Vegetables from the garden are used to make an impressive selection of pastas with original sauces. The herb bread is delicious, and the wine list includes some good choices. ⊠ *Camino al Volcan 5247, El Manzano* ☎ *2/871–1498* ▤ *No credit cards* ☉ *Closed Mon.–Wed.*

$

✕▥ **La Petite France.** You can't miss this attractive pink hotel with its Tudor-style frontage sitting high on a hillside just before the village of

San José de Maipo. The family that runs this small establishment, who returned to Chile after several years of living in France, keeps the hotel immaculate, including the inviting pool that fills one of the garden's many levels. The rooms are simple, spacious, and comfortable. Delight in unparalleled valley views from the restaurant's wide terrace while tucking into some delicious French-inspired cuisine like *caracoles* (snails). ⊠ *Camino al Volcan 16096* ☎ *2/861–1967* 🛏 *8 rooms* ⚭ *Restaurant, pool, bar* ▤ *AE, DC, MC, V* ⊗ *Restaurant closed Mon.*

San Alfonso

About 65 km (40 mi) south of Santiago is San Alfonso, a small but charming village with fantastic houses that look as though they've been stolen from a Chilean folktale. Look for the little details, such as a weather vane depicting two children running away with an enormous bunch of grapes.

Just past San Alfonso is the abandoned mining town of **El Volcán,** where you can visit the old abandoned copper-mine shafts and peer into the decaying, cramped miners' quarters. The visitor center in San José de Maipo has information about tours.

WHERE TO
STAY & EAT
¢–$
✗ **Los Ciervos.** At the restaurant, on San Alfonso's main drag, you can enjoy a filling lunch of traditional Chilean dishes such as pastel de choclo (a pie filled with ground beef, chicken, olives, and boiled eggs and topped with mashed corn) or *porotos granados* (a thick bean stew). There are also a few rooms that face a bright, airy pergola. ⊠ *Camino al Volcán 31411* ☎ *2/861–1581* ▤ *AE, DC, MC, V.*

$
Fodor'sChoice
★
🏨 **Cascada de las Animas.** Set on its own 10,000-acre nature reserve in the foothills of the Andes, just past the village of San Alfonso, Cascada de las Animas affords breathtaking views in all directions. The huge restaurant terrace, for example, overlooks the river below. You likely won't want to sit still for long, as the family-run establishment has excellent guides that take you white-water rafting down the Río Maipo and horseback riding high up into the mountains. The whimsical wood cabins are rustic but spacious, with wood-burning fireplaces for chilly evenings. Book ahead in the busy season. ⊠ *Camino al Volcan s/n* ☎ *2/861–1303* 🖷 *2/861–1833* ⊕ *www.cascada.net* 🛏 *9 cabins* ⚭ *Restaurant, kitchenettes, pool, sauna, hiking, horseback riding, Ping-Pong, bar, meeting room; no room TV* ▤ *No credit cards.*

$
🏨 **Santuario del Río.** A few miles north of San Alfonso, this resort enjoys a private perch above the Río Maipo. Its nine rustic cabins, each a discreet distance from its neighbors, sit right on the banks of the river. You can have your breakfast on your front porch, or head up the hill to the dining room in the beautiful main building. Massive windows overlook the pool and the mountains beyond. There are plenty of activities, from tennis to horseback riding. There's even a rock-climbing wall. ⊠ *Camino al Volcan s/n* ☎ *2/861–3175* 🖷 *2/861–3116* ⊕ *www.santuariodelrio.cl* 🛏 *9 cabins* ⚭ *Restaurant, kitchenettes, tennis court, pool, hiking, horseback riding, bar, meeting room; no room TV* ▤ *MC, V* ⧖ *BP.*

Lo Valdés

Past El Volcán, the gravel road leads higher into the jagged mountains. Green slopes give way to sheer mountain cliffs of gray and purple. Here you'll be able to spot layer upon layer of sedimentary rock, packed with fossils from the time when this whole area was under the ocean. About 12 km (7 mi) beyond El Volcán you'll pass the tiny town of Baños Morales, where Santiaguinos go to soak their tired muscles in the hot springs. Beyond Baños Morales, take the right fork to reach Lo Valdés, a charming village that makes an excellent place to stop for the night.

In Baños Morales you'll find the entrance to the **Monumento Natural El Morado,** named after the impressive purple peak. If it's a clear day you'll be privy to some stunning views of the snowcapped Andean peaks from the park. An exhilarating 8-km (5-mi), three-hour hike passes a glacier. There's an admission charge of 1,500 pesos.

About 11 km (7 mi) past Lo Valdés, along a poorly maintained road through an impressive moonscape of mauves, grays, and steely blues, are the isolated and picturesque **Baños de Colina.** These huge natural bowls, scooped out of the mountain edge, overflow with water from the hot springs. Here you can slip into a bathing suit (note, however, that there are no changing rooms) and choose the pool that has the temperature most to your liking. Let your body float gently in the mineral-rich waters and enjoy the view down the valley as your fellow soakers trade medical advice, offer salt and lemons to suck on, and speculate about the medicinal properties of the waters. Admission is 2,000 pesos.

WHERE TO STAY 🏨 **Lo Valdés Mountain Center.** Santiago's German Alpine Club built this
$ lodge, formerly the Refugio Alemán, in 1931 as a base camp for members scaling the Andes. The charming stone building looks as if it could be in the Alps. Wooden floors and walls exude a feeling of warmth, but accommodations are decidedly spartan. Its best selling point is its location at the base of the Andes. The restaurant terrace affords fabulous views. In summer this is a popular *paseo* (outing) for many Santiaguinos, who come to indulge not just in the clean air but also in the German-style *küchen* (fruit pie). ⊠ *Lo Valdés* ☎ *9/220–8525* ⊕ *www. refugiolovaldes.com* ⇢ *11 rooms without bath* ⌂ *Restaurant, mountain bikes, hiking, horseback riding* ▤ *No credit cards.*

Pomaire

You can easily spend a morning or afternoon wandering around the quaint village of Pomaire, a former settlement of indigenous people comprising nothing more than a few streets of single-story adobe dwellings. On weekends Pomaire teems with people who come to wander around, shop, and lunch in one of the picadas specializing in empanadas and other typical Chilean foods.

Pomaire is famous for its brown *greda,* or earthenware pottery, which you'll likely come across in one form or another throughout Chile. Order pastel de choclo and it will nearly always be served in a round, simple clay dish—they're heavy and retain the heat, so the food is brought to the table piping hot.

The village bulges with bowls, pots, and plates of every shape and size, not to mention other objects such as piggy banks, plant pots, vases, and figurines. You can purchase these items at shops and open-air markets around town. An average bowl will set you back no more than 200 to 300 pesos; an oven dish might cost between 2,000 and 3,000 pesos. The quality varies, so it's worth taking a look around before you buy. The workmanship at **Nativa** (⊠ Roberto Bravo 78 ☎ 2/832–5693) is among the best you'll find. Vases and other items are extremely delicate.

You can watch craftspeople at work at **Pumara** (⊠ Roberto Bravo 57 ☎ 2/832–5656). The shop echoes with the pretty wind chimes made from pieces of pottery.

Pomaire, which lies 70 km (43 mi) west of Santiago, is easy to find. It's clearly signposted to your right off the Autopista del Sol. You can also take any of the buses that depart frequently from Terminal San Borja in downtown Santiago.

Where to Eat

★ **$–$$$** ✕ **Los Naranjos.** An eclectic collection of gramophones could be reason enough to come and lunch here, but more than anything diners come back time and again for the excellent Chilean food. If you're hungry try the *pernil de chancho* (leg of pork)—it's succulent and fit for an army. This is also a good place to try one of the national staples such as pastel de choclo—a delicious concoction of minced beef, chicken, olives, and boiled egg, topped with a creamy layer of mashed corn. Sunday there's often a traditional Chilean dance show to entertain you while you eat. ⊠ *Roberto Bravo 44* ☎ *2/831–1791* ▤ *No credit cards.*

¢–$$ ✕ **La Greda.** Named for the earthenware pottery that made this village famous, La Greda is a great place for grilled meats. Try the *filete la grada,* a steak covered with a sauce of tomatoes, onions, and mushrooms and topped with cheese. The expansive outdoor dining room has vines winding around the thick wood rafters. If the weather is cool, the staff will light a fire in the woodstove to keep things toasty. ⊠ *Manuel Rodriguez 251, at Roberto Bravo* ☎ *2/831–1166* ▤ *AE, DC, MC, V.*

Ski Resorts

No wonder skiing aficionados from around the world head to Chile: the snowcapped mountains to the east of Santiago have the largest number of runs not just in Chile or South America, but in the entire Southern Hemisphere. The other attraction is that the season here lasts from June to September, so savvy skiers can take to the slopes when everyone else is hitting the beach.

There are three distinct ski areas within easy reach of Santiago—Farellones, La Parva, and Valle Nevado—with a total of 43 lifts that can carry you to the top of 1,260 acres of groomed runs. To reach these areas, follow Avenida Las Condes eastward until you leave Santiago. Here, you begin an arduous journey up the Andes, making 40 consecutive hairpin turns. The road forks when you reach the top, with one road taking the relatively easy 16-km (10-mi) route east to Valle Nevado, and the other following a more difficult road north to Farellones and La Parva.

About 160 km (100 mi) north of Santiago and close to the Argentine border is Portillo, the oldest ski area in South America. It's a three-hour drive from the city, so a day trip would be exhausting. The only accommodation is Hotel Portillo, which requires a minimum one-week stay. To reach Portillo from Santiago, head north on the Pan-American Highway, following signs to the town of Los Andes. From there take the International Highway (Ruta 60) east until you reach the resort.

Farellones & El Colorado

The closest ski area to Santiago is Farellones, at the foot of Cerro Colorado. This area, consisting of a couple of ski runs for beginners, is used mainly by locals out for a day trip. Facilities are scanty—just a couple of unremarkable restaurants and a few drink stands. Farther up the road is El Colorado, which has 568 acres of groomed runs—the most in Chile. There are 18 runs here: seven beginner, four intermediate, three advanced, and four expert. You'll find a few restaurants and pubs in the village. Ski season here runs mid-June to mid-October. ☎ 2/217–9101 ⊕ *www.elcolorado.cl* ✍ *22,000 pesos* ⊙ *Mid-June–mid-Oct.*

WHERE TO
STAY & EAT
★ $$

🏨 **La Cornisa.** This year-round hotel on the road to Farellones is great if you want to get to the slopes early, as there's free shuttle service to and from the nearby ski areas. The quaint old inn, run by the same family for years, has 10 rooms with wood floors and heaters to keep out the chill. The best are the two corner rooms, which are a bit larger and have wide windows with excellent views. The rate includes breakfast and dinner in the small restaurant, warmed by a fireplace and looking directly down the mountain to Santiago. ⊠ *Av. Los Cóndores 636, Farellones* ☎ 2/220–7581 🖷 2/220–7581 ⊕ *www.lacornisa.cl* ✍ *10 rooms* △ *Restaurant, babysitting, laundry service* ▤ *AE, DC, MC, V* ⭐ *MAP.*

La Parva

About 3 km (2 mi) up the road from Farellones, La Parva is a colorful conglomeration of private homes set along a handful of mountain roads. At the resort itself there are 14 ski runs, most for intermediate skiers. La Parva is positioned perfectly to give you a stunning view of Santiago, especially at night. The season here tends to be a little longer than at the neighboring resorts. The slopes usually open in May, meaning the season can sometimes last six months. ☎ 02/431–0420 ⊕ *www.laparva.cl* ✍ *22,000 pesos* ⊙ *May–Oct.*

WHERE TO STAY
$$$$

🏨 **Condominio Nuevo Parva.** The best place to stay in La Parva is this complex of spacious, modern apartments that sleep between six and eight people. Linens are provided, but maid service is extra. You can rent only by the week, so plan for a lot of skiing. Valle Nevado and the other ski areas are a short drive away. ⊠ *Nueva La Parva 77* ☎ 2/212–1363 ⊕ *www.laparva.cl* ✍ *32 apartments* △ *Cable TV, kitchenettes, microwaves, pool* ▤ *AE, MC, V* ⊙ *Closed Oct.–May.*

Valle Nevado

Valle Nevado, just 13 km (8 mi) beyond La Parva, is Chile's largest ski region—a luxury resort area with 11 ski lifts that take you up to 27 runs on more than 300 acres of groomed trails. More lifts are being built to provide skiing fanatics with even more options. There are a few slopes for beginners, but Valle Nevado is intended for skiers who like a challenge. Three of the extremely difficult runs from the top of Cerro Tres Puntas are labeled "Shake," "Rattle," and "Roll." If that doesn't intimidate you then you might be ready for some heliskiing. A Bell 407 helicopter whisks you to otherwise inaccessible peaks where you can ride a vertical drop of up to 2,500 meters (8,200 feet).

A ski school at Valle Nevado gives pointers to everyone from beginners to experts. As most of the visitors here are European, the majority of the 50 instructors are from Europe. Equipment rental runs about 25,000 pesos a day. ☎ *2/477–7700* 🌐 *www.vallenevado.cl* 🎫 *22,500 pesos* 🕒 *Mid-June–Oct.*

WHERE TO STAY Three hotels dominate Valle Nevado; staying at one gives you access to the facilities at the other two. The larger two—Puerta del Sol and Valle Nevado—are part of the same complex. The three hotels share restaurants, which serve almost every type of cuisine. Rates include lift tickets, ski equipment, and all meals. Peak season is July and August; you can often get the same room for half the price if you stay in June or September.

$$$$ **Puerta del Sol.** The largest of the Valle Nevado hotels, Puerta del Sol can be identified by its signature sloped roof. Rooms here are larger than those at Tres Puntas, but still rather small. One good option are the "altillo rooms," which have a loft bed that gives you more space. North-facing rooms cost more but have unobstructed views of the slopes. Since all three hotels share facilities, Puerta del Sol is your best value. ✉ *Valle Nevado* ☎ *2/206–0027, 800/669–0554 toll-free in U.S.* 📠 *2/208–0697* 🌐 *www.vallenevado.com* *124 rooms* *2 restaurants, room service, in-room data ports, in-room safes, minibars, cable TV, gym, massage, sauna, Ping-Pong, downhill skiing, cinema, dance club, recreation room, babysitting, laundry service, airport shuttle* 💳 *AE, DC, MC, V* 🕒 *Closed Oct.–June 14* 🍽 *MAP.*

$$$$ **Tres Puntas.** It bills itself as a hotel for young people, and Tres Puntas may indeed remind you of a college dormitory. The closet-size rooms come with either bunk beds or two single beds and maybe a night table. And the tiny wooden balconies are just big enough for two people. In short, these rooms are for people who intend to be on the slopes all day. Inside is a pub and an American-style restaurant complete with a jukebox. ✉ *Valle Nevado* ☎ *2/206–0027, 800/669–0554 toll-free in U.S.* 📠 *2/208–0697* 🌐 *www.vallenevado.com* *89 rooms* *Restaurant, cable TV, billiards, downhill skiing, pub, recreation room, laundry service* 💳 *AE, DC, MC, V* 🕒 *Closed Oct.–June 14* 🍽 *MAP.*

$$$$ **Valle Nevado.** Valle Nevado's most extravagantly priced lodge provides ski-in ski-out convenience. Rooms here are larger than at the other two hotels, and all have balconies. Off season, it's possible to trek by horse or on foot from here to the foot of El Plomo, which is more than 5,000 meters (16,400 feet) high. ✉ *Valle Nevado* ☎ *2/206–0027, 800/669–0554 toll-free in U.S.* 📠 *2/208–0697* 🌐 *www.vallenevado.com* *53 rooms* *2 restaurants, room service, in-room data ports, in-room safes, minibars, cable TV, indoor pool, gym, massage, sauna,* *mountain bikes, hiking, horseback riding, downhill skiing, bar, lobby lounge, dance club, laundry service, Internet, business services, meeting rooms ▤ AE, DC, MC, V ⼳⊘⼳ MAP.*

Portillo

This ski area north of Santiago is renowned for its slopes, where numerous world speed records have been recorded. It also has the best views of any of the area's ski resorts. The slopes here were discovered by engineers building the now-defunct railroad that linked Chile to Argentina. After the railroad was inaugurated in 1910, skiing aficionados headed here despite the fact that there were no facilities available. Hotel Portillo, the only accommodation in the area, opened its doors in 1949, making Portillo the country's first ski resort, and went on to host the World Ski Championships in 1966.

The facilities at the hotel are reserved for hotel guests, but you can dine in the *auto-servicio* (cafeteria-style) restaurant if you're here for the day. ☎ 2/263–0606 ⊕ *www.skiportillo.cl* ⊠ *22,000 pesos* ⊙ *Mid-June–mid-Oct.*

WHERE TO STAY

$$$$

⊞ **Hotel Portillo.** Staying here feels a bit like going off to camp: every Saturday a new group settles in for a week's worth of outdoor activities. Besides skiing there's skating on the Laguna del Inca and even swimming in the heated outdoor pool. The hotel has almost as many employees as guests, which means service is excellent and the mood relaxed. Big windows in the guest rooms showcase mountain views or the more prized view of the lake. Family-style apartments come with bunk beds for children. ⊠ *Los Andes* ☎ *2/361–7000, 2/263–0606, 800/829–5325 toll-free in U.S.* 🖷 *2/361–7080* ⊕ *www.skiportillo.com* ⇘ *150 rooms, 5 suites, 15 apartments* ⼳ *4 restaurants, in-room data ports, in-room safes, indoor-outdoor pool, gym, hair salon, massage, sauna, billiards, Ping-Pong, downhill skiing, ice-skating, ski shop, bar, dance club, recreation room, theater, babysitting, laundry service, Internet, business services, airport shuttle, helipad, travel services* ▤ *AE, DC, MC, V* ⼳⊘⼳ *AI.*

Wineries

The wineries in the valley below Santiago are some of the oldest in Chile. Here you'll find most of the biggest and best-known vineyards in the country. For years tourists were virtually ignored by these wineries, but they are finally getting attention. Now many wineries are throwing their doors open to visitors for the first time, often letting them see behind-the-scenes activities like harvesting and pressing.

One of the most recognizable of Chile's wine appellations is the Valle de Maipo, an area that stretches south from Santiago. Viña Santa Rita is the only vineyard in the area with a restaurant, and it's a good one. Others worth a visit are Viña Concha y Toro, the country's largest winemaker, and Viña Undurraga, known for its lovely grounds.

Don Francisco Undurraga Vicuña founded **Viña Undurraga** in 1885 in the town of Talagante, 34 km (21 mi) southwest of Santiago. The opulent mansion he built here has hosted various visiting dignitaries, from

CloseUp
WINE TOURS AROUND SANTIAGO

If you want to see the vineyards of Chile, there's no need to travel to the Central Valley. Some of the country's finest wineries are within an hour or so of Santiago, meaning that you have plenty of time to tour one or two early in the day and still be back in the capital in time to enjoy your favorite vintage at one of the city's excellent restaurants.

Many of the city's top tour companies offer half-day trips to the vineyards—a good idea if you want to avoid driving on Santiago's crowded streets. The rates vary quite a bit, but expect to pay between $50 and $74 per person, depending on the number of people in the tour and the number of stops along the way. *Chip Travel* ⊠ Av. Santa María 227, Bellavista ☎ 2/735-9044 ⊕ www.chipsites.com can put together customized tours of the usually including Viña Cousiño-Macul, on the eastern edge of Santiago. The company can also arrange visits to some of the smaller boutique wineries in the region.

Turismo Cocha ⊠ Av. El Bosque Norte 0430, Las Condes ☎ 2/464-1000 ᖴ 2/464-1010 ⊠ Pedro de Valdivia 0169, Providencia ☎ 2/464-1600 ᖴ 2/464-1699 ⊠ Huérfanos 653, Santiago Centro ☎ 2/464-1950 ⊕ www.cocha.com, one of the country's largest tour companies, brings you on daylong journeys either to Viña Cousiño-Macul or Concha y Toro for a tour and a tasting. On the way back you'll stop at a roadside stand to sample steaming hot empanadas or at a typical country restaurant.

— Mark Sullivan

the queen of Denmark to the king of Norway. Today you can tour the house and the gardens—designed by Pierre Dubois, who planned Santiago's Parque Forestal—take a look at the facilities, and enjoy a tasting. Reserve ahead for a spot on the tour. Viña Undurraga is along the way to Pomaire, so you might visit both in the same day. ⊠ *Camino a Melipilla Km 34, Talagante* ☎2/372-2811 ⊕*www.undurraga.cl* 🖃*4,000 pesos* ⊙ *Tours: weekdays 10, 11:30, 2, and 3:30; Sat. 10 and 11:30.*

Chile's largest winemaker, **Viña Concha y Toro** produces 11 million cases annually. Some of its table wines—identifiable by the short, stout bottles—are sold domestically for about $2. The best bottles, however, fetch sky-high prices abroad. This is one of the oldest wineries in the region. Melchor de Concha y Toro, who once served as Chile's minister of finance, built the *casona,* or main house, in 1875. He imported vines from Europe, significantly improving the quality of the wines he was able to produce. Hour-long tours begin with an introductory video, a stroll through the vineyards and the century-old gardens, a look at the modern facilities, and a tasting. Reserve a few days ahead for a weekday tour, or a week ahead for the popular Saturday tours. Since they are all in the same region, you might want to consider a side trip to Viña Concha y Toro and Viña Santa Rita when you visit the Cajón del Maipo.

✉ *Av. Virginia Subercaseaux 210, Pirque* ☎ *2/476–5269* ⊕ *www. conchaytoro.com* 🎫 *Tour: 3,000 pesos* ☉ *Weekdays 10:30–6, Sat. 10–noon. English tours weekdays at 11:30 and 3, Sat. at 11.*

Chile's third-largest winery, **Viña Santa Rita,** played an important historical role in Chile's battle for independence. In 1814, 120 soldiers led by revolutionary hero Bernardo O'Higgins hid here in the cellars. Paula Jaraquemada, who ran the estate, refused to let the Spanish enter, saving the soldiers. (Santa Rita's 120 label commemorates the event.) At the center of Santa Rita's Maipo Valley estate half an hour south of Santiago, the lovely colonial hacienda now serves as the winery's headquarters. Its restaurant, La Casa de Doña Paula, is a delightful place to have a bite after the tour.

Tours take you down into the winery's musty cellars, which are worthy of Edgar Allen Poe. Built by French engineers in 1875 using a lime-and-stone technique called *cal y canto,* the fan-vault cellars have been named a national monument. The wine was once aged in the barrels you'll see, which are more than 120 years old and are made of *raulí* wood; today the wine is aged in stainless-steel towers. Unfortunately, the wonderful gardens and the original proprietor's house, with its chapel steeple peeking out from behind a thick canopy of trees, are not part of the tour. Note that you must reserve ahead for these tours. ✉ *Camino Padre Hurtado 0695, Alto Jahuel-Buín* ☎ *2/362–2594* ⊕ *www.santarita.com* 🎫 *Tours: 6,500 pesos; tastings cost extra* ☉ *Tours in English and Spanish: Tues.–Fri. at 10, 11:30, and 4.*

WHERE TO EAT   ✗ **La Casa de Doña Paula.** A two-century-old colonial hacienda with thick
★ **$–$$**   adobe walls houses Viña Santa Rita's restaurant. Under a peaked wood ceiling, the restaurant is decorated with old religious sculptures and portraits, including one of Paula Jaraquemada, who once ran the estate. If you plan to lunch here, it's a good idea to arrange to take the winery's 12:15 tour. Locally raised meats are the draw here; try the delicious *costillar de cerdo* (pork ribs). For dessert, the house specialty is *ponderación,* a crisp swirl of fried dough atop vanilla ice cream and caramel syrup. ✉ *Viña Santa Rita, Camino Padre Hurtado 695, Alto Jahuel-Buín* ☎ *2/362–2594* 🍴 *Reservations essential* 💳 *AE, DC, MC, V* ☉ *Closed Mon. No dinner.*

SANTIAGO ESSENTIALS

Transportation

BY AIR

Santiago's Comodoro Arturo Merino Benítez International Airport, often referred to simply as Pudahuel, is about a 30-minute drive west of the city.

Among the U.S. carriers, American serves Santiago from Dallas and Miami, and Delta connects from Atlanta. Lan flies nonstop to Santiago from both Miami and Los Angeles and with a layover in Lima from New York. Air France flies nonstop from Paris, and Iberia has nonstop flights from Madrid.

Most of the major Central and South American airlines also fly to Santiago, including Aerolíneas Argentinas, Aeromexico, Avianca, Copa, Lloyd Aéreo Boliviano, Taca, and Varig.

Lan has daily flights from Santiago to most cities throughout Chile. Aerolíneas del Sur and Sky also fly to most large cities within Chile.

Airport Comodoro Arturo Merino Benítez International Airport ☎ 2/690-1900 ⊕ www.aeropuertosantiago.cl.

Carriers Aerolíneas Argentinas ☎ 2/210-9300. Aerolíneas del Sur ☎ 2/690-1422. Aeromexico ☎ 2/690-1038. Air France ☎ 2/690-9696. American Airlines ☎ 2/601-9272. Avianca ☎ 2/270-6613. Copa ☎ 2/690-1014. Delta Airlines ☎ 2/690-1555. Iberia ☎ 2/870-1070. Lan ☎ 2/565-2000. Lloyd Aéreo Boliviano ☎ 2/690-1140. Sky ☎ 600/600-2828. Taca ☎ 2/690-1276. Varig ☎ 2/690-1348 in Chile.

AIRPORT TRANSFERS You have several options for getting to and from the airport. The most expensive is taxi service through Taxiofficial, which should cost you around 10,000 pesos for a trip downtown.

Centropuerto, which runs buses every 10 minutes between the airport and Terminal Los Héroes, charges about 1,100 pesos. Tur-Bus has service between the airport and its own terminal near Los Héroes Metro station; it departs every half hour and costs 1,200 pesos. The buses stop en route at the Pajaritos Metro station. Many locals prefer to use this station to get to and from the airport, as there is less traffic than downtown.

Transvip and Tur Transfer operate minibus service between the airport and various locations in the city. The cost is about 3,800 pesos.

Note that there is no Metro service to the airport.

Centropuerto ☎ 2/695-5958. Taxiofficial ☎ 2/690-1381. Transvip ☎ 2/677-3000. Tur-Bus ☎ 2/270-7500. Tur Transfer ☎ 2/677-3000.

BY BUS

TO & FROM SANTIAGO All the country's major highways pass through Santiago, which means you won't have a problem catching a bus to almost any destination. Finding that bus, however, can be a problem. The city has several terminals, each with buses heading in different directions. Terminal Los Héroes is on the edge of Santiago Centro near Los Héroes Metro station. Several companies have buses to points north and south from this station. The other three stations are clustered around the Universidad de Santiago Metro station. The modern Terminal San Borja has buses headed north and west. Terminal Santiago is the busiest, with dozens of small companies going west to the coast and to the south. Terminal Alameda, which handles only Tur-Bus and Pullman Bus, is for coastal and southern traffic. Terminal Los Héroes and Terminal Santiago also handle a few international routes, heading to far-flung destinations such as Buenos Aires, Rio de Janeiro, and Lima.

Several bus companies run regularly scheduled service to the Andes in winter. Skitotal buses depart from the office on Avenida Apoquindo and head to all of the ski resorts except Portillo. Buses depart at 8:45 AM; a round-trip ticket costs 10,000 pesos. Also available for hire here are taxis— (65,000 pesos) and 12-person minibuses (90,000 pesos). Manzur Expediciones runs buses to Portillo on Wednesday, Saturday, and Sunday for about the same price. Buses leaves at 8:30 AM from the Plaza Italia in front of the Teatro Universidad de Chile.

Bus service to the Cajón del Maipo is frequent and inexpensive—Manzur offers a round-trip ticket to Lo Valdés Mountain Center for less than 8,000 pesos. Only the 8 AM bus makes the two-hour trek to Baños de Colina, however. Sit on the right side of the bus for a good view of the river.

🚌 **Bus Companies Manzur Expediciones** ✉ Sótero del Río 475, Santiago Centro ☎ 2/777-4284. **Pullman Bus** ✉ Terminal Alameda, Estación Central ☎ 2/779-2026. **Skitotal** ✉ Av. Apoquindo 4900, Las Condes ☎ 2/246-0156. **Tur-Bus** ✉ Terminal Alameda, Estación Central ☎ 2/270-7500.

🚌 **Bus Depots Terminal Alameda** ✉ La Alameda 3750, Estación Central ☎ 2/270-7500. **Terminal Los Héroes** ✉ Tucapel Jiménez 21, Estación Central ☎ 2/420-0099. **Terminal San Borja** ✉ San Borja 184, Estación Central ☎ 2/776-0645. **Terminal Santiago** ✉ La Alameda 3850, La Alameda ☎ 2/376-1750.

WITHIN SANTIAGO Bus service is confusing for most newcomers. (It's confusing for most residents, too.) Buses (called *micros*) operate on hundreds of routes along the city's main thoroughfares. At any given moment there might be a dozen buses at a corner, all of them honking their horns and gesturing you aboard.

What to do? There are signs at covered bus stops telling you which number bus is headed in which direction. You can also check on the front of the buses themselves. Above the windshield should be the end points of the route. On the windshield, often on placards that the driver changes frequently, are the intermediate stops. These are often streets, so a sign reading PROVIDENCIA means the bus runs along Avenida Providencia. If you don't see your particular destination listed, look for a nearby mall or subway station.

Bus fare is usually 350 pesos, paid upon boarding. Drivers give change for small bills—and they do it while they are whizzing through traffic.

BY CAR

You don't need a car if you're not going to venture outside the city limits, as most of the downtown sights are within walking distance of each other. To get to other neighborhoods, taxis are inexpensive and the subway system is safe and efficient. After you dodge a line of cars speeding through a red light or see the traffic snarls during rush hour, you may be glad you don't have to drive in the city.

A car is the best way to see the surrounding countryside, however. Although the highways around Santiago are generally well maintained, weather conditions can make them dangerous. Between May and August, rain can cause roads in low-lying areas to flood. Avoid driving if it has been raining for several hours. If you're headed north or south, you'll probably use the Pan-American Highway, also called Ruta 5. To reach Valparaíso, Viña del Mar, or the northernmost beach resorts on the Central Coast, take Highway 68; for the southern beaches, take Ruta 78.

It can take up to two hours to reach the region's three major ski resorts, which lie 48–56 km (30–35 mi) from Santiago. The road is narrow, winding, and full of Chileans racing to get to the top. If you decide to drive, make sure you have either a four-wheel-drive vehicle or snow chains, which you can rent along the way. The chains are installed for about 8,000 pesos. Don't think you need them? There's a police checkpoint just before the road starts to climb into the Andes, and if the weather is rough they'll make you turn back. To reach Valle Nevado, Farellones, and La Parva, take Avenida Kennedy or Avenida Las Condes east. Signs direct you once you get into the mountains. Portillo is three hours north of Santiago. Call the hotel there ahead of time to find out about road conditions.

To reach Cajón del Maipo, head south on Avenida José Alessandri until you reach the Rotonda Departamental, a large traffic circle. There you take Camino Las Vizcachas, following it south into the valley.

CAR RENTALS Renting a car is convenient in Santiago, as most companies have offices at the airport and downtown. The international agencies generally rent compact cars with unlimited mileage and insurance coverage for about 40,000 pesos a day. They can provide ski-equipped vehicles for climbs to the Andes. Reputable local agencies include Alameda, Chilean, and Rosselot, whose rates can be as low as 20,000 pesos a day.
🚗 **Agencies Alameda** ✉ Diego de Velásquez 2087, Providencia ☎ 2/415-2071. **Alamo** ✉ Airport ☎ 2/690-1370 ✉ Av. Francisco Bilbao 2846, Providencia ☎ 2/225-3061. **Avis** ✉ Airport ☎ 2/690-1382 ✉ Av. Santa María 1742, Providencia ☎ 2/274-7621 ✉ Av. San Pablo 9900, Pudahuel ☎ 2/601-9747. **Budget** ✉ Airport ☎ 2/690-1386 ✉ Av. Francisco Bilbao 1439, Providencia ☎ 2/690-1489. **Chilean** ✉ Bellavista 0183, Bellavista ☎ 2/737-9650. **Hertz** ✉ Airport ☎ 2/690-1029 ✉ Av. Andrés Bello 1469, Providencia ☎ 2/496-1000. **Rosselot** ✉ Airport ☎ 2/343-9058 ✉ Av. Francisco Bilbao 2032, Providencia ☎ 2/343-9058.

BY SUBWAY

Santiago's excellent subway system is the best way to get around town. The Metro is comfortable, inexpensive, and safe. The system operates Monday–Saturday 6:30 AM–10:30 PM and Sunday 8–10:30 PM. Línea 1 runs east–west along the axis of the Río Mapocho. This is the most popular line, and perhaps the most useful, because it runs past most of the heavily touristed areas. Línea 2 runs north–south; it's rarely used by nonresidents because it heads to residential areas. Línea 5 also runs north–south except at its northern tip, where it bends to the west to connect with the Bellas Artes and Plaza de Armas stations. At this writing Linea 4, which connects to the Tobalaba, Vicente Valdes, and La Cisterna stations, was scheduled to open in 2006.

Every station has an easy-to-read map of all the stations and the adjoining streets. Buy tickets in any station at the glass booths or at the nearby machines. Individual tickets cost 340 to 430 pesos, depending on the time of day. After depositing your ticket in the turnstile, pass through and retrieve it to use again later. Single-ride tickets are not returned.

When you wave a *Multivía* card in front of a sensor of the turnstiles, it automatically deducts the fare. These cards, available at all ticket windows, save you the hassle of buying single-ride tickets. You can put any amount over 500 pesos on a card.
🚇 **Subway Information Metro de Santiago** ☎ 600/422-3330 ⊕ www.metrosantiago.cl.

BY TAXI

With some 50,000 taxis in Santiago, you can easily flag one down on most streets. The average ride costs around 2,000 to 3,000 pesos. The driver will turn the taxi meter on when you start your journey; it should read 150 pesos, the minimum charge. Taxi drivers don't always know where they are going and frequently ask directions; it's a good idea to carry a map. Radio-dispatched cabs are slightly more expensive but will pick you up at your door.

⛴ Taxi Companies Alborada ☎ 2/246-4900. **Alto Oriente** ☎ 2/226-2116. **Andes Pacífico** ☎ 2/225-3064 or 2/204-0104. **Apoquindo** ☎ 2/211-6073.

BY TRAIN

Chileans once boasted about the country's excellent rail service, but there's little left today aside from the limited service from Santiago to points south. Santiago's Estación Central, in Santiago Centro at the Metro station of the same name, is where you catch trains headed to the Central Valley. Note that you can also purchase tickets for the trains at the Estación Metro Universidad de Chile.

Trains run from Santiago through the larger cities of Rancagua, Curicó, Talca, Chillán, Concepción, and Temuco.

⛴ Estación Central ✉ La Alameda 3170, Santiago Centro ☎ 2/376-8500 ⊕ www.efe.cl. **Estación Metro Universidad de Chile** ✉ Local 10, La Alameda ☎ 2/688-3284.

Contacts & Resources

BANKS & EXCHANGE SERVICES

Unlike other South American countries, Chile rarely accepts U.S. dollars. (The exception is larger hotels, where prices are often quoted only in dollars.) Credit cards and traveler's checks are accepted everywhere in Santiago's most touristy areas.

You can exchange money in many places in the city. Banks in Santiago are usually open weekdays 9–4, and *casas de cambio* (currency-exchange offices) are open weekdays 9–7 and Saturday 9–3. They normally cluster together; in Providencia, for example, along Pedro de Valdivia, just before La Costanera, there are three or four.

Automatic teller machines dispense only Chilean pesos. To use an ATM issued by a foreign bank, select the "foreign client" option from the menu. Santander Santiago, with the most ATMs in town, has instructions in English, as do most other ATMs, and is linked to both the Plus and Cirrus systems. ATMs in a few banks are linked only to Cirrus. There are two ATMs on the second floor of the airport, as well as in the train and bus stations.

⛴ Banks American Express ✉ Av. Andrés Bello 2711, Las Condes ☎ 2/350-6955 ✉ Av. Isidora Goyenechea 3621, Las Condes ☎ 2/350-6700. **Santander Santiago** ✉ Estado 171, Santiago Centro ☎ 600/320-3000 ✉ Av. Providencia 1414, Providencia ☎ 600/320-3000 ✉ Av. Apoquindo 4815, Las Condes ☎ 600/320-3000.

EMERGENCIES

Farmacias Ahumada is a chain with branches in every part of the city. Few are open 24 hours, but many are open until midnight. There's a good one downtown near the Plaza de Armas at Paseo Ahumada and Huérfanos.

🚹 **Emergency Numbers Ambulance** ☎ 131. **Fire** ☎ 132. **Police** ☎ 133.

🚹 **Hospitals Clinica Alemana** ✉ Av. Vitacura 5951, Las Condes ☎ 2/210-1334. **Clinica Las Condes** ✉ Lo Fontecilla 441, Las Condes ☎ 2/210-4000. **Clinica Santa María** ✉ Av. Santa María 0410, Providencia ☎ 2/461-2000.

🚹 **Late-Night Pharmacy Farmacias Ahumada** ✉ Ahumada 301, at Huérfanos, Santiago Centro ☎ 2/631-3003.

ENGLISH-LANGUAGE MEDIA

The Instituto Chileno-Norteamericano de Cultura has a selection of books in English, as well as English-language periodicals. Librería Inglesa sells new books, but the prices are high. For popular newspapers and magazines in English, check the kiosks on the pedestrian mall of Paseo Ahumada in Santiago Centro or the kiosk on the top floor of the Parque Arauco Mall (Avenida Kennedy 5413) in Las Condes.

🚹 **Bookstores Instituto Chileno-Norteamericano de Cultura** ✉ Moneda 1467, Santiago Centro ☎ 2/696-3215. **Librería Inglesa** ✉ Av. Pedro de Valdivia 47, Providencia ☎ 2/231-6270 ✉ Av. Vitacura 5950, Vitacura ☎ 2/219-3080 ✉ Huérfanos 669, Local 11, Santiago Centro ☎ 2/638-7118.

INTERNET, MAIL & SHIPPING

In Santiago there are plenty of Internet cafés; you're likely to find several around your hotel. Most larger hotels provide business services, but these can be expensive. Web boxes dotted around the second floor of the Parque Arauco Mall (Avenida Kennedy 5413) in Las Condes allow you to access the Internet free of charge.

Correo Central—Santiago's main post office—is housed in the ornate Palacio de los Gobernadores, in Santiago Centro on the north side of the Plaza de Armas. It is open weekdays 8:30–7 and Saturday 8:30–3. There is a second downtown branch near the Palacio de la Moneda, as well as one in Providencia near the Manuel Montt Metro stop and one in Las Condes at El Golf stop.

For overnight delivery, DHL and Federal Express both have offices in Santiago Centro.

🚹 **Internet Cafés Crossings** ✉ Londres 68, La Alameda ☎ 2/664-2025. **Cybercenter** ✉ General Holley 190, Providencia ☎ 2/233-4364. **Cyberia** ✉ Matías Cousiño 68, La Alameda ☎ 2/699-7297. **Easy@Net** ✉ Paseo Las Palmas 2213, Providencia ☎ 2/333-7112. **Saiber Café** ✉ San Antonio 333, Santiago Centro ☎ No phone.

🚹 **Post Office Correo Central** ✉ Catedral and Paseo Ahumada, Santiago Centro ☎ 2/697-1701 ⊕ www.correos.cl.

🚹 **Shipping Services DHL** ✉ San Francisco 301, Santiago Centro ☎ 2/124-2121 ✉ Bandera 204, Santiago Centro ☎ 2/697-1081 ✉ Av. 11 de Septiembre 2070, Providencia ☎ 2/234-1516. **Federal Express** ✉ San Camilo 190, Santiago Centro ☎ 2/361-6000 ✉ Av. Providencia 1951, Providencia ☎ 2/233-2564.

TOURS

Sernatur (⇨ Visitor Information), the national tourism agency, maintains a listing of experienced individual tour guides who will take you on a half-day tour of Santiago and the surrounding area for about

25,000 pesos. These tours are a great way to get your bearings when you have just arrived in the city. They can also greatly enrich your visit. In museums, for example, they often provide information not generally available to the public and are especially helpful in museums with little or no signage in English.

Altué Expediciones arranges adventure trips such as white-water rafting on nearby rivers and hiking to the mouths of volcanoes. Chilean Travel Services and Sportstour handle tours of both Santiago and other parts of Chile. Chip Travel has several interest tours available, including a "human rights legacy" tour of sites that are reminders of dictator Augusto Pinochet's 17-year regime.

With more than a dozen locations, Turismo Cocha, founded in 1951, is one of the city's biggest private tour operators. It arranges tours of the wineries of the Cajón del Maipo and the beach resorts of Valparaíso and Viña del Mar, in addition to the usual city tours. It also has offices in the domestic and international terminals of the airport as well as in some of the larger hotels.

⭐ Tour Operators Altué Expediciones ✉ Encomenderos 83, Las Condes ☎ 2/232-1103 🖷 2/233-6799 ⊕ www.altue.com. **Chilean Travel Services** ✉ Antonio Bellet 77, Office 101, Providencia ☎ 2/251-0400 🖷 2/251-0423 ⊕ www.ctsturismo.cl. **Chip Travel** ✉ Antonio Bellet 77, Office 101, Providencia ☎ 2/735-9044 🖷 2/735-2267 ⊕ www.chipsites.com.

Sportstour ✉ Moneda 970, Santiago Centro ☎ 2/549-5200 🖷 2/698-2981 ⊕ www.sportstour.cl. **Turismo Cocha** ✉ Av. El Bosque Norte 0430, Las Condes ☎ 2/464-1000 🖷 2/464-1010 ✉ Pedro de Valdivia 0169, Providencia ☎ 2/464-1600 🖷 2/464-1699 ✉ Huérfanos 653, Santiago Centro ☎ 2/464-1950 ⊕ www.cocha.com.

VISITOR INFORMATION

Sernatur, the national tourist service, stocks maps and brochures and has a large and friendly staff that speaks English. The Providencia office, in a building with saffron-color columns, is near the Manuel Montt Metro stop. It is open weekdays 8:45–6 and Saturday 9–2.

Santiago runs two tourist information offices, one downtown in the Casa Colorada, the other on Cerro Santa Lucía. They are open Monday–Thursday 10–6, Friday 10–5.

For information about the Cajón del Maipo, stop by the office on the main square in San José de Maipo. The eager-to-please staff won't let you leave without an armload of brochures. The office is open weekdays 8:30–5:30.

⭐ Sernatur Casa Colorada ✉ Merced 860, El Centro ☎ 2/632-7783 ⊕ www.ciudad.cl/turismo. **Cerro Santa Lucía** ✉ Terraza Neptune, El Centro ☎ 2/664-4206 ⊕ www.ciudad.cl/turismo. **Providencia** ✉ Av. Providencia 1550, Providencia ☎ 2/731-8336 or 2/731-8337 ⊕ www.sernatur.cl. **San José de Maipo** ✉ Comercio 19788 ☎ 2/861-1275.

The Central Coast

WORD OF MOUTH

"Each year Valparaíso welcomes the New Year with an awesome fireworks display. The Valparaíso New Year's Pyrotechnic Festival lights up the whole city, but some of the best views are on the city's hills like Cerro Alegre or Cerro Concepción. However, if you want a truly magnificent experience, reserve tickets early at the Muelle Prat visitor's center for a boat cruise underneath one of the brightest and most beautifully choreographed pyrotechnic shows in the world."

—macarena93

Updated by
Mark Sullivan

MOST PEOPLE HEAD TO THE CENTRAL COAST for a single reason: the beaches. Yes, some may be drawn by the rough grandeur of the windswept coastline, with its rocky islets inhabited by sea lions and penguins, but those in search of nature generally head south to Chiloé and Patagonia or north to the Atacama Desert. Yet this stretch of coastline west of Santiago has much more than sun and surf.

The biggest surprise is the charm of Valparaíso, Chile's second-largest city—known locally as Valpo. Valparaíso shares a bay with Viña del Mar but the similarities end there. Valparaíso is a bustling port town with a jumble of colorful cottages nestled in the folds of its many hills. Viña del Mar has lush parks surrounding neoclassical mansions and a long beach lined with luxury high-rises. Together they form an interesting contrast of working class and wealth at play.

The *balnearios* (small beach towns) to the north of the twin cities have their own character, often defined by coastal topography. Proximity to Santiago has resulted in the development—in some cases overdevelopment—of most of them as summer resorts. At the beginning of the 20th century, Santiago's elite started building vacation homes. Soon after, when trains connected the capital to beaches, middle-class families started spending their summers at the shore. Improved highway access in recent decades has allowed Chileans of all economic levels to enjoy the occasional beach vacation. Late December–mid-March, when schools let out for summer vacation and Santiago becomes torrid, the beaches are packed. Vacationers frolic in the chilly sea by day, and pack the restaurants and bars at night. The rest of the year, the coast is relatively deserted and, though often cool and cloudy, a pleasantly tranquil place to explore. Local *caletas*—literally meaning "coves," this is where fishing boats gather to unload their catch, and it's usually the site of local fishing cooperatives—are always colorful and lively.

Exploring the Central Coast

Valparaíso is the only city in the Central Coast capable of holding your attention for long; you could easily spend a few days exploring its winding streets and enjoying its varied nightlife. Viña del Mar has far less character but is still quite pleasant with its tree-lined streets and wide beach. The small towns along the coast, wherever the current has carved out a beach, have few museums or monuments. Most are little more than beaches and a chance to explore the rocky coastline between them—which can be exhilarating. Alternatives to lounging on the beach are tennis, golf, and horseback riding.

To reach the balnearios south of Valparaíso, take Highway 68 from Santiago to Casablanca, where a road leads to most of the coastal towns. (Quintay is reached via another road a few miles west of Casablanca.) It's a 1½-hour drive on Highway 68 from Santiago to either Valparaíso or Viña del Mar. Beach towns to the north of Viña del Mar are all accessible by the coastal highway, the *Costanera*, which winds its way past amazing scenery north to Papudo. Los Molles, on the other hand, is best reached by driving on the Pan-American Highway.

CENTRAL COAST FESTIVALS & SEASONAL EVENTS

The annual Festival Internacional de la Canción (International Song Festival) takes place during a week in mid-February in Viña del Mar. The concerts are broadcast live on television. Most towns have colorful processions on the Día de San Pedro on June 29. A statue of St. Peter, patron saint of fisherfolk, is typically hoisted onto a fishing boat and led along a coastal procession. Thousands turn out for the event in Valparaíso.

About the Restaurants

Dining is one of the great pleasures of visiting the Central Coast. It's not rare to see fishermen bringing the day's catch straight to the restaurants that inevitably line the shore. Your server will be happy to share with you which fish were caught fresh that day. With the exception of major holidays, reservations are almost never required for restaurants here. Most restaurants close between lunch and dinner: from 3 or 4 to 7 or 8.

About the Hotels

Because the central beach resorts were developed by and for the Santiago families who summer here, they are dominated by vacation homes and apartments. There's a shortage of hotels; the most common accommodation is the cabana, which is usually a somewhat rustic cabin with a kitchenette and one or more bedrooms designed to accommodate families on tight budgets. An even more affordable option is a *residencial* (guesthouse), often just a few rooms for rent in a private home. The exceptions to this trend are Viña del Mar and nearby Reñaca and Concón, which have a dozen or so hotels between them.

WHAT IT COSTS In pesos (in thousands)					
	$$$$	**$$$**	**$$**	**$**	**¢**
RESTAURANTS	over 11	8–11	5–8	3–5	under 3
HOTELS	over 105	75–105	45–75	15–45	under 15

Restaurant prices are for a main course at dinner. Hotel prices are for a double room in high season, excluding tax.

When to Go

It seems that all of Chile heads to the coast in the summer months of January and February. This can be a great time to visit, with the weather

SAMPLE ITINERARY

Plan to spend at least two days in **Valparaíso,** where you can ride a few funiculars and explore the cobbled streets. While you're here, a good day trip is an excursion to Pablo Neruda's waterfront home nearby in **Isla Negra.** You'll want to take a day or so to stroll around the bustling beach town of **Viña del Mar.** After that you can drive north along the coastal highway, stopping for lunch in either **Concón** or **Maitencillo.** From there you can return to Viña del Mar or continue on to spend a night in **Zapallar.**

2

at its warmest, and the nightlife hopping. It's also a tough time to find a room, especially on weekends. Make reservations as far in advance as possible. The climate is also nice in spring (September, October, and November) and fall (March, April and May), when the days are warm and breezy, and the nights cool. December and March are excellent months to visit—the weather is still good, but you can explore the coast's natural wonders in relative solitude.

VALPARAÍSO & VIÑA DEL MAR

Viña del Mar and Valparaíso (Vineyard of the Sea and Paradise Valley, respectively) each maintain an aura that warrants their dreamy appellations. Only minutes apart, these two urban centers are nevertheless as different as twin cities can be. Valparaíso won the heart of poet Pablo Neruda, who praised its "cluster of crazy houses," and it continues to be a disorderly, bohemian, charming town. Valparaíso's lack of beaches keeps its mind on matters more urban, if not urbane.

Viña del Mar, Valparaíso's glamorous sibling, is a clean, orderly city with miles of beige beach, a glitzy casino, manicured parks, and shopping galore. Viña, together with nearby Reñaca, is synonymous with the best of life for vacationing Chileans. Its beaches gleam, its casino rolls, and its discos sizzle.

Valparaíso

10 km (6 mi) south of Viña del Mar, 120 km (75 mi) west of Santiago.

Valparaíso's dramatic topography—45 *cerros,* or hills, overlooking the ocean—requires the use of winding pathways and wooden *ascensores* (funiculars) to get up many of the grades. The slopes are covered by candy-color houses—there are almost no apartments in the city—most of which have exteriors of corrugated metal peeled from shipping containers decades ago. Valparaíso has served as Santiago's port for centuries. Before the Panama Canal opened, Valparaíso was the busiest port in South America. Harsh realities—changing trade routes, industrial decline—have diminished its importance, but it remains Chile's principal port.

Most shops, banks, restaurants, bars, and other businesses cluster along the handful of streets called *El Plan* (the flat area) that are closest to the shoreline. *Porteños* (which means "the residents of the port") live in the

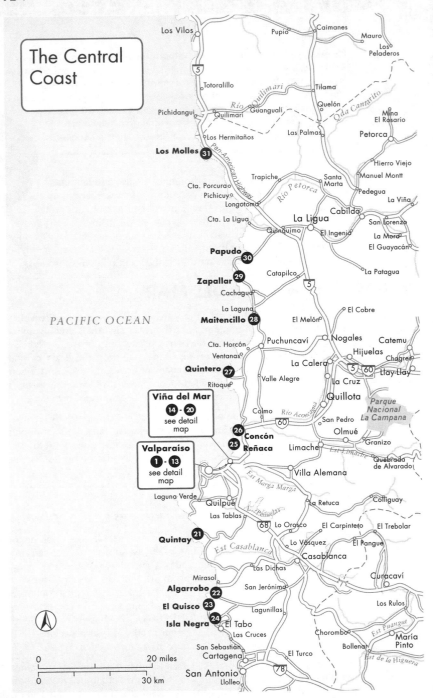

The Central Coast

PACIFIC OCEAN

Los Vilos

Pupio

Caimanes

Mauro

Los Peladeros

5

Totoralillo

Tilama

Quelón

Río Quilimari

Pichidangui

Quilimari

Guanguali

Las Palmas

Oda Canarito

Mina El Rosario

Petorca

Los Hermitaños

Los Molles 31

Pan-American Highway

Trapiche

Santa Marta

Hierro Viejo

Manuel Montt

Pedegua

La Viña

Río Petorca

Cabildo

San Lorenzo

Cta. Porcura

Pichicuy

Longotoma

Cta. La Ligua

La Ligua

Quinquimo

El Ingenio

La Mora

El Guayacán

Papudo 30

Zapallar 29

Catapilco

La Patagua

Cachagua

La Laguna

El Cobre

Maitencillo 28

El Melón

Cta. Horcón

Puchuncaví

Nogales

Catemu

Ventanas

Hijuelas

Chagres

Quintero 27

La Calera

5 60

Llay-Llay

Ritoque

Valle Alegre

La Cruz

Quillota

Viña del Mar

14 - 20

see detail map

Colmo

Río Aconcagua

60

San Pedro

Olmué

Parque Nacional La Campana

26

Concón

25

Reñaca

Limache

Granizo

Est Limache

Quebrada de Alvarado

Valparaíso

1 - 13

see detail map

Villa Alemana

Est Marga Marga

Laguna Verde

Quilpué

Las Tablas

La Retuca

Colliguay

L. Peñuelas

Quintay 21

Est Casablanca

68

Lo Orosco

El Carpinteto

El Trebolar

Lo Vásquez

El Pangue

Las Dichas

Casablanca

Curacaví

Mirasol

San Jerónimo

Algarrobo 22

El Quisco 23

Lagunillas

Los Rulos

Isla Negra 24

El Tabo

Las Cruces

Chorombo

Est Puangue

Bollenar

María Pinto

San Sebastián

Cartagena

El Turco

Est de la Higuera

0   20 miles

0   30 km

San Antonio

Llolleo

78

Riding the Ascensores

It's an uphill climb in Valparaíso, but the way is smoothed out a bit by the *ascensores,* or funiculars, that shuttle locals between their jobs near the port and their homes in the hills. The word means "elevator," though only the Ascensor Polanco travels vertically; the rest are pulled up steep inclines at an angle by steel cables. The views are unbelievable, and the ride is thrilling.

Beautiful Beaches

Thousands of Santiaguinos flock to the Central Coast's beaches every summer. To serve the hungry masses are dozens and dozens of seafood shacks, all serving freshly caught fish. The Humboldt Current, which flows northward along the coast of Chile, carries cold water to the Central Coast. If you plan to surf or skin-dive, you need a wet suit; if you plan to swim, you need thick skin.

2

Superb Shopping

The streets of Cerro Alegro and Cerro Concepción in Valparaíso are lined with shops selling everything from finely wrought jewelry to hand-tooled leather. There are also several crafts markets *artesanías,* including one right by the docks. Viña del Mar, Valparaíso's neighbor to the north, has everything from large department stores and outlet malls to trendy shops and boutiques.

---

surrounding hills in an undulating array of colorful abodes. At the top of any of the dozens of stairways, the *paseos* (promenades) have spectacular views; many are named after prominent Yugoslavian, Basque, and German immigrants. Neighborhoods are named for the hills they cover.

With the jumble of power lines overhead and the hundreds of buses that slow down—but never completely stop—to pick up agile riders, it's hard to forget you're in a city. Still, walking is the best way to experience Valparaíso. Be a careful where you step, though—locals aren't very conscientious about curbing their dogs.

a good walk

Take a taxi, or any bus that has ADUANA written on its windshield, to the Plaza Aduana, at the northwestern end of El Plan. Here is the scarlet Aduana de Valparaíso, the stately 19th-century customs house still in use today. Next door is the Ascensor Artillería, a funicular that carries you up to the **Paseo 21 de Mayo ❶ ▶**. Behind this promenade with a sweeping view of the bay is the **Museo Naval y Marítimo de Valparaíso ❷**. Take the funicular back down to the plaza, or walk down the stairway that ends near the base of the customs house. Walk south along Calle Cochrane, the first block of which has some tawdry bars—note the WELCOME SAILOR signs (needless to say, avoid this area at night). Along the way you'll pass the atmospheric **Mercado Central ❸**, where many of the locals come to do their shopping. When you reach Almirante Muñoz Hurtado, take a right. Across Calle Serrano is the entrance to Ascencor Cordillera. At the top of the hill is the lovely **Museo del Mar Lord Cochrane ❹**.

Valparaíso

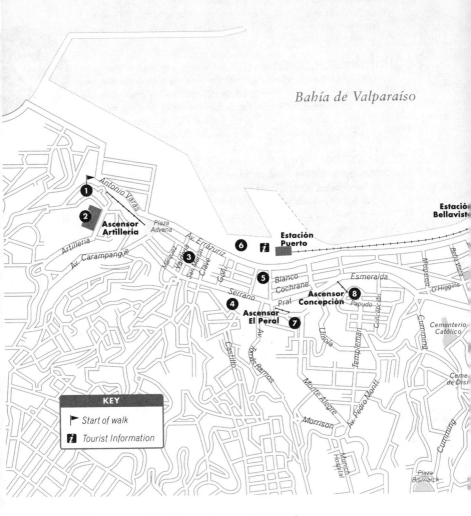

Bahía de Valparaíso

Estación Bellavist·

Estación Puerto

Ascensor Artillería

Plaza Advana

Antonio Varas

Artillería

Av. Carampangue

Márquez

Ibarra

San Martín

Clave

Cifré

Serrano

Blanco

Cochrane

Prat

Esmeralda

Ascensor Concepción

Papudo

D'Higgins

Cementerio Católico

Ascensor El Peral

Castillo

Av. Tomás Ramos

Urriola

Concepción

Templeman

Monte Alegre

Morrison

Av. Pedro Montt

Cumming

Ceme· de Disi·

Munic· Hospital

Plaza Bismarck

Cumming

KEY

▶ *Start of walk*

𝑖 *Tourist Information*

Cerro Concepción **8**

Galería Municipal
de Arte **12**

Mercado Central **3**

Muelle Prat **6**

Museo a
Cielo Abierto **10**

Museo de
Bellas Artes **7**

Museo de
Historia Natural
de Valparaíso **11**

Museo del
Mar Lord Cochrane **4**

Museo Naval y
Marítimo de
Valparaíso **2**

Paseo 21 de Mayo **1**

Plaza Sotomayor **5**

Plaza Victoria **13**

La Sebastiana **9**

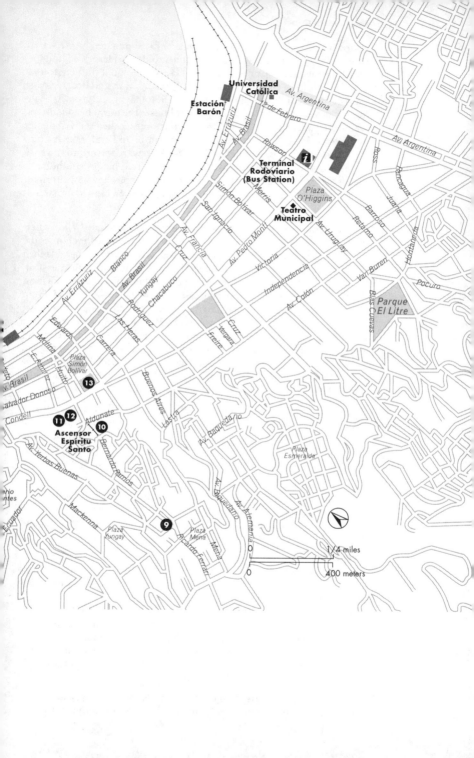

Follow Calle Cochrane to **Plaza Sotomayor** ❺, dominated by the stately Comandancia building and the Monumento de los Héroes de Iquique. North of the monument is **Muelle Prat** ❻, where you'll find the tourist office, the station for trains bound for Viña del Mar, and boats leaving for short tours of the bay. Return to Plaza Sotomayor and cross it, heading to the left of the grand building that houses the naval headquarters, where a smaller square lies before the courthouse called the Tribunales de Justicia. Hidden on your left is the Ascensor El Peral; take it up to the art nouveau **Museo de Bellas Artes** ❼. Afterward, return to the base of the hill, turn right on Calle Prat, and walk two blocks southeast to the Ascensor Concepción, at the end of a narrow passage on your right. Ride this up to the neighborhood of **Cerro Concepción** ❽, with its sweeping views of the city.

If you return to Calle Prat and continue right, it becomes Calle Esmeralda; follow this and you'll pass the neoclassical structure that houses the world's oldest Spanish-language newspaper, *El Mercurio*. Esmeralda then curves south to a small square called Plaza Anibal Pinto. Head east on Calle Condell to Calle Ecuador, where you can find some of the city's most popular nightspots. Taxis from here can take you to **La Sebastiana** ❾. From there you can walk down the narrow streets of Cerro Bellavista and get a look at a series of murals known as the **Museo a Cielo Abierto** ❿, near the top of the Ascensor Espíritu Santo. Then ride down to Calle Huito, which in turn leads back to Calle Condell. Turn left, and go to the old Palacio Lyon, which houses the **Museo de Historia Natural de Valparaíso** ⓫ and the **Galería Municipal de Arte** ⓬. A block east of the Palacio on Calle Condell is **Plaza Victoria** ⓭, across from which stands the city's cathedral.

TIMING & PRECAUTIONS You need a good pair of shoes to fully appreciate Valparaíso. Walking past all the sights, exploring the museums, and enjoying a meal and drinks makes for a long, full day. You might visit La Sebastiana the next morning to give yourself more time to linger. Definitely bring sunblock or a hat. Even if it's cloudy when you start, the sun often comes out by afternoon.

Like most port cities, Valparaíso has its share of street crime. Avoid deserted areas and be on the lookout for suspicious characters. It's best not to walk alone, especially after dark. Keep an eye on cameras and other valuables, or keep them in your hotel safe.

What to See

❽ **Cerro Concepción.** Ride the Ascensor Concepción to this hilltop neighborhood covered with houses and cobblestone streets. The greatest attraction is the view, which is best appreciated from Paseo Gervasoni, a wide promenade to the right when you exit the ascensor, and Paseo Atkinson, one block to the east. Over the balustrades that line those paseos lie amazing vistas of the city and bay. Nearly as fascinating are the narrow streets above them, some of which are quite steep. Continue uphill to Cerro Alegre, which has a bit of a bohemian flair. ✉ *Ascensor Concepción, Prat.*

⓬ **Galería Municipal de Arte.** This crypt in the basement of the Palacio Lyon is the finest art space in the city. Temporary exhibits by top-caliber Chilean artists are displayed on stone walls under a series of brick arches. It's easy to miss the entrance, which is on Calle Condell just beyond the Museo de Historia Natural de Valparaíso. ⊠ *Condell 1550* ☎ *32/939–562* ☜ *Free* ☉ *Weekdays 10–7, Sat. 10–5.*

❸ **Mercado Central.** Before *supermercados* became popular, locals did all their grocery shopping in markets such as this one topped by an enormous octagonal glass roof. On the ground floor you'll find produce piled high on tables and tumbling out of baskets, and upstairs is whatever types of fish the boats brought in that morning. A dozen different eateries serve up the catch of the day. Watch your wallet, as this place can get crowded. ⊠ *Cochrane between Valdivia and San Martín* ☎ *No phone.*

❻ **Muelle Prat.** Though its name translates as Prat Dock, the Muelle is actually a wharf with steps leading to the water. Sailors from the ships in the harbor arrive in *lanchas* (small boats), or board them for the trip back to their vessels. It's a great place to watch the activity at the nearby port, and the ships anchored in the harbor. To get a closer look, you can board one of the lanchas—it costs 2,000 pesos for the trip out to a ship and back, or 10,000 pesos for a 40-minute tour of the bay. Here you'll find the tourist information office and a row of souvenir shops. One of the city's best seafood restaurants, Bote Salvavidas, is a few steps away. ⊠ *Av. Errázuriz at Plaza Sotomayor.*

★ ❼ **Museo de Bellas Artes.** The art nouveau Palacio Baburizza houses the city's fine-arts museum. Former owner Pascual Baburizza donated his large collection of European paintings to the city. The fanciful decorative exterior is reminiscent of the style of Spanish architect Antoni Gaudí. Note the bronze children dancing around the portico. The museum was closed at this writing but was slated to open again by the end of 2006. ⊠ *Ascensor El Peral to Paseo Yugoslavo* ☎ *32/252–332* ⊕ *www.museobaburizza.cl.*

❿ **Museo a Cielo Abierto.** The Open Sky Museum is a winding walk past 20 official murals (and a handful of unofficial ones) by some of Chile's best painters. There's even one by the country's most famous artist, Roberto Matta. The path is not marked—there's no real fixed route—as the point is to get lost in the city's history and culture. ⊠ *Ascensor Espíritu Santo up to Cerro Buenavista.*

> **need a break?** While exploring Cerro Bellavista, be sure to stop for a coffee at **Gato Tuerto** (⊠ Hector Calvo Jofré 20 ☎ 32/220–867), the One-Eye Cat. This meticulously restored 1910 Victorian house, painted eye-popping shades of yellow and blue, affords lovely views. It's also a popular nightspot.

⓫ **Museo de Historia Natural de Valparaíso.** Within the Palacio Lyon, one of the few buildings to survive the devastating 1906 earthquake is this rather outdated natural history museum. Among the more unusual exhibits are a pre-Columbian mummy, newborn conjoined twins in formaldehyde, and stuffed penguins. ⊠ *Condell 1546* ☎ *32/257–441* ☜ *600 pesos* ☉ *Tues.–Sat. 10–1 and 2–6, Sun. 10–2.*

④ Museo del Mar Lord Cochrane. There's a small collection of naval paraphernalia, but the real reason for a visit is to the see the house itself, constructed for Lord Thomas Cochrane. The colonial-style house, with its red tile roof and stately wood columns, is one of the most beautiful in Valparaíso. As you might expect for an admiral's abode, it has wonderful views of the port. ⊠ *Merlet 195* ☎ *32/213–124* 💲 *600 pesos* ⊙ *Tues.–Sat. 10–1 and 2–6, Sun. 10–2.*

② Museo Naval y Marítimo de Valparaíso. Atop Cerro Artillería is the large neoclassical mansion that once housed the country's naval academy. It now contains a maritime museum, with displays that document the history of the port and the ships that once defended it. Cannons positioned on the front lawn frame the excellent view of the ocean. ⊠ *Ascensor Artillería up to Paseo 21 de Mayo* ☎ *32/437–651* 💲 *500 pesos* ⊙ *Tues.–Sun. 10–6.*

▶ **① Paseo 21 de Mayo.** Ascensor Artillería pulls you uphill to Paseo 21 de Mayo, a wide promenade surrounded by well-tended gardens and stately trees from which you can survey the port and a goodly portion of the city through coin-operated binoculars. A gazebo—a good place to escape the sun—seems to be hanging in midair. Paseo 21 de Mayo is in the middle of Cerro Playa Ancha, one of the city's more colorful neighborhoods. ⊠ *Ascensor Artillería at Plaza Advana.*

⎧ **need a**⎫
⎩ **break?**⎭   If you can't get enough of the views from Paseo 21 de Mayo, stroll down the stairs that run parallel to the ascensor to the small restaurant, **Poseidon** (⊠ Subida Artillería 99 ☎ 32/346–713). With a terrace superbly perched on a high corner overlooking the city, this makes a great spot for a cool drink.

⑤ Plaza Sotomayor. Valparaíso's most impressive square, Plaza Sotomayor, serves as a gateway to the bustling port. **Comandancia en Jefe de la Armada,** headquarters of the Chilean navy, is a grand, gray building that rises to a turreted pinnacle over a mansard roof. At the north end of the plaza stands the **Monumento de los Héroes de Iquique,** which honors Arturo Prat and other heroes of the War of the Pacific. In the middle of the square (beware of traffic—cars and buses come suddenly from all directions) is the **Museo del Sitio.** Artifacts from the city's mid-19th-century port, including parts of a dock that once stood on this spot, are displayed in the open under glass. ⊠ *Av. Errázuriz at Cochrane.*

🐌 **⑬ Plaza Victoria.** The heart of the lower part of the city is this green plaza with a lovely fountain bordered by four female statues representing the seasons. Two black lions at the edge of the park look across the street to the neo-Gothic cathedral and its unusual freestanding bell tower. Directly to the north is **Plaza Simon Bolívar,** which delights children with swings, slides, and simple carnival rides. ⊠ *Condell at Molina.*

★ **⑨ La Sebastiana.** Some say the views from the windows of Pablo Neruda's hillside house are the best in all of Valparaíso. People come to La Sebastiana to marvel at the same ocean that inspired so much poetry. The house is named for Sebastián Collado, a Spanish architect who began it as a home for himself but died before it was finished. The incomplete building stood abandoned for 10 years before Neruda finished it, revising the design (Neruda had no need for the third-floor aviary or the helicopter landing pad) and adding curvaceous walls, narrow stairways, a tower, and a polymorphous character.

A maze of twisting stairwells leads to an upper room where a video shows Neruda enunciating the five syllables of the city's name over and again as he rides the city's ascensores. His upper berth contains his desk, books, and some original manuscripts. What makes the visit to La Sebastiana memorable, however, is Neruda's nearly obsessive delight in physical objects. The house is a shrine to his many cherished things, such as the beautiful orange-pink bird he brought back embalmed from Venezuela. His lighter spirit is here also, in the carousel horse and the pink-and-yellow barroom stuffed with kitsch. ⊠ *Ferrari 692* ☏ *32/256–606* ⊕ *www.neruda.cl* ☜ *1,800 pesos* ⊙ *Jan. and Feb., Tues.–Sun. 10:30–6:50; Mar.–Dec., Tues.–Fri. 10:10–1:30 and 3:30–6, Sun. 10:30–6.*

Where to Stay & Eat

$$–$$$ ✕ **Bote Salvavidas.** This restaurant on Muelle Prat has great views of the harbor from its glass-walled dining room. As you might guess, it specializes in seafood. Dishes such as *congrio margarita* (conger eel with shellfish sauce), *salmón salsa espinaca y nueces* (salmon smothered in a spinach-and-walnut sauce), and *pastel de jaiba* (crab pie) are among the popular specialties. A three-course *menu ejecutivo* (set lunch), available on weekdays, is quite the deal. ⊠ *Muelle Prat* ☏ *32/251–477* ▤ *AE, DC, MC, V* ⊙ *No dinner Sun. and Mon.*

$$–$$$ ✕ **Café Turri.** Near the top of Ascensor Concepción, this 19th-century
Fodor's Choice mansion commands one of the best views of Valparaíso. It also has some
★ of the finest seafood. House specialties such as sea bass or shrimp in almond sauce are alone worth the effort of driving to the coast from Santiago. If you're a seafood lover, splurge on the *jardín de mariscos especial*, which is a huge platter of the catch of the day. Outside there's a terrace and inside are two floors of dining rooms. The old-fashioned service, overseen by the affable owner, is excellent. ⊠ *Templeman 147, at Paseo Gervasoni* ☏ *32/252–091* ▤ *32/259–198* ▤ *AE, DC, MC, V.*

$$–$$$ ✕ **La Colombina.** This restaurant is in an old home on Cerro Alegre, one of the city's most beautiful hilltop neighborhoods. Dining rooms on two floors are notable for their elegant furnishings, stained-glass windows, and impressive views of the city and sea. Seafood dominates the menu, with such inventive dishes as *albacora del bufón* (swordfish in a caper-and-mushroom cream sauce) and *trilogía del mar* (salmon, sea bass, and conger eel in a white wine, mushroom, and vegetable sauce). Choose from a list of 80 national wines. ⊠ *Paseo Yugoslavo 15* ☏ *32/236–254* ▤ *AE, DC, MC, V* ⊙ *No dinner Mon.*

$–$$$ ✕ **Coco Loco.** It takes a little more than an hour to turn 360 degrees in this impressive *giratorio* (revolving restaurant), meaning you can savor all the smashing views of the city. The vast menu ranges from *filete de ciervo salsa hongos* (venison in a mushroom sauce) to fettuccine with a squid-and-mussels sauce. ⊠ *Blanco 1781* ☏ *32/227–614* ⚑ *Reservations essential* ▤ *AE, DC, MC, V* ⊙ *No dinner Sun.*

CloseUp

CHILEAN COASTAL CUISINE

"In the turbulent sea of Chile lives the golden conger eel," wrote Chilean poet Pablo Neruda in a simple verse that leaves the real poetry for the dinner table. To many, dining is the principal pleasure of a trip to the Central Coast. Along with that succulent conger eel, congrio, menus here typically have corvina (sea bass), a whitefish called reineta, and the mild lenguado (sole). The appetizer selection, which is invariably extensive, usually includes ostiones (scallops), machas (razor clams), camarones (shrimp), and jaiba (crab). Because lobster is extremely rare in Chilean waters, it's more expensive here than just about anywhere in the world.

Fish and meat dishes are often served alone, which means that if you want french fries, mashed potatoes, a salad, or palta (avocado), you have to order it as an agregado (side dish). Bread, a bowl of lemons, and a sauce called pebre (a mix of tomato, onion, coriander, parsley, and often chili) are always brought to the table. Valparaíso is known for a hearty, cheap meal called chorillana—a mountain of minced steak, onions, cheese, and eggs on a bed of french fries.

— Mark Sullivan

$$ ✕ **Pasta y Vino.** Everything isn't black and white at this extremely popular restaurant on Cerro Concepción. The innovative food, served in the monochromatic dining room, comes in eye-popping colors. Even the fanciful breads, which seem to swirl out of the basket, are lovely shades of brown. Start with clams on the half shell flavored with ginger and lime, then move on to fettuccine tossed with ham, walnuts, and honey or ravioli filled with duck in a rich port wine reduction. The wine list, focusing on local vintages, is impressive. The hip young staff in floor-length black aprons couldn't be more accommodating. ✉ *Templeman 352* ☎ *32/496–187* ⌚ *Reservations essential* ▭ *AE, DC, MC, V.*

Fodor'sChoice
★

¢–$ ✕ **Brighton.** Nestled below the eponymous bed-and-breakfast on the edge of Cerro Concepción, this popular restaurant has an amazing view from its black-and-white-tiled balcony. Vintage advertisements hang on the walls of the intimate dining room. A limited menu includes such Chilean standards as *machas a la parmesana* (razor clams Parmesan) and seviche, as well as several kinds of crepes and a Spanish *tortilla* (egg-and-potato pie). An extensive wine list and cocktail selection make it a popular nightspot, especially on weekends, when there's live music. ✉ *Paseo Atkinson 151* ☎ *32/223–513* ▭ *AE, DC, MC, V.*

¢–$ ✕ **Donde Carlitos.** A stone's throw from the port are dozens of eateries specializing in whatever was caught that morning. You won't find any fresher fish than at this tiny storefront restaurant near Mercado Central. Through a window on the street you can watch the chefs prying open oysters and rolling razor clams into empanadas. The simple dining room has a half dozen tables under chandeliers shaped like—you guessed it—ships' wheels. ⊠ *Blanco 166* ☎ *32/217–310* ▤ *No credit cards* ⊘ *No dinner.*

¢   ✕ **Casino Social J. Cruz M.** This eccentric restaurant is a Valparaíso institution, thanks to its legendary status for inventing the *chorillana* (minced beef with onions, cheese, and an egg atop french fries), which is now served by most local restaurants. There is no menu—choose either a plate of chorillana for two or three, or *carne mechada* (stewed beef), with a side of french fries, rice, or tomato salad. Glass cases choked with dusty trinkets surround tables covered with plastic cloths in the cramped dining room. You may have to share a table. The restaurant is at the end of a bleak corridor off Calle Condell. ⊠ *Condell 1466* ☎ *32/211–225* ▤ *No credit cards.*

$$–$$$ ▥ **Casa Thomas Somerscales.** Perched high atop Cerro Alegre, this palm-
Fodor'sChoice   shaded mansion has an unobstructed view of the sea. As befits an ele-
★   gant home from the 19th century, its rambling hallways and wooden staircases lead to rooms of various shapes and sizes. Ask for Number 8, which has lovely French doors and a private terrace where you can enjoy your breakfast. All rooms at this boutique hotel are impeccably furnished with antique armoires and bureaus and beds piled high with imported linens. Dozens of trendy shops and restaurants are steps away. ⊠ *San Enrique 446* ☎ *32/331–379* 🖷 *32/331–006* ⊕ *www. hotelsomerscales.cl* ⤳ *8 rooms* ♢ *Dining room, in-room safes, mini-bars, cable TV, in-room DVD, shop, Internet, meeting room* ▤ *AE, DC, MC, V* ¦◉¦ *CP.*

$–$$$ ▥ **Ultramar.** No, you're not seeing spots. Those huge polka dots in the bathroom are part of the whimsical design at Ultramar, the city's first real boutique hotel. The candy-color stripes and bold geometric patterns are like nothing this country has ever seen. They come as a complete surprise, as the hotel is housed in a staid-looking brick building dating from 1907. There's a café on the first floor that hosts occasional art exhibits and a terrace with eye-popping views of the bay. Just about the only caveat is the location, which is a bit far from the action. ⊠ *Tomás Peréz 173, Cerro Cárcel* ☎ *32/210–000* ⊕ *www.hotelultramar.cl* ⤳ *17 rooms* ♢ *Café, cable TV* ▤ *AE, MC, V.*

$ ▥ **Brighton B&B.** This bright-yellow Victorian house enjoys an enviable
Fodor'sChoice   location at the edge of tranquil Cerro Concepción. The house is furnished
★   with brass beds and other antiques chosen by owner Nelson Morgado, who taught architecture for two decades at the University of Barcelona. The terrace of its restaurant and three of its six rooms have vertiginous views of the bay. One room has a private balcony that is perfect for a romantic breakfast. Room size varies considerably—only the so-called suite (just a larger room) is spacious—but all are charming. ⊠ *Paseo Atkinson 151* ☎ *32/223–513* 🖷 *32/598–802* ⊕ *www.brighton.cl* ⤳ *9*

rooms ⚄ *Restaurant, bar, laundry service; no a/c, no room phones* ▭ *AE, DC, MC, V* ⛾ *CP.*

$ ⊞ **Hostal La Colombina.** The location here is excellent: on a quiet street just up the hill from the Ascensor Concepción, near Paseo 21 de Mayo in the heart of Cerro Concepción. Dozens of shops and restaurants are on the nearby streets. Rooms in this old house may be sparsely furnished, but they are ample, with high ceilings and wooden floors. Most have big windows, though none of them have much of a view. ⊠ *Concepción 280* ☎ *32/236–254 or 32/234–980* ⊕ *www.lacolombina.cl* ⤳ *8 rooms without bath* ⚄ *Dining room, wine bar; no a/c, no room phones, no room TVs* ▭ *AE, DC, MC, V* ⛾ *CP.*

$ ⊞ **Puerta de Alcalá.** The rooms surround a five-story atrium flooded with light at this central hotel. They have little personality, but are clean and well equipped, with little extras like hair dryers. Those facing the street are bright, but can be noisy on weekends. If you're a light sleeper, take a room in the back. Try to get on the fourth floor—the lower floors get less sunlight because they are blocked by the building next door. There's a decent restaurant and bar on the ground level. ⊠ *Pirámide 524, at Condell* ☎ *32/227–478* 🖷 *32/745–642* ⊕ *www.hotelpuertadealcala.cl* ⤳ *21 rooms* ⚄ *Restaurant, room service, in-room data ports, minibars, cable TV, bar, laundry service, meeting room; no a/c* ▭ *AE, DC, MC, V* ⛾ *CP.*

Nightlife & the Arts

Valparaíso has an inordinate number of nocturnal establishments, which run the gamut from pubs to tango bars and salsa dance clubs. Thursday–Saturday nights, most places get crowded between 11 PM and midnight. Young people stay out until daybreak. The main concentrations of bars and clubs are on Subida Ecuador, near Plaza Anibal Pinto, and a block of Avenida Errázuriz nearby. Cerro Concepción, Alegre, and Bellavista have quieter options, many with terraces perfect for admiring the city lights.

BARS It's not surprising that there are a handful of bars surrounding the dock. The rougher ones west of Plaza Sotomayor are primarily patronized by sailors, whereas those to the east welcome just about anybody. A short walk east of Plaza Sotomayor, **Bar Inglés** (⊠ Cochrane 851 ☎ 32/214–625) has dark-wood paneling and the longest bar in town. You can also order decent food. The huge antique mirrors of **Bar La Playa** (⊠ Serrano 567 ☎ 32/218-011), just east of Plaza Sotomayor, give it a historic feel. It becomes packed with party animals after midnight on weekends in January and February. **Valparaíso Eterno** (⊠ Almirante Señoret 150 ☎ 32/228–374), one block from Plaza Sotomayor, is filled with paintings of Valparaíso and floor-to-ceiling graffiti lovingly supplied by patrons. It opens only on weekends.

DANCE CLUBS Some of the city's hottest dance clubs are found on the streets east of Plaza Sotomayor. Among the top dance clubs is **Aché Havana** (⊠ Av. Errázuriz 1042 ☎ 9/521–9872), which plays mostly salsa and other Latin rhythms. Nearby are several other large dance clubs: **Bulevar** (⊠ Av. Errázuriz 1154 ☎ No phone) has eclectic music on weekend nights. The basement **Eterno** (⊠ Blanco 698 ☎ 32/219–024) plays only Latin dance music, and opens weekends only.

There is also a cluster of bars along the streets that lead uphill from Plaza Anibal Pinto. The four-story **Mr. Egg** (⊠ Ecuador 50 ☎ No phone) has a bar on the ground floor and a dance club above it.

LIVE MUSIC   Tango dancing is so popular in Valparaíso that you might think you were in Buenos Aires. On Cerro Concepción, **Brighton** (⊠ Paseo Atkinson s/n ☎ 32/223–513) has live bolero music on Friday and tango on Saturday, starting at 11 PM. Its black-and-white tile terrace overlooks the city's glittering lights. Dance to live tango music weekends at **Cinzano** (⊠ Anibal Pinto 1182 ☎ 32/213–043), an old-fashioned watering hole facing Plaza Anibal Pinto. The walls above the bar are decorated with scenes of old Valparaíso, including some notable shipwrecks.

If you want to see the lights of the city, several of the most popular establishments are perched on the nearby hills. On Cerro Alegre, **La Colombina** (⊠ Papudo 526 ☎ 32/219–891) has live Latin music weekend nights. Tiny **Color Café** (⊠ Papudo 612 ☎ 32/251–183), on Cerro Concepción, serves up live Latin music on weekends. Cerro Bellavista's **Gato Tuerto** (⊠ Hector Calvo Jofré 205 ☎ 32/220–867) hosts live Latin music on weekends in a lovely Victorian mansion with a city view.

Weekends, **Entre Socios** (⊠ Ecuador 75), on the upper end of the Subita Ecuador, plays alternative music. Concert fans should check out **La Piedra Feliz** (⊠ Av. Errázuriz 1054 ☎ 32/256–788), which hosts performances by Chile's best bands Tuesday–Saturday. The music starts at 9 PM weeknights and 11 PM weekends. Wednesday is jazz night. There's live Latin music weekends at **El Triunfo** (⊠ Ecuador 27 ☎ 32/257–428).

FILM   **Cine Hoyts** (⊠ Av. Pedro Montt 2111 ☎ 32/594–709), across from Parque Italia, is a state-of-the-art theater showing American releases on five screens. The restaurant **Valparaíso Mi Amor** (⊠ Papudo 612 ☎ 32/219–891) screens 16-millimeter films about Valparaíso made by owner Nelson Cabrera, as well as European features.

THEATER   **Ex-Cárcel de Valparaíso** (⊠ El Castro s/n ☎ 32/250–891), a crumbling former prison on Cerro Cárcel, is a haunting space often used for plays and concerts. Off Plaza O'Higgins, the lovely old **Teatro Municipal de Valparaíso** (⊠ Uruguay 410 ☎ 32/214–654) hosts symphonies, ballet, and opera May–November.

Sports & the Outdoors

BEACHES   If it's beaches you're after, head to Viña del Mar or one of the other resort towns along the coast. Valparaíso has only one notable beach, **Playa Las Torpederas,** a sheltered crescent of sand east of the port. Though less attractive than the beaches up the coast, it does have very calm water. A short bus ride south of the city is **Laguna Verde,** a completely undiscovered stretch of shore that is absolutely gorgeous. There are no eateries, so make sure to pack a picnic.

BOATING   Informal boat operators at **Muelle Prat** take groups on a 40-minute circuit of the bay for 2,000 pesos per person. If you have several people, consider hiring your own boat for 10,000 pesos.

SOCCER   Valparaíso's first-division soccer team is the **Valparaíso Wanderers** (✉ Independencia 2061 ☎ 32/217–210). Matches are usually held Monday at the Estadio Municipal in Playa Ancha.

Shopping

Outside of Santiago, there are more shops in Valparaíso than anywhere else in Chile. The country's major department store chain, **Ripley** (✉ Condell 1646 ☎ 32/622–531), is across from Plaza Victoria. The fifth floor has a food court.

If it's handicrafts you're looking for, head to the bohemian neighborhoods of Cerro Concepción and Cerro Alegre. There are dozens of workshops where you can watch artisans ply their crafts. On Cerro Concepción, **Paraíso del Arte** (✉ Abtao 529 ☎ 32/239–357) has a wonderful collection of paintings and mosaics. Most days you'll find artists hard at work. In the same building as Paraíso del Arte, **Trio** (✉ Abtao 529-B ☎ 32/239–357) carries beaded handbags and funky jewelry. **Taller Arte en Plata** (✉ Pasaje Templeman 8 ☎ 9/315–0438) displays necklaces, bracelets, and rings, almost all made from silver.

On Cerro Alegre, **Taller Antiquina Artesania en Cero** (✉ San Enrique 510 ☎ 9/378–1006) has handmade leather items ranging from belts to satchels. **Paulina Acuña** (✉ Almirante Montt 64 ☎ 9/871–8388), a small boutique downhill from Cerro Alegre, sells an unusual collection of handicrafts, including painted glass, candles, jewelry, and clothing.

Cooperativa Artesanal de Valparaíso (✉ Av. Pedro Montt at Las Heras ☎ No phone) is a daily market where you can buy local crafts. The weekend flea market, **Feria de Antigüedades** (✉ Av. Argentina at Plaza O'Higgins ☎ No phone), has an excellent selection of antiques.

Viña del Mar

130 km (85 mi) northwest of Santiago.

Viña del Mar has high-rise apartment buildings that tower above its excellent shoreline. Here are wide boulevards lined with palms, lush parks, and mansions. Miles of beige sand are washed by heavy surf. The town has been known for years as Chile's tourist capital (a title being challenged by several other hot spots), and is currently in the midst of some minor refurbishment.

Viña, as it's popularly known, has the country's oldest casino, excellent hotels, and an extensive selection of restaurants. To some, all this means that Viña del Mar is modern and exciting; to others, it means the city is lacking in character. But there's no denying that Viña del Mar has a little of everything—trendy boutiques, beautiful homes, interesting museums, a casino, varied nightlife, and, of course, one of the best beaches in the country.

Downtown Viña del Mar is completely flat and organized on a grid. To make things even easier, almost all the street names are numbers in sequential order. For the streets running north–south, the numbers start on either side of Avenida Libertad. So you have 1 Poniente (west) and 1 Oriente (east).

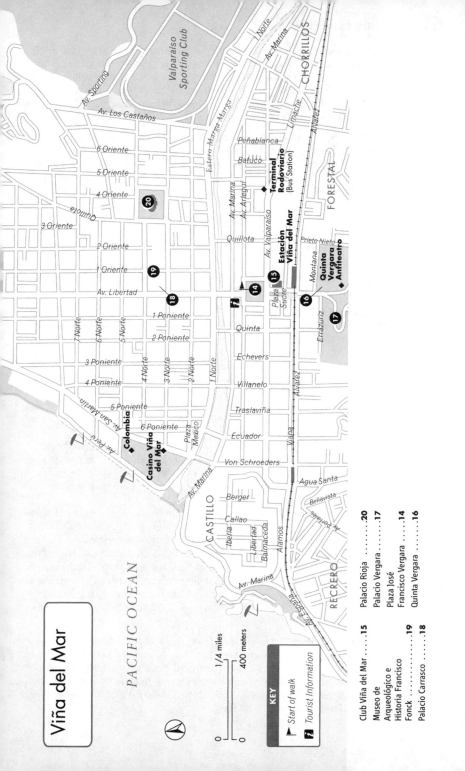

Viña del Mar

PACIFIC OCEAN

KEY

▲ Start of walk

🛈 Tourist Information

0   1/4 miles

0   400 meters

Club Viña del Mar **15**

Museo de
Arqueológico e
Historia Francisco
Fonck **19**

Palacio Carrasco **18**

Palacio Rioja **20**

Palacio Vergara **17**

Plaza José
Francisco Vergara **14**

Quinta Vergara **16**

Plaza José Francisco Vergara ⓮ ▶ is the heart of the city. Just to the south is a smaller square called Plaza Sucre. Grandly filling the east end of the square is the **Club Viña del Mar** ⓯. Walking south past Plaza Sucre you reach **Quinta Vergara** ⓰, one of the country's best botanical gardens. On the grounds you'll discover the **Palacio Vergara** ⓱, a magnificent mansion that is now home to the Museo de Bellas Artes.

Return to Plaza Vergara and head north across the Estero Marga Marga via the Puente Libertad. Gondolas once floated through the estuary, but today it's nearly dry outside of the rainy season (July and August). Walk north along Avenida Libertad then turn east on 4 Norte. Here you'll find the **Palacio Carrasco** ⓲, an Italianate structure that serves as the city's cultural center. Just beyond, another early-20th-century mansion houses the **Museo de Arqueológico e Historia Francisco Fonck** ⓳, renowned for its Easter Island artifacts. Continue east two more blocks until the street ends at a lush park, in the heart of which stands the lovely **Palacio Rioja** ⓴.

TIMING   The terrain in Viña del Mar is flat, so walking is easy. You can take in all the sights on this tour in a few hours. Save yourself for the beach—it's the main attraction.

What to See

⓯ **Club Viña del Mar.** It would be a shame to pass up a chance to see this private club's magnificent interior. The neoclassical building, constructed in 1901 of materials imported from England, is where wealthy locals come to play snooker. Nonmembers are usually allowed to enter only the grand central hall, but there are often tours of the building during the week. The club hosts occasional concerts during which you may be able to circumambulate the second-floor interior balcony. ⊠ *Plaza Sucre at Av. Valparaíso* ☎ *32/680–016.*

need a break? Even die-hard shoppers may be overwhelmed by the myriad shops along Avenida Valparaíso. Take a load off at **286 Rue Valparaíso** (⊠ Av. Valparaíso 286 ☎ 32/710–140), a café with tables on the sidewalk. Enjoy a cappuccino, a milk shake, or perhaps a crepe.

⓳ **Museo de Arqueológico e Historia Francisco Fonck.** A 500-year-old stone *moai* (a carved stone head) brought from Easter Island guards the entrance to this archaeological museum. The most interesting exhibits are the finds from Easter Island, which indigenous people call Rapa Nui, such as wood tablets displaying ancient hieroglyphics. The museum, named for groundbreaking archaeologist Francisco Fonck—a native of Viña del Mar—also has an extensive library of documents relating to the island. ⊠ *4 Norte 784* ☎ *32/686–753* 🖭 *1,000 pesos* ☉ *Tues.–Sat. 10–6, Sun. 10–1.*

⓲ **Palacio Carrasco.** Set in a shady park, this Italian-style mansion is now the home of the city's archives, library, and cultural center. The grand facade is its best feature, but the interior is also worth a look. A few rooms are set aside for temporary exhibits, usually of works by local artists. ⊠ *Av. Libertad 250* ☎ *32/269–708* 🖭 *Free* ☉ *Mon.–Sat. 10–6, Sun. 10–1.*

⑳ Palacio Rioja. This grand palace was built by Spanish banker Francisco Rioja immediately after the earthquake that leveled much of the city in 1906. It contains a decorative-arts museum showcasing a large portion of Rioja's belongings and a conservatory, so there's often music in the air. Performances are held in the main ballroom. The beautifully landscaped grounds are great for shady lounging or a picnic. ⊠ *Quillota 214* ☎ *32/689–665* 🖅 *300 pesos* ⊙ *Tues.–Sun. 10–1:30 and 3–5:30.*

★ **⑰ Palacio Vergara.** The neo-Gothic Palacio Vergara, erected after the 1906 earthquake as the residence of the wealthy Vergara family, houses the **Museo de Bellas Artes.** Inside is a collection of classical paintings dating from the 15th to the 19th century, including works by Rubens and Tintoretto. A highlight is the intricate parquet floor—you'll be given booties to wear over your shoes so as not to scuff it up. ⊠ *Av. Errázuriz 563* ☎ *32/680–618* 🖅 *600 pesos* ⊙ *Tues.–Sun. 10–2 and 3–6.*

⚑ **⑭ Plaza José Francisco Vergara.** Viña del Mar's central square, Plaza Vergara is lined with majestic palms. Presiding over the east end of the plaza is the patriarch of coastal accommodations, the venerable Hotel O'Higgins, which has seen better days. Opposite the hotel is the neoclassical Teatro Municipal de Viña del Mar, where you can watch a ballet, theater, or music performance. To the west on Avenida Valparaíso is the city's main shopping strip, a one-lane, seven-block stretch with extra-wide sidewalks and numerous stores and sidewalk cafés. You can hire a horse-drawn carriage to take you from the square past some of the city's stately mansions.

need a break? In search of a great place to watch the sunset? Head to **Enjoy Del Mar** (⊠ Av. Perú 100 ☎ 32/500–703), an ultramodern restaurant right on the beach. Locals eschew the food and come instead for coffee and a view of the sky turning various shades of pink, purple, and green.

⑯ Quinta Vergara. Lose yourself on the paths that wind amid soaring eucalyptus trees on the grounds that contain one of Chile's best botanical gardens. An amphitheater here holds an international music festival, *Festival Internacional de la Canción de Viña del Mar,* in February. ⊠ *Av. Errázuriz 563* ☎ *32/477–310* 🖅 *Free* ⊙ *Daily 7–6.*

Where to Stay & Eat

$–$$$ ✕ **Armandita.** Meat-eaters need not despair in this city of seafood saturation. A rustic restaurant half a block west of Avenida San Martín serves almost nothing but grilled meat, including various organs. The menu includes popular dishes such as *lomo a lo pobre* (flank steak served on a bed of french fries and topped with a fried egg). The *parrillada especial,* a mixed grill of steak, chicken, ribs, pork, and sausage, serves two or three people. ⊠ *6 Norte 119* ☎ *32/671–607* 🖃 *AE, DC, MC, V.*

$–$$$ ✕ **Calatrava.** The crimson-walled dining room is lovely, but the best tables at this elegant eatery are on the glassed-in terrace. The atmosphere is laid-back, but that doesn't mean they forgo nice touches like crisp linen tablecloths and extravagant floral displays. The staff is affable, always ready to explain the dishes on the menu. Start with cream of carrot soup, then move on to such entrées as ravioli stuffed with smoked salmon and ricotta cheese or braised sea bass served on a bed of saffron risotto. If you want something simple, choose one of the freshly caught fish and have it grilled with a little lemon. ⊠ *5 Norte 476* ☎ *32/691–714* ▭ *AE, DC, MC, V.*

$–$$$ ✕ **San Marcos.** More than five decades after Edoardo Melotti emigrated here from northern Italy, the restaurant maintains a reputation for first-class food and service. A modern dining room with abundant foliage and large windows overlooks busy Avenida San Martín. Farther inside, the two dining rooms in the house the restaurant originally occupied are elegant and more refined. The menu includes the traditional gnocchi and cannelloni, as well as *lasagna di granchio* (crab lasagna) and *pato arrosto* (roast duck). Complement your meal with a bottle from the extensive wine list. ⊠ *Av. San Martín 597* ☎ *32/975–304* ▭ *AE, DC, MC, V.*

$$ ✕ **Delicias del Mar.** Nationally renowned chef Raúl Madinagoitía, who
Fodor's Choice   has his own television program, runs the show here. The menu lists such
★   seafood delicacies as Peruvian-style seviche, stuffed sea bass, and *machas curadas* (steamed clams with dill and melted cheese). Oenophiles are impressed by the extensive, almost exclusively Chilean wine list. Save room for one of the excellent desserts, maybe crème brûlée, chocolate mousse, or cheesecake with a raspberry sauce. ⊠ *Av. San Martín 459* ☎ *32/901–837* ▭ *AE, DC, MC, V.*

$–$$ ✕ **Sushi Taro.** With so much fresh fish available, it's a wonder that it's taken so long for sushi and sashimi to catch on with locals. Now that it has, it's hard to find a block downtown that lacks a Japanese restaurant. A favorite with locals is Sushi Taro, which occupies a few black-and-red rooms on Avenida San Martín. The tempura is flavorful, especially when it incorporates juicy Ecuadorean shrimp. Sushi here is a group activity—you can order platters of anywhere from 17 to 80 pieces. ⊠ *Av. San Martín 419* ☎ *32/737–956* ▭ *AE, MC, V.*

★ **$$–$$$**   ✕▥ **Hotel Oceanic.** Built on the rocky coast between Viña and Reñaca, this boutique hotel has luxurious rooms with gorgeous ocean views. Rooms are cheerful, decorated in bright shades of pink and orange. The nicest ones have terraces, ideal for watching waves crash against the coast. The pool area, perched on the rocks below, is occasionally drenched by big swells. Although there's no beach access, the sands of Salinas are a short walk away. The restaurant is one of the area's best, serving French-inspired dishes such as shrimp crepes, *filete café de Paris* (tenderloin with herb butter), and congrio *oceanic* (conger eel in an artichoke mushroom sauce). ⊠ *Av. Borgoño 12925, north of town* ☎ *32/830–006* 🖷 *32/830–390* ⊕ *www.hoteloceanic.cl* ⇗ *22 rooms, 6 suites* △ *Restaurant, room service, in-room data ports, in-room safes, minibars, cable TV, pool, hot tub, massage, sauna, bar, business services, meeting rooms; no a/c* ▭ *AE, DC, MC, V* ⦿ *BP.*

$$ ✕▥ **Cap Ducal.** This ship-shape building on the waterfront was inspired by transatlantic ocean liners, but it takes a bit of imagination to see what the architect had in mind. Like the building, rooms are oddly shaped, but they are nicely decorated with plush carpets and pastel wallpaper.

Those on the third floor have narrow balconies. Be sure to ask for a view of Reñaca, or you may see, and hear, the highway. The three-level restaurant serves seafood that tops the view. Try the congrio *a la griega* (conger eel with a mushroom, ham, and cream sauce) or *pollo a la Catalana* (chicken with an olive, mushroom, and tomato sauce). ⊠ *Av. Marina 51* ☎ *32/626–655* 🖷 *32/665–478* ⊕ *www.capducal.cl* ⇌ *22 rooms, 3 suites* ⚿ *Restaurant, in-room safes, minibars, cable TV, bar, laundry service; no a/c* ▤ *AE, DC, MC, V* �|◯| *BP.*

$$$$
Fodor'sChoice
★
Hotel Del Mar. A rounded facade, echoing the shape of the adjacent Casino Viña del Mar, means that almost every room at this oceanfront hotel has unmatched views. The exterior is true to the casino's neoclassical design, but spacious guest rooms are pure 21st century, with sleek furnishings, original modern art, and sliding glass doors that open onto balconies. Marble floors, fountains, abundant gardens, and impeccable service make Hotel Del Mar one of Chile's most luxurious. An eighth-floor spa and infinity pool share the view. A stay here includes free access to the upscale casino, which evokes Monaco rather than Las Vegas. ⊠ *Av. San Martín 199* ☎ *32/500–800* 🖷 *32/500–801* ⊕ *www. hoteldelmar.cl* ⇌ *50 rooms, 10 suites* ⚿ *3 restaurants, café, in-room data ports, in-room safes, minibars, cable TV, indoor pool, exercise equipment, spa, bar, cabaret, casino, shop, babysitting, laundry service, concierge, Internet, business services, convention center* ▤ *AE, DC, MC, V* �|◯| *BP.*

$$
Hotel Gala. Modern rooms in this upscale 14-story hotel have panoramic views of the city. The rooms are spacious, and large windows let in lots of light. The bathrooms are crisp and clean and outfitted in white tile. There's a small heated pool next to the bar. One block from the Avenida Valparaíso shopping strip, Gala is near most of the city's attractions. One down point is the staff, which seems stretched a bit thin. ⊠ *Arlegui 273* ☎ *32/686–688* 🖷 *32/689–568* ⊕ *www.gala.cl* ⇌ *64 rooms, 13 suites* ⚿ *Restaurant, in-room data ports, minibars, cable TV, Wi-Fi, pool, massage, sauna, bar, laundry service, business services, convention center* ▤ *AE, DC, MC, V* �|◯| *BP.*

★ $
Residencia 555. A stay in this charming wooden house, dating from 1912, may just make you feel like a local. Antiques fill the high-ceilinged living room, and a wide, curvaceous staircase leads to rooms on the second floor, several with balconies overlooking the garden. Considering the inn's charm, cleanliness, and central location, it's no surprise that Residencia 555 has several times been named the city's top guesthouse. ⊠ *5 Norte 555* ☎🖷 *32/739–035* ⊕ *www.gratisweb.com/residencial555* ⇌ *12 rooms* ⚿ *Restaurant, minibars, cable TV, laundry service* ▤ *AE, DC, MC, V* �|◯| *BP.*

$
Tres Poniente. Come for the personalized service and for many of the same amenities as larger hotels at a fraction of their rates. Rooms are carpeted, nicely furnished, and impeccably clean. Two "apartments," larger rooms in back, are ideal for small families. Complimentary breakfast and light meals are served at the bright café in front, behind which is a small lounge with armchairs and a sofa. The small hotel is half a block from busy 1 Norte, but is remarkably quiet. ⊠ *3 Poniente 70, between 1 and 2 Norte* ☎ *32/977–822* 🖷 *32/478–576* ⊕ *www.*

hotel3poniente.com ⚏ *12 rooms* ⌂ *Café, room service, in-room safes, minibars, cable TV, bar, babysitting, laundry service, Internet, no-smoking rooms; no a/c* ▭ *AE, DC, MC, V* ⃝ *BP.*

Nightlife & the Arts

Viña's nightlife varies considerably according to the season, with the most glittering events concentrated in January and February. There are nightly shows and concerts at the casino and frequent performances at Quinta Vergara. During the rest of the year, things get going only on weekends. Aside from the casino, late-night fun is concentrated in the area around the intersection of Avenida San Martín and 4 Norte, the shopping strip on Avenida Valparaíso, and the eastern end of the alley called Paseo Cousiño. Viña residents tend to go to Valparaíso to party to live music, since it has a much better selection.

BARS Though it's surrounded by the dance clubs and loud bars of Paseo Cousiño, **Kappi Kua** (⊠ Paseo Cousiño 11-A ☎ 32/977–331) is a good place for a quiet drink. **Margarita** (⊠ Av. San Martín 348 ☎ 32/972–110) is a popular watering hole late at night. The namesake cocktail is a killer. **Rituskuan** (⊠ Av. Valparaíso at Von Schroeders ☎ 9/305–0340) is colorful and has excellent beer and electronic music.

CASINO With a neoclassical style that wouldn't be out of place in a classic James Bond movie, **Casino Viña del Mar** (⊠ Av. San Martín 199 ☎ 32/500–600) has a restaurant, bar, and cabaret, as well as roulette, blackjack, and 1,500 slot machines. It's open nightly until the wee hours of the morning most of the year. There's a 3,000-peso cover charge. People dress up to play here, especially in the evening.

DANCE CLUBS The popular **El Burro** (⊠ Paseo Cousiño 12-D ☎ No phone) opens only Friday and Saturday. **El Mezón con Zeta** (⊠ Paseo Cousiño 9 ☎ No phone) has a small dance floor. Viña's most sought-out dance club is **Scratch** (⊠ Bohn 970 ☎ 32/978–219), a long block east of Plaza Sucre.

The impossible-to-spell **Zeuz's** (⊠ Arlegui 829 ☎ No phone) is the hottest gay disco on the coast. Don't get here before 1:30 or 2, when the extravagant drag shows on the balcony stop all the action on the dance floor.

FILM **Cine Arte** (⊠ Plaza Vergara 142 ☎ 32/882–998) is an art-house theater on the west side of Plaza Vergara. **Cinemark Marina Arauco** (⊠ Av. Libertad 1348 ☎ 32/688–188) has four screens showing American flicks. You can catch newly released American films on eight screens at the **Cinemark Shopping Viña** (⊠ Av. 15 Norte 961 ☎ 32/993–388), but it's a little far from the center of town.

THEATER **Teatro Municipal de Viña del Mar** (⊠ Plaza José Francisco Vergara s/n ☎ 32/681–739), a lovely neoclassical auditorium in the center of the city, hosts frequent theatrical productions, as well as music and dance performances.

Sports & the Outdoors

BEACHES Just north of the rock wall along Avenida Peru is a stretch of sand that draws throngs of people December–March. Viña del Mar really has just one **main beach,** bisected near its southern end by an old pier, though its parts have been given separate names: Playa El Sol and Playa Blanca. South of town, on the far side of Cerro Castillo, the small **Playa Caleta Abarca** receives fewer sun worshippers than the main beach. A short drive north of town is the tiny **Las Salinas,** a crescent of sand that has the calmest water in the area.

GOLF   You can play 18 holes Tuesday–Sunday at the **Granadilla Country Club** (⊠ Camino Granadilla s/n ☏ 32/689–249). It's an established course in Santa Inés—a 10-minute drive from downtown. The greens fees are 56,000 pesos, and they rent clubs for 15,000 pesos, but you need to make a reservation.

HORSE RACING   **Valparaíso Sporting Club** (⊠ Av. Los Castaños 404 ☏ 32/689–393) hosts horse racing every Wednesday. The Clásico del Derby, Chile's version of the Kentucky Derby, takes place the first Sunday in February. Rugby, polo, cricket, and other sports are also played here.

SOCCER   Everton is Viña del Mar's soccer team. Matches are held at the 19,000-seat **Estadio Sausalito** (⊠ Laguna Sausalito ☏ 32/978–250), which hosted World Cup matches in 1962.

Shopping

Viña's main shopping strip is **Avenida Valparaíso** between Cerro Castillo and Plaza Vergara, where wide sidewalks accommodate throngs of shoppers. Stores here sell everything from shoes to cameras, and there are also sidewalk cafés, bars, and restaurants. South of Plaza Vergara is the city's largest department store, **Ripley** (⊠ Sucre 290 ☏ 32/384–480). **Falabella** (⊠ Sucre 250 ☏ 32/264–740) is a popular small department store south of Plaza Vergara. For one-stop shopping, locals head to the mall. **Viña Shopping** (⊠ Av. 15 Norte at 2 Norte ☏ No phone), on the north end of town, is a longtime favorite. Next door to Viña Shopping is **Mall Marina Arauco** (⊠ Av. 14 Norte at 2 Oriente ☏ No phone), which is even bigger.

Local crafts are sold at the **Cooperativa de Artesanía de Viña del Mar** (⊠ Quinta 220, between Viana and Av. Valparaíso ☏ No phone). On the beach, near the pier at Muelle Vergara, the **Feria Artesanal Muelle Vergara** is a crafts fair open daily in summer and on weekends the rest of the year. There are also collections of **handicraft stands** on the road to Reñaca.

THE SOUTHERN BEACHES

Once a dominion of solitude and sea, the stretch of coastline south of Valparaíso has seen much development, not all of it well planned, over the past few decades. A succession of towns here caters to the beach-bound hordes January and February. Though none of the towns is terribly attractive, a few of the beaches are quite nice. The main reason to visit—and it's a great one—is to take a look at poet Pablo Neruda's hideaway at Isla Negra. Here you can see the various treasures he collected during his lifetime.

Because large waves create dangerous undertows at some southern beaches, pay attention to warning flags: red means swimming is prohibited, whereas green, usually accompanied by a sign reading PLAYA APTA PARA NADAR (beach suitable for swimming), is a go-ahead signal.

Quintay

★ ㉑ *30 km (19 mi) south of Valparaíso.*

Not too long ago, migrating sperm whales could still be seen from the beaches at Quintay. The creatures were all but exterminated by the whaling industry that sprang up in Quintay in 1942. Whaling was banned in 1967, and Quintay returned to being a quiet fishing village. If you wonder what the coast used to be like before condos began springing up, head to this charming spot. Just past the handful of brightly colored fishing boats on the little beach is the nearly abandoned **whaling factory.** Walk around its skeletal remains—parts are now used as an open-air shellfish hatchery.

Escuela San Pedro de Quintay, the town's elementary school, serves as a makeshift museum dedicated to Quintay's whaling past. Jose Daniel Barrios, a former whaler, maintains the humble display; his whaling contract is among the exhibits. Others include photos of the plant, a whale gun, whale teeth, and a harpoon. Also here are some pottery and skeletons from the indigenous Aconcagua people, who inhabited the region around 1300. ⊠ *Escuela San Pedro s/n* ☎ *No phone* 💰 *Donation* ☾ *Jan. and Feb., daily 10–noon and 2–6; Mar.–Dec., hrs vary.*

Where to Eat

$–$$ ✕ **Los Pescadores.** Echoing the colors of the fishing boats below, this seafood restaurant is painted vivid shades of yellow, green, and red. Because of the restaurant's proximity to the caleta (cove), the fish on your plate was probably pulled from the water early that morning. The sea bass here is about the freshest around. Attentive servers will help you choose from the good wine selection. ⊠ *Costanera s/n* ☎ *32/362–068* 🚪 *AE, DC, MC, V.*

Sports & the Outdoors

BEACHES Vacation apartments have replaced the pine forest surrounding **Playa Grande,** which gets its fair share of sun worshippers in summer. There are two ways to reach the beach: through the town, following Avenida Teniente Merino, or through the gated community of Santa Augusta.

DIVING Chile's coastline has several interesting shipwrecks. Two are off the shores of Quintay, including *Indus IV,* a whaling ship that went down in 1947. There are no dive companies in Quintay, but in nearby Algarrobo, Cinco Oceanos dive operator runs trips to both Quintay shipwrecks. The Santiago-based **Poseidon** (⊠ Av. Andrés Bello 2909, Santiago ☎ 2/231–3597 ⊕ www.posseidon.cl) arranges dive excursions to the wrecks of Quintay.

Algarrobo

㉒ *35 km (22 mi) south of Quintay.*

The largest town south of Valparaíso, Algarrobo is the first in a string of balnearios spread along the coast to the south. Though Algarrobo isn't the prettiest, it has a winding coastline with several yellow-sand beaches, and consequently attracts throngs of sun worshippers.

Next to Playa San Pedro is the private yacht club, **Club de Yates Algarrobo.** In February, boats from all over the country participate in one of Chile's most important nautical events here: the Regata Mil Millas Náuticas.

The **Cofradía Náutica,** a private marina at the end of a point south of town, harbors some of the country's top yachts. Just offshore from the Cofradía Náutica is a tiny island called **Isla de los Pájaros Niños,** a penguin sanctuary that shelters more than 300 Humboldt and Magellan penguins. The upper crags of the island are dotted with hundreds of little caves dug by the penguins using their legs and beaks. Though only members are allowed in the marina, a path leads to the top of a nearby hill from which you can watch the flightless birds through binoculars.

Where to Stay & Eat

$–$$ ✕ **Algarrobo.** The only waterfront restaurant in Algarrobo has an expansive terrace overlooking the beach. The extensive menu is almost exclusively seafood, including half a dozen types of fish served with an equal number of sauces. Ostiones *pil pil* (spicy scallop scampi) and *loco apanado* (fried abalone) are popular starters. Finish with sole or sea bass steamed, grilled, or served *a lo probre* (topped with a fried egg). ⊠ *Av. Carlos Alessandri 1505* ☎☎ *35/481–078* ☰ *No credit cards.*

$$ ⌂ **Hotel Pacífico.** This older hotel in the heart of town, a block from Playa Las Cadenas, has bland but comfortable rooms. The main building dates from the 1940s, with polished wooden floors and a nice lounge with a fireplace. Spacious rooms on the second floor have seen better days, but a few in front overlook the sea. A newer—1960s—annex is stacked against the hillside. Rooms on the upper floors need some fresh paint, but they have nice ocean views. ⊠ *Av. Carlos Alessandri 1930* ☎ *35/482–818* 🖶 *35/481–040* ➟ *79 rooms* ⌂ *Restaurant, cable TV, pool, bar, playground, laundry service, business services, meeting rooms; no a/c* ☰ *AE, DC, MC, V* ⧫ *BP.*

★ $ ⌂ **Pao Pao.** Llamas trim the grass around the cabanas spread here across a forested ridge north of town. The octagonal pine cabanas range from cozy studios that sleep two to two-bedroom apartments complete with wooden decks and hot tubs that are great for families. Only some have views of the water at Playa Grande. All of the cabanas have giant windows and well-stocked kitchenettes; most have small fireplaces. The adjacent restaurant opens only on weekends outside of January and February. ⊠ *Camino Mirasol s/n* ☎☎ *35/482–145 or 35/481–264* ⊕ *www.turismopaopao.cl* ➟ *21 cabins* ⌂ *Restaurant, kitchenettes, minibars, cable TV, pool, babysitting, playground, laundry service; no a/c* ☰ *AE, DC, MC, V.*

Sports & the Outdoors

BEACHES   Algarrobo's nicest beach is **Playa El Canelo,** in a secluded cove south of town. It's an idyllic spot of fine yellow sand, calm blue-green water, and a backdrop of pines. Though quiet most of the year, it can get crowded in January and February. Follow Avenida Santa Teresita south to Avenida

El Canelo and the pine forest of Parque Canelo. Guarded parking there costs 2,000 pesos. If you want seclusion, follow the trail that leads southwest from Playa El Canelo, past the guano-splotched outcropping called Peñablanca, to the smaller **Playa Canelillo.**

The second-nicest beach in Algarrobo is **Playa Grande.** The beige sand stretches northward from town for several miles. There's usually rough surf, which can make it dangerous for swimming. Massive condominium complexes on either end of this beach spill thousands of vacationers onto it every summer. The most popular beach in town is tiny **Playa San Pedro;** a statue of Saint Peter in the sand next to the wharf marks the spot. It's small, but the waters are surrounded by a rocky barrier that keeps them calm and good for swimming. **Playa Las Cadenas,** on the north end of town, has a waterfront promenade. The name, Chain Beach, refers to the thick metal links lining the sidewalk, which were recovered from a shipwreck off Algarrobo Bay.

DIVING **Cinco Oceanos** (⊠ Hotel Pacífico, Av. Carlos Alessandri 1930 ☎ 9/720–7960 or 35/482–818) runs boat dives to half a dozen spots, including underwater cliffs and the two shipwrecks off Quintay.

El Quisco

㉓ *2 km (1 mi) south of Algarrobo.*

El Quisco is a gesture of summer, nothing but a long beach of pale sand guarded on either end by stone jetties. In the middle of the beach is a boulder with a 15-foot-high, six-pronged cactus sculpture perched atop it. South of the beach is the blue-and-yellow caleta, where boats anchored offshore create a picturesque composition. In summer, the beach is packed on sunny days, as visitors outnumber *Quisqueños* (locals) about 10 to 1.

Where to Stay & Eat

★ $ ✕⊡ **Der Münchner Hof.** This German-owned guesthouse on the north end of the bay stands just across the street from the beach, which gives its restaurant a lovely view. Simple but spotless accommodations are on the second floor, above the spacious dining room. Ask for Room 3, which has a terrace overlooking the beach, or Room 2, the only other room with an ocean view. Though the large restaurant, the best in town, serves mostly seafood, the menu does include a few Bavarian dishes, such as smoked ham and strudel. Weekends there's a lunch buffet. ⊠ *Costanera 111* ☎ 35/471–704 ⇔ *5 rooms* ⚙ *Restaurant, room service, cable TV, bar, laundry service; no a/c* ▤ *AE, DC, MC, V.*

Isla Negra

㉔ *6 km (4 mi) south of El Quisco.*

"I needed a place to work," Chilean poet and Nobel laureate Pablo Neruda wrote in his memoirs. "I found a stone house facing the ocean, a place nobody knew about, Isla Negra." Neruda, who bought the house in 1939, found much inspiration here. "Isla Negra's wild coastal strip, with its turbulent ocean, was the place to give myself passionately to the writing of my new song," he wrote.

NERUDA'S INSPIRATION

First of all, let's clear up one thing: Isla Negra may mean "Black Island," but this little stretch of rugged coastline is not black, and it is not an island. This irony must have appealed to Nobel Prize–winning poet Pablo Neruda, who made his home here for more than three decades.

Of his three houses, Pablo Neruda was clearly most attached to Isla Negra. "Ancient night and the unruly salt beat at the walls of my house," he wrote in one of his many poems about his home in Isla Negra. It's easy to see how this house, perched high above the waves crashing on the purplish rocks, could inspire such reverie.

Neruda bought this house in 1939. Like La Sebastiana, his house in Valparaíso, it had been started by someone else and then abandoned. Starting with the cylindrical stone tower, which is topped by

a whimsical weather vane shaped like a fish, he added touches that could only be described as poetic. There are odd angles, narrow hallways, and various nooks and crannies, all for their own sake.

What is most amazing about Isla Negra, however, is what he chose to place inside. There's a tusk from a narwhal in one room, and figureheads from the fronts of sailing ships hanging overhead in another. There are huge collections ranging from seashells to bottles to butterflies. And yet it is also just a house, with a simple room designed so he could gaze down at the sea when he needed inspiration.

— Mark Sullivan

Fodor's Choice ★ A must-see for Pablo Neruda's ardent admirers, **Casa-Museo Isla Negra** is a shrine to his life, work, and many passions. The house, perched on a bluff overlooking the ocean, displays the treasures—from masks and maps to seashells—he collected over the course of his remarkable life. Although he spent much time living and traveling abroad, Neruda made Isla Negra his primary residence later in life. He wrote his memoirs from the upstairs bedroom; the last pages were dictated to his wife here before he departed for the Santiago hospital where he died of cancer. Neruda and his wife are buried in the prow-shape tomb area behind the house.

Just before Neruda's death in 1973, a military coup put Augusto Pinochet in command of Chile. He closed off Neruda's home and denied all access. Neruda devotees chiseled their tributes into the wooden gates surrounding the property. In 1989 the Neruda Foundation, started by his widow, restored the house and opened it as a museum. Here his collections are displayed as they were while he lived. The living room contains—among numerous other oddities—a number of bowsprits from ships hanging from the ceiling and walls. Neruda called them his "girlfriends."

You can enter the museum only with a guide, but there are excellent English-language tours every half hour. The tour will help you understand Neruda's many obsessions, from the positioning of guests at the dinner table to the east–west alignment of his bed. Objects had a spiritual and symbolic life for the poet, which the tours make evident. ⊠ *Camino Vecinal s/n* ☎🖳 *35/461–284* ⊕ *www.neruda.cl* 🖳 *3,000 pesos* ⊙ *Tues.–Sun. 10–5.*

Where to Stay & Eat

$–$$ ✕ **El Rincón del Poeta.** Inside the entrance to the Neruda museum, this small restaurant has a wonderful ocean view, with seating both indoors and on a protected terrace. The name translates as Poet's Corner, a theme continued in the small but original menu. Corvina *Neruda* is a sea bass fillet in a mushroom, artichoke, and shrimp cream sauce, and congrio *Garcia Lorca* is conger eel topped with tomato, sausage, and melted cheese. The house specialty is *pastel de centolla* (king crab pie), and they have lighter dishes such as chicken crepes, salmon seviche, and a spicy squid scampi. ⊠ *Casa-Museo Isla Negra, Camino Vecinal s/n* ☎ *35/461–774* ▤ *No credit cards* ⊙ *Closed Mon.*

$–$$ ✕🖭 **La Candela.** Wander along the same rocky shore that Neruda once explored while staying at La Candela. The owner, Chilean folk singer Rosario "Charo" Cofré, was a good friend of the Nerudas—note the photos in the lobby. If there's a crowd, she'll often sing a few songs. Many of the large guest rooms have fireplaces, and about half overlook the sea through the pines. The restaurant serves a vast selection of clams, sea bass, shrimp, and other seafood in numerous sauces. Country-style rooms have pale-wood furnishings and beds piled high with comforters. ⊠ *De la Hostería 67* ☎ *35/461–254* 🖳 *35/462–531* ⊕ *www.candela. cl* ⇌ *16 rooms* ⚿ *Restaurant, bar, laundry service; no a/c, no room phones, no room TVs* ▤ *AE, DC, MC, V* ¶◎¶ *CP.*

THE NORTHERN BEACHES

To the north of Viña del Mar, the Pacific collides with the rocky offshore islands and a rugged coastline broken here and there by sandy bays. The coastal highway runs from Viña del Mar to Papudo, passing marvelous scenery along the way. Between Viña and Concón, it winds along steep rock faces, turning inland north of Concón, where massive sand dunes give way to expanses of undeveloped coastline. The farther north you drive, the greater the distance between towns, each of which is on a significantly different beach. Whether as a day trip from Viña, or on a series of overnights, this stretch of coast is well worth exploring.

Reñaca

㉕ *6 km (4 mi) north of Viña del Mar.*

Thousands of Chileans flock to Reñaca every summer for one, and only one, reason—the crashing waves. You need merely contemplate this wide stretch of golden sand pounded by aquamarine waves, glistening beneath an azure sky, to understand why it's so popular. Contemplate it on a January or February afternoon, though, and you're likely to have trouble discerning the golden sand for the numerous bodies stretched across it. Vacation apartments are stacked up the steep hillside behind the beach, and on summer nights the bars and restaurants are packed. If you're seeking solitude, continue up the coast.

Where to Stay & Eat

$–$$
Fodor'sChoice
★
✕ **Delicias del Mar.** At this seafood standout, you can watch through the wide windows as the waves crash against the rocks across the street. The second- and third-floor dining rooms are set back a bit so that everyone can enjoy the sun and surf. It's what comes out of the kitchen, however, that keeps people coming back. Start with seviche or *gratín de jaiba* (crab casserole), then feast on *salmón de rosita* (salmon on a bed of spinach), or corvina *rellena* (sea bass stuffed with crab, spinach, and mushrooms). ⊠ *Av. Borgoño 16000* ☎ *32/890–491* ⊟ *AE, MC, V.*

$$–$$$
Fodor'sChoice
★
🏨 **Club Hotel La Fayette.** You can take in some of the best views on the Central Coast from this 10-story hotel built onto the hillside north of the beach. Breakfast is served in a rooftop dining room with a vista to top all. The spacious apartments have two bedrooms, a living room, kitchenette, and large terraces that afford an amazing coastal panorama. Smaller corner rooms have less expansive views, but are still bright, spacious, and well equipped. Though a short walk from the beach, this is a remarkably quiet hotel. ⊠ *Subida el Encanto 280* ☎ *32/832–312* 🖷 *32/832–316* 🖅 *20 rooms, 28 apartments* ♨ *Dining room, in-room safes, kitchenettes, cable TV, laundry service; no a/c* ⊟ *AE, DC, MC, V* ⁍◎⁌ *BP.*

Nightlife & the Arts

The dance club **Kamikaze** (⊠ Av. Vicuña Mackenna 1106 ☎ 32/834–667), west of town, draws a young crowd. **Margarita** (⊠ Av. Central 150 ☎ 32/836–398) hosts live music on weekend nights.

Concón

㉖ *11 km (7 mi) north of Reñaca.*

How to explain the lovely name Concón? In the language of the Changos, *co* meant "water," and the duplication of the sound alludes to the confluence of the Río Aconcagua and the Pacific. When the Spanish arrived in 1543, Pedro de Valdivia created an improvised shipyard here that was destroyed by natives, leading to one of the first clashes between indigenous and Spanish cultures in central Chile.

Today, the town that holds the name is packed with high-rise apartment buildings, though it does have decent ocean views. The attraction lies to the north and south: the rugged coastal scenery along the road that connects it to Reñaca, and the sand dunes that rise up behind the beaches north of town.

North of town across from a large wooden restaurant is **Isla de Lobos,** a small rocky island that shelters a permanent population of sea lions, which can be viewed from shore. ⊠ *Costanera, 9 km (5½ mi) north of Concón.*

Roca Oceánico is a massive promontory covered with scrubby vegetation. Footpaths that wind over it afford excellent views of Viña del Mar and Valparaíso—and of the sea churning against black volcanic rock below. ⊠ *Costanera, 1 km (½ mi) north of Isla de Lobos.*

Where to Stay & Eat

$–$$
FodorśChoice
★

✕ **Aquí Jaime.** Owner Jaime Vegas is usually on hand, seating customers and scrutinizing the preparation of such house specialties as *lenguado almendrina* (sole in an almond white sauce), *arroz a la valenciana* (paella packed with seafood), and *albacora portuguesa* (grilled swordfish topped with shrimp-tomato flambé). Perhaps this is why the small restaurant perched on a rocky promontory next to Caleta Higuerillas has one of the best reputations in the region. Large windows let you watch the waves crashing just below, passing boats and pelicans, and the coast that stretches northward. ⊠ *Av. Borgoño 21303* ☎ *32/812–042* ▭ *No credit cards* ☉ *No dinner Sun. and Mon.*

$

✕▤ **Hostería Edelweiss.** Each accommodation in this Swiss-owned inn, nestled in a curve overlooking the rocky coast and sea south of town, consists of two floors: upstairs there's a bedroom, downstairs a sitting area with a wet bar and a small terrace. Breakfast is delivered to your room. The restaurant has one of the best wine lists on the coast, including French and Spanish labels, and an original menu that includes fondues, *salmón a la Florentina* (salmon in a spinach cream sauce), and *camarones* Bombay (prawns in a curried fruit sauce). ⊠ *Av. Borgoño 19200* ☎ *32/811–683* 🖷 *32/811–440* ⊕ *www.edelweiss.cl* ➟ *6 rooms* ⚄ *Restaurant, room service, refrigerators, cable TV, pool, bar, laundry service* ▭ *AE, DC, MC, V* ⑩ *BP.*

$
FodorśChoice
★

▤ **Bahía Bonita.** Perched on a hilltop overlooking Concón, this all-suites hotel is painted pale shades of yellows and oranges. All the rooms have flower-filled terraces—some more than one—overlooking the crashing waves. Living rooms with plenty of space to spread out and full-size kitchens packed with elegant plates and glassware make this a great place for a family or several friends. Some of the larger rooms can easily sleep five or six. To top it all off, the price is about what you'd pay for dinner for two. ⊠ *Av. Borgoño 22040* ☎ *32/818–757* ⊕ *www. aparthotelbahiabonita.cl* ➟ *12 suites* ⚄ *In-room safes, kitchens, cable TV, pool, Internet, laundry service* ▭ *AE, DC, MC, V* ⑩ *CP.*

Sports & the Outdoors

BEACHES
The southernmost beach in Concón, **Playa Los Lilenes** is a tiny yellow-sand cove with calm waters. After the wharf is **Playa Las Bahamas,** the beach favored by surfers and windsurfers. At the north end of town is the gray-sand **Playa La Boca.** It was named Mouth Beach because the Río Aconcagua flows into the Pacific here, which makes the water murky. Concón's nicest beach is **Playa Ritoque,** a long, wide, golden strand that starts several miles north of town and stretches northward for several miles. Access is good at Punta de Piedra, 5 km (3 mi) north of town, where guarded parking costs 2,000 pesos per day. You can reenact scenes from *The English Patient* 1 km (½ mi) north of here, where the vast sand dunes that resemble those in the movie rise up behind the beach.

HORSEBACK
RIDING
Sol y Mar (⊠ Camino a Quintero, Km 5 ☎ 32/813–675) has horseback excursions on the beach or to the sand dunes that can be combined with kayaking or boat trips on a nearby lake.

Quintero

27 *26 km (16 mi) north of Concón.*

The town of Quintero, with its dusty streets and many dilapidated houses, could easily be skipped if not for its impressive coastal scenery. The town has spread over a bluff that ends in a windswept coastline, where several bays hold small, yellow-sand beaches nestled against sheer rock faces. Quintero also has a good hotel, which is well positioned for contemplating the passing pelicans, waves crashing against rocks, and memorable sunsets.

The main strip in town, Avenida Normandie, leads directly to **Muelle Asimar,** a dock where you can watch fishermen unload their catch; you may be able to talk a boat owner into a trip around the bay.

Where to Stay & Eat

$ ✕⌷ **Hotel Yachting.** This old hotel's greatest asset is its exquisite view of the rocky coast from all of the guest rooms. The main building sits on the edge of a cliff, giving the restaurant an amazing coastal perspective enhanced by massive windows. Try the veal *cordon bleu* (stuffed with cheese and ham) or corvina *vasca* (sea bass in an onion-tomato sauce). Older, standard rooms are a bargain, opening onto terraces steps from the pool. The added-on superior rooms are more spacious, but only those on the ground floor have terraces. ⌷ *Luís Acevedo 1736* ☎ *32/930– 061* 🖷 *32/931–557* ⊕ *www.hotelyachting.cl* ⤳ *20 rooms, 2 suites* ⌷ *Restaurant, room service, minibars, cable TV, pool, sauna, boating, recreation room, meeting rooms* ▭ *AE, DC, MC, V* ¶◎¶ *CP.*

Beaches

Most of Quintero's beaches are in hidden coves and can be hard to find, or may require a bit of a hike to reach. **Playa Los Enamorados** is a short walk from the Parque Municipal. Surfing is popular at **Playa El Libro,** which is reached from Hermanos Carrera or Balmaceda via concrete stairs. Swimming is prohibited here, but kids play in the little pools that form behind the rocks. If you follow Avenida 21 de Mayo to its end, you come to **Playa Durazno,** a small, unattractive gray-sand beach that does have calm water. **Playa El Caleuche,** beyond the rocks at the end of Playa Durazno, is safe for swimming.

Maitencillo

28 *20 km (12 mi) north of Quintero.*

This town is a mass of cabanas and eateries spread out along the 4-km (2½-mi) Avenida del Mar. Two long beaches are separated by an extended rocky coastline that holds the local caleta. To complement the abundant sand and surf, there is a decent selection of restaurants, bars, and accommodations.

Off the coast from Cachagua, several miles north of Maitencillo, is the **Monumento Nacional Isla Cachagua,** a protected island inhabited by Magellan and Humboldt penguins. No one is allowed on the island, but you can ride around in a small boat that can be hired at the Caleta de La

Laguna or Caleta de Zapallar. You can also view the island from the beach below Cachagua, though you need binoculars to watch the penguins wobble around.

Where to Stay & Eat

$–$$ ✕ **La Tasca de Altamar.** Old nautical equipment decorates the interior of this spacious restaurant across the street from the ocean. The ample, almost exclusively marine menu ranges from such Chilean standards as *ostiones a la parmesana* (scallops in melted cheese) and *perol de machas* (steamed razor clams with onions and parsley) to delicious, but exorbitantly priced, half lobsters. A pair of fireplaces warm things up when wintry winds blow. ⊠ *Av. del Mar 3600* ☎ *32/772–132* ▤ *AE, DC, MC, V* ☺ *Closed Wed. Mar.–Dec.*

$ ✕ **La Canasta.** Serpentine bamboo tunnels connect rooms, and slabs of wood suspended by chains serve as tables: the scene could be straight from *The Hobbit*. A small menu changes regularly, but includes dishes such as *cordero a la ciruela* (lamb with a cherry sauce) and corvina *queso de cabra* (sea bass with goat cheese). Although it's across from the beach, there's no view. ⊠ *Av. del Mar 593* ☎ *32/771–028* ▤ *No credit cards.*

$$–$$$ ✕⌂ **Marbella.** Golf fairways, pine trees, and ocean vistas surround a four-story white-stucco resort building. Spacious, colorful rooms are decorated with original art and have large terraces with views of Maitencillo Bay. The circular Mirador restaurant has great views and interesting menu selections, such as salmon-filled ravioli in tomato cream, and *duo de lenguado y salmón* (sole and salmon mixed in a tarragon sauce with artichoke and carrot puree). The only drawback is the distance from the beach—you need a car if you also want to explore the coast. ⊠ *Carretera Concón–Zapallar, Km 38* ☎ *32/772–020 or 800/211–108* ▤ *32/772–030, 2/206–0554 in Santiago* ⊕ *www.marbella.cl* ⇔ *70 rooms, 4 suites* ⌂ *2 restaurants, room service, in-room data ports, in-room safes, minibars, cable TV, golf privileges, 4 tennis courts, 2 pools, exercise equipment, hair salon, hot tub, spa, bicycles, horseback riding, bar, recreation room, shop, playground, laundry service, business services, convention center* ▤ *AE, DC, MC, V* ⧖ *BP, FAP, MAP.*

★ $$ ⌂ **Altamar Aparthotel.** All the rooms in this brick-red building with a vaguely New England feel have ocean views, though those on the third floor have the best ones. They are spotless, bright, and nicely decorated, with sliding glass doors that open onto either a terrace or balcony, most of which are surrounded by flowers. All of them have well-stocked kitchenettes, but they range in size from studios to one-bedroom apartments with sofa beds and large furnished terraces with grills. ⊠ *Av. del Mar 3600* ☎▤ *32/772–150* ⊕ *www.altamaraparthotel.cl* ⇔ *18 apartments* ⌂ *Restaurant, kitchenettes, cable TV, pool, laundry service, meeting rooms; no a/c* ▤ *AE, DC, MC, V.*

$ ⌂ **Cabañas Hermansen.** Set in an overgrown garden, these cabanas feel far away from everything. (In reality, they're just across from the beach.) A jumble of walkways leads uphill to the rooms. Stone fireplaces and wood walls add to the rustic feel. Ask for one of the newer rooms at the top of the hill, as they have a few nice touches like river-rock showers. ⊠ *Av. del Mar 593* ☎ *32/771–028* ⊕ *www.hermansen.cl* ⇔ *16 rooms* ⌂ *Restaurant, some kitchenettes, bar, shop* ▤ *No credit cards.*

Sports & the Outdoors

BEACHES On the north side is the largest beach in town, the extra-wide **Playa Larga.** It's often pounded by big surf. The light-gray sand of **Playa Aguas Blancas** lies to the south of a rock outcropping, protected from the swells, and consequently is good for swimming.

GOLF The **Marbella Country Club** (⊠ Carretera Concón–Zapallar, Km 35 ☎ 32/772–403) has 27 holes of golf—without a doubt some of the best on the coast—in an exclusive environment. The tennis and paddle-tennis courts are available only to members and to guests of the Marbella resort. Greens fees for hotel guests are 22,000 pesos, whereas nonguests pay 42,000 pesos during the week and 52,000 pesos on weekends.

HANG GLIDING *Parapente,* a seated version of hang gliding, is popular here. **Parapente Aventura** (⊠ South entrance to Maitencillo, veer left ☎ 32/770–019 or 9/332–2426) has classes and two-person trips for beginners.

HORSEBACK RIDING In Cachagua, **Club Ecuestre Cachagua** (⊠ Costanera s/n, Cachagua ☎ 32/771–039) runs horseback tours to scenic overlooks.

Zapallar

★ ㉙ *48 km (30 mi) north of Concón.*

An aristocratic enclave for the past century, Zapallar doesn't promote itself as a vacation destination. In fact, it has traditionally been reluctant to receive outsiders. The resort is the brainchild of Olegario O'-Valle, who owned property here. In 1893, following an extended stay in Europe, O'Valle decided to re-create the Riviera on the Chilean coast. He allotted plots of land to friends and family with the provision that they build European-style villas. Today the hills above the beach are dotted with these extravagant summer homes. Above them are the small, tightly packed adobes of a working-class village that has developed to service the mansions.

Zapallar's raison d'être is **Playa Zapallar,** a crescent of golden sand kissed by blue-green waters, with a giant boulder plopped in the middle. Cropped at each end by rocky points and backed by large pines and rambling flower gardens, it may well be the loveliest beach on the Central Coast.

At the south end of Playa Zapallar is a rocky point that holds **Caleta de Zapallar,** where local fisherfolk unload their boats, sell their catch, and settle in for dominoes. The view of the beach from the caleta and adjacent restaurant, El Chiringuito, is simply gorgeous. On the other side of the point, a trail leads over the rocks to rugged but equally impressive views.

☾ Up the hill from Caleta de Zapallar is the **Plaza del Mar Bravo.** Rough Sea Square has a park with yet another ocean view and a large playground. In January and February, there are usually mule rides for kids.

Note: There are no signs pointing the way down to the beach, and few signs even telling you on what road you happen to be traveling. Locals are happy to point the way.

Where to Stay & Eat

$–$$

Fodor's Choice

★

✕ **El Chiringuito.** Pelicans, gulls, and cormorants linger among the fishing boats anchored near this remarkable seafood restaurant. Since it's next door to the fishermen's cooperative, the seafood is always the freshest. For starters choose from machas (razor clams), camarones (shrimp), or ostiones (scallops) cooked *al pil pil* (with chili sauce and garlic), *a la parmesana* (with cheese), or *a la crema* (with a cream sauce). Then sink your teeth into any of half a dozen types of fish, served with different sauces. The dining room—with a floor of crushed shells and hand-carved chairs resembling sea creatures—is a delight. ✉ *Caleta de Zapallar s/n* ☎ *33/741–024* ▭ No credit cards ⊘ *No dinner weekdays Mar.–Dec.*

$–$$

✕ **Restaurante Cesar.** There's no better way to escape the afternoon sun than to snag one of the bright red tables at this terrace restaurant. The thatched parasols above you sway gently in the breeze. In winter, cozy up to a large fireplace in the dining room. The menu has an ample seafood selection, including many different dishes using swordfish and sole, as well as beef and chicken dishes, and is complemented by an extensive wine list. ✉ *Playa Zapallar* ☎ *8/441–9795* ▭ *AE, DC, MC, V.*

$$–$$$

Fodor's Choice

★

▥ **Isla Seca.** Bougainvillea and cypress trees surround two identical moss-green buildings with well-appointed, spacious rooms. If you choose those with *terraza y vista al mar,* you get picture windows and narrow balconies with wonderful views of the rocky coast and blue Pacific. The suites on the corners have views on two sides, but lack terraces. The airy restaurant, with its black-and-white tile floor and original art, has style to rival anything in Miami Beach. It leads directly out to a terrace wrapping around a sparkling pool. A staircase leads down to the beach. ✉ *Costanera s/n* ☎ *33/741–224* 🖷 *33/741–228* ⊕ *www.hotelislaseca. cl* ➷ *34 rooms, 5 suites* ⌂ *Restaurant, in-room safes, minibars, cable TV, 2 pools, bicycles, bar, playground, business services, meeting rooms; no a/c* ▭ *AE, DC, MC, V.*

Tennis

Zapallar's **Club de Tenis** (✉ Costanera s/n ☎ 33/741–55) has 14 clay courts scattered around a forested hillside above town. Nonmembers pay 5,000 pesos per game.

Papudo

㉚ *11 km (7 mi) north of Zapallar.*

In a letter dated October 8, 1545, Spanish conquistador Pedro Valdivia wrote: "Of all the lands of the New World, the port of Papudo has a goodness above any other land. It's like God's Paradise: it has a gentle temperate climate; large, resounding mountains; and fertile lands."

Today a jumble of apartment buildings and vacation homes detracts from the view Valdivia once admired, but the beaches and coast north of town remain quite pleasant. For years Papudo was connected to Santiago by a train that no longer runs. You can still find bits of that history in the quiet resort town.

A block from the beach is the **Palacio Recart,** built in 1910. The yellow building, which now holds municipal offices, hosts occasional art and history exhibitions. ⊠ *Costanera s/n* ☎ *No phone.*

Near the south end of town is the lovely **Iglesia Parroquial de Papudo,** a 19th-century church. It was once part of a convent that has been replaced by vacation apartments. ⊠ *Costanera s/n* ☎ *No phone* ⊙ *Jan. and Feb., weekends.*

Where to Stay & Eat

$–$$ ✕ **El Barco Rojo.** In 1913, a French ship called the *Ville de Dijon* sank off the coast of Papudo. The beams, doors, portholes, and other sundry parts were salvaged to build The Red Ship. Poet Pablo Neruda once frequented the spot. The ceiling is papered with love letters to the restaurant written by patrons. Tables and chairs are a delightful hodgepodge of styles and colors, and the tiny bar is eclectically furnished with bric-a-brac. The menu is dominated by seafood, but includes such treats as fried empanadas filled with cheese and basil. ⊠ *Av. Irarrazaval 300* ☎ *33/791–488* ▤ *No credit cards* ⊙ *Closed Mon.–Thurs. Mar.–Dec.*

$ ▥ **Hotel Carande.** The only respectable hotel in town, Carande has carpeted rooms devoid of charm but just a short walk from the beach. It's worth paying the extra money for a room on the third floor to have a sea view over the rooftops. There's a restaurant on the second floor, and the lobby has a fireplace that usually has a fire burning in winter. ⊠ *Chorillos 89* ☎ *33/791–105* ▤ *33/791–118* ⇗ *30 rooms* ♨ *Restaurant, refrigerators, bar; no a/c* ▤ *No credit cards.*

Beaches

Chileans migrate to Papudo from Santiago every summer to play on its beaches. **Playa Chica,** the small beach on the south end of town, is well protected and safe for swimming. Papudo's most popular beach is **Playa Grande,** a wide strand that stretches northward from the Barco Rojo for more than a mile. You have to do a bit of walking to reach **Playa Durazno.** It's an attractive beach north of Playa Grande—past the condominiums—that is lined with pine trees and protected by a rocky barrier offshore.

Los Molles

㉛ *32 km (20 mi) north of Papudo.*

Upon first inspection, Los Molles seems rather drab: a row of houses on a street leading to the beach. But the nearby landscape—a desertlike collection of cacti and other hardy plants—is truly splendid. Hawks, turtledoves, gulls, and pelicans fly past. Grab your binoculars and follow Avenida Las Jaibas uphill to its end to watch.

A 15-minute walk north of town along the coast brings you within earshot of the **Isla de los Lobos Marinos,** a rocky island filled with boisterous sea lions—off-limits to humans. Hike north from the Isla de los Lobos Marinos, and your ears are likely to be assaulted by the terrifying sound of the ocean water forced up through **Puquén,** a blowhole whose name means "Mouth of the Devil." The spray can shoot 50 meters (150 feet) in the air on a wavy day. For a simpler natural encounter, follow Avenida Los Pescadores past the north end of the beach to **Las Terrazas.** These terraces of chiseled rock are a great vantage point from which to see the tempestuous swells below.

Where to Stay

$ ⌂ **Cabañas Los Molles.** If you find yourself in Los Molles, you might want to follow the lead of Chilean families and check out this oceanfront lodging. The cabanas are plain, but they do have umbrella-shaded terraces right on the sand. They sleep either four or six people, making them perfect for groups. The restaurant serves good seafood. ⊠ *Las Jaivas at O'Higgins* ☎ *33/791–787* ⊕ *turismolosmolles.mi-pagina.cl* ⤴ *12 rooms* ⌂ *Restaurant, kitchenettes, cable TV, bar, laundry service* ⊟ *No credit cards.*

Diving

Hernan Labarca at **H. L. Divers** (⊠ Neruda 11 ☎ 33/791–762 or 9/ 276–5562), one of only five authorized dive centers in Chile, runs scuba certification classes and dives along submarine cliffs adorned with giant sponges.

CENTRAL COAST ESSENTIALS

Transportation

BY AIR

The Central Coast is served by Lan Airlines via Santiago's Aeropuerto Comodoro Arturo Merino Benítez, an hour and a half from Viña del Mar and Valparaíso.

BY BUS

There is hourly bus service between Santiago and both Valparaíso and Viña del Mar. The two-hour trip costs about 2,100 pesos. Tur-Bus and other companies leave from Santiago's Terminal Alameda. Smaller companies serving the other beach resorts depart from Santiago's Terminal Santiago.

Regular buses between Viña del Mar and Valparaíso cruise the main north–south routes of those cities. Regular city-bus service also connects Viña del Mar, Reñaca, and Concón. Buses to more distant towns along the Central Coast depart from Valparaíso's Terminal Rodoviario, across from the Congreso Nacional, and Viña's Terminal Rodoviario, two blocks east of Plaza Vergara. Both have sporadically staffed tourist information booths and ATMs.

Pullman Bus serves most coastal towns south of Valparaíso. Tur-Bus heads north to Cachagua, Zapallar, Papudo, and other towns. Sol del Pacífico also runs buses to the northern beaches.

🚌 Bus Depots **Valparaíso** ⊠ Av. Pedro Montt 2800 ☎ 32/213–246. **Viña del Mar** ⊠ Av. Valparaíso at Quilpué ☎ 32/882–661.

🚌 Bus Lines **Pullman Bus** ☎ 32/24–025. **Sol del Pacífico** ☎ 32/213–776. **Tur-Bus** ☎ 32/ 212–028.

BY CAR

Since it's so easy to get around in Valparaíso and Viña del Mar, there's no need to rent a car to explore these cities. But if you want to travel to other towns on the coast, renting a car is advisable. Hertz, with an office in Viña del Mar, is the only international company in the region. The Chilean company Rosselot usually has much cheaper prices.

Rental Agencies Hertz ✉ Quillota 766, Viña del Mar ☎ 32/381-025 or 32/689-918. **Rosselot** ✉ Victoria 2675, Valparaíso ☎ 32/352-365 ✉ Av. Libertad 892, Viña del Mar ☎ 32/382-373.

BY TAXI

In Valparaíso and Viña del Mar you can hail a taxi on busy streets and at plazas. Most smaller towns have a taxi stand on the main road. If you prefer to phone a cab, have your hotel receptionist call a reputable company, such as Radio Taxis Turismo in Valparaíso, and Taxi Sucre in Viña del Mar.

Taxi Companies Radio Taxis Turismo ☎ 32/212-885. **Taxi Sucre** ☎ 32/687-136.

BY TRAIN

Merval, a commuter train linking Viña de Mar and Valparaíso, was closed as this book went to press. Improvements to the system, including underground stations in Viña de Mar, are expected to be finished in 2006. In Valparaíso the main station is at Muelle Prat. In Viña del Mar, it's south of Plaza Vergara.

Train Stations Estación Puerto ✉ Plaza Sotomayor, Valparaíso ☎ 32/217-108. **Estación Viña del Mar** ✉ Plaza Sucre ☎ No phone.

Contacts & Resources

BANKS & EXCHANGE SERVICES

All but the smallest Central Coast towns have at least one ATM, and both Valparaíso and Viña del Mar have dozens of them. ATMs at well-distributed Banco de Chile branches also give cash advances on international credit cards. All but the most humble restaurants and hotels accept major credit cards.

ATMs Banco de Chile ✉ Cochrane 785, Valparaíso ☎ 32/356-500 ✉ Av. Valparaíso 667, Viña del Mar ☎ 32/648-760 ✉ Av. Borgoño 14675, Reñaca ☎ 32/836-938 ✉ Olegario O'Valle 336, Zapallar ☎ 33/741-613 ✉ Carlos Alessandri 1666, Algarrobo ☎ 35/482-857.

INTERNET, MAIL & SHIPPING

Valparaíso and Viña del Mar each have dozens of Internet cafés, but many smaller towns on the Central Coast lack them. Valparaíso has several between Plazas Sotomayor and Anibal Pinto, among them the World Next Door and Café Riquet. Viña del Mar's Avenida Valparaíso shopping strip has several per block, including 286 Rue Valparaíso and OKA Comunicaciones.

Perhaps because it is so close to Santiago, the postal system along the Central Coast is fairly efficient. On average, letters take five to seven days to reach the United States or Europe.

If you need to send something pronto, DHL has offices in Valparaíso and Viña del Mar.

⚡ Internet Cafés Café Riquet ⊠ Plaza Anibal Pinto 1199, Valparaíso ☎ 32/213–171. **OKA Comunicaciones** ⊠ Av. Valparaíso 242, Viña del Mar ☎ 32/713–712. **286 Rue Valparaíso** ⊠ Av. Valparaíso 286, Viña del Mar ☎ 32/710–140. **World Next Door** ⊠ Blanco 692, Valparaíso ☎ 32/227–148.

⚡ Post Offices Valparaíso ⊠ Southeast corner of Plaza Sotomayor. **Viña del Mar** ⊠ North side of Plaza Vergara.

⚡ Shipping Services DHL ⊠ Plaza Sotomayer 95, Valparaíso ☎ 32/213–654 ⊠ Av. Libertad 715, Viña del Mar ☎ 32/213–654

TOURS

You need a tour guide to really get to know the twisting streets of Valparaíso. Enlace Turístico has several city tours and trips to the Central Coast's smaller towns. In Viña del Mar, Chile Guías has bilingual guides for city tours, and trips to beaches north and south.

⚡ Tour Operators Chile Guías ⊠ Av. Errázuriz 674, Viña del Mar ☎ 32/692–580 ⊕ www.chileguias.com. **Enlace Turístico** ⊠ Cerro Bellavista, Valparaíso ☎ 32/232–313 or 9/896–4887 ⊕ www.enlaceturistico.cl.

VISITOR INFORMATION

Viña del Mar has the best tourist office on the coast, offering fistfuls of helpful maps and brochures. It's north of Plaza Vergara at the corner of Avenida Libertad and Avenida Marina. It's open weekdays 9–2 and 3–7, weekends 10–2 and 3–7. There's also a friendly kiosk on Avenida Valparaíso that's open Monday–Saturday 10–2 and 3–7.

Valparaíso has two information booths: one at Muelle Prat that is supposedly open daily 10–2 and 3–6 (although in real life the hours vary wildly), and one at the Terminal Rodoviario bus station, with the same hours except it closes Monday.

⚡ Valparaíso Muelle Prat office ⊠ Muelle Prat, Valparaíso ☎ 32/939–489. **Valparaíso Terminal Rodoviario office** ⊠ Av. Pedro Montt 2800, Valparaíso ☎ 32/939–669. **Viña del Mar main office** ⊠ Av. Libertad at Av. Marina, Viña del Mar ☎ 32/269–330. **Viña del Mar branch office** ⊠ Av. Valparaíso at Villanelo ☎ 32/683–355.

El Norte Chico

WORD OF MOUTH

"La Serena was an incredible find. We were wowed by the colonial architecture—when we got to town it felt like we had stepped back in time. And the Japanese garden in the heart of town, although not quite in keeping with the colonial surroundings, was a great place to unwind with a leisurely stroll."

—Brian K.

Updated by
Brian Kluepfel

FOR HUNDREDS OF YEARS, people have journeyed to El Norte Chico—Chile's Little North—for the riches that lay buried deep within the earth. First came the Incas, who wandered the burnt hills in search of gold. A century later the Spanish arrived on these shores, also seeking this precious metal. Prospectors flocked here in the 19th century when the silver boom afforded great rewards. Today it is yet another metal, copper, that yields the majority of the region's income. No wonder locals once called this "the land of 10,000 mines."

But El Norte Chico's appeal isn't purely metallurgical. The coastline has some of the best beaches in the country. Offshore there are rocky islands that shelter colonies of penguins and sea lions. Shimmering mountain lakes are home to huge flocks of flamingos. Even the parched earth flourishes twice a decade in a phenomenon called *el desierto florido,* or the flowering desert. During these years, the bleak landscape gives way to a riot of colors—flowers of every hue imaginable burst from the normally infertile soil of the plain.

In a land where water is so precious, it's not surprising that the people who migrated here never strayed far from its rivers. In the south, La Serena sits at the mouth of the Río Elqui. El Norte Chico's most important city, La Serena is the region's cultural center as well, with colonial architecture and a European flavor. Nearby, in the fertile Elqui Valley, farmers in tiny villages grow the grapes to make *pisco,* the potent brandy that has become Chile's national drink. Those in search of the region's history head to Valle del Encanto, a large collection of ancient petroglyphs.

On El Norte Chico's northern frontier is the Río Copiapó. This is the region that grew up and grew rich during the silver boom. The town of Copiapó, this area's most important trade center, makes an excellent jumping-off point for exploring the hinterland. Inland lies Parque Nacional Nevado Tres Cruces, with its snowcapped volcanoes and dazzling white salt flats. Head to the ocean and you'll come to Parque Nacional Pan de Azúcar, where you'll find some of El Norte Chico's most stunning coastal scenery.

Exploring El Norte Chico

El Norte Chico is a vast region spreading some 700 km (435 mi) between Río Aconcagua and Río Copiapó. You'll need more than one base if you want to explore the entire area. In the south, La Serena is a good place to start if you're going to the Elqui Valley. Vallenar, on the Río Huasco, is where you'll want to be if your destination is the flowering desert. Copiapó, near the region's northern border, is a convenient stop if you're headed to Parque Nacional Nevado Tres Cruces.

About the Restaurants

El Norte Chico is not known for its gastronomy, but the food here is simple, unpretentious, and often quite good. Along the coast you'll find abundant seafood. Don't pass up the *merluza con salsa margarita* (hake with butter sauce featuring almost every kind of shellfish imaginable) or *choritos al vapor* (mussels steamed in white wine). Inland you come

Five days won't allow you enough time to explore all of El Norte Chico, so make **La Serena** your home base. Spend your first day exploring the white-washed churches and lively markets of this quaint colonial town. The next morning head inland to **Vicuña,** birthplace of poet Gabriela Mistral. In the afternoon stop by the idyllic village of **Pisco Elqui**. A pisco sour here is almost obligatory. Explore the cloud forest of **Parque Nacional Fray Jorge** on the fourth day. On your last day, head to **Ovalle** to see the petroglyphs of the Valle del Encanto. End the day by taking a relaxing dip in the hot springs at the Termas de Socos. If you have more time, consider taking a side trip to the **Parque Nacional Llanos de Challe, Parque Nacional Nevado Tres Cruces,** or **Parque Nacional Pan de Azúcar.**

3

across country-style *cabrito* (goat), *conejo* (rabbit), and *pinchones es-cabechadas* (baby pigeons). Don't forget to order a pisco sour, the frothy concoction made with the brandy distilled in the Elqui Valley.

People in El Norte Chico generally eat a heavy lunch around 2 PM that can last two hours, followed by a light dinner around 10 PM. Reservations are seldom needed, except in the fanciest restaurants. Leave a 10% tip if you enjoyed the service.

About the Hotels

The good news is that lodging in El Norte Chico is relatively inexpensive. Your best bet is often the beach resorts, which have everything from nice cabanas to high-rise hotels. The bad news is that away from the areas that regularly cater to tourists you may have to make do with extremely basic rooms with shared baths.

WHAT IT COSTS In pesos (in thousands)				
	$$$$	**$$$**	**$$**	**$**	**¢**
RESTAURANTS	over 11	8–11	5–8	3–5	under 3
HOTELS	over 105	75–105	45–75	15–45	under 15

Restaurant prices are for a main course at dinner. Hotel prices are for a double room in high season, excluding tax.

When to Go

During the summer months of January and February, droves of Chileans and Argentines flee their stifling hot cities for the relative cool of El Norte Chico's beaches. Although it is an exciting time to visit, prices go up and rooms are hard to find. Make your reservations at least a month in advance. For a little tranquillity, visit when the high season tapers off in March. Moving inland you'll find the weather is mild all year. The almost perpetually clear skies explain why the region has the largest concentration of observatories in the world. The temperatures drop quite a bit when you head to the mountains.

CloseUp

EL NORTE CHICO FESTIVALS & SEASONAL EVENTS

Every town in El Norte Chico celebrates various annual events, such as the days honoring certain patron saints. One fiesta that you should not miss is Andacollo's Fiesta Grande de La Virgen, in which some 150,000 devout pilgrims converge on the small town to celebrate its miraculous statue of the Virgen de Andacollo (December 23–26). Also in Andacollo, the more subdued Fiesta Chica takes place the first Sunday of October.

THE ELQUI VALLEY

It's hard to believe that hidden by the dusty brown hills of El Norte Chico is a sliver of land as lush and green as the Elqui Valley. The people who live along the Río Elqui harvest everything from olives to avocados. The most famous crop is the grapes distilled to make Chile's national drink: pisco. A village named after this lovely elixir, Pisco Elqui, sits high up the valley.

The Elqui Valley is renowned not only for its grapes, but also for its unusually clear skies, which have brought scientists from around the world to peer through the telescopes of the area's many observatories. The stars also attracted many New Agers who decided that the planet's spiritual center had shifted from the Himalayas to the Elqui Valley. Many who came here to check out the vibes decided to stay.

The Elqui Valley has been inhabited for thousands of years. First came the Diaguitas, whose intricate pottery is among the most beautiful of pre-Columbian ceramics. The Molles, who are believed to have carved the fascinating petroglyphs in the Valle del Encanto, followed. The Incas, who came here 500 years ago in search of gold, are relative newcomers. The clues these cultures left behind are part of what makes the Elqui Valley so fascinating.

La Serena

❶ *270 km (167 mi) north of Santiago.*

La Serena, Chile's second-oldest city, with several venerable churches and pleasant beaches, got off to a shaky start. Founded by Spanish conquistador Pedro de Valdivia in 1544, La Serena was destroyed by the Diaguitas only four years later. But the Spaniards weren't about to give

Ancient Landscapes

You'll pass heards of goats and their caretakers en route to Parque Nacional Fray Jorge, but the true enchantment is upon arrival and drifting, ghostlike, through the foggy forests that form when coastal clouds hit the park's ridge. Tiptoe through the fairy-tale foliage of cinnamon, myrtle, and olivillo trees. Northeast of Ovalle, the Enchanted Valley (El Valle del Encanto) is rich in examples of ancient hunting artifacts and petroglyphs. Another 30 km to the north is the national monument of Pichasca, a rugged volcanic-rock region whose terrain can tell stories 75 million years old; tales of volcanic eruptions, earth movement, and ancient animal and plant life. The Casa de Piedra (Rock House) is a fascinating example of how the ancients turned their surroundings into a utilitarian shelter.

3

Sugar-Sand Beaches

The sugary sand, turquoise water, and warm breezes make El Norte Chico's beaches among the best in the country. During the summer months of January and February, you may have to fight for a place in the sun. If tranquillity is what you seek, plan your trip for another part of the year, when the weather is fine, the prices are cheaper, and it's not hard to find a stretch of shoreline that's completely deserted.

Crafts & Jewelry

Unusual crafts are what you'll find in El Norte Chico. The Elqui Valley is known for the beautiful ceramics of the Diaguita people, which often come in zoomorphic shapes with intricate geometric patterns. In La Serena, jewelry and other items crafted from the locally mined marble called *combabalita* are particularly lovely. The best places to shop are usually the *ferias artesenales* (artisan fairs), where locals sell all types of handmade items.

---

in, so they rebuilt the city on its original site. Near the mouth of the Río Elqui, La Serena slowly grew until it was visited by British pirate Bartholomew Sharp, who sacked and burned it in a three-day rampage in 1680. Once again the city was rebuilt, and by the time of the silver boom in the late 19th century, it was thriving.

One of the most striking features of La Serena is the number of churches: there are more than 30, and many of them date as far back as the late 16th century. Most have survived fires, earthquakes, and pirate attacks. The largest church is the imposing **Iglesia Catedral,** which faces the beautiful Plaza de Armas. French architect Jean de Herbage built this behemoth in 1844, but it wasn't until the turn of the 20th century that the bell tower was added. On Cordovez stands the **Iglesia Santo Domingo,** an impressive church built in 1673 and then rebuilt after a pirate attack in 1755. Its Italian Renaissance-style facade is eye-catching, especially the elegant bell tower. One of La Serena's oldest churches, **Iglesia San Francisco,** on Balmaceda and de la Barra, has a baroque facade and thick stone walls. The exact date of the church's construction is not known, as the city archives were destroyed in 1680, but it's estimated that the structure was built sometime between 1585 and 1627.

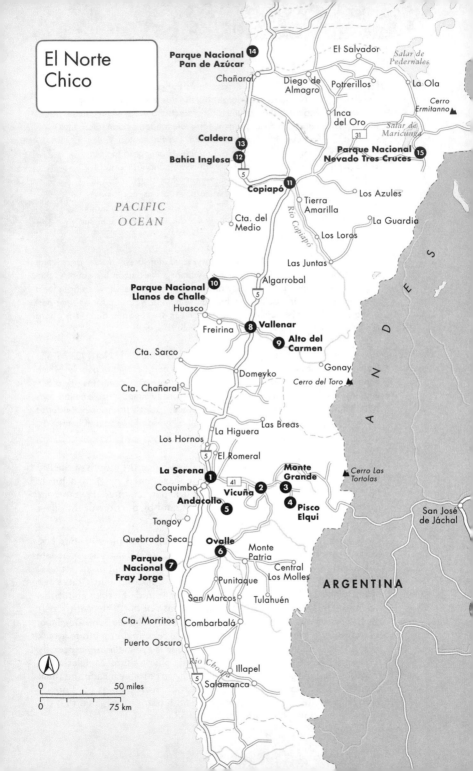

El Norte Chico

PACIFIC OCEAN

Parque Nacional Pan de Azúcar (14)

El Salvador

Salar de Pedernales

Chañaral

Diego de Almagro

Potrerillos

La Ola

Inca del Oro

Cerro Ermitanno ▲

31

Salar de Maricunga

Caldera (13)

Bahía Inglesa (12)

5

Parque Nacional Nevado Tres Cruces (15)

Copiapó (11)

Tierra Amarilla

Los Azules

La Guardia

Cta. del Medio

Río Copiapó

Los Loros

Las Juntas

Parque Nacional Llanos de Challe (10)

Algarrobal

5

Huasco

Freirina

Vallenar (8)

Alto del Carmen (9)

Cta. Sarco

Domeyko

Gonay

Cerro del Toro ▲

Cta. Chañaral

Las Breas

La Higuera

Los Hornos

El Romeral

5

La Serena (1)

Coquimbo

Monte Grande

Cerro Las Tortolas ▲

41

Vicuña (2)

(3)

Andacollo

(5)

(4) **Pisco Elqui**

Tongoy

San José de Jáchal

Quebrada Seca

Ovalle (6)

Monte Patria

Parque Nacional Fray Jorge (7)

Central Los Molles

ARGENTINA

Punitaque

San Marcos

Tulahuén

Cta. Morritos

Combarbalá

Puerto Oscuro

Río Choapa

Illapel

5

Salamanca

A N D E S

0   50 miles

0   75 km

La Serena's pleasant streets, hidden plazas, and well-preserved colonial buildings are the fruition of one man's dream. Gabriel González Videla, then president of Chile, instituted his "Plan Serena" in 1940. He mandated that all new buildings be in the colonial style. The **Museo Histórico Gabriel González Videla,** his former home, has exhibits about the ex-president as well as showings of works by Chilean artists. ⊠ *Matta 495* ☏ *51/217–189* ⊕ *www.dibam.cl* 🖅 *600 pesos* ⊙ *Tues.–Fri. 10–6, Sat. 10–1.*

Housing many fascinating artifacts—including an impressive collection of Diaguita pottery—the **Museo Arqueológico de La Serena** is a must-see for anyone interested in the history of the region. The Archaeology Museum contains one of the world's best collections of precolonial ceramics. Also here is a *moai* (a carved stone head) from Easter Island. ⊠ *Cordovez at Cienfuegos* ☏ *51/224–492* ⊕ *www.dibam.cl* 🖅 *600 pesos* ⊙ *Tues.–Fri. 9:30–5:50, Sat. 10–1 and 4–7.*

One of the most complete mineral collections in the world can be found at the **Museo Mineralógico.** Exhibits highlight fossils and minerals from the surrounding region. ⊠ *Anfión Muñoz 870* ☏ *51/204–096* 🖅 *300 pesos* ⊙ *Weekdays 9:30–12:30.*

A Japanese garden in the heart of Latin America, **Parque Japones** is a pleasant place to pass an afternoon. Here you will find koi-filled ponds, intricate bridges, and a network of paths. The park was built by a mining company as a goodwill gesture to its Japanese trading partners. ⊠ *Pedro Pablo Muñoz at Cordovez* ☏ *51/217–013* 🖅 *600 pesos* ⊙ *Daily 10–8.*

Where to Stay & Eat

★ **\$–\$\$** ✕ **Donde el Guatón.** This European-style steak house, also known as La Casona del Guatón, serves up everything from shish kebab to steak with eggs. With several intimate dining areas off the main salon, this is a great place to enjoy a romantic, candlelit meal. The service, although friendly, can be overly solicitous. ⊠ *Brasil 750* ☏ *51/211–519* ⚛ *Reservations essential* 🖃 *AE, DC, MC, V.*

¢–\$\$ ✕ **Restaurant Velamar Beach.** Enjoy a seaside *parrillada* (barbecue) of just about any cut of beef imaginable at this longtime favorite. The restaurant literally sits on the sand, so it's a great place to watch the sunset from inside or on the patio. ⊠ *Av. del Mar 2300* ☏ *51/215–461* 🖃 *MC, V.*

\$\$ 🏨 **Hotel Costa Real.** Despite its neoclassical design, Hotel Costa Real has all the modern touches you might expect from an executive-class hotel: business center, meeting rooms, and Internet access. Wood and glass furniture fill the spotless rooms. The staff is friendly and attentive. ⊠ *Av. Francisco de Aguirre 170* ☏ *51/221–010* 🖷 *51/221–122* ⊕ *www.costareal.cl* 🛏 *49 rooms, 2 suites* ⚭ *Restaurant, room service, some in-room data ports, in-room safes, minibars, cable TV, pool, bar, laundry service, business services, meeting rooms, free parking; no a/c* 🖃 *AE, DC, MC, V* ⧠ *BP.*

\$\$ 🏨 **La Serena Club Resort.** A large beachfront hotel in mauve-tinted adobe, this is a good bet for die-hard beachcombers. Yellow-and-blue comforters brighten up the smallish rooms, and upper-story suites have views of the ocean. There is a large pool with a fountain for kids. ⊠ *Av. del Mar*

1000 ☎ 51/221–262 🖷 51/217–130 ⊕ *www.laserenaclubresort.cl*
🖙 *49 rooms, 46 suites* ⟁ *Restaurant, in-room safes, minibars, cable
TV, tennis court, pool, bar, laundry service, meeting rooms, free parking; no a/c* ▭ *AE, DC, MC, V* ⵎ⚊ *BP.*

★ $ ▦ **Hotel del Cid.** Relax and catch some rays on a beach chair in the court-
yard of this great-value colonial-style bed-and-breakfast run by a Scot-
tish-Chilean couple. The rooms are warm, cozy, and welcoming. Breakfast
is served in the courtyard or in the tiny dining room. ⊠ *Av. Bernardo
O'Higgins 138* ☎ *51/212–692* 🖷 *51/222–289* ⊕ *www.hoteldelcid.cl*
🖙 *18 rooms* ⟁ *Cable TV, laundry service, free parking; no a/c* ▭ *AE,
DC, MC, V* ⵎ⚊ *BP.*

$ ▦ **Hotel Francisco de Aguirre.** A rambling three-story, colonial-style build-
ing houses this lovely hotel. La Serena's most venerable hotel, this charming establishment stands just a block away from the Plaza de Armas. Cool
off in the pool tucked away in a lush courtyard, or sweat away your wor-
ries in the sauna. ⊠ *Cordovez 210* ☎ *51/222–991* 🖷 *51/228–506*
⊕ *www.turismochile.cl/cristoinn/francisco/francingles.html* 🖙 *85 rooms*
⟁ *Restaurant, room service, minibars, cable TV, pool, sauna, bar, laundry service, Internet, free parking; no a/c* ▭ *AE, DC, MC, V* ⵎ⚊ *BP.*

Nightlife & the Arts

La Serena's nightlife is a little subdued, fitting perfectly with the city's
conservative nature. There are very few bars in the city proper—most
of La Serena's pubs and discos lie near the beach on glitzy Avenida del
Mar. **Brooklyn's** (⊠ Av. del Mar 2150 ☎ 51/212–891) is a big, impersonal pub with a dance floor. A huge palm dominates the central courtyard at **Café del Patio** (⊠ Arturo Prat 470 ☎ 51/210–759), a small pub
in the center of town. This is a great place to grab a snack and listen to
live jazz and blues. Just off Avenida del Mar is **Kamikaze** (⊠ Av. Cua-
tro Esquinas s/n ☎ 51/218–515). Part of a popular chain of Asian-theme
discos, it livens things up late at night. There's a Japanese fighter-plane
lodged inside.

Beaches

Playa Peñuelas, La Serena's attractive sandy beach, stretches all the way
south to the neighboring town of Coquimbo. It's overrun with tourists
during high season in summer. **La Herradura,** 2 km (1 mi) south of Coquimbo, has a small but excellent beach. **Playa Totoralillo,** 14 km (9 mi)
south of Coquimbo, has beautiful green waters and a white-sand beach.

Shopping

Mercado La Recova, on the corner of Cienfuegos and Cantournet, is a
modern market housed in a pleasant neoclassical building. Here you can
buy dried fruits and handicrafts. The Diaguita-style ceramics and the
trinkets made from *combabalita,* the locally mined marble, are particularly stunning.

Vicuña

❷ *62 km (38 mi) east of La Serena.*

As you head into the Elqui Valley, the first town you come to is Vicuña,
famous as the birthplace of one of Chile's most important literary fig-

ures, Gabriela Mistral. Her beautiful, haunting poetry often looks back on her early years in the Elqui Valley. Mistral's legacy is unmistakable as you wander through town. In the Plaza de Armas, for example, there ★ is a chilling stone replica of the poet's death mask. The **Museo Gabriela Mistral** houses various artifacts pertaining to the poet, such as original copies of her books as well as handwritten letters and poems. There's also a replica of the adobe house where Mistral was born. ⊠ *Gabriela Mistral 759* ☎ *51/411–223* 🖻 *600 pesos* ☉ *Jan. and Feb., daily 10–7; Mar.–Dec., Tues.–Sun. 10–1.*

A huge steeple tops the 1909 **Iglesia de la Inmaculada Concepción,** which faces the central square. **Torre Bauer,** next to the Iglesia de la Inmaculada Concepción, is a wooden tower painted fire-engine red. It was prefabricated in Germany in 1905 and named after a former mayor. On the central square is **Teatro Municipal,** a theater noted for its art deco flourishes.

The **Casa de los Madariaga** affords a look into a historic, colonial-era home of the region, complete with antique furnishings, including ornate furniture and pictures of the Madariaga family. ⊠ *Gabriela Mistral 683* ☎ *51/411–220* 🖻 *600 pesos* ☉ *Daily 10:30–6:30.*

As this is the Elqui Valley, you'll eventually come across vineyards growing the grapes used to make pisco. **Planta Capel,** a pisco distillery, is just across the Elqui River. Here you can tour the bottling facility and even taste the results. ⊠ *Camino a Peralillo s/n* ☎ *51/411–391* ⊕ *www. piscocapel.com* 🖻 *Free* ☉ *Jan. and Feb., daily 9:30–6:30; Mar.–Dec., weekdays 9:30–12:30 and 2:30–6, weekends and holidays 9:30–12:30.*

★ Known for its clear skies, the Elqui Valley has many observatories. **Observatorio Cerro Mamalluca** is Chile's only observatory specifically intended for public use. The facility, 9 km (5½ mi) north of Vicuña, holds nightly viewings through a 12-inch telescope. ⊠ *Tour office: Gabriela Mistral 260* ☎ *51/411–352* ⊕ *www.mamalluca.org* 🖻 *5,000 pesos* ☉ *Basic Astronomy tours daily at 6:30 PM, 8:30 PM, 10:30 PM, 12:30 AM and 2:30 AM; Andean Cosmology tours at 9:15 PM, 11:15 PM, and 1:15 AM.*

The **Cerro de la Virgen** is a place of pilgrimage for those devout to the Virgen de Lourdes, the town's patron saint. This hill overlooking the city affords a great view of Vicuña. It's a 2-km (1-mi) hike north of the city via a path on Baquedano between Independencia and Yungay.

Where to Stay & Eat

¢–$ ✕ **Restaurant Halley.** With open-air dining under a straw roof, this restaurant gives you the feeling that you're having a picnic. The menu focuses on hearty country fare. The *cabrito* (roasted goat) is especially succulent. ⊠ *Gabriela Mistral 404* ☎ *51/411–225* 🖃 *AE, DC, MC, V.*

$ ✕🏨 **Hosteria Vicuña.** This large hotel's claim to fame is that poet Gabriela Mistral once slept here. It also has an inviting parlor and bar area complete with piano, and a tree-shaded garden. The restaurant is quite good and serves Elqui Valley specialties such as goat and rabbit as well as international fare. The ambience is a step above most eateries in El Norte Chico—there are even cloth napkins. ⊠ *Sargento Aldea 101* ☎ *51/411–301* 🖷 *51/411–144* ⊕ *www.hosteriavicuna.cl* ⇗ *14 rooms*

⚘ *Restaurant, café, cable TV, tennis court, pool, bar, playground, laundry service, meeting room, free parking; no a/c* ▤ *AE, DC, MC, V* ⑩ *CP.*

★ **$** ▤ **Hotel Halley.** In a pretty colonial house with wood trim and white walls, this inn has carefully decorated rooms filled with authentic circa-1950s radios and more doilies than you could possibly imagine. There's a small, rather shallow swimming pool in the back. ⊠ *Gabriela Mistral 542* ☎ *51/412–070* 🖷 *51/412–070* ⌂ *11 rooms, 1 suite* ⚘ *Restaurant, minibars, cable TV, pool, Internet, free parking, no-smoking rooms; no a/c* ▤ *AE, DC, MC, V* ⑩ *CP.*

Nightlife & the Arts

Pub Kharma (⊠ Gabriela Mistral 417 ☎ 51/419–738) occasionally hosts live music. Otherwise, the bar plays Bob Marley almost exclusively and pays further homage to the reggae legend with posters.

Shopping

You can buy local handicrafts, especially ceramics and jewelry, at the **Poblado Artesenal**, a collection of artisan stands on the Plaza de Armas. It's open daily 10–5.

Monte Grande

❸ *34 km (21 mi) east of Vicuña.*

A tiny village in the rugged Elqui Valley, Monte Grande recalls a time of simpler pleasures. This picturesque village in the midst of rolling hills is home to two of the world's purest vices: pisco and poetry. On the neighboring hillsides and in the valley below, farmers cultivate the grapes used to make pisco. Gabriela Mistral, born in nearby Vicuña, grew up in Monte Grande. Her family lived in the old schoolhouse where her older sister taught. The **Casa Escuela** has been turned into a museum and displays some relics from the poet's life. Her tomb is on a nearby hillside. ⊠ *Central plaza* ☎ *51/451–015* 🖅 *600 pesos* ☉ *Tues.–Sun. 10–1 and 3–6.*

Pisco Elqui

❹ *10 km (6 mi) south of Monte Grande, 43 km (27 mi) east of Vicuña.*

Once known as La Unión, this pisco-producing village, perched on a sun-drenched hillside, received its current moniker in 1939. Gabriel González Videla, at that time the president of Chile, renamed the village in a shrewd maneuver to ensure that Peru would not gain exclusive rights over the term "pisco." The Peruvian town of Pisco also produces the heady brandy.

This idyllic village of fewer than 600 residents has two pisco plants. The

★ **Solar de Pisco Elqui** (☎ 51/198–2503, 51/198–2649), on the main road, is Chile's oldest distillery. It produces the famous Tres Erres brand, perhaps Chile's finest. In the older section of the plant, maintained strictly for show, you can see the antiquated copper cauldrons and wooden barrels. The distillery arranges free daily tours, followed by tastings where you can sample a pisco sour. About 4 km (2½ mi) past Pisco Elqui you come upon the **Los Nichos** (☎ 51/411–085) distillery, which hosts free daily tours and tastings.

CHILE'S NATIONAL DRINK

DISTILLED FROM MUSCAT GRAPES *grown in the sunbaked river valleys of El Norte Chico, pisco is indisputably Chile's national drink. This fruity, aromatic brandy is enjoyed here in large quantities—most commonly in a delightful elixir known as a pisco sour, which consists of pisco, lemon juice, and sugar. A few drops of bitters on top is optional. Some bars step it up a notch by adding whipped egg white to give the drink a frothy head. Another concoction made with the brandy is piscola—the choice of many late-night revelers—which is simply pisco mixed with soda. Tea with a shot of pisco is the Chilean answer to the common cold, and it may just do the trick to relieve a headache and stuffy nose. Whichever way you choose to take your pisco, you can expect a pleasant, smooth drink.*

Chileans have enjoyed pisco, which takes its name from pisku, the Quechuan word for "flying bird," for more than 400 years. The drink likely originated in Peru—a source of enmity between the two nations. In 1939, Chilean President Gabriel González Videla went so far as to change the name of the town of La Unión to Pisco Elqui in an attempt to gain exclusive rights over the name pisco. But Peru already had its own town south of Lima named Pisco. The situation is currently at a standoff, with both countries claiming they have the better product.

The primary spots for pisco distillation are the Huasco and Elqui valleys; the latter is particularly renowned for the quality of its grapes. The 300 days of sunshine per year here make these lush valleys perfect for cultivating muscat grapes. The distillation process has changed very little in the past four centuries. The fermented wine is boiled in copper stills, and the vapors are then condensed and aged in oak barrels for three to six months—pisco

makers call the aging process "resting." The result is a fruity but potent brandy with between 30% and 50% alcohol.

You're welcome to tour many of the region's pisco distilleries. Several of the distilleries are more than 100 years old— Chile's oldest distillery is in the idyllic town of Pisco Elqui in the verdant Elqui Valley. The Solar de Pisco Elqui has been entirely renovated since it began operations, but you can still take a tour of the old plant and learn a bit about how pisco is made. This is where the famous Tres Erres brand, arguably Chile's best pisco, is distilled. In Pisco Elqui you'll also find Los Nichos, a quaint 130-year-old distillery that is open to the public. Nearby Montegrande and Vicuña also have distilleries. To escape the pisco-loving crowds, head north to the Huasco Valley, with its less frequently visited pisco distilleries such as the Planta Pisquera Alto del Carmen. San Felix, a village nestled in the valley, has a 95-year-old plant that produces the Horcón Quemado brand.

Tours generally end with free tastings of different types of pisco, which will let you see why poetic Chileans call pisco "a million years of sunshine in a single drop."

— Gregory Benchwick

Where to Stay & Eat

★ ¢–$ ✕⊞ **El Tesoro de Elqui.** Beautiful gardens with flowers of every imaginable shape and size surround this hotel's nicely decorated cabanas. At the lovely pool you can laze around in the world-famous Elqui Valley sunshine and take in the panoramic view of the Andes. The restaurant, which serves as a meeting place for travelers, has an international menu. The tasty spaghetti Bolognese makes a welcome change from Chilean country cuisine. The owner also makes a mean pisco sour. ⊠ *Arturo Prat s/n* ☎ *51/451–069* ⊕ *www.tesoro-elqui.cl* ⤳ *5 rooms* ⛴ *Restaurant, pool; no a/c, no room phones, no room TVs* ▤ *AE, MC, V* ⦿ *BP.*

$$ ⊞ **Refugio Misterios de Elqui.** These six grass-roof cabanas surround a pleasant pool, where you can relax with a pisco sour and enjoy the delightful sunshine. The views of the mountains from the open-air restaurant are outstanding. ⊠ *Arturo Prat s/n* ☎☎ *51/451–126* ⊕ *www. misteriosdeelqui.cl* ⤳ *6 cabanas* ⛴ *Restaurant, pool, bar; no a/c, room phones, no room TVs* ▤ *DC, MC, V* ⦿ *BP.*

¢–$ ⊞ **Complejo Turístico Gabriela Mistral.** The cabanas at this hotel are comfortable, although some are a bit dark. The pool is shallow, but can be a great place to wallow after a day of exploring the sun-drenched valley. ⊠*Arturo Prat 59* ☎*51/451–086* ⊕*www.valledeelqui.cl* ⤳*12 rooms, 12 cabanas* ⛴ *Restaurant, pool, laundry service; no a/c, no room phones, no room TVs* ▤ *No credit cards.*

Nightlife & the Arts

There isn't much to do at night in Pisco Elqui but lie on your back and enjoy the brilliant stars. **Los Jugos** (☎ No phone), on the corner of the plaza, serves incredible fresh fruit drinks. Try the *jugo de frambuesa* (raspberry juice).

Shopping

Fresh fruit marmalade and preserves are sold in the town's main plaza. You can also head to the pisco distilleries to pick up a bottle of freshly brewed pisco.

Andacollo

❺ *54 km (34 mi) southeast of La Serena.*

The compact town of Andacollo, an important gold and silver mining center since the 16th century, makes a pleasant stopover between Ovalle and La Serena. Here you'll find one of Chile's most famous religious icons. The wooden image of the Virgen de Andacollo, deemed miraculous by the Vatican in 1901 for its putative power to cure disease, draws some 150,000 pilgrims to the town each year from December 23 to 26 for the Fiesta Grande de la Virgen. During the festival, the statue is decorated and paraded through the streets.

★ The Virgen de Andacollo sits on a silver altar in the small **Templo Antiguo,** on Plaza Videla, the town's main square. This church, built in the 17th century, has a museum of the offerings given to the virgin in hopes of her miraculous assistance. The **Basilica,** which was inaugurated in 1893 after nearly 20 years of construction, is by far the largest structure in the town. With a 40-meter-high (130-foot-high) dome and two giant steeples, it towers over everything else.

Ovalle

6 *34 km (21 mi) south of Andacollo.*

Ovalle, a modern town southeast of La Serena, serves as a good base for trips to the Monumento Natural Pichasca or the Valle del Encanto. The town's shady **Plaza de Armas** is a pleasant place to pass an afternoon. On the Plaza de Armas, the **Iglesia San Vicente Ferrer** is worth a visit. Constructed in 1849, the church was damaged by an earthquake in 1997 and remains in a semi-dilapidated state.

★ Unlike geoglyphs, which are large-scale figures chiseled into the landscape, petroglyphs are small pictures carved onto the rock surface. One of Chile's densest collections of petroglyphs can be found in **Valle del Encanto.** The 30 images in the Valley of Enchantment were most likely etched by the Molle culture between AD 100 and 600. The figures wear ceremonial headdresses hanging low over large, expressive eyes. On occasion a guide waits near the petroglyphs and will show you the best of the carvings for a small fee. To reach the site, take Ruta 45 west from Ovalle. About 19 km (12 mi) from the town head south for 5 km (3 mi) on a rough, dry road. ⊠ *24 km (15 mi) west of Ovalle* ☎ *No phone* ✆ *Free* ☉ *Daily 8–7:30.*

A tourist complex cut from the rough land, **Termas de Socos** is a very pleasant hot springs. The waters, which spout from the earth at 28°C (82°F), are said to have incredible healing powers. Curative or not, the waters here are extremely relaxing. ⊠ *24 km (15 mi) west of Ovalle on Ruta 45* ☎ *53/198–2505, 2/236–3336* ⊕ *www.termassocos.cl* ✆ *1,000 pesos* ☉ *Daily 8–8.*

Heading toward the Andes you come across **Monumento Natural Pichasca,** a forest of petrified tree trunks. These play host to dozens of fossils, such as imprints of leaves and outlines of small animals. Nearby is a cave beneath a stone overhang that housed indigenous peoples thousands of years ago. Inside you'll find some cave paintings by the Molle people. ⊠ *50 km (31 mi) northeast of Ovalle on Camino Ovalle–Río Hurtado* ☎ *No phone* ✆ *1,000 pesos* ☉ *Daily 8:30–4:30.*

Where to Stay & Eat

¢–$$ ✕**Bavaria.** Because of the country's large number of German immigrants, most Chilean cities have at least one Bavarian-theme restaurant. This one, part of a national chain, evokes the old country with wood beams and checkered yellow tablecloths. Entrées like *pollo a la plancha* (grilled chicken) are a bit bland, but wholesome and filling. ⊠ *Vicuña Mackenna 161-B* ☎ *53/630–578* ⊟ *AE, MC, V.*

$ ⊡ **Hotel Termas de Socos.** This rustic hotel, about 33 km (20 mi) west of Ovalle, allows you unlimited access to the hot springs at Termas de Socos. The rooms have large, comfortable beds, and many have expansive picture windows looking out over the surrounding desert. Also available are relaxing massages and private hot tubs. The service, unfortunately, is a little inattentive. ⊠ *Termas de Socos* ☎ *53/681–021* ⊕ *www. termasocos.cl* ⊅ *28 rooms* ⚭ *Restaurant, room service, cable TV, pool, bar, laundry service, meeting rooms; no a/c* ⊟ *AE, MC, V* ⦿⦿ *BP.*

$ ▦ **Hotel El Turismo.** A pleasant hotel in the center of town, Hotel El Turismo has spacious and well-kept rooms. Ask for a room facing the Plaza de Armas. ⊠ *Victoria 295* ☎ *53/623–536* ⊟ *53/623–536* ⊅ *30 rooms* ⚭ *Restaurant, minibars, laundry service; no a/c* ⊟ *MC, V* ⦿⦿ *CP.*

Parque Nacional Fray Jorge

❼ *110 km (68 mi) south of La Serena.*

Fodor'sChoice
★

The thought of a patch of land that is rich with vegetation and animal life in the heart of El Norte Chico's dry, desolate landscape seems to defy logic. But Parque Nacional Fray Jorge, a UNESCO world biosphere reserve since 1977, has a small cloud forest similar to those found in Chile's damp southern regions. The forest, perched 600 meters (1,968 feet) above sea level, receives its life-giving nourishment from the *camanchaca* (fog) that constantly envelops it. Within this forest you'll come across ferns and trees found nowhere else in the region. A slightly slippery boardwalk leads you on a half-hour tour. ⊠ *At Km 383 of Pan-American Hwy., take dirt road 18 km (11 mi) west* ☎ *No phone* ⊠ *1,600 pesos* ⊗ *Jan.–Mar., Thurs.–Sun. 8:30–6; Apr.–Dec., weekends 8:30–6.*

THE HUASCO VALLEY

At least twice a decade the desert bursts to life in a phenomenon called el desierto florido. If you are lucky enough to visit the area during these times, you'll see the desert covered with colorful flowers, some of which exist only in this region. Parque Nacional Llanos de Challe on the coast is an excellent place to view the flowering desert. When it occurs you can see the desierto florido in most of El Norte Chico, but the Huasco Valley in particular has a lovely and large variety of flora.

The Huasco Valley sees far fewer visitors than the Elqui Valley, giving you the feeling that you've beaten the crowds. Climbing into the Andes from Vallenar, the valley's largest city, you reach the Upper Huasco Valley. The Valle del Carmen, part of the Huasco Valley, has several quaint villages, such as Alto del Carmen and San Felix.

Vallenar

❽ *188 km (116 mi) north of La Serena.*

Vallenar, the transportation hub of the Huasco Valley, was founded in 1789 by Ambrosio O'Higgins, who named the town after his home in Ballinagh, Ireland. There aren't many sights that lure travelers off the highway—most who stop here are headed to the Parque Nacional Llanos de Challe. The large **Plaza O'Higgins** is a pleasant place for an early evening stroll. The **Iglesia Porroquial,** on the main square, is worth a visit to see its huge copper dome.

On display at the **Museo de Huasco** is a small collection of regional indigenous artifacts like pottery and textiles. There are also pictures of the flowering desert for those not lucky enough to see it in person. ⊠ *Sargento Aldea 742* ☎ *51/611-320* 🎫 *600 pesos* ⊙ *Weekdays 10–1 and 3–6, Sat. 10–12:30.*

Where to Stay & Eat

¢–$$ ✕ **Il Boccato.** Opposite the Plaza de Armas, this small, friendly corner pizza place with a brightly lighted interior is your best bet for a quick bite. Chose from myriad menu options, including a zesty pollo a la plancha. There's also a wide selection of seafood entrées. ⊠ *Plaza de Armas* ☎ *51/614–609* ⊟ *AE, DC, MC, V.*

¢–$$ ✕ **Moros y Christianos Restaurant.** This Mediterranean-style restaurant, named for the Spanish festivals commemorating the battle between the Moors and the Christians, serves flavorful fish and meat dishes. ⊠ *Pan-American Hwy. at entrance to Vallenar* ☎ *51/614–600* 🍴 *Reservations essential* ⊟ *AE, DC, MC, V* ⊙ *Closed Mon.*

$$ ▦ **Hostería de Vallenar.** The best lodging in Vallenar, this comfortable hostelry has basic rooms with wood furniture. The staff is friendly and helpful. The restaurant features some Brazilian specialties like *fejoida,* a hearty stew of black beans and sausage. ⊠ *Alonso de Ercilla 848* ☎ *51/614–195* 🖷 *51/614–538* 🖅 *johanacerda@mi.terra.cl* 🛏 *30 rooms* 🍴 *Restaurant, minibars, cable TV, pool, billiards, bar, laundry service, Internet; no a/c* ⊟ *AE, DC, MC, V* ⧗| *CP.*

$ ▦ **Hotel Cecil.** A pleasant garden with a pool makes Hotel Cecil a good budget lodging choice. The rooms are spotless, but the baths are a bit small. ⊠ *Arturo Prat 1059* ☎🖷 *51/614–400* ⊕ *www.hotelcecil.cl* 🛏 *18 rooms* 🍴 *Room service, cable TV, pool, laundry service, Internet; no a/c* ⊟ *No credit cards* ⧗| *CP.*

Nightlife & the Arts

La Casona (⊠ Serrano 1475 ☎ 51/611–600) caters to an older crowd and heats up with dancing on the weekends. You can dance to salsa and other Latin rhythms on the town's largest dance floor at **Cubaire** (⊠ Serrano 1398 ☎ No phone).

Alto del Carmen

⑨ *40 km (25 mi) southeast of Vallenar.*

Not far from where El Transito and El Carmen rivers join to form the Huasco you'll find Alto del Carmen, a quaint town whose inhabitants dedicate themselves to cultivating the muscat grapes used to make pisco. In addition to pisco, the town is famous for making *pajarete,* a sweet wine. The **Planta Pisquera Alto del Carmen,** just outside town, hosts free tours and tastings daily from 8 AM to 8 PM.

About 26 km (16 mi) east of Alto del Carmen in the Valle del Carmen you'll find the precious town of **San Felix,** whose central plaza, whitewashed church, and pleasant markets shouldn't be missed. There's also a pisco distillery here.

Parque Nacional Llanos de Challe

⑩ *78 km (48 mi) northwest of Vallenar, 99 km (61 mi) north of Huasco.*

There is no better place in El Norte Chico to view the desierto florido than this desolate coastal park. Every four or five years it is transformed into a carpet of reds, greens, and blues when there's sufficient rainfall to awaken the dormant bulbs below the dry, cracked earth. The park, spanning 450 square km (174 square mi), was formed to protect the *Garra de León,* a rare plant with an intoxicating red bloom that grows in only a few parts of the Huasco region. There are also a number of unusual species of cactus in the park—pacul, napina, and quisco flourish here. ⊠ *About 17 km (11 mi) north of Vallenar, turn west off Pan-American Hwy. Take this road 82 km (51 mi) to the coast* ☎ *No phone* 🎫 *Free.*

THE COPIAPÓ VALLEY

The region once known as Copayapu, meaning "cup of gold" in the Quechua language, was first inhabited by the Diaguitas around 1000. The Incas arrived several hundred years later in search of gold. Conquistador Diego de Almagro, who passed this way in 1535, was the first European to see the lush valley. Almagro didn't stop here for long; he continued on to Peru via the Inca Royal Road on his bloody conquest of the region.

During the 19th century the Copiapó Valley proved to be a true cup of gold when prospectors started large-scale mining operations in the region. But today, the residents of the valley make their living primarily from copper.

The northernmost city in the region, Copiapó, lies at the end of the world. Here the semiarid region of El Norte Chico gives way to the Atacama Desert. Continuing north from Copiapó there is little but barren earth for hundreds of miles.

Copiapó

⑪ *145 km (90 mi) north of Vallenar.*

Copiapó was officially founded in 1744 by Don Francisco Cortés, who called it Villa San Francisco de La Selva. Originally a *tambo,* or resting place, Copiapó was where Diego de Almagro recuperated after his grueling journey south from Peru in 1536. The 19th-century silver strikes solidified Copiapó's status as an important city in the region. In the center of Copiapó lies **Plaza Prat,** a lovely park lined with 100-year-old pepper trees. English architect William Rogers built the neoclassical **Iglesia Catedral Nuestra Señora del Rosario,** facing the central square, in the middle of the 19th century. The 1872 **Iglesia San Francisco** is a red-and-white candy cane of a church. The adjacent Plaza Godoy has a statue of goatherd Juan Godoy, who accidentally discovered huge silver deposits in nearby Chañarcillo.

The **Museo Mineralógico** offers a geological history of the region and what is perhaps the country's largest collection of rocks and minerals. There are more than 2,000 samples, including some found only in the Atacama Desert. The museum even displays a few meteorites that fell in the area. ⊠ *Colipí at Rodriguez* ☎ *52/206–606* ⊕ *www.unap.cl/museomin/index2.htm* 🎫 *500 pesos* ⊗ *Mon., Wed., Fri. 10:30–noon and 4–5:30; Tues. and Thurs. 10:30–noon and 6:30–8.*

A historic home that once belonged to the wealthy Matta family now houses the **Museo Histórico Regional,** dedicated to the natural history of the area. Regional archives suggest that the house was originally built by mining engineer Felipe Santiago Matta between 1840 and 1850. ⊠ *Atacama 98* ☎ *52/212–313* 🎫 *600 pesos* ⊗ *Mon. 2:30–6, Tues.–Thurs. 9–6, weekends 10–12:45.*

Where to Stay & Eat

¢–$ ✕ **El Cisne.** This locally recommended seafood restaurant specializes in shellfish. The *ostiones a la parmesana* (oysters with grated cheese) is particularly good. Chairs padded with black velvet, and prints of works by the old masters decorate the eclectic dining room. ⊠ *Colipí 220* ☎ *52/215–544* ▭ *No credit cards.*

★ $ 🏨 **Hotel La Casona.** Beautiful gardens surround this quaint country inn with a red facade and budget prices. Entering through wooden doors you reach the sunny lobby. To one side is a dining area with oak furniture and blue-and-white-checked tablecloths—an excellent place to enjoy your complimentary pisco sour. The rooms, decorated in blue, can get a little hot in summer. ⊠ *Av. Bernardo O'Higgins 150* ☎☎ *52/217–277* ⊕ *www.lacasonahotel.cl* 🛏 *10 rooms* ⚭ *Restaurant, minibars, cable TV, bar, laundry service; no a/c* ▭ *AE, DC, MC, V* ⵏ⚭ *BP.*

$ 🏨 **Hotel Chagall.** Although it appears a little run-down on the outside, this business hotel has clean, modern rooms. Ask to see a few before you decide, as some are very dark. The bar, decorated with lots of kelly green, is reminiscent of an Irish pub. You won't find Guinness on tap here, however, so you'll have to settle for a well-made pisco sour. ⊠ *Av. Bernardo O'Higgins 760* ☎ *52/213–775* ☎ *52/211–527* ⊕ *www.chagall.cl* 🛏 *34 rooms* ⚭ *Restaurant, minibars, cable TV, bar, laundry service; no a/c in some rooms* ▭ *AE, DC, MC, V* ⵏ⚭ *BP.*

$ 🏨 **Hotel Diego de Almeida.** A pleasant tiled entryway leads into an elegantly furnished lobby at this hotel a step above the rest. The Diego provides everything you would expect from a hotel catering to corporate travelers, from meeting rooms to business services. The rooms are pleasant, if a bit bland. Inquire about a room in the back, as those facing the street can be quite noisy. ⊠ *Av. Bernardo O'Higgins 656* ☎ *52/212–075* ☎ *52/218–688* ⊕ *www.diegodealmagrohoteles.cl* 🛏 *36 rooms* ⚭ *Restaurant, room service, in-room safes, cable TV, pool, sauna, bar, laundry service, business services, meeting rooms; no a/c* ▭ *AE, DC, MC, V* ⵏ⚭ *BP.*

$ 🏨 **Hotel Miramonti.** This central hotel has clean, modern rooms decorated in the same shade of mauve you'll find in the lobby and hallways. The staff here is friendly and helpful. Arched-back wooden chairs and blue tablecloths fill the country-style restaurant. The international menu here is heavy on seafood, and includes great merluza and ostiones. ⊠ *Ramón Freire 731* ☎☎ *52/210–440* ⊕ *www.miramonti.cl* 🛏 *47*

*rooms △ Restaurant, in-room safes, minibars, Internet, cable TV, bar,
recreation room, laundry service; no a/c ⊟ AE, DC, MC, V.*

Nightlife & the Arts

Because there are lots of students in town, nightlife in Copiapó can get
lively, with bars hosting bands, and a few dance clubs that rage all night
to salsa beats. **Discoteque Splash** (⊠ Juan Martinéz 46 ☎ 52/215–948)
is your best bet for late-night dancing. Outside town, the **Drive-In Esso
Pub** (⊠ Near exit ramp from Pan-American Hwy. ☎ 52/211–535) is perhaps the most innovative bar in northern Chile—it's in a converted gas
station. **La Tabla** (⊠ Los Carrera 895 ☎ 52/233–029), near Plaza Prat,
has live music, very expensive drinks, and good food.

Shopping

The **Casa de la Cultura** (⊠ Av. Bernardo O'Higgins 610, on Plaza Prat
☎ 52/210–824) has crafts workshops and a gallery displaying works
by local artists. On Friday there is a frenzied **fruit market** when locals
pack the normally tranquil Plaza Godoy.

Bahía Inglesa

⑫ *68 km (42 mi) northwest of Copiapó.*

Some of the most beautiful beaches in El Norte Chico can be found
at Bahía Inglesa, which was originally known as Puerto del Inglés because of the number of English buccaneers using the port as a hideaway. It's not just the beautiful white sand that sets these beaches apart,
however: it's also the turquoise waters, the fresh air, and the fabulous
weather. Combine all this with the fact that the town has yet to attract large-scale development and you can see why so many people flock
here in summer. If you are fortunate enough to visit during the low
season, you'll likely experience a tranquillity rarely felt in Chile's
other coastal towns.

Where to Stay & Eat

★ ¢–$ ✕ **El Pateao.** With ocean views and the region's best food, this bohemian
bistro is a must for anyone staying in the area. The innovative contemporary menu lists such culinary non sequiturs as curry dishes and *tal-
larines con mariscos* (a pan-Asian noodle concoction served with shellfish
and topped with cilantro). On the sand-covered porch you can sit in a
comfy chair and watch the sunset. ⊠ *Av. El Morro 756* ☎ *09/826–0007*
⊟ *No credit cards.*

$ 🏨 **Apart Hotel Playa Blanca.** If you are tired of indistinguishable chain
hotels, a cabana at Playa Blanca may just do the trick. These cabins are
more like condos, complete with comfortable living rooms and full
kitchens. Relax on a chaise longue by the pool, an asymmetrical beauty.
This is a great place for kids, as there is a play area with a slide and jungle gym. ⊠ *Camino de Martín 1300* ☎ *52/316–044* 🖷 *52/316–468*
🖉 *olivo.norte@ia.cl* ➷ *10 cabanas* △ *Kitchens, pool, playground; no
a/c* ⊟ *No credit cards.*

$ 🏨 **Hotel Rocas de Bahía.** This sprawling modern hotel, straight from *The
FodorśChoice   Great Gatsby,* has rooms with huge windows facing the sea. You'll also
★   find large beds and Southwestern-style furniture in the rooms. Take a

dip in the glistening waters of the bay, or head up to the rooftop pool. ⊠ *Av. El Morro 888* ☎ *52/316–005* 🖷 *52/316–032* ⊕ *www. rocasdebahia.cl* ⇄ *36 rooms* ⚲ *Restaurant, room service, in-room safes, pool, bicycles, billiards, Ping-Pong, playground, laundry service, meeting rooms; no a/c* ⊟ *AE, DC, MC, V* ⦿ *BP.*

Nightlife & the Arts

There are few true bars in Bahía Inglesa except in the hotels, but outside the city, on the way north to Caldera, you'll find several discos that are always packed during high season. You can dance at **Discoteque Loreto** (⊠ Camino Bahia Inglesa ☎ No phone), which lies midway between Bahía Inglesa and Caldera. Head to the funky **El Plateao** (⊠ Av. El Morro 756 ☎ 09/679–3016) to listen to reggae and Cuban tunes. **Takeo** (⊠ Camino Bahia Inglesa s/n ☎ No phone) attracts a mature, salsa-dancing crowd.

Sports & the Outdoors

BEACHES There are several easily accessible beaches around Bahía Inglesa. **Playa La Piscina** is the town's main beach. The rocky outcroppings and sugary sand are reminiscent of the Mediterranean. **Playa Las Machas**, the town's southernmost beach, is especially relaxing because few tourists have discovered it.

WATER SPORTS There are all types of water sports in the area. **Morro Ballena Expediciones** (⊠ El Morro s/n, on south end of beach ☎ No phone) arranges fishing, kayaking, and scuba-diving trips.

Caldera

⑬ *74 km (46 mi) northwest of Copiapó.*

An important port during the silver era, Caldera today is a slightly rundown town with decent beaches and friendly people. The echoes of piracy still haunt the port—a former pirate hideout—which is used today to export grapes and copper.

Near the beach is the **Estacion Ferrocarril,** once the terminus of Chile's first railroad. There's a tourist-information kiosk here. The large, Gothic-towered **Iglesia de San Vincente de Paul,** on the town's main square, was built in 1862.

Where to Stay & Eat

¢–$ ✕ **Nuevo Miramar.** Huge windows overlook the pier at this excellent seafood restaurant. One of the most elegant eateries in Caldera, the Nuevo Miramar has tables with fine linens and cloth napkins. Bow-tied waiters, all extremely attentive, will tell you the catch of the day. ⊠ *Gana 90* ☎ *52/315–381* ⚱ *Reservations essential* ⊟ *No credit cards.*

$ ⌂ **Hostería Puerta del Sol.** These A-frame cabanas have small kitchens and dining areas and a view of the bay. The showers pour out incredibly hot water, a nice touch after a long day of exploring. There is also a pool, which could be quite pleasant if it were filled to the top. ⊠ *Wheelwright 750* ☎ *52/315–205* 🖷 *52/315–507* ⇄ *7 cabanas* ⚲ *Kitchenettes, pool, bar, laundry service; no a/c, no room phones* ⊟ *AE, DC, MC, V.*

$ ▦ **Motel Portal del Inca.** This string of red cabanas has tennis courts and an inviting pool surrounded by lounge chairs. There's also a playground, making this an excellent choice if you are traveling with children. The rooms are simple, with furnishings that may have been popular back in the 1970s. ✉ *Carvallo 945* ☎ *52/315–252* ⊕ *www. portaldelinca.cl* ⟲ *34 cabanas* ⚴ *Coffee shop, kitchenettes, tennis court, pool, bar, playground, laundry service, business services, Internet, meeting rooms; no a/c* ▭ *MC, V.*

Nightlife & the Arts

Many of Caldera's bars are open only in summer, when the town is packed with vacationing South Americans. The funky **Bartolomeo** (✉ Wheelwright 747 ☎ 52/316–413) plays eclectic music. If you're hungry, chow down on the Asian and Mexican food. **Pub Entre Jotes** (✉ Wheelwright 485 ☎ No phone), with a terrace overlooking the port, is a good place to enjoy the sunset. The pub hosts live music on weekends, although it's often just a man playing a keyboard.

Beaches

The town's main beach is **Playa Copiapina.** North of the pier, **Playa Brava** stretches as far as you can see. About 4 km (2½ mi) to the south of town you come upon the pleasant sandy beach of **Playa Loreto.**

Parque Nacional Pan de Azúcar

★ ☾ ⑭ *91 km (56 mi) north of Caldera.*

Some of Chile's most spectacular coastal scenery is in Parque Nacional Pan de Azúcar, a national park that stretches for 40 km (25 mi) along the coast north of the town of Chañaral. Steep cliffs fall into the crashing sea, their ominous presence broken occasionally by white-sand beaches. These isolated stretches of sand make for excellent picnicking. Be careful if you decide to swim, as there are often dangerous currents.

Within the park you'll find an incredible variety of flora and fauna. Pelicans can be spotted off the coast, as can sea lions and sea otters, cormorants, and plovers (similar to sandpipers but with shorter beaks). There are some 20 species of cacti in the park, including the rare copiapoa, which resembles a little blue pincushion. The park also shelters rare predators, including the desert fox. In the pueblo of Caleta Pan de Azúcar, a tiny fishing village, you can get information from the CONAF-run kiosk (CONAF is the national forestry service, Corporación Nacional Forestal).

Offshore from Caleta Pan de Azúcar is a tiny island that a large colony of Humboldt penguins calls home. You can hire local fisherfolk to bring you here. Negotiate the price, which should be around 7,000 pesos. About 10 km (6 mi) north of the village, Mirador Pan de Azúcar affords spectacular views of the coastline. Another 30 km (19 mi) to the north is Las Lomitas. This 700-meter (2,296-foot) cliff is almost always covered with the *camanchaca* (fog), which rolls in from the sea. A huge net here is used to catch the fog and condense it into water. ✉ *An unpaved road north of the cemetery in Chañaral leads to Caleta Pan de Azúcar* ☎ *No phone* ⊕ *www.conaf.cl* ▨ *1,000 pesos* ☾ *Park daily, ranger kiosk daily 8–1 and 2–6.*

Where to Stay & Eat

$ ⌸ **Hostería Chañaral.** Leaps and bounds above the other places in Chañaral, where you will mostly likely stay the night when visiting the park, the Hostería Chañaral has well-maintained rooms and clean baths with plenty of hot water. A restaurant on the premises serves good seafood. ⊠ *Muller 268* ☎ *52/480–050* 🖷 *52/480–554* 🛏 *34 rooms* ⚨ *Restaurant, bar, laundry service; no a/c* ▤ *AE, MC, V* ⧠ *CP.*

Parque Nacional Nevado Tres Cruces

⑮ *200 km (124 mi) east of Copiapó.*

Heading inland from Copiapó you climb high into the Andes before reaching Parque Nacional Nevado Tres Cruces. The national park lies in the inhospitable altiplano some 4,000 meters (13,000 feet) above sea level, and for some time few tourists dared to venture here. Three of the world's four species of flamingos make their home here, and guanacos and vicuñas roam the arid region in search of food.

Two beautiful Andean lakes lie within the park's borders. At Laguna San Francisco, at the main entrance, you'll find flamingos as well as some species of ducks. Along the grassy banks it is not uncommon to come across an occasional Andean fox. Farther into the park you come to Laguna Santa Rosa and the salt flat of El Salar de Maricunga.

Near the border of Argentina are the beautiful waters of Laguna Verde. This shallow lagoon, colored green by microorganisms, is the lifeblood of the region. Many species of birds and animals—including flamingos, guanacos, and desert foxes—live along its banks. On the southern shore of the lake there is a natural hot-springs pool, which is free and open to the public. To the south is Ojos del Salado, the world's highest active volcano. Rising 6,893 meters (22,609 feet) above sea level, it's an awe-inspiring sight.

To visit the park you will need a four-wheel-drive vehicle. Be sure to bring extra fuel, as gas stops are few and far between in this region. An ambitious project to create a linked trail system from Tierra del Fuego to Chile's northernmost tip is under way and scheduled for completion around 2015. Sections of the trail are already in place here. Check with **CONAF** (☎ 56/390–000 ⊕ www.conaf.cl) officials for details of the trail in the Tres Cruces region. ⊠ *Take Ruta 31 from Copiapó to Paso de San Francisco, then head south on the rough road marked* QUEBRADA CIENAGA REDONDA ☎ *No phone* 🖅 *1,000 pesos.*

EL NORTE CHICO ESSENTIALS

Transportation

BY AIR

Because there are no international airports in El Norte Chico, you can't fly here directly from North America, Europe, or Australia. You can fly into Santiago and transfer to an Avant or Lan flight to La Serena or Copiapó. Round-trip flights from Santiago to El Norte Chico can run up to

200,000 pesos. Round-trip flights between cities in the north range from 25,000 to 100,000 pesos.

🛪 Airlines **Avant** ⊠ Colipí 510 ☎ 52/217-285 in Copiapó ⊠ Aeropuerto La Florido ☎ 51/220-943 in La Serena ⊕ www.avant.cl. **Lan** ⊠ Colipí 101 ☎ 52/213-512 in Copiapó ⊠ Balmaceda 400 ☎ 51/221-551 in La Serena ⊕ www.lan.com.

🛪 Airports **Aeropuerto Chamonate** ☎ 51/214-360. **Aeropuerto La Florido** ☎ 51/200-900.

BY BUS

Every major city in El Norte Chico has a bus terminal, and there are frequent departures to other cities as well as smaller towns in the area. Keep in mind that there may be no bus service to the smallest villages or the more remote national parks.

No bus company has a monopoly, so there are often several bus stations in each city. Because many companies may be running buses along the same route, shop around for the best price. The fare for a 300-km (186-mi) trip usually runs around 3,500–7,000 pesos. For longer trips find a bus that has a *salon semi-cama,* with comfortable seats that make all the difference.

🚌 Bus Stations **Copiapó** ⊠ Chañarcillo 680 ☎ 52/213-793. **Ovalle** ⊠ Maestranza 443 ☎ 53/626-707. **La Serena** ⊠ Av. El Santo and Amunátegui ☎ 51/224-573. **Vallenar** ⊠ Av. Matta and Arturo Prat ☎ No phone.

BY CAR

Because of the distances between cities, a car is the best way to truly see El Norte Chico. Many national parks can be visited only by car, preferably a four-wheel-drive vehicle.

Driving can be a little hectic in Copiapó and La Serena, where drivers don't always seem to observe the rules of the road. But once you get out on the open road, driving is considerably easier. Ruta 5, more familiarly known as the Pan-American Highway, bisects all of northern Chile. Ruta 41 snakes along from La Serena through the Elqui Valley to Vicuña. Ruta D485 will take you to Pisco Elqui. Ruta 31 takes you inland from Copiapó.

There are car-rental agencies in La Serena and Copiapó at the airport and in the city, and most hotels will help you arrange for a rental.

🚗 Rental Agencies **Avis** ⊠ Rómulo Peña 102, Copiapó ☎ 52/210-413 ⊠ Av. Francisco de Aguirre 68, La Serena ☎ 51/227-171 ⊕ www.avis.com. **Budget** ⊠ Ramón Freire 50, Copiapó ☎ 52/216-272 ⊠ Francisco Aguirre 15, La Serena ☎ 51/218-272 ⊕ www.budget.cl. **Hertz** ⊠ Copayapu 173, Copiapó ☎ 52/213-522 ⊠ Av. Francisco de Aguirre 225, La Serena ☎ 51/226-171 ⊕ www.hertz.cl.

BY TAXI

Taxis are the most efficient way to get around any city in El Norte Chico. They're easy to hail on the streets, but late at night you might want to ask someone at a hotel or restaurant to call one for you. Taxis often function as *colectivos,* meaning they will pick up anybody going in the same direction. The driver will adjust the price accordingly. Almost no taxis have meters, but many have the price posted on the windshield. Make sure you establish the price before getting inside. Prices range from

700 to 3,500 pesos, depending on the distance traveled and whether the taxi is a colectivo. Prices rise an average of 20% at night. Taxi drivers often will rent out their services for the day for a flat fee.

Contacts & Resources

MAIL & SHIPPING

Although most cities in El Norte Chico have a post office, you'll often encounter long lines that move at a snail's pace. Your best bet is to ask your hotel to post a letter for you. But don't expect your letter to reach its destination quickly. Mail headed out of the country can often take weeks.

If you need to send something right away, there's a DHL office in La Serena.

🏢 Post Offices **Copiapó** ⊠ Los Carreras 691. **Ovalle** ⊠ Plaza de Armas. **La Serena** ⊠ Arturo Prat at Matta. **Vallenar** ⊠ Plaza O'Higgins.

🏢 Shipping Services **DHL** ⊠ Arturo Prat 540 La Serena.

TOURS

El Norte Chico has travel agencies in most major cities, as well as in some of the smaller ones. Shop around to make sure that you are getting the best itinerary and the best price. In La Serena check out Talinay and Diaguitas Tour for tours to national parks and the interior. In Copiapó you can arrange trips to the antiplano through Turismo Atacama and Cobre Tour. Ovalle Tour runs trips in the Ovalle area.

🏢 Tour Operators **Cobre Tour** ⊠ Av. Bernardo O'Higgins 640, Copiapó ☎ 52/211-072. **Diaguitas Tour** ⊠ Av. del Mar 3000, La Serena ☎ 51/214-129. **Ovalle Tour** ⊠ Libertad 456, Ovalle ☎ 53/626-696. **Talinay** ⊠ Arturo Prat 470, La Serena ☎ 51/218-658. **Turismo Atacama** ⊠ Carreras 716, Copiapó ☎ 52/214-767.

VISITOR INFORMATION

Every major city in El Norte Chico has an office run by Sernatur, the Chilean tourism agency. The offices provide informative brochures of the region and other assistance for travelers. The staff often speaks some English.

CONAF—the Corporacíon Nacional Forestal de Chile—maintains Chile's national parks and forests, and can provide information on El Norte Chico's more remote regions.

🏢 **CONAF** ☎ 56/390-000 ⊕ www.conaf.cl. **Copiapó** ⊠ Los Carrera 691 ☎ 52/231-510. **La Serena** ⊠ Matta 461 ☎ 51/225-199. **Vallenar** ⊠ Plaza de Armas ☎ 51/619-215.

El Norte Grande

WORD OF MOUTH

"I had always associated the *altiplano* with Peru and Bolivia, but discovering the beauty of Chile's high plains, just a few hours from the coast, was a real treat! I could hardly believe my eyes when I saw pale pink flamingos soaring over the lakes at 5,000 meters above sea level. It was also a blast taking a muddy thermal bath while staring at Chungura and the other snow-capped peaks . . . while keeping a sharp eye out for the graceful vicuñas scampering by."

—Brian K.

Updated by
Brian Kluepfel

A LAND OF ROCK AND EARTH, terrifying in its austerity and vastness, El Norte Grande is one of the world's most desolate regions. Spanning some 1,930 km (1,200 mi), Chile's Great North stretches from the Río Copiapó to the borders of Peru and Bolivia. Here you will find the Atacama Desert, the driest place on Earth—so dry that in many parts no rain has ever been recorded.

Yet people have inhabited this desolate land since time immemorial, and indeed the heart of El Norte Grande lies not in its geography but in its people. The indigenous Chinchorro people eked out a meager living from the sea more than 8,000 years ago, leaving behind the magnificent Chinchorro mummies, the oldest in the world. High in the Andes, the Atacameño tribes traded livestock with the Tijuanacota and the Inca. Many of these people still cling to their way of life, though much of their culture was lost during the colonial period.

Although the Spanish first invaded the region in the 16th century, El Norte Grande was largely ignored by Europeans until the 1800s, when huge deposits of nitrates were found in the Atacama region. The "white gold" brought boom times to towns like Pisagua, Iquique, and Antofagasta. Because most of the mineral-rich region lay beyond its northern border, Chile declared war on neighboring Peru and Bolivia in 1878. Chile won the five-year battle and annexed the land north of Antofagasta, a continuing source of national pride for many Chileans. With the invention of synthetic nitrates, the market for these fertilizers dried up and the nitrate barons abandoned their opulent mansions and returned to Santiago. El Norte Grande was once again left on its own.

What you'll see today is a land of both growth and decay. The glory days of the nitrate era are gone, but copper has stepped in to help fill that gap (the world's largest open-pit copper mine is here). El Norte Grande is still a land of opportunity for fortune-seekers, as well as for tourists looking for a less-traveled corner of the world. It is a place of beauty and dynamic isolation, a place where the past touches the present in a troubled yet majestic embrace.

Exploring El Norte Grande

Only if you enjoy the solitude and desolation of the desert should you venture into El Norte Grande. On rare occasions only will you see a swath of green cutting through the empty landscape. The driest desert in the world, the Atacama is barren until it explodes in a riot of color known as *el desierto florido*. The flowering desert takes place every four or five years when unusual amounts of rain awaken dormant bulbs.

Don't worry if you're not lucky enough to see the flowering desert while you're here: there are more mysteries to behold in the desert, along the barren coastline, and among the peaks of the world's longest mountain chain. The *altiplano*, or high plains, rests between two giant branches of the Andes and houses such natural marvels as crystalline salt flats, geysers, and volcanoes. You'll also spot flocks of flamingos and such mammals as the vicuña, a cousin to the llama. At coastal ports like Arica

CloseUp

EL NORTE GRANDE FESTIVALS & SEASONAL EVENTS

Every town in the region celebrates the day honoring its patron saint. Most are small gatherings attended largely by locals, but a few are huge celebrations that attract people from all over the country. One fiesta not to be missed takes place in La Tirana from July 12 to 18. During this time some 80,000 pilgrims converge on the town to honor the Virgen del Carmen with riotous dancing in the streets.

and Iquique, you can get close up and personal with sea lions and pelicans at the *muelles,* or fishing piers, and take short boat trips to visit colonies of Humboldt penguins.

The best bases for exploration of El Norte Grande are San Pedro de Atacama, Iquique, and Arica. San Pedro is close to some of the most breathtaking scenery of the region, and it's within a day's reach of the coastal town of Iquique. Iquique is the best place to stay if you want to visit the Gigante de Atacama and the nearby hot springs at Pica and Mamiña. From Arica you can head inland to explore the altiplano or stay close to the sea, taking in the Chinchorro mummies.

About the Restaurants

The food of El Norte Grande is simple but quite good. Along the coast you can enjoy fresh seafood and shellfish, including *merluza* (hake), *corvina* (sea bass), *ostiones* (oysters), and *machas* (similar to razor clams but unique to Chile), to name just a few. Seviche (a traditional Peruvian dish made with raw, marinated fish) is also available in much of El Norte Grande, but make sure you sample it in a place where you are confident that the fish is fresh. Fish may be ordered *a la plancha* (grilled in butter and lemon) or accompanied by a sauce such as *salsa margarita* (a butter-based sauce comprising almost every shellfish imaginable). As you enter the interior region you'll come across heartier meals such as *cazuela de vacuno* (beef stew served with corn on the cob and vegetables) and *chuleta con arroz* (beef with rice). More heavily touristed areas, such as San Pedro de Atacama, also serve international fare.

People in the north generally eat a heavy lunch around 2 PM that can last two hours, followed by a light dinner around 10 PM. Reservations are seldom needed, except in the poshest of places. Leave a 10% tip if you enjoyed the service.

You'll have to hustle to see much of El Norte Grande in less than a week. You can spend at least two days in **San Pedro de Atacama,** visiting the incredible sights such as the bizarre moonscape of the Valle de la Luna and the desolate salt flats of the Salar de Atacama. For half a day soak in the hot springs in the tiny town of **Pica,** then head to the nitrate ghost town of Humberstone. On the way to Iquique, take a side trip to the **Gigante de Atacama,** the world's largest geoglyph. After a morning exploring Iquique, head up to **Arica,** the coastal town that bills itself as the "land of eternal spring." Be sure to visit the Museo Arqueológico de San Miguel de Azapa to see the Chinchorro mummies. Stop in **Purte** to catch your breath before taking in the flamingos at **Parque Nacional Lauca** or the vicuñas, llamas, and alpacas of **Reserva Nacional Las Vicuñas.**

4

About the Hotels

Lodging in El Norte Grande is relatively inexpensive. Hotels in the larger cities provide all the amenities you might expect from similar establishments back home, such as business centers, laundry service, pools, cable television, and minibars. However, some accommodations that bill themselves as "luxury" hotels haven't been remodeled or painted in years. Ask to look at a room before deciding. Few small towns have hotels, so you will have to make do with guesthouses with extremely basic rooms and shared bathrooms.

WHAT IT COSTS In pesos (in thousands)				
$$$$	**$$$**	**$$**	**$**	**¢**
RESTAURANTS over 11	8–11	5–8	3–5	under 3
HOTELS over 105	75–105	45–75	15–45	under 15

Restaurant prices are for a main course at dinner. Hotel prices are for a double room in high season, excluding tax.

When to Go

In the height of the Chilean summer, January and February, droves of Chileans and Argentines mob El Norte Grande's beaches. Although this is a fun time to visit, prices go up and finding a hotel can be difficult. Book your room a month or more in advance. The high season tapers off in March, an excellent time to visit if you're looking for a bit more tranquillity. If you plan to visit the altiplano, bring the right clothing. Winter can be very cold, and summer sees a fair amount of rain.

THE NITRATE PAMPA

The vast *pampa salitrera* is an atmospheric introduction to Chile's Great North. Between 1890 and 1925 this region was the site of more than

80 *oficinas de salitre,* or nitrate plants. The invention of synthetic nitrates spelled the end for all but a few. Crumbling nitrate works lay stagnant in the dry desert air, some disintegrating into dust, others remaining a fascinating testament to the white gold that for a time made this one of Chile's richest regions.

Snowcapped volcanoes dominate the landscape to the east, making mornings in this region especially memorable. The vast lunar landscapes around San Pedro de Atacama make for days' worth of fascinating trekking. Just watching the sun—or moon—rise over the dunes is worth the trip itself. And bird-lovers will find the Reserva Nacional de Flamencos well worth the high-altitude adjustment for a chance to see hundreds of pink flamingos against the backdrop of shimmering blue and green lakes.

Antofagasta

❶ *565 km (350 mi) north of Copiapó.*

Antofagasta is the most important—and the richest—city in El Norte Grande. It was part of Bolivia until 1879, when it was annexed by Chile in the War of the Pacific. The port town became an economic powerhouse during the nitrate boom. With the rapid decline of nitrate production, copper mining stepped in to keep the city's coffers filled.

Many travelers end up spending a night in Antofagasta on their way to the more interesting destinations like San Pedro de Atacama, Iquique, and Arica, but a few sights here are worth a look. Around two in the afternoon the city shuts down most of the streets in the center of town, making for pleasant afternoon shopping and strolling. High above Plaza Colón is the **Torre Reloj,** the clock tower whose face is a replica of London's Big Ben. It was erected by British residents in 1910.

The historic customs house, the town's oldest building, dates from 1866. Housed inside is the **Museo Regional de Antofagasta,** which displays clothing and other bric-a-brac from the nitrate era. ⊠ *Bolívar 1888* ☎ *55/227–016* ⊕ *www.dibam.cl* ⊠ *600 pesos* ☺ *Tues.–Fri. 9–5, weekends 11–2.*

Where to Stay & Eat

$$–$$$$ ✕ **Club de Yates.** This seafood restaurant with nice views of the port caters to yachting types, which may explain why the prices are a bit higher than at other restaurants in the area. The food is quite good, especially the *ostiones a la parmesana* (oysters with Parmesan cheese). The maritime theme is taken to the extreme—the plates, curtains, tablecloths, and every decoration imaginable come in the mandatory navy blue. The service is excellent. ⊠ *Av. Balmaceda 2705* ☎ *55/263–942* ⚓ *Reservations essential* ▤ *AE, DC, MC, V.*

★ $–$$ ✕ **Restaurant Arriero.** Serving up traditional dishes from Spain's Basque country, Arriero is the place to go for delicious barbecued meats. A healthful selection of national wines supplements the menu. The restaurant is in a pleasant Pyrenees-style inn decorated with traditional cured hams hanging from the walls. The owners play jazz on the piano almost every evening. ⊠ *Condell 2644* ☎ *55/264–371* ▤ *AE, DC, MC, V.*

4

Flora & Fauna
Yes, the Atacama Desert is one of the driest places on earth. But head to the Chilean Altiplano just a few hours east of Arica and you'll find an abundance of fauna and, depending on the season, flora. Pink flamingos dot the edges of volcanic lakes like Lago Chungará on the Bolivian border, and slender brown vicuñas—treasured for their fur, the finest of the American camelids—run in small herds through the sparse grasslands. Keep an eye out for the strange *vizcacha* a rabbitlike creature. Close to the town of Putre you can luxuriate in the thermal springs of Jurasi, and, in springtime, enjoy the riotous blooms of desert flowers.

Pristine Beaches
Pristine sands line the shore near Arica and Iquique. During the summer months of January and February they are packed with vacationing South Americans. Outside of these months, you just might have the beach to yourself.

Markets & Art Fairs
Handmade jewelry and expertly tanned leather are the items to look for in the *mercados* (markets) and *ferias artesenales* (artisan fairs) of El Norte Grande. Traditional Andean clothing and textiles are available in most cities, but tend to be more authentic farther off the beaten path. Though bargaining is acceptable, it is less common than in other parts of South America.

¢ ✕ **Don Pollo.** This rotisserie restaurant prepares some of the best chicken in Chile—a good thing, because it's the only item on the menu. The thatched-roof terrace is a great place to kick back after a long day of sightseeing. ⊠ *Ossa 2594* ☎ *No phone* ⊟ *No credit cards.*

★ $$$–$$$$ 🏨 **Hotel Antofagasta.** Part of the deluxe Panamericana Hoteles chain, this high-rise on the ocean comes with all the first-class luxuries, from an elegant bar with a grand piano to a lovely kidney-shape pool. The rooms, which have ample bathrooms and plenty of closet space, are comfortably furnished, and some have ocean views. A semiprivate beach is just steps from the hotel's back door. ⊠ *Av. Balmaceda 2575* ☎ *55/228–811* 🖷 *55/268–415* ⊕ *www.hotelantofagasta.cl* ⌁ *145 rooms, 18 suites* ⚭ *Restaurant, room service, in-room safes, minibars, cable TV, Wi-Fi, pool, health club, hair salon, billiards, bar, shop, laundry service, business services, meeting rooms* ⊟ *AE, DC, MC, V* ⭗ *BP.*

$ 🏨 **Marsal Hotel.** This modern and clean hotel faces busy Calle Arturo Prat, so be sure to ask for one of the pleasant rooms in the back. All the rooms have nice touches like desks. The service here is quite friendly—the staff goes out of its way to recommend restaurants and arrange excursions. ⊠ *Arturo Prat 867* ☎ *55/268–063* 🖷 *55/221–733* ⊕ *www.marsalhotel.cl* ⌁ *18 rooms* ⚭ *Minibars, cable TV, laundry service, business services, meeting rooms; no a/c* ⊟ *AE, DC, MC, V* ⭗ *CP.*

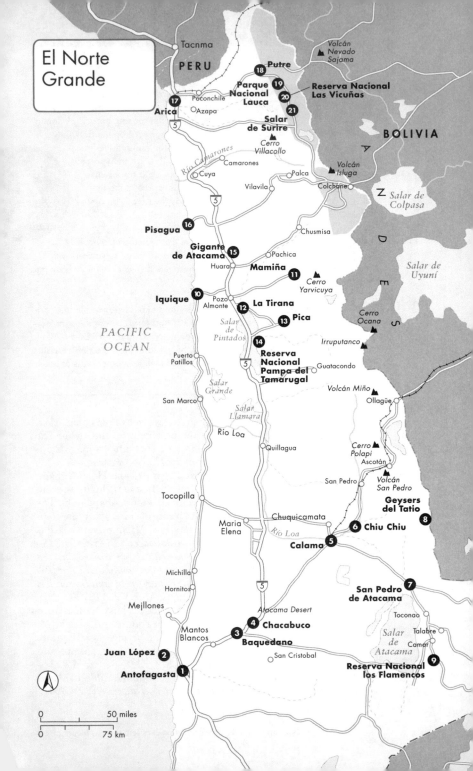

El Norte Grande

PERU

Tacnma

Volcán
Nevado
Sajama

Poconchile

18 Putre

Parque
Nacional   19
Lauca   20   Reserva Nacional
Las Vicuñas

Azapa

17
Arica

5

21

Salar
de Surire

BOLIVIA

Cerro
Villacollo

Río Camarones

Camarones

Cuya

Palca

Vilavila

Colchane

Volcán
Isluga

Salar de
Colpasa

5

Chusmisa

Salar de
Uyuní

Pisagua 16

Gigante
de Atacama 15

Pachica

Huara

Mamiña

11

Cerro
Yarvicuya

Iquique 10

Pozo
Almonte

12   La Tirana

13   Pica

Salar
de
Pintados

Cerro
Ocana

PACIFIC
OCEAN

14

Reserva
Nacional
Pampa del
Tamarugal

Irruputanco

Puerto
Patillos

5

Guatacondo

Salar
Grande

Volcán Miño

San Marco

Salar
Llamara

Ollagüe

Río Loa

Quillagua

Cerro
Polapi

Ascotán

Tocopilla

San Pedro

Volcán
San Pedro

Chuquicamata

Geysers
del Tatio

Maria
Elena

Río Loa

6   Chiu Chiu

8

Calama 5

Michilla

San Pedro
de Atacama   7

Hornitos

5

Mejllones

Atacama Desert

Toconao

Mantos
Blancos

4   Chacabuco

Talabre

Salar
de
Atacama

Camar

Juan López 2

3

Baquedano

San Cristobal

Reserva Nacional
los Flamencos   9

Antofagasta 1

0   50 miles

0   75 km

Nightlife & the Arts

Nightlife in El Norte Grande often means heading to the *schoperias,* beer stands where the almost entirely male clientele downs *schops* (draft beers) served by scantily clad waitresses. The drinking generally continues until everyone is reeling drunk. If this is your idea of fun, check out the myriad schoperias in the center of town around the Plaza Colón.

If you're not quite ready for the schoperia experience (and for many these are not the most pleasant places to spend an evening), don't worry: there are also a few bars where you can have a quiet drink. With its swinging saloon-style doors and a great waitstaff donning cowboy hats and blue jeans, the **Country Pub** (⊠ Salvador Reyes 1025 ☎ 55/371–751) is lots of fun. The music doesn't go country, however, staying instead on the modern side of pop (think lots of Cindy Lauper videos). Antofagasta's elite head to **Wally's Pub** (⊠ Antonino Toro 982 ☎ 55/223–697), an American-style grill with American-style prices.

Shopping

On the corner of Manuel A. Matta and Maipú you'll find the **Mercado Central,** a fruit and vegetable market with blue-and-yellow walls. Behind the market is the **Plaza del Mercado,** where artisans sell handmade jewelry and healing crystals, and where the occasional outdoor performance takes place.

Juan López

2 *38 km (24 mi) north of Antofagasta.*

Those turned off by the hustle and bustle of Antofagasta will likely be charmed by Juan López, a hodgepodge of pastel-color fishing shacks and a picturesque *caleta* (cove). In high season, January and February, the beaches are crowded and dirty. The rest of the year you may have the white, silken sand to yourself.

On the coast about 13 km (8 mi) south of Juan López lies **La Portada,** an offshore volcanic rock that the sea has carved into an arch. It's one of the most photographed natural sights in the country. Many local travel agencies include La Portada as part of area tours.

Where to Stay & Eat

$ ✕ **Restaurant Vitoco.** This restaurant, decorated with native textiles, serves a fixed meal of chicken or grilled fish. The food is good and the kitchen is spotless. ⊠ *Manzana 8* ☎ *55/383–071* ▭ *No credit cards.*

¢ ▦ **Hosteria Sandokan.** An airy garden complete with chirping caged birds surrounds the nicest place to stay in Juan López. Hosteria Sandokan has basic but clean rooms with shared baths. The hotel's terrace restaurant, which serves excellent seafood, affords great views of the pelicans going about their business. ⊠ *Fernando Bull s/n* ☎ *55/223–302* ➾ *6 rooms without bath* ⌂ *Restaurant; no a/c, no room phones, no room TVs* ▭ *No credit cards.*

Beaches

People come to Juan López for the beaches, and there are plenty from which to choose, both around town and in the surrounding area, where there are several larger beaches easily reached by car. The most popular beach is **Balneario Juan López,** a small strip of white sand near the center of town. It can get uncomfortably crowded in summer. If you want a bit more elbow room, head to the beaches outside town. Picturesque **Playa Acapulco** is in a small cove north of Balneario Juan López. **Playa Rinconada,** about 5 km (3 mi) south of Juan López, is lauded by locals for its warm water.

Baquedano

❸ *72 km (45 mi) northeast of Antofagasta.*

Once an important railway transfer station, Baquedano today sees only a fraction of the freight that passed through during its heyday. With the exception of an open-air railroad museum that hints at the village's past importance, there are few reasons to linger here. The **Museo Ferroviario,** in a dusty railroad yard, is a testament to the greatness of the nitrate era. Old locomotives from a century ago sit silently, waiting for the next boom. Hop aboard one of these paralyzed monsters and relive the days when they roared across the barren pampa. ☒ *South of the current depot* ☎ *No phone* ✆ *Free* ☉ *Daily 8–12:30 and 2–7.*

Chacabuco

★ **❹** *26 km (16 mi) northeast of Baquedano.*

In this region locals refer to as the *pampa salitrera* (literally "saltpeter plains"), there were some 80 nitrate plants in operation between 1890 and 1925. Many of the plants, as well as the company towns that housed their workers, still survive. A mysterious dot on the desert landscape, the ghost town of Chacabuco is a decidedly eerie place. More than 7,000 employees and their families lived here when the Oficina Chacabuco (a company mining town that was made a National Monument in 1971) was in operation between 1922 and 1944. Today you'll find tiny houses, their tin roofs flapping in the wind and their walls collapsing. You can wander through many of the abandoned buildings and take a look inside the theater, which has been restored to the way it looked when this was a boomtown.

Chacabuco did not remain closed forever. During the first years of Augusto Pinochet's military regime, it was used as a concentration camp for political dissidents. The artwork of prisoners still adorns many of the walls. Do not walk around the town's exterior, as land mines from this era are still buried here. ☒ *26 km (16 mi) northeast of Baquedano on Pan-American Hwy.* ☎ *No phone* ✆ *1,000 pesos* ☉ *Daily 7 AM–8 PM.*

en route Founded by a British company in 1926, **María Elena** is a dusty place that warrants a visit if you want to see a functioning nitrate town. It's home to the employees of the region's last two nitrate plants. The 8,000 people who live in María Elena are proud of their history—nearly every house has a picture of the town hanging inside. A tiny but informative museum on the town's main square houses many artifacts from the nitrate boom as well as a few from the pre-

Columbian era. The town is about 148 km (92 mi) north of Chacabuco.

Calama

5 *141 km (87 mi) northeast of Baquedano.*

The discovery of vast deposits of copper in the area turned Calama into the quintessential mining town, and therein lies its interest. People from the length of Chile flock to this dusty spot on the map in hopes of striking it rich. A modern-day version of the boomtowns of the 19th-century American West, Calama is rough around the edges, but it does possess a certain energy.

Founded as a *tambo,* or resting place, at the crossing of two Inca trails, Calama still serves as a stopover for people headed elsewhere. Most people traveling to San Pedro de Atacama end up spending the night here, but the town does have a few attractions of its own.

The gleaming copper roof of **Catedral San Juan Bautista** (⊠ Ramírez at Av. Granaderos), on Plaza 23 de Marzo, the city's main square, testifies to the importance of mining in this region.

The **Museo Arqueológico y Etnológico,** a natural history museum in the well-manicured Parque El Loa, depends heavily on dioramas to explain the region's pre-Columbian past. Nearby is a replica of the quaint church in neighboring Chiu Chiu. ⊠ *Parque El Loa, south of town on Av. Bernardo O'Higgins* ☎ *55/340–112* ⌦ *200 pesos* ⊙ *Tues.–Fri. 10–1 and 3–5:30, weekends 3–6.*

One of the world's largest open-pit mines, **Chuquicamata** is the lifeblood of Chile's copper industry. Heavy machinery roars in the bottom of the pit, producing 600,000 metric tons of copper yearly. Chiquicamata's immense size—4 km (2½ mi) long and 3 km (2 mi) wide—is the result of nearly a century of continuous mining. Experts say the mine will continue to yield copper for the next several decades. There is a small museum at the mine's entrance where you can get a close-up view of the machinery used to make such big holes. Tours are in Spanish, though your guide may also speak some English. Reserve in advance by phone or by e-mail. ⊠ *16 km (10 mi) north of Calama* ☎ *55/322–122* ⊕ *www. codelco.cl* ⌦ *1,000 pesos* ⊙ *Tours weekdays at 2 PM.*

Where to Stay & Eat

$–$$ ✕ **Cactus Restaurant & Bar.** An after-work crowd haunts this Mexican-theme restaurant, where a mandatory cow skull adorns one of the walls. South-of-the-border favorites like flautas, taquitos, and chimichangas dominate the menu. Many regulars crowd around the tables for the two-for-one mojitos and Cuba libres. ⊠ *Sotomayor 1901* ☎ *55/312–367* ⊟ *AE, DC, MC, V.*

$–$$ ✕ **Café Caruso.** This little slice of the Mediterranean coast in the Chilean desert is tastefully appointed with rich wood furniture and walls painted in muted copper-red tones. Caruso hits the high notes with a delicious set lunch (the roast pork is delectable). If you prefer, you can just hang out with a cup of coffee or glass of wine and check out the old photos of Calama's proud past. ☒ *Avaroa 1702* ☎ *55/ 364–872* 🖃 *No credit cards.*

$$$ 🏨 **Park Hotel Calama.** It's easy to see why international mining consultants frequent this top-notch hotel. The rooms have giant beds made up with luxurious linens, and the steaming showers feel great after a day of exploring the surrounding desert. A pool, a lovely garden, and an excellent restaurant serving international cuisine round out the hotel's attractions. ☒ *Camino Aeropuerto 1392* ☎ *55/319–900* 🖷 *55/319–901* ⊕ *www.parkplaza.cl* ⤴ *104 rooms* ☖ *Restaurant, room service, in-room safes, minibars, cable TV, tennis court, pool, health club, bar, piano, laundry service, business services, meeting rooms, airport shuttle* 🖃 *AE, DC, MC, V* ⚏ *BP.*

★ $ 🏨 **Hotel El Mirador.** This friendly bed-and-breakfast around the corner from Plaza 23 de Marzo is set in a colonial-style house built in the 19th century. Inside it's a charmer, with cheerful yellow rooms that are both clean and comfortable. A tasteful, antiques-filled salon leads to an enclosed courtyard where a Continental breakfast is served. ☒ *Sotomayor 2064* ☎☎ *55/340–329* ⊕ *www.hotelmirador.cl* ⤴ *14 rooms* ☖ *Cable TV, laundry service, Internet; no a/c, no room phones* 🖃 *AE, DC, MC, V* ⚏ *CP.*

Nightlife & the Arts

Calama is the land of the schoperia—locals say there are more schoperias than people. Come payday at the mine, these drinking halls fill up with beer-swilling workers. The schoperias near Plaza 23 de Marzo are less raucous. The **Afogata Bar** (☒ MacKenna 1977 ☎ No phone), from the Spanish word for bonfire, lives up to its name with a blazing fireplace. A twentysomething crowd packs into this cavelike setting, highlighted by mock petroglyphs on the walls. On weekends head to **Pub Anaconda** (☒ Granaderos 2663 ☎ 55/345–834), an upscale bar that attracts foreigners and locals alike. Pop and cumbia are played here at top volume, so bring your earplugs

Cine Teatro Municipal (☒ Ramírez 2034 ☎ 55/342–864) screens recent Hollywood movies. It also stages the occasional play or concert.

Shopping

Locals sell clothing and jewelry at the covered markets off the pedestrian mall of Calle Ramírez. There are also markets on Calle Vargas between Latorre and Vivar.

Chiu Chiu

❻ *33 km (20 mi) northeast of Calama.*

In contrast to the nearby, sprawling industrial center of Calama, Chiu Chiu, in a lush valley near the Río Loa, is a vision of the region's agrarian past. Inhabitants still make their living growing carrots and other vegetables in this pastoral town. Across from Chiu Chiu's main square is the **Iglesia de San Francisco.** Built in 1674, it's one of the oldest churches in the altiplano. A cactus-shingle roof tops the squat building's whitewashed adobe walls. No nails were used in its construction—rafters and beams are lashed together with leather straps. On October 4, things get lively when the 500 inhabitants congregate in the nearby central plaza to celebrate the town's patron saint, St. Francis of Asissi.

SAN PEDRO & THE ATACAMA DESERT

The most popular tourist destination in El Norte Grande (and perhaps all of Chile), San Pedro de Atacama sits in the midst of some of the most breathtaking scenery in the country—the heart of the Atacama Desert. A string of towering volcanoes, some of which are still active, stands watch to the east. To the west is La Cordillera de Sal, a mountain range composed almost entirely of salt. Here you'll find such marvels as the Valle de la Luna (Valley of the Moon) and the Valle de la Muerte (Valley of Death), part of the Reserva Nacional los Flamencos. The desolate Salar de Atacama, Chile's largest salt flat, lies to the south. The number of attractions in the Atacama area does not end there: alpine lakes, steaming geysers, colonial villages, and ancient fortresses all lie within easy reach.

The area's history goes back to pre-Columbian times, when the Atacameño people scraped a meager living from the fertile delta of the San Pedro River. By 1450 the region had been conquered by the Incas, but their reign was cut short by the arrival of the Europeans. Spanish conquistador Pedro De Valdivia, who eventually seized control of the entire country, camped here in 1540 while waiting for reinforcements. By the 19th century San Pedro had become an important trading center and was a stop for llama trains on their way from the altiplano to the Pacific coast. During the nitrate era, San Pedro was the main resting place for cattle drives from Argentina.

San Pedro de Atacama

★ ❼ *100 km (62 mi) southeast of Calama.*

With its narrow streets lined with whitewashed and mud-color adobe houses, San Pedro centers around a small Plaza de Armas teeming with artisans, tour operators, and others who make their living catering to tourists. The 1744 **Iglesia San Pedro,** to the west of the square, is one of the altiplano's largest churches. It was miraculously constructed without the use of a single nail—the builders used cactus sinews to tie the roof beams and door hinges. ⊠ *Padre Le Paige s/n* ☎ *No phone* ⊙ *Daily 8–8.*

Fodor'sChoice
★ The **Museo Arqueológico Gustavo Le Paige** exhibits an awe-inspiring collection of artifacts from the region, including fine examples of textiles and ceramics. The museum traces the history of the area from pre-Columbian times through the Spanish colonization. The most impressive exhibit is the well-preserved, fetal-positioned Atacameño mummy with her swatch of twisted black hair. Most of the items on display were gathered by the founder, Jesuit missionary Gustavo Le Paige. ⊠ *Padre Le Paige 380, at Paseo Artesenal* ☎ *55/851–002* 🎟 *2,000 pesos* ⊙ *Weekdays 9–noon and 2–6, weekends 10–noon and 2–6.*

San Pedro de Atacama & Environs

TO ANTOFAGASTA

Machuca

Volcán Apagado

Termas de Puritama

Volcán Sairecabur

Valle de la Muerte

Guatin

Volcán Licancabur

CORDILLERA DE LA SAL

Pukará de Quitor

San Pedro de Atacama

BOLIVIA

Cerro Toco

Salar de Tara

Valle de la Lune

Tulor

Toconao

Salar de Loyoques o Quisquiro

Laguna Chaxa

Volcán Aguas Calientes

Salar de Aguas Calientes

Salar de Atacama

Laguna Lejía

Socaire

Laguna Miscanti

Laguna Miñiques

Salar El Laco

ARGENTINA

Laguna Tuyajto

0   20 miles
0   30 km

need a break?

Although it sometimes seems unlikely, it does get hot in San Pedro, so stop in at **Babalu Heladeria** (⌧ Caracoles 160 ☎ No phone) to sample one of 52 flavors of ice cream. Stop at **Café Cuna** (⌧ Tocopilla 359 ☎ 55/851–999) for sweet, fresh juices and excellent specials for lunch or dinner. The dining area is in a huge courtyard with chañar trees.

Just 3 km (2 mi) north of San Pedro lies the ancient fortress of **Pukara de Quitor.** This group of stone structures at the entrance to the Valle de Catarpe was built in the 12th century to protect the Atacameños from invading Incas. It wasn't the Incas but the Spanish who were the real threat, however. Spanish conquistador Pedro de Valdivia took the fortress by force in 1540. The crumbling buildings were carefully reconstructed in 1981 by the University of Antofagasta. ⌧ *On road to Valle Catarpe* ☎ *No phone* 🎫 *1,200 pesos* ⊘ *Daily 8–8.*

The archaeological site of **Tulor,** 9 km (5½ mi) southwest of San Pedro, marks the remains of the oldest known civilization in the region. Built around 800 BC, the village of Tulor was home to the Linka Arti people, who lived in small mud huts resembling igloos. The site was uncovered only in the middle of the 20th century, when Jesuit missionary Gustavo Le Paige excavated it from a sand dune. Archaeologists hypothesize that the inhabitants left because of climatic changes and a possible sand storm. Little more about the village's history is known, and only one of the huts has been completely excavated. As one of the well-informed guides will tell you, even this hut is sinking back into the obscurity of the Atacama sand. ⊠ *9 km (5½ mi) southwest of San Pedro, then 3 km (2 mi) down the road leading to the Valle de la Luna* ☎ *No phone* ⊠ *1,500 pesos* ⊙ *Daily 8–8.*

Where to Stay & Eat

★ **$–$$**   ✕ **Café Adobe.** With a lattice-covered dining area surrounding a blazing fire and a terrace that is open to the stars, Café Adobe is San Pedro's finest eatery. The regional and international cuisine is excellent, and the animated (at times downright frenetic) waitstaff makes for a unique dining experience. At night, a white-capped chef grills meat in the center courtyard. Try the perfectly seasoned steaks, the cheesy quesadillas, or any of the pasta dishes. There's an Internet café in the rear. ⊠ *Carcoles 211* ☎ *55/851–132* ⊟ *AE, DC, MC, V.*

$–$$ ✕ **Casa Piedra.** This rustic stone structure (*piedra* means "stone") affords views of the cloudless desert skies from its central courtyard. As at most San Pedro eateries, a blazing fire keeps you company. The sea bass and shrimp are among the best choices on the menu, which includes international and local dishes. Specialty sauces spice up any dinner. ⊠ *Caracoles 225* ☎ *55/851–271* ⊟ *AE, DC, MC, V.*

★ **$$$$**   ▥ **Hotel Explora.** Is it a modern monstrosity or an expressionist showpiece? Hotel Explora, built by the same company that constructed the much-lauded Hotel Explora in Parque Nacional Torres del Paine, attracted much criticism for not fitting in with the local architecture. On the other hand, it has also won architectural prizes for its skewed lines and sleek courtyard. The hotel, which has three-, four-, and seven-day all-inclusive stays—with tours, meals, and drinks included—delivers the best service and amenities of any lodging in northern Chile. The wood-and-tile floors and wall-to-wall windows make the views from each room more enjoyable. ⊠ *Domingo Atienza s/n* ☎ *55/851–110* ⊟ *55/851–115* ⊕ *www.explora.com* ⇥ *52 rooms* ⚭ *Restaurant, fans, in-room safes, in-room hot tubs, 4 pools, massage, sauna, mountain bikes, horseback riding, bar, shop, babysitting, laundry service, Internet, meeting rooms, airport shuttle, free parking, no-smoking rooms; no a/c, no room TVs* ⊟ *AE, DC, MC, V* ⊚ *AI.*

$$$ ▥ **Lodge Andino Terrantai.** An architectural beauty with river-stone walls, **Fodor's Choice** Lodge Andino Terrantai has high-ceilinged rooms highlighted by beautiful tile floors and big beds piled with down comforters. Hand-carved ★ furnishings add a rustic feel. Throw open the huge windows to let in the morning breeze. The candlelit restaurant, perfect for a romantic dinner, serves international fare. There's also a tiny, natural-rock plunge pool in the center. The hotel is just a block away from the Plaza de Armas. ⊠ *Tocopilla 411* ☎ *55/851–140* ⊟ *55/851–037* ⊕ *www.terrantai.cl* ⇥ *21 rooms* ⚭ *Restaurant, room service, fans, pool, laundry service; no room TVs* ⊟ *AE, DC, MC, V* ⊚ *BP.*

$$ ▥ **Hotel Altiplánico.** This boutique hotel just outside the center of San Pedro has the look and feel of an altiplano pueblo. A river-stone walkway leads you from room to room, each with its own private terrace. Muted whites decorate the guest chambers, making them quite welcoming. Some rooms have private watchtowers for stargazing. ✉ *Domingo Atienza 282* ☎ *55/851–212* 📠 *55/851–238* ⊕ *www.altiplanico.cl* 🛏 *14 rooms, 12 with bath* ♨ *Restaurant, pool, massage, laundry service, Internet, travel services; no a/c, no room phones, no room TVs* ⊟ *AE, DC, MC, V* ⧀ *BP.*

$$ 🏨 **Hotel Kimal.** This adobe-walled dwelling has comfortable rooms and a cheery central courtyard dotted with islands of desert shrubbery. The rooms are pleasantly airy, with skylights and reed ceilings. The excellent restaurant serves Chilean fare. The pool is ideal for cooling off after your desert exploration. ✉ *Domingo Atienza 452* ☎ *55/851–030* 📠 *55/851–152* ⊕ *www.kimal.cl* 🛏 *11 rooms* ♨ *Restaurant, minibars, pool, shop, laundry service; no a/c, no room TVs* ⊟ *AE, DC, MC, V* ⧀ *BP.*

$ 🏨 **Hotel Tambillo.** A good budget alternative, Hotel Tambillo has simple, rather drab rooms along a long, outdoor walkway. The outdoor garden, with a thatched-roof sitting area, is a nice place to relax. There's also a good restaurant. ✉ *Gustavo Le Paige 159* ☎ *55/851–078* ⊕ *www.hoteltambillo.cl* 🛏 *15 rooms* ♨ *Restaurant; no a/c, no room phones, no room TVs* ⊟ *No credit cards.*

Nightlife & the Arts

The bohemian side of San Pedro gets going after dinner and generally ends around 1 AM. Most of the bars are on Caracoles. **Café Export** (✉ Caracoles at Toconao ☎ 55/851–547) is smaller and more intimate than the other bars in town. There's a pleasant terrace out back. **La Estaka** (✉ Caracoles 259B ☎ 55/851–201) is a hippie bar with funky decor, including a sculpted dragon hanging on one of the walls. Reggae music rules, and the international food isn't half bad either.

Sports & the Outdoors

San Pedro is an outdoors-lover's dream. There are great places for biking, hiking, and horseback riding in every direction. Extreme-sports enthusiasts can try their hand at sand-boarding on the dunes of the Valle de la Muerte. Climbers can take on the nearby volcanoes. The only trouble is the crowds. At the Valle de la Luna, for example, you'll sometimes encounter a caravan of 20 or 30 tourists scurrying toward the top of the large sand dune to watch the sunset.

Whatever your sport, keep in mind that San Pedro lies at 2,400 meters (7,900 feet). If you're not acclimated to the high altitude, you'll feel tired much sooner than you might expect. Also remember to slather on the sunscreen and drink plenty of water.

BIKING   An afternoon ride to the Valle de la Luna is unforgettable, as is a quick trip to the ruins of Tulor. You can also head to the Salar de Atacama. Bike rentals can be arranged at most hotels and tour agencies.

HIKING   There are hikes in all directions from San Pedro. Good hikes include trips through the Valle de la Muerte, as well as to the ruins of Pukara de Quitor. **Cosmo Andino Expediciones** (✉ Caracoles s/n ☎ 55/851–069) runs excellent treks with well-informed guides.

HORSEBACK RIDING San Pedro has the feeling of a Wild West town, so why not hitch up your horse and head out on an adventure? Although the sun is quite intense during the middle of the day, sunset is a perfect time to visit Pukara de Quitor or Tulor. An overnight journey to the Salar de Atacama or the Valle de La Luna is a great way to see the region at a relaxed pace. **Herradura** (⌧ Tocopilla s/n ☎ 55/851–087) provides horses and guides.

Shopping

Just about the entire village of San Pedro is an open-air market. The **Feria Artesenal,** just off the Plaza de Armas, is bursting at the seams with artisan goods. Here, you can buy high-quality knits from the altiplano, such as sweaters and other woolen items. **Galeria Cultural de Pueblos Andinos** (⌧ Caracoles s/n ☎ No phone) is an open-air market selling woolens and crafts. **Mallku** (⌧ Caracoles s/n ☎ No phone) is a pleasant store carrying traditional altiplano textiles, some up to 20 years old. **Rayo de La Luna** (⌧ Caracoles 378 ☎ 09/473–9018) sells jewelry made by local artisans.

Geysers del Tatio

8 *95 km (59 mi) north of San Pedro.*

The world's highest geothermal field, the Geysers del Tatio are a breathtaking natural phenomenon. The sight of dozens of *fumaroles,* or geysers, throwing columns of steam into the air is unforgettable. A trip to El Tatio usually begins at 4 AM, on a guided tour, when San Pedro is still cold and dark (any of the tour agencies in San Pedro can arrange this trip). After a three-hour bus trip on a relentlessly bumpy road you reach the high plateau about daybreak. The jets of steam are already shooting into the air as the sun slowly peeks over the adjacent cordillera. The rays of light illuminate the steam in a kaleidoscope of chartreuses, violets, reds, oranges, and blues. The vapor then silently falls onto the sulfur-stained crust of the geyser field. As the sun heats the cold, barren land, the force of the geysers gradually diminishes, allowing you to explore the mud pots and craters formed by the escaping steam. Be careful, though—the crust is thin in places and people have been badly burned falling into the boiling-hot water. On your way back to San Pedro, you may want to stop at the **Termas de Puritama** (⌦ 5,000 pesos) hot springs. A hot soak may be just the thing to shake off that early-morning chill.

Reserva Nacional los Flamencos

9 *10 km (6 mi) south and east of San Pedro.*

Many of the most astounding sights in El Norte Grande lie within the boundaries of the protected Reserva Nacional los Flamencos. This sprawling national reserve to the south and east of San Pedro encompasses a wide variety of geographical features, including alpine lakes, salt flats, and volcanoes. You can get information about the park at the station run by CONAF, the Chilean forestry service. *⌧ CONAF station near Laguna Chaxa ☎ No phone ⊕ www.conaf.cl ⌦ 2,000 pesos ⊙ Daily 8:30–1 and 2:30–6:30.*

★ About 10 km (6 mi) south of San Pedro you arrive at the edge of the **Salar de Atacama,** Chile's largest salt flat. The rugged crust measuring 3,000 square km (1,158 square mi) formed when salty water flowing down from the Andes evaporated in the stifling heat of the desert. Unlike other salt flats, which are chalkboard-flat surfaces of crystalline salt, the Salar de Atacama is a jumble of jagged rocks. **Laguna Chaxa,** in the middle of Salar de Atacama, is a very salty lagoon that is home to three of the world's four species of flamingos. The elegant pink-and-white birds are mirrored by the lake's glassy surface. Near Laguna Chaxa, beautiful plates of salt float on the calm surface of **Laguna Salada.**

It's possible to take a three- to five-day, four-wheel-drive excursion from San Pedro into Bolivia's massive and mysterious **Salar de Uyuni.** Beware: the accommodations—usually clapboard lodgings in small oasis towns—are rustic to say the least, but sailing along the world's largest salt flat, which is chalkboard flat, is a treat. Around the Salar de Uyuni are geysers, small Andean lagoons, and islands of cactus that sit in sharp contrast to the sea-like salt flat. The number of tour agencies in San Pedro can be a bit overwhelming: shop around, pick a company you feel comfortable with, ask questions, and make sure the company is willing to cater to your needs.

★ One of the most impressive sights in Reserva Nacional los Flamencos is the 4,350-meter-high (14,270-foot-high) **Laguna Miscanti,** an awe-inspiring blue lake that merits a few hours of rest and repose. **Laguna Miñeques,** a smaller lake adjacent to Laguna Miscanti, is spectacular. Here you will find vicuña and huge flocks of flamingos attracted by the warm waters.

★ Very few places in the world can compare to the **Valle de la Luna** (✉ 14 km [9 mi] west of San Pedro). This surreal landscape of barren ridges, soaring cliffs, and pale valleys could be from a canvas by Salvador Dalí. Originally a small corner of a vast inland sea, the valley rose up with the Andes. The water slowly drained away, leaving deposits of salt and gypsum that were folded by shifting of the Earth's crust and then worn away by wind and rain. It's best to visit Valle de la Luna in the late afternoon to take advantage of the incredible sunsets visible from atop the immense sand dune. Not far from the Valle de la Luna are the reddish rocks of the **Valle de la Muerte.** Jesuit missionary Gustavo Le Paige, who in the 1950s was the first archaeologist to explore this desolate area, discovered many human skeletons. These bones are from the indigenous Atacameño people, who lived here before the arrival of the Spanish. He hypothesized that the sick and the elderly may have come to this place to die.

IQUIQUE AREA

The waterside town of Iquique itself is rather dreary, but the area holds many sights that merit a visit. Wander down to the port and watch the fishing boats come in; while you're there, imagine the key battle of the War of the Pacific being waged offshore in 1879, or Sir Francis Drake and his gang of brigands arriving to sack the town in 1577. (You can find out more about this history at the Museo Naval.)

A stone's throw from Iquique, nitrate ghost towns like Humberstone sit in eternal silence. Farther inland you encounter the charming hot spring oases of Pica and Mamiña and the enigmatic Gigante de Atacama, the world's largest geoglyph.

Iquique

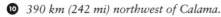 *390 km (242 mi) northwest of Calama.*

Iquique is the capital of Chile's northernmost region, but it wasn't always so important. For hundreds of years it was a tiny fishing community. After the arrival of the Spanish the village grew slowly, eventually becoming a shipping port. The population, however, never totaled more than 100. It was not until the great nitrate boom of the 19th century that Iquique became a major port. Many of those who grew rich on nitrate moved to the city and built opulent mansions, almost all of which still stand today. Many of the old mansions are badly in need of repair, however, giving the city a rather worn-down feeling. The boom went bust, and those who remained turned again to the sea to make a living. Today Iquique is the world's largest exporter of fish meal.

At the base of a coastal mountain range, Iquique is blessed with year-round good weather. This may explain why it's popular with vacationing Chilean families, who come for the long stretches of white beaches as well as the *zona franca,* or duty-free zone. Life in the city revolves around the **Plaza Prat,** where children ride bicycles along the sidewalks and adults chat on nearly every park bench. The 1877 **Torre Reloj,** with its gleaming white clock tower and Moorish arches, stands in the center of the plaza.

Leading out from Plaza Prat is **Calle Baquedano,** a pedestrian mall with wooden sidewalks. This is a great place for an afternoon stroll past some of Iquique's salitrera-era mansions, or a leisurely cappuccino in one of the many sidewalk cafés. An antique trolley runs the length of the mall.

Unlike most cities, Iquique does not have a cathedral on the main plaza. Here instead you'll find the sumptuous **Teatro Municipal,** built in 1890 as an opera house. The lovely statues on the Corinthian-columned facade represent the four seasons. If you're lucky you can catch a play or musical performance here. ⊠ *Plaza Prat* ☎ *57/411–292* 🎫 *Tickets 1,500–5,000 pesos* ☾ *Daily 8–7.*

★ For a tantalizing view into the opulence of the nitrate era, visit the Georgian-style **Palacio Astoreca.** This palace, built in 1903, include such highlights as the likeness of Dionysus, the Greek god of revelry; a giant billiards table; and a beautiful skylight over the central hall. An art and natural history museum on the upper level houses modern works by Chilean artists and such artifacts as pottery and textiles. ⊠ *Av. Bernardo O'Higgins 350* ☎ *57/425–600* 🎫 *Free* ☾ *Tues.–Fri. 10–1 and 4–7:30, Sat. 10–1:30, Sun. 11–2.*

Along the historic Calle Baquedano is the **Museo Regional,** a natural history museum of the region. It showcases pre-Columbian artifacts such as deformed skulls and arrowheads, as well as an eclectic collection from the region's nitrate heyday. ⊠ *Baquedano 951* ☎ *57/411–214* ⊠ *Free* ⊙ *Mon.–Sat. 9:30–1 and 3–6:30.*

Inside **Museo Naval,** in the old customs house, are displays about the Battle of Iquique in 1879, when the Chileans claimed Iquique from their neighbors to the north. Here you can get a glimpse at what the soldiers wore during the war and at the antiquated English arms used by Chilean soldiers. ⊠ *Sotomayor and Anibal Pinto* ☎ *57/402–121* ⊠ *Free* ⊙ *Mon.–Sat. 9–1 and 4–6, Sun. 10–1.*

Where to Stay & Eat

$–$$$

Fodor's Choice

★

✕ **Casino Español.** This venerable gentleman's club on Plaza Prat has been transformed into a palatial Spanish restaurant, with beautiful Moorish architecture that calls to mind the Alhambra in Granada. The service is good, though rather fussy, and the food is extravagant in the traditional Andalucian style. The paella *Valenciana* is quite good, as is the variety of sauces that accompany the freshly caught fish. Don't miss the *salsa Carolina,* a rich combination of garlic and fresh herbs. Try a side of *pure catalan* (mashed potatoes with bacon, onion, and grilled peppers). ⊠ *Plaza Prat 584* ☎ *57/423–284* ⚉ *Reservations essential* ▤ *AE, DC, MC, V.*

$–$$$ ✕ **Nautico Cavancha.** Located away from the center of the city, this seafood restaurant treats you to views of Playa Cavancha. It's very stylish, right down to the cloth napkins (a rarity in El Norte Grande). Try the sole stuffed with shrimp in a lemon-cognac sauce, the shrimp in a pepper-whiskey sauce, or the paella for two, served by friendly bow-tied waiters. ⊠ *Los Rieles 110* ☎ *57/432–896* ⚉ *Reservations essential* ▤ *DC, MC, V.*

★ $$ ✕ **Taberna Barracuda.** An immensely popular bar and grill, Taberna Barracuda serves everything from tapas to rib-eye steak. The wine list is good, making this an ideal place to sample some of Chile's labels. A general sense of joviality and merriment here hearkens to the decadent days of the nitrate boom. Antiques ranging from brass instruments to time-stained photos decorate the labyrinthine, salitrera-era house. ⊠ *Gorostiaga 601* ☎ *57/427–969* ⚉ *Reservations essential* ▤ *AE, DC, MC, V* ⊙ *Closed Sun. mid-June–early Sept.*

¢–$$ ✕ **Boulevard.** Excellent seafood is served in a variety of ways at this intimate, candlelit restaurant. The cuisine is an interesting mélange of French and international recipes—try hake served in a creamy sauce or the *tagine,* a savory Moroccan stew. There's live music on weekends. ⊠ *Baquedano 790* ☎ *57/413–695* ⚉ *Reservations essential* ▤ *MC, V.*

¢–$ ✕ **Restaurant Protectora.** A soaring molded ceiling and a huge chandelier overlook this elegant contemporary restaurant next to the Teatro Municipal. The international menu includes such succulent items as lamb cooked in mint sauce and merluza con salsa margarita. The service, though a bit doting, is top-notch. ⊠ *Thompson 207* ☎ *57/421–923* ▤ *AE, DC, MC, V.*

¢–$ ✕ **Split Café.** This café, on the lower floor of the Croatian Community Center on Plaza Prat, pays tribute to the thousands of immigrant workers from the Dalmatian coast who came to work the mines in the late 19th and early 20th century. Teas, coffees, and seven-flavor cake—a Croatian specialty—highlight the menu. There are also tasty sandwiches. Replicas of the coats of arms from Croatia, Slovenia, and Dalmatia sit proudly above the counter. ⊠ *Plaza Prat 310* ☎ *57/316–541* ⊟ *No credit cards.*

$$ ▦ **Sunfish.** On Playa Cavancha, Sunfish has very large, very modern rooms, many with views of the beach. Though the hotel lacks character, the royal-blue exterior will certainly catch your eye. There's a small rooftop pool, but it's surrounded by a tacky artificial-grass terrace. ⊠ *Amunategui 1990* ☎ *57/419–000* 🖷 *57/419–001* ⊕ *www.sunfish.cl* ⇩ *45 rooms* ⚭ *Restaurant, in-room safes, minibars, cable TV, pool, bar, laundry service, business services, meeting rooms* ⊟ *AE, DC, MC, V* ⑩ *BP.*

$$ ▦ **Terrado Suites.** A skyscraper at the southern end of Playa Cavancha, the Terrado is Iquique's most upscale hotel. A marble entryway leads you down to the comfortable lounge and restaurant area. Overstuffed sofas, Andean prints, and hardwood accents decorate the large suites, which have private balconies. The pool and underground sauna are a delight after a day in the desert. ⊠ *Los Rieles 126* ☎ *57/437–878* 🖷 *57/437–755* ⊕ *www.terrado.cl* ⇩ *91 suites* ⚭ *2 restaurants, room service, in-room data ports, in-room safes, minibars, cable TV, 2 pools, gym, hot tub, massage, sauna, bar, babysitting, laundry service, business services, meeting rooms, airport shuttle, car rental; no a/c in some rooms* ⊟ *AE, DC, MC, V* ⑩ *BP.*

$ ▦ **Hotel Arturo Prat.** The only thing this luxury hotel in the heart of Iquique's historic district lacks is access to the ocean. To make up for this, it has a very pleasant rooftop pool area decorated with white umbrellas and navy-blue sails. The rooms are all comfortable and modern, though some look out onto the parking lot. Ask for one of the newer rooms, which are several notches above the rooms in the older section of the hotel. The Arturo faces the central square, and the restaurant, which serves good but somewhat uninspired fare, sits right on Plaza Prat. ⊠ *Anibal Pinto 695* ☎ *57/427–000* 🖷 *57/429–088* ⊕ *www.hotelarturoprat.cl* ⇩ *83 rooms, 9 suites* ⚭ *Restaurant, room service, in-room safes, minibars, cable TV, pool, exercise equipment, sauna, billiards, bar, laundry service, business services, meeting rooms; no a/c in some rooms* ⊟ *AE, DC, MC, V* ⑩ *BP.*

★ $ ▦ **Hotel Atenas.** Housed in a venerable nitrate-era mansion on the beach, Hotel Atenas is truly a taste of the city's history. Antiques and wood furnishings fill most of the rooms. There are more modern rooms in the back, but these are not nearly as charming. The honeymoon suite has a giant tub where you can imagine the nitrate barons bathing in champagne. There's also a pleasant pool in the garden. ⊠ *Los Rieles 738* ☎ *57/431–100* 🖷 *57/431–100* ⇩ *40 rooms, 3 suites* ⚭ *Restaurant, room service, fans, in-room safes, minibars, cable TV, pool, hot tub, laundry service, Internet; no a/c* ⊟ *AE, DC, MC, V* ⑩ *CP.*

Nightlife & the Arts

Iquique really gets going after dark. Young vacationers stay out all night and then spend the next day lazing around on the beach.

BARS   Bars, most of which feature folk and jazz performances, get crowded around midnight. **Bar Sovia** (⊠ Tarapaca 173 ☎ 57/517–015), perhaps the North's only microbrewery, is a relaxed place for a frothy brew. For sunset drinks and excellent empanadas head to **Choza Bambu** (⊠ Arturo Prat s/n, Playa Cavancha ☎ 57/519–002). One of the city's most popular bars is **Van Gogh** (⊠ Ramirez 805 ☎ 57/319–847), with impressive murals of the Dutch master's work filling the walls and live music on weekends.

DANCE CLUBS At about 2 AM the beachfront discos start filling with a young, energetic crowd. Check out the dance clubs along Playa Brava and just south of town. **Kamikaze** (⊠ Bajo Molle, Km 7 ☎ No phone), part of a popular chain of discos, is jam-packed on weekends with young people dancing to salsa music. **Timber House** (⊠ Bolívar 553 ☎ 57/422–538) has a disco upstairs and an Old West–style saloon downstairs.

Beaches

Just south of the city center on Avenida Balmaceda is **Playa Cavancha,** a long stretch of white, sandy beach that's great for families. You can stroll along the boardwalk and touch the llamas and alpacas at the petting zoo. There's also a walk-through aquarium housing a group of *yacares,* small crocodiles that inhabit the rivers of Bolivia, Argentina, and Uruguay. Because it's so close to town, the beach is often crowded. If you crave solitude, follow the coast south of Playa Cavancha for about 3 km (2 mi) on Avenida Balmaceda to reach **Playa Brava,** a pretty beach that's often deserted. The currents here are quite strong, so swimming is not recommended. **Playa Blanca,** 13 km (8 mi) south of the city center on Avenida Balmaceda, is a sandy spot that you can often have all to yourself.

Shopping

Many Chileans come to Iquique with one thing on their minds—shopping. About 3 km (2 mi) north of the city center is the **Zona Franca**— known to locals as the Zofri—the only duty-free zone in the country's northern tip. This big, unattractive mall is stocked with cheap cigarettes, alcohol, and electronic goods. Remember that large purchases, such as personal computers, are taxable upon leaving the country. ⊠ *Av. Salitrera Victoria* ☎ *57/515–100* ⊕ *www.iquique.cl* ⊙ *Mon. 4–9, Tues.–Fri. 10–9, Sat. 10–2 and 5–9.*

en route One of the last nitrate plants in the region, **Humberstone** closed in 1960 after operating for nearly 200 years. Now it's a ghost town where ancient machines creak and groan in the wind. You can wander through the central square and along the streets of the company town, where almost all of the original buildings survive. The theater, with its rows of empty seats, is particularly eerie. ⊠ *45 km (28 mi) east of Iquique on the Pan-American Hwy.* ☎ *57/324– 642* ⊑ *1,000 pesos* ⊙ *Daily 9–5.*

Mamiña

⓫ *125 km (78 mi) east of Iquique.*

An oasis cut from the brown desert, the tiny village of Mamiña has hundreds of hot springs. Renowned throughout Chile for their curative powers, these springs draw people from around the region. Every hotel in the town has the thermal water pumped into its rooms, so you can enjoy a soak in the privacy of your own *tina,* or bathtub. The valley also has several public pools fed by thermal springs. The town itself is perched on a rocky cliff above the terraced green valley where locals grow alfalfa.

If you'd like to wallow in the mud, try a soothing mud bath in a secluded setting at **Barros El Chino** (⌗ Near the Mamiña bottler ☎ No phone 🎫 1,000 pesos). After your bath you can bake in the sun on one of the drying racks. Leap into one of the plunge pools to wash the stinky brown stuff off your skin. **Baños Ipla** (⌗ Near the Mamiña bottler ☎ No phone 🎫 1,000 pesos) lets you soak in large public tinas. A fountain near the Baños Ipla called the **Vertiente del Radium,** with slightly radioactive spring water, is said to cure every type of eye malady.

The simple, charming **Iglesia Nuestra Señora del Rosario** in the central plaza dates to 1632. The church's twin bell towers are unique in Andean Chile. A garish electric sign mars the front of the building.

A two-hour hike from Mamiña will bring you to **Pukara del Cerro Inca,** a great place to watch the sunset. Here you'll find interesting petroglyphs left by the Incas and an excellent view of the valley. To find it, head west on the trail a block west of the bottler.

Where to Stay & Eat

★ **$$** ✕⌗ **Hotel los Cardenales.** Two highlights of this hotel are its lovely garden and its pool, which is covered by an awning to protect you from the fierce rays of the sun. All rooms have private tubs that fill with spring water—most tubs are on the small side, but the one in the honeymoon suite is big enough for two. At the pleasant restaurant terrace you can enjoy views of the valley. A fixed menu includes a soup or cazuela, and grilled meat. ⌗ *Camino Barros El Chino s/n* ☎ *57/517-000, 09/553–0934* 🛏 *10 rooms, 1 suite* ⚂ *Restaurant, pool; no a/c, no room phones, no TV in some rooms* ⊟ *No credit cards* ⦿| *AI.*

$ ✕⌗ **Hotel Refugio del Salitre.** You reach the Hotel Refugio del Salitre, on the hill in the northern part of the valley, by a series of flower-lined walkways. Although the rooms here have seen better days (the carpets are a bit threadbare), the tubs are big and the king-size towels are luxurious. The views of the alfalfa-laden valley from your bath are also quite nice. Your stay includes all meals, including dinners of grilled fish or meat that are served in the wood-floor restaurant. ⌗ *Av. El Tambo 1* ☎ *57/751–203* 🖷 *57/751–203* ⊕ *www.refugiodelsalitre.cl* 🛏 *40 rooms* ⚂ *Restaurant, pool, bar; no a/c, no room phones* ⊟ *No credit cards* ⦿| *AI.*

La Tirana

⑫ *72 km (45 mi) southeast of Iquique.*

Bushlike tamarugo trees and a hodgepodge of adobe and concrete houses make up this town in the forbidding Atacama Desert. La Tirana, a village of 250 people, is usually a quiet place. The sleepy town awakens each year from July 12 to 18, when 80,000 people in colorful masks and costumes converge here, filling the square with riotous dancing. The object of all this merriment is one of Chile's most important religious icons, the Virgen del Carmen (also known as the Virgen de la Tirana). The statue is found inside the rather run-down **Santuario de la Tirana,** on the main plaza.

The **Museo del Salitre,** on Tirana's main plaza, is a family-run museum that houses artifacts from the nitrate era, including ice-cream makers and a film projector. There are also other odd items, such as a stuffed condor. ⊠ *Opposite Santuario de la Tirana on the main plaza* 🕾 *No phone* 🖃 *Free* ⊙ *Mon.–Sat. 8:30–1 and 3–8.*

Pica

⑬ *42 km (26 mi) southeast of La Tirana, 114 km (71 mi) southeast of Iquique.*

From a distance, Pica appears to be a mirage. This oasis cut from the gray and brown sand of the Atacama Desert is known for its fruit—the limes used to make pisco sours are grown here. A hint of citrus hangs in the air, because the town's chief pleasure is sitting in the Plaza de Armas and sipping a *jugo natural,* fresh-squeezed juice of almost any fruit imaginable, including mangoes, oranges, pears, and grapes. You can buy a bag of any of those from a vendor for the bus trip back to Iquique.

Most people come to Pica not for the town itself but for the incredible hot springs at **Cocha Resbaladero.** Tropical green foliage surrounds this lagoonlike pool cut out of the rock, and nearby caves beckon to be explored. It is quite a walk, about 2 km (1 mi) north of town, but well worth the effort. You can also drive here. ⊠ *Gen. Ibañez* 🕾 *No phone* 🖃 *1,000 pesos* ⊙ *Daily 8–8.*

Where to Stay & Eat

$ ✕ **Los Naranjos.** This is a popular place among the locals because of the inexpensive lunch specials, usually featuring a meat or fish dish. It's nothing fancy, little more than long tables in a low-slung dining room. ⊠ *Barboza 200, at Esmeralda* 🕾 *57/741–318* 🖃 *No credit cards.*

¢–$ ✕ **San Andres.** Locals speak highly of this family-style restaurant at the Hotel San Andres serving a fixed lunch. The northern Chilean fare, which usually includes a cazuela and chicken or beef entrée, is delicious. ⊠ *Av. Balmaceda 197* 🕾 *57/741–319* 🖃 *No credit cards.*

★ ¢ 🏨 **Hotel los Emelios.** Birds chirping in the garden and a refreshing plunge pool make this comfortable, homey, family-owned B&B your best bet in Pica. The small rooms have nice linens on the somewhat lumpy beds. Breakfast is served on the terrace in the back, where you'll enjoy bread with marmalade and tea or coffee. ⊠ *L. Cochrane 213* 🕾 *57/741–126* 🖷 *57/741–126* 🛌 *7 rooms* 🖆 *Restaurant, pool, laundry service; no a/c, no room phones* 🖃 *No credit cards* 🍽 *CP.*

Reserva Nacional Pampa del Tamarugal

⑭ *96 km (60 mi) southeast of Iquique.*

The tamarugo tree is an anomaly in the almost lifeless desert. These bushlike plants survive where most would wither because they are especially

ETCHED IN STONE

FOR WHATEVER REASON THEY WERE CONSTRUCTED, *the geoglyphs of El Norte Grande are a beautiful testament to the sophistication and aesthetic sensibility of the indigenous cultures that created them more than 1,000 years ago. Huge pictures drawn on the sides of mountains with stone, these geoglyphs are sometimes so big that they can be seen properly only from the air.*

The motive behind the creation of these immense geoglyphs still remains a mystery, but some invaluable clues can be found from the region's history. Nearly 8,000 years ago, the Chinchorro people lived in coastal villages around Arica and Iquique, dedicating themselves primarily to fishing. Later, two of the world's great ancient civilizations, the Tijuanacota and the Inca, were building pyramids high in the Andes. The two cultures flourished, exchanging both ideas and material goods. This intercultural exchange left a lasting impression on the region, and long trade routes were established through the mountains down to the coast. On the sides of some of these mountains along the trade routes the ancients constructed huge figures representing animals, people, and geometric designs.

Various theories exist to explain the purpose of these figures. They may have been built, for example, as offerings to the gods; many of the geoglyphs do seem to depict high priests within the cultures. Or perhaps they were used as giant road signs for navigation along the trade routes—as landmarks in the vast wasteland of the Atacama Desert.

In addition to the Gigante de Atacama, the world's largest geoglyph at 86 meters (282 feet) high, there are geoglyphs throughout El Norte Grande. The rock art at Cerros Pintados comprises the largest collection of geoglyphs in South America.

More than 400 images adorn this hill in Reserva Nacional Pampa del Tamarugal. Figures representing birds, animals, people, and geometric patterns appear to dance along the hill. Farther north, the Tiliviche geoglyphs decorate a hill sitting not far from the modern-day marvel of the Pan-American Highway. These geoglyphs, most likely constructed between AD 1,000 and 1,400, during the Inca reign, depict a large caravan of llamas. All of these llamas are headed in the same direction— toward the sea—a testament, perhaps, to the geoglyphs' navigational use during the age when llama trains brought silver down to the coast in exchange for fish.

— Gregory Benchwick

adapted to the saline soil of the Atacama. Over time they developed extensive root systems that search for water deep beneath the almost impregnable surface. Reserva Nacional Pampa del Tamarugal has dense groves of tamarugos, which were almost wiped out during the nitrate era when they were felled for firewood. At the entrance to this reserve is a CONAF station. ⊠ *24 km (15 mi) south of Pozo Almonte on Pan-American Hwy.* ☎ *57/751–055* 🖀 *Free.*

Fodor's Choice ★   The amazing **Cerros Pintados** (Painted Hills), within the Reserva Nacional Pampa del Tamarugal, are well worth a detour. Here you'll find the largest group of geoglyphs in the world. These figures, which scientists believe ancient peoples used to help them navigate the desert, date from AD 500 to 1400. They are also enormous—some of the figures are decipherable only from the air. Drawings of men wearing ponchos were probably intended to point out the route to the coast to the llama caravans coming from the Andes. More than 400 figures of birds, animals, and geometric patterns adorn this 4-km (2½-mi) stretch of desert. There is a CONAF kiosk on a dirt road 2 km (1 mi) west of the Pan-American Highway. ⊠ *45 km (28 mi) south of Pozo Almonte* ☎ *57/751–055* 🖀 *1,000 pesos* ⊗ *Daily 9:30–6.*

Gigante de Atacama

🔟 *84 km (52 mi) northeast of Iquique.*

The world's largest geoglyph, the Gigante de Atacama, measures an incredible 86 meters (282 feet). The Atacama Giant, thought to represent a chief of an indigenous people or perhaps created in honor of Pachamama (Mother Earth), looks a bit like a space alien. It is adorned with a walking staff, a cat mask, and a feathered headdress that resembles rays of light bursting from his head. The exact age of the figure is not known, but it certainly hails from before the arrival of the Spanish, perhaps around AD 900. The geoglyph, which is on a hill, is best viewed just before dusk, when the long shadows make the outline clearer. ⊠ *Cerro Unita, 13 km (8 mi) west of the turnoff to Chusmiza* ☎ *No phone* 🖀 *Free.*

Pisagua

🔟 *132 km (82 mi) north of Iquique.*

Pisagua, one of the region's most prominent ports during the nitrate era, at one time sustained a population of more than 8,000 people. Many of the mansions built at that time are still standing, although others have fallen into disrepair. During Pinochet's regime Pisagua was the site of a concentration camp, now used as a hotel. Today, there are only around 100 inhabitants in Pisagua—fisherfolk and guano harvesters primarily. The echoes of the Pinochet massacres and the bygone era of decadence still permeate the oceanfront village, giving it a haunted air.

The town's most famous sight, the **Torre Reloj,** built in 1887 from Oregon pine, stands on a hill overlooking the city, its blue and white paint peeling in the hot coastal sun. This clock tower, which was constructed by Alexandre Gustave Eiffel, is an excellent place to catch views of the town and its port.

The **Teatro Municipal** testifies to the wealth the town once possessed. Built in 1892 at the height of the nitrate boom, the once-lavish theater has grand touches, such as the painted cherubs dancing across the ceiling. The theater sits right on the edge of the sea, and waves crash against its walls, throwing eerie echoes through the empty, forgotten auditorium. Get the key to the theater and a very informative free tour from a woman in the tourist kiosk opposite the theater.

Where to Eat

★ ¢–$ ✕ **Restaurant La Picada de Don Gato.** This terrace restaurant, recommended by locals, serves simple but exquisite seafood. The shellfish dishes, especially the ostiones a la parmesana, are particularly delicious. Don't let the plastic chairs, which look like they belong in a bus station, distract you from the great food. ⊠ *Arturo Prat 127* ☎ *57/731–511* ▤ *No credit cards.*

ARICA AREA

At the very tip of Chile, Arica is the country's northernmost city. This pleasant community on the rocky coast once belonged to Peru. In 1880, during the War of the Pacific, Chilean soldiers stormed El Morro, a fortress set high atop a cliff in Arica. Three years later, much of the land north of Antofagasta that was once part of Peru and Bolivia belonged to Chile. Though the Arica of today is fervently Chilean, you can still see the Peruvian influence in the streets and market stalls of the city. Indigenous women still sell their goods and produce in the town's colorful markets.

Inland from Arica, the Valle Azapa cuts its way up into the mountains, a strip of green in a land of brown. Here, the excellent Museo Arqueológico de San Miguel de Azapa contains the world's oldest mummies. They were left behind by the Chinchorro people who inhabited Chile's northern coast during pre-Hispanic times. Ascending farther up the mountains toward the Bolivian border you pass through the pleasant indigenous communities of Socoroma and Putre. These towns, though far from picturesque, are good resting points if you're planning to make the journey to the 4,000-meter-high (13,120-foot-high) Parque Nacional Lauca and the neighboring Reserva Nacional Las Vicuñas. The beautiful Lago Chungará, part of Parque Nacional Lauca, lies near Bolivia, creating what is probably the country's most impressive border crossing.

Arica

🔟 *301 km (187 mi) north of Iquique.*

Arica boasts that it is "the land of the eternal spring," but its temperate climate and beaches are not the only reason to visit this small city. On Plaza Colón is the **Iglesia de San Marcos,** constructed entirely from iron. Alexandre Gustave Eiffel, designer of that famed eponymous Parisian tower, had the individual pieces cast in France before erecting them in Arica in 1876. Across from Parque General Baquedano, the **Aduana de Arica,** the city's former customs house, is one of Eiffel's creations. It currently contains the town's cultural center, where you can find ex-

CloseUp

EIFFEL'S OTHER TOWER

AN EXTREMELY AMBITIOUS MAN, *Alexandre Gustave Eiffel designed buildings and bridges all over the world, so when Peruvian President José Balta invited him to construct a new church, Eiffel leaped at the chance. (Before the War of the Pacific, much of what is northern Chile was part of Peru or Bolivia.) The structure was originally intended for the coastal town of Ancón, but when a great earthquake felled Arica's cathedral in 1868, the parts that had already been fabricated in Eiffel's Parisian workshop were rerouted.*

Eiffel took advantage of new building materials—for example, iron—in constructing the Iglesia de San Marcos, a job that took five years. The plates and girders were cast in an iron foundry in Paris and transported to Arica, where they were carefully assembled. The only part of this marvel of Gothic-style architecture that is wood is the massive front door. Eiffel's structure withstood a harrowing test just

two years after completion, when an earthquake and storm surge pummeled the town. In 2001, it stood tall again when parts of Arica succumbed to yet another temblor.

In addition to the church and customs house in Arica, Eiffel also designed a clock tower in the Chilean town of Pisagua. In neighboring Peru you can see the cathedral—made of more traditional stone—that Eiffel designed for the town of Tacna in 1870 and the bridge he designed for Arequipa in 1882. All this happened before his famed Parisian tower was built in 1889.

— Brian Kluepfel

hibits about northern Chile, old photographs of Arica, and works by local painters and sculptors. ☎ *No phone* ✉ *Free* ⊙ *Daily 10–6.*

North of Parque General Baquedano is the defunct **Estacíon Ferrocarril,** the train station for the Arica–La Paz railroad. Though trains no longer run across the mountains to the Bolivian capital, there are round-trip journeys four times a week to the antiplano. The 1913 building houses a small museum with a locomotive and other remnants of the railroad. ☎ *No phone* ✉ *Free* ⊙ *Daily 10–6.*

Hanging over the town, the fortress of **El Morro de Arica** is impossible to ignore. This former Peruvian stronghold was the site of one of the key battles in the War of the Pacific. The fortress now houses the **Museo de las Armas,** which commemorates that battle. As you listen to the proud drumroll of military marches you can wander among the uniforms and weapons of past wars. ✉ *Reached by footpath from Calle Colón* ☎ *58/ 254–091* ⊕ *www.infoarica.cl/morro* ✉ *500 pesos* ⊙ *Daily 8–8.*

Fodor's Choice ★ A must for any visitor to El Norte Grande is the **Museo Arqueológico de San Miguel de Azapa.** In an 18th-century olive-oil refinery, this museum houses an impressive collection of artifacts from the cultures of the Chinchorros (a coastal people) and Tijuanacotas (a group that lived in the antiplano). Of particular interest are the Chinchorro mummies, the oldest in the world, dating to 6,000 BC. The incredibly well-preserved mummies are arranged in the fetal position, which was traditional in this area. To look into their wrinkled, expressive faces is to get a glimpse at a history that spans more than 8,000 years. The tour ends at an olive press that functioned until 1956, a reminder of the still-thriving industry in the surrounding valley. The museum is a short drive from Arica. You can also make the 20-minute journey by colectivo from Patricio Lynch for about 600 pesos. ⊠ *12 km (7 mi) south of town on the route to Putre* ☎ *58/205–555* ⊕ *www.uta.cl-masmas* ☜ *1,000 pesos* ⊘ *Jan. and Feb., daily 10–7; Mar.–Dec., daily 10–6.*

Where to Stay & Eat

$–$$ ✕ **Maracuyá.** Wicker furniture enhances the cool South Pacific atmosphere of this pleasant, open-air restaurant that literally sits above the water on stilts. The international menu focuses on fish. The seafood, lauded by locals, is always fresh; ask the waiter what the fishing boats brought in that day. House specialties include octopus grilled in lemon and olive oil, salmon in an orange sauce, and sea bass in the pineapple-flavored *salsa amazonia*. ⊠ *Av. Comandante San Martin 0321* ☎ *58/227–600* ▤ *AE, DC, MC, V.*

¢–$ ✕ **Casino La Bomba.** In the old fire station, Casino La Bomba is more of a cultural curiosity than a culinary one. That said, the traditional food isn't bad, and the service is friendly. You'll have to maneuver around the parked fire trucks to get inside, where you are greeted by wagon-wheel furnishings and a menu heavy on grilled fish and roasted chicken. ⊠ *Colon 357* ☎ *58/231–312* ▤ *No credit cards.*

¢–$ ✕ **Club de Deportes Náuticos.** This old yacht club with views of the port serves succulent seafood dishes in a relaxed terrace setting. One of the friendliest restaurants in town, this former men's club is a great place to meet the old salts of the area. Bring your fish stories. ⊠ *Thompson 1* ☎ *58/234–396* ▤ *MC, V.*

¢–$ ✕ **El Rey de Mariscos.** Locals call this the best seafood restaurant in town, for good reason. The corvina con salsa margarita is a winner, as is the *paila marina*, a hearty soup stocked with all manner of fish. The dreary fluorescent lights and faux-wood paneling give this restaurant on the second story of a concrete-block building an undeserved down-at-the-heels air. ⊠ *Colon 565* ☎ *58/229–232* ▤ *AE, MC, V.*

★ **$$–$$$** ✕▥ **Hotel Arica.** The finest hotel in Arica, this first-class establishment sits on the ocean between Playa El Laucho and Playa Las Liseras. The rooms, which are elegant if a bit dated, have views of the ocean and great showers with plenty of hot water. The courteous and attentive staff can help set up sightseeing tours or book a table at a local eatery. The hotel's tony restaurant ($–$$), which takes advantage of the ocean views, serves fresh seafood cooked to order, including crab, octopus, and tuna. Don't pass up the conger eel chowder. ⊠ *Av. Comandante San Martin 599* ☎ *58/254–540* 🖷 *58/231–133* ⊕ *www.panamericanahoteles. cl* ⇱ *108 rooms, 13 suites, 20 cabanas* ⧉ *Restaurant, room service, in-room safes, minibars, cable TV, tennis court, pool, gym, bar, shop, children's programs (ages 2–10, summer only), laundry service, business*

---

services, convention center, meeting rooms, car rental ⊟ *AE, DC, MC, V* ⭕ *BP.*

$–$$ 🏨 **Hotel El Paso.** This modern lodging in the center of Arica surrounds a landscaped courtyard and a pool with a swim-up bar. Though not on the ocean, it's a short walk from any of the city's beaches. The superior rooms, with newer furnishings and larger televisions, are a far better value than the standard ones. ⊠ *Av. General Velasquez* ☎ *58/230–808* 📠 *58/231–965* ⊕ *www.hotelelpaso.cl* 🛏 *71 rooms, 10 suites* ⭗ *Restaurant, in-room safes, minibars, cable TV, tennis court, pool, bar, laundry service, Internet, free parking; no a/c* ⊟ *AE, DC, MC, V* ⭕ *BP.*

$ 🏨 **Hotel Plaza Colon.** This small hotel is a good option if you don't mind being so far from the beach. You are close to the downtown attractions, including the historic Iglesia de San Marcos. The pink-wall rooms are small but clean. ⊠ *San Marcos 261* ☎ *58/254–424* 📠 *58/231–244* 📧 *hotel_plaza_colon@entelchile.net* 🛏 *39 rooms* ⭗ *Restaurant, room service, minibars, cable TV, babysitting, laundry service, free parking; no a/c* ⊟ *AE, DC, MC, V* ⭕ *CP.*

$ 🏨 **Hotel Saint Gregory.** Although it's quite a hike from Arica's city center, this pleasant oceanfront hotel is great for weary travelers who simply want to relax on the beach. Some of the rooms and common areas have dated decor, but the hotel is still a good value. Many rooms have their own hot tubs. ⊠ *Av. Comandante San Martin 1020* ☎ *58/257–697* 📠 *58/233–320* ⊕ *www.hotelsaintgregory.cl* 🛏 *28 rooms, 8 suites* ⭗ *Restaurant, some kitchenettes, cable TV, indoor-outdoor pool, exercise equipment, massage, billiards, bar, dance club, Internet, airport shuttle, free parking* ⊟ *AE, DC, MC, V* ⭕ *CP.*

Nightlife & the Arts

You can join the locals for a beer at one of the cafés lining the pedestrian mall of 21 de Mayo. These low-key establishments, many with outdoor seating, are a great place to spend an afternoon watching the passing crowds. An oddity in Arica is the attire of the servers in various tranquil cafés and tea salons: women serve coffee and tea dressed in lingerie. You might just want to check out the uniform of your server before you sit down.

In the evening you won't have trouble finding the city's many watering holes. For a more refined setting, try the lively, funky **Barrabas** (⊠ 18 de Septiembre 520 ☎ 58/230–928), a bar and adjoining disco that attracts Arica's younger set. **Discoteca SoHo** (⊠ Buenos Aires 209 ☎ 58/ 215–892), near Playa Chinchorro, livens things up weekends with the sounds of pop and cumbia. The beachfront **Puesta del Sol** (⊠ Raul Pey 2492 ☎ 58/216–150) plays '80s tunes and appeals to a slightly older crowd. Weekends you can enjoy live music on the pleasant terrace.

Beaches

Part of the reason people flock to Arica is the beaches. The surf can be quite rough in some spots, so look for—and heed—signs that say NO APTA PARA BAÑARSE (no swimming). South of El Morro, **Playa El Laucho** is the closest to the city, and thus the most crowded. It's also a bit rocky at the bottom. South of Playa El Laucho you'll find **Playa Brava,** with a pontoon that keeps the kids occupied. At the somewhat secluded white-sand **Playa Chinchorro,** 2 km (1 mi) north of the city, you can rent Jet Skis in high season.

Shopping

Calle 21 de Mayo is a good place for window-shopping. **Calle Bolognesi,** just off Calle 21 de Mayo, is crowded with artisan stalls selling handmade goods. The length of **Calle Chacabuco,** four blocks north of Calle 21 de Mayo, is closed to traffic on Sunday for a market featuring everything from soccer jerseys to bootleg CDs.

The **Feria Internacional** on Calle Máximo Lira sells everything from bowler hats (worn by Aymara women) to blankets to batteries. The Terminal Pesquero next door offers an interesting view of fishing, El Norte Grande's predominant industry. Located outside the city in the Azapa Valley, the **Poblado Artesenal** (⊠ Hualles ☎ 58/222–683) is an artisan cooperative designed to resemble an altiplano community. This is a good place to pick up traditionally styled ceramics and leather.

Putre

18 *145 km (90 mi) east of Arica.*

In a valley protected by two snowcapped mountains, Putre can be described only as *tranquilo*—tranquil. As tourism has yet to take root in this Andean village, it's still possible to witness traditional Aymara culture, such as women wearing traditional hats and shawls. On an ancient Inca trail later used by the Spanish to transport gold from Bolivia, Putre is still a stop along the road for people heading elsewhere, such as to Parque Nacional Lauca and Reserva Nacional Las Vicuñas. Worth a visit is the lovely **Iglesia de Putre,** on the northeast corner of the main plaza. The church was built in 1670 but had to be reconstructed in 1871 after an earthquake destroyed the interior.

Where to Stay & Eat

¢ ✕ **Pub Kuchu Marka.** The funky, eclectic Pub Kuchu Marka is a nice place to pass an evening playing a game of *cacho* (a popular local dice game) or sipping a *mate de coca* (medicinal tea made with leaves from the coca plant). Grab a cold beer and plan your excursion for the next day. The pub serves local specialty dishes such as cazuela and, on certain days, llama steaks. ⊠ *Baquedano* ☎ *No phone* ☰ *No credit cards.*

$$ ✕⊡ **Hotel Las Vicuñas.** This row of older buildings, originally used as a miners' camp, is the best lodging in town. The rooms are clean and basic and have space heaters, which are essential because it gets chilly in the Andes. With Andean textiles serving as tablecloths, the restaurant (¢) serves typical fare for the region: expect a fixed menu with cazuela followed by a meat dish. Breakfast and your choice of lunch or dinner are included. ⊠ *Baquedano* ☎ *58/228–564* ✎ *ukg@entelchile.net* ⟷ *112 rooms* ⌂ *Restaurant, Ping-Pong, bar; no a/c, no room phones, no room TVs* ☰ *No credit cards* ¶⊙¶ *MAP.*

$ ⊡ **Casa Barbarita.** Comfy flannel sheets and heaters keep you warm on chilly nights at this friendly B&B, and the baths have steaming hot showers. You can get the scoop on the area from the owner, naturalist Barbara Knapton, and you can prepare your own food in the kitchen.

⌦ *Baquedano 294* ☎ *9/282–6195* ⊕ *www.birdingaltoandino.com*
⌦ *2 rooms* ⚭ *Kitchen, library, Internet; no a/c, no room phones, no
room TVs* ▭ *No credit cards* ⑩ *BP.*

Parque Nacional Lauca

★ ⑲   *47 km (29 mi) southeast of Putre.*

On a plateau more than 4,000 meters (13,120 feet) above sea level, the
magnificent Parque Nacional Lauca shelters flora and fauna found in
few other places in the world. Cacti, grasses, and a brilliant emerald-
green moss called *llareta* dot the landscape. Playful vizcacha—rabbitlike rodents with long tails—laze in the sun, and llamas, graceful vicuñas,
and alpacas make their home here as well. About 10 km (6 mi) into the
park you come upon a CONAF station with informative brochures. ⌦ *Off
Ruta 11* ☎ *58/250–570 in Arica* ⊕ *www.conaf.cl* ✉ *Free.*

Within the park, off Ruta 11, is the altiplano village of **Parinacota,** one
of the most beautiful in all of Chile. In the center of the village sits the
whitewashed **Iglesia Parinacota,** dating from 1789. Inside are murals depicting sinners and saints and a mysterious "walking table," which
parishioners have chained to the wall for fear that it will steal away in
the night. An interesting Aymara cultural commentary can be found in
the Stations of the Cross, which depict Christ's tormenters not as Roman
soldiers, but as Spanish conquistadors. Opposite the church you'll find
crafts stalls run by Aymara women in the colorful shawls and bowler
hats worn by many altiplano women. Only 18 people live in the village,
but many more make a pilgrimage here for annual festivals such as the
Fiesta de las Cruces, held on May 3, and the Fiesta de la Virgen de la
Canderlaria, a three-day romp that begins on February 2.

About 8 km (5 mi) east of Piranacota are the beautiful **Lagunas Cotacotani,** which means "land of many lakes" in the Quechua language. This
string of ponds—surrounded by a desolate moonscape formed by volcanic eruptions—attracts many species of bird, including Andean geese.

Lago Chungará sits on the Bolivian border at an amazing altitude of 4,600
meters (15,100 feet) above sea level. Volcán Parinacota, at 6,330 meters (20,889 feet), casts its shadow onto the lake's glassy surface. Hundreds of flamingos make their home here. There is a CONAF-run office
at Lago Chungará on the highway just before the lake. ⌦ *From Ruta
11, turn north on Ruta A-123* ☎ *No phone* ⊕ *www.conaf.cl* ✉ *Free*
☉ *CONAF office daily 8–8.*

Reserva Nacional Las Vicuñas

★ ⑳   *121 km (75 mi) southeast of Putre.*

Although it attracts far fewer visitors than neighboring Parque Nacional
Lauca, Reserva Nacional Las Vicuñas contains some incredible sights—
salt flats, high plains, and alpine lakes. And you can enjoy the vistas without running into buses full of tourists. The reserve, which stretches some
100 km (62 mi), has a huge herd of graceful vicuñas. Although quite similar to their larger cousins, llamas and alpacas, vicuñas have not been

domesticated. Their incredibly soft wool, among the most prized in the world, led to so much hunting that these creatures were threatened with extinction. Today it is illegal to kill a vicuña. Getting to this reserve, unfortunately, is quite a challenge. There is no public transportation, and the roads are passable only in four-wheel-drive vehicles. Many people choose to take a tour out of Arica. ⊠ *From Ruta 11, take Ruta A-21 south to park headquarters* ☎ *58/250–570 in Arica* ⊕ *www.conaf.cl.*

Salar de Surire

㉑ *126 km (78 mi) southeast of Putre.*

After passing through the high plains, where you'll spot vicuña, alpaca, and the occasional desert fox, you'll catch your first glimpse of the sparkling Salar de Surire. Seen from a distance, the salt flat appears to be a giant white lake. Unlike its southern neighbor, the Salar de Atacama, it's completely flat. Three of the world's six species of flamingos (Andean, Chilean, and James') live in the nearby lakes. ⊠ *South from Reserva Nacional Las Vicuñas on Ruta A-235* ☎ *58/250–570* ⊕ *www. conaf.cl* ⊠ *Free.*

EL NORTE GRANDE ESSENTIALS

Transportation

BY AIR

Since there are no international airports in El Norte Grande, you can't fly here directly from the United States, Canada, Europe, or Australia. You must fly into Santiago and transfer to a flight headed to Antofagasta, Calama, Iquique, or Arica. Avant and Lan fly from Santiago to El Norte Grande. Round-trip flights can run up to 300,000 pesos or more.

You can also get here from other South American countries. Lan runs direct flights between El Norte Grande and neighboring Bolivia and Peru.

Since the cities in El Norte Grande are far apart, taking planes between them can save you both time and a lot of hassle. Avant, Sky Airline, and Lan offer service between the major cities. Prices range from 28,000 to 105,000 pesos.

🛪 **Airlines Avant** ☎ 55/452-050 in Antofagasta ⊕ www.avant.cl. **Lan** ☎ 55/265-151 in Antofagasta, 55/313-927 in Calama, 57/427-600 in Iquique, 58/251-641 in Arica ⊕ www.lan.com. **Sky Airline** ☎ 600/600-2828 ⊕ www.skyairline.com.

🛪 **Airports Antofagasta** ☎ 55/269-077. **Arica** ☎ 58/211-116.

Calama ☎ 55/312-348. **Iquique** ☎ 57/407-000.

BY BUS

Getting around by bus in El Norte Grande is easy. There is a terminal in every major city with frequent departures to the other cities as well as smaller towns in the area. Keep in mind that there may be no bus service to the smaller villages or the more remote national parks.

No bus company has a monopoly, so there are often several bus stations in each city. Because many companies may be running buses along the same route, shop around for the best price. The fare for a 300-km (186-mi) trip usually runs around 8,000 pesos. For longer trips find a bus that has a *salon semi-cama,* with seats that recline halfway; the extra comfort will make all the difference.

BY CAR

A car is definitely the best way to see El Norte Grande. If you want to get far off the beaten path, there are few options. You can get everywhere in this chapter by public transport, however, with some patience.

Driving in the cities can be a little hectic, but once you get on the highway it is usually smooth sailing. The roads of the north are generally well maintained. The farther from major population centers you travel—such as the remote national parks like Parque Nacional Lauca and Reserva Nacional Las Vicuñas—the worse the roads become. Destinations like these require a four-wheel-drive vehicle. Ruta 5, more familiarly known as the Pan-American Highway, bisects all of northern Chile. Ruta 1, Chile's answer to California's Highway 101, is a beautiful coastal highway running between Antofagasta and Iquique. Calama is reached by Ruta 25.

You can rent cars in Antofagasta, Calama, Iquique, and Arica at both the airport and downtown. Most hotels will also help you arrange a rental. Avis, Budget, and Hertz have offices in most major cities in northern Chile. The best deals are probably in Iquique. However, cars rented here cannot be taken out of the Iquique area.

🚗 **Rental Agencies Avis** ✉ Av. Balmaceda 2556, Antofagasta ☎ 55/319-797 ✉ Latorre 1498, Calama ☎ 55/319-797 ✉ Manuel Rodriguez 734, Iquique ☎ 57/472-392 ⊕ www.avis.com.

Budget ✉ Av. Pedro Aguirre Cerda 13, Antofagasta ☎ 55/214-445 ✉ Hotel Arica, Av. Comandante San Martín 599, Arica ☎ 58/258-911 ✉ Parque Industrial Apia Sitio 1-C, Calama ☎ 55/361-072 ✉ Bulnes 542, Iquique ☎ 57/416-322 ⊕ www.budget.cl.

Hertz ✉ Av. Balmaceda 2492, Antofagasta ☎ 55/269-043 ✉ Granaderos 1416, Calama ☎ 55/341-380 ✉ Anibal Pinto 1303, Iquique ☎ 57/510-136 ✉ Hotel El Paso, Baquedano 999, Arica ☎ 58/231-487 ⊕ www.hertz.cl.

BY TAXI

Taxis are the most efficient way to get around any city in El Norte Chico. They're easy to hail on the streets, but late at night you might want to ask someone at a hotel or restaurant to call one for you. Taxis often function as *colectivos,* meaning they will pick up anybody going in the same direction. The driver will adjust the price accordingly. Almost no taxis have meters, but many have the price posted on the windshield. Make sure you establish the price before getting inside. Prices range from 700 pesos to 2,800 pesos, depending on the distance traveled and whether the taxi is a colectivo. Prices rise an average of 20% at night. Taxi drivers often will rent out their services for the day for a flat fee.

Contacts and Resources

INTERNET, MAIL & SHIPPING

Mailing letters and packages from El Norte Grande is a formidable task. Although most cities have a post office, you often are faced with long lines that move at a snail's pace. Your best bet is to ask your hotel to post a letter for you. But don't expect your letter to reach its destination quickly. Mail headed out of the country can often take weeks. If you need quicker service, DHL has offices in Antofagasta, Arica, Calama, and Iquique.

🖪 **Post Offices Antofagasta** ✉ Washington 2613. **Arica** ✉ Arturo Prat 305. **Calama** ✉ Mackenna at Granaderos. **Iquique** ✉ Bolívar 485.

🖪 **Shipping Services DHL** ✉ Arturo Prat 260, Antofagasta ☎ 55/260-209 ✉ Colón 351, Arica ☎ 58/256-753 ✉ Sotomayor 1952, Calama ☎ 55/340-570 ✉ Anibel Pinto 695, Iquique ☎ 57/472-820.

TOURS

Tours can be arranged in the major cities and a number of the smaller towns. It's a good idea to shop around to make sure that you're getting the best itinerary and the best price.

In Antofagasta, Desertica Expediciones arranges trips into the interior, including excursions to Parque Nacional Pan de Azucar in El Norte Chico.

There are myriad tour agencies in San Pedro de Atacama. Cosmo Andino Expediciones offers excellent tours with well-informed guides to the Salar de Uyuni and other destinations. Herradura runs horseback tours.

In Arica and Iquique, a well-respected agency called Geotour arranges trips to Parque Nacional Lauca, the Salar de Surire, and the Reserva Nacional Las Vicuñas. Most Arica-based companies can arrange a one-day altiplano tour for about 15,000 pesos. One company near Plaza Colon, Raices Andinas, has two- and three-day options, which allow for a more expansive visit. The tour includes a stop at a Hari Krishna ashram in the Azapa Valley for a delicious vegetarian lunch.

In Putre, Birding Alto Andino has an Alaskan naturalist who leads birding expeditions.

🖪 **Tour Operators Birding Alto Andino** ✉ Baquedano, Putre ☎ 9/ 282-6195 ⊕ www.birdingaltoandino.com. **Cosmo Andino Expediciones** ✉ Caracoles s/n, San Pedro de Atacama ☎ 55/851-069. **Desertica Expediciones** ✉ La Torre 2732, Antofagasta ☎ 55/386-877 ⊕ www.desertica.cl. **Geotour** ✉ Bolognesi 421, Arica ☎ 58/253-927 ✉ Baquedano 982, Iquique ☎ 57/428-984 ⊕ www.geotour.cl. **Herradura** ✉ Tocopilla s/n, San Pedro de Atacama ☎ 55/851-087. **Raices Andinas** ✉ Sotomayor 195, Arica ☎ 58/233-305 ⊕ www.raicesandinas.com.

VISITOR INFORMATION

Most major cities in El Norte Grande have an office of Sernatur, Chile's tourism agency (www.sernatur.cl). Here you'll find helpful information about the region, including maps and brochures. Some staff members speak English.

🖪 **Sernatur Antofagasta** ✉ Maipú 240 ☎ 55/264-044. **Arica** ✉ San Marcos 101 ☎ 58/252-054. **Calama** ✉ Latorre at Vicuña ☎ 55/364-176. **Iquique** ✉ Anibal Pinto 436 ☎ 57/312-238. **San Pedro de Atacama** ✉ Toconao at Gustavo Le Paige ☎ 55/851-420.

The Central Valley

5

Updated by
Brian Kluepfel

A QUIET NOBILITY is maintained by the people of the Central Valley. Perhaps it is because they have had to work so hard to cultivate the arid region, irrigating their farmland with the runoff from distant Andean snow. Perhaps it's because their tradition of industriousness has paid off—the region produces wine to rival that of any nation. Though it has ties to other great wine regions, the area has a personality all its own. If Bordeaux has its châteaux, the Central Valley has its haciendas. Here the traditional hacienda—the main structure on a farm—has become more than an economic and agricultural center; it is a manifestation of a family's honor. Some of these grand manor houses have been preserved as museums, and one of them is a luxury hotel.

The Central Valley is also home to the *huaso,* a cousin of the Argentine gaucho and a distant relation of the American cowboy. Chilean rodeo began here, and you're likely to see horses being ridden in the countryside and sometimes even in the area's major cities.

As you head south, or east into the mountains, the relatively dry foliage gives way to pine forests and more verdant pastures. Follow any of various valleys into the high country, and you'll encounter gorgeous mountain scenery, patches of which are protected in nature reserves, and one corner of which holds one of the country's best ski areas: Termas de Chillán.

Exploring the Central Valley

Bordered on the east by the volcanic cones of the Andes and on the west by smaller mountain ranges running along the Pacific coast, the Central Valley is a straight shot down the Pan-American Highway. The landscape in between is unpredictably hilly. It's about a six-hour drive from Santiago south to Concepción, although most people choose to stop somewhere along the way.

About the Restaurants

Even the most informal meal in the Central Valley is likely to revolve around an excellent local wine. Lunch in Santa Cruz may be accompanied by a cabernet from Viña Santa Laura, and dinner in Curicó might mean a merlot from Viña San Pedro. Knowing a handful of wine-related words will doubtless come in handy. *Vino* is the Spanish word for wine; red is *tinto* (never *rojo*) and white is *blanco. Degustación* and *cata* both refer to a formal wine tasting.

Cuisine in the Central Valley is not unlike what you'll find in other parts of the country. Though much of the region is ranching country, seafood forms an integral part of many menus, even in the mountain resorts. Although most restaurants in the region serve uninspired food, enough of them stand apart from the crowd to provide some memorable dining experiences. Note that many restaurants don't open for dinner until 8 or so.

About the Hotels

Each sizable town in this region has one or two respectable hotels, usually near the central square. But with the notable exception of Hacienda

CloseUp
CENTRAL VALLEY FESTIVALS & SEASONAL EVENTS

The Fiesta de la Vendimia, the annual harvest festival, is celebrated with particular zest in Santa Cruz and Curicó. The four-day fiesta, which takes place the first weekend in March, includes grape-stomping contests and the selection of a grape queen, whose weight is measured out in grapes on a massive scale. In the religious festival called the Fiesta de San Francisco, held October 4 in the small town of Huerta de Maule, 38 km (24 mi)

southwest of Talca, more than 200 huasos gather from all over Chile for a day of horseback events, including races around the central square.

Los Lingues outside Rancagua, the lodgings in the Central Valley can't match those you'll find in Santiago. It may be an unfair comparison, however, as the smaller hotels here often have a charm all their own.

WHAT IT COSTS In pesos (in thousands)					
	$$$$	$$$	$$	$	¢
RESTAURANTS	over 11	8–11	5–8	3–5	under 3
HOTELS	over 105	75–105	45–75	15–45	under 15

Restaurant prices are for a main course at dinner. Hotel prices are for a double room in high season, excluding tax.

When to Go
There is no real high season in the Central Valley except in the Termas de Chillán, where snow attracts skiers between June and September. The activities here shift to hiking and horseback riding from December to April. Most people head to the Central Valley for its wineries. Grapes are picked in February and March, which is the best time to visit a vineyard, since you can see everything from crushing to bottling.

THE WINE COUNTRY

Within the vast Región del Valle Central are the four subregions that you'll most commonly find on a bottle of Chilean wine: Valle del Maipo (south of Santiago), Valle del Rapel (west of Rancagua), Valle de Curicó (around Curicó), and Valle del Maule (south of Talca). These four subregions are further subdivided, but save for moments of inspired snobbery these aren't found on labels. An exception is the Valle del Rapel, which is divided into the Valle del Cachapoal and the Valle de Colchagua.

5

If you can afford it, spend at least one night at Hacienda Los Lingues. The restored ranch near **Rancagua** gives you a sense of what life was like for the aristocrats who lived here centuries ago. Otherwise head to **Santa Cruz,** where you can explore another perfectly preserved hacienda outside town at the Museo San José del Carmen de El Huique. There are plenty of vineyards around Santa Cruz, in the Valle de Colchagua. Then head south through **Curicó,** to the lovely city of **Talca,** from which you can visit the wineries of Domaine Oriental and Balduzzi, the rodeo at San Clemente, and the nearby mountains. **Chillán** has markets selling handicrafts from all over the country. Drive east to **Termas de Chillán,** which has hot springs, skiing in winter, hiking in summer, and amazing mountain scenery year-round. Finish up in **Concepción,** the region's biggest city, which has a couple of nice museums, fine dining, and regular flights to Santiago.

The Pan-American Highway bisects the Central Valley, passing through most of the wine-growing areas. Just south of Santiago is the Valle del Rapel, where you'll find some of the area's most prestigious wineries. After exploring the valley's vineyards, you can head into the mountains and relax in the hot springs at the Termas de Cauquenes.

Don't overlook the wineries along the banks of the Río Maule—the Valle de Curicó and the Valle del Maule. Also here are the pleasant city of Talca and such wonderful protected areas as the Reserva Nacional Radal Siete Tazas.

Rancagua

❶ *87 km (54 mi) south of Santiago.*

The Rancagua region was first settled by the indigenous Picunche people and then by the Incas. A hanging bridge built over the Río Cachapoal by the Incas was later used by Spanish colonists led by José Antonio Manso de Velasco. He founded Villa Santa Cruz de Triana, later renamed Rancagua, here in 1745.

In 1814, the hills around the city were the site of a battle in the War of Independence known as the *Desastre de Rancagua* (Disaster of Rancagua). Chilean independence fighters, including Bernardo O'Higgins, held off the powerful Spanish army for two days before being captured. In the resulting blaze, much of the town was destroyed.

Today's Racagüinos spend their evenings in the city's central square, the **Plaza de los Héroes.** This plot of land, the site of a bloody battle, is marked with a statue of a valiant O'Higgins on horseback. A block north of the plaza along Calle Estado is **Iglesia de la Merced,** a church that has been declared a national monument. It was in this bell tower that O'Higgins waited in vain for reinforcements during the battle for independence. The twin spires, in a somber neoclassical style, are a fitting memorial.

The Central Valley

0   50 miles
0   75 km

PACIFIC OCEAN

ARGENTINA

Valparaíso
San Antonio
Santiago
Talagante
Melipilla
Paine
Graneros
Sewell
Rancagua 1
Coya
Termas de Cauquenes
Peumo
Reserva Nacional Río los Cipreses
Pichilemu
San Fernando
Cerro Sosneado
Bucamlemu
Santa Cruz 2
Chimbarongo
Llico
Vichuquén 4
Hualañé
Iloca
Curicó 3
Las Leñas
Molina
Reserva Nacional Radal Siete Tazas
Gualleco
Peteroa
Constitución
Río Maule
Talca 5
San Clemente
Descabezado Grande
San Javier 6
7 **Colbún**
Reserva Nacional Altos del Lircay
Villa Allegre
Chanco
Longaví
Río Chico
Linares
Cauquenes
Parral
Cobquecura
Nevado Longaví
Quirihue
San Carlos
Coelemu
8 **Chillán**
Tomé
Pinto
Chillán
Talcahuano
Butnes
10 **Concepción**
Recinto
9 **Termas de Chillán**
San Pedro
Pemuco
Las Ovejas
Isla Santa María
Cabrero
Lota
Río Bío Bío
Yungay
Arauco
Parque Nacional Nahuelbula
La Laja
Parque Nacional Laguna del Laja 11
Curanilahue
Nacimiento
Quilleco
Antuco
Lebú
Los Angeles
Cañete
Munchen
Copahue
Angol
Copahue
Puren
Termas de Pemehue
Contulmo
Collipulli

5

Rowdy Rodeos
Ride high in the saddle between September and April, because San Clemente, a town 16 km (10 mi) southeast of Talca, hosts the best rodeo in the region. Besides riding and roping, you'll find food, dances, and beauty-queen competitions. Beyond San Clemente there are important *medialunas* (corrals) in Talca, Pelarco, Curicó, Molina, Pencahue, Los Niches, and Linares.

Sublime Skiing
A skier's paradise is how many downhill enthusiasts describe the country's varied topography. Termas de Chillán offers the best of both worlds—more than two dozen exhilarating ski lifts and the option of soaking in the neighboring hot springs afterward to relieve those tired muscles.

Scenic Train Rides
Chugging along in one of the continent's last passenger trains may be slow, but the scenery can't be beat. You wind through some of the country's most varied terrain. As you go you can stop for some shopping at the small villages or cruising along the coastal sand dunes.

The three rooms of the **Museo Regional de Rancagua** re-create a typical 18th-century home, complete with period furniture and religious artifacts. A small collection of 19th-century weaponry is the type that would have been used in the momentous Battle of Rancagua. Dioramas re-create this dramatic moment in the country's quest for independence. The whitewashed colonial building is a few blocks south of Plaza de los Héroes. ✉ *Estado 685, at Ibieta* ☎ *72/230–976* ⊕ *www.museorancagua.cl* ✉ *600 pesos, includes Casa de Pilar de Esquina* ⊗ *Tues.–Fri. 10–6, weekends 9–1.*

Casa del Pilar de la Esquina, across the street from the Museo Regional de Rancagua, belonged to Fernando Errázuriz Aldunate, who helped to draft the country's constitution. In addition to displays on the area's history, including the daily lives of its indigenous cultures, there are often modern-art exhibits on the first floor. ✉ *Estado 682, at Ibieta* ☎ *72/221–524* ✉ *500 pesos* ⊗ *Tues.–Sun. 10–5.*

Numerous trails lead through thick forests of cypress trees at **Reserva Nacional Río los Cipreses,** a 15,000-acre national reserve 54 km (33 mi) east of Rancagua. Occasionally you'll reach a clearing where you'll be treated to great views of the mountains above. CONAF, the national parks service, has an office here with informative displays and maps. Just south of the park is the spot where a plane carrying Uruguayan university students crashed in 1972. The story of the group, part of which survived three months in a harsh winter by resorting to cannibalism, was told in the book and film *Alive.* ✉ *Carretera del Cobre* ☎ *72/297–505* ⊕ *www.conaf.cl* ✉ *1,700 pesos* ⊗ *Dec.–Mar., daily 8:30–8; Apr.–Nov., daily 8:30–6.*

On the southern banks of the Río Cachapoal about 31 km (19 mi) east of Rancagua, the **Termas de Cauquenes** spout mineral-rich water that

CloseUp

THROUGH THE GRAPEVINE

FANS OF CHILEAN WINES *owe a debt to missionaries who arrived here in the 16th century. Spanish priests, who needed wine to celebrate the Catholic Mass, cultivated the country's first vines in the Maule Valley. Their initial efforts demarcated the modern boundaries of Chile's wine-producing region, from Copiapó in the north to Concepción in the south.*

Fast-forward three centuries to Santiago's Quinta Normal, today called the University of Chile, where Claudio Gay imported more than 60 varieties of French grapes. He found that varietals such as cabernet sauvignon, malbec, and carmenère thrived in the rich soil of the Central Valley. The country's near-perfect growing climate didn't hurt, either.

While other countries suffered from phylloxera, a deadly insect that destroyed many European vineyards in the 19th century and California vineyards in the

20th century, Chile avoided it altogether. Isolation, in this case, was a good thing. To this day pesticides are rarely used in the country's vineyards.

As the 20th century progressed, Chilean wineries did not keep pace with the rest of the world. But with the introduction of more modern methods in the 1990s, the country soon garnered the notice of wine enthusiasts. Investment from abroad made Chilean wines a tasty and affordable option. By the early 21st century, Chile was exporting more than $600 million worth of wine to more than 90 countries.

— Brian Kluepfel

has been revered for its medicinal properties since colonial days. The Spanish discovered the 48°C (118°F) springs in the late 1500s, and basic visitor facilities have existed since the 1700s. José de San Martín, who masterminded the defeat of Spanish forces in Chile, is said to have relaxed here before beginning his campaign. Naturalist Charles Darwin, who visited in 1834, wrote that the springs were situated in "a quiet, solitary spot, with a good deal of wild beauty." The current bathhouse, which resembles a church, was built in 1867. It holds about two dozen rooms with small marble tubs that are filled with spring water for 20-minute baths. There's a hotel here, and its guests have exclusive access to a naturally heated swimming pool outside that is considerably cooler. To reach the springs, take Ruta 32 to Coya and then head south. ✉ *Carretera del Cobre* ☎ 72/899–010 💰 *4,500 pesos* ⊙ *Daily 8–6:30.*

Mina El Teniente, in the mountains north of Termas de Cauquenes, 60 km (37 mi) northeast of Rancagua, is the world's largest subterranean copper mine. The mine can be visited on guided tours arranged by Hacienda Los Lingues (☎ 2/235–2458 ⊕ www.loslingues.cl) and the Rancagua tour operator **VTS** (☎ 72/210–290 ⊕ www.vts.cl).

Where to Stay & Eat

$$$$
Fodor'sChoice
★
✕⌂ **Hacienda Los Lingues.** One of Chile's best-preserved colonial haciendas, this estate southeast of Rancagua has remained in the same family for four centuries. Staying here is a bit like traveling back in time: 17th- and 18th-century adobe buildings hold spacious rooms furnished with brass beds and heated by woodstoves. The hacienda is part of a 20,000-acre working ranch with extraordinary horses and miles of trails through the foothills. Manicured gardens, timeless porticos, and plush living rooms provide idyllic spots for relaxation. Four-course Continental dinners, served in the garden or sumptuous dining room, make use of fine china, crystal, and silverware and are complemented by the definitive Chilean wine list. ⊠ *Panamericana Sur Km 124, San Fernando* ☎ *2/235–5466* 🖷 *2/235–7604* ⊕ *www. loslingues.com* ⤶ *17 rooms* ⌂ *Restaurant, room service, in-room safes, tennis court, pool, fishing, mountain bikes, horseback riding, bar, recreation room, shop, laundry service, travel services; no a/c, no room TVs* ▤ *AE, DC, MC, V.*

$$
✕⌂ **Hotel Termas de Cauquenes.** The main attractions of this hotel are the mineral baths, the thermal swimming pool, and one of the region's best restaurants, serving Continental and Chilean dishes. Despite its great location overlooking the Río Cachapoal, the hotel doesn't have much of a view. Only the restaurant and a few rooms in the *pabellón del río* (river building) afford glimpses of the boulder-strewn river. Dating from the 1960s, the pabellón's rooms are smallish and slightly spartan. Rooms in the older *patio central* building are spacious but lack views. Everything is timeworn, and the decor is uninspired. ⊠ *Carretera del Cobre* ☎ *72/899–010* 🖷 *72/899–009* ⊕ *www.termasdecauquenes.cl* ⤶ *38 rooms, 12 suites* ⌂ *Restaurant, room service, some minibars, pool, massage, bar, recreation room, playground, laundry service; no a/c* ▤ *AE, DC, MC, V* �| BP, FAP, MAP.*

Horseback Riding

A working ranch with more than 200 horses, **Hacienda Los Lingues** (☎ 02/235–5446) offers mountain rides on world-class steeds. The rides, which cost $25 per hour (about 14,000 pesos), take you past flora like the *lingue* (a tree from which the ranch's name was derived) and the *quillay,* a plant whose dried leaves are used for making medicinal teas. Farther from the ranch you might spot owls high in the trees.

Santa Cruz

❷ *104 km (64 mi) southwest of Rancagua.*

Reminiscent of many small towns in the grape-growing regions of Spain, Santa Cruz has a central square surrounded by a mix of modern and traditional architecture, a few streets lined with shops, and vineyards radiating out in all directions. In the center of the palm-lined **Plaza de Armas** is a colonial-style bell tower with a carillon that chimes every 15 minutes; inside the tower you'll find the town's tourist office. Facing the central square is the fortresslike **Iglesia Parroquial**, an imposing white stucco structure built in 1817.

★ The attractive **Museo de Colchagua,** built in colonial style at the end of the 20th century, focuses on the history of the region. It's the largest private natural history collection in the country, and second only in size to Santiago's Museo Nacional de Historia Natural. Exhibits include pre-Columbian mummies; extinct insects set in amber that must be viewed through special lenses; the world's largest collection of silver work by the indigenous Mapuche; and the only known original copy of Chile's proclamation of independence. A few early vehicles and wine-making implements surround the building. The museum is the creation of Santa Cruz native Carlos Cardoén, who has made millions from the global arms trade. The placards are only in Spanish, but a video provides some information in English about the museum's collection. ⊠ *Av. Errázuriz 145* ☎ *72/821–050* ⊕ *www.museocolchagua.cl* ⊠ *3,000 pesos* ☉ *Tues.–Sun. 10–6.*

★ **Museo San José del Carmen de El Huique,** a 2,600-acre country estate, is one of Chile's most important national monuments. Built in 1756, the hacienda belonged to the Errázuriz family until the government turned it into a museum in 1975. The rooms are preserved exactly as they were when Federico Errázuriz Echaurren, president of Chile from 1896 to 1901, lived here. Sumptuous suites contain collections of opal glass, lead crystal, bone china, and antique furniture as well as photographs and family portraits evoking aristocratic life in Chile a century ago. Today's tour guides know a lot about the estate, as many are descendants of the hundreds of people who worked for the Errázuriz family. A highlight of a tour of the grounds is the 1852 chapel, which has Venetian blown-glass balustrades ringing the altar and the choir loft. Sunday-morning Mass is held here at 11:30. Call ahead to arrange for an English-speaking guide. ⊠ *16 km (10 mi) north of Santa Cruz; follow road to Pichidegua and make a right onto dirt road leading to museum* ☎ *72/933–083* ⊠ *2,000 pesos* ☉ *Wed.–Sun. 11–5.*

Unlike most other small towns in the Central Valley, Santa Cruz has capitalized on the burgeoning interest in the region's viticulture. The **Ruta del Vino** office provides basic information about Colchagua's 14 vineyards and arranges guided tours in English to 10 of them. Though most vineyards have their own guides, few of them speak English, and some accept only visits arranged by Ruta del Vino. The office arranges tours to two or three vineyards, which cost 21,000 to 58,000 pesos per person and can include lunch at a vineyard; reserve at least one day in advance. One of the best times to visit the area is in early March, when the Fiesta de la Vendimia celebrates the harvest. Around that time of year, you can see much of the process of turning the grapes into wine. ⊠ *Plaza de Armas 298* ☎ *72/823–199* ⊕ *www.colchaguavalley.cl* ☉ *Weekdays 9–7:30, weekends 10–6:30.*

Another great way to explore the wine region around Santa Cruz is by taking the 1913 steam engine known as the **Tren del Vino.** The train leaves from the nearby town of San Fernando every Saturday morning (transfers are also available from Santiago), and chugs through the scenic Colchagua Valley, home to more than a dozen wineries. As well as making vineyard visits and tasting wine on board, you can also opt to stop for lunch at the Santa Cruz Plaza Hotel, or visit the Colchagua Museum. The trains leave the San Fernando Station at 10:30 AM; the tours are approximately 8 hours long (12 if you're transfering from Santiago). You must pre-book by phone or online. ☎ *2/470–7403* ⊕ *www.trendelvinochile.cl* ☒*42,000 pesos; 50,000 pesos with transfer from Santiago.*

One of the most attractive wineries in the Valle de Colchagua is **Viña Bisquertt,** where a 200-year-old farmhouse with a Spanish-tile roof makes you feel as though you've stepped back in time. The property once belonged to Federico Errázuriz Zañartu, Chile's president from 1871 to 1876, and his carriage is part of a beautiful collection of 19th-century coaches here. This family-run business oversees 1,200 acres of plantings. A tour will take you through the cellars, which hold 16 15-foot-tall wooden casks dating from the 1940s. The guides here lead tours in Spanish only, so you may want to arrange for an English-language tour through the Ruta del Vino office. ☒ *Camino a Lihueimo s/n* ☎ *72/821–692* ⊕ *www.bisquertt.cl* ☒ *7,000 pesos* ☉ *Wed.–Mon. 9–6.*

Viña Laura Hartwig is a small winery on lands where grapes have been grown for more than a century. The likeness of Laura Hartwig, the elegant owner of the estate, is beautifully drawn on the winery's labels by the famous Chilean artist Claudio Bravo. Hartwig's brother owns Viña Bisquertt, a family tie not uncommon among Chilean wineries. After a tour of the facilities, you should have a chance to sample the carmenère, a type of grape grown only in Chile. It has more character than merlot but is not as full-bodied as cabernet sauvignon. Also worth trying is the malbec, which has a lasting finish, a sensation compared by a winery guide to "kissing Sean Connery." Tours must be arranged through the Ruta del Vino office. ☒ *Camino Barreales s/n* ☎ *72/823–179* ⊕ *www.laurahartwig.cl* ☉ *Daily 9–6.*

Where to Stay & Eat

★ **$–$$$** ✕**Los Varietales.** The lovely Hotel Santa Cruz Plaza houses the best restaurant in town. The name refers to varieties of grapes, a motif reflected in the magnums above the fireplace mantel, and on the wine list, which includes all the Valle de Colchagua's labels. You have a choice of meat dishes, seafood, and sandwiches. Try the rack of lamb or the tuna. In warmer months, the trellised terrace in back is a great spot for lunch. ☒ *Plaza de Armas 286* ☎ *72/821–010* ▤ *AE, DC, MC, V.*

$–$$ ✕ **Club Social de Santa Cruz.** This simple restaurant overlooking the town's main square is known for its meat dishes. The house specialties are *conejo guisada finas herbas* (rabbit stewed with herbs) and *codornicez salsa cazador* (quail in a bacon-and-mushroom sauce), but there are also plenty of beef, chicken, and fish dishes. In summer, the courtyard fills with locals lunching under the shady pergola. ☒ *Plaza de Armas 178* ☎ *72/824–548* ▤ *AE, DC, MC, V.*

★ **$$$** ▥ **Hotel Santa Cruz Plaza.** This beautiful, colonial-style hotel on the Plaza de Armas may look historic, but it's less than a decade old. Behind the yellow facade adorned with wooden columns are Spanish-style arches, hand-painted tiles, antique reproductions, and stained glass. Guest rooms are small but charming, with orange stucco walls and French doors that open onto balconies. Those in back are quieter; they overlook a creek crossed by wooden footbridges, and a curvaceous pool surrounded by lush foliage. The nearby wineshop sells all the Valle de Colchagua wines. ⊠ *Plaza de Armas 286* ☎ *72/821–010, 2/470–7474 in Santiago* 📠 *72/823–445, 2/242–1044 in Santiago* ⊕ *www.hotelsantacruzplaza.cl* 🛏 *85 rooms, 9 suites* ⚹ *2 restaurants, room service, in-room data ports, in-room safes, cable TV, pool, sauna, 2 bars, babysitting, laundry service, business services, convention center, meeting rooms* ▤ *AE, DC, MC, V* ⦿️ *BP, FAP.*

Horseback Riding

Punta del Viento Cabalgatas (⊠ Fundo El Arrayán ☎ 09/728–4784) runs horseback tours to the top of a peak that affords a panoramic view of the vineyards that make up much of the Valle de Colchagua.

Shopping

The **Asociación de Artesanos** (⊠ Av. Rafael Casanova ☎ No phone), near the Viña La Posada, sells high-quality leather goods, embroidered tapestries, and clay figurines. About 5 km (3 mi) west of the plaza on the road to San Fernando is a colorful adobe house that holds the **Doña Selina** (⊠ Ruta I-50 ☎ 072/931–166) boutique, where you can buy local jams, straw hats, ceramics, wood carvings, and other unique handicrafts. If you want a souvenir you can't find elsewhere, head to **La Lajuela,** a hamlet 8 km (5 mi) southeast of Santa Cruz. Residents here weave *chupallas,* straw hats made from a fiber called *teatina* that is cut, dyed, dried, and braided by hand.

Curicó

❸ *113 km (71 mi) south of Rancagua.*

Curicó, founded in 1743, is the gateway to the Valle de Curicó. The bustling industrial town has a few sights of its own, but its main attraction is its proximity to surrounding vineyards. The lovely **Plaza de Armas** has a pretty fountain ringed by statues of dancing nymphs. Nearby is an elaborate bandstand that was constructed in New Orleans in 1904. The **Iglesia San Francisco,** five blocks east of the central plaza, houses a statue of the Virgen de la Velilla that was brought from Spain in 1734. It has been named a national monument.

The local **Ruta del Vino** (⊠ Arturo Prat 299 📠 75/328–972 ⊕ www.rvvc.cl) office, inside the Hotel Turismo, provides basic information and arranges tours with English-speaking guides to a dozen nearby wineries.

The Molina Vineyard that surrounds **Viña San Pedro** is the largest in Latin America. Viña San Pedro is one of Chile's oldest wineries, as the first vines were planted here in 1701. It's also among the most modern, with 28 half-million-liter stainless-steel tanks producing more wine than any other competitor except Concha y Toro. San Pedro makes the premium lines of Cabo de Horbos and Castillo de Molino as well as the ubiquitous Gato Negro and Gato Blanco brands. The bottling plant has a sleek glass dome and a second-floor viewing platform. Tours can be arranged through the Ruta del Vino office in Curicó. ⊠ *Ruta 5 S, Km 205* ☎ *75/492–770, 2/477–5300 in Santiago* ⊕ *www.vinosdechile.cl* ⊗ *Weekdays 9:30–5:30.*

Immediately off the Pan-American Highway is **Viña Miguel Torres,** one of Chile's most visitor-savvy vineyards. An orientation video providing a glossy overview of the winery all but nominates owner Don Miguel Torres for sainthood. The Spanish vintner may actually deserve the honor, as he single-handedly started the wine revolution in Chile. When he set up shop here in 1972, he had to import from Spain all the equipment needed to make wine. Now the methods he introduced to the region are taken for granted. He also brought another tradition from his native Iberia: the wine harvest festival that takes place in Curicó's main square each year. ⊠ *Ruta 5 S, Km 195* ☎ *75/564–100* ⊕ *www. migueltorres.cl* ☜ *Free* ☾ *Daily 10–7.*

A 13,000-acre national reserve 70 km (43 mi) southeast of Curicó, **Reserva Nacional Radal Siete Tazas** is famous for the unusual "Seven Teacups," a series of pools created by waterfalls along the Río Claro. From the park entrance, where you'll find a CONAF station, the falls are a short hike away. Farther along the trail are two other impressive cascades: the Salto Velo de la Novia (Bride's Veil Falls) and Salto de la Leona (Lioness Falls). Visible throughout the park is the *loro tricahue,* an endangered species that is Chile's largest and most colorful parrot. Camping is permitted in the park, which is snowed over in winter. October–March is the best time to visit. ⊠ *Camino Molina–Parque Inglés* ☎ *71/228–029* ⊕ *www.conaf.cl* ☜ *1,500 pesos* ☾ *Daily 8–8.*

Vichuquén

❹ *112 km (69 mi) west of Curicó.*

An hour's drive from Curicó, this once isolated community was a popular country retreat for Santiago business executives rich enough to helicopter in for the weekend. There is now a paved road almost all the way to the lake; nevertheless, the town retains a remote feeling, with just a few streets and very little traffic. Black-necked swans are a common sight on meandering Lago Vichuquén and nearby Laguna Torca, which is a protected area. Popular pastimes include swimming, windsurfing, boating, and fishing.

The **Museo Colonial de Vichuquén** displays ceramics, stone tools, and other artifacts collected from pre-Hispanic peoples. ⊠ *Av. Manuel Rodríguez s/n* ☎ *75/400–045* ☜ *700 pesos* ☾ *Daily 10–1 and 4–6.*

Where to Stay & Eat

$$ ✕⌂ **La Hostería.** This two-story structure constructed entirely of native woods affords unmatched views of Lago Vichuquén, with many rooms overlooking the lake from private decks. The hotel has excellent watersports facilities. The discotheque is a popular nightspot, and the restaurant is the best on the lake—many people from nearby accommodations arrive by motorboat. ⊠ *Sector Aquelarre, Lago Vichuquén* ☎ *75/400–018* 🖷 *75/400–030* ⊕ *www.lagovichuquen.cl* ⇥ *12 rooms* ⚹ *Restaurant, boating, bicycles, bar, dance club, laundry service; no a/c, no room TVs* ▤ *AE, DC, MC, V* ⧫ *BP.*

$$ ⌂ **Marina Vichuquén.** The comfortable Marina Vichuquén has an enviable location right on the shore, and makes use of it with its own marina. Many rooms have nice views of the lake and the surrounding pine forests. There are plenty of opportunities for water sports, including a sailing school for children. If you want to explore the nearby countryside, you can rent horses or mountain bikes. ☒ *Sector Aquelarre, Lago Vichuquén* ☎ *75/400–265* 🖷 *75/400–274* ⊕ *www.marinavichuquen. cl* ⤶ *18 rooms* ᐃ *Restaurant, tennis court, pool, exercise equipment, boating, jet skiing, marina, bicycles, horseback riding, volleyball, bar, recreation room, shop, babysitting, playground, laundry service, Internet; no a/c, no room TVs* 🖃 *AE, DC, MC, V* ¶◎¶ *BP.*

Talca

⑤ *56 km (35 mi) south of Curicó.*

Straddling the banks of the Río Claro, Talca is one of the most attractive towns in the Central Valley. Founded in 1692, it is laid out on a regimented grid pattern extending out from the Plaza de Armas. It's divided into quadrants—*poniente* means west and *oriente* east; *sur* means south and *norte* north. You can make out the city's orderly colonial design from **Cerro de la Virgen,** a hill that affords a panoramic view of Talca and the vineyards in the distance. One of the most pleasant stretches of green is **Avenida Bernardo O'Higgins,** a cedar-lined boulevard popular with joggers, skaters, and strolling couples. At its western tip is the Balneario Río Claro, where you can hire a boat to paddle down the river.

The **Museo O'Higginiano,** one block east of the Plaza de Armas, is a pink colonial mansion that belonged to Albano Pereira, a tutor of national hero Bernardo O'Higgins. As Chile's first president, O'Higgins signed the country's proclamation of independence in this house in February 1818. Declared a national monument in 1971, it now houses the city's fine-arts museum, which has a collection of more than 500 paintings by local artists. There's also an impressive armory of 19th-century *carabinas* (carbines) from Europe and America. The Chilean name for the police force, *carabineros,* is derived from this word. ☒ *1 Norte at 2 Oriente* ☎ *71/227–330* ⊕ *www.dibam.cl* 🖃 *Free* ☯ *Tues.–Fri. 10–7, weekends 10–2.*

Talca is the capital of the Valle del Maule, one of Chile's most important wine-producing regions, and a dozen wineries are scattered along the Maule River valley between Talca and San Javier. The **Valle del Maule Ruta del Vino** office, east of town, arranges visits to nearly a dozen wineries. It can provide transportation and an English-speaking guide, which simplifies and enriches a visit. The office is in the **Villa Cultural Huilquilem,** a hacienda built in 1850 that also holds a small museum of religious art and a restaurant. ☒ *Camino a San Clemente, Km 7* ☎ *71/246–460* ⊕ *www.chilewineroute.com* ☯ *Weekdays 10–1 and 3–7, Sat. 10–1.*

The **Domaine Oriental** winery was named for its location east of the city. A five-minute drive east out of Talca on a dirt road takes you to a massive iron gate bearing the winery's initials, beyond which stands a red hacienda with a barrel-tile roof. The vineyards themselves climb up into the Andean foothills. It is also known as Casa Donoso, since the Donoso family owned the estate for many generations before it was purchased in 1989 by four Frenchmen. The enological work is done by a skilled

Chilean staff, and the results are auspicious. The Casa Donoso label's blend of cabernet sauvignon, which lends the structure, and carmenère, which brings out the soft edges, is one of Chile's most promising reserves. ⊠ *Camino a Palmira, Km 3.5* ☎ *71/242–506* ⊕ *www.domaineoriental. cl* ⊠ *Free* ⊙ *Wed.–Sun. 8:30–1:30 and 3–6:30.*

There may be no better way to get to know the Central Valley than by taking a ride on Chile's only remaining *ramal* (branch-line railroad), which runs from Talca to the coastal city of Constitución. The 100-km (62-mi) **Ramal Talca–Constitución** makes a slow trip to the coast—it's 2½ hours each way—stopping for about 15 minutes at each of the small towns en route. In Constitución you'll be able to admire the coastal cliffs and rock formations. The train departs Talca's Estación de Tren daily at 7:30 AM, returning at 4 PM. In high season (December–April) a train also leaves at 11 and returns at 9. A good option is to arrange a tour on which you take the train to Constitución, then board a van to visit nearby sand dunes and other natural attractions. Contact **EFE, the national train service** (☎71/ 674–824 ⊕ www.efe.cl) for more information on the train tour.

The town of **San Clemente,** 16 km (10 mi) southeast of Talca, hosts the best rodeo in the region September–April, with riding, roping, dances, and beauty-queen competitions. The events take place weekends 11–6. The national championship selections are held here toward the end of the season.

Where to Stay & Eat

$–$$ ✕ **Vivace.** Hardwood, tiles, and brick decorate the warm dining room, and window tables overlook the lovely tree-lined boulevard at Vivace, one of Talca's most popular restaurants. The Italian menu includes the familiar, such as lasagna Bolognese, but also original entrées, such as *conejo mediterraneo* (rabbit with vegetables in a sherry sauce), fettuccine *con ragú de ciervo* (with a venison sauce), and fettuccine *con ragú de cordero* (with a curried lamb–and–pistachio sauce). The restaurant occupies a refurbished home half a block northwest of the Plaza de Armas, on the diagonal road. ⊠ *Isodoro del Solar 50* ☎ *71/238–337* ⊟ *AE, DC, MC, V* ⊙ *Closed Sun.*

¢–$$ ✕ **Rubén Tapío.** One of the best restaurants in the Central Valley, Rubén
Fodor's Choice Tapío is renowned for its refined service and outstanding cuisine. The
★ elegant dining rooms make you feel like a guest in someone's home. The spacious bar, which displays most local wines, is a nice spot for a cocktail. Signature dishes include a *caldillo de congrio dorado* (conger eel stew) that is reputed to be Pablo Neruda's recipe, curried salmon, *lomo estilo corralero* (tenderloin in a shellfish sauce), and *chupe de locos* (abalone casserole topped with shredded cheese). Even more unusual is the jambalaya, made with shrimp, chicken, and ham and served in a leaf of red lettuce. ⊠ *2 Oriente 1339* ☎ *71/237–875* ⊟ *AE, DC, MC, V* ⊙ *Closed Sun.*

$ 🏨 **Hostal del Puente.** This quiet, family-run hotel, at the end of a dusty street two blocks west of the Plaza de Armas, is quite a bargain. Simple carpeted rooms have small desks and windows that open onto a portico or overlook the parking area in back. Ask for one of the older rooms in the front, where a narrow garden holds níspero and cherry trees. The owners provide inexpensive breakfasts and free travel advice. ✉ *1 Sur 407* 🖨 *71/220–930* ⊕ *www.backpackersbest.cl* 🛏 *14 rooms* ⚭ *Dining room, cable TV, no-smoking rooms; no a/c, no room phones* 🚫 *No credit cards.*

$ 🖥 **Hotel Terrabella.** Half a block west of the Plaza de Armas, this hotel has rooms that although neither especially bright nor spacious, are tasteful and spotless. The ground floor holds a small lounge and a restaurant enclosed in glass walls with a view of the backyard and swimming pool. The shady lawn is hemmed by gardens, and the friendly staff make this a pleasant, if not luxurious, place to stay. ✉ *1 Sur 641* 🖨 *71/226–555* ⊕ *www.amarillas.cl/hotelterrabella* 🛏 *29 rooms, 2 suites* ⚭ *Restaurant, room service, in-room data ports, in-room safes, minibars, cable TV, pool, laundry service, business services, meeting room; no a/c* 🚫 *AE, DC, MC, V* 🍴 *BP.*

Nightlife

Pura Candela (✉ Isidoro del Solar 38 ☎ 41/236–505), in a colorful house just northwest of the Plaza de Armas, draws a young professional crowd Wednesday to Saturday. There's live Latin music on Friday and Saturday evenings, as well as a cover charge.

Horseback Riding

Horseback-riding tours are an excellent way to explore the amazing mountain scenery east of Talca. **Achibueno Expediciones** (✉ Ruta L-45, Km 8, Linares 🖨 73/375–098) runs 2- to 10-day horseback trips through the Andes that pass waterfalls, hot springs, and mountain lakes. **Expediciones Quizapu** (✉ Casilla 421 ☎ 71/621–592) arranges three- to seven-day horseback expeditions that combine camping and overnight stays in rustic farmhouses.

Shopping

The **Centro Artesanal Antumapu** (✉ 1 Sur 1330, Galería Bavaria ☎ No phone) sells work by 17 local artisans, including ceramics, jewelry, leather, and woolen goods. The **Mercado Central** (✉ 1 Sur, between 4 and 5 Oriente ☎ No phone) has stands filled with ceramics, copperware, baskets, and other handicrafts.

San Javier

❻ *21 km (13 mi) south of Talca.*

The small, bustling town of San Javier serves as the gateway to half a dozen Valle del Maule vineyards. Most of these wineries are family-run establishments, where the owners hand-label each bottle. In San Javier itself is **Viña Balduzzi.** Albano Balduzzi, who came from generations of winemakers in Italy, built the 40-acre estate here in 1906. His grandson, Jorge Balduzzi, still lives here, making a million liters of wine each year. The premium label features varietals such as cabernet sauvignon, sauvignon blanc, carmenère, merlot, and a sweet late-harvest chardonnay. Tours include a peek at the cellars that stretch underneath the property, and the collection of antique machinery, as well as a tasting. Within the estate is a beautiful expanse of oak and cedar trees that's perfect for a picnic. ⊠ *Av. Balmacaeda 1189* ☎ *73/322–138* ⊕ *www. balduzzi.cl* ⊠ *5,000 pesos* ⊙ *Mon.–Sat. 9–6.*

Colbún

❼ *50 km (31 mi) southeast of Talca.*

The tiny town of Colbún sits near a 93-square-km (36-square-mi) lake formed after a hydroelectric dam was built on the Río Maule in 1985. The largest such plant in Chile, it produces half the country's electrical power. The lake, stocked with trout, is an especially popular destination for fly-fishing aficionados. You can also rent motorboats and Jet Skis.

Hikers love the **Reserva Nacional Alto de Lircay,** with its lengthy trails that cut through native oak forest on their way to the volcanic cones of the Andes. To reach the CONAF-administered park, head east on Ruta 115, which is called the Camino Internacional Paso Pehuenche. Turn left at the signs past the hamlet of Corralones. About 25 km (16 mi) farther is the reserve. The park is snowed over July–September. ☎ *71/228–029* ⊕ *www.conaf.cl* ⊠ *1,700 pesos* ⊙ *Daily 8:30–5:30.*

Where to Stay

$ ▦ **Casas el Colorado.** Fields of grazing horses surround this lovingly re-stored 19th-century hacienda, not far from Colbún's lake. On the grounds is the simple wood-and-brick chapel of Santa Teresita de los Andes, where Mass is still celebrated on Sunday. It was constructed over the foundations of a Jesuit church dating from 1790; you can visit the ruins in the basement. The restaurant here is the best in the area; grilled salmon and filet mignon are house specialties. If you're going to spend some time here, pay for the full meal plan—otherwise there are additional charges for use of the spa and other facilities. ⊠ *Km 46, Colorado* ☎☎ *71/221–750* ⌦ *25 rooms* ⚭ *Restaurant, 6-hole golf course, tennis court, pool, exercise equipment, spa, horseback riding, bar, recreation room, shop, meeting rooms, helipad; no a/c* ⊟ *AE, DC, MC, V* ⑩ *BP, FAP.*

RÍO BÍO BÍO

The mighty Río Bío Bío empties into the Pacific Ocean at the regional capital of Concepción, a pleasant city of about 500,000 people with an important university but few attractions. The area's other major community, Chillán, is known for its attractive handicrafts market. It is also the gateway to the mountains of Termas de Chillán. Here, skiing rules in winter, hiking and horseback riding are possible in summer, and hot springs draw people year-round.

Chillán

❽ *157 km (97 mi) south of Talca.*

Friendly, tranquil Chillán isn't much to look at, but it's worth a stop for its colorful market. At the sprawling **Feria de Chillán** (⊠ Av. 5 de Abril between Calles Maipón and Arturo Prat) dozens of vendors sell crafts from all over Chile, including woven clothing, pottery, jewelry, and handicrafts. It's open daily until sunset. Across the street is the main market, where vendors sell locally produced sausages called *longaniza,* which you'll see hanging from stalls. The sight of thousands of these dangling rings of pork makes it clear that this delicacy is a staple of the local diet.

The heart of Chillán is the verdant **Plaza de Armas,** the city's pretty main square. A plaque honors Bernardo O'Higgins, who was born here in 1778. The modern **Catedral de Chillán,** on the east side of the main square, is constructed of nine parabolic arches. All ornamentation is eschewed inside and out, except for a crucifix above the altar, the stations of the cross in the spaces between the arches, and the mosaic above the entrance. A huge cement cross, even taller than the church itself, stands outside.

After an earthquake devastated Chillán in 1939, prompting a major reconstruction effort in the city, Pablo Neruda, then Chile's ambassador to Mexico, arranged a visa allowing Mexican painter David Alfaro Siquieros to travel to Chile. He painted an incendiary mural in the **Escuela México** (⊠ Av. Bernardo O'Higgins at Vega de Saldias), about five blocks from the Plaza de Armas. The mural depicts indigenous peoples being murdered by the Spanish conquistadors. Neruda lost his job because of the resulting scandal, but the mural remains.

Where to Stay & Eat

¢–$$ ✕ **Centro Español.** The narrow dining room of this small restaurant on the Plaza de Armas curves gracefully, as if reacting to the sinuous form of the adjacent cathedral, and its large windows overlook the plaza's massive trees. The menu has a good selection of local seafood—try the *zarzuela de mariscos,* a hearty seafood stew—as well as such traditional Spanish favorites as paella and *arroz a la valenciana,* a comparable seafood-and-rice dish. The building here also houses the Spanish Friends Society, a group that pays tribute to the Spanish legacy in the New World. ⊠ *Arauco 555* ☎ *42/430–433* ⊟ *AE, DC, MC, V* ☉ *Closed Sun.*

$ ⊞ **Hotel Las Terrazas.** The carpeted rooms here are on the small side, with tiny desks, but they have large baths and picture windows—those on the east side of the building afford memorable views of the Andes. The lounge has pillowy furniture that invites you to linger over the pisco sour that greets you when you arrive. Steps from the Plaza de Armas, Las Terrazas occupies the fifth and sixth floors of a small shopping center. ⊠ *Constitución 664, 5th fl.* ☎ *42/227–000* 🖷 *42/227–001* ⊕ *www. lasterrazas.cl* ⤳ *59 rooms, 2 suites* ⚴ *Restaurant, room service, in-room safes, minibars, cable TV, Wi-Fi, laundry service, Internet, meeting room; no a/c* ⊟ *AE, DC, MC, V* ¶⊙¶ *BP.*

Termas de Chillán

❾ *78 km (49 mi) east of Chillán.*

Billed as the continent's "most complete ski resort," Termas de Chillán has a mountainside location that rivals Valle Nevado and Portillo. Nine lifts carry skiers to 28 groomed runs, including one that is the longest in South America. There are snowmobiling and snowboarding, as well as more unusual activities such as Alaskan malamute sledding. Come summertime the activities switch to hiking and horseback riding. Ski lifts are still used to take people to the top of the mountain, from which they can hike down. Year-round, you can soak in the waters of the hot springs for which the resort was named—they are funneled into several swimming pools.

Where to Stay & Eat

During the ski season, rooms at the two resort hotels here can be arranged only in three-, four-, and seven-night packages, which include half-board (breakfast and dinner), lift tickets, use of the hot springs, and transportation from Chillán or Concepción. They also offer nightly rates when available. Rates change weekly during the ski season, varying considerably over the course of four months and peaking in mid-July. Hotels in nearby Las Trancas rent rooms by the night year-round.

★ **$$$$** ▦ **Gran Hotel Termas de Chillán.** This impressive facility offers skiing June–October, hiking and other outdoor activities December–April, and a state-of-the-art spa year-round. A stepped, seven-story building contains colorful, carpeted rooms with picture windows that take in either the ski hill and granite peaks, or a tree-lined mountainside. Rooms on the seventh floor are slightly cramped, but cost less. The spacious lobby and bar overlook the thermal pool and forested grounds. Shangri La has a host of options, from Pacific salmon in a butter sauce to wild boar in chocolate sauce. There's also a children's menu. ⊠ *Termas de Chillán* ☎ *42/223–887, 42/366–8726, 2/233–1313 in Santiago* ⊕ *www. termaschillan.cl* ⇨ *109 rooms* ⚹ *Restaurant, room service, in-room safes, minibars, cable TV, 2 tennis courts, 3 pools (1 indoors), gym, hair salon, spa, mountain bikes, hiking, horseback riding, squash, downhill skiing, ski shop, bar, dance club, recreation room, shop, babysitting, laundry service, Internet, meeting rooms* ▤ *AE, DC, MC, V* ⃝ *AI.*

$$$$ ▦ **Hotel Pirigallo.** Though dwarfed by the nearby Gran Hotel and lacking its sweeping views, the Pirigallo provides access to the same outdoor diversions for a little less money. Guest rooms and the restaurant surround a pool fed by the hot springs. Rooms are on the small side, but have large windows overlooking either the pool or surrounding forest; a few of them have tiny balconies. Room rates cover meals, lift tickets, spa service, and summer activities. ⊠ *Termas de Chillán* ☎ *42/223–887, 2/233–1313 in Santiago* ⊕ *www.skichillan. com* ⇨ *48 rooms* ⚹ *Restaurant, room service, some minibars, cable TV, pool, spa, downhill skiing, bar, babysitting, laundry service* ▤ *AE, DC, MC, V* ⃝ *AI, MAP.*

★ **$** ▦ **Parador Jamón, Pan y Vino.** Though 6 km (4 mi) short of the Termas proper, in the community of Las Trancas, this small lodge has a great location near the mountains and an impressive waterfall. Wooden buildings give the place a frontier feel, especially the lobby and restaurant, with their fireplace and various woodstoves. Guest rooms are rustic but spacious and have woodstoves and a porch overlooking verdant grounds. The restaurant ($–$$) serves a good selection of seafood and a few meat dishes; try the house specialty, *jamón serrano* (smoked ham) or the rich *chupe de guasitos* (tripe). ⊠ *Km 73, Termas de Chillán* ☎ *42/222–682* 🖷 *42/221–054* ⊕ *www.paradorjamonyvino.cl* ➷ *8 rooms, 15 cabanas* ☖ *Restaurant, pool, hot tub, sauna, billiards, bar, recreation room* ▤ *AE, DC, MC, V.*

Concepción

🔟 *112 km (70 mi) southwest of Chillán.*

Earthquakes have devastated this coastal city since it was founded in 1551. The latest few, in 1939 and 1960, destroyed pretty much any historic building still standing. The regional capital is a mishmash of modern buildings, many in disrepair and most aesthetically awry. The city straddles the Río Bío Bío, with two mile-long bridges (Puente Viejo and Puente Nuevo) crossing to the other side. **Plaza de la Independencia,** also called Plaza de Concepción, is the heart of the city, with pedestrian shopping streets radiating from its borders. To the west of the plaza stands the **Catedral de Concepción,** a massive gray structure built in the 1940s to replace a church destroyed by the 1939 earthquake.

Cerro Caracol, or Conch Hill, overlooks the city from the southeast, and is popular with joggers, hikers, and mountain bikers. You can reach the pine-tree-covered hill by heading south on Calle Tucapel. Park along the mossy cobblestone streets and wander among the many footpaths that lead into the woods.

The **Galería de la Historia de Concepción** depicts regional history through a dozen dioramas, including the 1939 earthquake that devastated the city; battles between the Spanish invaders and the indigenous Mapuche people; and Alonso de Ercilla writing the epic poem *La Araucana* in 1557. Rooms upstairs are dedicated to changing art exhibitions. The museum is in Parque Ecuador, at the foot of Cerro Caracol. ⊠ *Lamas at Lincyán* ☎ *41/231–830* ⊟ *Free* ☉ *Mon. 3–6:30, Tues.–Fri. 10–1:30 and 3–6.*

★ The **Casa del Arte,** at the Universidad de Concepción, contains the country's largest, and arguably best, collection of classical Chilean paintings. The museum is most famous for the striking mural by Mexican artist Jorge González Camarena. Unaware of the presence of a protruding staircase until he saw the room, González incorporated it into the work. It now bears the snaky form of Quetzalcoatl, a symbol of Aztec culture. Climb Quetzalcoatl to the galleries displaying selections from the collection of more than 1,600 works, including major canvases by Alfredo Valenzuela Puelma. Past exhibits in the three halls downstairs have included works by Picasso and the promising young painter, sculptor, and designer José Fernández Covich. ⊠ *Av. Chacabuco at Av. Paicavi* ☎ *41/ 204–126* ⊟ *Free* ☉ *Weekdays 10–6, Sat. 10–4, Sun. 10–1.*

Where to Stay & Eat

¢–$$$ ✕ **El Faro Belén.** Although it may not appear like much from the outside, this nautically themed restaurant serves some of the best seafood in Concepción. A towering wooden mermaid surveys the dining room, which overflows with locals on weekday afternoons. If you're a big eater, try the *plato americano,* a selection of seven seafood dishes including sea bass, shrimp, salmon, and clams, all served cold. For a hot entrée, you can't beat the *locos en salsa de camaron* (abalone in a creamy white shrimp sauce). A more intimate dining room is tucked away upstairs. ⊠ *Av. Bulnes 382* ☎ *41/243–430* ▭ *AE, DC, MC, V* ⊗ *No dinner Sun.*

¢–$$$ ✕ **Solo Carne.** Serious carnivores enjoy this popular *parrilla,* which serves everything from steak to lamb to *jabalí* (wild boar). Complement your grilled meat with any of a dozen fresh sauces, including sauces made from pesto, Roquefort, pepper, and capers. The name, which translates as "Meat Only," isn't entirely accurate: the restaurant also serves inexpensive pastas, including spinach or crab cannelloni, as well as seafood starters such as seviche. Dining is in several rooms with high wooden ceilings and paintings on the walls. It's a 10-minute drive from downtown, behind the Holiday Inn. ⊠ *Av. San Andres 78, Lomas de San Andrés* ☎ *41/480–199* ▭ *AE, DC, MC, V* ⊗ *Closed Sat.*

★ ¢–$$ ✕ **Canto de Luna.** This popular restaurant is perched over the water on Laguna Chica, a small lake in San Pedro, on the south side of the river. Giant windows and a wraparound deck overlook the surrounding lake, hemmed in by forested hills. The food rivals the view, with an enticing mix of grilled meat and seafood and an eclectic collection of European dishes such as *risotto de mariscos* (seafood risotto) and salmon *al papillote* (baked in paper). The wine list is extensive. There's a buffet at night and at lunch on Sunday, when reservations are a must. ⊠ *Av. Costanera 825, San Pedro* ☎ *41/284–545* ▭ *AE, DC, MC, V* ⊗ *No dinner Sun.*

$$ ⌂ **Hotel El Araucano.** Though a bit run-down, Hotel El Araucano is still a good choice for its excellent location next to the Plaza de la Independencia. The bathrooms are on the small side and the minibars are clearly relics from an earlier era, but the rooms have large windows with great city views—those on the upper floor on the west side overlook the Río Bío Bío. Because the hotel primarily serves business travelers, rooms here are half price on weekends. ⊠ *Caupolicán 521* ☎ *41/740–606* 🖷 *41/740–623* 🖙 *138 rooms, 6 suites* ⌂ *Restaurant, room service, in-room safes, minibars, cable TV, indoor pool, sauna, shops, laundry service, business services, meeting rooms, airport shuttle, free parking, no-smoking rooms; no a/c* ▭ *AE, DC, MC, V* ⧌ *BP.*

$ ⌂ **Hotel San Sebastian.** This hotel, spread over several floors in an old building on busy Calle Rengo, behind the Catedral, is quite likely Concepción's best lodging deal. Simple, clean rooms have large windows, high ceilings, and prints of modern art on the walls. Some have private bathrooms, but half share baths. There's a comfortable lounge next to the reception. ⊠ *Rengo 463* ☎ *41/243–412* 🖙 *10 rooms, 5 with bath* ⌂ *Cable TV, laundry service; no a/c* ▭ *AE, DC, MC, V* ⧌ *BP.*

$ ⌂ **Hotel Terrano.** From Avenida Bernardo O'Higgins, this hotel looks small and uninviting, but don't be fooled. It's actually quite spacious, with a taller wing hidden in the back that provides room for a restaurant and even a cavernous convention hall. Inside are bright and cheerful rooms with comfortable beds. The baths are fairly large, with extras like hair dryers and phones. Windows in upper-floor rooms overlook the surrounding hills. ⊠ *Av. Bernardo O'Higgins 340* ☎🖶 *41/240–078* ⊕ *www.hotelterrano.com* ↘ *68 rooms, 2 suites* ⚭ *Restaurant, room service, in-room safes, minibars, cable TV, exercise equipment, billiards, bar, laundry service, business services, convention center, free parking; no a/c* ⊟ *AE, DC, MC, V* ⦿ *BP.*

Nightlife

Nearly all this city's bars and dance clubs are clustered in the Barrio de la Estación, several blocks along Arturo Prat across from the Estación Ferrocarriles. Within walking distance of the train station are dozens of nocturnal lairs, which run the gamut from cozy pubs to crowded discotheques. **Treinta y Tantos** (⊠ Arturo Prat 402 ☎ 41/251–516), one of the Barrio de la Estación's more bohemian spots, is famous for its extensive selection of empanadas, which make it a good option for a light dinner or late-night snack.

Shopping

The best selection of handicrafts and other gift items can be found in the gallery of small shops surrounding the Hotel El Araucano. Head to the underground **Artesanias Yanara** (⊠ Caupolicán 521, Local 64 ☎ 41/242–617) for various souvenirs, including wool sweaters, decorative copper plates, mugs, jewelry, and knickknacks. **El Carro** (⊠ Caupolicán 521, Local 43 ☎ 41/232–543) carries ceramics, copper work, and jewelry made of local lapis lazuli and *piedra cruz,* a crystal-like stone common to the Andes, set in silver. The jewelry store **Itacolor** (⊠ Caupolicán 521, Local 36-A ☎ 41/229–178) sells lapis lazuli, jade, and other semiprecious stones set in silver and gold.

Parque Nacional Laguna del Laja

⓫ *225 km (140 mi) southeast of Concepción.*

A few hours' drive southeast of Concepción is a hiker's paradise, the Parque Nacional Laguna del Laja. It encompasses part of the Sendero de Chile, or Chilean Trail, which officials hope will one day run the length of the country. Several different routes are open for activities such as hiking, biking, and horseback riding. Some parts have gentler grades that make them a good choice for people with mobility problems.

Perhaps the most impressive of the trails is the 36-km (22-mi) path that rings Laguna del Laja, the country's largest natural reservoir. It crosses dozens of wooden footbridges before arriving at a valley carpeted with hardened lava—a sign of the last eruption of the now-dormant Antuco Volcano. About four dozen different species of birds can be spotted in the park, including the condor and black-headed Andean gull. Predators like the Andean fox and the puma prowl the perimeter in silent anticipation.

To get to Parque Nacional Laguna del Laja, take Ruta 5 south to Los Angeles, then Route Q45 east toward Antuco. The last 11 km (7 mi) of the road are not paved, so you want to avoid this route in rough weather. ⊠ *Ruta Q45* ☎ *No phone* ⊕ *www.conaf.cl* ⛝ *750 pesos.*

THE CENTRAL VALLEY ESSENTIALS

Transportation

BY AIR

Concepción's Aeropuerto Carriel Sur—5 km (3 mi) northwest of town—is the only major airport in the region. It's a good choice if you plan to explore the area around the Río Bío Bío. Otherwise it may be more convenient to fly into Santiago.

Lan runs half a dozen flights per day from Santiago to Concepción.
🔎 **Airline Lan** ✉ Barros Arana 600, Concepción ☎ 41/521-092 or 41/229-138 ⊕ www.lan.com.
🔎 **Airport Aeropuerto Carriel Sur** ☎ 41/732-000.

BY BUS

The two big bus companies in the region, Pullman Bus and Tur-Bus, offer hourly departures during the day between Santiago and Rancagua, Talca, Curicó, Chillán, and Concepción. There is less frequent service to Santa Cruz. The fare from Santiago to Concepción is around 5,000 pesos.
🔎 **Bus Lines Pullman Bus** ☎ 2/779-2026 ⊕ www.Pullman.cl. **Tur-Bus** ☎ 2/270-7500 ⊕ www.turbus.com.
🔎 **Bus Terminals Chillán Terminal María Teresa** ✉ Av. Bernardo O'Higgins 10 ☎ 42/272-149. **Concepción Terminal Puchacay** ✉ Terminal Principal Collao, Tegualda 860 ☎ 41/311-511. **Curicó Terminal** ✉ Arturo Prat 788 ☎ 72/100-141. **Rancagua Terminal Sur** ✉ Dr. Salinas 1165 ☎ 72/230-340. **Santa Cruz Terminal** ✉ Casanova 480 ☎ 72/822-191. **Talca Terminal** ✉ 12 Oriente at 2 Sur ☎ 71/243-270.

BY CAR

The Central Valley is sliced in half by Chile's major highway, the Pan-American Highway. With the exception of Concepción, it passes through all of the major towns in the region. Since so many of the sights are off the beaten path, traveling by car is often the most convenient way to see the region. The speed limit here is 100 km/h (62 mph). Be aware that road conditions vary greatly. Many of the secondary roads in the region remain unpaved.

Most visitors to the Central Valley who rent a vehicle do so in Santiago. If you find you need a car while traveling in the region, you can rent one from Avis or Hertz, both of which have offices in Aeropuerto Carriel Sur and downtown Concepción. The Chilean company Rosselot has agencies in Concepción and Talca.
🔎 **Rental Agencies Avis** ✉ Aeropuerto Carriel Sur ☎ 41/480-089 ✉ Av. Chacabuco 726, Concepción ☎ 41/235-837. **Hertz** ✉ Aeropuerto Carriel Sur ☎ 41/480-088 ✉ Arturo Prat 248, Concepción ☎ 41/230-341. **Rosselot** ✉ Aeropuerto Carriel Sur, Concepción ☎ 41/732-010 ✉ Av. San Miguel 2710, Talca ☎ 71/247-979.

BY TRAIN

Although service in much of the rest of the country has been gutted, the train remains an excellent way to travel among towns in the Central Valley. Express trains from Estación Central in Santiago to the cities of

Rancagua, Curicó, Talca, Chillán, and Concepción are faster than taking the bus or driving. Local trains are slower, but they stop in the smaller towns along that route.

For a complete schedule of trains to the Central Valley, contact the Empresa de Los Ferrocarriles del Estado, the national rail service better known as EFE.

🚊 Train Information **EFE** ☎ 600/737-62887 ⊕ www.efe.cl.

🚊 Train Stations **Chillán** ✉ Av. Brasil at Libertad ☎ 42/222-424. **Concepción** ✉ Arturo Prat at Barros Arana ☎ 41/226-925. **Curicó** ✉ Maipú 567 ☎ 75/310-028. **Rancagua** ✉ Av. Viña del Mar at Carrera Pinto ☎ 72/225-239. **Santiago** ✉ Av. Bernardo O'Higgins 3170, Santiago Centro ☎ 2/376-8500. **Talca** ✉ 11 Oriente at 2 Sur ☎ 71/232-721.

Contacts & Resources

BANKS & EXCHANGE SERVICES

Traveler's checks can be used at nearly all hotels and many restaurants. Every town has at least one bank with an ATM on its central plaza or main commercial street, and ATMs are also common in shopping centers, bus stations, large gas stations, and other spots where people congregate. The following are central banks in major towns.

🏦 Banks **Banco Concepción** ✉ Constitución 550, Chillán ☎ 42/221-306. **Banco del Estado** ✉ 1 Sur 971, Talca ☎ 71/223-285. **Banco Sudamericano** ✉ Independencia at Bueras, Rancagua ☎ 72/230-413. **BCI** ✉ Plaza de Armas 286-A, Santa Cruz ☎ 72/825-059. **Citibank** ✉ Av. Bernardo O'Higgins 499, Concepción ☎ 41/233-870.

INTERNET, MAIL & SHIPPING

In the major cities in the Central Valley, there are always one or two Internet cafés. In smaller towns, however, they are a bit harder to find. Cyber Planet Café, across from the tourist information office in Talca, is open daily 9:30 AM–11:30 PM. Concepción has various Internet cafés, among them Cyber C@fé, a block north of the Catedral, which is open daily 9:30 AM–midnight. Also here is Moonblass Café, which is open Monday–Saturday 9:30 AM–10:30 PM and Sunday 4 PM–9 PM.

There's at least one post office in every town in the Central Valley. Because of the proximity to Santiago, mail service is quicker here than in other regions. For the fastest service, DHL has branches in Chillán and Concepción.

🖥 Internet Cafés **Cyber C@fé** ✉ Caupolican 588, Concepción ☎ 41/238-394. **Cyber Planet Café** ✉ 1 Poniente 1282, Talca ☎ 71/210-775. **Moonblass Café** ✉ Aureliano Manzano 538, Concepción ☎ 41/910-233.

📮 Post Offices **Chillán** ✉ Libertad 505 ☎ 42/223-272. **Concepción** ✉ Colo Colo 417 ☎ 41/235-666. **Curicó** ✉ Carmen s/n ☎ 75/310-000. **Rancagua** ✉ Campos at Cuevas ☎ 72/230-413. **Talca** ✉ 1 Oriente 1150 ☎ 71/227-271.

📦 Shipping Services **DHL** ✉ 18 de Setiembre 565 Chillán ☎ 42/222-131 ✉ Salas 25 Concepción ☎ 41/220-843.

TOURS

In addition to the Ruta del Vino offices, which specialize in vineyard tours, there are several operators in the region that arrange day trips and overnight excursions. Casa Chueca, a guesthouse and outdoor outfitter near Talca, runs day trips to Constitución and the Reserva Nacional Radal Siete Tazas, white-water rafting trips, and hiking expeditions. Maule Ando Tours arranges various city tours of Talca.

RAM offers tours of Concepción and environs as well as excursions to Chillán, the waterfall and protected area of Salto del Laja, and the upper Río Bío Bío. Ecoturismo Puelche, in Chillán, runs one- to seven-day horseback tours in the nearby mountains.

⚑ Tour Operators Casa Chueca ✉ Talca ☎ 71/370-096 ⊕ www.trekkingchile.com. **Ecoturismo Puelche** ✉ Vegas de Saldía 688, Chillán ☎ 42/224-829 ⊕ www.chilesat. net/puelche. **Maule Ando Tours** ✉ 1 Poniente 1282, Talca ☎ 71/210-775 ⊕ maule-ando.galeon.com. **RAM** ✉ Martinez de Roca 869-E, Concepción ☎ 41/733-007.

VISITOR INFORMATION

Sernatur has outstanding offices with English-speaking staff in Concepción, Rancagua, and Talca. The offices are open weekdays 8:30–6.

⚑ Sernatur Concepción ✉ Anibal Pinto 460, Plaza de Armas ☎ 41/227-976. **Rancagua** ✉ German Riesco 277, Offices 2 and 3 ☎ 72/230-413. **Talca** ✉ 1 Poniente 1281 ☎ 71/226-940.

The Lake District

6

Updated by
Jeffrey Van
Fleet

AS YOU TRAVEL THE WINDING ROADS of the Lake District, the snow-capped shoulders of volcanoes emerge, mysteriously disappear, then materialize again, peeping through trees or towering above broad valleys. The sometimes difficult journey through breathtaking mountain passes is inevitably rewarded by views of a glistening lake, vibrant and blue. You might be tempted to belt out "The hills are alive . . . ," but this is southern Chile, not Austria. With densely forested national parks, a dozen large lakes, easy access to transportation and facilities, and predominantly small, family-run lodgings, this area has come pretty close to perfecting tourism.

The Lake District is the historic homeland of Chile's indigenous Mapuche people, who revolted against the early Spanish colonists in 1598, driving them out of the region. They kept foreigners out of the area for nearly three centuries. Though small pockets of the Lake District were controlled by Chile after it won its independence in 1818, most viewed the forbidding region south of the Río Bío Bío as a separate country. After a treaty ended the last Mapuche war in 1881, Santiago began to recruit waves of German, Austrian, and Swiss immigrants to settle the so-called "empty territory" and offset indigenous domination. The Lake District took on the Bavarian-Tyrolean sheen still evident today.

Exploring the Lake District

The Lake District's altitude descends sharply from the towering peaks of the Andes on the Argentine border, to forests and plains, and finally to sea level, all in the space of about 200 km (120 mi). The Pan-American Highway (Ruta 5) runs straight down the middle, making travel to most places in the region relatively easy. It connects the major cities of Temuco, Osorno, and Puerto Montt, but bypasses Valdivia by 50 km (30 mi). A drive from Temuco to Puerto Montt should take less than four hours. Flying between the hubs is a reasonable option. A Temuco–Puerto Montt ticket, for example, costs 18,000 pesos.

About the Restaurants

Meat and potatoes characterize the cuisine of this part of southern Chile. The omnipresent *cazuela* (a plate of rice and potatoes with beef or chicken) and *pastel de choclo* (a corn, meat, and vegetable casserole) are solid, hearty meals. Though more associated with Chiloé, the southern Lake District dishes up its own *curanto,* a fish stew served with lots of bread.

Arguably the greatest gifts from the waves of German immigrants were their tasty *küchen,* rich fruit-filled pastries. (Raspberry is a special favorite here.) Sample them during the late-afternoon *onces,* the coffee breaks locals take to tide them over until dinner. The Germans also brought their beer-making prowess to the New World; Valdivia, in particular, is recognized as Chile's brewing center, home to the popular Kunstmann brand.

About the Hotels

If you've traveled in Europe, you may feel at home in the Lake District, where most of the lodgings resemble old-world hotels. Many hostelries, even the newly built ones, are constructed in Bavarian-chalet style echoing the region's Germanic heritage. A handful of lodgings—Temuco's Hotel Continental, Pucón's Hotel Antumalal, and Puerto Octay's Hotel Centinela—are also historic landmarks that shouldn't be missed. The owners of many smaller places are couples in which one spouse is Chilean and the other is German, combining what one such pair calls "the best of both worlds: Chilean warmth and Germanic efficiency."

Central heating is a much-appreciated feature in most lodgings here in winter and on brisk summer evenings. Air-conditioning is unheard of, but then it's rarely necessary this far south. Rates usually include a Continental breakfast of coffee, cheese, bread, and jam. Although most of the places listed here stay open all year, call ahead to make sure the owners haven't decided to take a well-deserved vacation during the March–November off-season.

WHAT IT COSTS In pesos (in thousands)				
$$$$	**$$$**	**$$**	**$**	**¢**
RESTAURANTS over 11	8–11	5–8	3–5	under 3
HOTELS over 105	75–105	45–75	15–45	under 15

Restaurant prices are for a main course at dinner. Hotel prices are for a double room in high season, excluding tax.

When to Go

Seemingly everyone heads here during southern Chile's glorious summer, between December and February. Visiting during the off-season is no hardship, though, and lodging prices drop dramatically. An increasing number of smog-weary Santiaguinos flee the capital in winter to enjoy the Lake District's brisk, clear air. Just be prepared for rain and some snow at higher elevations.

LA ARAUCANÍA

The tourism industry uses "Lake District" to denote the 400-km (240-mi) stretch of land beginning in Temuco and running south to Puerto Montt, but Chileans call only the southern part of this region *Los Lagos* (The Lakes). To the north is the fiercely proud La Araucanía, whose regional government seems to emblazon its name on everything possible.

La Araucanía is the historic home of the Araucano, or Mapuche, culture. The Spanish both feared and respected the Mapuche. This nomadic society, always in search of new terrain, was a moving target that the Spaniards found impossible to defeat. Beginning with the 1598 battle against European settlers, the Mapuche kept firm control of the region for almost 300 years. After numerous peace agreements failed, a treaty signed near Temuco ended hostilities in 1881 and paved the way for the German, Swiss, and Austrian immigration that would transform the face of the Lake District.

It may not be called Los Lagos, but La Araucanía contains some of Chile's most spectacular lake scenery. Several volcanoes, among them Villar-

On your arrival into **Temuco,** spend the afternoon shopping for Mapuche hand-icrafts at the city's Mercado Municipal. Rise early the next morning and drive to **Villarrica** or **Pucón,** where you can spend the day exploring a beautiful area, maybe taking a dip in one of the nearby thermal springs. The next day take a hike up Volcán Villarrica. Day 4 means a drive south to **Valdivia,** where you can spend the afternoon visiting the modern-art and history museums on Isla Teja. Catch an evening cruise along the Río Valdivia. Rise early the next day and drive to the Bavarian-style village of **Frutillar** on Lago Llanquihue. Visit the Museo Colonial Alemán and wind up the afternoon partaking of the Chilean *onces* ritual with a cup of coffee and *küchen*. Head for **Puerto Varas** the next day for a thrilling rafting excursion on the nearby Río Petrohué. Save **Puerto Montt** for your final day, and spend the afternoon shopping for handicrafts in the Angelmó market stalls. Finish with a seafood dinner at one of the market's lively restaurants.

6

---

rica and Llaima, two of South America's most active, loom over the region. Burgeoning Pucón, on the shore of Lago Villarrica, has become the tourism hub of southern Chile. Other quieter alternatives exist, however. Lago Calafquén, farther south, begins the seven-lake Siete Lagos chain that stretches across the border to Argentina.

Temuco

❶ *675 km (405 mi) south of Santiago.*

This northern gateway to the Lake District acquired a bit of pop-culture cachet as the setting for a segment in 2004's *The Motorcycle Diaries,* a film depicting the early 1950s, prerevolutionary travels of Che Guevara through South America. But with its office towers and shopping malls, today's Temuco would hardly be recognizable to Guevara. The city has a more Latin flavor than the communities farther south. (It could be the warmer weather and the palm trees swaying in the pleasant central park.) It's also an odd juxtaposition of modern architecture and indigenous markets, of traditionally clad Mapuche women darting across the street and business executives talking on cell phones, but, oddly enough, it all works. This is big-city life Chilean style, and it warrants a day if you have the time.

Bustling **Plaza Aníbal Pinto,** Temuco's central square, is ringed with imported palm trees—a rarity in this part of the country. A monument to the 300-year struggle between the Mapuche and the Spaniards sits in the center. The small subterranean **Galería de Arte** displays rotating exhibits by Chilean artists. ⊠ *Plaza Aníbal Pinto* ☎ *45/236–785* 🖙 *Free* ☺ *Mon.–Sat. 10–8, Sun. 1–8.*

The city's modern **Catedral de Temuco** sits on the northwest corner of the central square, flanked by an office tower emblazoned with a cross.

CloseUp

LAKE DISTRICT FESTIVALS & SEASONAL EVENTS

Summer, with its better weather and ample presence of vacationers, means festival season in the Lake District. In late January and early February, Semanas Musicales de Frutillar brings together the best in classical music. Verano en Valdivia is a two-month-long celebration centered on the February 9 anniversary of the founding of Valdivia. Villarica hosts a Muestra Cultural Mapuche in January and February that shows off Mapuche art and music.

Lined with lime and oak trees, a shady secondary square called **Plaza Teodoro Schmidt** lies six blocks north of the Plaza Aníbal Pinto. It's ruled over by the 1906 Iglesia Santa Trinidad, an Anglican church that is one of the city's oldest surviving structures.

Housed in a 1924 mansion, the **Museo Regional de la Araucanía** covers the history of the area. It has an eclectic collection of artifacts and relics, including musical instruments, utensils, and the country's best collection of indigenous jewelry. Upstairs, exhibits document the Mapuche people's three-century struggle to keep control of their land. The presentation could be more evenhanded: the rhetoric glorifies the Central European colonization of this area as the *pacificación de la Araucanía* (taming of the Araucanía territories). But the museum gives you a reasonably good Spanish-language introduction to Mapuche history, art, and culture. ⊠ *Av. Alemania 84* ☏ *45/211–108* 🖅 *500 pesos* ⊙ *Weekdays 9–5, Sat. 11–5, Sun. 11–1.*

★ Author Pablo Neruda was Chile's most famous train buff. (Neruda spent his childhood in Temuco and his father was a rail worker.) Accordingly, the city has transformed its old rail yard into the **Museo Nacional Ferroviario Pablo Neruda**, a well-laid-out museum documenting Chile's rail history and dedicated to the author's memory. Thirteen locomotives (1 diesel and 12 steam) and nine train carriages are housed in the round engine building. Scattered among the exhibits are snippets from Neruda's writings: "Trains were dreaming in the station, defenseless, sleeping, without locomotives," reads one wistful reflection. Exhibits are labeled in Spanish, but an English-speaking guide is on hand if you need translation. The museum lies a bit off the beaten path, but if trains fascinate you, as they did Neruda, it's worth the short taxi ride from downtown. This new museum is a work in progress, with further acquisitions and transformation of other rail-yard buildings under way at this writing.

Fabulous Volcanoes
Volcán Villarrica and Volcán Osorno are the conical, iconic symbols of the northern and southern Lake District respectively, but some 50 other volcanoes loom and fume in this region. And not to worry: that's all they usually do; you can even climb many of them.

Stunning Summer Nights
Southern Chile's austral summer doesn't get more glorious than those January and February evenings when everyone is out dining, shopping, strolling, and enjoying the sunsets that don't fade until well after 10 PM.

6

Amazing Water Sports
There's good reason this is called "the Lake District." The region may sport a long Pacific coastline, but everyone flocks to the inland lakes. This far south, they're calmer and the water is warmer than the ocean.

Soothing Hot Springs
Chile counts some 280 thermal springs, and a good many of the well-operated ones are in the Lake District, the perfect place to pamper yourself after a day of outdoor adventure and sightseeing.

Shopping for Crafts
The Lake District is one of the best places to purchase traditional crafts. The best selection of woolen blankets and ponchos of the indigenous Mapuche people is sold in the markets of Temuco, most notably in the Mercado Municipal. Chilote woolens come from nearby Chiloé, but the best place to buy these handicrafts is not the island itself, but at the market stalls of Caleta Angelmó near Puerto Montt.

Twice-monthly tourist rail excursions to Valdivia, using the museum's restored 1940 steam locomotive, three cars, and a dining coach, are scheduled to begin in 2006. ⊠ *Av. Barros Arana 565* ☎ *45/227–613* 💰 *1,000 pesos* ☉ *Tues.–Sun. 9–6.*

The imposing **Monumento Natural Cerro Ñielol** is the hillside site where the 1881 treaty between the Mapuche and the Chilean army was signed, allowing for the city of Temuco to be established. Trails bloom with bright red *copihues* (a bell-like flower with lush green foliage), Chile's national flower, in autumn (March–May). The monument, not far from downtown, is part of Chile's national park system. ⊠ *Av. Arturo Prat, 5 blocks north of Plaza Teodoro Schmidt* 💰 *700 pesos* ☉ *Jan.–Mar., daily 8 AM–11 PM; Apr.–Nov., daily 8:30–12:30 and 2:30–6.*

Where to Stay & Eat

$$–$$$ ✕ **El Fogón.** Decorated with primary colors—yellow walls, red tablecloths, and blue dishes—this place certainly stands out in pastel-hue Temuco. The Chilean-style *parrillada*, or grilled beef, is the specialty of the house. Barbecue here has subtler spices than its better-known Argentine counterpart. The friendly owners will gladly take the time to explain the menu

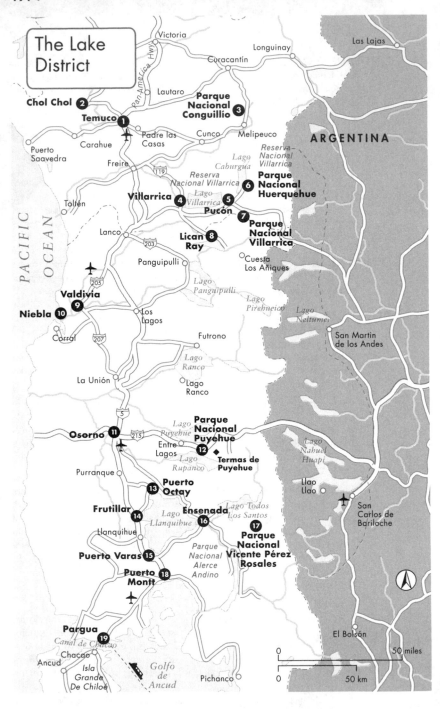

The Lake District

Victoria
Longuinay
Las Lajas
Curacantín
Pan-America Hwy.
Lautaro
Chol Chol ❷
Parque Nacional Conguillio ❸
Temuco ❶
Padre las Casas
Cunco
Melipeuco
ARGENTINA
Puerto Saavedra
Carahue
Freire
119
Reserva Nacional Villarrica
Lago Caburgua
Toltén
Reserva Nacional Villarrica
Villarrica ❹
Lago Villarrica
❺
Parque Nacional Huerquehue ❻
Pucón
❼
Parque Nacional Villarrica
Lanco
203
Lican Ray ❽
Panguipulli
Cuesta Los Añiques
Lago Pirehueico
Lago Panguipulli
205
Lago Neltume
Valdivia ❾
Niebla ❿
Los Lagos
San Martín de los Andes
Corral
207
Futrono
Lago Ranco
La Unión
Lago Ranco
Lago Puyehue
Parque Nacional Puyehue
Osorno ⓫
215
Entre Lagos
⓬
5
Lago Rupanco
♦ **Termas de Puyehue**
Lago Nahuel Huapi
Purranque
Puerto Octay ⓭
Llao Llao
Frutillar ⓮
Lago Llanquihue
Ensenada ⓰
Lago Todos Los Santos
San Carlos de Bariloche
Llanquihue
⓱
Parque Nacional Vicente Pérez Rosales
Parque Nacional Alerce Andino
Puerto Varas ⓯
Puerto Montt ⓲
El Bolsón
Pargua ⓳
Canal de Chacao
Chacao
Ancud
Isla Grande De Chiloé
Golfo de Ancud
Pichanco

PACIFIC OCEAN

0   50 miles
0   50 km

to the uninitiated. Even though this is close to downtown, you should splurge on a cab if you're coming to this dark street at night. ✉ *Aldunate 288* ☎ *45/737–061* ▤ No *credit cards.*

$$–$$$ ✕ **La Pampa.** Wealthy local professionals frequent this upscale modern steak house for its huge, delicious cuts of beef and the best *papas fritas* (french fries) in Temuco. Although most Chilean restaurants douse any kind of meat with a creamy sauce, this is one of the few exceptions: the entrées are served without anything but the simplest of seasonings. ✉ *Caupolicán 0155* ☎ *45/329–999* ⌂ *Reservations essential* ▤ *AE, DC, MC, V* ☺ *No dinner Sun.*

$–$$ ✕ **Centro Español.** The basement dining room of Centro Español, an association that promotes Spanish culture in Temuco, is open to all for lunch and dinner. You have your choice of four or five rotating prix-fixe menus. There will always be something Spanish, something seafood, and something meaty to choose from. *Jamón de Serrano,* a salty type of ham, is a specialty. ✉ *Av. Bulnes 483* ☎ *45/217–700* ▤ *AE, DC, MC, V.*

$–$$ ✕ **Confitería Central.** Coffee and homemade pastries are the specialties of this café, but sandwiches and other simple dishes are also available. Steaming-hot empanadas are served on Sunday and holidays, and during the week you'll swear all of Temuco stops by for a quick bite for lunch among the clattering of dishes and the army of waitresses maneuvering their way around the tables. ✉ *Av. Bulnes 442* ☎ *45/210–083* ▤ *DC, MC, V.*

$–$$ ✕ **Mercado Municipal.** In the central market around the produce stalls are small stands offering such typical Chilean meals as cazuela and pastel de choclo. Many have actually taken on the trappings of sit-down restaurants, and a few even have air-conditioning. The complex closes at 8 in summer and 6 the rest of the year, so late-night dining is not an option. ✉ *Manuel Rodríguez 960* ☎ No *phone* ▤ No *credit cards.*

$–$$ ✕▦ **Hotel Frontera.** This lovely old hotel is really two in one, with *nuevo* (new) and *clásico* (classic) wings facing each other across Avenida Bulnes. Tastefully decorated rooms have double-pane windows to keep out the street noise. Opt for the less expensive rooms in the newer wing—they're nicer anyway. La Taberna, the downstairs restaurant on the clásico side ($$–$$$), has excellent steak and seafood dining. An orchestra plays and people dance on weekends. ✉ *Av. Bulnes 733–726* ☎ *45/200–400* 🖷 *45/200–401* ⊕ *www.hotelfrontera.cl* 🛏 *60 rooms, 2 suites* ⌂ *Restaurant, minibars, cable TV, bar, laundry service, business services, convention center, meeting room; no a/c* ▤ *AE, DC, MC, V* ⭐️ *BP.*

★ $ ✕▦ **Hotel Continental.** If you appreciate faded elegance and don't mind an uneven floorboard or two, some peeling paint, and few conveniences, the 1890 Continental is for you. Checkered in black-and-white tiles, the lobby has leather furniture, antique bronze lamps, and handsome *alerce* and *raulí* (native wood) trims. Rooms, painted in ash-blue and cream tones, have hardwood floors and lofty ceilings. The hotel has hosted Nobel laureates Pablo Neruda and Gabriela Mistral, and former president Salvador Allende. The restaurant ($$–$$$) serves delicious French cuisine. Good choices include the steak au poivre and the salade niçoise. ✉ *Antonio Varas 708* ☎ *45/238–973* 🖷 *45/233–830* ⊕ *www.*

CloseUp

THE PEOPLE OF THE LAND

THE MAPUCHE PROFOUNDLY AFFECTED the history of southern Chile. For almost 300 years this indigenous group fought to keep colonial, then Chilean powers out of their land. The Spanish referred to these people as the Araucanos, from a word in the Quechua language meaning "brave and valiant warriors." In their own Mapudungun language, today spoken by some 400,000 people, the word Mapuche means "people of the land." In colonial times only the Spanish missionaries, who were in close contact with the Mapuche, seemed to grasp what this meant. "There are no people in the world," one of them wrote, "who so love and value the land where they were born."

Chilean schoolchildren learning about the Mapuche are likely to read about Lautaro, a feared and respected young chief whose military tactics were instrumental in driving out the Spanish. He cunningly adopted a know-thy-enemy strategy that proved tremendously successful in fending off the colonists. Students are less likely to hear about the tightly knit family structure or nomadic lifestyle of the Mapuche. Even the region's two museums dedicated to Mapuche culture, in Temuco and Valdivia, traditionally focused on the three-century war with the Spaniards. They toss around terms like pacificación (meaning "to pacify" or "to tame") to describe the waves of European immigrants who settled in the Lake District at the end of the 1800s, the beginning of the end of Mapuche dominance in the region.

Life has been difficult for the Mapuche since the signing of a peace treaty in 1881. Their land was slowly taken by the Chilean government. Some 200,000 Mapuche today are living on 3,000 reducciones (literally meaning "reductions"), operated much like the system of reservations in the United States. Other Mapuche have migrated to the cities, in particular fast-growing Temuco, in search of employment. Many have lost their identity in the urban landscape, scraping together a living as handicraft vendors.

A resurgence in Mapuche pride these days takes several forms, some peaceful, some militant. Mapuche demonstrations in Temuco are now commonplace, many calling attention to deplorable conditions on the reducciones. Some are seeking the return of their land, although others are fighting against the encroachment of power companies damming the rivers and logging interests cutting down the forests. News reports occasionally recount attacks and counterattacks between indigenous groups and farmers in remote rural areas far off the beaten tourist path. The courts have become the newest battleground as the Mapuche seek legal redress for land they feel was wrongfully taken.

Awareness of Mapuche history is rising. (Latest census figures show that about 1 million of Chile's population of 15 million can claim some Mapuche ancestry.) Both major museums have devoted more of their space to the art, language, and culture of this people. Both institutions spend ample time these days discussing the group's distinctive textiles, with their bold rhomboid, triangular, and zigzagging lines. Both museums also devote considerable space to traditional animal-shape pottery.

There is also a newfound interest in the Mapuche language and its seven dialects. Mapudungun poetry movingly describes the sadness and dilemma of integration into modern life and of becoming lost in the anonymity of urban life. Never before really understood by others who shared their land, the Mapuche may finally make their cause known.

—Jeffrey Van Fleet

turismochile.cl/continental/ ⇖ *40 rooms, 20 with bath* ⚿ *Restaurant, bar, meeting room; no a/c, no TV in some rooms* ⊟ *AE, DC, MC, V* †◎ *CP.*

$$–$$$ ⊞ **Hotel Terraverde.** Temuco's most luxurious lodging combines all the comforts of a modern hotel with the style of a hunting lodge. The dramatic, glass-enclosed spiral staircase leads off the stone-wall lobby with its huge fireplace and has a view of Cerro Ñielol. Cheerful rooms have lovely wood furnishings. Rates include a huge breakfast buffet, a nice change from the roll and coffee served at many other lodgings in the region. It's part of Chile's Panamericana Hoteles chain. ⊠ *Av. Arturo Prat 220* ☎ *45/239–999, 2/234–9610 in Santiago* 🖷 *45/239–455, 2/234–9608 in Santiago* ⊕ *www.panamericanahoteles.cl* ⇖ *64 rooms, 10 suites* ⚿ *Restaurant, in-room safes, minibars, cable TV, some Wi-Fi, pool, sauna, piano bar, laundry service, Internet room, business services, convention center, meeting rooms, airport shuttle, travel services, no a/c, no-smoking rooms* ⊟ *AE, DC, MC, V* †◎ *BP.*

$ ⊞ **Holiday Inn Express.** This hotel is one of five of the chain's outlets in Chile. If you're looking for something uniquely Chilean about the place, you won't find it, but you will find all the U.S.-style amenities, including the do-it-yourself breakfast for which the chain is known, and that's its selling point for guests who stay here. You're quite a way from downtown, but it's a good option if you have a vehicle. ⊠ *Av. Rudecindo Ortega 1800* ☎ *45/223–300* 🖷 *45/224–100* ⊕ *www.hiexpress.com* ⇖ *62 rooms* ⚿ *Coffee shop, dining room, in-room safes, cable TV, some Wi-Fi, pool, gym, hot tub, dry cleaning, laundry service, business services, no-smoking rooms; no a/c* ⊟ *AE, MC, V* †◎ *BP.*

$ ⊞ **Don Eduardo Hotel.** Orange inside and out, this pleasant nine-story hotel is made up entirely of cozy furnished apartments, with comfortable chairs and dining area. All have two or three bedrooms and kitchenettes. The many business travelers who frequent the place appreciate the work areas, with desks and shelves, although you do need to go downstairs to log on to the Internet. An eager-to-please staff tends to your needs. ⊠ *Bello 755* ☎ *45/214–133* 🖷 *45/215–554* ⊕ *www. hoteldoneduardo.cl* ⇖ *33 apartments* ⚿ *Restaurant, cable TV, Internet room, business services, meeting room; no a/c* ⊟ *AE, DC, MC, V* †◎ *BP.*

$ ⊞ **Hotel Aitué.** The exterior of this hotel is unimposing; in fact, its covered drive-up entry, set back from the road, might cause you to drive right past it. Once you're in, though, you'll find that this small, pleasant business-class hotel has bright, airy rooms with a tan-and-lavender color scheme. They're on the smallish side, but cozy and comfortable, and come complete with minibars and music systems. ⊠ *Antonio Varas 1048* ☎ *45/212–512* 🖷 *45/212–608* ⊕ *www.hotelaitue.cl* ⇖ *35 rooms* ⚿ *Coffee shop, minibars, cable TV, bar, laundry service, Internet room, business services, meeting rooms; no a/c* ⊟ *AE, DC, MC, V* †◎ *CP.*

$ ⊞ **Hotel Turismo.** Originally established as a budget accommodation, this three-story hotel retains its bland facade. The interior has been upgraded, however, with a comfortable lobby and rooms with their own music systems, cushy beds, and tables and chairs. A lime-green color scheme permeates throughout. ⊠ *Av. Lynch 563* ☎🖷 *45/911–090*

⊕ *www.hotelturismotemuco.cl* ↩ *30 rooms* ⌂ *Restaurant, cable TV, bar, laundry service; no a/c* ⊟ *AE, DC, MC, V.*

Sports & the Outdoors

CONAF (✉ Bilbao 931 ☎ 45/298–221) administers Chile's national parks and provides maps and other information about them. In summer it also organizes hikes in Parque Nacional Conguillío. The agency is strict about permits to ascend the nearby volcanoes, so expect to show evidence of your climbing ability and experience.

Shopping

The **Mercado Municipal** (✉ Manuel Rodríguez 960 ☎ No phone) is one of the best places in the country to find Mapuche woolen ponchos, pullovers, and blankets. The interior of the 1930 structure has been extensively remodeled, and is quite open and airy. The low-key artisan vendors share the complex with butchers, fishmongers, and fruit sellers. There is no bargaining, but the prices are fair. It opens daily at 8, but closes around 3 on Sunday.

A little more rough-and-tumble than the Mercado Municipal is the **Feria Libre** (✉ Barros Arana at Miraflores). You can bargain hard with the Mapuche vendors who sell their crafts and produce in the blocks surrounding the railroad station and bus terminal. Leave the camera behind, as the vendors aren't happy about being photographed. It's open from about 7 to 2 Monday–Saturday.

Casa de la Mujer Mapuche (✉ Portales 1190 ☎ 45/233-886), an indigenous women's center, lets you shop for textiles, ponchos, and jewelry in its display room, with a minimum of fuss. (The organization even handles catalog sales.) Proceeds support social development programs. It's open weekdays 9:30–1 and 3–6.

Across the Río Cautín from Temuco is the suburb of **Padre Las Casas** (✉ 2 km [1 mi] southeast of Temuco), a Mapuche community whose center is populated by artisan vendors selling locally crafted woodwork, textiles, and pottery under the auspices of the town's rural development program. You can purchase crafts here weekdays 9–5.

Chol Chol

② *29 km (18 mi) northwest of Temuco.*

The Chol Chol experience begins the moment you board the bus in Temuco. Expect to share space with Mapuche vendors and their enormous sacks and baskets of fruits and vegetables, all returning from market. A trip in your own vehicle is much less wearing, but infinitely less colorful, too. Regardless of your chosen mode of transport, you'll arrive to the sight of *rucas,* traditional indigenous thatch huts, plus claptrap wooden houses, horse-drawn carts, and artisan vendors lining the dusty streets—all of whom sell their wares from 9 until about 6. Photo opportunities are plentiful, but be unobtrusive and courteous with your camera. Locals dislike being treated as merely part of the scenery.

The small **Museo de Chol Chol** exhibits a collection of animal-shape ceramics and textiles with bold rhomboid and zigzag designs—both are distinctively

OUTDOOR ADVENTURES

AWASH IN RIVERS, *mountains, forests, gorges, and its namesake lakes, this part of the country is Chile's outdoor capital. Outfitters traditionally have concentrated in the northern resort town of Pucón and the southern Puerto Varas, but firms up and down this 400-km-long (240-mi-long) slice of Chile can rent you equipment or guide your excursions.*

You can—take a deep breath—go white-water rafting, canoeing, kayaking, mountain biking, fishing, volcano climbing, rappelling, rock climbing, canyoning, horseback riding, skiing, snowshoeing, snowboarding, waterskiing, bird-watching, hiking, swimming, sailing, and skydiving. The most recent addition to the activities mix is the canopy tour: you can make like a bird and glide through the treetops, courtesy of zip lines, helmets, and a very secure harness.

The increasing popularity of such excursions means that everybody and their brother and sister seem to want a slice of the adventure küchen. Quality varies widely, especially in everybody's-an-outfitter destinations such as Pucón. Ask questions about safety and guide-to-client ratios. (A few unscrupulous businesses might take 20 climbers up the Villarrica volcano with a single guide.) Also, be brutally frank with yourself about your own capabilities: Are you really in shape for rappelling? Or is bird-watching more your style? This is nature at its best and sometimes at its most powerful.

Mapuche specialties—as well as old black-and-white photographs. A *fogón*, the traditional cooking pit, graces the center of the museum. ⊠ *Balmaceda s/n* ☏ *45/611–034* 💷 *300 pesos* ☉ *Tues.–Sun. 9–6.*

Parque Nacional Conguillío

❸ *91 km (54 mi) east of Temuco.*

Volcán Llaima, which erupted as recently as 1994 and has shown constant, but not dangerous, low levels of activity since 2002, is the brooding centerpiece of Parque Nacional Conguillío. The 3,125-meter (10,200-foot) monster, one of the continent's most active volcanoes, has altered the landscape—much of the park's southern portion is a moonscape of hardened lava flow. But in the 610-square-km (235-square-mi) park's northern sector there are thousands of umbrella-like araucaria pines, often known as monkey puzzle trees.

The Sierra Nevada trail is the most popular for short hiking. The three-hour trek begins at park headquarters on Laguna Conguillío, continuing northeast to Laguna Captrén. One of the inaugural sections of the Sendero de Chile, a hiking and biking trail, passes through the park. Modeled on the Appalachian Trail in the United States, the project will eventually span the length of the country. Completion is expected around 2010.

Heavy snow can cut off the area in winter, so November to March is the best time to visit the park's eastern sector. Conguillío's western sector, Los Paraguas, comes into its own in winter because of a small ski center. ⊠ *Entrances at Melipeuco and Curacautín* ☎ *45/298–213 in Temuco* 🎫 *2,500 pesos* ⊙ *Dec.–Mar., daily 8 AM–10 PM; Apr.–Nov., daily 8–5.*

Where to Stay

$–$$ 🏨 **Cabañas Conguillío.** The only accommodation available close to the park, this property rents basic four-person cabins built around the trunks of araucaria trees. All come with kitchen utensils, stoves, and cooking fuel. Also here are an on-site restaurant and a small store where you can stock up on provisions. ⊠ *Laguna Conguillío* ☎ *45/213–299 in Temuco* 🛏 *6 cabins* 🍴 *Restaurant, grocery; no a/c, no room phones, no room TVs* ▭ *No credit cards* ⊙ *Closed Apr.–Nov.*

Villarrica

❹ *87 km (52 mi) southeast of Temuco.*

Villarrica was founded in 1552, but the Mapuche wars prevented extensive settlement of the area until the early 20th century. Today, the pleasant town on the lake of the same name is in one of the loveliest, least-spoiled areas of the southern Andes, and has stunning views of the Villarrica and Llaima volcanoes. To its eternal chagrin, Villarrica lives in the shadow of Pucón, its flashier neighbor a few miles down the road. Many travelers drive through without giving Villarrica a glance, but they're missing out. Villarrica has some wonderful hotels that won't give you a case of high-season sticker shock. Well-maintained roads and convenient public transportation make the town a good base for exploring the area.

The municipal museum, **Museo Histórico y Arqueológico de Villarrica,** displays an impressive collection of Mapuche ceramics, masks, leather, and jewelry. A replica of a ruca graces the front yard. It's made of thatch so tightly entwined that it's impermeable to rain. ⊠ *Pedro de Valdivia 1050* ☎ *45/413–445* 🎫 *100 pesos* ⊙ *Jan. and Feb., Mon.–Sat. 9–1 and 4–10; Mar.–Dec., Mon.–Sat. 9–1 and 3–7:30.*

Where to Stay & Eat

$–$$$ ✕ **The Travellers.** Hui, Martin, and Juan came from China, Germany, and Chile respectively, met by happenstance, and decided to open a place serving food from their homelands and several others. The result is a place that serves one or two dishes from Germany, Thailand, China, Italy, Mexico, and many countries in between. While you chow down on an enchilada, your companions might be having spaghetti with meatballs or sweet-and-sour pork. Dining on the front lawn under umbrella-covered tables is the best option on a summer evening. ⊠ *Valentín Letelier 753* ☎ *45/413–617* ▭ *AE, DC, MC, V.*

$–$$ ✕ **Café 2001.** For a filling sandwich, a homemade küchen, and an espresso or cappuccino brewed from freshly ground beans, this is the

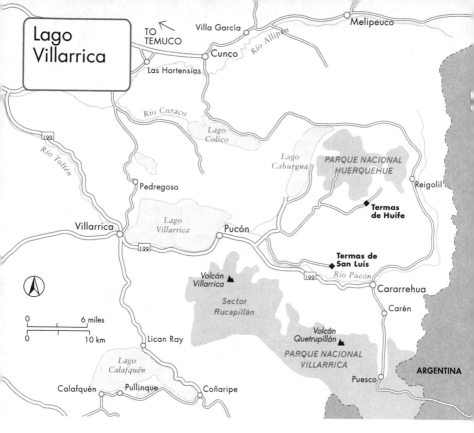

place to stop in Villarrica. Pull up around a table in front or slip into one of the quieter booths by the fireplace in the back. The *lomito completo* sandwich—with a slice of pork, avocado, sauerkraut, tomato, and mayonnaise—is one of the best in the south. ⊠ *Camillo Henríquez 379* ☎ *45/411–470* 🖃 *AE, DC, MC, V.*

$$$$ 🏨 **Villarrica Park Lake Hotel.** This sumptuous old European spa with modern touches is the perfect mix of old-world plush and clean, uncluttered design. There's ample use of hardwood in the bright, spacious common area and the rooms—each with its own balcony and lake view—that descend down a hill toward Lago Villarrica. ⊠ *13 km (8 mi) east of Villarrica on the road to Pucón* ☎ *45/450–000, 2/207–7070 in Santiago, 888/790–5264 in North America* 🖷 *45/450–202, 2/207–7020 in Santiago* ⊕ *www.villarricaparklakehotel.cl/* 🛏 *61 rooms, 9 suites* 🍴 *Restaurant, in-room data ports, in-room safes, minibars, cable TV, 2 pools (1 indoors), gym, hair salon, hot tub, sauna, spa, 2 bars, babysitting, library, shop, dry cleaning, laundry service, Internet room, business services, meeting rooms, airport shuttle* 🖃 *AE, DC, MC, V* 🍽 *BP.*

$$ 🏨 **Hostería de la Colina.** The friendly American owners of this hostería, **Fodor'sChoice** Glen and Beverly Aldrich, provide attentive service as well as special little touches like homemade ice cream. Rooms in the half-century-old main house are a mix of large and small, carpets and hardwood floors, all tastefully decorated with wood furnishings. Two bright, airy hillside cottages are carpeted and wood paneled and have private patios. There's a hot tub heated by a wood-burning stove, and a serene *vivero* (greenhouse) and garden that attracts birds. The terrace has stupendous views of Lago Villarrica. ⊠ *Las Colinas 115* ☏ *45/411–503* ⊕ *www. hosteriadelacolina.com* ➟ *8 rooms, 2 cabins* ⚒ *Dining room, hot tub, massage, croquet, horseshoes, Ping-Pong, bar; no a/c, no room phones, no room TVs* ▤ *AE, DC, MC, V* ⦿⏐ *BP.*

$ ▥ **Hotel El Ciervo.** Villarrica's oldest hotel is an unimposing house on a quiet street, but inside are elegant details such as wrought-iron fixtures and wood-burning fireplaces. Spacious rooms, some with their own fireplaces, have huge beds and sparkling bathrooms. Just outside is a lovely pool and a secluded patio. Rates include an enormous German breakfast with loads of fruit, muesli, and fresh milk. El Ciervo also has all-inclusive seven-day tour packages. ⊠ *General Körner 241* ☏ *45/411– 215* 🖷 *45/413–884* ⊕ *www.hotelelciervo.cl* ➟ *12 rooms* ⚒ *Restaurant, cable TV, pool, bar, laundry service, Internet room, meeting rooms; no a/c* ▤ *AE, DC, MC, V* ⦿⏐ *BP.*

$ ▥ **El Parque.** You can take in the commanding views of Lago Villarrica from just about anywhere at this 70-year-old, rustic and quaint retreat—the comfy lobby, the sitting area, the restaurant, or the warmly colored guest rooms. Eleven modern cabins amble down the hill to a private beach and dock. Each cabin, which accommodates two–eight people, comes with a kitchen, fireplace, and terrace. You are on your own here, but lots of personalized attention is yours for the asking. ⊠ *Camino Villarrica–Pucón, Km 2.5* ☏ *45/411–120* 🖷 *45/411–090* ⊕ *www.hotelelparque.cl* ➟ *8 rooms, 12 cabins* ⚒ *Restaurant, cable TV, tennis court, pool, beach, laundry service, meeting room; no a/c* ▤ *AE, DC, MC, V* ⦿⏐ *BP.*

$ ▥ **Montebianco Hotel.** The owner makes many of the wood furnishings that fill this central lodging. The pleasant rooms upstairs all have small balconies. The tiled bathrooms are clean and bright, but the showers are tiny, with barely enough room to turn around. ⊠ *Pedro de Valdivia 1011* ☏ *45/411–798* 🖷 *45/411–586* ⊕ *www.hotelmontebianco.cl* ➟ *16 rooms* ⚒ *Restaurant, cable TV, bar, meeting room; no a/c* ▤ *AE, DC, MC, V* ⦿⏐ *CP.*

Horseback Riding

The friendly, knowledgeable folks at **Flor del Lago** (⊠ Camino a Pedregoso, Km 9 ☏ 45/415–455 ⊕ www.flordellago.cl) will take you on half- or full-day horseback-riding excursions in the forests surrounding Lago Villarrica.

Pucón

❺ *25 km (15 mi) east of Villarrica.*

The trendy resort town of Pucón, on the southern shore of Lago Villarrica, attracts wealthy, fashionable Chileans. Like their counterparts in the Colorado ski resort of Vail, they come to enjoy their luxurious vacation homes, stroll along the main strip, and flock to the major nightspots. For

Pucón

Lago
Villarrica

Playa Grande

La Peninsula

Clemente Holzapfel

Carlos Ansorena

Pasaja Luck

Pedro de Valdivia

Alderete

General Urrutia

O'Higgins

Caupolican

Lincoyan

Fresia

Miguel Ansorena

Palguin

Peru

Arauco

Colo Colo

Camino Internacional

Brasil

Chile

Uruguay

Paraguay

Peru

Ecuador

TO VILLARRICA

Sebastian Engler

Pablo Nappe

TO ARGENTINA

Hotels ▼		Restaurants ▼
Apart Hotel Del Volcán .. **11**	Hotel del Lago **3**	Arabian Restaurant **10**
¡École! **8**	Hotel Huincahue **5**	En Alta Mar **7**
Gran Hotel Pucón **1**	Hotel Malalhue **15**	La Maga **4**
Gudenschwager Hotel ... **2**	Kila Leufu **13**	Patagonia Express **6**
Hotel del Antumalal **12**	Termas de San Luis **14**	¡Viva Perú! **9**

every fan, Pucón has a detractor who laments the town's meteoric rise to fame. "Trendy" translates as "pricey," and your pesos will not go as far here in summer as they do elsewhere in the Lake District. Pucón has a few genuinely wonderful hotels, and several others that, although acceptable, charge dearly for their well-known "everyone wants to stay here" reputation among Chileans. But that doesn't stop visitors from coming; one summer-night stroll along Avenida Bernardo O'Higgins and Fresia, the main streets, and you might be hooked, too.

With Volcán Villarrica looming south of town, a color-coded alert system on the Municipalidad (city hall) on Avenida Bernardo O'Higgins' signals volcanic activity, and signs around town explain the colors' meanings: green—that's where the light almost always remains—signifies "normal activity," indicating steam being let off from the summit with sulfuric odors and constant, low-level rumblings; yellow and red indicate more dangerous levels of activity. Remember: the volcano sits 15 km (9 mi) away, and you'll scarcely be aware of any activity. Indeed, ascending the volcano is the area's most popular excursion.

Where to Stay & Eat

$$–$$$$ ✕ **La Maga.** Argentina claims to prepare the perfect parrillada, or grilled beef, but here's evidence that Uruguayans just might do it best. Watch the beef cuts or salmon turn slowly over the wood fire at the entrance. That, rather than charcoal, is the key, says the owner, a transplant from Punta del Este. The product is a wonderfully smoked, natural taste, accented with a hint of spice in the mild *chimichurri* (a tangy steak sauce). ✉ *Fresia 125* ☎ *45/444–277* ▤ *AE, DC, MC, V* ☾ *Closed Mon. Apr.–Dec.*

$$–$$$$ ✕ **¡Viva Perú!** As befits the name, Peruvian cuisine reigns supreme at this restaurant with rustic wooden tables. Try the *ají de gallina* (hen stew with cheese, milk, and peppers) or the seviche, thoroughly cooked but served cold. You can dine on the porch, a nice option for a pleasant summer night—and take advantage of the two-for-one pisco sours nightly until 9 PM. You can also order to carry out. ✉ *Lincoyan 372* ☎ *45/444–025* ▤ *AE, DC, MC, V.*

$$–$$$ ✕ **En Alta Mar.** The best seafood in Pucón is served here, so don't be frightened off by the nondescript dining room: basic wooden tables and the ubiquitous nautical theme. You'll receive a free welcoming pisco sour when you arrive. ✉ *Fresia at Urrutia* ☎ *45/442–294* ▤ *AE, DC, MC, V.*

¢–$ ✕ **Arabian Restaurant.** The Apara family knows how to whip up tasty falafel or *shawarma* (a pita-bread sandwich filled with spicy beef or lamb). Most everyone opts for the outdoor tables over the tiny indoor dining area. ✉ *Fresia 354* ☎ *45/443–469* ▤ *No credit cards.*

¢–$ ✕ **Patagonia Express.** Argentine owner Marina Secco operates this wonderful café, where yummy fruit-filled pastries are baked fresh all day long. In winter, you can enjoy one, along with a coffee or hot chocolate, at a table near the cozy woodstove; if it's summer, head for one of the tables outside on the sidewalk. This place stays quite lively on summer nights until about 3 AM. ✉ *Fresia 233* ☎ *45/443–165* ▤ *AE, DC, MC, V.*

**$** ✕▥ **¡école!** It's part hostel and part beach house—and takes its name from a Chilean expression meaning "Great!" Cozy two-, three-, and four-person rooms can be shared or private. The vegetarian restaurant ($–$$), a rarity in the Lake District, merits a trip in itself. You can choose among truly international options, such as lasagna, burritos, and moussaka, and eat in the sunny courtyard or small dining room. The environmentally conscious staff can organize hiking and horseback-riding trips and expeditions to volcanoes and hot springs, as well as arrange for Spanish lessons and massages. ⊠ *General Urrutia 592* ☎ *45/441–675* ⊕ *www.ecole.cl* ➟ *21 rooms, 9 with bath* ⌂ *Restaurant, bar, travel services; no a/c, no room phones, no room TVs, no smoking* ⊟ *AE, DC, MC, V.*

$$$$ ▨ **Hotel del Lago.** Short on charm, this glitzy hotel has everything else you could hope for—an indoor pool, a health spa, even a movie theater. Enter through the five-story atrium lobby, then let one of the glass elevators whisk you upstairs. The rooms are simple and elegant, with blond wood and crisp white linens. The hotel is known as "the Casino" for its Las Vegas–style ground floor, complete with rows of one-arm bandits and tables for roulette and poker. ⊠ *Miguel Ansorena 23* ☎ *45/291–000, 2/462–1900 in Santiago* 🖷 *45/291–200, 2/370–5942 in Santiago* ⊕ *www.hoteldellago.cl* ➟ *81 rooms, 2 suites* ⌂ *Restaurant, snack bar, in-room safes, minibars, cable TV, 2 pools, gym, hair salon, massage, sauna, bar, casino, theater, shops, business services, convention center, meeting room; no a/c* ⊟ *AE, DC, MC, V* ⦿ *BP, MAP.*

$$$–$$$$ ▨ **Gran Hotel Pucón.** The outside of Pucón's largest hotel is quite *gran* and imposing in true alpine-lodge style, with wonderful views of Lago Villarrica. Its location right on the shore provides direct access to the beach. The rooms, although perfectly acceptable, are disappointingly contemporary; the exterior gets your hopes up for something more old world. Depending on which side of the building you are on, though, you do get stupendous views of either the lake or of Volcán Villarrica. The hotel is enormously popular among Chileans who come here for the slate of activities, so you won't find much peace and quiet here, especially in summer. ⊠ *Clemente Holzapfel 190* ☎ *45/441–001, 2/353–0000 in Santiago* 🖷 *2/207–4586 in Santiago* ⊕ *www.granhotelpucon.cl* ➟ *145 rooms* ⌂ *2 restaurants, in-room safes, minibars, cable TV, 2 pools, massage, sauna, squash, bar, theater, laundry service, business services, convention center, meeting room, travel services; no a/c* ⊟ *AE, DC, MC, V* ⦿ *BP, MAP.*

★ $$$ ▨ **Hotel Antumalal.** A young Queen Elizabeth stayed here in the 1950s, as did actor Jimmy Stewart—and the Antumalal hasn't changed very much since. The décor, styles, and colors from that decade have all been maintained at this family-run hotel, which has the feel of a country inn. It's perched atop a cliff just outside town overlooking Lago Villarrica, and its cozy rooms have fireplaces and huge windows overlooking the spectacularly landscaped grounds. If you tire of relaxing with a refreshing pisco sour on the wisteria-shaded deck, just ask owner Rony Pollak to arrange an adventure for you. Favorites include fly-fishing, white-water rafting, and volcano climbing. ⊠ *Casilla 84* ☎ *45/441–011* 🖷 *45/441–013* ⊕ *www.antumalal.com* ➟ *16 rooms, 2 suites* ⌂ *Restaurant, cable TV, 2 tennis courts, pool, massage, sauna, spa, bar, travel services; no a/c* ⊟ *AE, DC, MC, V* ⦿ *BP.*

$$$
Fodor'sChoice
★

▣ **Hotel Huincahue.** In a town whose motto could be "Bigger is better" when it comes to lodging, the elegant Huincahue is a refreshing find, and deserves to be Pucón's real prestige address. The place sits close to the center of town on the main plaza and has the attentive service that only a small hotel can offer. Lots of windows brighten the lobby and library of the German-style building, which is warmed by a roaring fire. Bright, airy rooms come furnished with wrought-iron and blond-wood furniture, as well as extras, such as Wi-Fi, that are rarely seen in lodgings of this size. Rooms on the second floor have small balconies. Rates include a hearty American breakfast. ⊠ *Pedro de Valdivia 375* ☏ *45/443–540* 🖷 *45/442–728* ⊕ *www.hotelhuincahue.cl* ⇆ *20 rooms* ⌂ *Coffee shop, in-room data ports, cable TV, Wi-Fi, pool, bar, laundry service; no a/c* ▤ *AE, DC, MC, V* ⦿*BP.*

$$–$$$

▣ **Termas de San Luis.** The famous San Luis hot springs are the main attraction of this hideaway east of Pucón. Here you can rent a rustic cabin that sleeps up to six people. Rates include the option of all or some meals—cabins are not kitchen equipped—and free use of the baths. If you're not staying, 5,500 pesos gets you a day of soaking in the thermal springs and mud baths. ⊠ *Carretera Internacional, Km 27, Catripulli* ☏☏ *45/412–880* ⊕ *www.termasdesanluis.cl* ⇆ *6 cabins* ⌂ *2 restaurants, cable TV, 2 pools, massage, sauna, horseback riding, bar; no a/c* ▤ *No credit cards* ⦿*BP, MAP, FAP.*

$$

▣ **Apart Hotel Del Volcán.** In keeping with the region's immigrant heritage, the furnishings of this chalet-style hotel look like they come straight from Germany. Checked fabrics cover carefully fluffed duvets in the guest apartments. Many of the generously proportioned apartments also have balconies. Each unit in this centrally located hotel sleeps up to six people. ⊠ *Fresia 420* ☏ *45/442–055* 🖷 *45/442–053* ⊕ *www.aparthoteldelvolcan.cl* ⇆ *18 apartments* ⌂ *Dining room, in-room safes, kitchenettes, cable TV, gym, free parking; no a/c* ▤*AE, DC, MC, V* ⦿*BP.*

$$
Fodor'sChoice
★

▣ **Hotel Malalhue.** Dark wood and volcanic rock make up the construction of this built-in-2004 building at the edge of town on the road to Calburga. It's about a 15-minute walk from the hubbub of downtown Pucón, but Malalhue's many fans see that as a selling point. The cozy sitting room just off the lobby with fireplace and couches is so inviting you may want to linger there for hours. But the guest rooms, with their plush comforters and pillows, beckon, too. The top-floor "superior" rooms under the gables are more spacious and contain vaulted ceilings; they're a few thousand pesos more than the "standard" rooms, perfectly acceptable in their own right, smaller, but with exactly the same style. ⊠ *Camino Internacional 1615* ☏ *45/443–130* 🖷 *45/443–132* ⊕ *www.malalhue.cl* ⇆ *24 rooms* ⌂ *Dining room, in-room safes, cable TV, bar, babysitting, laundry service, Internet room, travel services, no-smoking rooms; no a/c* ▤ *AE, DC, MC, V* ⦿*BP.*

$

▣ **Gudenschwager Hotel.** The Chilean-born, Los Angeles–raised owners of this property have taken one of Pucón's oldest lodgings and given it a complete (and much appreciated) overhaul, stripping the paint and reexposing the original wood walls and the old radiators. They've placed queen beds in every room and installed little touches, such as Wi-Fi and safety rails in the bathtubs, which you rarely see in large hotels in Chile, let alone small inns of this size. They bill a few of the more simply furnished rooms on the top floor as "backpacker" rooms, and they are a definite cut above Pucón's typical budget lodgings. Location is everything here: sitting on the peninsula that juts out into Lago Villarrica, the deck affords both lake and volcano views. ⊠ *Pedro de Valdivia 12* ☎ *45/442–025* 🖷 *45/442–326* ⊕ *www.hogu.cl* ⤳ *20 rooms* ⋆ *Restaurant, Wi-Fi, hot tub, bar; no a/c, no room phones, no room TVs, no smoking* ⊟ *AE, DC, MC, V* ⏐⊙⏐ *BP.*

¢ 🔲 **Kila Leufu.** As part of a growing agro-tourism trend in Chile, a Mapuche family has opened this red farmhouse, 15 minutes from Pucón, to temporary urban refugees eager to partake of rural life. You can bake bread and milk the cows if you like, or just relax and read. Horseback-riding excursions cost an extra 14,000 pesos. ⊠ *Camino a Curarrehe, Puente Cabedane* ☎ *09/711–8064* ⊕ *www.kilaleufu.homestead.com* ⤳ *5 rooms, 2 with bath* ⋆ *Dining room, BBQs, fishing, horseback riding; no a/c, no room phones, no room TVs* ⊟ *No credit cards* ⏐⊙⏐ *FAP.*

Nightlife

Most of Pucón's traditional-style nightlife consists of rowdy bars south of Avenida Bernardo O'Higgins; they're best avoided. Feel welcome to make an appearance at the friendly **Mamas & Tapas** (⊠ Av. Bernardo O'Higgins 597 ☎ 45/449–002). It's de rigueur among the expat crowd. Light Mexican dining morphs into DJ-generated or live music lasting into the wee hours. Across the street from Mamas & Tapas is the equally welcoming **El Bosque** (⊠ Av. Bernardo O'Higgins 524 ☎ 45/444–025), a popular bar among locals.

Sports & the Outdoors

At first glance Pucón's myriad outfitters look the same and sell the same slate of activities and rentals; quality varies, however. The firms listed below get high marks for safety, professionalism, and friendly service. Although a given outfitter might have a specialty, it usually offers other activities as well. Pucón is the center for rafting expeditions in the northern Lake District, with Río Trancura just 15 minutes away, making for easy half-day excursions on Class III–V rapids.

Friendly, French-owned **Aguaventura** (⊠ Palguín 336 ☎ 45/444–246 ⊕ www.aguaventura.com) outfits for rafting, as well as canoeing, kayaking, snowshoeing, and snowboarding.

Anden Sport (⊠ Av. Bernardo O'Higgins 535 ☎ 45/441–048 ⊕ www.andensport.cl) is a good bet for bikes, snowboards, snowshoes, and skis.

Huepil Malal (⊠ Km 27, Carretera a Huife ☎ 09/643–2673 ⊕ www.huepilmalal.cl) arranges horseback riding in the nearby Cañi mountains, with everything from half-day to six-day excursions.

Highly regarded **Outdoor Experience** (⊠ General Urrutia 592 ☎ 45/441–675) specializes in mountain-bike rental in summer, as well as rafting, volcano ascents, rappelling, trekking, and some pretty demanding rock-climbing excursions, and outdoor-survival courses.

Politur (⊠ Av. Bernardo O'Higgins 635 ☎ 445/441–373 ⊕ www.politur.com) can take you rafting on the Río Trancura, trekking in nearby Parque Nacional Huerquehue, on ascents of the Volcán Villarrica, and skydiving.

William Hatcher of **Sol Y Nieve** (⊠ Av. Bernardo O'Higgins and Lincoyan 🕾 45/441–070 ⊕ www.chilesolnieve.com) runs rafting trips and hiking and skiing expeditions.

Parque Nacional Huerquehue

❻ *35 km (21 mi) northeast of Pucón.*

Unless you have a four-wheel-drive vehicle, this 124-square-km (48-square-mi) park is accessible only in summer. (And even then, a jeep isn't a bad idea.) It's worth a visit for the two-hour hike on the Lago Verde trail beginning at the ranger station near the park entrance. You head up into the Andes through groves of araucaria pines, eventually reaching three startlingly blue lagoons with panoramic views of the whole area, including distant Volcán Villarrica. 🕾 *45/298–221 in Temuco* 🖭 *2,800 pesos* ⊙ *Dec.–Mar., daily 8 AM–10 PM; Apr.–Nov., daily 8–6.*

Where to Stay

$$$ 🏨 **Termas de Huife.** Just outside Parque Nacional Huerquehue, this resort lets you relax in three steaming pools set beside an icy mountain stream. At the spa you can enjoy an individual bath, a massage, or both. The complex includes a handful of luxurious cabins, all of which have enormous tubs you can fill with water from the hot springs. Those just visiting for the day—hours are 9 AM–10 PM—pay 7,500 pesos for entry. If you lack your own wheels, the office in Pucón offers twice-daily shuttle service for 13,000 pesos round-trip. There's also a country house past the spa where you can soak in privacy. ⊠ *33 km (20 mi) from Pucón on the road to Caburga* 🕾 *45/441–222, 449–570 in Pucón* ⊕ *www.termashuife.cl* 🛏 *11 cabins* ⚭ *Restaurant, coffee shop, minibars, cable TV, pool, hot tub, massage, sauna, bar, meeting room; no a/c* ⊟ *AE, DC, MC, V* ❙�◉❙ *BP.*

Parque Nacional Villarrica

❼ *15 km (9 mi) south of Pucón.*

Fodor'sChoice
★

One of Chile's most popular national parks, Parque Nacional Villarrica has skiing, hiking, and many other outdoor activities. The main draw, however, is the volcano that gives the 610-square-km (235-square-mi) national park its name. You don't need to have any climbing experience to reach Volcán Villarrica's 3,116-meter (9,350-foot) summit, but a guide is a good idea. The volcano sits in the park's Sector Rucapillán, a Mapuche word meaning "house of the devil." That name is apt, as the perpetually smoldering volcano is one of South America's most active. CONAF closes off access to the trails at the slightest hint of volcanic activity they deem to be out of the ordinary. It's a steep uphill walk to the snow line, but doable any time of year. All equipment will be supplied by any of the Pucón outfitters that organize daylong excursions for about 30,000 pesos per person. Your reward for the six-hour climb is the rare sight of an active crater, which continues to release clouds of sulfur gases and explosions of lava. You're also treated to superb views of the nearby volcanoes, the less-visited Quetrupillán and Lanín. ⊠ *15 km (9 mi) south of Pucón* ☎ *45/298–221 in Temuco* 🎫 *1,100 pesos* ⊙ *Daily 8–6.*

Where to Stay

$ 🏕 **Volcán Villarrica.** This camping area run by CONAF is in the midst of a forest of *coigué,* Chile's massive red oaks. The site charges 8,800 pesos per person and provides very basic toilets. ⊠ *Sector Rucapillán* ☎ *45/298–221 in Temuco* ▭ *No credit cards.*

Skiing

The popular **Ski Pucón** (⊠ Parque Nacional Villarrica ☎ 45/441–901 ⊕ www.skipucon.cl), in the lap of Volcán Villarrica, is one of the best-equipped ski areas in southern Chile, with 20 runs for varying levels of experience, nine rope tows, three double-chair tows, and equipment rental as well as instruction. The facility offers snowboarding, too. High-season rates run 16,000 pesos per day; 12,000 pesos per half day. There's also a restaurant and coffee shop. Information about the facility can be obtained from the Gran Hotel Pucón.

Lican Ray

❽ *30 km (18 mi) south of Villarrica.*

In the Mapuche language, Lican Ray means "flower among the stones." This pleasant, unhurried resort town is on Lago Calafquén, the first of a chain of seven lakes that spills over into Argentina. You can rent rowboats and sailboats along the shore. Lican Ray lacks Pucón's perfect manicure. With but one paved street, a lot of dust gets kicked up on a dry summer day.

Where to Stay & Eat

$–$$$$ ✕ **Cábala Restaurant.** Impeccable service is the hallmark of this Italian restaurant on Lican Ray's main street. The brick-and-log building has plenty of windows where you can watch the summer crowds stroll by as you enjoy pizza and pasta. ⊠ *General Urrutia 201* ☎ *45/431–176* ▭ *AE, DC, MC, V* ⊙ *Closed Apr.–Nov.*

$–$$$ ✕ **The Ñaños.** Hearty meats and stews are the offerings at Lican Ray's most popular eatery. Most people partake of cazuela or pastel de choclo on the plain covered terrace on the main street, but the wood-trimmed dining room is a lot cozier, especially if the place is doing one of its trout fries on a summer evening. ⊠ *General Urrutia 105* ☎ *45/431–021* ▭ *DC, MC, V.*

$ 🏨 **Hostal Hoffman.** Owner Maria Hoffman keeps attentive watch over this little house just outside town. You can get lost in the plush chairs as you read a book in the sitting room. Equally plush and comfy are the bright, airy rooms with lots of pillows and thick, colorful quilts on the beds. Rates include a huge breakfast with lots of homemade breads and pastries. ⊠ *Camino a Coñaripe 100* ☎ *45/431–109* 🛏 *4 rooms* 🍴 *Dining room; no a/c, no room phones, no room TVs* ▭ *No credit cards* 🍽 *BP.*

$ **⊞ Hotel Inaltulafquen.** This rambling old house sits in a garden on a quiet street fronting Playa Grande. The rooms are simple, but bright and airy and filled with plants. The cozy restaurant serves Chilean dishes. There's soft music playing in the background, but someone is bound to sit down at the piano and encourage the crowd to sing along. ⊠ *Punulef 510* ☎ *45/431–115* ⊙ *Closed Mon. Apr.–Dec.* ⟿ *6 rooms* ⚹ *Restaurant, bar; no a/c, no room phones, no room TVs* ⊟ *DC, MC, V* ⑩| *BP.*

Beaches
The peninsula on which Lican Ray sits has two gray-sand beaches. **Playa Chica,** the smaller of the beaches near Lican Ray, is south of town. It's popular for swimming. **Playa Grande** stretches along a few blocks on the west side of Lican Ray and has choppy water. Swimming is best avoided here.

LOS LAGOS

Los Lagos, the southern half of the Lake District, is a land of snowcapped volcanoes, rolling farmland, and, of course, the shimmering lakes that give the region its name. This landscape is literally a work in progress, as it's part of the so-called Ring of Fire encircling the Pacific Rim. Most of Chile's 55 active volcanoes are here.

For a region so conscious of its heritage, history is not much in evidence. Some of Chile's oldest cities are in Los Lagos, yet you may be disappointed if you come looking for colonial grandeur. Wars with indigenous peoples kept the Spaniards, then Chileans, from building here for 300 years. An earthquake of magnitude 9.5, the largest recorded in history, was centered near Valdivia and rocked the region on May 22, 1960. It destroyed many older buildings in the region and produced a tsunami experienced as far away as Japan.

Eager to fill its *tierras baldías* (uncultivated lands) in the 19th century, Chile worked tirelessly to promote the country's virtues to German, Austrian, and Swiss immigrants looking to start a new life. The newcomers quickly set up shop, constructing breweries, foundries, shipyards, and lumberyards. By the early part of the 20th century, Valdivia had become the country's foremost industrial center, aided in large part by the construction of a railroad from Santiago. To this day the region retains a distinctly Germanic flair, and you might swear you've taken a wrong turn to Bavaria when you pull into towns such as Frutillar or Puerto Octay.

Valdivia

⑨ *120 km (72 mi) southwest of Villarrica.*

If you have time for just one of the Lake District's four hub cities, make it Valdivia. The city gracefully combines Chilean wood-shingle construction with the architectural style of the well-to-do German settlers who colonized the area in the late 1800s. But the historic appearance is a bit of an illusion, as the 1960 earthquake destroyed all but a few old riverfront structures. The city painstakingly rebuilt its downtown area, seamlessly mixing old and new buildings. Today you can enjoy evening strolls through its quaint streets and along its two rivers, the Valdivia and the Calle Calle.

Various tour boats leave from the docks at Muelle Schuster along the Río Valdivia for a one-hour tour around nearby Isla Teja. Expect to pay about 3,000 pesos. If you have more time, a five-hour excursion takes you to Niebla near the coast for a visit to the colonial-era forts. A four-hour tour north transports you to Puncapa, the site of a 16th-century Jesuit church and a nature sanctuary at San Luis de Alba de Cruces. Most companies charge 10,000–12,000 pesos for either of the longer tours. Each tour company offers all three excursions daily during the December–March high season, and you can always sign on to one at the last minute. Most will not operate tours for fewer than 15 passengers, however, which makes things a bit iffy during the rest of the year. **Bahía Princesa** (⊠ Philippi at San Martín ☎65/348–727). **Marques de Mancera** (⊠Philippi at San Martín ☎ 65/249–191). **M/N Neptuno** (⊠ Philippi at San Martín ☎ 65/215–889). **Reina Sofia** (⊠ Philippi at San Martín ☎ 65/207–120).

Valdivia's imposing modern **Catedral de Nuestra Señora del Rosario** faces the west side of the central plaza. A small museum inside documents the evangelization of the region's indigenous peoples from the 16th through 19th century. ⊠ *Independencia 514* ☎ *63/232–040* 🖭 *Free* 🕙 *Masses: weekdays 7 AM and noon, Sat. 8 AM and 7 PM, Sun. 10:30 AM, noon, and 7 PM; museum: Dec.–Mar., Tues.–Sun. 10–1 and 3–7; Apr.–Nov., Tues.–Fri. 10–1 and 3–7.*

The awning-covered **Mercado Fluvial,** in the southern shadow of the bridge leading to Isla Teja, is a perfect place to soak up the atmosphere of a real fish market. Vendors set up early in the morning; you hear the thwack of fresh trout and the clatter of oyster shells as they're piled on the side of the market's boardwalk fronting the river. If the sights, sounds, and smells are too much for you, fruit and vegetable vendors line the other side of the walkway opposite the river. ⊠ *Av. Arturo Prat at Libertad* 🖀 *No phone* 🕙 *Mon.–Sat. 8–3.*

The city's 1918 **Mercado Municipal** barely survived the 1960 earthquake intact, but it thrives again after extensive remodeling and reinforcement as a shopping-dining complex. A few restaurants, mostly hole-in-the-wall seafood joints, but some quite nice, share the three-story building with artisan and souvenir vendors. ⊠ *Block bordered by Av. Arturo Prat, Chacabuco, Yungay, and Libertad* 🖀 *No phone* 🕙 *Dec.–Mar., daily 8 AM–10 PM; Apr.–Nov., daily 8 AM–8:30 PM.*

For a historic overview of the region, visit the **Museo Histórico y Antropológico Maurice van de Maele,** on neighboring Isla Teja. The collection focuses on the city's colonial period, during which it was settled by the Spanish, burned by the Mapuche, and invaded by Dutch corsairs. Downstairs, rooms re-create the interior of the late-19th-century Anwandter mansion that belonged to one of Valdivia's first immigrant families; the upper floor delves into Mapuche art and culture. ⊠ *Los Laureles, Isla Teja* 🖀 *63/212–872* 🖭 *1,200 pesos* 🕙 *Dec.–Feb., Tues.–Sun. 10–1 and 2–6; Mar.–Nov., Tues.–Sun. 10–1 and 2–8.*

The **Museo Philippi,** under construction at this writing, sits behind the history and anthropology museum. It bears the name of 19th-century Chilean explorer and scientist Bernardo Philippi and will be designed to foster an interest in science among young people. ⊠ *Los Laureles, Isla Teja* ☎ *63/212–872* ⊗ *1,200 pesos* ☉ *Dec.–Feb., Tues.–Sun. 10–1 and 2–6; Mar.–Nov., Tues.–Sun. 10–1 and 2–8.*

Fondly known around town as the "MAC," the **Museo de Arte Contemporáneo** is one of Chile's foremost modern-art museums. This Isla Teja complex was built on the site of the old Anwandter brewery destroyed in the 1960 earthquake. The minimalist interior, formerly the brewery's warehouses, contrasts sharply with ongoing construction of a modern glass wall fronting the Río Valdivia, a project slated for completion by 2010, Chile's bicentennial. The museum has no permanent collection; it's a rotating series of temporary exhibits by contemporary Chilean artists. ⊠ *Los Laureles, Isla Teja* ☎ *63/221–968* ⊕ *www.macvaldivia.uach.cl* ⊗ *600 pesos* ☉ *Tues.–Sun. 10–1 and 3–7.*

A walk south of downtown on Yungay and General Lagos takes you through a neighborhood of late-19th- and early-20th-century houses that were spared the ravages of the 1960 earthquake. One of these houses dates from 1870 and accommodates the **Centro Cultural El Austral.** It's worth the stop if you have an interest in period furnishings. ⊠ *Yungay 733* ☎ *63/213–6588* ⊕ *www.macvaldivia.uach.cl* ⊗ *Free* ☉ *Tues.–Sun. 10–1 and 4–7.*

Just south of the Centro Cultural El Austral lies the **Torreón Los Canelos,** one of two fortress towers constructed in 1774 to defend Valdivia from constant indigenous attacks. Both towers—the other sits on Avenida Picarte between the bus terminal and the bridge entering the city over the Río Calle Calle—were built in the style of those that guarded the coasts of Andalusia, in southern Spain. A wall and moat connected the two Valdivia towers in the colonial era, effectively turning the city into an island. ⊠ *General Lagos at Yerbas Buenas.*

The **Jardín Botánico,** north and west of the Universidad Austral campus, is awash with 1,000 species of flowers and plants native to Chile. It's a lovely place to wander among the alerce, cypress, and laurel trees whatever the season—and if you can't make it to Conguillío National Park to see the monkey puzzle trees, this is the place to see them—but it's particularly enjoyable in spring and summer. ⊠ *Isla Teja* ☎ *63/216–964* ⊗ *Free* ☉ *Dec.–Feb., daily 8–8; Mar.–Nov., daily 8–4.*

Valdivia means beer to many Chileans, and **Cervecería Kunstmann** brews the country's beloved lager. The Anwandter family immigrated from Germany a century-and-a-half ago, bringing along their beer-making know-how. The *cervecería* (brewery), on the road to Niebla, hosts interesting guided tours by prior arrangement. There's also a small museum and a souvenir shop where you can buy the requisite caps, mugs, and T-shirts, plus a pricey restaurant serving German fare. ⊠ *Ruta 350 No. 950* ☎ *63/222–560* ⊗ *Free* ☉ *Restaurant and museum, daily noon–midnight.*

Catedral de
Nuestra Señora
del Rosario **1**

Centro Cultural
El Austral **8**

Cervecería
Kunstmann ... **10**

Jardín
Botánico **7**

Mercado
Fluvial **3**

Mercado
Municipal **2**

Museo de Arte
Contemporáneo . **4**

Museo Histórico
y Antropológico
Maurice van de
Maele **6**

Museo
Philippi **5**

Torreón los
Canelos **9**

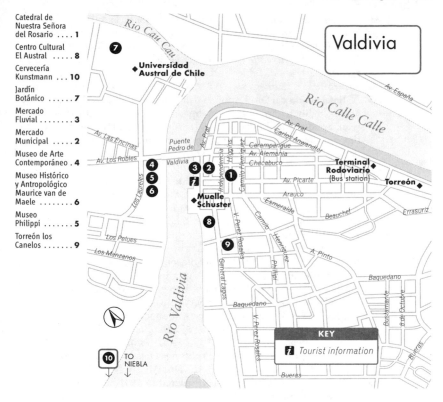

Where to Stay & Eat

$$–$$$$ ✕ **Salón de Té Entrelagos.** This swanky café caters to Valdivian business executives, who come here to make deals over sandwiches (try the Isla Teja—with grilled chicken, tomato, artichoke hearts, asparagus, olives, and red peppers), decadent crepes, and desserts. In the evenings, the atmosphere feels less formal—the menu is exactly the same—as the Entrelagos becomes a place to meet friends and converse well into the night. ⊠ *Vicente Pérez Rosales 640* ☎ *63/218–333* ▤ *AE, DC, MC, V.*

$–$$$ ✕ **Café Haussmann.** The excellent *crudos* (steak tartare), German-style sandwiches, and delicious küchen here are testament to the fact that Valdivia was once a mecca for German immigrants. The place is small—a mere four tables and a bar—but it's that rarest of breeds in Chile: a completely nonsmoking restaurant. ⊠ *Av. Bernardo O'Higgins 394* ☎ *63/213–878* ▤ *AE, DC, MC, V* ☉ *Closed Sun.*

$–$$$ ✕ **La Calesa.** Head to this centrally located, well-known restaurant for a good introduction to Peruvian cuisine. Try the *ají* (chicken stew with cheese, milk, and peppers), but be careful not to burn your mouth. Peruvian dishes, particularly the stews, are spicier than their Chilean counterparts. ⊠ *Yungay 735* ☎ *63/225–467* ▤ *AE, DC, MC, V* ☉ *Closed Sun. No lunch Sat.*

$–$$ ✗ **Camino de Luna.** The Way of the Moon floats on a barge on the Río Valdivia, just north of the Pedro de Valdivia bridge. As the city is only a few miles from the ocean, it's no surprise that seafood is a specialty here. The *congrío calle calle* (conger eel in a cheese-and-tomato sauce) is particularly good. Tables by the windows offer views of Isla Teja. ⊠ *Av. Arturo Prat Costanera s/n* ☎ *63/213–788* ⊟ *AE, DC, MC, V.*

$$$ ▦ **Hotel Puerta del Sur.** Expect lavish pampering with top-notch service at this highly regarded lodging. Spacious rooms, all with views of the river, are decorated in soft lavender tones. Play a few games of tennis, then hit the pool or relax in the hot tub. You're near the edge of town here, so this is a good place to stay if you have your own car. ⊠ *Los Lingues 950, Isla Teja* ☎ *63/224–500, 2/633–5101 in Santiago* 🖷 *63/ 211–046, 2/633–6541 in Santiago* ⊕ *www.hotelpuertadelsur.com* ⤙ *40 rooms, 2 suites* ⚴ *Restaurant, in-room safes, some Wi-Fi, tennis court, pool, gym, outdoor hot tub, sauna, dock, volleyball, 2 bars, Internet room, meeting room, travel services; no a/c* ⊟ *AE, DC, MC, V* ⭑◯⭑ *BP.*

★ **$$** ▦ **Hotel Naguilán.** You can relax at this charming hotel's poolside gar- den while watching the boats pass by on the Río Valdivia. Rooms in the property's newer building are bigger, with balconies and more mod- ern furnishings; the older rooms, in a building that dates from 1890, are smaller and a bit dated, with lime-green carpeting, but they have more character, and are cheaper. Service-wise, you're in good hands here: as soon as you check in, a waiter will appear to offer you a welcome pisco sour. ⊠ *General Lagos 1927* ☎ *63/212–851* 🖷 *63/219–130* ⊕ *www.hotelnaguilan.com* ⤙ *33 rooms, 3 suites* ⚴ *Restaurant, cable TV, Wi-Fi, pool, dock, bar, babysitting, laundry service, business ser- vices, meeting room; no a/c* ⊟ *AE, DC, MC, V* ⭑◯⭑ *BP.*

$ ▦ **Hostal Torreón.** Originally constructed in 1918 for a family of Ger- man settlers, this architecturally appealing German-style home set back from the street now offers basic lodgings to guests. A stairway of *pel- lín* (oak) twists up to the bright second-story rooms. José Retamales Prelle, the hotel's amiable proprietor, gives discounts to Hosteling Interna- tional members. ⊠ *Vicente Pérez Rosales 783* ☎ *63/212–622* 🖷 *63/ 203–217* ✑ *hctorreon@entelchile.net* ⤙ *15 rooms, 8 with bath* ⚴ *Din- ing room, cable TV, laundry service; no a/c* ⊟ *No credit cards* ⭑◯⭑ *BP.*

$ ▦ **Hotel Isla Teja.** This affordable hotel doubles as student housing for the nearby Universidad Austral, though a section is always open for non- university guests. The rooms are quiet and comfortable, with modern amenities. ⊠ *Las Encinas 220, Isla Teja* ☎ *63/215–014* 🖷 *63/214–911* ⊕ *www.hotelislateja.cl* ⤙ *70 rooms* ⚴ *Restaurant, in-room data ports, cable TV, bar, meeting room, Internet room, business services, meeting room, travel services; no a/c* ⊟ *AE, DC, MC, V* ⭑◯⭑ *CP.*

$ ▦ **Hotel Palace.** The exterior could benefit from a fresh coat of paint, but this solid, friendly, midrange lodging in downtown Valdivia has bright, cheerful rooms. They're all simply furnished, with blue or pink bedspreads and a chair and table. ⊠ *Chacabuco 308* ☎ *63/213–319 or 213–029* 🖷 *63/219–133* ✑ *hotelpalace@surnet.cl* ⤙ *30 rooms* ⚴ *Coffee shop, dining room, cable TV, bar, laundry service, meeting room; no a/c* ⊟ *AE, DC, MC, V.*

HIER IST ALLES SO DEUTSCH

YOU'LL MEET PEOPLE in the Lake District with names like María Schmidt or Pablo Gudenschwager. At first, such juxtapositions sound odd, but, remember, this melting pot of a country was liberated by a man, good Irishman that he was, named Bernardo O'Higgins.

The Lake District's Germanic origins can be traced to one Vicente Pérez Rosales. (Every town and city in the region names a street for him, and one of Puerto Montt's more fabulous lodgings carries his name.) Armed with photos of the region, Don Vicente, as everyone knew him in his day, made several trips on behalf of the Chilean government to Germany, Switzerland, and Austria in the mid-19th century. His mission? Recruit waves of European immigrants to settle the Lake District and end 300 years of Mapuche domination in the region once and for all.

Thousands signed on the dotted line and made the long journey to start a new life in southern Chile. It was a giant leap of faith for the original settlers, but it didn't hurt that the region looked just like the parts of Central Europe that they'd come from. The result was küchen, sausage, and a good old-fashioned work ethic mixed with a Latin-spirited, oom-pah-pah gemütlichkeit. But don't bother to dust off that high-school German for your trip here; few people speak it these days.

— Jeffrey Van Fleet

¢ ⚠ **Complejo Turístico Isla Teja.** The campsites at this facility sit in the middle of an apple orchard with an attractive view of the Río Valdivia. There's electricity and hot showers. ⊠ *Los Cipreses 1125, Isla Teja* ☎ *63/213–584* 🖷 *63/225–855.*

Sports & the Outdoors

Valdivia-based tour operator **Jumping Chile** (⊠ Pasaje 11 No. 50 ☎ 63/217–810) organizes marvelous fly-fishing trips for two to six people on the nearby rivers. An astonishing variety of wetland birds inhabits this part of the country. **Hualamo** (☎ 63/215–135 ⊕ www.hualamo.com) lets you get a close look if you join its bird-watching and natural-history tours based out of a lodge 20 km (12 mi) upriver from Valdivia.

Shopping

Affiliated with the restaurant of the same name next door, **Entrelagos** (⊠ Vicente Pérez Rosales 622 ☎ 63/212–047) has been whipping up sinfully rich chocolates for more than three decades, and arranging them with great care in the storefront display windows. Most of what is sold here is actually made at Entrelagos' factory outside town, but a small army of chocolate makers is on-site to let you see, on a smaller scale, how it's done, and to carefully package your purchases for your plane ride home.

Niebla

10 *18 km (11 mi) southwest of Valdivia.*

To protect the all-important city of Valdivia, the Spanish constructed a series of strategic fortresses at Niebla, where the Valdivia and Torna-galeones rivers meet. Portions of the 1671 **Fuerte de Niebla** and its 18 cannons have been restored. The ground on which the cannons sit is unstable; you can view them from the ramparts above. The old com-mander's house serves as a small museum documenting the era's mili-tary history. ⊠ *1 km (½ mi) west of entrance to Niebla* ☎ *No phone* 🖅 *600 pesos, Wed. free* ⊗ *Nov.–Mar., daily 10–7; Apr.–Oct., Tues.–Sun. 10–5:30.*

Across the estuary from the Fuerte de Niebla, the 1645 **Castillo San Se-bastián de la Cruz** is large and well preserved. In the January–February summer season, historic reenactments of Spanish military maneuvers take place daily at 4 and 6. ⊠ *1 km (½ mi) north of Corral* 🖅 *Free* ⊗ *Dec.–Mar., daily 8:30 AM–10 PM; Apr.–Nov., daily 9–5.*

$ ▦ **Hotel El Castillo.** A grand, old 1920s German-style house sits at Niebla's main intersection on the riverfront and has been converted into this lovely bed-and-breakfast with lots of knickknacks, antiques, and cuckoo clocks in the common areas. Rooms have more modern amenities, but retain the old wood finishing, and overlook either the river or the pool and back gardens. A new wing has been added, but so seamlessly blends with the original house that you can't tell where one ends and the other begins. ⊠ *Antonio Ducce* ☎ *63/282–061* 🖷 *63/219–133* ✉ *hotel-castillo@hotmail.com* 🛏 *11 rooms, 2 cabins* ⚭ *Dining room, BBQ, cable TV, 2 pools; no a/c* ▤ *AE, DC, MC, V (Jan. and Feb only)* ⚏ *BP.*

Beaches

The Lake District is still a region that looks to its inland lakes rather than out to the sea, so the beaches near the Pacific coast don't draw quite the crowds you find on Lagos Villarrica or Llanquihue. Just north of Niebla is the green-blue water of the popular **Playa Los Molinos.** A few miles past the villages of Loncollén and Calfuco is **Playa Curiñanco.** The waves can be a bit strong, so be cautious.

en route **Isla Huapi.** Some 20% of Chile's 1 million Mapuche live on *reducciones,* or reservations. One of the most welcoming communities is on Isla Huapi, a leafy island in the middle of deep-blue Lago Ranco. It's out of the way—about 80 km (48 mi) southeast of Valdivia—but worth the trip for those interested in Mapuche culture. A boat departs from Futorno, on the northern shore of the lake, at 7 AM Monday, Wednesday, and Friday, returning at 5 PM. The pastoral quiet of Isla Huapi is broken once a year in January or February with the convening of the island council, in conjunction with the Lepún harvest festival. You are welcome during the festival, but be courteous and unobtrusive with your camera.

Osorno

⓫ *107 km (65 mi) southeast of Valdivia.*

Workaday Osorno is the least visited of the Lake District's four major cities. It's one of the oldest in Chile, but the Mapuche prevented foreigners from settling here until the late 19th century. Like other communities in the region, it bears the imprint of the German settlers who came here in the 1880s. Osorno, situated in a bend of the Río Rahue, makes a convenient base for exploring the nearby national parks.

Osorno's friendly **tourist office** arranges free daily tours in summer. Each day has a different focus: walks around the city, fruit orchards, or nearby farms are a few of the offerings. ⊠ *North side of Plaza de Armas* ☎ *64/264–250* ⌦ *Free* ⊙ *Office: Dec.–Feb., daily 8–8; Mar.–Nov., weekdays 9–1 and 2:30–6. Tours: daily 10:30.*

The 1960 earthquake left Osorno with little historic architecture, but a row of **19th-century houses** miraculously survived on Calle Juan Mackenna between Lord Cochrane and Freire. Their distinctively sloped roofs, which allow adequate drainage of rain and snow, are replicated in many of Osorno's newer houses.

The modern **Catedral de San Mateo Apostol** fronts the Plaza de Armas and is topped with a tower resembling a bishop's mitre. "Turn off your cell phone," the sign at the door admonishes those who enter. "You don't need it to communicate with God." ⊠ *Plaza de Armas* ☎ *No phone* ⊙ *Mass: Mon.–Sat. 7:15 PM; Sun. 10:30, noon, and 8:15.*

The **Museo Municipal Osorno** contains a decent collection of Mapuche artifacts, Chilean and Spanish firearms, and exhibits devoted to the German settlement of Osorno. Housed in a pink neoclassical building dating from 1929, this is one of the few older structures in the city center. ⊠ *Manuel Antonio Matta 809* ☎ *64/238–615* ⌦ *Free* ⊙ *Mon.–Thurs. 9:30–5:30, Fri. 9:30–4:30, Sat. 2–6.*

Where to Stay & Eat

$–$$$ ✕ **Club Alemán.** This was the first in a network of German associations in southern Chile. Established in 1862, it predated the first big waves of European immigration. Despite the exclusive-sounding name, anyone can dine here. Options are limited, however. There's usually a choice of four or five rotating prix-fixe menus for lunch and dinner, often including a seafood stew or a hearty cazuela, and lots of tasty küchen and other pastries for dessert. ⊠ *Av. Bernardo O'Higgins 563* ☎ *64/232–784* ⊟ *AE, DC, MC, V.*

$–$$ ✕ **Café Central.** You can dig into a hearty American-style breakfast in the morning, and burgers and sandwiches the rest of the day, at this diner on the Plaza de Armas. The friendly, bustling staff speaks no English, but if it's clear you're North American, an English menu will be presented to you with great fanfare. ⊠ *Av. Bernardo O'Higgins 610* ☎ *64/257–711* ⊟ *DC, MC, V.*

$$ ⌂ **Hotel García Hurtado de Mendoza.** This stately hotel two blocks from the Plaza de Armas is one of Osorno's nicest lodgings. Classical lines

grace the traditional furnishings and complement the subdued fabrics of the bright and airy guest rooms. ⊠ *Juan Mackenna 1040* ☎ *64/237-111* ⊟ *64/237-115* ⊕ *www.hotelgarciahurtado.cl* ⊃ *31 rooms* ⑁ *Restaurant, cable TV, gym, hair salon, hot tub, sauna, bar, meeting room; no a/c* ⊟ *AE, DC, MC, V* ⏀ *BP.*

$ ⊞ **Gran Hotel Osorno.** Osorno's grande dame, built in the era when art deco was all the rage, has stood the test of time. The five-story hotel has an unbeatable location on the Plaza de Armas. The rooms, although a tad dark, are clean and comfortable. Mercifully, the hotel's Power Disco has closed, though the neon sign still blinks out front. ⊠ *Av. Bernardo O'Higgins 615* ☎ *64/232-171* ⊟ *64/239-311* ✎ *granhotelosorno@entelchile.net* ⊃ *57 rooms* ⑁ *Restaurant, cable TV, bar, laundry service, meeting room; no a/c* ⊟ *AE, DC, MC, V.*

$ ⊞ **Hotel Innsbruck.** Osorno's most Germanic hotel, the Innsbruck has half-timbered walls and cheery flower boxes in the windows. Rooms are small and simply furnished with little more than beds, nightstands, and televisions, but the vaulted ceilings make them seem spacious. ⊠ *Manuel Rodríguez 941* ☎☎ *64/242-000* ✎ *hinnsbruck@telsur.cl* ⊃ *18 rooms* ⑁ *Dining room, coffee shop, cable TV, bar; no a/c* ⊟ *AE, DC, MC, V* ⏀ *CP.*

$ ⊞ **Hotel Lagos del Sur.** Business travelers frequent Osorno more than leisure travelers do, and this place near the Plaza de Armas provides attentive service and a quiet place to work. Warm golds and greens make a splash in sparkling white guest rooms. The color scheme echoes the building's dark green exterior. Doubles include a small sitting room off to one side. ⊠ *Av. Bernardo O'Higgins 564* ☎ *64/243-244* ⊟ *64/243-696* ⊕ *www.hotelagosdelsur.cl* ⊃ *20 rooms* ⑁ *Coffee shop, cable TV, Wi-Fi, bar, laundry service; no a/c* ⊟ *AE, DC, MC, V* ⏀ *CP.*

Shopping

Osorno's city government operates the **Centro de Artesanía Local** (⊠ Juan MacKenna at Ramón Freire), a complex of 46 artisan vendors' stands built with steeply sloped roofs in the style of the Calle MacKenna houses. Woodwork, leather, and woolens abound. Prices are fixed but fair. It's open January and February, daily 9 AM–10 PM, and March–December, daily 10–8.

en route An Osorno business executive's love for tail fins and V-8 engines led him to establish the **Auto Museum Moncopulli.** His particular passion is the little-respected Studebaker, which accounts for 50 of the 80 vehicles on display. Elvis and Buddy Holly bop in the background to put you in the mood. ⊠ *Ruta 215, 25 km (16 mi) east of Osorno Puyehue* ☎ *64/204-200* ⊕ *www.moncopulli.cl* ⏃ *1,500 pesos* ☺ *Dec.–Mar., daily 10–8; Apr.–Nov., daily 10–6.*

Parque Nacional Puyehue

⑫ *81 km (49 mi) east of Osorno.*

Chile's most popular national park, Parque Nacional Puyehue draws crowds who come to bask in its famed hot springs. Most never venture beyond them, and that's a shame. A dozen miles east of the Aguas Calientes sector lies a network of short trails leading to evergreen forests with dramatic waterfalls. Truly adventurous types attempt the five-hour hike to the summit of 2,240-meter (7,350-foot) Volcán Puyehue. As with most climbs in this region, CONAF rangers insist on ample documentation of experience before allowing you to set out. Access to the 1,070-square-km (413-square-mi) park is easy: head due east from Osorno on the highway leading to Argentina. ⊠ *Ruta 215* ☎ *64/374–572* ⌸ *800 pesos* ⊙ *Nov.–Mar., daily 8* AM*–9* PM; *Apr.–Oct., daily 8–7.*

Where to Stay

★ **$$–$$$** ⌸ **Gran Hotel Termas de Puyehue.** Probably Chile's most famous hot-springs resort, this grandiose stone-and-wood lodge sits on the edge of Parque Nacional Puyehue. Make no mistake: the place is enormous, with a slate of activities to match, offering everything from darts to skiing. Yet, despite its enormous popularity, and the fact that something is always going on, it can be a surprisingly nice place to relax. Most people come for a soak in the thermal pools. All-day use of the springs is 9,000 pesos for nonguests. The rooms and common areas here mix starkly modern and 19th-century Germanic features: chrome, hardwoods, and even some modern art happily share the same space. ⊠ *Ruta 215, Km 76, Puyehue* ☎ *64/232–881, 2/293–6000 in Santiago* 🖷 *64/236–988, 2/283–1010 in Santiago* ⊕ *www.puyehue.cl* ⌸ *140 rooms* ⌂ *3 restaurants, in-room safes, minibars, miniature golf, tennis courts, 2 pools, gym, sauna, spa, fishing, bicycles, billiards, horseback riding, Ping-Pong, downhill skiing, library, theater, shop, laundry service, Internet room, meeting room, travel services; no a/c, no room TVs* ▤ *AE, DC, MC, V* ⑩ *BP.*

Puerto Octay

🔞 *80 km (48 mi) southwest of Parque Nacional Puyehue, 50 km (30 mi) southeast of Osorno.*

The story goes that a German merchant named Ochs set up shop in this tidy community on the northern tip of Lago Llanquihue. A phrase uttered by customers looking for a particular item, "¿Ochs, hay . . . ?" ("Ochs, do you have . . . ?"), gradually became "Octay." With spectacular views of the Osorno and Calbuco volcanoes, the town was the birthplace of Lake District tourism: a wealthy Santiago businessman constructed a mansion outside town in 1912, using it as a vacation home to host his friends. (That structure is now the area's famed Hotel Centinela.) Puerto Octay doesn't have the frenetic energy of neighboring Frutillar and Puerto Varas, but its many fans enjoy its less-frenzied, more-authentic nature.

The **Museo El Colono** displays great old photographs and maps documenting the town's turn-of-the-20th-century German settlers. An annex in a barn outside town at the turnoff to Centinela exhibits farm machinery. At this writing both locales are open but undergoing extensive expansion and remodeling, a project scheduled for completion by the start of the January 2007 high season. ⊠ *Independencia 591* ☎ *64/391–523*

⛁ *500 pesos* ⏱ *Dec.–Mar., daily 10–1 and 3–7; Apr.–Nov., Tues.–Sun. 10–1 and 3–7.*

Where to Stay & Eat

$–$$ ✕ **Restaurant Baviera.** Because it's on the Plaza de Armas, this is a popular lunch stop for tour groups. Baviera serves solid German fare—schnitzel, sauerkraut, sausage, and küchen are among the favorites. Beer steins and other Bavarian paraphernalia lining the walls evoke the old country. ✉ *German Wulf 582* ☎ *64/391–460* 🚫 *No credit cards.*

★ $$ 🏨 **Hotel Centinela.** Simple and elegant, the venerable 1912 Hotel Centinela remains one of Chile's best-known accommodations. This imposing wood-shingled lodge with a dramatic turret sits amid 20 forested acres at the tip of Península Centinela jutting into Lago Llanquihue. Britain's Edward VII, then Prince of Wales, was the most famous guest (but there's some mystery as to whether his future wife, American divorcée Wallis Simpson, accompanied him). Imposing beds and armoires fill the huge rooms in the main building. The cabins, whose rates include three meals a day delivered to the door, are more modern than the rooms in the lodge. ✉ *Península de Centinela, 5 km (3 mi) south of Puerto Octay* ☎🖷 *64/391–326* ⊕ *www.hotelcentinela.cl* 🛏 *11 rooms, 1 suite, 18 cabins* ⚒ *Restaurant, sauna, beach, dock, bar; no a/c, no TV in some rooms* 🚫 *AE, DC, MC, V* ❄ *BP, FAP.*

★ $ 🏨 **Zapato Amarillo.** Backpackers make up the majority of the clientele here, but this is no scruffy youth hostel. This modern alerce-shingled house with wood-panel rooms affords a drop-dead gorgeous view of Volcán Osorno outside town. Armin Dubendorfer and Nadi Muñoz, the eager-to-please Chilean-Swiss couple that owns it, will arrange guided horseback-riding, hiking, and cycling tours, as well as cheese-fondue evening gatherings. Rates include an excellent buffet breakfast that uses local fruits and dairy products. You also have access to the kitchen. ✉ *2 km (1 mi) north of Puerto Octay on road to Osorno* ☎🖷 *64/391–575* ⊕ *zapatoamarillo.8k.com* 🛏 *7 rooms, 2 with bath* ⚒ *Dining room, bicycles, horseback riding, library, laundry facilities, Internet, travel services; no a/c, no room phones, no room TVs* 🚫 *No credit cards* ❄ *BP.*

Frutillar

⑭ *30 km (18 mi) southwest of Puerto Octay.*

Halfway down the western edge of Lago Llanquihue lies the small town of Frutillar, a destination for European immigrants in the late 19th century and, today, arguably the most picturesque Lake District community. The town—actually two adjacent hamlets, Frutillar Alto and Frutillar Bajo—is known for its perfectly preserved German architecture. Don't be disappointed if your first look at the town is the nondescript neighborhood (the Alto) on the top of the hill; head down to the charming streets of Frutillar Bajo that face the lake, with their picture-perfect view of Volcán Osorno.

Each year, in late January and early February, the town hosts **Semanas Musicales de Frutillar,** an excellent series of mostly classical concerts (and a little jazz) in the lakeside Centro de Conciertos y Eventos, a semi-outdoor venue inaugurated for the 2006 festival. Ticket prices are a reasonable 2,000–5,000 pesos. ⊠ *Av. Phillipi 1000* ☎ *65/421–290* ⊕ *www. semanasmusicales.cl.*

Culture in Frutillar is not only about Semanas Musicales these days. In the Centro de Conciertos y Eventos is also housed the **Teatro del Lago**, with a year-round schedule of concerts, art shows, and film. Events take place every week. ⊠ *Av. Phillipi 1000* ☎ *65/422–954* ⊕ *www. teatrodellago.cl.*

★ You step into the past when you step into one of southern Chile's best museums, the **Museo Colonial Alemán.** Besides displays of the 19th-century agricultural and household implements, this open-air museum has full-scale reconstructions of buildings—a smithy and barn, among others—used by the original German settlers. Exhibits at this complex administered by Chile's Universidad Austral are labeled in Spanish and, *natürlich*, German, but there are also a few signs in English. A short walk from the lake up Avenida Arturo Prat, the museum also has beautifully landscaped grounds and great views of Volcán Osorno. ⊠ *Av. Vicente Pérez Rosales at Av. Arturo Prat* ☎ *65/421–142* ⊠ *1,600 pesos* ⊙ *Dec.–Feb., daily 10–7; Mar.–Nov., daily 10–2 and 3–5.*

Where to Stay & Eat

$$ ✕ **Club Alemán.** One of the German clubs that dot the Lake District, this restaurant in the center of town has a selection of four or five rotating prix-fixe menus that cost 3,500 pesos. There will always be a meat and seafood option—often steak and salmon—with soup, salad, and dessert. Don't forget the küchen. ⊠ *Philippi 747* ☎ *65/421–249* ⊟ *AE, DC, MC, V.*

$–$$ ✕ **Fogón del Lago.** Friendly, attentive service and good, solid food are the hallmark of this casual semicircular restaurant just up the hill from the beach road. *Carne a la braza* (meats prepared on the grill) is the specialty here, and you choose from beef, chicken, pork, and poultry. Accompany your meal with a great selection of Chilean wines. ⊠ *Antonio Varas 24* ☎ *65/421–164* ⊟ *AE, DC, MC, V.*

★ ¢ ✕ **Café Capuccini.** Sink into one of the plush couches here and write some postcards while you nurse a gourmet coffee drink on a chilly evening. If the couches are taken—they are in demand—grab one of the small tables adorned with a musical-score lampshade. All have superb lake and volcano views out the curving, sweeping picture window. This café in the new Centro de Conciertos y Eventos complex caters mostly to a pre- and post-theater crowd, but it serves up light fare (sandwiches, küchen, and desserts) on brown stoneware to anyone, any day. ⊠ *Av. Phillipi 1000* ☎ *65/421–164* ⊟ *No credit cards.*

$ ✕⌂ **Hotel Salzburg.** Rooms at this Tyrolean-style lodge command excellent views of the lake. Cozy cabins and slightly larger bungalows, all made of native woods, are fully equipped with kitchens and private terraces. The staff will gladly organize fishing trips. The restaurant ($$–$$$) serves some of the best smoked salmon in the area. ⊠ *Costanera Norte* ☎ *65/421–589* 🖷 *65/421–599* ⊕ *www.salzburg.cl* ⌦ *31 rooms, 9 cabins, 5 bungalows* ⌂ *Restaurant, pool, sauna, billiards, Ping-Pong,* *volleyball, bar, laundry service, meeting rooms, travel services; no a/c, no room TVs* ⊟ *AE, DC, MC, V* ⦿⦿ *BP.*

$ ⌗ **Hotel Elun.** From just above every vantage point at this hillside lodging just south of town—the lobby, the library, and, of course, the guest rooms—you have a spectacular view of Lago Llanquihue. Each room has huge bay windows framing Volcán Osorno. The blue of the facade is repeated in the rooms, which have polished wood furniture. Add the exceptionally attentive owners to the mix, and you have a real find. ✉ *Costanera Sur* ☎ *65/420–055* 🖷 *65/420–170* ⊕ *www.hotelelun.cl* ⟳ *14 rooms* ⌂ *Restaurant, cable TV, sauna, bicycles, bar, library, Internet room, meeting rooms, no-smoking rooms; no a/c* ⊟ *AE, DC, MC, V* ⦿⦿ *BP.*

$ ⌗ **Hotel Frau Holle.** Norma Bonomett, the friendly owner of this 1930s German-style house, may not be Frau Holle (a character out of the Grimm brothers' fairy tales)—but her attentive service will help you to have a storybook lodging experience. Rooms here are bright and cheery, with hardwood floors and period furnishings; a few have views of Lago Llanquihue and both volcanoes. The hearty German breakfast includes fresh fruit grown in the property's orchard. ✉ *Antonio Varas 54* ☎🖷 *65/421–345* ✎ *frauholle@frutillarsur.cl* ⟳ *8 rooms* ⌂ *Dining room, laundry service; no a/c, no room phones, no room TVs* ⊟ *AE, DC, MC, V* ⦿⦿ *CP.*

$ ⌗ **Hotel Kaffee Bauernhaus.** Gingerbread cutouts and swirls adorn this cozy 1911 home-turned-inn. You couldn't ask for a much better location—the property is right on the lake, although only one guest room has a lake view. All, however, are wood paneled and tastefully decorated with flowered bedspreads and curtains. The German breakfast is substantial. ✉ *Av. Philippi 663* ☎ *65/421–201* 🖷 *65/421–750* ⊕ *www.salzburg.cl* ⟳ *8 rooms* ⌂ *Coffee shop; no a/c, no TV in some rooms* ⊟ *AE, DC, MC, V* ⦿⦿ *BP.*

$ ⌗ **Hotel Serenade.** The names of the guest rooms here reflect musical compositions—like *Fantasia* and *Wedding March*—and each door is painted with the first few sheet-music bars of the work it's named for. Inside are plush quilts and comforters, hardwood floors, and throw rugs. The cozy sitting room, overlooking a quiet side street, is another lovely place to relax. The musical theme makes this an especially appropriate place to stay during the Semanas Musicales de Frutillar in late January. ✉ *Pedro Aguirre Cerda 50* ☎ *65/420–332* ⟳ *6 rooms* ⌂ *Meeting room; no a/c, no room TVs* ⊟ *No credit cards* ⦿⦿ *CP.*

Beaches

Packed with summer crowds, the gray-sand **Playa Frutillar** stretches for 15 blocks along Avenida Philippi. From this point along Lago Llanquihue you have a spectacular view due east of the conical Volcán Osorno, as well as the lopsided Volcán Puntiagudo.

Puerto Varas

⓯ *27 km (16 mi) south of Frutillar.*

A small resort town on the edge of Lago Llanquihue, Puerto Varas is known for the stunning rose arbors that bloom from December to

March. Often described as the "Lucerne of Chile," the town has ice-cream shops, cozy cafés, and trendy restaurants. The view of the Osorno and Calbuco volcanoes graces dozens of postcards and travel brochures for the Lake District. The town isn't quite there yet, but it could someday soon mount a serious challenge to Pucón as the region's top vacation spot.

Where to Stay & Eat

★ **$$–$$$$** ✕ **Merlin.** A perennial favorite for diners in southern Chile, this charming old restaurant on a side street in Puerto Varas is known for its unusual fish and vegetables dishes. Specialties include razor clams with vegetable strips in a curry vinaigrette and beef tenderloin in a morel-mushroom sauce. For dessert, try peaches packed with almond cream. ✉ *Imperial 605* ☎ *65/233–105* ▭ *AE, DC, MC, V* ☺ *No lunch.*

$–$$$ ✕ **Pim's.** This restaurant just a couple of blocks from the center of town evokes an old-fashioned American bar. There's nothing particularly Southwestern about the decor, but you can chow down here on good, filling Tex-Mex dishes. The hot, spicy chili—perfect for a chilly night in Chile—is best enjoyed in front of the fireplace. ✉ *San Francisco 712* ☎ *65/233–998* ▭ *AE, DC, MC, V.*

$–$$ ✕ **Govinda.** It's impossible to pin down the small but ever-changing menu here. This place takes great pride in using the freshest in-season, organic ingredients available, and that might mean a curry lasagna, lobster in garlic sauce, or cod in tomato sauce. You can always count on little touches like goat cheese, organic wine, and wild-apple vinegar for your salad, and wonderful fruit in summer. The restaurant occupies a house on a busy lakefront intersection, and the wood deck is the place to survey the passing scene. In the cozy dining room, with its blond-wood tables and woven place mats, you get the same lake views out the big picture window without the noise of passing traffic. After dinner, grab your cup of coffee and sink into one of the couches in front of the fireplace. ✉ *Santa Rosa 218* ☎ *65/233–080* ▭ *AE, DC, MC, V.*

Fodor'sChoice
★

$$–$$$ ▥ **Hotel Cabañas del Lago.** It's the pine-panel cabins, hidden among carefully tended gardens, that make this place special. Each A-frame unit, which can accommodate five people, is decorated with lace curtains and floral-pattern bedding, and has a woodstove and full kitchen. Most rooms in the main hotel are a little on the small side, but they're cozy and have lovely views of Volcán Osorno. ✉ *Klenner 195* ☎ *65/232–291* ▤ *65/232–707* ⊕ *www.cabanasdellago.cl* ⇱ *134 rooms, 13 cabins, 2 suites* ⏦ *Restaurant, cable TV, indoor pool, massage, sauna, billiards, bar, babysitting, meeting rooms; no a/c* ▭ *AE, DC, MC, V.*

$$ ▥ **Hotel Bellavista.** This hotel, an eclectic mix of traditional Bavarian and modern architectural styles, sits right on the lake. Most of the bright rooms have views of the nearby volcanoes, and some have their own balconies. Stylish contemporary furnishings are upholstered in tailored stripes. ✉ *Vicente Pérez Rosales 60* ☎ *65/232–011* ▤ *65/232–013* ⊕ *www.hotelbellavistachile.cl* ⇱ *51 rooms* ⏦ *Restaurant, in-room safes, minibars, cable TV, Wi-Fi, sauna, bar, laundry service, meeting room; no a/c* ▭ *AE, DC, MC, V* ⏝ *BP.*

$$ ▥ **Hotel Colonos del Sur.** This five-story building, with peaked gables that give it a Germanic look, dominates the waterfront in Puerto Varas. The views from the upper floors are magnificent. If you can, look at a few rooms before you decide which to book: some have views of the lake, and others overlook the casino across the street. Warm alerce and pine dominate the interior, including the paneled guest rooms. Even if you're not staying here, make a point to stop by for the late-afternoon onces (coffee breaks). The hotel does them up big. ⊠ *Del Salvador 24* ☎ *65/ 233–369* 🖷 *65/233–394* ⊕ *www.colonosdelsur.cl* ⤴ *64 rooms* ♧ *Restaurant, coffee shop, minibars, cable TV, indoor pool, massage, sauna, bar, meeting room; no a/c* ⊟ *AE, DC, MC, V* ¶⚬ *BP.*

$$ 🖼 **Hotel Licarayén.** Ask for a room with a balcony overlooking Lago Llanquihue at this rambling Bavarian-style chalet. Carpeted rooms are bright and have wood paneling. The standard rooms lack views of the lake but overlook the garden. It's worth the splurge for the superior rooms with balconies and lake and volcano views. There's a fireplace in the common sitting room. ⊠ *San José 114* ☎ *65/232–305* 🖷 *65/232–955* ⊕ *www.hotellicarayen.cl* ⤴ *23 rooms* ♧ *Dining room, cable TV, gym, sauna, Internet room; no a/c* ⊟ *AE, DC, MC, V* ¶⚬ *CP.*

★ $ 🖼 **The Guest House.** The aroma of fresh coffee greets you all day long, and little homemade chocolates wait on your pillow at this B&B, a restored 1926 mansion just a couple of blocks from downtown. Period furnishings and antiques fill the rooms, which are bright and cheery. Vicky Johnson, the exuberant American owner, a longtime resident of Chile and a fount of information, truly treats you like a valued guest. ⊠ *Av. Bernardo O'Higgins 608* ☎ *65/231–521* 🖷 *65/232–240* ⊕ *www.vickijohnson.com* ⤴ *9 rooms* ♧ *No a/c, no room TVs, no smoking* ⊟ *No credit cards* ¶⚬ *BP.*

Nightlife

The flashy **Casino de Puerto Varas** (⊠ Del Salvador 21 ☎ 65/346–600) dominates the center of town these days. It has all the Vegas-style trappings, from slot machines to roulette, along with weekly Vegas-style entertainment.

Cozy, intimate café by day, seafood restaurant by evening, **Barómetro** (⊠ San Pedo 418 ☎ 65/346–100) becomes a live music venue by night— well into the night. Expect a DJ most of the year, but live music during the peak summer season.

Sports & the Outdoors

Al Sur Expediciones (⊠ Del Salvador 100 ☎ 65/232–300 ⊕ www. alsurexpeditions.com) is known for rafting and kayaking trips on the Class III Río Petrohué. It also runs horseback-riding and fly-fishing trips. **Aqua Motion** (⊠ San Francisco 328 ☎ 65/232–747 ⊕ www.aquamotion.com) leads rafting and kayaking excursions on the nearby Río Petrohué, as well as trekking, horseback riding, helicopter rides, birdwatching, and fly-fishing tours. Based in nearby Cochamó, **Campo Aventura** (⊠ Valle Cochamó ☎ 65/232–910) leads 1- to 10-day horseback and trekking expeditions to its base camp in Parque Nacional Vicente Pérez Rosales.

Pachamagua (⊠ San Pedo 418 ☎ 65/346–100) specializes in half- and full-day canyoning and rappelling trips near Volcán Calbuco, in addition to kayaking and horseback-riding excursions. **Tranco Expediciones** (✉ San Pedro 422 ☎ 65/311–311 ⊕ www.trancoexpediciones.cl) leads photo hikes up Volcánes Osorno and Calbuco, in addition to rafting trips on the Río Petrohué, and bike excursions.

Ensenada

⑯ *47 km (28 mi) east of Puerto Varas.*

A drive along the southern shore of Lago Llanquihue takes you through the heart of Chile's *murta*-growing country. Queen Victoria is said to have developed a fondness for these tart, red berries, and today you'll find them used as ingredients in the region's syrups, jams, and küchen. Frutillar, Puerto Varas, and Puerto Octay might all boast about their views of Volcán Osorno, but you can really feel up close and personal with the volcano when you arrive in the town of Ensenada, which also neighbors the jagged Volcán Calbuca. The lake drive also illustrates how volcanoes play hide-and-seek on you: you'll see neither along a given stretch of road; then suddenly, you round a bend, or the clouds will part, and there they are.

$-$$ ✕ **Club Alemán.** The country setting distinguishes this German club from its other Lake District counterparts. The elegant, dark alerce-wood building sits on a small knoll with stupendous lake views and has a 1904 water mill on the grounds; it's great for taking a stroll before or after your meal. This place specializes in lamb and *jabalí* (wild pig), roasted over wood *asado al palo*-style. Make a point to stop by for the late-afternoon onces; these folks do it up big with küchen, pasta salad, and lots of cheesecake. ✉ *Ruta 225, Km 21* ☎ *65/330–140 or 9/869–9914* ⊟ *AE, DC, MC, V.*

$-$$ ✕ **Las Tranqueras.** What the menu at this place near the entrance to the town of Ensenada lacks in breadth, it makes up for in depth. Order off the regular menu, and you are limited to sandwiches and kúchen. Opt instead for the 6,000-peso prix-fixe dinner of pork, beef, trout, or wood-roasted salmon. The price includes salad, dessert, and a glass of house wine, and it's all served on dark-wood tables with emerald-green tablecloths. There's a souvenir shop for browsing while you wait. ✉ *Ruta 225, Km 41* ☎ *65/212–056* ⊟ *AE, DC, MC, V.*

$ 🏨 **Hotel Puerto Pilar.** Set on the shore of Lago Llanquihue, this hotel's many activities and perfect volcano views make it immensely popular among Chileans in summer. If you want a bit more of the get-away-from-it-all feel for which the place was originally intended, opt for one of the completely furnished cabins. Eight of them are constructed in *palafito*-style, held up with stilts right on the lakeshore (a style most commonly seen on the island of Chiloé); you can even fish right from your deck. Carpeted rooms in the main lodge all come with king beds and enormous windows. ✉ *Ruta 225, Km 27* ☎ *65/335–378, 2/650–8118 in Santiago* 🖷 *65/335–344, 2/650–8111 in Santiago* ⊕ *www. hotelpuertopilar.cl* ⤳ *18 rooms, 2 suites, 13 cabins* ⚭ *Restaurant, in-room safes, minibars, cable TV, tennis court, indoor pool, hot tub, massage, marina, fishing, bar, laundry service, Internet room, business services, meeting room; no a/c* ⊟ *AE, DC, MC, V* ⑩ *BP.*

Horseback Riding

The friendly folks at **Quinta del Lago** (⊠ Ruta 225, Km 25 ☏ 65/338–275 or 9/299–9302 ⊕ www.quintadellago.cl) farm rent horses for 6,000 pesos per hour and offer five-hour guided excursions to the foothills of Volcán Calbuco for 48,000 pesos.

Kayaking

KoKayak (⊠ Ruta 225, Km 25 ☏ 65/346–433 ⊕ www.kokayak.cl) can take you on guided kayaking and rafting excursions of the nearby Río Petrohue.

Parque Nacional Vicente Pérez Rosales

⑰ *3 km (2 mi) east of Ensenada.*

Chile's oldest national park, Parque Nacional Vicente Pérez Rosales was established in 1926. South of Parque Nacional Puyehue, the 2,538-square-km (980-square-mi) preserve includes the Osorno and lesser-known Puntiagudo volcanoes, as well as the deep blue Lago Todos los Santos. The visitor center opposite the Hotel Petrohué provides access to some fairly easy hikes. The Rincón del Osorno trail hugs the lake; the Saltos de Petrohué trail runs parallel to the river of the same name. Rudimentary campsites are available for 10,000 pesos per person. ☏ 65/290–711 ⊞ 1,000 pesos ⊗ Dec.–Feb., daily 9–8; Mar.–Nov., daily 9–6.

The Volcán Osorno begins to appear in your car window soon after you drive south from Osorno and doesn't disappear until shortly before your arrival in Puerto Montt. (The almost-perfectly conical volcano has been featured in a Samsung television commercial shown in the United States.) The mountain forms the foundation for Chile's newest ski area, **Ski & Outdoors Volán Osorno** (⊠ San Francisco 333, Puerto Varas ☏ 65/233–445 or 09/262–3323 ⊕ www.volcanosorno.com), which offers ski and snowboard rentals and lessons. Adults pay 14,000 pesos for a full day of skiing; 10,000 pesos for a half day, with transportation offered from the office in the center of Puerto Varas.

One of the Lake District's signature excursions is a binational one. The **Cruce de Lagos** takes in a combination of bus and boat transport from Puerto Varas to San Carlos de Bariloche, Argentina, via the park's Lago Todos los Santos and Argentina's Lago Nahuel Huapi. **Andina del Sud** (⊠ Del Salvador 72, Puerto Varas ☏ 65/232–811 ⊕ www.crucedelagos.cl) offers the trip starting from Puerto Varas or Puerto Montt.

Where to Stay

$$–$$$$ ⊞ **Hotel Petrohué.** The common areas in this stately, rustic orange chalet have vaulted ceilings and huge fireplaces. Guest rooms are a mix of dark woods and stone and have brightly colored drapes and spreads. Cabins echo the design of the main building and have their own fireplaces. The hotel's tour office can set you up with cruises on nearby lakes or take you to scale Volcán Osorno if you're an experienced climber. ⊠ *Ruta 225, Km 64, Petrohué s/n* ☏☏ *65/212–025* ⊕ *www.petrohue. com* ⌇ *20 rooms, 4 cabins* ⌂ *Restaurant, coffee shop, pool, fishing, bicycles, horseback riding, bar, shop, laundry service, meeting room, travel services; no a/c, no room TVs* ⊟ *AE, DC, MC, V* ⏐⚬⏐ *BP, MAP, AI.*

Sports & the Outdoors

Make like Tarzan (or Jane) and swing through the treetops in the shadow of Volcán Osorno with **Canopy Chile** (☎ 65/233–121 or 09/750–1040 ⊕ www.canopychile.com). A helmet, a very secure harness, 2 km (1 mi) of zip line strung out over 12 platforms, and experienced guides give you a bird's-eye view of the forest below.

Puerto Montt

⑱ *20 km (12 mi) south of Puerto Varas.*

For most of its history, windy Puerto Montt was the end of the line for just about everyone traveling in the Lake District. Now the Carretera Austral carries on southward, but for all intents and purposes Puerto Montt remains the region's last significant outpost, a provincial city that is the hub of local fishing, textile, and tourist activity. Today the city center is quickly sprouting malls, condos, and office towers, but away from downtown, Puerto Montt consists mainly of low clapboard houses perched above its bay, the Seno de Reloncaví. If it's a sunny day, head east to Playa Pelluco or one of the city's other beaches. If you're more interested in exploring the countryside, drive along the shore for a good view of the surrounding hills.

Latin America's ornate church architecture is nowhere to be found in the Lake District. More typical of the region is Puerto Montt's stark 1856 **Catedral.** The alerce-wood structure, modeled on the Pantheon in Paris, is the city's oldest surviving building. ⊠ *Plaza de Armas* ☎ *No phone* ☯ *Mass: Mon.–Sat. noon and 7 PM; Sun. 8:30, 10, and noon.*

The **Museo de Puerto Montt,** east of the city's bus terminal, has a collection of crafts and relics from the nearby archipelago of Chiloé. Historical photos of Puerto Montt itself give a sense of the area's slow and often difficult growth and the impact of the 1960 earthquake, which virtually destroyed the port. Pope John Paul II celebrated Mass on the grounds during his 1987 visit. One exhibit documents the event. ⊠ *Av. Diego Portales 991* ☎ *65/344–457* 🎫 *500 pesos* ☯ *Daily 9–7.*

About 3 km (2 mi) west of downtown along the coastal road lies the **Caleta Angelmó,** Puerto Montt's fishing cove. This busy port serves small fishing boats, large ferries, and cruisers carrying travelers and cargo southward through the straits and fjords that form much of Chile's shoreline. On weekdays small launches from Isla Tenglo and other outlying islands arrive early in the morning and leave late in the afternoon. The fish market here has one of the most varied selections of seafood in all of Chile.

Barely a stone's throw from Puerto Montt, the mountainous 398-square-km (154-square-mi) **Parque Nacional Alerce Andino,** with more than 40 small lakes, was established to protect some 20,000 endangered alerce trees. Comparable to California's hardy sequoia, alerce grow to average heights of 40 meters (130 feet), and can reach 4 meters (13 feet) in diameter. Immensely popular for construction of houses in southern Chile, they are quickly disappearing from the landscape. Many of these are

3,000–4,000 years old. ⊠ *Carretera Austral, 35 km (21 mi) east of Puerto Montt* ☎ 65/212–036 🎟 *1,700 pesos* ◷ *Daily 9–6.*

Where to Stay & Eat

$–$$$ ✕ **Café Haussmann.** Its pale-wood-and-chrome decor might make this place seem trendy, but it's actually a fun, friendly place. The great sandwiches and light meals of crudos, cakes, and küchen make it a great destination for late-night noshing. ⊠ *San Martín 185* ☎ *65/293–980* ▤ *AE, DC, MC, V.*

$–$$$ ✕ **Club Alemán.** As befitting an old German association, Puerto Montt's Club Alemán exhibits a huge collection of beer steins on dark-wood shelving and serves delicious küchen and other pastries, but the rest of the menu is more local. Seafood—delicious clams, oysters, and lobster—as well as freshwater trout are the specialties here. ⊠ *Antonio Varas 264* ☎ *65/252–551* ▤ *AE, DC, MC, V* ◷ *No dinner Sun.*

$–$$$ ✕ **Club de Yates.** There are no yachts here, despite the tony-sounding name, and prices are reasonable—you can feast on lobster for just a few dollars. The arresting yellow exterior contrasts sharply with the subdued elegance of the interior, which has crisp linens and candlelight. You can't miss this place, as it sits on a high pier jutting out into the bay. The various fish and seafood dishes are prepared grilled or barbecued. ⊠ *Av. Juan Soler Manfredini 200* ☎ *65/284–000* ▤ *AE, DC, MC, V* ◷ *No dinner Sun.*

$–$$$ ✕ **Feria Artesanal Angelmó.** Several kitchens here prepare *mariscal* (shellfish soup) and *caldillo* (seafood chowder), as well as *almejas* (clams), *machas* (razor clams), and *ostiones* (scallops) with Parmesan cheese. Separate tables and counters are at each kitchen in this enclosed market, which is 3 km (2 mi) west of Puerto Montt along the coast road. Don't expect anything as formal as set hours, but most open around 11 AM for lunch and serve for about three hours, and then from about 6 to 9 PM for dinner every day in the January–March high season. The rest of the year, most close during varying days of the week. ⊠ *Caleta Angelmó* ☎ *No phone* ▤ *No credit cards.*

$–$$ ✕ **Restaurant Kiel.** Hospitable German-born proprietor Helga Birkir stands guard at this Chilean-Teutonic seafood restaurant on the coast west of Puerto Montt. Helga offers a little bit of everything else, but it's her curanto that draws crowds. Fresh produce from her well-kept garden makes lunch here a delight. ⊠ *Camino Chinquihue, Km 8, Chinquihue* ☎ *65/255–010* ▤ *AE, DC, MC, V.*

¢–$$ ✕ **Café Central.** This old-style café in the heart of Puerto Montt retains the spirit of the 1920s and 1930s. It's a good place for a filling afternoon tea, with its menu of sandwiches, ice cream, and pastries. The raspberry küchen is a particular favorite here. ⊠ *Rancagua 117* ☎ *65/254–721* ▤ *AE, DC, MC, V.*

$$–$$$ ▥ **Don Luis Gran Hotel.** This modern lodging down the street from the cathedral, a favorite among upscale business travelers, has panoramic vistas of the Seno de Reloncaví. (Rooms on the seventh and eighth floors have the best views.) The carpeted rooms have undergone a welcome renovation and have either queen-size beds or doubles with two full-size beds. A big American-style breakfast, served in a cozy salon, is included in the rate. ⊠ *Urmeneta at Quillota* ☎ *65/259–001* 🖷 *65/259–*

005 ⊕ *www.hoteldonluis.com* ⌐ *60 rooms, 1 suite* ⚄ *Restaurant, coffee shop, snack bar, cable TV, gym, sauna, bar, laundry service, business services, meeting rooms; no a/c* ▤ *AE, DC, MC, V.*

$$ ⊞ **Gran Hotel Don Vicente.** The grandest of Puerto Montt's hotels underwent a much needed face-lift in 2002–2003 and, more than ever, it retains its Gstaad-by-the-sea glory. Its Bavarian-style facade resembles that of countless other Lake District lodgings, but the lobby's huge picture window overlooking the Seno de Reloncaví lets you know this place is something special. The modern guest rooms are comfy, with carpets and contemporary wood furniture—but do yourself a favor and spring for a standard room, rather than an economy one. The difference in price is tiny, but the difference in quality of the rooms is substantial. ⊠ *Diego Portales 450* ☎ *65/432–900, 2/953–5037 in Santiago* ⎙ *65/437–699, 2/953–5900 in Santiago* ⊕ *www.granhoteldonvicente.cl* ⌐ *77 rooms, 4 suites* ⚄ *Restaurant, coffee shop, in-room safes, minibars, cable TV, bar, laundry service, concierge, business services, meeting rooms, airport shuttle, travel services; no a/c* ▤ *AE, DC, MC, V* ⑩ *BP.*

$$ ⊞ **Viento Sur.** This old Victorian house sits proudly on a hill, offering a majestic view of both the city and the sea. Rooms in the original 1920s building have high ceilings and huge picture windows. Those in the newer wing below the house are smaller, but all are comfortably furnished with generous use of native Chilean blond woods. The restaurant serves excellent Chilean seafood and a huge buffet breakfast (included in the rate) that just may keep you going until dinner. ⊠ *Ejército 200* ☎ *65/258–700* ⎙ *65/314–732* ⊕ *www.hotelvientosur.cl* ⌐ *27 rooms, 2 suites* ⚄ *Restaurant, in-room safes, cable TV, sauna, bar, laundry service, Internet room, business services, meeting room; no a/c* ▤ *AE, DC, MC, V* ⑩ *BP.*

$ ⊞ **Hostal Pacífico.** European travelers favor this solid budget option up the hill from the bus station. The rooms are small, but they have comfy beds with lots of pillows. Look at a few before you pick one, as some of the interior rooms have skylights rather than windows. The staff is exceptionally friendly and helpful. ⊠ *Juan J. Mira 1088* ☎☎ *65/256–229* ⊕ *www.hostalpacifico.cl* ⌐ *30 rooms* ⚄ *Dining room, cable TV, Internet room, travel services; no a/c* ▤ *No credit cards* ⑩ *CP.*

$ ⊞ **O'Grimm.** The warmth and charm of this four-story inn evokes a small town in Germany. The helpful staff makes you feel right at home. Muted shades of gray, rose, and green decorate the simple rooms, which are furnished with double beds, small tables, and chairs. ⊠ *Guillermo Gallardo 211* ☎ *65/252–845* ⎙ *65/258–600* ⊕ *www.ogrimm.com* ⌐ *26 rooms, 1 suite* ⚄ *Restaurant, minibars, cable TV, Wi-Fi, bar, laundry service, meeting rooms; no a/c* ▤ *AE, DC, MC, V* ⑩ *BP.*

¢ ⛺ **Los Alamos.** You can camp here at a site with fine views of the Seno de Reloncaví and Isla Tenglo. Sites have electricity and water, and hot showers are nearby. There's also a dock with boats you can rent. The campground is 11 km (7 mi) west of Caleta Angelmó. ⊠ *Costanera, highway to Chinquihue* ☎ *65/264–666* ▤ *No credit cards.*

Nightlife & the Arts

The **Casa de Arte Diego Rivera** (⊠ Quillota 116 ☎ 65/261–859), a gift of the government of Mexico, commemorates the famed muralist of the same name. It hosts art exhibitions in the gallery, as well as evening theater productions and occasional music and film festivals.

Shopping

An excellent selection of handicrafts is sold at the best prices in the country at the **Feria Artesanal Angelmó**, on the coastal road near Caleta Angelmó. Chileans know there's a better selection of crafts from Chiloé for sale here than in Chiloé itself. Baskets, ponchos, figures woven from different kinds of grasses and straws, and warm sweaters of raw, hand-spun, and hand-dyed wool are all offered. Much of the merchandise is geared toward tourists, so look carefully for more authentic offerings. Haggling is expected. It's open daily 9–dusk.

Pargua

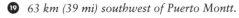 *63 km (39 mi) southwest of Puerto Montt.*

Pargua is the Lake District's end of the line, the jumping-off point for ferries to nearby Chiloé. This is where you catch the boats leaving every 30 minutes to Chacao on the northern tip of Chiloé's Isla Grande.

THE LAKE DISTRICT ESSENTIALS

Transportation

BY AIR

None of the Lake District's airports—Osorno, Puerto Montt, Temuco and Valdivia—receives international flights; flying here from another country means connecting in Santiago. Of the four cities, Puerto Montt has the greatest frequency of domestic flights. (When flying south to this region from Santiago, the left side of the plane affords the best views of the Andes.)

At this writing, plans are mapped out for the new Aeropuerto de la Araucanía to serve the northern Lake District, and to be built near the town of Freire, 25 km (15 mi) south of Temuco. The $40 million project is scheduled to open in 2008 and will receive international flights, providing faster access from abroad to the region, and especially to Pucón and Villarrica. The post-2008 status of the aging airports in Temuco and Valdivia remains uncertain.

Lan and its domestic affiliate LanExpress fly from Santiago to Temuco, Valdivia, Osorno, and Puerto Montt. A few of the flights south make an intermediate stop in Concepción. Some flights to Puerto Montt continue onward to Balmaceda and Punta Arenas. Sky Airline connects Puerto Montt to Santiago with an intermediate stop in Concepción and continues south to Balmaceda and Punta Arenas. Aerolineas del Sur flies from Santiago to Puerto Montt, with flights continuing south to Punta Arenas. Aerotaxis del Sur flies daily between Puerto Montt and Chaitén.

🛪Airlines **Aerolineas del Sur** ✉ Antonio Varas 464, Puerto Montt ☎ 65/319-450. **Aerotaxis del Sur** ✉ Aeropuerto El Tepual, Puerto Montt ☎ 65/252-523. **Lan/LanExpress** ✉ Eleuterio Ramírez 802, Osorno ☎ 64/204-119 ✉ Av. Bernardo O'Higgins 167, Puerto Montt ☎ 65/253-315 ✉ Bulnes 687, Temuco ☎ 45/211-339 ✉ Maipú 271, Valdivia ☎ 63/213-042. **Sky Airline** ✉ Benavente 405, Puerto Montt ☎ 65/437-555.

⚡ Airports Aeropuerto Cañal Bajo ⊠ Osorno ☎ 64/247-555. **Aeropuerto El Tepual** ⊠ Puerto Montt ☎ 65/488-203. **Aeropuerto Maquehue** ⊠ Temuco ☎ 45/554-801. **Aeropuerto Pichoy** ⊠ Valdivia ☎ 63/272-295.

AIRPORT TRANSFERS ETM provides bus transfers between Puerto Montt's Aeropuerto El Tepual and the city's bus terminal. Transfer & Turismo de la Araucanía vans meet arriving flights at Temuco's Aeropuerto Maquehue and transport passengers to various sites in the city. Reservations for transportation to the airport should be made a day in advance.
⚡ ETM ⊠ Puerto Montt ☎ 65/256-253.

Transfer & Turismo de la Araucanía ⊠ Temuco ☎ 45/339-900.

BY BOAT & FERRY

To drive much farther south than Puerto Montt, you've got to take a boat or ferry. Cruz del Sur operates a ferry connecting the mainland town of Pargua with Chacao on the northern tip of Chiloé's Isla Grande. Boats run every 30 minutes from early morning until after midnight. The trip takes about a half hour.

Navimag operates a cargo and passenger fleet throughout the region. The M/N *Evangelistas,* a 324-passenger ferry, sails round-trip from Puerto Montt to the popular tourist destination of Laguna San Rafael, stopping in both directions at Puerto Chacabuco on the Southern Coast. The 200-passenger M/N *Alejandrina* and M/N *Puerto Edén* sail from Puerto Montt to Chaitén, Quellón, and Puerto Chacabuco before making the trip in reverse.

Transmarchilay operates a cargo and passenger ferry service similar to that of Navimag, with ships that start in Puerto Montt and sail to Chaitén. From early January through late February, Transmarchilay's M/N *El Colono* sails weekly from Puerto Montt into Laguna San Rafael and back to Puerto Montt.

Naviera Río Cisnes operates twice-weekly passenger and auto ferry service each way between Puerto Montt and Chaitén and Puerto Montt and Puerto Chacabuco.

If it's speed you're after, Catamaranes del Sur provides twice-weekly catamaran service between Puerto Montt and Chaitén at a relatively quick 4½ hours. In January and February you can continue on from Chaitén for three more hours to Castro, on the Chiloe's Isla Grande.
⚡ Boat & Ferry Companies Catamaranes del Sur ⊠ Diego Portales and Guillermo Gallardo, Puerto Montt ☎ 65/267-533 ⊕ www.catamaranesdelsur.cl. **Cruz del Sur** ⊠ Puerto Montt ☎ 64/254-731 ⊕ www.busescruzdelsur.cl. **Naviera Río Cisnes** ⊠ Puerto Montt ☎ 64/432-700 ⊕ www.navierariocisnes.cl. **Navimag** ⊠ Angelmó 2187, Puerto Montt ☎ 65/432-300 ⊕ www.navimag.cl. **Transmarchilay** ⊠ Angelmó 2187, Puerto Montt ☎ 65/270-421 ⊕ www.transmarchilay.cl.

BY BUS

There's no shortage of bus companies traveling the Pan-American Highway (Ruta 5) from Santiago south to the Lake District. The buses aren't overcrowded on these long routes, and seats are assigned. Tickets may be purchased in advance, always a good idea if you're traveling in summer. Cruz del Sur and Tur-Bus connect the major cities. Buses JAC connects the resort towns of Pucón and Villarrica with Temuco and Valdivia. Buses Vía Octay runs between Osorno and Puerto Octay.

Representative bus fares are Temuco–Pucón, 2,200 pesos; Pucón–Villarrica, 600 pesos; Valdivia–Temuco, 2,600 pesos; Puerto Montt–Osorno, 1,600 pesos; Puerto Montt–Puerto Varas, 700 pesos.

Osorno, Puerto Montt, and Valdivia have their own central terminals. About half the bus companies serving Temuco use a joint terminal, called the Rodoviario, near the Holiday Inn Express on the north edge of town; several other companies have their own terminals close together along Vicuña Mackenna and Lagos.

🚌 Bus Depots **Osorno** ✉ Errázuriz 1400 ☎ 64/234–149. **Puerto Montt** ✉ Av. Diego Portales ☎ No phone. **Temuco** ✉ Av. Rudecindo Ortega ☎ 45/257–904. **Valdivia** ✉ Anfión Muñoz 360 ☎ 63/212–212.

🚌 Bus Lines **Buses JAC** ✉ Vicuña Mackenna 798, Temuco ☎ 45/210–313 ✉ Bilbao 610, Villarrica ☎ 45/411–447 ✉ Anfión Muñoz 360, Valdivia ☎ 63/212–925. **Buses Vía Octay** ✉ Errázuriz 1400, Osorno ☎ 64/237–043. **Cruz del Sur** ✉ Vicuña Mackenna 671, Temuco ☎ 45/210–701 ✉ Anfión Muñoz 360, Valdivia ☎ 63/213–840 ✉ Errázuriz 1400, Osorno ☎ 64/232–777 ✉ Av. Diego Portales, Puerto Montt ☎ 65/254–731. **Tur-Bus** ✉ Lagos 538, Temuco ☎ 45/239–190.

BY CAR

It's easier to see more of the Lake District if you have your own vehicle. The Pan-American Highway (Ruta 5) through the region is a well-maintained four-lane toll highway. You pay tolls of 1,500 pesos each at Púa (Km 623), Quepe (Km 695), Lanco (Km 775), La Unión (Km 888), and Purranque (Km 961); the southernmost toll plaza at Puerto Montt (Km 1,019) levies a 500-peso toll. Tollbooths at many exits charge 400 pesos as well.

Once you're this far south, driving is easy because there's little traffic, even on the major highways. Roads to most of the important tourist centers are paved, but many of the routes through the mountains are gravel or dirt, so a four-wheel-drive vehicle is ideal.

For a drop-off charge, a few rental-car companies, including Hertz, will allow you to rent a car in one city and return it in another.

🚗 Rental Agencies **Autovald** ✉ Portales 1330, Puerto Montt ☎ 65/256–355 ✉ Vicente Pérez Rosales 660, Valdivia ☎ 63/212–786. **Avis** ✉ Benavente 670, Puerto Montt ☎ 65/258–199 ✉ Aeropuerto El Tepual, Puerto Montt ☎ 65/255–164 ✉ Vicuña Mackenna 448, Temuco ☎ 45/237–575 ✉ Aeropuerto Maquehue, Temuco ☎ 45/337–715 ✉ Holzapfel 190, Pucón ☎ 45/444–351 ✉ Beaucheff 619, Valdivia ☎ 63/278–455 ✉ Aeropuerto Pichoy, Valdivia ☎ 63/278–458. **Budget** ✉ Antonio Varas 162, Puerto Montt ☎ 65/286–277 ✉ Aeropuerto El Tepual, Puerto Montt ☎ 65/294–100 ✉ Vicuña Mackenna 399, Temuco ☎ 45/232–715 ✉ Aeropuerto Maquehue, Temuco ☎ 45/338–836 ✉ Picarte 1348, Valdivia ☎ 63/340–060 ✉ Aeropuerto Pichoy, Valdivia ☎ 63/272–293. **Hertz** ✉ Antonio Varas 126, Puerto Montt ☎ 65/259–585 ✉ Aeropuerto El Tepual, Puerto Montt ☎ 65/268–944 ✉ Las Heras 999, Temuco ☎ 45/318–585 ✉ Aeropuerto Maquehue, Temuco ☎ 45/337–019 ✉ Ansorena 123, Pucón ☎ 45/441–664 ✉ Picarte 640, Valdivia ☎ 63/218–613 ✉ Aeropuerto Pichoy, Valdivia ☎ 63/272–273.

BY TAXI

As elsewhere in Chile, solid black or solid yellow cabs operate as *colectivos*, or collective taxis, following fixed routes and picking up to four people along the way. A sign on the roof shows the general destination. The cost is little more than that of a city bus. A black cab with a yellow roof will take you directly to your requested destination for a metered fare. Hail these in the street.

BY TRAIN

Chile's State Railway Company, the Empresa de los Ferrocarriles del Estado, has daily service southward from Santiago's Alameda station as far as Temuco on its Terra Sur trains. It's a far cry from the journey Paul Theroux recounted in *The Old Patagonian Express*. Trains run daily all year; the overnight trip takes about nine hours. Shuttle-bus service to and from Pucón and Villarrica runs in conjunction with the trains. Prices range from 10,000 pesos for an economy-class seat to 70,000 pesos for a sleeper with all the trimmings. If you prefer to rent a vehicle in Santiago, you can use the Autotren service from there to Temuco. The price is an extra 50,000–70,000 pesos each way, with surcharges assessed for vehicles longer than 16 feet.

🚆 Train Information **Empresa de los Ferrocarriles del Estado (EFE)** ☎ 2/585-5000 in Santiago, 45/233-416 in Temuco ⊕ www.efe.cl.

🚆 Train Station **Estación de Ferrocarriles** ✉ Av. Barros Arana 191, Temuco ☎ 45/233-416.

Contacts & Resources

BANKS & EXCHANGE SERVICES

All of the major cities in the Lake District have several banks that will exchange U.S. dollars. Most banks will not touch traveler's checks, which are best cashed at most *casas de cambio* (exchange offices). Inter Money Exchange offices sell and cash American Express traveler's checks. Many larger hotels will also exchange currency and a few will exchange traveler's checks. ATMs at Banco Santander and Banco de Chile, part of the omnipresent Redbanc network, accept both Cirrus- and Plus-affiliated cards. The district's four main airports have ATMs and casas de cambio.

🏦 Exchange Office **Inter Money Exchange** ✉ Claro Solar 780, Temuco ☎ 45/236-650 ✉ Del Salvador 257, Puerto Varas ☎ 65/232-019 ✉ Talca 84, Puerto Montt ☎ 65/253-745.

EMERGENCIES

🚨 Emergency Services **Ambulance** ☎ 131. **Fire (Bomberos)** ☎ 132. **Police (Carabineros)** ☎ 133.

🏥 Hospitals **Hospital Base Osorno** ✉ Dr. Guillermo Bühler, Osorno ☎ 64/235-571. **Hospital Base Puerto Montt** ✉ Seminario s/n, Puerto Montt ☎ 65/261-100. **Hospital Regional Valdivia** ✉ Simpson 850, Valdivia ☎ 63/297-000. **Hospital de Temuco** ✉ Manuel Montt, Temuco ☎ 45/296-100.

💊 Pharmacies At least one branch of Farmacias Ahumada in the Lake District's four cities stays open nightly until midnight and, in Temuco, 24 hours.

Farmacias Ahumada ✉ Eleuterio Ramírez 981, Osorno ☎ 64/421-561 ✉ Antonio Varas 651, Puerto Montt ☎ 65/344-419 ✉ Av. Alemania 505, Temuco ☎ 45/231-553 ✉ Av. Ramón Picarte 310, Valdivia ☎ 63/257-889.

INTERNET, MAIL & SHIPPING

You can check your e-mail at hotels in the larger towns and cities. Most towns also have Internet cafés, which are generally open until at least 10 PM, charging 500–600 pesos per hour.

Reasonably efficient, Correos de Chile has post offices in most towns. They are generally open weekdays 9–7 and Saturday 9–1. Mail posted from the Lake District's four hub cities takes up to two weeks to reach North America and three to reach Europe. Anything of value (or that looks valuable) should be sent via courier. DHL has offices in Temuco, Osorno, and Puerto Montt.

🏢 Internet Cafés **Café Phonet** ⊠ Libertad 127, Valdivia ☎ 63/341-054. **Comunic@te** ⊠ Pedro de Valdivia 651, Villarrica ☎ 45/416-785. **Cybercafé Mundosur** ⊠ San Martín 232, Puerto Montt ☎ 65/344-773. **Gea.com** ⊠ Av. Bernardo O'Higgins 520, Osorno ☎ 64/207-700. **Internet** ⊠ Del Salvador 257, Puerto Varas ☎ 65/237-667. **Net & Cofee** ⊠ Portales 873, Temuco ☎ 45/940-001. **Unid@d G** ⊠ Av. Bernardo O'Higgins 415, Pucón ☎ 45/444-918.

🏢 Post Offices **Correos de Chile** ⊠ Av. Bernardo O'Higgins 645, Osorno ⊠ Av. Rancagua 126, Puerto Montt ⊠ Av. Diego Portales 801, Temuco ⊠ Av. Bernardo O'Higgins 575, Valdivia.

🏢 Shipping Service **DHL** ⊠ Diego Portales 864, Temuco ☎ 45/218-720 ⊠ Bulnes 698, Osorno ☎ 64/222-021 ⊠ Av. Bernardo O'Higgins 175, Puerto Montt ☎ 65/268-740.

TOURS

The Lake District is the jumping-off point for luxury cruises. Many companies that offer trips to the fjords of Chilean Patagonia are based in Puerto Montt. Skorpios, with a trio of luxurious ships, has first-class cruises from Puerto Montt to the Laguna San Rafael. The ships carry between 70 and 130 passengers.

A number of companies offer cruises on the region's lakes. Andina del Sud operates between Puerto Varas and San Carlos de Bariloche, and traverses the Lago Todos los Santos.

🏢 Boat Tours **Andina del Sud** ⊠ Del Salvador 72, Puerto Varas ☎ 65/232-811. **Skorpios** ⊠ Augosto Leguia Norte 118, Santiago ☎ 2/231-1030 ⊕ www.skorpios.cl.

VISITOR INFORMATION

The Lake District's four major cities have offices of Sernatur, Chile's national tourist office. The Osorno, Temuco, and Valdivia branches are well staffed with friendly people, full of good advice; the Puerto Montt branch is on the second floor of an out-of-the-way building and doesn't lend itself well to walk-in visitors. City tourist offices, run by the government or a chamber of commerce, are in most communities catering to tourists. They are valuable resources but cannot book rooms or tours. Many city tourist offices keep sharply abbreviated hours in the April–November off-season.

🏢 **Frutillar Tourist Office** ⊠ Philippi at San Martín ☎ 65/420-198. **Lican Ray Tourist Office** ⊠ General Urrutia 310 ☎ 45/431-201. **Osorno Tourist Office** ⊠ Plaza de Armas ☎ 64/264-250. **Pucón Tourist Office** ⊠ Av. Bernardo O'Higgins 483 ☎ 45/293-002. **Puerto Montt Tourist Office** ⊠ San Martín at Diego Portales ☎ 65/261-823. **Puerto**

Octay Tourist Office ✉ La Esperanza 55 ☎ 64/391–491. **Puerto Varas Tourist Office** ✉ Costanera at San José ☎ 65/233–315. **Sernatur** ✉ Av. Bernardo O'Higgins 667, Osorno ☎ 64/237–575 ✉ Av. de la Décima Región 480, Puerto Montt ☎ 65/254–850 ✉ Claro Solar and Bulnes, Temuco ☎ 45/211–969 ✉ Av. Arturo Prat 555, Valdivia ☎ 63/342–300. **Temuco Tourist Office** ✉ Mercado Municipal ☎ 45/216–360. **Valdivia Tourist Office** ✉ Terminal de Buses, Anfión Muñoz 360 ☎ 63/212–212. **Villarrica Tourist Office** ✉ Pedro de Valdivia 1070 ☎ 45/206–618.

Chiloé

7

WORD OF MOUTH

"Getting to Chiloé seems difficult, but this is not Easter Island. Your reward for the half-hour ferry ride is a quiet, get-away-from-it-all place that, I swear, only Chileans seem to know about. Bundle up—there are plenty of woolens for sale here if you didn't bring your own—and visit the markets and the simple Jesuit churches leftover from the colonial era."

—Jeff V.

Updated by
Jeffrey Van Fleet

STEEPED IN MAGIC, SHROUDED IN MIST, the 41-island archipelago of Chiloé is that proverbial world apart, isolated not so much by distance from the mainland—it's barely more than 2 km (1 mi) at its nearest point—but by the quirks of history. Some 130,000 people populate 35 of these rainy islands, with most of them living on the 8,394-square-km (3,241-square-mi) Isla Grande de Chiloé. Almost all are descendants of a seamless blending of colonial and indigenous cultures, a tradition that entwines farming and fishing, devout Catholicism and spirits of good and evil, woolen sweaters and wooden churches.

Originally inhabited by the indigenous Chono people, Chiloé was gradually taken over by the Huilliche. Though Chiloé was claimed as part of Spain's empire in the 1550s, colonists dismissed the archipelago as a backwater. The 1598 rebellion by the Mapuche people on the mainland drove a contingent of Spanish settlers to the isolated safety of Chiloé. Left to their own devices, Spaniards and Huilliche lived and worked side by side. Their society was built on the concept of *minga,* a help-thy-neighbor spirit in the best tradition of the barn raisings and quilting bees in pioneer America. The outcome was a culture neither Spanish nor indigenous, but Chilote, a quintessential mestizo society.

Isolated from the rest of the continent, islanders had little interest in or awareness of the revolutionary fervor sweeping Latin America in the early 19th century. In fact, the mainland Spaniards recruited the Chilote to help put down rebellions in the region. When things got too hot in Santiago, the Spanish governor took refuge on the island, just as his predecessors had done two centuries earlier. Finally defeated, the Spaniards abandoned Chiloé in 1826, surrendering their last outpost in South America, and the island soon joined the new nation of Chile.

These days, the isolation is more psychological than physical. Some 40 buses per day and frequent ferries make the half-hour crossing between Chiloé and Pargua, near Puerto Montt in the Lake District on the mainland. Construction has begun on the long-discussed but controversial Puente Bicentenario de Chiloé, a 2½-km (1½-mi) bridge spanning the Gulf of Ancud and connecting Isla Grande with the mainland. The $306 million project remains one of the most contentious issues here. (Many islanders maintain the funds could be better used to improve infrastructure within Chiloé itself.) Completion is scheduled for 2010, Chile's bicentennial year. Meanwhile, a $10 million grant from the Inter-American Development Bank will be used for improvement of sustainable tourism here, with a portion slated to restore Chiloé's historic Jesuit churches.

Exploring Chiloé

If you're like most people, you'll explore Chiloé by car. The Pan-American Highway (Ruta 5) that meanders through northern Chile ends at the Golfo de Ancud and continues again on Isla Grande. It connects the major cities of Ancud, Castro, and Chonchi before coming to its anticlimactic end in Quellón. Paved roads also connect the Pan-American to Quemchi and Dalcahue, and Achao on Isla Quinchao.

CloseUp
CHILOÉ FESTIVALS & SEASONAL EVENTS

As elsewhere in southern Chile, Chiloé's festivals usually take place in summer, when there's the best chance of good weather. Fiestas Costumbritsas, which celebrate Chilote customs and folklore, take place over several weekends during January and February in Ancud and Castro. Ancud hosts a small open-air film festival the first few days in February. Every community celebrates its patron saint's day. Although they are local affairs, outsiders are always welcome.

About the Restaurants

As befits an island culture, seafood reigns in Chiloé. The signature Chilote dish is *curanto,* a hearty stew of fish and shellfish with chicken, beef, pork, and lamb thrown in. It's served with plenty of potato bread. Most restaurants here serve curanto, though not every day of the week. *Salmón ahumado* (smoked salmon) is another seafood favorite.

The archipelago is also known for its tasty fruit liqueurs, usually from the central Chiloé town of Chonchi. Islanders take mangoes, grapes, and apples and turn them into the *licor de oro* that often greets you as you check into your hotel.

About the Hotels

There are three or four good hotels on Chiloé, but none would pass for luxury lodgings on the mainland. That said, the islands have perfectly acceptable, reasonably priced hotels. Castro and Ancud have the most varied choices; Chonchi, Achao, and Quellón less so. As in the Lake District to the north, a number of the hotels look as if they were transplanted from Germany. Many are sided with shingles made from a type of local wood called *alerce.* Much-appreciated central heating and a light breakfast are standard in most better hostelries. Few places here are equipped to handle credit cards, but with ATMs readily available in Castro and Ancud, paying in cash isn't as inconvenient as you might expect.

Outside the major cities, the pickings are slim. *Hospedaje* ("lodging") signs seem to sprout in front of every other house in Castro and Ancud in summer as home owners rent rooms to visitors. Quality varies, so inspect the premises before agreeing to take a room from someone who greets you at the bus station.

Following a trend seen elsewhere in Chile, Chiloé has developed a system of so-called agro-tourism lodgings called the Red Agroturismo Chiloé (☎ 65/628–333), headquartered in the northern community of

After crossing the Golfo de Ancud on the morning ferry on your first day, drive south to ⛴ **Ancud.** Soak up the port town's atmosphere that afternoon. Head to **Dalcahue** the next day; if it's Sunday you can wander among the stalls of the morning market. Take the short ferry ride to **Isla Quinchao** and visit the colorful church of Santa María de Loreto. Back on Isla Grande, head to **Castro.** Spend the next day visiting the capital's historical and modern-art museums and the lovely church. The following day, head south to **Chonchi,** known to locals as the "City of Three Stories." From there it's a rough but doable drive to the sparsely populated Pacific coast to visit the **Parque Nacional Chiloé,** where you can enjoy one of the short hikes through the forest. On your last day head to Chiloé's southernmost town, ⛴ **Quellón.**

7

Ancud. The network of 19 farms, most of them on Isla Grande, gives the adventurous Spanish-speaking traveler a chance to partake of rural life, helping to milk the cows, churn the butter, or just relax. Rates run 10,000–12,000 pesos per person, including breakfast. Accommodations are in no-frills farmhouses, but plenty of smog- and traffic-weary Santiago residents are lapping up the experience.

WHAT IT COSTS In pesos (in thousands)				
$$$$	**$$$**	**$$**	**$**	**¢**
RESTAURANTS over 11	8–11	5–8	3–5	under 3
HOTELS over 105	75–105	45–75	15–45	under 15

Restaurant prices are for a main course at dinner. Hotel prices are for a double room in high season, excluding tax.

When to Go

When best to visit Chiloé? In one word, summer. The islands get only 60 days of sunshine a year, most during December–February. Chiloé receives some 157 inches of rain annually, and most of that falls between April and November. You should be prepared for rain any time of year, however. The high-season crowds are never overwhelming, and they make the island look festive. Off-season Chiloé is beguilingly forlorn. Though admittedly not for everyone, the mist and fog and sunless days deepen the mystery of the island.

Ancud

❶ *90 km (54 mi) southwest of Puerto Montt.*

Unless you're one of those rare visitors who approaches the archipelago from the south, Ancud is the first encounter you'll have with Chiloé. Founded in 1769 as a fortress city on the northern end of Isla Grande, Ancud was repeatedly attacked during Chile's war for independence. It remained the last stronghold of the Spaniards in the Americas, and the

Chiloé

PACIFIC OCEAN

Canal Chacao

Carelmapu

Pargua

Calbuco

Gaubún

Quetalmahue

1 Ancud

Chacao

Chepu

Linao

Lliuco

Río Pudeto

Golfo de Ancud

Río Butalcura

2 Quemchi

Sector Chepu

Alto Butalcura

3 Quicaví

Parque Nacional Chiloé 10

4 Tenaún

5 Dalcahue

Aldachildo

6 Isla Quinchao

Curaco de Velez

Achao

Sector Anay

Castro 7

Chonchi 8

9 Isla Lemuy

Cucao

Lago Cucao

Huillinco

Detif

Lago Tepuhueico

Pan-American Highway

Compú

11 Queilén

Chadmo Central

Isla Tranqui

Golfo Corcovado

Isla Grande de Chiloé

Río Medina

Huildad

Coinco

Lago Chaiguata

Yaldad

12 Quellón

Isla Cailin

Punta Roble

Isla Quilán

Isla San Pedro

Fantastic Folklore

Spirits benevolent and malevolent inhabit Chiloé—or at least populate its colorful folklore. Old-timers can regale you with stories of trolls, witches, mermaids and ghost ships. Who knows if there's a word of truth to any of the tales? But don't let curmudgeonly disbelief spoil your fun on a misty, foggy night here.

Charming Churches

Chiloé is its churches, simple in their elegance, elegant in their simplicity. Some 150 of these stark wooden structures dot Isla Grande. They were constructed by Jesuit missionaries during the colonial era and were key to the evangelization of the indigenous peoples. A few are open to the public, and a visit to one is essential to understanding the island's austere history.

7

Sports & the Outdoors

Small means manageable in Chiloé's adventure-tourism scene. The pickings might seem slim if you've just arrived from the mainland Lake District, but what the archipelago lacks in sheer number of outfitters, it makes up in the high quality of services offered by those that are here. Hiking, sailing, sea kayaking, and horseback riding are the best and most popular activities.

Traditional Crafts

Warm, wooly and wonderful are the sweaters and ponchos you can buy in Chiloé. Islanders process their hand-spun, hand-dyed wool to retain the fabric's natural oils and keep it water-resistant. Castro's waterfront Feria Artesanal is the most popular place to shop for such traditional goods, as is Dalcahue's Sunday-morning market.

---

seat of their government-in-exile after fleeing from Santiago, a distinction it retained until Chiloé was finally annexed by Chile in 1826.

Although it's the largest city in Chiloé, Ancud seems like a smaller town than perpetual rival Castro. Both have their fans. Castro has more activities, but Ancud, with its hills, irregular streets, and commanding ocean views, gets raves for its quiet charm.

Statues of mythical Chilote figures, such as the Pincoya and Trauco, greet you on the terrace of the fortresslike **Museo Regional de Ancud,** just uphill from the Plaza de Armas. The ship *La Goleta Ancud,* the museum's centerpiece, carried Chilean settlers to the Strait of Magellan in 1843. Inside is a collection of island handicrafts. ⊠ *Libertad 370* ☎ *65/622–413* 🖅 *600 pesos* ☺ *Jan. and Feb., daily 10–7:30; Mar.–Dec., weekdays 10–5:30, weekends 10–2.*

Northwest of downtown Ancud, the 16 cannon emplacements of the **Fuerte de San Antonio** are nearly all that remain of Spain's last outpost in the New World. The fort, constructed in 1786, was a key component in the defense of the Canal de Chacao, especially after the Spanish colonial government fled to Chiloé during Chile's war for independence. ⊠ *Lord Cohrane at San Antonio* ☎ *No phone* 🖅 *Free.*

Where to Stay & Eat

$$–$$$ ✕ **Restaurant La Pincoya.** According to Chilote legend, the presence of the spirit La Pincoya signals an abundant catch. La Pincoya does serve up abundant fresh fish and usually whips up curanto on the weekends. This friendly waterfront restaurant is nothing fancy—plain wooden tables and chairs—but the views are stupendous. ⊠ *Arturo Prat 61* ☎ *65/ 622–613* ▤ *No credit cards* ⊘ *Closed Aug.*

$$–$$$ ✕ **Retro's Pub.** This cozy, intimate place makes a nice break from Chiloé's ubiquitous seafood. Instead, chow down on fajitas, burritos, and nachos. Portions are ample. The dining room is dark and casual. Around the corner on Pudeto, the same owners operate Cafe Retro's, which is much brighter with lighter sandwich-and-dessert fare. ⊠ *Maipú 615* ☎ *65/ 626–410* ▤ *AE, DC, MC, V.*

$$ ✕▥ **Hostería Ancud.** Ancud's finest hotel—some say the best in Chiloé—
Fodor's Choice sits atop a bluff overlooking the Fuerte de San Antonio. It's part of Chile's
★ Panamericana Hoteles chain, but that doesn't mean it lacks individuality. The rooms in the rustic main building, for example, have log-cabin walls. The wood-paneled lobby, with a huge fireplace inviting you to linger, opens into the town's loveliest restaurant, which feels spacious thanks to its vaulted ceilings and picture windows. Try the *salmón del caicavilú* (salmon stuffed with chicken, ham, cheese, and mushrooms). ⊠ *San Antonio 30* ☎ *65/622–340* 🖨 *65/622–350* ⊕ *www. panamericanahoteles.cl* ⇨ *24 rooms* ⌂ *Restaurant, coffee shop, bar, meeting room, travel services, no-smoking rooms; no a/c* ▤ *AE, DC, MC, V* ▥ *CP.*

$$ ▥ **Hotel Galeón Azul.** Formerly a Catholic seminary, the Blue Galleon is actually painted bright yellow. Perched like a ship run aground on a bluff overlooking Ancud's waterfront, this modern hotel has pleasantly furnished rooms with big windows and great views of the sea. It's owned by the same folks who own the Hotel Unicornio Azul in Castro, and it has the same personalized service. ⊠ *Libertad 751* ☎ *65/622–567* 🖨 *65/622–543* ✉ *galeonazul@surnet.cl* ⇨ *15 rooms* ⌂ *Restaurant, bar, cable TV; no a/c* ▤ *No credit cards* ▥ *CP.*

$ ▥ **Hostal Lluhay.** Don't let this hostal's drab exterior fool you: inside is a charming lobby filled with knickknacks, and a dining room dominated by a 200-year-old rosewood piano. Rooms are plain, but pleasant considering the reasonable rates. The amiable owners include a buffet breakfast in the price. ⊠ *Lord Cochrane 458* ☎ *65/622–656* ⊕ *www. hostal-lluhay.cl* ⇨ *18 rooms* ⌂ *Cable TV, bar, Internet, travel services; no a/c, no room phones* ▤ *No credit cards* ▥ *BP.*

¢ ▥ **Hospedaje O'Higgins.** The nicest of the many hospedajes in Ancud, this 60-year-old home sits on a hillside overlooking the bay. You have your pick of eight bright rooms. The furniture in the common areas is a bit worn, but the whole place has a cozy, lived-in feel. The friendly service will make you overlook any inadequacies. ⊠ *Av. Bernardo O'Higgins 6* ☎ *65/622–266* ⇨ *8 rooms, 2 with bath* ⌂ *Laundry service; no a/c, no room phones, no room TVs* ▤ *No credit cards* ▥ *CP.*

Quemchi

2 *62 km (37 mi) southeast of Ancud.*

On the protected inside of the Golfo de Ancud, Quemchi is a small, picturesque fishing village with a church in one of the best structural conditions on the island. The **Iglesia de San Antonio de Padua,** on the Plaza de Armas, was constructed in the late 19th century, replacing the original Jesuit structure, and painstakingly restored in 1996. Sunday-morning Mass is the only time to get a glimpse inside.

A block uphill from the church is a typical old Chilote **cemetery,** almost a town in miniature. Each tomb is a small mausoleum, topped and sided with alerce shingles and made to look like a little house, with a door and windows.

Some 4 km (2½ mi) east of Quemchi is the tiny **Isla de Aucar,** a forested islet reached only by a wooden pedestrian bridge. The Jesuit chapel here dates from 1761.

Quicaví

3 *25 km (15 mi) southeast of Quemchi.*

The center of all that is magical and mystical about Chiloé, Quicaví sits forlornly on the eastern coast of Isla Grande. More superstitious locals will strongly advise you against going anywhere near the coast to the south of town, where miles of caves extend to the village of Tenaún. They believe that witches, and evil ones at that, inhabit them. On the beaches are mermaids that lure fishermen to their deaths. (These are not the beautiful and benevolent Pincoya, also a legendary kelp-covered mermaid. A glimpse of her is thought to portend good fishing for the day.) And many a Quicaví denizen claims to have glimpsed Chiloé's notorious ghost ship, the *Caleuche,* roaming the waters on foggy nights, searching for its doomed passengers. Of course, a brief glimpse of the ship is all anyone dares admit, as legend holds that a longer gaze could spell death.

In an effort to win converts, the Jesuits constructed the enormous **Iglesia de San Pedro** on the Plaza de Armas. The original structure survives from colonial times, though it underwent extensive remodeling in the early 20th century. It's open for services the first Sunday of every month at 11 AM, which is the only time you can get a look inside.

Tenaún

4 *12 km (7 mi) south of Quicaví.*

A small fishing village, Tenaún is notable for its 1861 neoclassical **Iglesia de Tenaún,** on the Plaza de Armas, which replaced the original 1734 structure built by the Jesuits. The style differs markedly from that of other Chilote churches, as the two towers flanking the usual hexagonal central bell tower are painted a striking deep blue. You can see the interior during services on Sunday at 9:30 AM and the rest of the week at 5 PM.

CloseUp

WITCHES AND GHOST SHIPS

AS THE SOUTHERNMOST OUTPOST OF SPAIN'S EMPIRE, *Chiloé was also the "end of Christendom," as naturalist Charles Darwin wrote after his 1834 visit. But Chilote Catholicism was also tied up in magic and legend. Much of what is identified as Chilean folklore originated here, though the rest of the country happily embraces it as its own. Mythical creatures are thought to populate the coasts of these foggy green islands. On the beach you might spot the beautiful blonde Pincoya, signaling good fishing that day. Beware the troll-like Trauco, seducer of young women. Don't go poking around caves for fear of stumbling upon a brujo, or witch; that encounter could bode good or evil. And don't gaze too intently out at the ocean on a foggy night, lest you catch a glimpse of the Caleuche, the ill-fated ghost ship that sank on its maiden voyage and forever cruises the dark waters looking for its passengers lost at sea.*

These days, your encounter with such characters will more likely take the form of a woven-straw figure for sale in a market in Castro or Dalcahue. But you just might run into a self-proclaimed brujo in that same market offering an herbal cure for whatever ails you.

— Brian Kluepfel

Dalcahue

⑤ *40 km (24 mi) west of Tenaún, 74 km (44 mi) southeast of Ancud.*

Most days travelers in Dalcahue stop only long enough to board the ferry that deposits them 15 minutes later on Isla Quinchao. But everyone lingers in Dalcahue if it's a Sunday morning, when they can visit the weekly artisan market. Dalcahue is a pleasant coastal town—one that deserves a longer visit.

The 1850 **Iglesia de Nuestra Señora de los Dolores,** modeled on the churches constructed during the Jesuit era, sits on the main square. A portico with nine arches, an unusually high number for a Chilote church, fronts the structure. The church, which is on Plaza de Armas, holds a small museum and is open daily 9–6.

A *fogón*—a traditional indigenous cooking pit—sits in the center of the small *palafito* (a shingled house built on stilts and hanging over the water) housing the **Museo Histórico de Dalcahue,** which displays historical exhibits from this part of the island. ⊠ *Av. Pedro Montt 105* ☎ *65/642–375* ⌫ *Free* ⊙ *Oct.–Mar., daily 8–2 and 2:30–6; Apr.–Sept., weekdays 8–2 and 2:30–5.*

Where to Stay

$ 🖼 **Hotel La Isla.** One of Chiloé's nicest lodgings, the wood-shingled Hotel La Isla greets you with a cozy sitting room and big fireplace off the lobby. Huge windows and vaulted ceilings make the wood-panel rooms bright and airy. Comfortable mattresses with plush pillows and warm comforters invite you to sleep tight. ✉ *Mocopulli 113* 🕿 *65/641–241* ✎ *hotellaisla@hotmail.com* ➦ *16 rooms* ⌂ *Cable TV, bar, laundry service; no a/c* ⊟ *No credit cards* ⑩ *CP.*

Shopping

Dalcahue's Sunday-morning art market, **Feria Artesanal,** on Avenida Pedro Montt near the waterfront municipal building, draws crowds who come to shop for Chilote woolens, baskets, and woven mythical figures. Things get under way about 8 AM and begin to wind down about noon. Bargaining is expected, though the prices are already quite reasonable. There's fun to be had and bargains to be found, but the market is more touristy than the ramshackle daily market in nearby Castro.

Isla Quinchao

6 *1 km (½ mi) southeast of Dalcahue.*

For many visitors, the elongated Isla Quinchao, the easiest to reach of the islands in the eastern archipelago, defines Chiloé. Populated by hardworking farmers and fisherfolk, Isla Quinchao provides a glimpse into the region's past. Head to Achao, Quinchao's largest community, to see the alerce-shingle houses, busy fishing pier, and colonial church.

Fodor'sChoice ★ On Achao's Plaza de Armas, the town's centerpiece is its 1706 **Iglesia de Santa María de Loreto,** the oldest remaining house of worship on the archipelago. In addition to the alerce so commonly used to construct buildings in the region, the church also uses wood from cypress and *mañío* trees. Its typically unadorned exterior contrasts with the deep-blue ceiling embellished with gold stars inside. Rich baroque carvings grace the altar. Mass is celebrated Sunday at 11 AM and Tuesday at 7 PM, but docents give guided tours in Spanish while the church is open. An informative Spanish-language museum behind the altar is dedicated to the period of Chiloé's Jesuit missions. All proceeds go to much-needed church restoration—termites have taken their toll. ✉ *Delicias at Amunategui* 🕿 *65/661–881* 🎟 *500 pesos* ☉ *Daily 10:30–1 and 2:30–7.*

About 10 km (6 mi) south of Achao is the archipelago's largest church, the 1869 **Iglesia de Nuestra Señora de Gracia.** As with many other Chilote churches, the 200-foot structure sits in solitude near the coast. The church has no tours, but may be visited during Sunday Mass at 11 AM.

Where to Stay & Eat

$–$$ ✕ **Mar y Velas.** Scrumptious oysters and a panoply of other gifts from the sea are served in this big wooden house at the foot of Achao's dock. You might not pick it out as a restaurant at first, as there's sometimes laundry hanging outside the windows, but the place has the friendliest service in town. ✉ *Serrano 2, Achao* 🕿 *65/661–375* ⊟ *AE, DC, MC, V.*

$–$$ ✕ **Restaurant La Nave.** On the beach, Restaurant La Nave serves seafood in a rambling building that arches over the street. The matter-of-fact staff

CloseUp

CHILOÉ'S CHAPELS

MORE THAN 150 WOODEN CHURCHES ARE SCATTERED across the eastern half of Chiloé's main island. Built by Jesuit missionaries who came to the archipelago after the 1598 Mapuche rebellion on the mainland, the chapels were an integral part of the effort to convert the indigenous peoples. Pairs of missionaries traveled the region by boat, making sure to celebrate Mass in each community at least once a year. Franciscan missionaries continued the tradition after Spain expelled the Jesuits from its new-world colonies in 1767.

The architectural style of the churches calls to mind those in rural Germany, the home of many of the missionaries. The complete lack of ornamentation is offset only by a steep roof covered with wooden shingles called tejuelas and a three-tier hexagonal bell tower. An arched portico fronts most of the churches. Getting to see more than the outside of many of the churches can be a challenge. Many stand alone on the coast, forlorn in their solitude and locked

most of the year; others are open only for Sunday services. The exceptions: Castro's orange-and-lavender Iglesia de San Francisco, dating from 1906—it's technically not one of the Jesuit churches but was built in the same style—opens its doors to visitors. Achao's Iglesia de Santa María de Loreto gives daily guided Spanish-language tours.

A nonprofit support organization, the Fundación de Amigos de las Iglesias de Chiloé, raises funds for restoration of the archipelago's churches, many of which are in urgent need of repair. A March 2002 storm toppled the tower of Chonchi's Iglesia de San Carlos, prompting studies to evaluate the structural integrity of several other churches. Help is on the way in the form of a $2.8 million grant from the Inter-American Development Bank. Funds are earmarked for repair and restoration in a project expected to be completed by 2009.

— Brian Kluepfel

dishes up curanto most days during the January–March high season, but usually only on weekends and for groups the rest of the year (call in advance). ⊠ *Arturo Prat at Sargento Aldea, Achao* ☎ *65/661–219* ▤ *No credit cards.*

¢ ▥ **Hostal La Plaza.** This cozy private home is close to the hubbub of the Plaza de Armas, but being down an alley and behind a chocolate shop affords it a degree of privacy and quiet. Simply furnished rooms have private baths, which is surprising considering the very reasonable rates. The owners are warm and friendly. ⊠ *Amunategui 20, Achao* ☎▤ *65/661–283* ⤶ *7 rooms* ⌂ *Dining room, cable TV; no a/c, no room phones* ▤ *No credit cards* ⵙ *CP.*

Castro

7 *45 km (27 mi) southeast of Achao, 88 km (53 mi) south of Ancud.*

Founded in 1567, Castro is Chile's third-oldest city. Its history has been one of destruction, with three fires and three earthquakes laying waste to the city over four centuries. The most recent disaster was in 1960, when a tidal wave caused by an earthquake on the mainland engulfed the city.

Castro's future as Isla Grande's governmental and commercial center looked promising after the 1598 Mapuche rebellion on the mainland drove the Spaniards to Chiloé, but then Dutch pirates sacked the city in 1600. Many of Castro's residents fled to the safety of more isolated parts of the island. It wasn't until 1982 that the city finally became Chiloé's administrative capital.

With a population of 20,000, Castro is Chiloé's second-largest city. Although Ancud is larger, Castro is more cosmopolitan. Though hardly an urban jungle, this is big-city life Chiloé-style. Residents of more rural parts of the island who visit the capital—no more often than necessary, of course—return home with tales of traffic so heavy that it has to be regulated with stoplights.

Next to its wooden churches, palafitos are the best-known architectural symbol of Chiloé. These shingled houses are all along the island's coast. Avenida Pedro Montt, which becomes a coastal highway as it leads out of town, is the best place to see palafitos in Castro. Many of these ramshackle structures have been turned into restaurants and artisan markets.

Any tour of Castro begins with the much-photographed 1906 **Iglesia de San Francisco,** constructed in the style of the archipelago's wooden churches, only bigger and grander. Depending on your perspective, terms like "pretty" or "pretty garish" describe the orange-and-lavender exterior, colors chosen when the structure was spruced up before Pope John Paul II's 1987 visit. It's infinitely more reserved on the inside. The dark-wood interior's centerpiece is the monumental carved crucifix hanging from the ceiling. In the evening, a soft, energy-efficient external illumination system makes the church one of Chiloé's most impressive sights. ⊠ *Plaza de Armas* ☎ *No phone* ☉ *Dec.–Feb., daily 9–12:30 and 3–11:30; Mar.–Nov., daily 9–12:30 and 3–9:30.*

Fodor'sChoice ★ The **Museo Regional de Castro,** just off the Plaza de Armas, gives the best Spanish-language introduction to the region's history and culture. Packed into a fairly small space are artifacts from the Huilliche era (primarily rudimentary farming and fishing implements) through the 19th century (looms, spinning wheels, and plows). One exhibit displays the history of the archipelago's wooden churches; another shows black-and-white photographs of the damage caused by the 1960 earthquake that rocked southern Chile. The museum has a collection of quotations about the Chiloé culture made by outsiders: "The Chilote talks little, but thinks a lot. He is rarely spontaneous with outsiders, and even with his own countrymen he isn't too communicative," wrote one ethnographer. The portrait is dated, of course, but even today, residents have been compared with the stereotypical taciturn New Englander. ⊠ *Esmeralda 205* ☎ *65/635–967* ▨ *Free* ☉ *Jan. and Feb., daily 9:30–8; Mar.–Dec., daily 9:30–1 and 3–6:30.*

All that remains of Chiloé's once-thriving Castro–Ancud rail service is the locomotive and a few old photographs displayed on the outdoor **Plazuela del Tren** down on the waterfront road. Nobel laureate Pablo Neruda called the narrow-gauge rail service "a slow, rainy train, a slim, damp mushroom." Service ended with the 1960 earthquake. ⊠ *Av. Pedro Montt s/n.*

Northwest of downtown, the **Museo de Arte Moderno de Chiloé** is housed in five refurbished barns. Referred to locally as the MAM, this modern-art complex in a city park exhibits works by Chilean artists. The museum opens to the public only in summer, but holds occasional temporary exhibitions the rest of the year. ⊠ *Pasaje Díaz 181* ☎ *65/635–454* 🎫 *Free* ⊙ *Jan.–Mar., daily 10–6.*

Conozca Castro Caminando, or "Get to Know Castro Walking," runs two-hour historical walking tours in English, Spanish, or German, at least four times weekly December–February and at other times by request. The folks here are quite flexible about accommodating your schedule. ⊠ *Plaza de Armas* ☎ *09/411–6198* 🎫 *7,000 pesos.*

Where to Stay & Eat

★ **$–$$$** ✕ **Octavio.** A devoted tourist clientele flocks to waterside Octavio for its well-known curanto, seafood stews, and some of the most attentive service around. And unlike at other restaurants in town, you can also chow down on steak and pork chops here. The well-maintained alerce-shingled palafito-style building, which is much nicer than most in town, has wonderful views over the water. ⊠ *Av. Pedro Montt 261* ☎ *65/632–855* 🚫 *No credit cards.*

$–$$ ✕ **Café la Brújula del Cuerpo.** Next to the fire station on the Plaza de Armas, this little place, whose name translates oddly as "the body's compass," bustles with all the commotion of a big-city diner. Sandwiches are standard fare—burgers and clubs are favorites. Don't leave without trying one of the mouthwatering ice-cream sundaes or banana splits. ⊠ *Av. Bernardo O'Higgins 308* ☎ *65/633–229* 🚫 *AE, DC, MC, V.*

$–$$ ✕ **1 Palafito Restaurant.** This is the first of five palafitos on Castro's downtown waterfront that have been converted into seafood restaurants. You really can't go wrong with any of them, but locals swear this one is the best. It's no place to escape the crowds, though: the cavernous restaurant can easily seat a few hundred on a bright summer night. The portions are huge; it's a hard task to finish the tasty curanto. If you have a light appetite, order something smaller, such as clams or salmón ahumado. ⊠ *Eusebio Lillo 30* ☎ *65/635–476* 🚫 *No credit cards.*

$$ 🛏 **Hostería de Castro.** Looming over downtown near the estuary, this *hostería* has a sloped chalet-style roof with a long skylight, which makes the interior seem bright and airy even on a cloudy day. Modern rooms have simple furnishings and cheery flowered bedspreads. The downstairs seafood restaurant has huge windows with great views of the Golfo de Corcovado. ⊠ *Chacabuco 202* ☎ *65/632–301* 🖨 *65/635–688* ⊕ *www.hosteriadecastro.cl* ➷ *29 rooms* ⚭ *Restaurant, bar, cable TV, laundry service, Internet, meeting room; no a/c* 🚫 *AE, DC, MC, V* 🍴 *BP.*

★ **$$** 🛏 **Hotel Unicornio Azul.** Taking its name from a popular song by Cuban singer Silvio Rodríguez, the Blue Unicorn is actually pink, though it does have a bright blue roof. The rambling hotel, dating from 1910, climbs the hill from the waterfront. There are lots of stairs, and many twists and turns as you make your ascent, but you'll find a sitting room and reading alcove at every landing and big windows to catch the view. Furnishings in the bright rooms echo the facade's pastel hues. ⊠ *Av. Pedro Montt 228* ☎ *65/632–359* 🖨 *65/632–808* ✍ *hotelunicornioazul@*

hotmail.com ↘ *17 rooms, 1 cabin* ⌂ *Restaurant, bar, cable TV; no a/c* ⊟ *No credit cards* ¡⊙¡ *CP.*

$ ▦ **Hostal Kolping.** Great inexpensive lodging is yours at this alerce-shingled building with a big porch in the center of town. Paneled rooms are bright, sunny, spacious, and sparkling clean, with comfortable beds and lots of pillows. ⊠ *Chacabuco 217* ▦▦ *65/633–273* ↘ *11 rooms* ⌂ *Dining room; no a/c, no room phones, no TV* ⊟ *No credit cards* ¡⊙¡ *CP.*

$ ▦ **Hostal Quelcun.** An unpromising alley between two downtown storefronts opens onto a green, leafy courtyard around which you'll find this two-story wooden building, one of Castro's nicest budget lodgings. Some of the wood-paneled rooms have improbable layouts, requiring a bit of maneuvering to get into the second bed, but all are pleasantly furnished. The staff here is friendly and eager to please. ⊠ *San Martín 581* ▦▦ *65/632–396* ✍ *quelcun@telsur.cl* ↘ *16 rooms* ⌂ *Dining room, cable TV, travel services; no a/c, no room phones* ⊟ *No credit cards* ¡⊙¡ *CP.*

$ ▦ **Hotel Esmeralda.** This hot-pink storefront hotel sits just off the bustling Plaza de Armas. The compact four-story building has lots of windows and all the amenities that you would expect from such a modern place. It's popular among corporate travelers because of its meeting rooms and business services. ⊠ *Esmeralda 266* ☎ *65/637–900* 🖷 *65/637–910* ⊕ *www.hotelesmeralda.cl* ↘ *32 rooms, 2 suites* ⌂ *Restaurant, cable TV, pool, bar, recreation room, laundry service, business services, meeting rooms; no a/c* ⊟ *AE, DC, MC, V* ¡⊙¡ *BP.*

Shopping

The city's **Feria Artesanal,** a lively, often chaotic artisan market on Eusebio Lillo, is regarded by most as the best place on the island to pick up the woolen sweaters, woven baskets, and the straw figures for which Chiloé is known. Prices are already quite reasonable, but vendors expect a bit of bargaining. The stalls share a ramshackle collection of palafitos with several seafood restaurants. It's open daily 9–dusk.

Chonchi

❽ *23 km (14 mi) south of Castro.*

The colorful wooden houses of Chonchi are on a hillside so steep that it's known in Spanish as the *Ciudad de los Tres Pisos* (City of Three Stories). The town's name means "slippery earth" in the Huilliche language, and if you tromp up the town's steep streets on a rainy day you'll understand why. Arranged around a scenic harbor, Chonchi wins raves as Chiloé's most picturesque town.

The town's centerpiece is the **Iglesia de San Carlos,** on the Plaza de Armas. Started by the Jesuits in 1754, it was left unfinished until 1859. Rebuilt in the neoclassical style, the church is now a national monument. An unusually ornate arcade with five arches fronts the church, and inside are an intricately carved altar and wooden columns. The church contains Chonchi's most prized relic, a statue of the Virgen de la Candelaria. According to tradition, this image of the Virgin Mary protected the town from the Dutch pirates who destroyed neighboring Castro in 1600. Townspeople celebrate the event every February 2 with fireworks and gunpowder symbolizing the pirate attack. A March 2002 storm felled the church's tower; fund-raising for reconstruction has been painfully slow, but an infusion of funds from the Inter-American Development Bank means restoration is expected to be completed by 2008. Tower or no tower, the building is open for Mass Sunday at 11 AM.

The small **Museo de las Tradiciones Chonchinas** documents life in Chonchi through furnishings and photos in a 19th-century house. ⊠ *Centenario 116* ☎ *No phone* 🔊 *Free* ⊙ *Sept.–May, weekdays 9–7; June–Aug., weekdays 9–1.*

Where to Eat

$ ✕ **El Trébol.** This seafood restaurant sits next to Chonchi's waterfront market. The decorations are basic, but the food is good, and the prices are very reasonable. You have a better chance of getting curanto or salmón ahumado if you're here in high season. ⊠ *Irarrázaval 187* ☎ *65/671–203* 🖭 *No credit cards* ⊙ *Closed Sun.*

Isla Lemuy

❾ *3 km (2 mi) east of Chonchi.*

Though easily reached by a 15-minute ferry ride from Chonchi, Isla Lemuy seems miles away from anything. It's the third-largest of Chiloé's islands, just slightly smaller than Isla Quinchao to the north. Jesuit churches dominate three of its villages—Ichuac, Aldachildo, and Detif—none of which is more than a handful of houses. Ichuac's church is in a sorry state of disrepair, as funds for restoration are in short supply. The Aldachildo chapel is locked most of the year, though the folks in the local telephone office can help track down someone who can open it up for you. Detif's church, open only for Sunday-morning Mass, is noteworthy for its "votive boats," small wooden ship models hung in thanksgiving for a safe journey. From here there's a stunning view of Volcán Michinmahuida on the mainland.

Where to Stay

$ 🏨 **Lidia Pérez.** The Pérez family of Puchilco operates one of the nicer lodgings in Red Agroturismo Chiloé, the 19-member agro-tourism network. The only accommodation on Isla Lemuy, it's just a wooden farmhouse painted a distinctive orange and green, but it gives you a chance to see rural Chilote life up close—in this case, life on a sheep farm. Rooms are spartan, but pleasantly furnished with cheery green bedspreads and drapes. ⊠ *Puchilco* ☎ *09/444–0252, 65/628–333 in Ancud* 🔊 *3 rooms without bath* ⚫ *Dining room; no a/c, no room phones, no room TVs* 🖭 *No credit cards* ⊙ *BP.*

Parque Nacional Chiloé

❿ *35 km (21 mi) west of Chonchi.*

The 430-square-km (166-square-mi) Parque Nacional Chiloé hugs Isla Grande's sparsely populated Pacific coast. During his 1834 visit, Charles Darwin, the park's most famous visitor, marveled at the indigenous families who scratched out a living from this inhospitable land.

The park's two sectors differ dramatically in terms of landscape and access. Heavily forested with evergreens, Sector Anay, to the south, is most easily entered from the coastal village of Cucao. An unpaved but passable road heads west to the park from the Pan-American Highway at Notuco, just south of Chonchi. Sector Anay is popular among backpackers, who hike the short El Tepual trail, which begins at the Chanquín Visitor Center 1 km (½ mi) north of the park entrance. The longer Dunas trail also begins there and leads through the forest to the beach dunes near Cacao. Hiking through the park will give you the best chance of seeing the Chiloé fox, native to Isla Grande; more reclusive is the *pudú,* a miniature deer found throughout southern Chile. Some 3 km (2 mi) north of the Cucao entrance is a Huilliche community on the shore of Lago Huelde. Unobtrusive visitors are welcome.

Accessible only during the drier months of January through March, the northern Sector Chepu of Chiloé National Park is primarily wetlands created by the tidal wave that rocked the island in 1960. The sector now shelters a large bird population (most notably penguins) as well as a sea lion colony. Reaching this portion of the park is difficult—take a gravel road turnoff at Coipomó, about 20 km (12 mi) south of Ancud on the Pan-American Highway, to Chepu on the Pacific coast. From there, it's about a 90-minute hike to the park's northern border. ⊠ *North of Cucao and south of Chepu* ☎ *65/637–266 in Castro* ✆ *Each sector, 1,000 pesos* ⊙ *Daily 7–5.*

Queilén

⑪ *47 km (29 mi) southeast of Chonchi.*

This town named for the red cypress trees that dot the area sits on an elongated peninsula and, as such, is the only town on Isla Grande with two seafronts. Two of Isla Grande's best bathing beaches are the town's central **Playa de Queilén,** and the **Playa Lelbun,** 15 km (9 mi) northwest of the city.

The **Refugio de Navegantes** serves as the town's cultural center and contains a small museum with artifacts and old black-and-white photographs. Nothing is very colorful here—the muted tones of the pottery, the fabrics, and the farm implements reflect the stark life of colonial Chiloé. ⊠ *Pedro Aguirre Cerda s/n* ☎ *No phone* ✆ *Free* ⊙ *Weekdays 9–12:30 and 2:30–6.*

Uphill on Calle Presidente Kennedy is a **mirador.** The observation point has stupendous views of the Golfo de Ancud, the smaller islands in the archipelago, and, on a clear day, the Volcán Corcovado on the mainland.

Quellón

⑫ *99 km (60 mi) south of Castro.*

The Pan-American Highway, which begins in Alaska and stretches for most of the length of North and South America, ends without fanfare here in Quellón, Chiloé's southernmost city. The Carretera Austral continues south on the mainland. Quellón was the famed "end of Christendom" described by Charles Darwin during his 19th-century visit. Just a few years earlier it had been the southernmost outpost of Spain's empire in the New World. For most visitors today, Quellón is also the end of the line. But if you're truly adventurous, it's the starting point for ferries that head to the Southern Coast.

Taking its name from a Huilliche phrase meaning "from our past," the **Museo Inchin Cuivi Ant** stands apart from other museums in Chiloé because of its "living" exhibitions: Chilote women spin woolens on their looms, make empanadas in a traditional fogón, and cultivate a botanical garden with herbs, plants, and trees native to Chiloé. ✉ *Ladrilleros 225* ☎ *No phone* 💵 *500 pesos* ☉ *Daily 9–1 and 2:30–8.*

Where to Stay & Eat

$–$$ ✕ **Hostería Romeo Alfa.** This imposing seafood restaurant, which resembles a Bavarian chalet, sits right on Quellón's pier. Choose one of the tables along the window and watch all the comings and goings while you dine on the delectable curanto. The white tablecloths and candles give the dining room an elegant appearance, but the atmosphere is informal and very friendly. ✉ *Capitán Luis Alcazar 554* ☎ *65/680–177* 🖃 *No credit cards.*

$ ▥ **Hotel Los Suizos.** The owners pride themselves on providing Swiss-style service to their lodgers, which means you can expect efficiency and friendliness. The bright upstairs rooms have light-wood paneling. The intimate downstairs restaurant serves Swiss cuisine as well as seafood. ✉ *Ladrilleros 399* ☎ *65/681–787* 🖷 *65/680–747* ✆ *dianaoberlin@hotmail.com* ⇩ *6 rooms* ⚘ *Restaurant, bar, cable TV, laundry service; no a/c, no room phones* 🖃 *No credit cards.*

¢–$ ▥ **Hotel Tierra del Fuego.** This rambling alerce-shingle house, dating from the 1920s, is on Quellón's waterfront. The light clues you as to when you've crossed the threshold between the original rooms, with their small windows, and those added in the past decade. Opt for one of the wood-paneled rooms in the newer wing or on the third floor; they maintain the style of the original house, but sunlight streams in through big windows. Everyone in town seems to stop by for lunch at the bustling restaurant downstairs. ✉ *Av. Pedro Montt 445* ☎🖷 *65/682–079* ⇩ *30 rooms, 21 with bath* ⚘ *Restaurant, bar, cable TV; no a/c, no room phones* 🖃 *No credit cards.*

Shopping

Quellón's **Feria Artesanal Llauquil,** on Avenida Gómez García, doesn't have the hustle and bustle of similar artisan markets in Castro and Dalcahue, but there are some good buys on woolens and straw folkloric figures at this restored complex of artisan shops. Don't bother to bargain; you'll find the prices are already extremely reasonable. The market is open daily until 7 December–February, and Monday–Saturday until 6 the rest of the year.

CHILOÉ ESSENTIALS

Transportation

BY AIR

Chiloé has a small military airstrip, but there's no airport for either national or international flights. Most people flying to the region head to Aeropuerto El Tepual, 90 km (54 mi) northeast of Ancud in Puerto Montt. Lan maintains an office in Castro.

▸ Airlines **Lan** ✉ Blanco 299, Castro ☎ 65/632-866.

BY BOAT & FERRY

Since Chiloé is an archipelago, the only way to drive here is by taking one of the frequent ferries across the Golfo de Ancud. Most people arrive by crossing from the mainland to the tiny town of Chacao in the north. Cruz del Sur operates the frequent ferry service connecting mainland Pargua with Chacao on the northern tip of Isla Grande. Boats leave twice an hour from early morning until after midnight, and trips take about 30 minutes (8,000 pesos for a car, no passenger fee).

Many fewer arrive via Quellón in the south. Navimag connects Quellón with Chaitén eight times a month during the January–February summer season, less frequently the rest of the year. Departure time varies. The cost is 50,000 pesos for a vehicle shorter than 13 feet in length. Each passenger pays 10,000 pesos for the crossing.

Catamaranes del Sur provides twice-weekly catamaran service during January and February between Castro and mainland Chaitén at a relatively quick three hours, with continuing service to Puerto Montt. Pehuén Expediciones is the sales agent in Castro.

▸ **Catamaranes del Sur** ✉ Pehuén Expediciones, 299 Blanco, Castro ☎ 65/632-361 ✉ Diego Portales at Guillermo Gallardo, Puerto Montt ☎ 65/267-533 ⊕ www.catamaranesdelsur.cl. **Cruz del Sur** ✉ Chacabuco 672, Ancud ☎ 65/622-265. **Navimag** ✉ Av. Pedro Montt 457, Quellón ☎ 65/682-207 ⊕ www.navimag.com.

BY BUS

Cruz del Sur and its subsidiary Transchiloé operate some 30 buses per day between Ancud and the mainland, usually terminating in Puerto Montt. Many of the routes continue north to Temuco, and a few travel all the way to Santiago. Bus service is timed to coincide with the company's frequent ferries between Pargua and Chacao. Buses arriving from the mainland provide *very* local service once they reach the island, making frequent stops.

Cruz del Sur and Transchiloé also operate hourly service along the Pan-American Highway between Ancud, Castro, Chonchi, and Quellón. Queilén Bus has service between Chiloé's major cities about 10 times daily. It also makes twice-daily runs between Castro and Quemchi.

Many other companies operate small buses or comfortable minivans. Dalcahue Expreso connects Castro with Dalcahue every half hour during the week, less often on weekends. Buses Gallardo runs buses between Castro and Isla Lemuy three times a day during the week, less often on weekends. Buses Arroyo has twice-a-day service between Castro and Cucao, the gateway to Parque Nacional Chiloé.

🚌 Bus Information **Buses Arroyo** ⊠ San Martín s/n, Castro ☎ 65/635-604. **Buses Gallardo** ⊠ San Martín 667, Castro ☎ 65/634-521. **Cruz del Sur** ⊠ Chacabuco 672, Ancud ☎ 65/622-265 ⊠ San Martín 486, Castro ☎ 65/632-389 ⊠ Av. Portales at Lota, Puerto Montt ☎ 64/254-731. **Dalcahue Expreso** ⊠ Ramírez 233, Castro ☎ 65/635-164. **Queilén Bus** ⊠ San Martín 667, Castro ☎ 65/632-173.

BY CAR

Rather than terminating in Puerto Montt, the Pan-American Highway skips over the Golfo de Ancud and continues through Ancud, Castro, and Chonchi before stopping in Quellón. The Carretera Austral continues on down the mainland Southern Coast. Paved roads also lead to Quemchi, Dalcahue, and Achao on Isla Quinchao. You can reach a few other communities by *ripios,* rough gravel roads. Plan ahead, as it's often slow going during the long rainy season. Most of the western half of the island is inaccessible by car.

Most visitors who rent a vehicle do so on the mainland, but if you decide you need wheels after your arrival, try the local firm of ADS Rent-a-Car in Castro.

🚗 Rental Agency **ADS Rent-a-Car** ⊠ Esmeralda 260, Castro ☎ 65/637-777.

BY TAXI

As is true elsewhere in the region, solid black or solid yellow cabs operate as *colectivos,* or collective taxis. They follow fixed routes with fixed stops, picking up to four people along the way. A sign on the roof shows the general destination. The cost (usually less than 700 pesos within town) is little more than that of a city bus. Black cabs with yellow roofs take you directly to your requested destination for a metered fare. You can hail them on the street.

Colectivos also operate between many of Isla Grande's communities. They may look like regular cabs, or they may be minivans. They have fixed stops, often near a town's central bus station.

Contacts & Resources

BANKS & EXCHANGE SERVICES

With few businesses equipped to handle credit cards, Chiloé is primarily a cash-and-carry economy. Banks will gladly change U.S. dollars for Chilean pesos, but most will not touch traveler's checks. The situation is not as frustrating as it sounds; ATMs are popping up everywhere in larger cities like Castro and Ancud. You can use your Plus- or Cirrus-affiliated card to get cash at the going rate at any of the ATMs on the Redbanc network.

EMERGENCIES

Chiloé has no hospital for emergency attention. The nearest such facility is in mainland Puerto Montt.

🚨 Emergency Services **Ambulance** ☎ 131. **Fire (Bomberos)** ☎ 132. **Police (Carabineros)** ☎ 133.

🏥 Hospital **Hospital Base Puerto Montt** ⊠ Seminario s/n, Puerto Montt ☎ 65/261-100.

INTERNET & MAIL

Internet access is not as common in Chiloé as on the mainland. The places here charge around 800 pesos per hour. Chiloé Virtual is a small Internet café in Castro. The Café la Brújula del Cuerpo restaurant has one computer for public use. Entel telephone offices in Castro and Ancud have a few public computers.

Mail sent from Chiloé can take a few weeks to reach North America or Europe. Posting from mainland Puerto Montt is a quicker option. You can find a Correos de Chile office in most larger cities. They are generally open weekdays 9–6 and Saturday 9–noon.

⚑ Internet Cafés Café la Brújula del Cuerpo ✉ Av. Bernardo O'Higgins 308, Castro ☎ 65/633-229. **Chiloé Virtual** ✉ Esmeralda 232, Castro ☎ 65/633-427. **Entel** ✉ Av. Bernardo O'Higgins 480, Castro ✉ Pudeto 219, Ancud.

⚑ Post Offices Correos de Chile ✉ Av. Bernardo O'Higgins 388, Castro ✉ Pudeto at Blanco Encalada, Ancud ✉ 22 de Mayo and Ladrilleros, Quellón.

TOURS

Highly regarded Dalcahue sea kayaking expert Francisco Valle is the local contact for Santiago tour operator Altue Sea Kayaking. He leads kayakers on two- to nine-day tours through the region. Two- and four-day excursions November–March focus on Chiloé itself; longer tours incorporate travel into the mainland fjords.

Austral Adventures, the region's best tour operator—it's actually one of the best in the country—runs intimate guided tours of Chiloé and neighboring Patagonia. The agency's own 50-foot vessel, the *Cahuella,* plies the archipelago and the Chilean fjords in three-, four-, and eight-day tours. Austral Adventures can custom-design tours of Chiloé itself, whether your tastes run to sea kayaking, church visits, farm stays, or hikes in Chiloé National Park, and can take you farther afield to the Lake District and Parque Pumalín on the mainland.

Pehuén Expediciones has guided tours of the archipelago, in particular land tours to Dalcahue and Isla Achao and the island churches, as well as horseback riding and hiking in Parque Nacional Chiloé.

The M/N *Skorpios II,* a luxury cruise liner operating between Puerto Montt and Laguna San Rafael, calls at Castro on its return trip.

⚑ Tour Operators Altue Sea Kayaking ✉ Encomenderos 83 Santiago ☎ 2/232-1103 ⊕ www.seakayakchile.com. **Austral Adventures** ✉ Lord Cochrane 432, Ancud ☎ 65/625-977 ⊕ www.austral-adventures.com. **Pehuén Expediciones** ✉ Blanco 299, Castro ☎ 65/635-254 ⊕ www.turismopehuen.cl. **Skorpios** ✉ Augosto Leguía Norte 118, Santiago ☎ 2/477-1900 ⊕ www.skorpios.cl.

VISITOR INFORMATION

Sernatur, Chile's national tourist office, operates a friendly, well-staffed information office on the Plaza de Armas in Ancud. It's open January and February, daily 9–8; March–December, Monday–Saturday 9–noon and 2–6.

A small, locally run information kiosk on the Plaza de Armas in Castro keeps irregular hours.

⚑ Sernatur ✉ Libertad 665, Ancud ☎ 65/622-800.

The Southern Coast

WORD OF MOUTH

"Watching your breath turn to a frosty steam is one thing—but watching a giant hunk of glacier 'calve' off and splash into the water is unforgettable. Riding around on the local ferries was about the most peaceful part of our Chile trip . . . really soothing. Waterfalls, fjords . . . almost like being in Spanish-speaking Scandinavia."

—Brian K.

Updated by
Brian Kluepfel

THE SLIVER OF LAND known as the Southern Coast stretches for more than 1,000 km (620 mi) in the administrative district of Aisén (locally spelled Aysén). Sandwiched between the tranquil valleys of the Lake District and the wondrous ice fields of Patagonia, it largely consists of heavily forested mountains, some of which rise dramatically from the shores of shimmering lakes, others directly out of the Pacific Ocean. Slender waterfalls and nearly vertical streams, often seeming to emerge from the rock itself, tumble and slide from neck-craning heights. Some dissipate into misty nothingness before touching the ground, others flow into the innumerable rivers—large and small, wild and gentle—heading westward to the sea. Chile has designated vast tracts of this truly magnificent landscape as national parks and reserves, but most are accessible only on foot. The few roads available to vehicles are slightly widened trails or the occasional logging route navigable only by the most rugged of four-wheel-drive vehicles.

The Southern Coast is one of the least-populated areas remaining in South America: the population density here is said to be lower than that of the Sahara Desert. The infrequent hamlets scattered along the low-lying areas of this rugged region exist as fishing villages or small farming centers. The gradual increase of boat and ferry service to some of these towns and the expansion of the major highway called the Carretera Austral have begun to encourage migration to the region. Coyhaique, the only town here of any size, with a population of 50,000, has lots of dining, lodging, and shopping. Meanwhile, a few intrepid entrepreneurs have established world-class accommodations in remote locations near spectacular mountain peaks, ancient volcanoes, and glaciers, with their concomitant fjords and lakes.

Planning a visit to the region's widely separated points of interest can be challenging, as getting from place to place is often difficult. Creating a logical itinerary in southern Chile is as much about choosing how to get here as it is about choosing where you want to go. The most rewarding mode of transport through this area is a combination of travel by boat and by plane, with an occasional car rental if you want to journey a little deeper into the hinterlands.

Exploring the Southern Coast

The Southern Coast is an expansive region covered with vast national parks and reserves. By and large, this is territory for adventurous types who come for the unparalleled fishing, kayaking, and white-water rafting. The region rewards intrepid explorers with relatively untrammeled trails and rarely viewed vistas.

Part of the challenge of traveling within this region of Chile is the country's narrow north–south orientation. The distances between sights can be daunting. Circuits, per se, are virtually impossible. Traveling by air is a good option if your time is limited. Ferries are slow and not always scenic, particularly if skies are the least bit clouded. There are, however, a few firms offering sightseeing cruises.

The key to enjoying the Southern Coast is knowing that your trip probably won't always go as planned. Itineraries cannot be too tight, as schedules are not always reliable. Meet with a professional tour operator familiar with the region and focus on your priorities.

About the Restaurants

The Southern Coast's ecology means that fish and shellfish can be found just about anywhere. Lamb and beef dishes are almost as common. Rice is usually available as an alternative to the ubiquitous french fries. By and large, entrées are simple and hearty. Locally grown vegetables and fruits abound. The variety on most menus is extensive, so many dishes are prepared from scratch when you order. Just sit back and sip your wine or beer while you wait.

Having food and drink on hand when driving along the Carretera Austral is necessary because of the distances between points of interest. The tiniest rural town has at least one *supermercado*. These markets are rarely "super," but the shelves typically sag under all manner of canned and packaged foods and bottled drinks. Bread of one type or another is rarely out of stock, and many stores carry a small selection of deli meats and cheeses.

Traveling by road throughout the region, you may see crudely printed signs with an arrow pointing to a nearby farmhouse advertising *küchen* (rich, fruit-filled pastries)—clear evidence of the many pockets of German influence.

About the Hotels

This region offers a surprisingly wide choice of accommodations, including some of the finest resorts in the country. What you won't find is the blandness of chain hotels. Most of the region's establishments reflect the distinct personalities and idiosyncrasies of their owners.

Some of the most humble homes in villages along the Carretera Austral have supplemented their family income by becoming bed-and-breakfasts. A stay in one of these *hospedajes* is an ideal way to meet the people and experience the culture. These accommodations are not regulated, so inquire about the availability of hot water and confirm that breakfast is included. Don't hesitate to ask to see the room—you may even get a choice.

WHAT IT COSTS In pesos (in thousands)					
	$$$$	$$$	$$	$	¢
RESTAURANTS	over 11	8–11	5–8	3–5	under 3
HOTELS	over 105	75–105	45–75	15–45	under 15

Restaurant prices are for a main course at dinner. Hotel prices are for a double room in high season, excluding tax.

When to Go

Midsummer—late November to early February—is considered high season in southern Chile; demand for accommodations is keen, and ad-

Unless you fly, the only way to reach the Southern Coast is by boat or ferry. On your first day head to the port town of **Chaitén**. Devote a day to visiting **Parque Pumalín,** which has some of the most pristine landscape in the region. The third day, take the Carretera Austral to **Puerto Puyuhuapi.** A stay at Puyuhuapi Lodge & Spa, a resort accessible only by boat, is a must. Head out the next morning to see the famous "hanging glacier" of **Parque Nacional Queulat.** On your fifth day travel down to **Coyhaique,** the only city of any size in the region. The next morning head to **Puerto Chacabuco,** where you can board a boat bound for the unforgettable **Parque Nacional Laguna San Raphael.** On your last day make your way back up the highway.

8

vance reservations at high-end lodgings are vital. In spring (September into November) and fall (March to May) the weather is delightfully cool and hotel rooms are easier to come by. However, ferry service is reduced and sometimes even canceled.

Chaitén

❶ *201 km (125 mi) south of Puerto Montt.*

A century ago, Chaitén wasn't even on the map. Today it's a small port town, with a population of barely more than 3,000. Although it's not really a destination itself, Chaitén serves as a convenient base for exploring the area, including Parque Pumalín.

Getting there is fairly easy: both Navimag (www.navimag.com) and Transmarchilay (www.transmarchilay.com) operate regular ferry service between Chaitén and Puerto Montt in the Lake District and Quellón on Chiloé. Flying is also an option; a few small airlines offer flights between Chaitén and Puerto Montt.

It's also possible to drive to Chaitén from Puerto Montt via the Carretera Austral, but you have to make use of two car ferries. The first is fine, as Transmarchilay ferries make nine daily trips between La Arena and Puelche all year. The second leg is tougher because Transmarchilay's ferries between Hornopirén and Caleta Gonzalo operate only in January and February.

Isla Puduguapi, home to some 150 noisy sea lions, is an hour-long boat ride away. Toninas, a resident dolphin, may escort your boat. Half-day tours are the only way to see the island. Try Chaitur Excursions (*See* ⇨ Tours *in* The Southern Coast Essentials).

The emerald-green **Lago Yelcho,** one of the best places in the region to fish for brown trout, runs along the Carretera Austral south of Chaitén. Just past the village of Puerto Cárdenas is Puente Ventisquero Yelcho (Glacier Bridge), the beginning of a challenging two-hour hike to Ventisquero Cavi (Hanging Glacier). ⊠ *Off Carretera Austral, 2 km (1 mi) past Puerto Cardenas.*

The much-lauded **Termas del Amarillo,** a modest hot springs about 25 km (16 mi) southeast of Chaitén, offers a nice respite for weary muscles. The setting, along a river running through a heavily forested valley, is lovely. ⊠ *Off Carretera Austral, 6 km (4 mi) inland from Puerto Cardenas* ☎ *No phone* 🎫 *2,000 pesos* ☉ *Daily 8 AM–9 PM.*

Where to Stay & Eat

$–$$ ✕ **Brisas del Mar.** This cheerful little eatery overlooks the sea from its perch on the second floor. The sheer number of items on the menu is astounding. Try excellent fish dishes such as *salmón en mantequilla* (salmon braised in butter), *congrio* (conger eel), and *loco* (abalone). ⊠ *Corcovado 278* ☎ *65/731–284* ▭ *No credit cards.*

$ ▥ **Hotel Schilling.** Of the town's numerous family-run hospedajes, Hotel Shilling is the most professional and hospitable. Rooms are simple, enlivened by bedspreads in a rainbow of colors. Its location, just across from the ocean, is a major draw. ⊠ *Corcovado 230* ☎ *65/731–295* ⤶ *12 rooms* ⚹ *Dining room; no a/c, no room phones, no room TVs* ▭ *No credit cards* ⵁ CP.

★ $ ▥ **Puma Verde.** This adorable, wood-shingled B&B is run by Parque Pumalín, which explains why it's in a class of its own. Locally crafted furniture sits atop polished wood floors. Woolen blankets and piles of pillows add to the coziness. Puma Verde has three rooms (one double, two triples), and one apartment that sleeps five. The large apartment, filled with hand-carved wood furniture, rents for a bargain 60,000 pesos without breakfast. ⊠ *Av. Bernardo O'Higgins 54* ☎ *65/232–300* ⊕ *www.parquepumalin.cl* ⤶ *3 rooms, 1 apartment* ⚹ *No a/c, no room TVs* ▭ *AE, DC, MC, V* ⵁ BP.

¢–$ ✕ **Corcovado.** Here's one place where you won't leave hungry: the portions of the seafood dishes and *asado a la brasa* (mixed grilled meats), served with a baked potato and salad, are huge, but the prices are small. This wooden building sits near the water, so you are treated to great views. ⊠ *Corcovado 408* ☎ *65/731–221* ▭ *No credit cards.*

Parque Pumalín

❷   *56 km (35 mi) north of Chaitén.*

Fodor$**Choice**
★

Parque Pumalín is an extraordinary venture that began when conservationist Doug Tompkins bought a 42,000-acre *araucaria* (an indigenous evergreen tree) forest south of Puerto Montt. Since 1988, he has spent more than $15 million to purchase the nearly 800,000 acres that make up Parque Pumalín. The region shelters one of the last remaining temperate rain forests in the world. The Chilean government declared the park a nature sanctuary in August 2005.

Tompkins, an American who made his fortune founding the clothing company Esprit, owns two strips of land that stretch from one side of the country to the other. He tried to buy the parcel between the two halves that would have connected them, but the sale was fiercely opposed by

Magnificent Glaciers

Watching as chunks of ice break off the glaciers near Mount San Valentín, and fall with a thundering splash into the lake below, is reason enough to take a trip to Laguna San Rafael National Park (which has 19 different glaciers). Wildlife lovers can also glimpse black-browed albatross and elegant black-necked swans here, as well as sea lions, dolphins, elephant seals, and *chungungos*—the Chilean version of the sea otter.

8

Fabulous Fishing

Fly-fishing fanatics, among the first to explore the area thoroughly, found an abundance of fish—from brown and rainbow trout to silver and steelhead salmon—in the region's icy rivers and streams (there are more than 50 in the area). At numerous mountain lodges you can step right outside your door for great fishing. A short boat trip will bring you to isolated spots where you won't run into another soul for the entire day.

Unusual Crafts

Unique finds abound in this part of the country. A small artisans' market on the Plaza de Armas in Coyhaique sells locally produced handicrafts such as leather goods and pottery. Interesting regional items to be on the lookout for are the pottery bowls and small jugs with animal skin shrunken onto their bases to keep liquids from seeping out. Woolen items are sold everywhere.

---

some government officials who questioned whether a foreigner should own so much of Chile. The Pan-American Highway, which trundles all the way north to Alaska, is interrupted here. No public roads, with their accompanying pollution, pass through the preserve.

Parque Pumalín encompasses some of the most pristine landscape in the region, if not the world. There are a dozen or so trails that wind past lakes and waterfalls. Stay in log cabins at traditional or covered campsites, or put up your tent on one of the local farms scattered across the area that welcome travelers. The entrance to the park is at Caleta Gonzalo, where the ferries from Hornopirén arrive. Buses run from Chaitén January and February. ⊠ *Information centers: Buín 356, Puerto Montt* ☎ *65/250–079* 🖷 *65/255–145* ⊠ *Av. Bernardo O'Higgins 62, Chaitén* ☎ *65/731–341* ⊕ *www.parquepumalin.cl* 🗐 *Free* ⊙ *Daily.*

Where to Stay

★ $$ 🏨 **Cabañas Caleta Gonzalo.** Nine gray-shingled cabanas, each designed to be distinct from its neighbor, sit high on stilts against the backdrop of the misty mountains. Broad front porches and tall windows let in lots of light. The interiors are rustic yet luxurious, with handcrafted furniture and handwoven woolen blankets. The complex includes an attractive visitor center and handicraft shop stocking books, guides, and maps, as well as organic honey and jams. A copper-hooded corner fireplace wel-

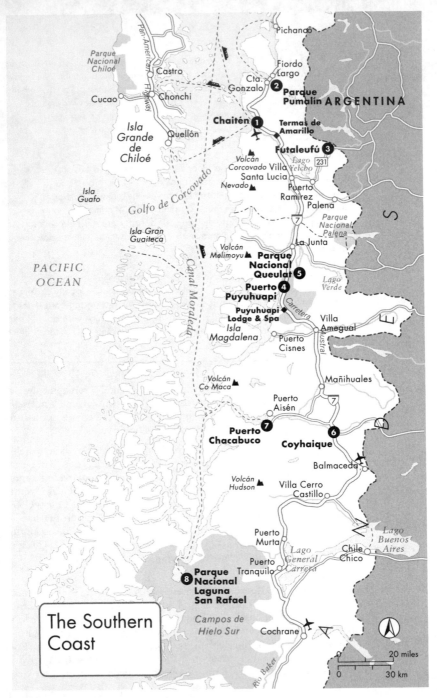

Parque
Nacional
Chiloé

Pan-American Highway

Castro

Cucao

Chonchi

Quellón

Isla
Grande
de
Chiloé

Isla
Guafo

Isla Gran
Guaiteca

PACIFIC
OCEAN

Golfo de Corcovado

Canal Moraleda

Pichanao

Fiordo
Largo

Cta.
Gonzalo

2

**Parque
Pumalín**

ARGENTINA

Chaitén **1**

**Termas de
Amarillo**

Volcán
Corcovado Villa
Santa Lucía
Nevado

Futaleufú **3**

Lago
Yelcho

231

Puerto
Ramírez

Palena

Parque
Nacional
Palena

7

La Junta

Volcán
Melimoyu

**Parque
Nacional
Queulat** **5**

Lago
Verde

**Puerto
Puyuhuapi** **4**

**Puyuhuapi
Lodge & Spa**

Isla
Magdalena

Puerto
Cisnes

Villa
Amengual

Carretera Austral

Volcán
Co Maca

Mañihuales

Puerto
Aisén

7

**Puerto
Chacabuco** **7**

Coyhaique **6**

Balmaceda

Volcán
Hudson

Villa Cerro
Castillo

Puerto
Murta

Lago
General
Carrera

Chile
Chico

Lago
Buenos
Aires

8 **Parque
Nacional
Laguna
San Rafael**

Puerto
Tranquilo

Campos de
Hielo Sur

Cochrane

Río Baker

The Southern
Coast

0   20 miles
0   30 km

comes you at the adjacent café for meals from early morning until midnight year-round. ⊠ *Caleta Gonzalo* ☎ *65/232–300* ➾ *9 rooms* & *Café, shop; no a/c, no room TVs* ⊟ *AE, DC, MC, V* ⦿ *BP.*

Futaleufú

③ *159 km (99 mi) east of Chaitén.*

Near the town of Villa Lucia, Ruta 231 branches east from the Carretera Austral and winds around Lago Yelcho. About 159 km (99 mi) later, not far from the Argentine border, it reaches the tiny town of Futaleufú. Despite being barely five square blocks, Futaleufú is on many travelers' itineraries. World-class adventure sports await here, where the Río Espolón and the Río Futaleufú collide. It's the staging center for serious river and sea kayaking, white-water rafting, and mountain biking, as well as fly-fishing, canyon hiking, and horseback riding. Daylong trips for less-experienced travelers are available.

Where to Stay

$$$ ⬚ **Hostería Río Grande.** The biggest and best lodging in Futaleufú, this sleek wooden hotel is adventure-travel headquarters for the area. It hosts the Futaleufú Adventure Center, a branch of Expediciones Chile (www.exchile.com) operated by former U.S. Olympic paddler Chris Spelius. December–March it offers four- to seven-night packages that include kayaking, rafting, and hiking trips throughout the region. There is cable TV in the salon. ⊠ *Manuel Rodriguez 315; office: Gabriel Mistral 296* ☎ *65/721–386, 888/488–9082 in U.S.* ⊕ *www.exchile.com* ➾ *12 rooms* & *Restaurant, room service, boating, fishing, hiking, bar, Internet, laundry service; no a/c, no room TVs* ⊟ *AE, DC, MC, V* ⦿ *BP.*

Puerto Puyuhuapi

④ *196 km (123 mi) south of Chaitén.*

This mossy fishing village of about 500 residents is one of the oldest along the Carretera Austral. It was founded in 1935 by German immigrants fleeing the economic ravages of post–World War I Europe. As in much of Patagonia, Chile offered free land to settlers with the idea of making annexation by Argentina more difficult. Those early immigrants ventured into the wilderness to clear the forests to make way for farms.

Today this sleepy town is a convenient stopover for those headed farther south in the region. It has a few modest guesthouses, as well as some markets and a gas station.

Where to Stay & Eat

$$$$ ✕⬚ **Puyuhuapi Lodge & Spa.** If you arrive at night, your catamaran pulls
Fodor'sChoice past a dark fjord to a spectacular welcome—drums, bonfires along the
★ shore, and fireworks illuminating the grounds. Accessible only by water (it's a five-hour boat ride from Puerto Chacabuco to the south), the property is remote and profoundly secluded. Luckily, your every need is taken care of here, whether you're in the mood for hiking and kayaking, excursions to glaciers, or just relaxing with a massage or

CloseUp

CHILE'S ROAD TO RICHES

THE PAN-AMERICAN HIGHWAY, *which snakes its way through the northern half of Chile, never quite makes it to the Southern Coast. To connect this remote region with the rest of the country, former President Augusto Pinochet proposed a massive public works project to construct a highway called the Carretera Austral. But the $300 million venture had another purpose as well. Pinochet was afraid that without a strong military presence in the region, neighboring Argentina could begin chipping away at Chile's territory. The highway would allow the army easier access to an area that until then was accessible only by boat.*

Ground was broken on the Carretera Austral in 1976, and in 1982 the first section, running from Chaitén to Coyhaique, opened to great fanfare. The only trouble was that you still couldn't get there from the mainland. It took another five years for the extension from Chaitén north to Puerto Montt to be completed. An extension from Coyhaique south to Cochrane was finished the following year.

The word finished is misleading, as construction continues to this day. Although the Carretera Austral is nicely paved near Puerto Montt, it soon reveals its true nature as a two-lane gravel surface that crawls inexorably southward for 1,156 km (718 mi) toward the outpost of Villa O'Higgins. And the highway isn't even contiguous. In places the road actually ends abruptly at water's edge (ferries link these broken stretches of highway), and it is interrupted by Parque Pumalín, a preserve where the road is not allowed to pass. The segment from Chaitén to Coyhaique is scheduled for completion this year.

The Carretera Austral is lauded in tourism brochures as "a beautiful road studded with rivers, waterfalls, forests, lakes, glaciers, and the occasional hamlet." This description is accurate—you may live the rest of your life and never see anything half as beautiful as the scenery. However, the highway itself is far from perfection. The mostly unpaved road has dozens of single-lane, wide-board bridges over streams and rivers. Shoulders are nonexistent or made of soft, wheel-grabbing gravel. Periodically, traffic must wend its way through construction, amid heavy equipment and workers.

As you drive south along the Carretera Austral, Chile's southernmost reaches seem to simply disintegrate into a tangle of sounds and straits, channels and fjords. Here you'll find lands laden with lush vegetation or layered in fields of ice. The road struggles valiantly along this route, connecting tiny fishing towns and farming villages all the way from Puerto Montt to Villa O'Higgins. There, the huge Campo de Hielo Sur (Southern Ice Field) forces it to a halt.

Navigating the Carretera Austral requires some planning, as communities along the way are few and far between. Some parts of the highway, especially in the southernmost reaches, are deserted. Check out your car thoroughly, especially the air in the spare tire. Make sure you have a jack and jumper cables. Bring along enough food in case you find yourself stuck far from the nearest restaurant.

What the Carretera Austral offers adventurous travelers is a chance to see a part of the world where few have ventured. The views from the highway are truly amazing, from the conical top of Volcán Corcovado near Chaitén to the sprawling valleys around Coyhaique. Here you'll find national parks where the trails are virtually deserted, such as Parque Nacional Queulat and Reserva Nacional Río Simpson. The region's crowning glory, of course, is the vast glacier at Laguna San Raphael. It may be a tough journey today, but when it is eventually finished, the Carretera Austral could rival the most spectacular scenic roadways in the world.

— Pete Nelson

in one of the many indoor and outdoor hot-spring pools. Pathways wind among flower beds, where hummingbirds hover, and between the low-roofed but spacious accommodations, with decks extending over the lakefront. The dining room *($$$)* has terrific views of the fjord, and a wonderful selection of wines. ✉ *Bahia Dorita s/n, Carretera Austral, 13 km (8 mi) south of Puerto Puyuhuapi* ☎ *2/225–6489 in Santiago* 📠 *2/274–8111 in Santiago* 🌐 *www.termasdepuyuhuapi.cl* *28 rooms, 2 cabins* *Restaurant, 3 pools, saltwater pool, health club, sauna, spa, boating, waterskiing, fishing, hiking, bar, lounge, recreation room, shop, laundry service, Internet; no room TVs* 💳 *AE, DC, MC, V* 🍽 *BP.*

$ **Hosteria Alemana.** The home of Ursula Flack, last of the town's original German settlers, is a great choice for budget-minded travelers who want to explore the beautiful countryside. Flack moved here in 1958, 10 years after her husband, who built this large Bavarian-style home with gardens in the middle of town. Rooms with functional baths are simple but charming. Fresh flowers fill the quaint dining room. Ursula also runs the best eatery in town, Café Rossbach, just a five-minute walk down the road, next to the carpet workshop run by her son, Helmut. ✉ *Puerto Puyuhuapi s/n* ☎ *67/325–118* *6 rooms* *Laundry facilities; no a/c, no room phones, no room TVs* 💳 *No credit cards* 🍽 *BP.*

Fishing

More than 50 rivers are within easy driving distance of Puerto Puyuhuapi, making this a cherished destination among fishing enthusiasts. Here are rainbow and brown trout, silver and steelhead salmon, and local species such as the robalo. The average size is about 6 pounds, but it's not rare to catch monsters twice that size. Daily trips are organized by the staff at the resort hotel, Puyuhuapi Lodge & Spa.

Shopping

Carpets at **Alfombras de Puyuhuapi** (✉ E. Ludwig s/n ☎ 67/325–131 🌐 www.puyuhuapi.com) are handwoven by three generations of women from Chiloé who use only natural wool thread and cotton fibers. The rustic vertical looms, designed and built specifically for this shop, allow the weavers to make carpets with a density of 20,000 knots per square meter. Trained by his father and grandfather, who opened the shop here in the 1940s, proprietor Helmut E. Hopperdietzel proudly displays the extensive stock of finished carpets of various sizes and designs. Carpets can be shipped. The shop is closed in June.

Parque Nacional Queulat

❺ *175 km (109 mi) south of Chaitén.*

The rugged 350,000-acre Parque Nacional Queulat begins to rise and roll to either side of the Carretera Austral some 20 km (12 mi) south of the town of La Junta. Rivers and streams that crisscross dense virgin forests attract fishing aficionados from all over the world. At the higher altitudes brilliant blue glaciers can be found in the valleys between snowcapped peaks. If you're lucky you'll spot a pudú, one of the diminutive deer that make their home in the forest.

Less than 1 km (½ mi) off the east side of the Carretera Austral you are treated to a close-up view of the hanging glacier, **Ventisquero Colgante**. This sheet of ice slides forward between a pair of gentle rock faces. Several waterfalls cascade down the cliffs to either side of the glacier's foot. There is an easy 15-minute walk leading to one side of the lake below the glacier, which is not visible from the overlook. Another, longer hike takes you deeper into the park's interior.

A short drive farther south, where the Carretera Austral makes one of its sharp switchback turns as it climbs higher, a small sign points into the undergrowth, indicating the trailhead for the **Salto Padre García**. There is no parking area, but you can leave your car on the shoulder. This short hike through dense forest is well worth attempting for a close-up view of this waterfall of striking proportions.

There are two CONAF stations (the national forestry service), one at the Ventisquero Colgante overlook, the other a few miles north of the southern park gateway. ⊠ *Carretera Austral, 20 km (12 mi) south of La Junta* ☎ *67/231–065 or 67/232–599* ⊕ *www.conaf.cl* ☎ *1,500 pesos* ⊙ *Daily 8:30–6:30.*

Where to Stay

$$ ⊞ **Hotel El Pangue.** Follow the driveway to the sprawling complex of reddish buildings on the sheltered shores of Lake Risopatrón. Several shingle-roofed cabanas, all with central heating and ample hot water, were constructed by local craftspeople from native wood. The clubhouse has a fireplace and a panoramic view of the lake. The dining room serves barbecued lamb prepared on a traditional *quincho* (grill). Activities include trolling and fly-fishing on the lake and nearby rivers. Canoes, mountain bikes, and horses are available for exploring the lake and park trails. It's 5 km (3 mi) south of the entrance of Parque Nacional Queulat. ⊠ *Carretera Austral, Km 240* ☎ *67/325–128* ⊕ *www.elpangue.cl* ⤳ *10 rooms, 15 cabanas* ⚭ *Restaurant, pool, lake, hot tub, sauna, boating, fishing, hiking, horseback riding, bar; no a/c, no room TVs* ⊟ *AE, MC, V* ⦿ *BP.*

Coyhaique

❻ *224 km (140 mi) south of Puerto Puyuhuapi.*

Where Río Simpson and Río Coyhaique come together you'll find Coyhaique, the only community of any size on the Carretera Austral. Calling itself "the capital of Patagonia," Coyhaique has some 50,000 residents—more than half of the region's population.

Ten streets radiate from the central plaza. Horn, one of the most colorful, holds the crafts stands of the Feria Artesenal. Balmaceda connects the central square with the smaller Plaza Prat. Navigating the area around the plaza is confusing at first, but the streets, bearing those traditional names used throughout the country, soon yield to a simple grid system.

The pentagonal **Plaza de Armas** is the center of town and the nexus for its attractions, including the town **Catedral** and **Intendencia**, the government building.

The Carretera Austral leads into the northeastern corner of town and to the **Monumento al Ovejero.** On the broad median of the Avenida General Baquedano a solitary shepherd with his horse and his dog lean motionless into the wind behind a plodding flock of sheep. ⊠ *Av. General Baquedano.*

The **Museo Regional de la Patagonia** is worth the small fee for the black-and-white photos of early-20th-century pioneering in this region, as well as for the collections of household, farming, and early industrial artifacts from the same era. A visit is a reminder of how recently many parts of southern Chile began to develop. ⊠ *Av. General Baquedano 310* ☎ *No phone* 🖃 *1,000 pesos* ⊙ *Daily 8:30–1 and 2:30–6:30.*

The 5,313-acre **Reserva Nacional Coyhaique,** about 4 km (2½ mi) north of Coyhaique, provides hikers with some stunning views when the weather cooperates. If it's raining you can drive a 9-km (5½-mi) circuit through the park. ⊠ *54 km (34 mi) east of Coyhaique* ☎ *No phone* ⊕ *www.conaf.cl* 🖃 *600 pesos* ⊙ *Jan. and Feb., daily 8 AM–9 PM; Mar.–Dec., daily 8:30–5.*

The evergreen forests of **Reserva Nacional Río Simpson,** just north of Reserva Nacional Coyhaique, are filled with waterfalls tumbling down steep canyon walls. A lovely waterfall called the Cascada de la Virgen is a 1-km (½-mi) hike from the information center, and another called the Velo de la Novia is 8 km (5 mi) farther. ⊠ *Carretera Austral, Km 32* ☎ *No phone* ⊕ *www.conaf.cl* 🖃 *400 pesos* ⊙ *Jan. and Feb., daily 8 AM–9 PM; Mar.–Dec., daily 8:30–5.*

The only skiing in northern Patagonia can be had 32 km (20 mi) outside town at **El Fraile.** You can rent equipment for the three trails here. There are no accommodations and it's wise to bring food and water with you. The season runs May–September. ⊠ *Camino Lago Pollux* ☎ *67/210–210.*

off the beaten path ★ **LAGO GENERAL CARRERA.** It takes a 280 km (174 mi) drive from Coyhaique along the rutted, unpaved Carretera Austral to reach this beautiful, almost surreally blue lake, the biggest in Chile (and the second-largest in South America, after Lake Titicaca). But this spectacular place is more than worth the trip. Tourism has only just started developing here, but already, travelers have been making the pilgrimage in four-wheel-drive vehicles to fish, hike, and gasp at the mountains, glaciers and waterfalls that dot the landscape. The best place to stay in the area is **Terra Luna,** which occupies 15 peaceful acres at the southeastern edge of the lake. The property is serene, with charming (very basic) redwood cabins, grazing horses, and a beautiful main lodge where all meals are served. Excursion packages are offered; you can trek in nearby mountains, raft or kayak on the lake or more lively rivers, or take scenic flights over ice fields and glaciers. The remoteness and changeable weather of the region mean these excursions aren't always guaranteed to happen as planned—but if it's too windy for your plane ride, you can always borrow a mountain bike, or relax in the waterfront Jacuzzi. ⊠ *Km 1.5, Carretera Austral, Puerto Guadal* ☎ *67/ 431–263* 🖷 *67/ 431–264* ⊕ *www.terraluna.cl.*

Where to Stay & Eat

¢–$$ ✕ **Cafetería Alemana.** Whether you're seated in one of the dining rooms or outside at a table on the sidewalk, Cafetería Alemana is a great place for people-watching. The menu lists light fare, including tiny *empanaditas* (small meat-filled pies). Challenge your dietary willpower by taking a look at the case full of authentic küchen. ⊠ *Condell 119* ☎ *67/231–731* ▤ *AE, MC, V.*

★ ¢–$$ ✕ **Casona.** A fire crackles in the corner wood-burning stove in this tidy little restaurant. Vases filled with fresh flowers adorn tables covered with white linen. The place is run by the González family—the mother cooks, her husband and son serve—who exude a genuine warmth to everyone who walks in the door. There's plenty of traditional fare on the menu, but the *centolla* (king crab) and *langostino* (lobster) are the standouts. ⊠ *Obispo Vielmo 77* ☎ *67/238–894* ▤ *AE, DC, MC, V.*

$–$$ ✕ **Restaurant Histórico Ricer.** Operated by the same family for decades, this popular restaurant is a Coyhaique institution. The stairs in the back lead to a wooden dinner parlor; the walls are covered with fascinating sepia photos from the town's archives. An upper loft here makes a cozy place for tea. Among the most popular items on the extensive menu are salmon, rabbit, and grilled leg of lamb. Lighter fare includes excellent empanadas filled with *locate* (a local mollusk). The pottery and crocheted hangings that decorate the restaurant were created by the family's matriarch. ⊠ *Horn 40 at 48* ☎ *67/232–920 or 67/237–950* ▤ *AE, DC, MC, V.*

$ ✕ **La Olla.** Starched linen tablecloths lend an unmistakable aura of European gentility to this modest restaurant, operated by a courtly Spaniard and his son. Among the specialties are a fine paella and a hearty *estofado de cordero* (lamb stew). ⊠ *Àv. Arturo Prat 176* ☎ *67/242–588* ▤ *AE, DC, MC, V.*

★ $$ ▥ **Hostal Belisario Jara.** You realize how much attention has been paid to the detail here when the proprietor points out that the weather vane on the peak of the single turret is a copy of one at Chilean poet Pablo Neruda's home in Isla Negra. In the quaint lodging's various nooks and crannies, wide windows and natural woods are abundant. In the small but tasteful rooms, terra-cotta floors complement the rustic carved-pine beds, spread with nubby cream linens. ⊠ *Francisco Bilbao 662* ☎ *67/234–150* ⊕ *www.belisariojara.itgo.com* ⇱ *8 rooms* ⚴ *Dining room, bar* ▤ *No credit cards* ▯◯▮ *BP.*

$$ ▥ **Hotel Coyhaique.** This nicely landscaped lodging is in a quiet corner of town, but it's within easy walking distance of the Plaza de Armas. Rooms are a bit motel-like, with flat pale-green comforters and drapes, a bed, a TV, and not much else. But they are clean and spacious. ⊠ *Magallanes 131* ☎ *67/231–137 or 67/231–737* ⊕ *www.hotelcoyhaique.cl* ⇱ *40 rooms* ⚴ *Restaurant, room service, minibars, cable TV, pool, bar, laundry service, Internet, convention center, airport shuttle* ▤ *AE, MC, V* ▯◯▮ *CP.*

$ ▥ **El Reloj.** Simple, very clean, wood-paneled rooms contain just the basic pieces of furniture. But the salon is warmly decorated with antiques and wood furnishings, and it has a large fireplace. Request a second-floor room for a view of the Coyhaique River. ⊠ *Av. General Baquedano 828*

☎ 67/231–108 ⊕ *www.aisen.org* ⤶ *9 rooms* ⚭ *Restaurant, cable TV, laundry service, Internet; no a/c* ▤ *AE, DC, MC, V* ¶⊘¶ *CP.*

Nightlife & the Arts

The outrageous stylishness of **Piel Roja** (⊠ Moraleda 495 ☎ 67/237–832) is refreshingly amplified, given its remote location. The bar-disco, whose name translates into "Red Skin," opens relatively early, at 7 PM. Nosh on pizza and explore the four levels of sculptural decor, several bars, a large dance floor, and a private nook. The furnishings are over-size and slightly surreal, a mix of motifs from art nouveau to Chinese. The weekend cover price of 6,000 pesos for men and 3,000 pesos for women is credited toward drinks or food.

Shopping

The **Feria Artesenal** (⊠ Plaza de Armas between Dussen and Horn ☎ No phone) has stalls selling woolen clothing, small leather items, and pottery.

Puerto Chacabuco

❼ *68 km (43 mi) northwest of Coyhaique.*

It's hard to imagine a drive more beautiful—anywhere in the world—than the one from Coyhaique to Puerto Chacabuco. The mist hangs low over farmland, adding a dripping somnolence to the scenery. Dozens of waterfalls and rivers wend their way through mountain formations. Yellow poplars surround charming rustic lodges. And sheep and cattle graze on mossy, vibrant fields. The picture of serenity terminates at the sea, where the nondescript port town of Chacabuco, Coyhaique's link to the ocean, sits, a conduit to further beauty. This harbor ringed by snowcapped mountains is where you board the ferries that transport you north to Puerto Montt in the Lake District and Quellón on Chiloé, as well as boats headed south to the spectacular Laguna San Raphael.

A hanging bridge leads from Chacabuco to **Puerto Aisén**, founded in 1928 to serve the region's burgeoning cattle ranches. Devastating forest fires that swept through the interior in 1955 filled the once-deep harbor with silt, making it all but useless for transoceanic vessels. The busy main street is a good place to stock up on supplies for boat trips to the nearby national parks.

Where to Stay & Eat

$$$ ✕▨ **Hotel Loberías del Sur.** On a hill overlooking the port, Hotel Loberías del Sur is a luxurious hotel in an unlikely place. The owner, who runs a catamaran service to Parque Nacional Laguna San Rafael, needed a place to pamper foreign vacationers for the night (running a nice tab in the process). The hotel provides real comforts after a blustery day at sea, such as firm queen-size beds and separate showers and bathtubs. The restaurant ($$$), as you might expect, has the finest service in town. ⊠ *Carrera 50* ☎ *67/351–112* 🖶 *67/351–188* ⊕ *www.catamaranesdelsur.cl* ⤶ *60 rooms* ⚭ *Restaurant, room service, cable TV, pool, gym, sauna, bar, lounge, recreation room, shop, laundry service, Internet, business services, convention center* ▤ *AE, DC, MC, V* ¶⊘¶ *BP.*

Parque Nacional Laguna San Rafael

8 *5 hrs by boat from Puerto Chacabuco.*

Fodor'sChoice
★
Nearly all of the 101,000-acre Parque Nacional Laguna San Rafael is fields of ice, totally inaccessible. But only a handful of the people who come here ever set foot on land. Most travel by boat from Puerto Chacabuco or Puerto Montt through the maze of fjords along the coast to the expansive San Rafael Lagoon. Floating on the surface of the brilliant blue water are scores of icebergs that rock from side to side as boats pass. Most surprising is the variety of forms and colors in each iceberg, including a shimmering, translucent cobalt blue.

Massive Ventisquero San Rafael extends 4 km (2½ mi) from end to end. The glacier is receding about 600 feet a year: paint on a bordering mountain marks the location of the glacier in past years. It's a noisy beast, roaring like thunder as the sheets of ice shift. If you're lucky you'll see huge pieces of ice calve off, causing violent waves that should make you glad your boat stayed at a safe distance.

Several different companies make the trip to Laguna San Rafael. The cheapest are Navimag and Transmarchilay, which offer both two-night trips from Puerto Chacabuco and four-night trips from Puerto Montt. More luxurious are the three-night cruises from Puerto Chacabuco and the six-night cruises from Puerto Montt run by Skorpios. For those with less time, Patagonia Connection has day trips from Chacabuco on a deluxe catamaran. (See *Tours* in Southern Coast Essentials, below, for more information.

THE SOUTHERN COAST ESSENTIALS

Transportation

BY AIR

Lan has flights to the regions from Santiago, Puerto Montt, and Punta Arenas. They arrive at the Southern Coast's only major airport, 55 km (34 mi) south of Coyhaique in the town of Balmaceda.

Booking air travel through a good tour company or travel agency can be invaluable. Unforeseen delays may occur when traveling this challenging region, and an informed agent is best equipped to rearrange your plans at the last minute.

🛪 **Airline Lan** ✉ General Parra 215, Coyhaique ☎ 67/231-188 ⊕ www.lan.com.

AIRPORT
TRANSFERS
A minivan ride from Balmaceda airport to Coyhaique using Transfer Valencia costs about 2,500 pesos.

🛪 **Transfer Valencia** ✉ Balmaceda Airport, Coyhaique ☎ 67/233-030.

BY BOAT & FERRY

Ferry lines operating in southern Chile sail the interwoven fjords, rivers, and lakes of the region. Fares in high season (January and February) are dramatically higher than other times.

Navimag (short for "Navigación Magallanes") operates a rather inelegant, but highly serviceable, cargo and passenger fleet throughout the region. The M/V *Evangelistas*, a 324-passenger ferry, sails round-trip from Puerto Montt to the Laguna San Rafael, stopping in both directions in Coyhaique's port of Puerto Chacabuco. The 200-passenger M/V *Alejandrina* sails from Puerto Montt to Chaitén, Quellón on Chiloé, and Puerto Chacabuco before making the trip in reverse.

Transmarchilay operates a cargo and passenger ferry fleet similar to that of Navimag, with ships that start in Puerto Montt and sail either to Chaitén or Puerto Chacabuco. It also sails between Quellón and Chaitén. Transmarchilay operates the ferry M/V *El Colono* from early January through late February, sailing weekly from Puerto Montt into Laguna San Rafael and back to Puerto Montt. Tour companies offer more luxurious transport to similar destinations.

🚢 **Boat & Ferry Information Navimag** ✉ Presidente Ibáñez 347, Coyhaique ☎ 67/233-306 ⊕ www.navimag.cl. **Transmarchilay** ✉ Corcovado 266, Chaitén ☎ 65/731-272 ✉ Av. Bernardo O'Higgins s/n, Puerto Chacabuco ☎ 67/351-144 ✉ General Parra 86, Coyhaique ☎ 67/231-971 ⊕ www.transmarchilay.cl.

BY BUS

Service between Puerto Montt and Cochrane is by private operators such as Tur-Bus. Travel along the Carretera Austral is often agonizingly and inexplicably slow, so don't plan on getting anywhere on schedule.

🚌 **Bus Information Tur-Bus** ✉ Magallanes 303, Coyhaique ☎ 67/237-571.

BY CAR

Renting a car in the Southern Coast can be expensive, and driving the Carretera Austral can be a hassle. But if you want to see the parts of the Southern Coast that are off the beaten path, there's no better way than in your own four-wheel-drive vehicle: you can stop in any of the little fishing villages and farming communities that the tour buses whiz past. A four-wheel-drive vehicle runs about 60,000 pesos, including tax and insurance. A car costs less than 40,000 pesos.

At Balmaceda airport there are three rental agencies, Budget, AGS Rent A Car, and Int'l Rent A Car. Automotriz Los Carrera rents four-wheel-drive vehicles. Make certain to understand the extent of your liability for any damage to the vehicle, including routine events such as a chipped or cracked windshield. If you want to visit one of the more popular parks, check out prices of tours. They might prove far cheaper than driving yourself.

🚗 **Rental Agencies AGS Rent A Car** ✉ Av. Ugana 1298, Coyhaique ☎ 67/231-511. **Automotriz Los Carrera** ✉ Carrera 330, Coyhaique ☎ 67/231-457. **Budget** ✉ Balmaceda Airport, Coyhaique ☎ 67/255-177. **Int'l Rent A Car** ✉ Balmaceda Airport, Coyhaique ☎ 67/214-770.

Contacts & Resources

BANKS & EXCHANGE SERVICES

Converting cash can be a bureaucratic headache, particularly in smaller towns like Chaitén. A better option is using your ATM card at numerous local banks connected to Cirrus or Plus networks.

When you're anticipating smaller purchases, try to have coins and small bills on hand at all times, even though your pockets and purses will seem to bulge a bit. Small vendors do not always have change for large bills.

INTERNET, MAIL & SHIPPING

Some hotels offer Internet access, either for free or for a small fee. Internet access is often available at telephone company offices such as CTC, but this is generally a more expensive option. Usually cheaper are the Internet cafés that have sprung up around Coyhaique as well as in smaller towns.

Mail service is poky here, so you might want to save that letter for home until you get to a bigger city. The post office in Coyhaique is on the south side of the Plaza de Armas. It's open weekdays 9–12:30 and 2:30–6, Saturday 8:30–noon. If you need a courier service, DHL has an office in Cayhaique.

🖪 **Post Office Correos** ⊠ Lord Cochrane 202, Coyhaique.

🖪 **Overnight Services DHL** ⊠ 12 de Octubre 208, Coyhaique ☎ 67/234-196.

TOURS

Willy Stone in Coyhaique takes up a small charter plane for tours of San Rafael and the surrounding countryside. Reservations are required.

Austral Adventures offers a personalized approach to seeing the waterways of the northern Southern Coast, especially the fjords around Parque Pumalín. Three- to seven-day tours include trips to natural and hidden hot springs. The deluxe catamaran *Patagonia Express* is operated by Patagonia Connection, the same company that owns the beautiful Puyuhuapi Lodge & Spa. During the peak-season months of January and February, the vessel operates a full-day tour to the Laguna San Rafael from Puerto Chacabuco daily. Out of season the boat makes the same trip on Friday. The onboard service is excellent, and includes meals, cocktails, and even a video "lounge" for warming up. Catamaranes del Sur also offers luxury catamaran trips to San Rafael from Puerto Chacabuco, as well as trips to other coastal destinations.

If it's Laguna San Rafael you want to see, there are several different types of boats to take you there, but most do not operate during the winter months of June, July, and August. Skorpios's trio of luxurious ferries carry between 70 and 130 passengers in first-class style to the Laguna San Rafael. You can sail round-trip either from Puerto Chacabuco or Puerto Montt.

In Coyhaique, Andes Patagónicos is adjacent to the Restaurant Histórico Ricer and owned by the same family. Gregarious Patricia Chiblé and her staff are knowledgeable and helpful. Among the regional tours they offer are flights over Laguna San Rafael and its glacier. American-born Nicholas La Penna runs Chaitur Excursions, the best place in Chaitén for tours, trekking, and general information about the region. Among his itineraries are full-day trips into Parque Pumalín as well as a half-day trip to the sea lion colony on Isla Puduguapi.

In Santiago, SportsTour has more than 30 years of experience. It puts together individual itineraries, as well as offering half- and full-day city tours and multiday excursions throughout the Southern Coast and the rest of the country. Most staff members speak excellent English.

A knowledgeable tour operator or travel agent is a must for travel to the Southern Coast. In the United States, a number of companies are experienced with travel here. Among them is the Georgia-based Lost World Adventures, whose staff specializes in tailoring itineraries around your specific interests.

🚹 **Air Tours** **Willy Stone** ☎ 9/817-2172.

🚹 **Boat Tours** **Austral Adventures** ✉ Lord Cochrane 432, Chiloé ☎ 65/625-977 🌐 www.austral-adventures.com. **Catamaranes del Sur** ✉ Carrera 50, Puerto Chacabuco ☎ 67/351-112 🌐 www.catamaranesdelsur.cl. **Patagonia Connection** ✉ Puerto Puyuhuapi ☎ 2/225-6489 🌐 www.patagonia-connection.com. **Skorpios** ✉ Augusto Leguia Norte 118, Santiago ☎ 2/477-1900 🌐 www.skorpios.cl.

🚹 **Regional Tours** **Andes Patagónicos** ✉ Horn 40 and 48, Coyhaique ☎🖨 67/232-920 or 67/237-950 🌐 www.patagoniachile.cl/ap. **Chaitur Excursions** ✉ Diego Portales 350, Chaitén ☎ 65/731-439. **SportsTour** ✉ Moneda 790, 14th fl., Santiago ☎ 2/549-5200 🖨 2/698-2981 🌐 www.chilnet.cl/sportstour.

🚹 **U.S.-Based Tours** **Lost World Adventures** ✉ 337 Shadowmoor Dr., Decatur, GA 30030 ☎ 404/373-5820 or 800/999-0558 🖨 404/377-1902 🌐 www.lostworldadventures.com.

VISITOR INFORMATION

Sernatur, the national tourist office, is one-stop shopping (so to speak) for all information: you can pick up brochures, book tours, and get general advice. The area is so rich in natural beauty that you're sure to learn something new. Stop in before exploring.

🚹 **Sernatur** ✉ Av. Region X 480, Puerto Montt ☎ 65/259-615 ✉ Bulnes 35, Coyhaique ☎ 67/231-752.

Patagonia & Tierra del Fuego

9

Updated by
Robin
Goldstein

TRADITIONAL BOUNDARIES CANNOT DEFINE Patagonia. This vast stretch of land east of the Andes, at the southern tip of South America, is mostly a part of Argentina. Chile, however, shares its southern extremity—a stretch of land that almost kisses Antarctica.

This is not a landscape of friendly snowcaps, but of towering, menacing cones of white ice, torturously shaped by glaciers and studded with jagged protrusions of brown rock. The few blankets of smooth snow seem almost out of place against this tableau, as do the many lakes; the placid pools of glacial turquoise appear to have been intimidated into pale submission by the soaring cliffs above.

Navigating the channel that today bears his name, conquistador Hernando de Magallanes arrived on these shores in 1520, claiming the region for Spain. Although early attempts at colonization failed, the forbidding landscape continued to fascinate explorers. Naturalist Charles Darwin, who sailed through the Estrecho de Magallanes (Straits of Magellan) in 1833 and 1834, called it a "mountainous land, partly submerged in the sea, so that deep inlets and bays occupy the place where valleys should exist."

Because of the region's remote location, much of what Darwin described is still relatively undisturbed. North from Punta Arenas the land is flat and vast; this terrain gave rise to the book of poems *Desolation* by Nobel Prize–winning, Chilean poet Gabriela Mistral. The road peters out to the north at Parque Nacional Torres del Paine, a natural wonder, where snow-covered pillars of stone seem to rise vertically from the plains below. To the east, across the Argentine border, is the only glacier in the world that is still growing after 30,000 years—Glaciar Perito Moreno, one of Argentina's national landmarks. To the south is Tierra del Fuego, the storm-lashed island at the continent's southernmost tip. This bleak wilderness, which still calls out to explorers today, is literally the end of the Earth.

Exploring Patagonia & Tierra del Fuego

Patagonia is the most southerly destination you can travel to without boarding a boat. Whereas South Africa's Cape of Good Hope lies near the 35th parallel (about the same latitude as Montevideo, Uruguay), and the southernmost point of New Zealand touches the 47th parallel, Chile's Punta Arenas is even farther south, near the 53rd parallel. The southernmost town on the globe, Puerto Williams, is just above the 55th. It's closer to the South Pole than to the northern border of Chile. Bigger, and just to the northeast of Puerto Williams, is Ushuaia, Argentina, the world's southernmost *city.*

Working out a rewarding itinerary can be relatively easy. If you want to begin your trip in Chile, it's best to fly into Punta Arenas, the region's principal city. If you'd rather begin your Patagonian jaunt in Argentina, El Calafate and Ushuaia are the two most popular jumping-off points. From any of these locations, you can travel to most of the other destinations by bus or car (or take the ferry from Punta Arenas to Tierra del Fuego). A few remote spots, such as Isla Magdalena or Puerto Williams, can be reached only by boat or airplane.

About the Restaurants

Chilean Patagonia is no gourmet haven, but the aura of sophistication that lingers in Punta Arenas, the region's largest city, is reflected in the variety of restaurants you can find here. In Puerto Natales, it's harder, but still possible, to find a good meal. All around the region, service is courteous and attentive, even in informal eateries.

Menus tend to be extensive, although two items in particular might be considered specialties, especially in Tierra del Fuego: *centolla* (king crab), and moist, tender *cordero magallánico* (Magellanic lamb). King crab is always expensive; it's worth the splurge only if it's fresh, rather than frozen (the waiters will be honest with you if you ask). Some hotels also often have tantalizing breakfast spreads that, if you choose to indulge, will carry you comfortably well past noon. Be warned: many restaurants close for several hours in the afternoon and early evening (3–8).

If you hop the border into Argentina, the dining options are cheaper and often tastier. You'll find the same fire-roasted centolla and cordero (in Argentina it's *cordero a la cruz* or *al asador*—slow-roasted on wooden spits over an open fire) but you'll also get a chance to try the famous Argentine *parrillas* (grilled-meat restaurants). These serve excellent steaks like *bife de chorizo* (bone-in sirloin), as well as *asado de tira* (a rib roast), and delicious *mollejas* (grilled sweetbreads).

About the Hotels

Because of its prosperous past, Punta Arenas has many historic hotels offering luxurious amenities and fine service. A night or two in one of them should be part of your trip. For its size, Puerto Natales has a surprising number of options: though most tend to be small, bland, aging inns, some of them are charming, too. There are also several good resorts and lodges within Parque Nacional Torres del Paine. Rates can be half price out of peak season. Some hotels in the park turn off electricity during night hours, such as midnight–6 AM. Almost absent in the region are foreign chains. In Argentine Patagonia, hotels tend to be a bit cheaper—but there, too, you'll find a few ultraluxurious options.

The terms *hospedaje* and *hostal* are used interchangeably in the region, so don't make assumptions based on the name. Many hostals are fine hotels—not youth hostels with multiple beds—just very small. By contrast, some *hospedajes* are little more than a spare room in someone's home.

WHAT IT COSTS IN CHILEAN PATAGONIA: Chilean Pesos (in thousands)				
$$$$	**$$$**	**$$**	**$**	**¢**
RESTAURANTS over 11	8–11	5–8	3–5	under 3
HOTELS over 105	75–105	45–75	15–45	under 15

Restaurant prices are for a main course at dinner. Hotel prices are for a double room in high season, excluding tax.

9

If you have a limited amount of time, you should head to the mountains as soon as possible. Factor in the weather and dedicate days that promise sunshine to Torres del Paine park. Assuming the weather is clear each day, spend your first day driving from **Punta Arenas** north to **Puerto Natales,** where you can spend the night. Head another three hours (a slow drive along gravel roads) north to see the magnificent soaring peaks of **Parque Nacional Torres del Paine,** and spend a day or three there if you can. Then head back toward Punta Arenas, stopping along the way at the **Pingüinera de Seno Otway.**

Alternatively, you can keep your base in Puerto Natales, doing one day trip to Torres del Paine and a second one- or two-day (overnight) trip to the stunning **Glaciar Perito Moreno** in Argentina.

If you have more time to spend, consider seeing more of the region by boat. The Cruceros ships *Mare Australis* and *Via Australis* make four- and five-day trips between Punta Arenas and Argentine **Ushuaia.** Along the way, the boats stop at such sights as Ainsworth Bay, the Pia and Garibaldi glaciers, and colonies of elephant seals and penguins. Alternatively, beginning in **Puerto Montt,** take the four-day Navimag trip to Natales; then spend three days hiking Torres del Paine and two days based in Argentina's **El Calafate,** seeing the unforgettable Glaciar Perito Moreno.

WHAT IT COSTS IN ARGENTINE PATAGONIA: Argentine Pesos				
	$$$$	$$$	$$	$	¢
RESTAURANTS	over 35	25–35	15–25	8–15	under 8
HOTELS	over 400	250–400	150–250	80–150	under 80

Restaurant prices are for one main course at dinner. Hotel prices are for two people in a standard double room in high season.

When to Go

Late November to early March—summer in the Southern Hemisphere—is considered high season in Patagonia. Demand for accommodations is highest in January and February, so advance reservations are vital. Summer weather in these latitudes is by no means warm, but rather pleasantly cool. Bring an extra layer or two, even when the sun is shining. Windbreakers are essential. On or near these Antarctic waters, stiff breezes can be biting. In spring (September to November) and fall (March to May) the weather is usually delightfully mild, but can also be downright cold, depending on clouds and wind. The region goes into virtual hibernation in the winter months of June, July, and August.

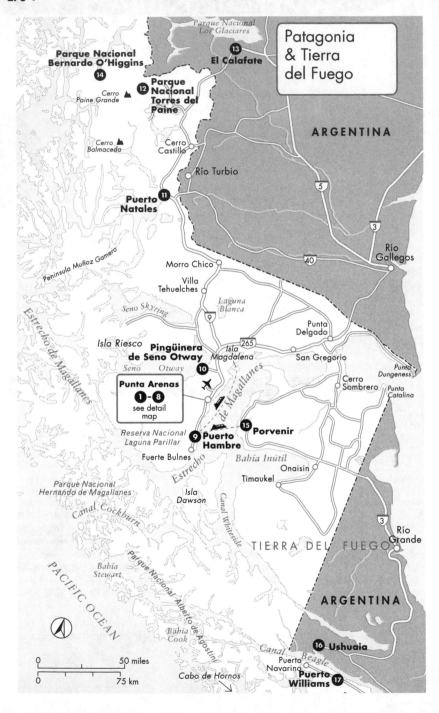

Patagonia
& Tierra
del Fuego

Parque Nacional
Los Glaciares

Parque Nacional
Bernardo O'Higgins
14

13
El Calafate

12 Parque
Nacional
Torres del
Paine

Cerro
Paine Grande ▲

ARGENTINA

Cerro
Balmaceda ▲

Cerro
Castillo

Río Turbio

5

Puerto **11**
Natales

3

Río
Gallegos

Península Muñoz Gamero

Morro Chico

Villa
Tehuelches

Laguna
Blanca

40

Seno Skyring

9

Isla Riesco

Punta
Delgado

Pingüinera
de Seno Otway

265

Isla
Magdalena

San Gregorio

Punta
Dungeness

Seno Otway

10

Cerro
Sombrero

Punta
Catalina

Punta Arenas
1-**8**
see detail
map

Estrecho de Magallanes

Reserva Nacional
Laguna Parillar

9 Puerto
Hambre

15 Porvenir

Fuerte Bulnes

Bahía Inútil

Estrecho

Onaisin

Parque Nacional
Hernando de Magallanes

Isla
Dawson

Timaukel

Canal Whiteside

Estrecho de Magallanes

Canal Cockburn

TIERRA DEL FUEGO

3

Río
Grande

Bahía
Stewart

Parque Nacional Alberto de Agostini

PACIFIC OCEAN

ARGENTINA

Bahía
Cook

16 Ushuaia

Canal Beagle

Puerto
Navarino

Cabo de Hornos

Puerto **17**
Williams

0   50 miles
0   75 km

Unforgettable Boat Cruises

Patagonia's unusual topography makes it optimal for travel by water. Several boat tour companies make journeys through the region, ranging from a day or two to a week or more. The vistas you'll see from on board, such as fantastic glaciers and icebergs, are breathtaking, and most boat tours also visit colonies of elephant seals and penguins.

Wild Wooliness

Wool may no longer be king of the economy, but vast flocks of sheep still yield a high-quality product that is woven into the clothing here. Leather products are also common, but the prices are not necessarily low.

9

Spectacular Glaciers

Patagonia's glaciers—miles-wide sheets of moving ice that are actually forging the topography before your eyes—are awesome to behold. Argentina's Glaciar Perito Moreno, from which chunks of ice fall off and crash into the glacial lake below, is the most arresting, but you'll also see glaciers all over Chile's Parque Nacional Torres del Paine and in Tierra del Fuego.

Cordero al Asador

In Argentine and Chilean Patagonia, lamb is deliciously prepared in the traditional manner: spit-roasted whole over an open fire. Restaurants offering *cordero al asador* often have grills positioned in their front windows to tempt you; you can smell, as well as see, the meat roasting to a delectable crispness.

PATAGONIA

Patagonia held little appeal for the earliest explorers. Discouraged by the inhospitable climate, they continued up the coast of South America in search of gold among the Aztec and Inca civilizations. The first Spanish settlements, given only halfhearted support from the crown, were soon abandoned. The newly formed nation of Chile showed little interest in Patagonia until 1843, when other countries began to eye the region, and Chilean President Manuel Bulnes sent down a ragtag group of soldiers to claim some of it for Chile. Five years later the town of Punta Arenas was founded.

And it wasn't a moment too soon; shortly thereafter, Punta Arenas became a major stop on the trade route around the tip of South America. Steam navigation intensified the city's commercial importance, leading to its short-lived age of splendor from 1892 to 1914, when its population rose from approximately 2,000 to 20,000. The opening of the Panama Canal all but bumped Punta Arenas off the map. By 1920 many of the founding families decided to move on, leaving behind the lavish mansions and the impressive public buildings they'd built.

Massive ranches once dominated the area around Punta Arenas. The vast flocks of sheep that dot the landscape still contribute to the local economy, but not as before. Today exploration for oil and natural gas is making the region prosperous again. Another source of income is tourism, as more and more people are drawn to this beautiful, if forbidding, land at the bottom of the Earth.

Punta Arenas

Founded a little more than 150 years ago, Punta Arenas (Point of Sands) was Chile's first permanent settlement in Patagonia. Great developments in cattle-keeping, mining, and wood production led to an economic and social boom here at the end of the 19th century; today, though the port is no longer an important stop on trade routes, it exudes an aura of faded grandeur. Plaza Muñoz Gamero, the central square, is surrounded by evidence of its early prosperity: buildings whose then-opulent brick exteriors recall a time when this was one of Chile's wealthiest cities.

The newer houses here have colorful tin roofs, best appreciated when seen from a high vantage point such as the Mirador Cerro la Cruz. Although the city as a whole may not be particularly attractive, look for details: the pink-and-white house on a corner, the bay window full of potted plants, parking attendants wearing the regional blue and yellow colors, and schoolchildren in identical naval peacoats that remind you that the city's fate is tied to the sea.

Although Punta Arenas is 3,141 km (1,960 mi) from Santiago, daily flights from the capital make it an easy journey. As the transportation hub of southern Patagonia, Punta Arenas is within reach of Chile's Parque Nacional Torres del Paine (about a six-hour drive) and Argentina's Parque Nacional los Glaciares. It's also a major base for penguin-watchers and a key point of embarkation for travel to Antarctica.

Numbers in the text correspond to numbers in the margins and on the Punta Arenas map.

a good walk

You can get an idea of the layout of the city at **Mirador Cerro la Cruz ❶** ⌐, an observation deck with a stunning view of the city. Head down the stairs and continue for three blocks to reach the cedar-lined **Plaza Muñoz Gamero ❷**, the center of the city. Here you'll find a monument honoring explorer Hernando de Magallanes. In deference to the many historical and political figures they honor, streets change their names as they pass by this square. The venerable **Palacio Sara Braun ❸** overlooks Plaza Muñoz Gamero. A block east is the **Museo Regional de Magallanes ❹**, commonly known as the Braun-Menéndez Palace for the family that built and occupied the mansion that houses the museum. Farther along Avenida Pedro Montt is the **Museo Naval y Marítimo ❺**, with its overview of the all-important role of the Chilean Navy in the region's history.

A block north you reach Avenida Colón, one of four intersecting avenues designed to accommodate large flocks of sheep. Today, the parks that run down the centers make pleasant places to stroll. Head north

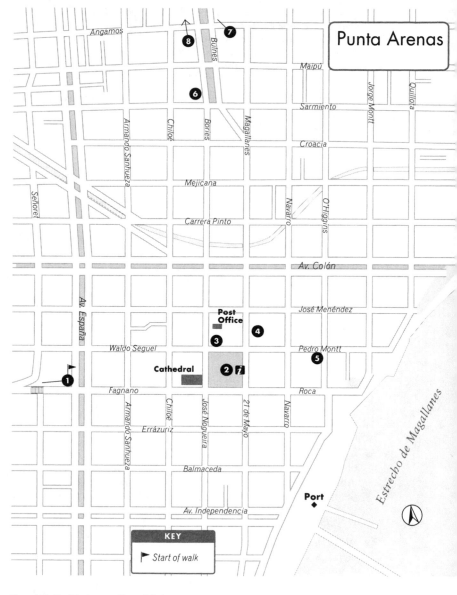

Punta Arenas

Cementerio Municipal . . .**7**
Mirador Cerro la Cruz . . .**1**
Museo del Recuerdo **8**
Museo Naval y
Marítímo **5**
Museo Regional
de Magallanes **4**

Museo Salesiano
de Maggiorino
Borgatello **6**
Palacio Sara Braun **3**
Plaza Muñoz Gamero . . .**2**

on Calle Bories for four blocks to reach the **Museo Salesiano de Maggiorino Borgatello** ❻. Three blocks north on Avenida Bulnes is the main entrance to the **Cementerio Municipal** ❼. Here among the manicured gardens and tall cypress trees are the grand mausoleums the town's wealthiest citizens erected in memory of themselves. Farther north on Avenida Bulnes is the **Museo del Recuerdo** ❽.

TIMING   The walk itself will take at least 1½ hours, but budget in extra time if you wish to explore the museums. Remember that most of the museums, as well as many businesses, close for lunch about noon and reopen a few hours later. You might want to save a visit to Cerro la Cruz or the Cementerio Municipal for these times.

What to See

❼ **Cementerio Municipal.** The fascinating history of this region is chiseled into stone at the Municipal Cemetery. Bizarrely ornate mausoleums honoring the original families are crowded together along paths lined by sculpted cypress trees. In a strange effort to recognize Punta Arenas's indigenous past, there's a shrine in the northern part of the cemetery where the last member of the Selk'nam tribe was buried. Local legend says that rubbing the statue's left knee brings good luck. ⊠ *Av. Bulnes 949* 🕾 *No phone* 🎫 *Free* 🕓 *Daily dawn–dusk.*

Isla Magdalena. Punta Arenas is the launching point for a boat trip to see the more than 120,000 Magellanic penguins at the **Monumento Natural Los Pingüinos** on this island. A single trail, marked off by rope, is accessible to humans. The trip to the island, in the middle of the Estrecho de Magallanes, takes about two hours. To get here, you must take a tour boat. If you haven't booked in advance, you can stop at any one of the local travel agencies and try to get on a trip at the last minute, which is often possible. You can go only from December to February; the penguin population peaks in January and February. However you get here, make sure to bring along warm clothing, even in summer; the island can be chilly, particularly if a breeze is blowing across the water.

❶ **Mirador Cerro la Cruz.** From a platform beside the white cross that gives this hill lookout its name, you have a panoramic view of the city's colorful corrugated rooftops leading to the Strait of Magellan. Stand with the amorous local couples gazing out toward the flat expanse of Tierra del Fuego in the distance. ⊠ *Fagnano at Señoret* 🕾 *No phone* 🎫 *Free* 🕓 *Daily.*

❺ **Museo Naval y Marítimo.** The Naval and Maritime Museum extols Chile's high-seas prowess, particularly concerning Antarctica. Its exhibits are worth a visit by anyone with an interest in ships and sailing, merchant and military alike. The second floor is designed in part like the interior of a ship, including a map and radio room. Aging exhibits include an account of the 1908 visit to Punta Arenas by an American naval fleet. Ask for a tour or an explanatory brochure in English. ⊠ *Av. Pedro Montt 981* 🕾 *61/205–558* 🎫 *700 pesos* 🕓 *Tues.–Sat. 9:30–5.*

❽ **Museo del Recuerdo.** In the gardens of the Instituto de la Patagonia, part of the Universidad de Magallanes, the Museum of Memory is an envi-

PATAGONIA'S PENGUINS

AS THE FERRY SLOWLY APPROACHES Isla Magdalena, you begin to make out thousands of black dots along the shore. You catch your breath, knowing that this is your first look at the 120,000 seasonal residents of Monumento Natural Los Pingüinos, one of the continent's largest penguin sanctuaries, a population that is at its height during the breeding season, which peaks in January in February.

But the squat little birds are much closer than you think. You soon realize that on either side of the ferry are large groups of penguins catching their breakfast. They are amazingly agile swimmers, leaping almost entirely out of the water before diving down below the surface once again. A few swim alongside the boat, but most simply ignore the intrusion.

Several different types of penguins, including the Magellanic penguins found on the gentle hills of Isla Magdalena, make their homes along the Chilean coast. Although most favor cooler climates, small colonies can be found in the warmer waters north of Santiago. But for the thrill of seeing tens of thousands in one place, nothing beats Monumento Natural Los Pingüinos, open only from December to February. At this reserve, a two-hour trip by boat from Punta Arenas, the birds can safely reproduce and raise their young.

Found only along the coast of Chile and Argentina, Magellanic penguins are named for Spanish explorer Hernando de Magallanes, who spotted them when he arrived on these shores in 1520. They are often called jackass penguins because of the braying sound they make when excited. Adults, with the characteristic black-and-white markings, are easy to distinguish from the adolescents, which are a mottled gray. Also gray are the chicks, which hide inside their burrows when their parents are searching for food.

A good time to get a look at the fluffy little fellows is when their parents return to feed them regurgitated fish.

A single trail runs across Isla Magdalena, starting at the dock and ending on a hilltop at a red-and-white lighthouse. Ropes on either side keep humans from wandering too far afield. The penguins, however, have the run of the place. They waddle across the path, alone or in small groups, to get to the rocky beach. Familiar with the boatloads of people arriving two or three times a week, the penguins usually don't pay much attention to the camera-clutching crowds. A few of the more curious ones will walk up to people and inspect a shoelace or pants leg. If someone gets too close to a nest, however, they cock their heads sharply from side to side as a warning.

An easier way to see penguins in their natural habitat is to drive to Pingüinera de Seno Otway, on the mainland about an hour northwest of Punta Arenas. It's open longer than Isla Magdalena—from October to March. Founded in 1990, the reserve occupies 2 km (1 mi) of coastline. There are far fewer penguins here—only about 4,000—but the number is still astounding. The sanctuary is run by a nonprofit group, which can provide English-language guides. Travel companies from Punta Arenas arrange frequent tours to the reserve.

— Pete Nelson

able collection of machinery and heavy equipment used during the late-19th- and early-20th-century pioneering era. There are exhibits of rural employment, such as a carpenter's workshop, and displays of typical home life. ✉ *Av. Bulnes, Km 4 Norte* ☎ *61/207–056* 🎫 *Free* ⊙ *Weekdays 8:30–11:30 and 2:30–6:30, Sat. 8:30–1.*

4 **Museo Regional de Magallanes.** Housed in what was once the mansion
Fodor'sChoice of the powerful Braun-Menéndez family, the Regional Museum of Ma-
★ gallanes is an intriguing glimpse into the daily life of a wealthy provincial family at the beginning of the 20th century. Lavish Carrara marble hearths, English bath fixtures, and cordovan leather walls are among the original accoutrements. The museum also has an excellent group of displays depicting Punta Arenas's past, from the moment of European contact to its decline with the opening of the Panama Canal. The museum is half a block north of the main square. ✉ *Av. Magallanes 949* ☎ *61/244–216* 🎫 *1,000 pesos* ⊙ *Oct.–Mar., Mon.–Sat. 10:30–5, Sun. 10:30–2; Apr.–Sept., daily 10:30–2.*

6 **Museo Salesiano de Maggiorino Borgatello.** Commonly referred to simply as "El Salesiano," this museum is operated by Italian missionaries whose order arrived in Punta Arenas in the 19th century. The Salesians, most of whom spoke no Spanish, proved to be daring explorers. Traveling throughout the region, they collected the artifacts made by indigenous tribes that are currently on display. They also relocated many of the indigenous people to nearby Dawson Island, where they died by the hundreds (from diseases like influenza and pneumonia). The museum contains an extraordinary collection of everything from skulls and native crafts to stuffed animals. ✉ *Av. Bulnes 336* ☎ *61/241–096* 🎫 *1,500 pesos* ⊙ *Oct.–Mar., Tues.–Sun. 10–6; Apr.–Sept., Tues.–Sun. 10–1 and 3–6.*

★ **3** **Palacio Sara Braun.** This resplendent 1895 mansion, a national landmark and architectural showpiece of southern Patagonia, was designed by French architect Numa Meyer at the behest of Sara Braun (the wealthy widow of wool baron José Nogueira). Materials and craftsmen were imported from Europe during the home's four years of construction. The city's central plaza and surrounding buildings soon followed, ushering in the region's golden era. The Club de la Unión, a social organization that now owns the building, opens its doors to nonmembers for tours of some of the rooms and salons, which have magnificent parquet floors, marble fireplaces, and hand-painted ceilings. After touring the rooms, head to the cellar tavern for a drink or snack. ✉ *Plaza Muñoz Gamero 716* ☎ *61/241–489* 🎫 *1,000 pesos, free Sun. and May* ⊙ *Tues.–Fri. 10:30–1 and 6:30–8:30, Sat. 10:30–1 and 8–10, Sun. 11–2.*

need a break? Tea and coffee house, chocolate shop, and bakery, **Chocolatta** (✉ Bories 852 ☎ 61/268–606) is the perfect place to refuel during a day of wandering Punta Arenas. The interior is cozy, the staff
★ friendly, and you can hang out, perhaps over a creamy hot chocolate, for as long as you like.

2 **Plaza Muñoz Gamero.** A canopy of pine trees shades this square, which is surrounded by splendid baroque-style mansions from the 19th century. A bronze sculpture commemorating the voyage of Hernando de Magallanes dominates the center of the plaza. Local lore has it that a kiss on the shiny toe of Calafate, one of the Fuegian statues at the base of the monument, will one day bring you back to Punta Arenas. ⊠ *José Nogueira at 21 de Mayo.*

Where to Stay & Eat

$$–$$$ ✕ **La Pérgola.** In what was once the sunroom and winter garden of Sara Braun's turn-of-the-20th-century mansion, La Pérgola has one of the city's most refined settings. A 100-year-old vine festoons the glass windows and ceiling. The photo-illustrated menu lists mainly Chilean seafood and meat dishes; you might start with fried calamari and then have whitefish in garlic sauce. The service is formal and attentive as in the rest of the Hotel José Nogueira, to which the restaurant belongs. ⊠ *Bories 959* ☎ *61/248–840* ▤ *AE, DC, MC, V.*

★ $–$$$ ✕ **Sotito's Bar.** A virtual institution in Punta Arenas, Sotito's has dining rooms that are warm and cozy, with exposed-brick walls and wood-beamed ceilings. Locals gather here to enjoy some of the best centolla (king crab) in the area. It's prepared in several imaginative ways, including a dish called *chupé,* with bread, milk, cream, and cheese. The restaurant is near the water, a few blocks east of Plaza Muñoz Gamero. ⊠ *Av. Bernardo O'Higgins 1138* ☎ *61/243–565* ▤ *AE, DC, MC, V.*

$–$$$ ✕ **La Tasca.** Inside the Sociedad Española, on Punta Arena's main square, is this rustically elegant Spanish restaurant, operated by the same owners as the legendary Taberna Club de la Unión. You can look out the windows of the gracious, wood-ceilinged dining room onto the plaza while enjoying a typical Chilean *vaina* (port, sherry, chocolate, cinnamon, and egg whites), followed by paella *con centolla* (with king crab). If you're ordering fish, keep it simple; some of the heavy cream sauces can be overwhelming. ⊠ *Sociedad Española, Plaza Muñoz Gamero 771, 2nd fl.* ☎ *61/242–807* ▤ *AE, DC, MC, V.*

★ ¢–$$$ ✕ **Los Ganaderos.** You'll feel at home on the range in this enormous restaurant resembling a rural *estancia* (ranch). The manager and waiters, dressed in gaucho costumes, serve up spectacular *cordero al ruedo* (spit-roasted lamb) cooked in the *salón de parilla* (grill room); a serving comes with three different cuts of meat. You can wash down your meal with a choice from the long list of Chilean wines. Interesting black-and-white photographs of past and contemporary ranch life are displayed along the walls. The restaurant is several blocks north of the center of town, but it's worth going out of the way for. ⊠ *Av. Bulnes 0977, at Manantiales* ☎ *61/214–597* ▤ *AE, MC, V* ⊗ *Closed Sun.*

$$ ✕ **Restaurant Asturias.** Rough-hewn wood beams and white stucco walls at this restaurant evoke the Asturias region of Spain. The warmly lighted dining room is an inviting place to linger over *salmón papillote* (salmon poached in white wine with cured ham, cream cheese, and tomatoes), paella, or *congrio a la vasca* (conger eel—Chile's ubiquitous whitefish—in cream sauce). ⊠ *Lautaro Navarro 967* ☎ *61/243–763* ▤ *AE, DC, MC, V.*

$–$$ ✕ **El Estribo.** Centered around a large fireplace used to grill the meats, this narrow restaurant is filled with intimate little white-clothed tables. The name means "The Stirrup," and the walls are adorned with tastefully arranged bridles, bits, lariats, and—of course—all manner of stirrups. The longtime popularity of the place, however, has more to do with its excellent regional food (which it ambitiously dubs *platos exóticos patagónicos*) than novelty decor. The more unusual preparations include rabbit stroganoff and fillet of guanaco (a local animal that resembles a llama) in sherry sauce. There's also delicious spit-roasted lamb. For dessert try rhubarb pie—uncommon in these parts. ⊠ *Ignacio Carrera Pinto 762 at Av. Magallanes* ☎ *61/244–714* ▭ *No credit cards.*

$–$$ ✕ **El Remezón.** This cheerful little restaurant stands out because of its deliciously seasoned grilled fish and meats. The dining room is unpretentious and homey, and the day's menu is scrawled onto a chalkboard; if you're lucky, it might include a delicious *pisco*-marinated goose. Although it's near the port, away from the main part of town, the terrific food and potent pisco sours (brandy mixed with lemon, egg whites, and sugar) make it worth the walk (at night, it's best to spring for a short taxi ride). ⊠ *21 de Mayo 1469* ☎ *61/241–029* ▭ *AE.*

$–$$ ✕ **Taberna Club de la Unión.** A jovial, publike atmosphere prevails in this
Fodor'sChoice   wonderful, labyrinthine cellar redoubt down the side stairway of Sara
★   Braun's old mansion on the main plaza. A series of nearly hidden rooms are walled in cozy stone and brick, and black-and-white photos of historical Punta Arenas adorn the walls. You're likely to hear ragtime and jazz on the stereo while you enjoy beers served cold in frosted mugs, tapas-style meat and cheese appetizers, sandwiches, tacos, pizza, fajitas, and carpaccio (the menu has more bar snacks than dinner entrées). The bar is affiliated with the Club de la Unión headquartered upstairs, and many members relax down here. ⊠ *Plaza Muñoz Gamero 716* ☎ *61/ 241–317* ▭ *AE, DC, MC, V* ☉ *Closed Sun. No lunch.*

¢–$ ✕ **Santino Bar.** This downtown bar has a winning combination of friendly service, good pizzas and crepes, and an excellent assortment of Chilean cocktails. It's most popular for its drinks; perhaps the most interesting libation is the beer that's frothed up with egg whites. It was nicknamed the "Shourtney" after a young couple from Texas and Uruguay, who declared their undying love for the egg beer—and for each other—at Santino. ⊠ *Av. Colón 657, between Bories and Chiloé* ☎ *61/220–511* ▭ *AE, DC, MC, V* ☉ *Closed Sun.*

¢   ✕ **Lomit's.** A fast-moving but friendly staff serves Chilean-style blue-plate specials at this bustling deli. In addition to traditional hamburgers, you can try the ubiquitous *completos*—hot dogs buried under mounds of toppings, from spicy mayonnaise to guacamole—or try the Uruguayan-style *chivitos* (sandwiches with meat, lettuce, tomato, egg, and other trimmings). Locals gather here from morning to midnight. ⊠ *José Menéndez 722 between Bories and Av. Magallanes* ☎ *61/243–399* ▭ *No credit cards.*

$$$ ▤ **Hotel Finis Terrae.** A Best Western affiliate, this contemporary hotel has a good location (it's a couple of blocks from the main square) and a very professional staff. Guest rooms are comfortable, with traditional floral-print bedcovers and overstuffed chairs, and the baths are spacious and modern. There's a pleasant lounge with a fireplace, and the sixth-floor restaurant and bar has panoramic views. Stick with the superior rooms or, better yet, the junior suites, and avoid the tiny standard rooms; if you need two beds in a room, look elsewhere. Discounts are considerable March–September. ⊠ *Av. Colón 766* ☎ *61/228–200* 🖷 *61/ 248–124* ⊕ *www.hotelfinisterrae.com* 🛏 *60 rooms, 4 suites* ⚖ *Restaurant, in-room safes, minibars, cable TV, 2 bars, Internet, business services, airport shuttle* ⊟ *AE, DC, MC, V* ⭐ *BP.*

★ **\$\$\$** ⌨ **Hotel José Nogueira.** Originally the home of Sara Braun, this opulent 19th-century mansion also contains a museum. The location—steps off the main plaza—couldn't possibly be better. Carefully restored over many years, the building retains the original crystal chandeliers, marble floors, and polished bronze accents that were imported from France. Rooms are rather small—some smaller than others—but compensate with high ceilings, thick carpets, and period furniture. Suites have hot tubs and in-room faxes. ⊠ *Bories 959* ☎ *61/248–840* 🖷 *61/248–832* ⊕ *www. hotelnogueira.com* 🛏 *25 rooms, 3 suites* ⚖ *Restaurant, in-room data ports, in-room safes, minibars, cable TV, bar, laundry service, business services* ⊟ *AE, DC, MC, V.*

\$\$ ⌨ **Hotel Isla Rey Jorge.** Lofty wood windows let lots of light into the intimate rooms, decorated in mint and deep rose, at this English-style hotel with impeccable service. The hotel's richly toned *linga* and *coigué* woodwork in the lobby continues down into the popular basement pub, El Galeón. The hotel is just one block from Plaza Muñoz Gamero. ⊠ *21 de Mayo 1243* ☎☎ *61/248–220 or 61/222–681* ⊕ *www.islareyjorge. com* 🛏 *21 rooms, 4 suites* ⚖ *Restaurant, cable TV, bar, Internet, airport shuttle, travel services* ⊟ *AE, DC, MC, V.*

\$\$ ✕⌨ **Hotel Los Navegantes.** This unpretentious older hotel, just a block from the Plaza de Armas, has spacious burgundy-and-green rooms and a nautical theme (maritime maps cover the walls). There's a charming dark-wood bar and a restaurant that serves delicious roast lamb. ⊠ *José Menéndez 647* ☎ *61/244–677* 🖷 *61/247–545* ⊕ *www.hotellosnavegantes.com* 🛏 *50 rooms, 2 suites* ⚖ *Restaurant, in-room safes, minibars, bar, airport shuttle, travel services* ⊟ *AE, DC, MC, V.*

\$\$ ✕⌨ **Hotel Tierra del Fuego.** Just a couple of blocks from the main plaza, this hotel is aging with grace. The place is clean and simple, with an old-world pub that serves sandwiches and drinks into the wee hours. Rooms are brightened by pretty rugs and marble bathroom sinks; some even have kitchenettes. The prices are reasonable; it's a good value in this category, especially given the amount of space you get. ⊠ *Av. Colón 716* ☎☎ *61/ 226–200* ⊕ *www.puntaarenas.com/tierradelfuego* 🛏 *26 rooms* ⚖ *Some kitchens, minibars, cable TV, pub, Internet* ⊟ *AE, DC, MC, V* ⭐ *BP.*

\$ ⌨ **Hostal de la Avenida.** The rooms of this pea-green guesthouse all overlook a garden lovingly tended by the owner, a local of Yugoslav origin. Flowers spill out from a wheelbarrow and a bathtub, birdhouses hang from trees, and a statue of Mary rests in a shrine with a grotto. The rooms offer modest comforts for those on a budget. The ones across the garden, away from the street, are the newest. Beside them is a funky bar that Chilean poet Pablo Neruda would have approved of; it seems hunkered down for blustery winters. ⊠ *Av. Colón 534* ☎ *61/ 247–532* 🛏 *10 rooms, 6 with bath* ⚖ *Dining room, in-room safes, minibars, cable TV, bar, laundry service* ⊟ *AE, DC, MC, V* ⭐ *CP.*

★ **\$** ⌨ **Hostal Oro Fueguino.** On a sloping cobblestone street near the observation deck at Cerro la Cruz, this charming little hostelry—tall, narrow, and rambling—welcomes you with lots of color. The first thing you notice is the facade, painted bright orange and blue. Inside are homey wall hangings and lamp shades made of eye-catching fabrics from as far off as India. The dining and living rooms are cheerful, and there's a wealth of tourist information. The warmth is enhanced by the personal zeal of the proprietor, Dinka Ocampo. ⊠ *Fagnano 365* 🖶🖶 *61/249–401* ⊕ *www.orofueguino.cl* ⤴ *12 rooms* ⌂ *Cable TV, laundry service, Internet; no a/c* 🖃 *AE, DC, MC, V* ⦿⦿ *BP.*

$ 🖼 **Hotel Condor de Plata.** The idiosyncratic decor at the Silver Condor includes scale models of ships and photographs of old-fashioned airplanes that once traversed the region. Like a handful of other small hotels on this busy, tree-lined avenue, it offers basic amenities for those on a budget—simple, clean rooms that have a bed and a TV. ⊠ *Av. Colón 556* 🖀 *61/241–078* 🖶 *61/241–149* ⊕ *www.condordeplata.cl* ⤴ *14 rooms* ⌂ *Cafeteria, in-room safes, minibars, bar, laundry service* 🖃 *AE, DC, MC, V.*

Nightlife & the Arts

During the Chilean summer, because Punta Arenas is so far south, the sun doesn't set until well into the evening. That means that locals don't think about hitting the bars until midnight. If you can't stay up late, try the hotel bars, such as Hotel Tierra del Fuego's **Pub 1900** (⊠ Av. Colón 716 🖀 61/242–759), which attract an early crowd. The city's classic speakeasy, **La Taberna Club de la Unión,** hops into the wee hours with a healthy mix of younger and older patrons. If you're in the mood for dancing, try **Abracadabra** (⊠ Bories 546 🖀 61/224–144), where the younger set goes to party until dawn.

Shopping

Almacén de Antaño (⊠ Av. Colón 1000 🖀 61/227–283) offers a fascinatingly eclectic selection of pewter, ceramics, mirrors, and graphics frames. **Dagorret** (⊠ Bories 587 🖀 61/228–692 ⊕ www.dagorret.cl), a Chilean chain with other outlets in Puerto Montt and Puerto Natales, carries top-quality leather clothing, including *gamuza* (suede) and *gamulán* (buckskin), some with wool trim. **Quilpué** (⊠ José Nogueira 1256 🖀 61/220–960) is a shoe-repair shop that also sells *huaso* (cowboy) supplies such as bridles, bits, and spurs. Pick up some boots for folk dancing.

Puerto Hambre

9 *50 km (31 mi) south of Punta Arenas.*

In an attempt to gain a foothold in the region, Spain founded Ciudad Rey Don Felipe in 1584. Pedro Sarmiento de Gamboa constructed a church and homes for more than 100 settlers. But just three years later, British navigator Thomas Cavendish came ashore to find that all but one person had died of hunger. He renamed the town Port Famine. Today a tranquil fishing village, Puerto Hambre still has traces of the original settlement, a sobering reminder of the often unbridled zeal of early European explorers.

About 2 km (1 mi) west of Puerto Hambre is a small white **monolith** that marks the geographical center of Chile, the midway point between northernmost Arica and the South Pole.

In the middle of a Chilean winter in 1843, a frigate under the command of Captain Juan Williams Rebolledo sailed southward from the island of Chiloé carrying a ragtag contingent of 11 sailors and eight soldiers. In October, on a rocky promontory called Santa Ana overlooking the Estrecho de Magallanes, they built a wooden fort, which they named **Fuerte Bulnes,** thereby founding the first Chilean settlement in the southern reaches of Patagonia. Much of the fort has been restored. ⊠ *5 km (3 mi) south of Puerto Hambre* 🕾 *No phone* 💷 *Free* 🕓 *Weekdays 8:30–12:30 and 2:30–6:30.*

The 47,000-acre **Reserva Nacional Laguna Parrillar,** west of Puerto Hambre, is centered around a shimmering lake in a valley flanked by hills. It's a great place for a picnic, if the weather cooperates. There are a number of well-marked paths that offer sweeping vistas over the Estrecho de Magallanes. ⊠ *Off Ruta 9, 52 km (32 mi) south of Punta Arenas* 🕾 *No phone* 💷 *650 pesos* 🕓 *Oct. 16–Mar. 15, weekdays 8:30–5:30, weekends 8:30–8:30.*

Pingüinera de Seno Otway

➓ *65 km (40 mi) northwest of Punta Arenas.*

Magellanic penguins, which live up to 20 years in the wild, return repeatedly to their birthplace to mate with the same partner. For about 2,000 penguin couples—no singles make the trip—home is this desolate and windswept land off the Otway Sound. In late September the penguins begin to arrive from the southern coast of Brazil and the Falkland Islands. They mate and lay their eggs in early October, and brood their eggs in November. Offspring are hatched mid-November through early December. If you're lucky, you may catch sight of one of the downy gray chicks that stick their heads out of the burrows when their parents return to feed them. Otherwise you might see scores of the ungainly adult penguins waddling to the ocean from their nesting burrows. They swim for food every eight hours and dive up to 30 meters (100 feet) deep. The penguins depart from the sound in late March.

The road to the sanctuary begins 30 km (18 mi) north of Punta Arenas, where the main road, Ruta 9, diverges near a checkpoint booth. A gravel road then traverses another fierce and winding 30 km (18 mi), but the rough trip (mud will be a problem if there's been a recent rain) should reward you with the sight of hundreds of sheep, cows, and birds, including, if you're lucky, rheas and flamingos. The sanctuary is a 1-km (½-mi) walk from the parking lot. It gets chilly, so bring a windbreaker.

If you don't have a car, Comapa, like many other tour companies based in Punta Arenas, offers tours to the Pingüinera (⇨ *By Boat in* Patagonia & Tierra del Fuego Essentials). The tours generally leave from Punta Arenas and return about 3½ hours later. ⊠ *Off Ruta 9* 💷 *1,200 pesos* 🕓 *Oct.–Mar., daily 8:30–8:30.*

Puerto Natales

⑪ *242 km (150 mi) northwest of Punta Arenas.*

The land around Puerto Natales held very little interest for Spanish explorers in search of riches. A not-so-warm welcome from the indigenous peoples encouraged them to continue up the coast, leaving only a name for the channel running through it: Seno Última Esperanza (Last Hope Sound).

The town of Puerto Natales wasn't founded until 1911. A community of fading fishing and meat-packing enterprises, with some 20,000 friendly residents, it's seen a large increase in tourism in recent years; it's now rapidly emerging as the staging center for visits to Parque Nacional Torres del Paine, Parque Nacional Bernardo O'Higgins, and other attractions, including the Perito Moreno Glacier across the border in Argentina. There is also a lot of tourism generated by the scenic **Navimag cruise** that makes four-day journeys between here and Puerto Montt, to the north. (⇨ By Boat *in* Patagonia & Tierra del Fuego Essentials.)

Aside from the numerous tour operators, everything here still feels more rustic and isolated than in cosmopolitan Punta Arenas. Hotels and restaurants are simpler, and shops older and more basic. On a clear day, an early-morning walk along Avenida Pedro Montt, which follows the shoreline of the Seno Última Esperanza (or Canal Señoret, as it is called on some maps), can be a soul-cleansing experience. The rising sun gradually casts a glow on the mountain peaks to the west.

Serious hikers often come to this area and spend four or five days—or more—hiking and camping in **Torres del Paine,** either before or after stopping in Puerto Natales. Others choose to spend a couple of nights in one of the park's luxury hotels, and take in the sights during day hikes from that base.

If you have less time, however, it's quite possible to spend just one day touring the park, as many people do, with Puerto Natales as your base. In that case, rather than drive, you'll want to book a one-day Torres del Paine tour with one of the many tour operators in Natales. Most tours pick you up at your hotel between 8 and 9 AM, and most go along the same route, visiting several lakes and mountain vistas, seeing Lago Grey and its glacier, and stopping for lunch in Hostería Lago Grey or one of the other hotels inside the park. These tours return around sunset.

Argentina's magnificent **Perito Moreno Glacier,** near El Calafate, can also be visited in a popular (long) one-day tour, leaving at the crack of dawn and returning late at night—don't forget your passport. It's a four-hour-plus trip in each direction. (Some tours instead include overnights in El Calafate.) For some recommended tour agencies, *see* Tours *in* Patagonia & Tierra del Fuego Essentials, but there are many in town, most of them booking the same vans. A few blocks east of the Seno Ultima Esperanza is the not-quite-central **Plaza de Armas.** An incongruous railway engine sits prominently in the middle of the square. ⊠ *Arturo Prat at Eberhard.*

Across from the Plaza de Armas is the squat little **Iglesia Parroquial.** The ornate altarpiece in this church depicts the town's founders, indigenous peoples, and the Virgin Mary all in front of the Torres del Paine.

A highlight in the small but interesting **Museo Historico Municipal** is a room of photos of indigenous peoples. Another room is devoted to the exploits of Hermann Eberhard, a German explorer considered the region's first settler. ⊠ *Av. Bulnes 285* ☎ *61/411–263* ⊠ *Free* ☉ *Weekdays 8:30–12:30 and 2:30–6, weekends 2:30–6.*

In 1896, Hermann Eberhard stumbled upon a gaping cave that extended 200 meters (650 feet) into the earth. Venturing inside, he discovered the bones and dried pieces of hide of an animal he could not identify. It was later determined that what Eberhard had discovered were the extraordinarily well-preserved remains of a prehistoric herbivorous mammal, *mylodon darwini,* about twice the height of a man, which they called a *milodón.* The cave and a somewhat kitschy life-size fiberglass rendering of the creature are at the **Monumento Natural Cueva de Milodón.** ⊠ *Off Ruta 9, 28 km (17 mi) northwest of Puerto Natales* ☎ *No phone* ⊠ *1,500 pesos* ☉ *Daily 8:30–6.*

Where to Stay & Eat

★ **$$** ✕ **Asador Patagónico.** This bright spot in the Puerto Natales dining scene is zealous about meat. Incredible care is taken here with the excellent *lomo* and other grilled steaks, as well as the steak tartare starter. Try the soupy, yummy *arroz con leche* (rice pudding) for dessert. Though the wine list is serious, the atmosphere is less so—there's good music, dim lighting, an open fire, and a friendly buzz. ⊠ *Prat 158* ☎ *61/413–553* ⊕ *www.asadorpatagonico.cl* ⊟ *AE, DC, MC, V.*

$–$$ ✕ **Centro Español.** Tables swathed in bright red, and hardwood floors that would be perfect for flamenco dancing create this restaurant's subtly Spanish style. It's a bit formal, but never stuffy. There's a wide selection of simply prepared meat and fish entrées, including succulent squid, served in ample portions. ⊠ *Av. Magallanes 247* ☎ *61/411–181* ⊟ *AE, MC, V.*

$–$$ ✕ **Restaurant Edén.** Grilled lamb sizzles prominently near the entrance of this eatery, while Chilean folk music plays softly in the background. The expansive dining room, with tables generously spaced on the white terrazzo floor, has floor-to-ceiling windows on two sides that give you the feeling of dining alfresco. ⊠ *Blanco Encalada 345* ☎ *61/414–120* ⊟ *AE, MC, V.*

$–$$ ✕ **Restaurant Última Esperanza.** Named for the strait on which Puerto Natales is located, the Last Hope Restaurant sounds as if it might be a bleak place. It's known, however, for its attentive service and top-quality dishes from chefs Miguel Risco and Manuel Marín. *Cordero* (lamb) and *salmón a la plancha* (grilled salmon) are specialties. The room is big and a bit impersonal. ⊠ *Av. Eberhard 354* ☎ *61/413–626* ⊟ *No credit cards.*

★ **¢–$$** ✕ **Concepto Indigo.** Eco-friendly vibes waft from this bright café, setting it apart from nearly every other eatery in Patagonia. Fossils collected from the nearby fjord, piles of *National Geographic*s and informational brochures about area attractions, Internet access, and an English-speaking staff make Indigo a de facto tourist office, museum, and library. The homemade pizzas are good—ask which toppings are fresh and which are canned—as are the sandwiches served on homemade wheat bread. The corner location, overlooking the water and a backdrop of snowy peaks, makes this a pleasant place to visit, even if you come just for a cup of coffee. ⊠ *Ladrilleros 105* ☎ *61/413–609* ⊟ *MC, V* ☺ *Closed in winter; months vary.*

★ ¢–$$ ✕ **El Rincón del Tata.** It's all about the atmosphere at this dimly lighted, funky little spot. In the evenings a strolling guitarist entertains with Chilean folk songs, encouraging diners to join in. Artifacts, mainly household items, from the town's early days fill the dining room, which has a working wood-burning stove to keep you warm, and Internet access. Pizza is a specialty here, and it's not bad by Chilean standards; the *salmón à la mantequilla* (salmon baked in butter and black pepper) is also decent, and the grilled lamb with garlic sauce is a Patagonian highlight. The waiters' ridiculous gaucho outfits, however, are not. ⊠ *Arturo Prat 236* ☎ *61/413–845* ⊟ *AE, DC, MC, V.*

¢–$ ✕ **Café Melissa.** The best espresso in town can be found at this café, which also serves pastries and cakes baked on the premises. In the heart of downtown, this is a popular meeting place for residents and visitors alike, and there's Internet access, too. It's open until 9 PM. ⊠ *Blanco Encalada 258* ☎ *61/411–944* ⊟ *No credit cards.*

$$$ ▥ **Hotel CostAustralis.** Designed by a local architect, this venerable three-story hotel has one of the most distinctive buildings in Puerto Natales; its peaked, turreted roof dominates the waterfront. Rooms have wood-paneled entryways and Venetian and Czech furnishings. Some have a majestic view of the Seno Última Esperanza and the snowcapped mountain peaks beyond, and others look out over the city. ⊠ *Av. Pedro Montt 262, at Av. Bulnes* ☎ *61/412–000* ⊟ *61/411–881* ⊕ *www.costaustralis.com* ⇴ *72 rooms, 2 suites* ⚭ *Restaurant, café, room service, in-room safes, minibars, cable TV, bar, laundry service, Internet, travel services* ⊟ *AE, DC, MC, V* ⓞ *BP.*

$$ ▥ **Hotel Alberto de Agostini.** The Agostini is one of the modern hotels that have cropped up in Puerto Natales in the past few years. Small rooms—some with hot tubs—are unremarkable in decor, but a comfortably furnished lounge on the second floor looks out over the Seno Última Esperanza. ⊠ *Av. Bernardo O'Higgins 632* ☎ *61/410–060* ⊟ *61/410–070* ⇴ *25 rooms* ⚭ *Restaurant, café, room service, minibars, cable TV, sauna, bar, laundry service, Internet, travel services* ⊟ *AE, DC, MC, V.*

$$ ▥ **Hotel Martín Gusinde.** Part of Chile's modern AustroHoteles chain, this intimate inn possesses an aura of sophistication that contrasts with the laid-back atmosphere of Puerto Natales. The hotel is named after an Austrian ethnologist who studied the native inhabitants of Tierra del Fuego. Rooms are decorated with wood furniture and colorfully patterned wallpaper. It's across from the casino, a block south of the Plaza de Armas. In low season, prices drop by almost two-thirds. ⊠ *Carlos Bories 278* ☎ *61/412–770* ⊟ *61/412–820* ⊕ *www.austrohoteles.cl/martingusinde.html* ⇴ *20 rooms* ⚭ *Restaurant, room service, in-room safes, cable TV, bar, Internet* ⊟ *AE, MC, V* ⓞ *CP.*

$-$$ ⊞ **Hostal Lady Florence Dixie.** Named after an aristocratic English immigrant and tireless traveler, this modern hostel with an alpine-inspired facade is on the town's main street. Its bright, spacious lounge is a great people-watching perch. Guest rooms are a bit spartan—not much more than a bed—although the "superior" rooms are bigger and have bathtubs. ⊠ *Av. Bulnes 655* ☎ *61/411–158* 🖷 *61/411–943* ⊕ *www. chileanpatagonia.com/florence* 🛏 *18 rooms* 🖴 *Café, in-room safes, Internet, laundry service* 🞔 *AE, MC, V* ⋔ *CP.*

★ **¢** ⊞ **Concepto Indigo.** Rooms in this restored old home have amazing views down the Canal Señoret, stretching as far as the Mt. Balmaceda glacier and the Paine Grande. Ask for one of the corner rooms, which have windows along two walls. The walls are sponge-painted in bright reds, yellows, and blues, and hung with local art. The quirky and friendly café downstairs has an eclectic collection of artifacts. English is spoken well, as exhibited in the nightly slide shows about Torres del Paine park. ⊠ *Ladrilleros 105* ☎ *61/413–609* 🖷 *61/410–169* ⊕ *www. conceptoindigo.com* 🛏 *7 rooms* 🖴 *Restaurant, laundry service, Internet, travel services; no room phones, no room TVs* 🞔 *MC, V* ⊗ *Closed in winter; months vary.*

$ ⊞ **Hostal Francis Drake.** Toss a coin in the wishing well out front before you enter this half-timbered house near the center of town. The proprietor is a delightful European lady who dotes on her guests and carefully maintains cleanliness. Rooms are small and basic. The beds are not the world's most comfortable. ⊠ *Philippi 383* ☎☎ *61/411–553 or 61/ 410–852* ⊕ *www.chileaustral.com/francisdrake* 🛏 *12 rooms* 🖴 *Café, cable TV, lounge, Internet; no a/c* 🞔 *DC, MC, V* ⋔ *CP.*

Parque Nacional Torres del Paine

⑫ *125 km (75 mi) northwest of Puerto Natales.*

Fodor'sChoice
★
Some 12 million years ago, lava flows pushed up through the thick sedimentary crust that covered the southwestern coast of South America, cooling to form a granite mass. Glaciers then swept through the region, grinding away all but the ash-gray spires—nicknamed *torres* or "towers"—that rise over the landscape of one of the world's most beautiful natural phenomena, now the Parque Nacional Torres del Paine (established in 1959). Snow formations dazzle along every turn of road, and the sunset views are spectacular.

Among the 2,420-square-km (934-square-mi) park's most beautiful attractions are its lakes of turquoise, aquamarine, and emerald green waters. (Don't bother looking for the torres themselves from within the confines of the park—you can see them only from the outside on a clear day; in any case, it is the glaciers, mountain lakes, and snowcapped peaks—especially at sunset—that are the true highlights here.)

Another draw is the park's unusual wildlife. Creatures like the guanaco (a woollier version of the llama) and the *ñandú* (resembling a small ostrich) abound. They are used to visitors, and don't seem to be bothered by the proximity of automobile traffic and the snapping of cameras. Predators like the gray fox make less-frequent appearances. You may also spot

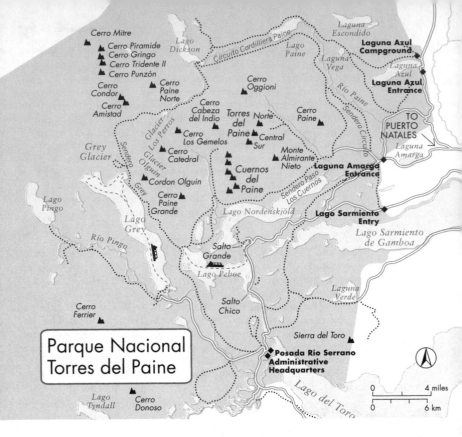

Parque Nacional
Torres del Paine

the dramatic aerobatics of falcons and the graceful soaring of endangered condors. The beautiful puma, celebrated in a National Geographic video filmed here, is especially elusive, but sightings have grown more and more common. Pumas follow the guanaco herds and eat an estimated 40% of their young.

Although considerable walking is necessary to take full advantage of Parque Nacional Torres del Paine, you need not be a hard-core backpacker. Many people choose to hike the so-called **"W" route,** which takes four days, but others prefer to stay in one of the comfortable lodges and hit the trails for the morning or afternoon. **Glaciar Grey,** with its fragmented icebergs, makes a rewarding and easy hike; equally rewarding is the spectacular boat ride across the lake, past icebergs, and up to the glacier, which leaves from Hostería Lago Grey (⇨ *below*). Another great excursion is the 900-meter (3,000-foot) ascent to the sensational views from **Mirador Las Torres,** four hours one way from Hostería Las Torres (⇨ *below*). Even if you're not staying at the Hostería, you can arrange a morning drop-off there, and a late-afternoon pickup, so that you can see the Mirador while still keeping your base in Puerto Natales or elsewhere in the park; alternatively, you can drive yourself to the Hostería and park there for the day.

If you do the "W," you'll begin (or end, if you reverse the route) at Laguna Amarga and continue to Mirador Las Torres and Los Cuernos, then continue along a breathtaking path to Valle Frances and finally Lago Grey. An even more ambitious route is the "Circuito," which essentially leads around the entire park and takes up to a week. Along the way, some people sleep at the dozen or so more humble *refugios* (shelters) found along the trails, and still others in tents. Driving is another way to enjoy the park: most of the more than 100 km (62 mi) of roads leading to the most popular sites are safe and well maintained, though unpaved.

The vast majority of visitors come during the summer months, which means the trails can get congested. Early spring, when wildflowers add flashes of color to the meadows, is an ideal time to visit because the crowds have not yet arrived. The park is open all year, and trails are almost always accessible. Storms can hit without warning, however, so be prepared for sudden rain or snow. The sight of the Paine peaks in clear weather is stunning; if you have any flexibility in your itinerary, be sure to visit the park on the first clear day.

There are three entrances to the park: Laguna Amarga, Lago Sarmiento, and Laguna Azul. You are required to sign in when you arrive. *Guardaparques* (park rangers) staff six stations around the reserve; they request that you inform them when setting out on a hike. CONAF, the national forestry service, has an office at the northern end of Lago del Toro with a scale model of the park, and numerous exhibits (some in English) about the flora and fauna. ⊠ *CONAF station in southern section of the park past Hotel Explora* ☎ *61/691–931* ✉ *8,000 pesos* ☉ *Ranger station: Nov.–Feb., daily 8–8; Mar.–Oct., daily 8–12:30 and 2–6:30* ⊠ *Punta Arenas Branch, Av. Bulnes 0309* ☎ *61/238–581* ⊠ *Puerto Natales Branch, Av. Bernardo O'Higgins 584* ☎ *61/411–438.*

Where to Stay & Eat

$–$$ ✕🏠 **Posada Río Serrano.** A welcoming staff will show you a selection of rooms, including those with bunk beds and those with regular beds. Rooms are small, but clean, and have colorful bedspreads. A few actually have lake views. A warm and cheerful salon with a fireplace makes a nice place to relax. Don't expect pampering—besides camping, this is the cheapest dining and lodging in the park. The restaurant serves filling fish dishes *a lo pobre* (with fried eggs and french fries), as well as lamb; in summer there might be an outdoor asado. The inn also has a general store where you can find basic necessities such as batteries and cookies. ⊠ *Lago Toro* ☎ *61/412–911 for reservations (Puerto Natales)* ⊕ *www.baqueanozamora.com* 🛏 *14 rooms, 4 with bath* ⚂ *Restaurant, grocery, bar; no a/c, no room phones, no room TVs* ▤ *No credit cards* ⌑ *CP.*

$$$$ 🏠 **Hostería Lago Grey.** The panoramic view past the lake to the glacier beyond is worth the journey here, which doesn't change the fact that this older hotel is overpriced and not very attractive. Rooms seem cheaply built, but are comfortable and inexpensive, with small baths. There's a TV with a VCR in the lounge. The view—and it's one you're not likely to forget—can also be enjoyed through the picture windows in the dining room (breakfast is included; lunch costs about 10,000 pesos

per person, and dinner about 20,000 pesos per person with wine). The food is mediocre; though—simple sandwiches are your best bet. The hotel operates its own sightseeing vessel, the *Grey II*, for close-up tours to Glaciar Grey. ⊠ *Lago Grey* 🏨 *61/225–986* ⊕ *www.lagogrey.com* ➷ *30 rooms* ⚹ *Restaurant, boating, fishing, hiking, horseback riding, bar, lounge, laundry service; no room TVs* ▤ *AE, DC, MC, V* ⦿ *BP.*

$$$$ 🏨 **Hosteria Tyndall.** A boat ferries you from the end of the road the few minutes along the Serrano River to this wooden lodge. The simple rooms in the main building are small but cute, with attractive wood paneling. The lodge can be noisy, a problem solved by renting a log cottage (a great value for groups of four). There's also a much more basic refugio with dorm-style rooms that are very cheap. Owner Christian Bore is a wildlife enthusiast and bird-watcher; ask him for a tour of the grassy plain looking out toward the central cluster of snowy peaks. Or go fishing—the kitchen staff will cook your catch for free. The prix-fixe dinner costs 11,900 pesos. ⊠ *Ladrilleros 256, Lago Tyndall, Puerto Natales* 🏨 *61/413–139* ⊕ *www.hosteriatyndall.com* ➷ *24 rooms, 6 cottages* ⚹ *Restaurant, boating, fishing, hiking, horseback riding, lounge, laundry service; no room phones, no room TVs* ▤ *AE, DC, MC, V* ⦿ *CP.*

$$$$ 🏨 **Hotel Explora.** On the southeast corner of Lago Pehoé, this lodge is
Fodor'sChoice one of the most luxurious—and the most expensive—in Chile. Although
★ there may be some debate about the aesthetics of the hotel's low-slung minimalist exterior, the interior is impeccable: it's Scandinavian in style, with local woods used for ceilings, floors, and furniture. No expense has been spared—even the bed linens were imported from Spain. A dozen full-time guides (for a maximum of 60 guests) tailor all-inclusive park outings to guests' interests. A four-night minimum stay is required, for which you'll pay a minimum of US$3,120 (1,648,000 pesos) for two people, including airport transfers, three meals a day, drinks, and excursions. Rooms with better views go up to almost double that. Nonguests may also enjoy a pricey prix-fixe dinner at the restaurant. ⊠ *Lago Pehoé* ☎ *2/206–6060 in Santiago* 📠 *2/228–4655 in Santiago* ⊕ *www.explora.com* ➷ *26 rooms, 4 suites* ⚹ *Restaurant, indoor pool, gym, outdoor hot tub, massage, sauna, boating, hiking, horseback riding, piano bar, library, shop, babysitting, laundry service, Internet, business services, meeting rooms, airport shuttle; no room TVs* ▤ *AE, DC, MC, V* ⦿ *AI.*

$$$–$$$$ 🏨 **Hostería Las Torres.** This is one of the (relatively) less-expensive choices in the park, but it's still comfortable and the location makes it perfect if you want to day-hike to Mirador Torres, one of the park's highlights. Rooms are simple, clean, and comfortable. The Hostería also offers hostel-style rooms for a bargain-basement 25 pesos, but they come without sheets and towels. Hiking excursions can be arranged through the hotel. ⊠ *Lago Grey* 🏨 *61/710–050* ⊕ *www.lastorres.com* ➷ *57 rooms* ⚹ *Restaurant, spa, bar* ▤ *AE, MC, V.*

$$$–$$$$ 🏨 **Hosteria Pehoé.** Cross a 100-foot footbridge to get to this hotel on its own island in the middle of glistening Lake Pehoé, across from the beautiful Torres del Paine mountain peaks. Upon seeing the setting, nonguests are often tempted to cancel other reservations. Unfortunately, rooms at Pehoé—built in 1970 as the first hotel in the park—are dark, poorly furnished, and windowless, and they face an interior lawn. Management built a new wing (completed in early 2003) with newly obstructed views. However, it is a delight to walk over the footbridge and have a drink at the ski lodge–like bar, where the views are jaw-dropping. ⊠ *Lago Pehoé* ☎ *61/244–506* 🖷 *61/248–052* ⊕ *www.pehoe.com* ⇥ *25 rooms* ⚘ *Restaurant, café, bar, laundry service; no room phones, no room TVs* ▤ *AE, DC, MC, V* ⦿ *CP.*

El Calafate, Argentina & the Parque Nacional los Glaciares

⑬ *253 km (157 mi) east of Río Turbio on Chilean border via R40, 362 km (225 mi) east of Puerto Natales.*

Founded in 1927 as a frontier town, El Calafate is the base for excursions to Argentina's Parque Nacional los Glaciares (Glaciers National Park), which was created in 1937 as a showcase for one of South America's most spectacular sights, the Perito Moreno Glacier. It's quite accessible from Chile—just five hours by bus from Puerto Natales, via Río Gallegos, and including a brief delay for passport control at the border. In fact, the park itself is sometimes visited on a very long day trip from Natales, but it's far more enjoyable to include at least one or two nights in El Calafate.

Because of its location on the southern shore of Lago Argentino, the town enjoys a microclimate much milder than the rest of southern Patagonia. During the long summer days between December and February (when the sun sets around 10 PM), and during Easter vacation, thousands of visitors come to see the glaciers and fill the hotels and restaurants; you'll need to make reservations well in advance if you plan to travel here during those times. October, November, March, and April are less crowded, and lodging prices are less expensive. March through May can be rainy and cool, but also less windy and often quite pleasant. Winter goes from June to September; you really don't want to visit in June, July, or August.

To call El Calafate a boomtown would be to put it mildly. Between 2001 and 2005, the town's population exploded from 4,000 to 15,000, and it shows no signs of slowing down; at every turn you'll see new construction. As such, the downtown has a very new feel to it, although most buildings are constructed of wood, with a rustic aesthetic that seems to respect the majestic natural environment. As the paving of the road between El Calafate and the Perito Moreno Glacier nears completion, the visitors continue to flock in—whether luxury-package tourists bound for the legendary Hostería Los Notros, backpackers over from Chile's Parque Nacional Torres del Paine, or *porteños* (Buenos Aires residents) in town for a long weekend.

Daily flights from Buenos Aires, Ushuaia, and Río Gallegos, as well as direct flights from Bariloche, transport tourists in a few hours to El Calafate's 21st-century glass-and -steel airport—an island of modernity surrounded by the lonely expanse of Patagonia—with the promise of adventure and discovery in distant mountains and unseen glaciers. El Calafate is so popular that the flights are selling out weeks in advance, so don't plan on booking at the last minute.

Driving or busing from Puerto Natales, via Río Gallegos, takes about four hours across desolate plains, enlivened occasionally by the sight of a gaucho, his dogs, and a herd of sheep, as well as *ñandú* (rheas), shy llamalike guanacos, silver-gray foxes, and fleet-footed hares the size of small deer. **Esperanza** is the only gas, food, and bathroom stop halfway between the two towns.

Avenida del Libertador San Martín (known locally as Libertador or San Martín) is the main street, with tour offices, restaurants, and shops selling regional specialties, sportswear, camping and fishing equipment, souvenirs, and food. A staircase in the middle of San Martín ascends to Avenida Julio Roca, where you'll find the bus terminal and a very busy **Oficina de Turismo** (⊠ Av. Julio Roca 1004 ☏☏ +54 2902/491–090 ⊕ www.elcalafate.gov.ar) with a bulletin board listing available accommodations and campgrounds; you can also get brochures and maps, and there's a multilingual staff to help plan excursions. It's open daily 7 AM–10 PM. The **Parques Nacionales** (⊠ Av. del Libertador San Martín 1302 ☏ +54 2902/491–005), open weekdays 7–2, has information on the entire park, the glaciers, area history, hiking trails, and flora and fauna.

Where to Stay & Eat

$$$–$$$$ ✕ **Toma Wine Bar y Restó.** This hip restaurant represents the new, yuppie face of El Calafate, with creative preparations like *ojo de bife con calabazas confitadas* (rib eye with pumpkin confit), and *papas Toma* (french fries with melted cheese, smoked bacon, spring onion, and cream). Wine pairings are suggested with each entrée, and to finish, there's good ol' apple pie à la mode, and perhaps a glass of port-style Malamado, made from Malbec grapes. The atmosphere is cool, dark, and trendy, and the service deferential. ⊠ *Av. del Libertador San Martín 1359* ☏ *+54 2902/492–993* ⊟ *AE, MC, V* ⊙ *Closed Sun. No lunch.*

$–$$$ ✕ **Casimiro Biguá.** This restaurant and wine bar has a hipper-than-thou interior, which is a great place to enjoy such delectable delights as Patagonian lamb with *Calafate* sauce (made with a local wild berry). The *cordero al asador* (spit-roasted lamb) displayed in the window, though, is a bit of a traditional throwback. There's an outdoor garden in the back, and a great wine list. ⊠ *Av. del Libertador San Martín 963* ☏ *+54 2902/492–590* ⊟ *AE, DC, MC, V* ⊙ *Closed Sun. No lunch.*

★ $$ ✕ **Pura Vida.** Modernity merges with tradition at this hippieish, veggie-friendly restaurant a few blocks out of the center of El Calafate. It's a real treat to find such creative fare, funky decor, cool candles, and modern art in such a frontier town. The beef stew is charmingly served inside a *calabaza* (pumpkin); although it's excellently seasoned, the beef isn't particularly tender. Even if, technically speaking, the cooking isn't quite top-flight, Pura Vida is more than the sum of its parts, drawing in backpackers and older folks alike with an almost mystical allure. ⊠ *Av. del Libertador San Martín 1876* ☏ *+54 2902/493–356* ⊟ *AE, MC, V.*

$$ ✕ **Rick's Café.** It's *tenedor libre* (all you can eat) for 22 pesos at this immensely popular parrilla in a big yellow building on El Calafate's main street. It's a great value, and accordingly the place is packed full of locals and tourists day and night. The room is big and bustling, if not particularly interesting, and the spread includes lamb and *vacío* (flank

EL PARQUE NACIONAL LOS GLACIARES

THE HIELO CONTINENTAL *(Continental Ice Cap)* spreads its icy mantle from the Pacific Ocean across Chile and the Andes into Argentina, covering an area of 21,700 square km (8,400 square mi). Approximately 1.5 million acres of it are contained within the **Parque Nacional los Glaciares,** a UNESCO World Heritage site. Extending along the Chilean border for 350 km (217 mi), the park is 40% covered with ice fields that branch off into 47 major glaciers. These glaciers feed two lakes: the 15,000-year-old Lago Argentino *(Argentine Lake, the largest body of water in Argentina and the third largest in South America)* in the southern end of the park, where you'll see the occasional group of flamingos; and Lago Viedma *(Lake Viedma)* at the northern end near Cerro Fitz Roy, which rises 3,395 meters (11,138 feet). Plan on a minimum of two to three days to see the glaciers and enjoy the town—more if you plan to visit El Chaltén or any of the other lakes. Entrance to the park costs 30 pesos.

One of the few glaciers in the world still growing after 3,000 years, the **Glaciar Perito Moreno** lies 80 km (50 mi) away on R11, which is paved from El Calafate to the national park entrance. From there, a road that's partly paved winds through hills and forests of lenga and ñire trees, until suddenly, the startling sight of the glacier comes into full view. Descending like a long white tongue through distant mountains, it ends abruptly in a translucent blue wall 3 km (2 mi) wide and 50 meters (165 feet) high at the edge of frosty green Lago Argentino.

Although it's possible to rent a car and go on your own, virtually everyone visits the park on day-trip tours that are booked in El Calafate (unless, that is, you're staying in Los Notros, the only hotel inside the park itself). The most basic of these tours just take you to see the glacier up close from a viewing area composed of a series of platforms that are wrapped around the point of the Península de Magallanes. The viewing area, which might ultimately provide the most impressive view of the glacier, allows you to wander back and forth, looking across the Canal de los Tempanos *(Iceberg Channel).* Here you listen and wait for nature's number one ice show—first, a cracking sound, followed by tons of ice breaking away and falling with a thunderous crash into the lake. As the glacier creeps across this narrow channel and meets the land on the other side, an ice dam sometimes builds up between the arm-shape inlet of Brazo Rico on the left and the rest of the lake on the right. As the pressure on the dam increases, everyone waits for the day it will rupture again. The last time was in March 2004, when the whole thing collapsed in a series of explosions that lasted hours and could be heard in El Calafate.

Glaciar Upsala, the largest glacier in South America, is 60 km (37 mi) long and 10 km (6 mi) wide, and accessible only by boat. Daily cruises depart from Puerto Banderas (40 km [25 mi] west of El Calafate via R11) for the 2½-hour trip. While dodging floating icebergs (tempanos), some as large as small islands, the boats maneuver as close as they dare to the wall of ice rising from the aqua-green water of Lago Argentino. The seven glaciers that feed the lake deposit their debris into the runoff, causing the water to cloud with minerals ground to fine powder by the glacier's moraine (the accumulation of earth and stones left behind in the glacier's path). Condors and black-chested buzzard eagles build their nests in the rocky cliffs above the lake. When the boat stops for lunch at Onelli Bay, don't miss the walk behind the restaurant into a wild landscape of small glaciers and milky rivers carrying chunks of ice from four glaciers into Lago Onelli.

— *Robin Goldstein*

steak). ⊠ *Av. del Libertador San Martín 1091* ☎ *+54 2902/492–148* ⊟ *MC, V.*

$–$$ ✕ **La Lechuza.** This cozy, bustling local place is known for having some of the best pizza in town. The brick-oven-baked, thin-crust pies have an Italian-style taste and texture (unlike most Chilean pizza, which has a thick crust and very little tomato). ⊠ *Av. del Libertador San Martín at 1 de Mayo* ☎ *+54 2902/491–610* ⊟ *No credit cards* ☺ *No lunch Sun.*

$–$$ ✕ **La Tablita.** It's a couple of extra blocks away from downtown, across
Fodor'sChoice a little white bridge, but this bustling parrilla is where all the locals go
★ for a special night out. You can watch your food as it's prepared: Patagonian lamb and beef ribs are cooked gaucho-style on an asador; the grilled-meat choices also include steaks, chorizo, and excellent *morcilla* (blood sausage). The enormous *parrillada* for two is an excellent way to sample it all, and the wine list is well priced and well chosen. ⊠ *Coronel Rosales 28* ☎ *+54 2902/491–065* ⊟ *AE, DC, MC, V* ☺ *No lunch Mon.–Thurs. in June and July.*

$$$$ ✕⌂ **Hostería los Notros.** The weathered wood buildings of this inn cling
Fodor'sChoice to the mountainside that overlooks the Perito Moreno Glacier as it de-
★ scends into Lago Argentino. Although it's 73 km (45 mi) west of El Calafate, it could just as well be at the end of the world. With the glacier framed in the windows of the rooms (some of which have fireplaces), inside is as nice as out. A path, through the garden and over a bridge spanning a canyon with a waterfall, connects rooms to the main lodge. Appetizers and wine are served in full view of sunset (or moonrise) over the glacier, followed by an absolutely spectacular menu that spotlights game, including delicious venison and creative preparations of Argentine classics. Herbs used in the recipes come from the garden. Note that a two-night minimum stay is required; prices include all meals, cocktails, park entry, and a glacier excursion. If you don't feel like spending that much, you can always come just for a meal. ⊠ *Reservations in Buenos Aires: Arenales 1457, 7th fl., 1961* ☎ *+54 11/4814–3934 in Buenos Aires, +54 2902/ 499–510 in El Calafate* 🖷 *+54 11/4815–7645 in Buenos Aires, +54 2902/499–511 in El Calafate* ⊕ *www.losnotros.com* ⇥ *32 rooms* ⌂ *Restaurant, fishing, hiking, horseback riding, bar, recreation room, playground, Internet, airport shuttle, travel services; no room phones, no room TVs* ⊟ *AE, DC, MC, V* ☺ *Closed June–mid-Sept.* ⦿ *AI.*

$$$ ⌂ **Hotel Kau-Yatun.** Books, games, and magazines clutter the tables in the large living room of this former ranch house; guests congregate at the bar or in front of the fireplace. Rooms vary in size, shape, and decor, with all following a casual ranch theme. Country cuisine (meat, pasta, and vegetables) is served in the dining room, and wild-game dishes are available at La Brida restaurant. On weekends, steaks and chorizo sizzle on a large open grill in the *quincho* (combination kitchen, grill, and dining room), while lamb or beef cooks gaucho-style on an asador. ⊠ *25 de Mayo* ☎ *+54 2902/491–059* 🖷 *+54 2902/491–260* ✉ *kauyatun@cotecal.com.ar* ⇥ *45 rooms* ⌂ *Restaurant, horseback riding, bar, Internet, airport shuttle* ⊟ *AE, MC, V* ☺ *Closed May–Sept.* ⦿ *CP.*

$$$ ⌂ **Kosten Aike.** The stone-and-brick accents and wood balconies outside, and the slate floors, wood-beamed ceilings, and unfailing attention to detail inside, will please aficionados of Andean Patagonian architecture. Tehuelche (an indigenous local tribe) symbols and designs are used in everything from the curtains to the room plaques. A lobby bar and living room with fireplace, card tables, magazines, and a large TV is conducive to lounging about indoors anytime of day. ⊠ *Gobernador Moyano at 25 de Mayo* ☎ *+54 2902/492–424, +54 11/4811–1314 in Buenos Aires* 🖷 *+54 2902/491–538* ⊕ *www.kostenaike.com.ar* ⇒ *58 rooms, 2 suites* ⚭ *Restaurant, gym, bar, shop, Internet, business services, meeting room, car rental* ▤ *AE, DC, MC, V* ⊗ *Closed May–Sept.*

$$$ ⌱ **Posada los Alamos.** Surrounded by tall, leafy alamo trees and constructed of brick and dark *quebracho* (ironwood), this attractive country-manor house uses rich woods, leather, and handwoven fabrics to produce conversation-friendly furniture groupings in the large lobby. Plush comforters and fresh flowers in the rooms, and a staff ready with helpful suggestions, make this a top-notch hotel. Lovingly tended gardens surround the building and line a walkway through the woods to the restaurant and the shore of Lago Argentino. ⊠ *Gobernador Moyano 1355, at Bustillo* ☎ *+54 2902/491–144* 🖷 *+54 2902/491–186* ⊕ *www.posadalosalamos.com* ⇒ *140 rooms, 4 suites* ⚭ *Restaurant, 3-hole golf course, tennis court, 2 bars, travel services* ▤ *AE, MC, V* ⧦ *CP.*

$$–$$$ ⌱ **Michelangelo.** Bright red and yellow native flowers line the front of this low log-and-stucco building, with its distinctive A-frames extending over rooms, restaurant, and reception area. A fine collection of local photographs is displayed on the walls next to a sunken lobby, where easy chairs and a banquette surround the fireplace. Motel-style rooms have individual heaters, and there's an excellent restaurant on-site. ⊠ *Gobernador Moyano 1020* ☎ *+54 2902/491–045* 🖷 *+54 2902/491–058* ✍ *michelangelohotel@cotecal.com.ar* ⇒ *20 rooms* ⚭ *Restaurant, café, cable TV* ▤ *AE, MC, V* ⊗ *Closed June* ⧦ *CP.*

¢–$ ⌱ **América del Sur.** The only downside to this new hostel, which caters largely to young backpackers, is its location (a 10-minute uphill walk from downtown), but beautiful views of the lake and mountains, and a free shuttle service compensate for the distance. Otherwise, the place is simple but spectacular—sparklingly clean and legendarily friendly. Some rooms have two beds, others have four; the four-person rooms are a particularly good deal. ⊠ *Puerto Deseado* ☎ *+54 2902/493–525* ⊕ *www.americahostel.com.ar* ⇒ *4 rooms* ⚭ *Restaurant, bar, Internet, travel services; no room TVs* ▤ *No credit cards.*

¢–$ ⌱ **Calafate Hostel.** This lodgelike structure caters to every demographic, with hostel-style accommodations for backpackers in one building, and well-kept private rooms with private baths—and, believe it or not, Internet-connected desktop computers in every room—in a separate structure next door. Both buildings share the bar-lounge and breakfast room. The bar is something of a hangout; this might not be the most upscale accommodation in town, but it's very comfortable, and it's right downtown. ⊠ *Gobernador Moyano 1226* ☎ *+54 2902/492–450* ⊕ *www.calafatehostels.com* ⚭ *Kitchen, Internet, travel services* ▤ *AE, MC, V.*

Sports & the Outdoors

BOAT RIDES There are two extremely popular scenic boat rides in the Parque Nacional los Glaciares. The first is the hour-long **Safari Náutico**, in which your boat cruises just a few feet away from the face of the Glaciar Perito Moreno. There's also the full-day **Upsala Glacier Tour,** in which you navigate through a more extensive selection of glaciers, including Upsala (the biggest in South America) and Onelli, as well as several lakes within the park that are inaccessible by land. The Safari Náutico is offered through several local tour companies, including **René Fernández Campbell** (⊠ Av. del Libertador San Martín 867, El Calafate ☎ +54 2902/491–155). It costs 60 pesos, which includes transportation from El Calafate, making it a half-day excursion, or 25 pesos from in front of the glacier. The full-day Upsala trip, including lunch, costs around 175 pesos. The tours are run by **Upsala Explorer** (⊠ 9 de Julio 69, El Calafate ☎ +54 2902/491–034 📠 +54 2902/491–292 ⊕ www.upsalaexplorer.com.ar), among other local tour operators.

ICE TREKKING   A two-hour minitrek on the Perito Moreno Glacier involves transfer from
★   El Calafate to Brazo Rico by bus and a short lake crossing to a dock and refugio, where you set off with a guide, put crampons over your shoes, and literally walk right across a stable portion of the glacier, scaling ridges of ice and ducking through bright blue ice tunnels. It is one of the most unique experiences in Argentina. The entire outing lasts about five hours, culminating with whiskey over 1,000-year-old ice cubes. Hotels generally arrange minitreks through **Hielo y Aventura** (⊠ Av. del Libertador San Martín 935 ☎ +54 2902/492–205 📠 +54 2902/491–053 ⊕ www.hieloyaventura.com), which also organizes much longer, more difficult trips of eight hours to a week to other glaciers; you can also arrange the trek directly through their office in downtown El Calafate. Minitrekking runs about 250 pesos for the day.

Parque Nacional Bernardo O'Higgins

⑭ *Southwest of Parque Nacional Torres del Paine.*

Bordering the Parque Nacional Torres del Paine on the southwest, Parque Nacional Bernardo O'Higgins is composed primarily of the southern tip of the vast Campo de Hielo Sur (Southern Ice Field). As it is inaccessible by land, the only way to visit the park is to take a boat up the Seno Última Esperanza. The Puerto Natales tour company Turismo 21 de Mayo (⇨ By Boat *in* Patagonia & Tierra del Fuego Essentials) operates two boats here, the *21 de Mayo* and the *Alberto de Agostini.* On your way to the park you approach a cormorant colony with nests clinging to sheer cliff walls, venture to a glacier at the foot of Mt. Balmaceda, and finally dock at Puerto Toro for a 1-km (½-mi) hike to the foot of the Serrano Glacier. On the trip back to Puerto Natales the crew treats you to a pisco sour served over a chunk of glacier ice. As with many full-day tours, you must bring your own lunch. Warm clothing, including gloves, is recommended year-round, particularly if there's even the slightest breeze.

TIERRA DEL FUEGO

Tierra del Fuego, a vaguely triangular island separated from the southernmost tip of South America by the twists and bends of the Estrecho de Magallanes, is indeed a world unto itself. The vast plains on its northern reaches are dotted with trees bent low by the savage winds that frequently lash the coast. The mountains that rise in the south are equally forbidding, traversed by huge glaciers slowly making their way to the sea.

The first European to set foot on this island was Spanish explorer Hernando de Magallanes, who sailed here in 1520. The smoke that he saw coming from the fires lighted by the native peoples prompted him to call it Tierra del Humo (Land of Smoke). King Charles V of Spain, disliking that name, rechristened it Tierra del Fuego, or Land of Fire.

Tierra del Fuego is split in half. The island's northernmost tip, well within Chilean territory, is its closest point to the continent. The only town of any size here is Porvenir. Its southern extremity, part of Argentina, points out into the Atlantic toward the Falkland Islands. Here is Ushuaia, on the shores of the Canal Beagle. Farther south is Cape Horn, the southernmost bit of land before you reach Antarctica.

Porvenir

⑮ *30 km (18 mi) by boat from Punta Arenas.*

A short trip eastward across the Estrecho de Magallanes, Porvenir is the principal town on Chile's half of Tierra del Fuego. It's not much to speak of, as its population is just more than 6,000. Located at the eastern end of narrow Bahia Porvenir, it was born during the gold rush of the 1880s. After the boom went bust, it continued to be an important port for the burgeoning cattle and sheep industries.

Porvenir's small **Museo Provincial Fernando Cordero Rusque** includes collections of memorabilia about subjects as eclectic as early Chilean filmmaking and the culture of the indigenous peoples. There are interesting photos of the gold rush and the first sheep ranches. The museum is the only sight of particular interest in this otherwise quiet port of entry to Tierra del Fuego. ⌧ *Plaza de Armas* ☏ *No phone* ⌦ *Free* ☺ *Weekdays 9–5, weekends 11–5.*

Ushuaia, Argentina

⑯ *41 km (25 mi) east of Puerto Williams.*

At 55 degrees latitude south, Ushuaia is the capital and tourism base for Argentine Tierra del Fuego, and bigger than any town on the Chilean side of the island. It was claimed by Argentina in 1902 with the opening of a penal colony, establishing the permanent settlement of its most southern territories and, by implication, everything in between.

At first, only political prisoners were sent to Ushuaia. Later, however, fearful of losing Tierra del Fuego to its rivals, the Argentine state sent increased numbers of more dangerous criminals. When the prison, El Presidio, closed in 1947, Ushuaia had a population of about 3,000, made up mainly of former inmates and prison staff. Another population boom occurred after Argentina's 1978 industrial incentives law, which attracted electronics manufacturers like Philco and Grundig to Ushuaia.

Today, the 50,000 residents of Ushuaia are hitching their star to tourism; the city rightly, if perhaps too loudly, promotes itself as the southernmost city in the world. (Chile's Puerto Williams, a few miles south on the Chilean side of the Beagle Channel, is but a tiny town.) Ushuaia still feels a bit like a frontier boomtown, with the heart of a rugged, weather-beaten fishing village and the frayed edges of a city that quadrupled in size in the 1970s and '80s. Unpaved portions of R3, the last stretch of the Pan-American Highway, which connects Alaska to Tierra del Fuego, are finally, albeit slowly, being paved. The summer months—December to March—draw 120,000 visitors, and the city is trying to extend those visits with events like March's Marathon at the End of the World.

Above the city, the last mountains of the Andean Cordillera rise, and just south and west of Ushuaia they finally vanish into the often stormy sea. Snow whitens the peaks well into summer. Nature is the principal attraction here, with trekking, fishing, horseback riding, and sailing among the most rewarding activities, especially in the Parque Nacional Tierra del Fuego (Tierra del Fuego National Park).

The **tourist office** (⊠ Av. San Martín 674 ☎ +54 2901/432–000 or 0800/ 333–1476 ⊕ www.e-ushuaia.com) is a great resource for information on the town's and Tierra del Fuego's attractions. It's open weekdays 8 AM–10 PM, weekends 9–8. Several people on the cheerful staff speak English. Although the office also has a stand (☎ +54 2901/437–666) at the airport that greets all flights, it's worth a stop into the main office to plan a stay in the area.

The **Antigua Casa Beben** (Old Beben House) is one of Ushuaia's original houses, and long served as the city's social center. Built between 1911 and 1913, Fortunato Beben is said to have ordered the house through a Swiss catalog. In the 1980s the Beben family donated the house to the city to avoid demolition. It was moved to its current location along the coast and restored, and is now a cultural center with art exhibits. ⊠ *Maipú at Pluschow* ☎ *No phone* 🎫 *Free* ⊙ *Tues.–Fri. 10–8, weekends 4–8.*

Rainy days are a reality in Ushuaia, but two museums give you an avenue for urban exploration and a glimpse into Tierra del Fuego's fascinating past. Part of the original penal colony, the Presidio building was built to hold political prisoners, street orphans, and a variety of other **Fodor'sChoice** social undesirables from the north. Today it holds the **Museo Marítimo** ★ (Maritime Museum), within Ushuaia's naval base, which has exhibits on the town's extinct indigenous population, Tierra del Fuego's navigational past, Antarctic explorations, and life and times in an Argentine penitentiary. You can enter cell blocks and read the stories of the prisoners who lived in them (and gape at the eerie mannequins that recreate their presence). Well-presented tours (in Spanish only) are conducted at 3:30 daily. ⊠ *Gobernador Paz at Yaganes* ☎ *+54 2901/437– 481* 🎫 *15 pesos* ⊙ *Daily 10–8.*

At the **Museo del Fin del Mundo** (End of the World Museum), you can see a large stuffed condor, as well as other native birds, indigenous artifacts, maritime instruments, and such seafaring-related objects as an impressive mermaid figurehead taken from the bowsprit of a galleon. There are also photographs and histories of El Presidio's original inmates, such as Simon Radowitzky, a Russian immigrant anarchist who received a life sentence for killing an Argentine police colonel. The museum is in the 1905 residence of a Fuegonian governor. The home was later converted into a bank, and some of the exhibits are showcased in the former vault. ⊠ *Maipú 173 at Rivadavía* ☎ *+54 2901/421–863* ⌸ *5 pesos* ⊙ *Oct.–Mar., daily 10–8; Apr.–Sept., daily noon–7.*

The **Tren del Fin del Mundo** or End of the World Train, takes you to Estación Ande, inside the Parque Nacional Tierra del Fuego, 12 km (7 mi) away to the east. The train ride, which lasts 50 minutes each way, is a simulation of the trip on which El Presidio prisoners were taken into the forest to chop wood; but unlike them, you'll also get a good presentation of Ushuaia's history (in Spanish and English). The train departs daily at 9:30 AM, noon, and 3 PM in summer, and just once a day, at 10 AM, in winter, from a stop near the national park entrance. If you have a rental car, you'll want to do the round-trip, but if not, one common way to do the trip is to hire a *remis* (car service) that will drop you at the station for a one-way train ride, pick you up at the other end, and then drive you around the Parque Nacional for two or three hours of sightseeing (which is more scenic than the train ride itself). ⊠ *Ruta 3, Km 3042* ☎ *+54 2901/431–600* ⌸ *+54 2901/437–696* ⊕ *www.trendelfindelmundo.com.ar* ⌸ *95 pesos 1st-class ticket, 50 pesos tourist-class ticket, 20 pesos national park entrance fee (no park fee in winter).*

Tour operators run trips along the **Canal Beagle,** on which you can get a startling close-up view of all kinds of sea mammals and birds on **Isla de los Lobos, Isla de los Pájaros,** and near **Les Eclaireurs Lighthouse.** There are catamarans that make three-hour trips, generally leaving from the Tourist Pier at 3 PM, and motorboats and sailboats that leave twice a day, once at 9:30 AM and once at 3 PM (all of these weather allowing; few trips go in winter). Prices range from 60 pesos to 140 pesos; some include hikes on the islands. Check with the tourist office for the latest details; you can also book through any of the local travel agencies.

One good excursion in the area is to **Lago Escondido** (Hidden Lake) and **Lago Fagnano** (Fagnano Lake). The Pan-American Highway out of Ushuaia goes through deciduous beech-wood forest and past beavers' dams, peat bogs, and glaciers. The lakes have campsites and fishing and are good spots for a picnic or a hike. This can be done on your own or as a seven-hour trip, including lunch, booked through the local travel agencies (75 pesos without lunch, 95 pesos with lunch). One recommended operator, with a comfortable bus with a bilingual guide and lunch at Las Cotorras, is **All Patagonia** (⊠ Juana Fadul 26 ☎ +54 2901/433–622 or +54 2901/430–725 ⌸ +54 2901/433–622 or +54 2901/1556–5758).

A rougher, more unconventional tour of the lake area goes to **Monte Olivia,** the tallest mountain along the Canal Beagle, rising 1,360 meters (4,455 feet) above sea level. You also pass the **Cerros Cinco Hermanos,** or Five Brothers Mountains, and go through the **Garibaldi Pass,** which begins at the Rancho Hambre, climbs into the mountain range, and ends with a spectacular view of Lago Escondido. From here you continue on to Lago Fagnano through the countryside, past sawmills and lumberyards. To do this tour in a four-wheel-drive truck with an excellent bilingual guide, contact **Canal Fun** (⊠ Rivadavía 82 ☎ +54 2901/ 437–395); you'll drive *through* Lago Fagnano (at a point about 1 meter [3 feet] deep) to a secluded cabin on the shore and have a delicious asado, complete with wine and dessert.

If you've never butted heads with a glacier, and especially if you won't be covering El Calafate on your trip, then you should check out **Glaciar Martial,** in the mountain range just above Ushuaia. Named after Frenchman Luís F. Martial, a 19th-century scientist who wandered this way aboard the warship *Romanche* to observe the passing of planet Venus, the glacier is reached via a panoramic *aerosilla* (ski lift). Take the Camino al Glaciar (Glacier Road) 7 km (4½ mi) out of town until it ends. This route is also served by the local tour companies, including **Transportes Kaupen** (⇨ By Bus *in* Patagonia & Tierra del Fuego Essentials). Even if you don't plan to hike to see the glacier, it's a great pleasure to ride the 15-minute lift, which is open daily 10–5, weather allowing (it's often closed mid-May–August) and costs 10 pesos round-trip. If you're afraid of heights, you can instead enjoy a small nature trail here, and a teahouse. You can return on the lift, or continue on to the beginning of a 1-km (½-mi) trail that winds its way over lichen and shale straight up the mountain. After a strenuous 90-minute hike, you can cool your heels in one of the many gurgling, icy rivulets that cascade down water-worn shale slopes, or picnic while you wait for sunset (you can walk all the way down if you want to wait until after the aerosilla closes). When the sun drops behind the glacier's jagged crown of peaks, brilliant rays beam over the mountain's crest, spilling a halo of gold-flecked light on the glacier, valley, and channel below. Moments like these are why this land is so magical. Note that temperatures drop dramatically after sunset, so come prepared with warm clothing.

★ The pristine **Parque Nacional Tierra del Fuego,** 21 km (13 mi) west of Ushuaia, offers a chance to wander through peat bogs; stumble upon hidden lakes; trek through native *canelo, lenga,* and wild-cherry forests; and experience the wonders of Tierra del Fuego's rich flora and fauna. Everywhere, too, you'll see *castoreros* (beaver dams) and lodges. Fifty beaver couples were first brought in from Canada in 1948 so that they could breed and create a fur industry. In the years since, however, the beaver population has grown to more than 50,000 and now represents a major threat to the forests, as the dams flood the roots of the trees; you can see their effects on the gnawed-down trees everywhere. Believe it or not, the government now pays hunters a bounty of 30 pesos for each beaver they kill (they need to show a tail and head as proof).

Visits to the park, which is tucked up against the Chilean border, are commonly arranged through tour companies. Trips range from bus tours to horseback riding to more adventurous excursions, such as canoe trips across Lapataia Bay. Another way to get to the park is to take the Tren del Fin del Mundo (⇨ *above*). **Transportes Kaupen** (☎ +54 2901/434–

015), one of several private bus companies, has buses that travel through the park, making several stops within it; you can get off the bus, explore the park, and then wait for the next bus to come by or trek to the next stop (the service operates only in summer). Yet one more option is to drive to the park on R3 (take it until it ends and you see the famous sign indicating the end of the Pan-American Highway, which starts 17,848 km [11,090 mi] away in Alaska, and ends here). If you don't have a car, you can also hire a private remis to spend a few hours driving you through the park, including the Pan-American terminus, and perhaps also combining the excursion with the Tren del Fin del Mundo. Trail and camping information is available at the park-entrance ranger station or at the Ushuaia tourist office. At the entrance to the park is a gleaming new restaurant and teahouse set amid the hills, **Patagonia Mia** (✉ Ruta 3, Entrada Parque Nacional ☎ +54 2901/1560–2757 🖷 +54 2901/430–707 ⊕ www.patagoniamia.com); it's a great place to stop for tea or coffee, or a full meal of roast lamb or Fuegian seafood.

A nice excursion in the park is by boat from lovely **Bahía Ensenada** to **Isla Redonda** (Round Island), a wildlife refuge where you can follow a footpath to the western side and see a wonderful view of the Canal Beagle. This is included on some of the day tours; it's harder to arrange on your own, but you can contact the tourist office to try. While on Isla Redonda you can send a postcard and get your passport stamped at the world's southernmost post office. You can also see the Ensenada bay and island (from afar) from a point on the shore that is reachable by car. Other highlights of the park include the spectacular mountain-ringed lake, **Lago Roca,** as well as **Laguna Verde,** a lagoon whose green color comes from algae at its bottom. Much of the park is closed from roughly June through September, when the descent to Bahía Ensenada is blocked by up to 2 meters (6 feet) of snow. Even in May and October, chains for your car are a good idea. Tours to the park are run by **All Patagonia** (✉ Juana Fadul 26 ☎ +54 2901/433–622 or +54 2901/430–725 🖷 +54 2901/430–707).

Where to Stay & Eat

Dotting the perimeter of the park are five free campgrounds, none of which has much more than a spot to pitch a tent and a fire pit. Call the **park office** (☎ +54 2901/421–315) or consult the ranger station at the park entrance for more information. **Camping Lago Roca** (✉ South on R3 for 20 km [12 mi] ☎ No phone), within the park, charges 8 pesos per person per day and has bathrooms, hot showers, and a small market. Of all the campgrounds, **La Pista del Andino** (✉ Av. Alem 2873 ☎ +54 2901/435–890) is the only one within the city limits. Outside town, **Camping Río Pipo** (☎ +54 2901/435–796) is the closest to Ushuaia (it's 18 km [11 mi] away).

Choosing a place to stay depends in part on whether you want to spend the night in town or 5 km (3 mi) uphill. Las Hayas Resort, Cumbres de Martial, and Los Yámanas have stunning views, but require a taxi ride to reach Ushuaia.

$$–$$$$ ✕ **Chez Manu.** *Herbes de Provence* in the greeting room tip French
Fodor'sChoice owner-chef Manu Herbin's hand: he uses local seafood with a French
★ touch to create some of Ushuaia's most memorable meals. Perched a
couple of miles above town, across the street from the Hotel Glaciar,
the expensive, glass-front restaurant has grand views of the Canal Bea-
gle. The rest of the restaurant is understated, with an aquarium in the
center of the dining room, a kind of throne to the king crab. The good
wine list includes Patagonian selections. Don't miss the local trout in
white wine sauce, served with buttery rice cooked in fish stock. The cen-
tolla (king crab) au gratin is also a standout. ⊠ *Camino Luís Martial
2135* ☎ *+54 2901/432–253* ▤ *AE, MC, V* ⊘ *Closed Mon.*

$–$$$$ ✕ **La Estancia.** Set in a pleasant wooden A-frame dining room, this is one
of the classiest of the good-value *tenedor libre* (all-you-can-eat) paril-
las on the main strip—nobody here orders à la carte. Skip the Italian
buffet and fill up instead on the mouthwatering spit-roasted Patagonian
lamb, grilled meats, and delicious *morcilla* (blood sausage). It's all you
can eat for 21 pesos. Sit by the glass wall to see the *parrillero* artfully
coordinate the flames and spits. ⊠ *Av. San Martín 247* ☎ *+54 2901/
1556–8587* ▤ *AE, DC, MC, V.*

$–$$$$ ✕ **Tía Elvira.** On the street that runs right along the Beagle Channel, this
is an excellent place to sample the local catch. Garlicky shellfish appe-
tizers and centolla are delicious, and even more memorable is the dreamy,
meltingly tender *merluza negra* (black sea bass). The room is decked out
with nautical knickknacks that are maybe a bit tacky for the fairly high
price point; the service, however, is friendly and familial. ⊠ *Maipú 349*
☎ *+54 2901/424–725* ▤ *AE, DC, MC, V* ⊘ *Closed July.*

★ **$–$$$** ✕ **Volver.** A giant plastic king crab sign beckons you into this red tin restau-
rant, which provides some major relief from Avenida del Libertador San
Martín's row of all-you-can-eat parrillas. The name means "return" and
it's the kind of place that calls for repeat visits. Newspapers from the
1930s line the walls in this century-old home; informal table settings
have place mats depicting old London landmarks; and fishing nets hang
from the ceiling, along with hams, a disco ball, tricycles, and antique
lamps. The culinary highlight is, of course, centolla, which comes served
with a choice of five different sauces. ⊠ *Maipú 37* ☎ *+54 2901/423–
977* ▤ *AE, DC, MC, V* ⊘ *No lunch in winter.*

$$$$ ▦ **Cumbres de Martial.** This charming wood complex, painted fire-engine red, is high above Ushuaia at the foot of the ski lift that leads to
the Martial Glacier. Depending on your take, the hostería can seem
desolate and removed from town, or a peaceful sanctuary close to glacier
hiking. Each spacious room has an extremely comfortable bed and a
small wooden deck with terrific views down to the Beagle Channel.
The cabanas are beautiful self-contained log cabins. A teahouse and
a small nature trail beside the Martial River are also here. There is,
however, no complimentary shuttle service to town, so you'll need to
take a (cheap) taxi to access Ushuaia. ⊠ *Camino Luís Martial 3560*
☎ *+54 2901/424–799* ⊕ *www.cumbresdelmartial.com.ar* ⇗ *6
rooms, 4 cabins* ⌂ *Restaurant, tea shop, in-room safes, bar, lounge,
laundry service, airport shuttle* ▤ *AE, DC, MC, V* ⊘ *Closed Apr. and
May* ⏹ *BP.*

$$$$ ⌂ **Hotel y Resort Las Hayas.** Las Hayas is in the wooded foothills of the
Fodor'sChoice Andes, overlooking the town and channel below. Ask for a *canal* view.
★ Rooms are all decorated differently, and feature Portuguese linen, solid
oak furnishings, and fabric-padded walls. A suspended glass bridge
connects the hotel to a spectacular health spa, which includes a heated
pool and even a squash court. The delicious restaurant prepares an excellent version of *mollejas de cordero* (lamb sweetbreads) with scallops.
Frequent shuttle buses take you into town. ⊠ *1650 Camino Luís Martial, Km 3* ☎ *+54 2901/430–710, 11/4393–4750 in Buenos Aires* ⊟ *+54
2901/430–710 or +54 2901/430–719* ⊕ *www.lashayashotel.com* ↩ *85
rooms, 7 suites* ⌂ *Restaurant, coffee shop, in-room safes, golf privileges,
indoor pool, health club, hot tub, massage, sauna, squash, bar, laundry
service, convention center, meeting rooms, airport shuttle, travel services*
⊟ *AE, DC, MC, V* ⋈ *CP.*

$$$ ⌂ **Hotel Los Yámanas.** This gleaming but cozy new hotel 4 km (2½) from
the center of town, named after a local indigenous tribe, blends a rus-
tic mountain aesthetic with impeccably elegant comfort. Some rooms
have stunning views over the Beagle Channel, and all have wrought-iron
bed frames and are furnished with simple good taste. There are rooms
for people with disabilities, too. The expansive lobby and the second-
floor restaurant are just as welcoming, and services offered include
catamaran trips. ⊠ *Los Ñires 1850, Km 3* ☎ *+54 2901/445–960*
⊕ *hotelyamanas.com.ar* ↩ *18 rooms* ⌂ *Restaurant, in-room safes,
minibars, cable TV, gym, bar, recreation room, shop, laundry service,
Internet* ⊟ *AE, DC, MC, V* ⋈ *CP.*

★ **$$** ⌂ **Hostería Patagonia Jarké.** Jarké means "spark" in the local language
of the indigenous Yamana tribe, and indeed this B&B is a vibrant ad-
dition to Ushuaia proper. The two-story lodge, on a dead-end street in
the heart of town, is an amalgam of alpine and Victorian styles on the
outside; inside, a spacious contemporary design incorporates a glass-roof
lobby, lounge, and breakfast room. Rooms have polished wood floors,
peaked-roof ceilings, artisanal soaps, woven floor mats, and lovely
views. ⊠ *Sarmiento 310* ☎⊟ *+54 2901/437–245* ⊕ *www.
hosteriapatagoniaj.com* ↩ *10 rooms* ⌂ *Café, in-room safes, cable TV,
bar, library, laundry service, Internet* ⊟ *AE, DC, MC, V* ⊗ *Closed Apr.
and May* ⋈ *BP.*

$$ ⌂ **Hotel Cabo de Hornos.** Cabo de Hornos is a cut above other down-
town hotels in the same price category. The rooms are clean and sim-
ple, and all have cable TV and telephones. The lobby lounge is kitschy
and cheerful, decorated with currency and postcards from all over the
world. Its old ski-lodge feel makes it a nice place to relax and watch
fútbol with a cup of coffee or a beer. ⊠ *San Martín at Rosas* ☎ *+54
2901/430–677* ⊟ *+54 2901/422–313* ⌸ *cabodehornos@arnet.com.ar*
↩ *30 rooms* ⌂ *Restaurant, bar* ⊟ *AE, MC, V* ⋈ *CP.*

Bars and Cafés

Ushuaia has a lively nightlife scene in summer, with its casino, discos,
and cozy cafés all within close proximity of each other. The biggest and
most popular pub is **El Náutico** (⊠ Maipú 1210 ☎+54 2901/430–415).
For more traditional Argentine entertainment, **Hotel del Glaciar** (⊠ 2355
Camino Glaciar Martial, Km 3.5 ☎+54 2901/430–640) has tango

shows Saturday at 11 PM. **Bar Ideal** (⊠ San Martín 393) is a cozy and historic bar and café. **Tante Sara** (⊠ San Martín 701 ☏ +54 2901/433–710 ⊕ cafebartantesara.com.ar) is a popular café-bar with a casual, old-world feel, in the very heart of town, where locals kick back with a book or a beer (they pour Beagle, the local artisanal brew).

Sports & the Outdoors

SCENIC FLIGHTS The gorgeous scenery and island topography of the area is readily appreciated on a Cessna tour. A half-hour flight (US$35, or 102 pesos per passenger; US$50, or 145 pesos for one passenger alone) with a local pilot takes you over Ushuaia and the Beagle Channel with views of area glaciers and snowcapped islands south to Cape Horn. A 60-minute flight (US$70 or 203 pesos per passenger; US$100 or 290 pesos for one passenger alone) crosses the Andes to the Escondida and Fagnano lakes. **Aero Club Ushuaia** (⊠ Antiguo Aerpuerto ☏ +54 2901/421–717 ⊕ www. aeroclubushuaia.org.ar) offers half-hour and hour-long trips.

SKIING Ushuaia is the cross-country skiing (*esqui de fondo* in Spanish) center of South America, thanks to enthusiastic **Club Andino** (☏ +54 2901/422–335) members who took to the sport in the 1980s and made the forested hills of a high valley about 20 minutes from town a favorite destination for skiers. **Hostería Tierra Mayor** (☏ +54 2901/423–240), **Hostería Los Cotorras** (☏ +54 2901/499–300), and **Haruwen** (☏ +54 2901/424–058) are three places where you can ride in dog-pulled sleds, rent skis, go cross-country skiing, get lessons, and eat; contact the Ushuaia tourist office for more information. **Glaciar Martial Ski Lodge** (☏ +54 2901/243–3712), open year-round, Tuesday–Sunday 10–7, functions as a cross-country ski center from June to October. Skis can also be rented in town, as can snowmobiles.

For downhill (or *alpino*) skiers, Club Andino has bulldozed a couple of short, flat runs directly above Ushuaia. The area's newest downhill ski area, **Cerro Castor** (☏ +54 2901/422–244 ⊕ www.cerrocastor.com), is 26 km (17 mi) northeast of Ushuaia on R3, and has 19 trails and four high-speed ski lifts. More than half the trails are at the beginner level, six are intermediate, and three are expert trails, but none of this terrain is very challenging for an experienced skier. You can rent skis and snowboards and take ski lessons. **Transportes Kaupen** (⇨ *above*) and other local bus companies run service back and forth from town.

Puerto Williams

⓱ *75-min flight southeast from Punta Arenas; 42 km (25 mi) southeast of Ushuaia, Argentina.*

On an island southeast of Ushuaia, the town of Puerto Williams is the southernmost permanent settlement in the world. Originally called Puerto Luisa, it was renamed in 1956 in honor of the military officer who took possession of the Estrecho de Magallanes for the newly founded nation of Chile in 1843. Most of the 2,500 residents are troops at the naval base, but there are several hundred civilians in the adjacent village. A tiny community of indigenous peoples makes its home in the nearby Ukika village.

For a quick history lesson on how Puerto Williams evolved and some insight into the indigenous peoples, visit the **Museo Martin Gusinde,** named for the renowned anthropologist who traveled and studied in the region between 1918 and 1924. ✉ *Aragay 1* ☎ *No phone* 💲 *500 pesos* ☉ *Weekdays 10–1 and 3–6, weekends 3–6.*

Weather permitting, **Aerovís DAP** (✉ Av. Bernardo O'Higgins 891, Punta Arenas ☎ 61/223–340 ⊕ www.aeroviasdap.cl) offers charter flights over Cabo de Hornos, the southernmost tip of South America. Although the water looks placid from the air, strong westerly winds make navigating around Cape Horn treacherous. Over the last few centuries, hundreds of ships have met their doom here trying to sail to the Pacific.

Where to Stay & Eat
When you arrive in Puerto Williams, your airline or ferry company will recommend a few of the hospedajes available, then take you around to see them. All are rustic inns that also serve meals.

$ 🏠 **Hostal Pusaki.** Run with Chilean hospitality, this humble hospedaje has comfortable rooms with up to four beds (including bunks). The dining room serves fine local fare. Dinner is especially pleasant if the fresh *ensalada de centolla* (king crab salad) is on the changing menu. ✉ *Piloto Pardo 242* ☎ *61/621–020* 📠 *61/621–116* 🛏 *3 rooms without bath* ⚴ *Restaurant; no a/c, no room phones, no room TVs* ═ *No credit cards* ▯◯▮ *CP.*

Nightlife
Permanently moored at the main town dock is a small Swiss freighter listing slightly to port called the *Micalvi.* It's home to the rustic **Club de Yates** (✉Dockside ☎61/621–041). Sailors stop off here for good company, strong spirits, and hearty food as they travel between the Atlantic and Pacific around Cape Horn. Stop by and mingle; you might meet Aussies, Brits, Finns, Russians, Swedes, or even the occasional American.

A world away from the cosmopolitan clubs of Santiago, **Pub El Pingüino** (✉ Centro Commercial ☎ No phone) is a watering hole patronized by the town's civilians. Hours are irregular, but closer to the weekend it opens earlier and closes later.

Hiking
A hike to the top of nearby **Cerro Bandera** is well worth the effort if you have the stamina. The trail is well marked, but very steep. The view from the top toward the south to the Cordón Dientes del Perro (Dog's Teeth Range) is impressive, but looking northward over the Beagle Channel to Argentina—with Puerto Williams nestled below and Ushuaia just visible to the west—is truly breathtaking.

PATAGONIA & TIERRA DEL FUEGO ESSENTIALS

Transportation
BY AIR
Lan and its subsidiary, Ladeco, operate a number of flights daily between Punta Arenas and Santiago, Coihaique, and Puerto Montt. Another do-

mestic airline, Aerovís DAP, has regularly scheduled flights between Punta Arenas, Porvenir, Puerto Williams, and the Argentine city of Ushuaia. Aerolíneas Argentinas has service between Buenos Aires and Ushuaia, Argentina, and Buenos Aires and El Calafate, Argentina.

It's a good idea to make air-travel arrangements through a reliable tour company, if possible. That way you can rely on the company if you need to make last-minute changes in your itinerary.

🛪 Airlines **Aerolíneas Argentinas** ✉ Roger de Flor 2915, Santiago ☎ 800/610-200 in Chile, 2/210-9300 in Santiago, 0810/2228-6527 24-hr reservations and sales in Argentina, 11/4317-3000 in Buenos Aires.

Aerovís DAP ✉ Av. Bernardo O'Higgins 891, Punta Arenas ☎ 61/223-340 ⊕ www. aeroviasdap.cl. **Lan** ✉ Lautaro Navarro 999, Punta Arenas ☎ 600/526-2000, +56 2526-2000 from outside Chile ⊕ www.lan.com.

AIRPORT   Public bus service from the airport into Punta Arenas is 1,500 pesos.
TRANSFERS   Private transfers by small companies running minivans out of the airport (with no other pickup points or call-in service) run 3,000 pesos per person.

BY BOAT

Boat tours are a popular way to see otherwise inaccessible parts of Patagonia and Tierra del Fuego. The four-day Navimag trips from Puerto Montt to Puerto Natales, which pass the Amalia Glacier, are immensely popular with backpackers and other visitors. The ship isn't luxurious, but it has a restaurant, pub, and lectures on local culture. Depending on which sort of cabin you choose, cabins are priced US$720–$845 (380,000 pesos–446,000 pesos) per person for double occupancy in high season, and US$340–$410 (180,000 pesos–216,500 pesos) per person in low season. Prices include all meals. The boat calls at Puerto Edén, where you can get off and visit the town for a few hours. Navimag tickets can be bought online or at local travel agencies.

If you prefer to travel through the region's natural wonders in comfort, Comapa's affiliate Cruceros Australis runs two ships, the elegant 55-cabin *Mare Australis,* built in 2002, and the even newer 63-cabin *Vía Australis,* constructed in 2005. Both ships have the classic, wood-and-polished-brass design of old-world luxury liners, and both sail round-trip between Punta Arenas and Ushuaia (there are 4-day and 5-day options). On the way, the ships stop at a number of sights, including the Garibaldi Glacier, a breathtaking mass of blue ice. You also ride smaller motorboats ashore to visit Isla Magdalena's colony of 120,000 penguins, and Ainsworth Bay's family of elephant seals. The cruises include lectures in English, German, and Spanish on the region's geography and history, flora and fauna; all multi-course meals and cocktails (including some formidable pisco sours) are included. Comapa also runs a ferry three times a week between Punta Arenas and Porvenir, and the *Barcaza Melinka,* which makes thrice-weekly trips to Isla Magdalena (during penguin season).

Turismo 21 de Mayo operates two ships, the *Cutter 21 de Mayo* and the *Alberto de Agostini,* to the Balmaceda and Serrano glaciers in Parque Nacional Bernardo O'Higgins. Passengers on these luxurious boats are treated to lectures about the region as the boat moves up the Seno Última Esperanza. Lago Grey Tours offers boat trips to Glaciar Grey inside the Parque Nacional Torres del Paine (35 pesos).

In El Calafate, Upsala Explorer combines a day at an estancia and a boat trip to Upsala Glacier.

🚢 **Boat & Ferry Lines Comapa** ✉ Av. Magallanes 990, Punta Arenas ☎ 61/200-200 🌐 www.comapa.cl ✉ Av. Bulnes 533 Puerto Natales ☎ 61/414-300. **Cruceros Australis** ✉ Av. El Bosque Norte 0440, Piso 11, Santiago ☎ 2/442-3110 🖷 2/203-5173 🌐 www.australis.com. **Lago Grey Tours** ✉ Lago Grey ☎🖷 61/225-986 🌐 www.lagogrey.com. **Navimag** ✉ Av. El Bosque Norte 0440, Santiago ☎ 2/442-3120 🖷 2/203-5025 🌐 www.navimag.com. **Turismo 21 de Mayo** ✉ Ladrilleros 171, Puerto Natales ☎ 61/411-176. **Upsala Explorer** ✉ 9 de Julio 69, El Calafate ☎ +54 2902/491-034 🖷 +54 2902/491-292 🌐 www.upsalaexplorer.com.ar.

BY BUS

The four-hour trip between Punta Arenas and Puerto Natales is serviced by small, private companies. One of the best is Buses Fernández, which has a fleet of first-class coaches and its own terminals in both towns. To travel between Punta Arenas, Río Gallegos, and Ushuaia, Argentina, your best bet is Tecni-Austral, based in Argentina.

🚌 **Bus Companies Bus Sur** ✉ At the bus station, Av. Julio A. Roca 1004, Río Gallegos, Argentina ☎ 2966/442-687, 2902/491-631 in El Calafate. **Buses Fernández** ✉ Armando Sanhueza 745, Punta Arenas ☎ 61/221-429 ✉ Eleuterio Ramirez 399, Puerto Natales ☎ 61/411-111 🌐 www.busesfernandez.com. **Tecni-Austral** ✉ Lautaro Navarro 975, Punta Arenas ☎ 61/222-078 or 61/223-205 ✉ Roca 157, Ushuaia, Argentina ☎ +54 2901/431-408.

Transportes Kaupen ☎ +54 2901/434-015.

BY CAR

Driving in Patagonia isn't as difficult as you might think. Highways are paved. Secondary roads, including those in the more popular parks, are well maintained. Be careful of gravel roads—broken windshields are a common hazard when driving on them.

Renting a car in Patagonia is not cheap—most companies charge about 70,000 pesos per day. Compare rental rates to the cost of tours; you may find a tour is far cheaper than driving yourself. Make sure you don't rent a more expensive car than you need. Four-wheel-drive vehicles are popular and readily available, but they often aren't necessary if you're not leaving the major roads. (They're extremely useful, however, in Torres del Paine or El Calafate.) Make certain to understand the extent of your liability for any damage to the vehicle, including routine accidents such as a chipped or cracked windshield. Puerto Williams is a 12-hour drive from Punta Arenas and some agencies have daily surcharges (typically 21,000 pesos a day) for a foreign license, so flying to southern Tierra del Fuego is an attractive option.

Of the international chains, Budget, Avis, and Hertz have offices in Punta Arenas. At the Punta Arenas airport, there are four rental agencies: Avis, Budget, Hertz, and International Rent A Car. Check prices with each, as any one may be considerably lower than the other three. Avis also has a branch in Puerto Natales. Additional drivers are free. Reputable local companies in Punta Arenas include RUS and Payne.

Rental Agencies Avis ✉ Roca 1044, Punta Arenas ☎ 61/241–182 ✉ Aeropuerto Presidente Ibañez, Punta Arenas ☎ 61/241–182 ✉ Av. Bulnes 632, Puerto Natales ☎ 61/410–775. **Budget** ✉ Av. Bernardo O'Higgins 964, Punta Arenas ☎ 61/241–696 ✉ Aeropuerto Presidente Ibañez, Punta Arenas ☎ 61/241–696. **Hertz** ✉ Av. Bernardo O'Higgins 987, Punta Arenas ☎ 61/248–742 ✉ Aeropuerto Presidente Ibañez, Punta Arenas ☎ 61/210–096. **International Rent A Car** ✉ Aeropuerto Presidente Ibañez, Punta Arenas ☎ 61/212–401. **Payne** ✉ José Menéndez 631, Punta Arenas ☎ 61/240–852. **RUS** ✉ Av. Colón 614, Punta Arenas ☎ 61/221–529.

BY TAXI

Taxis are readily available in Punta Arenas, Puerto Natales, El Calafate, and Ushuaia. Ordinary taxis, with yellow roofs, are the easiest. *Colectivos,* with black roofs, run on fixed routes. They cost less, but figuring them out can be tricky if you're not a fluent Spanish speaker. You can flag down one of these along the set route, but stops are unmarked. Ask at your hotel to find out which car number to look for.

Contacts & Resources

BANKS & EXCHANGE SERVICES

There are a number of banks in Punta Arenas, Puerto Natales, El Calafate, and Ushuaia where you can exchange cash and withdraw money from ATMs that accept cards on the Cirrus or Plus systems. Do not count on banking services outside these main cities.

When you're anticipating smaller purchases, try to have coins and small bills on hand at all times. Many vendors do not always have appropriate change for large bills.

INTERNET, MAIL & SHIPPING

Some hotels offer Internet access for a small fee. Some telephone company offices also offer Internet services, but it's generally more expensive. Your best bet is usually the Internet cafés that are now found on almost every block in Punta Arenas and Puerto Natales. In Ushuaia and El Calafate, Argentina, the Internet cafeß are so ubiquitous that it's hard to walk 100 feet without finding one.

In Punta Arenas, one of the most welcoming Internet cafés is El Calafate, on Avenida Magallanes. It's open 24 hours. Rates are about 2,100 pesos per hour. Another Internet site in Punta Arenas is Cyber Café. In Puerto Natales, El Rincón del Tata has one computer terminal; Concepto Indigo has two.

Mail takes weeks and weeks to get from the end of the earth to the United States or the United Kingdom. It's best to send it from the airport in Santiago. Important packages can be sent via DHL in Punta Arenas.

Internet Cafés El Calafate ✉ Av. Magallanes 922, Punta Arenas ☎ 61/241–281. **Concepto Indigo** ✉ Ladrilleros 105, Puerto Natales ☎ 61/413–609 ⊕ www.conceptoindigo.com. **Cyber Café** ✉ Av. Colón 778, 2nd fl., Punta Arenas ☎ 61/200–610. **El Rincón del Tata** ✉ Arturo Prat 23, Puerto Natales ☎ 61/413–845.

7 Shipping Service DHL ✉ Pedro Montt 840 Local 4, Punta Arenas ☎ 61/228462 ⊕ www. dhl.com.

TOURS

AIR TOURS Air tours are often a little more expensive than cruises, but they provide an entirely different perspective, and may take you farther than you could otherwise go. Aerovís DAP operates charter flights over Cape Horn for about US$75 (39,500 pesos) per person. DAP was the first airline to have regular commercial flights to the Antarctic, beginning in 1987. In the austral summer (December–February) they fly small groups to comfortable refuges in the Chilean Antarctic, where you can stay in a lodge for up to three nights. DAP staffs a resident guide in Antarctica, and visits include trips to the air force bases of Russia, China, and Chile. Single-day visits begin at US$2,500 (1,320,000 pesos). The flight is 3½ hours. DAP also has helicopter service across Patagonia.

7 **Aerovís DAP** ✉ Av. Bernardo O'Higgins 891, Punta Arenas ☎ 61/223-340 ⊕ www. aeroviasdap.cl.

LAND-BASED TOURS & EXCURSIONS SportsTour, based in Santiago, offers half- and full-day city tours and multiday excursions throughout the region; the company also arranges individual tour itineraries. Most staff members speak excellent English. In Puerto Natales, TourExpress operates a fleet of small vans for comfortable tours into Parque Nacional Torres del Paine. The bilingual guides are well versed not only on the area's culture and history but on its geology, fauna, and flora.

The U.S.-based Lost World Adventures specializes in tailoring Patagonia and Tierra del Fuego itineraries around your specific interests.

In El Calafate, Hielo y Aventura specializes in glacier tours with "minitrekking" (walking on the Perito Moreno or Upsala glaciers with crampons). Horseback riding treks can be arranged by Gustavo Holzman or through the El Calafate tourist office. Interlagos Turismo arranges tours between Río Gallegos and El Calafate to the glaciers. Tur Aiké Turismo organizes tours in and around Río Gallegos.

In Ushuaia and the Tierra del Fuego, All Patagonia and Tolkar both offer a wide variety of adventurous treks through the Parque Nacional Tierra del Fuego and around the Canal Beagle. Tolkeyén Patagonia organizes tours of the Canal Beagle and bus trips that give an overview of the national park. All Patagonia organizes bus trips to Lago Escondido and other spots in the area.

7 **Tour Operators All Patagonia** ✉ Juana Fadul 26, Ushuaia ☎ +54 2901/433-622 or 2901/1556-5758 🖷 +54 2901/430-707 ⊕ www.allpatagonia.net. **Gustavo Holzman** ✉ J. A. Roca 2035, El Calafate ☎ +54 2902/491-203. **Hielo y Aventura** ✉ Av. del Libertador San Martín 935, El Calafate ☎ +54 2902/492-205. **Interlagos Turismo** ✉ Fagnano 35, Río Gallegos ☎ +54 2966/422-614 ✉ Av. Libertador 1175, El Calafate ☎ +54 2902/491-175 🖷 +54 2902/491-241. **Lost World Adventures** ✉ 337 Shadowmoor Dr. South, Decatur, GA 30030 ☎ 404/373-5820 or 800/999-0558 🖷 404/377-1902 ⊕ www. lostworldadventures.com. **SportsTour** ✉ Moneda 970, 18th fl., Santiago ☎ 2/549-5200 🖷 2/698-2981 ⊕ www.sportstour.cl. **Tolkar** ✉ Roca 157, Ushuaia ☎ +54 2901/431-408 or +54 2901/437-421. **Tolkeyén Patagonia** ✉ Maipú 237, Ushuaia ☎ +54

2901/437–073 or +54 2901/424–504. **TourExpress** ✉ Av. Bulnes 769, Puerto Natales ☎ 61/410–734. **Tur Aiké Turismo** ✉ Zapiola 63, Río Gallegos ☎ +54 2902/422–436.

VISITOR INFORMATION

The border between Chile and Argentina is still strictly maintained, but crossing it doesn't present much difficulty beyond getting out your passport and waiting in a line to get the stamp. Most travelers end up crossing the border by bus, which means getting out of the vehicle for 30–45 minutes to go through the bureaucratic proceedings, then loading back in. (Be sure to bring your valuables with you when you leave the bus.) Crossing by car is also quite manageable (check with your car-rental company for restrictions on international travel). Traveling between Chile's Puerto Natales and Torres del Paine and Argentina's Río Gallegos, you'll cross at Cancha Carrera. From the border crossing, it's 129 km (80 mi) east on PR7 to La Esperanza, then 161 km (100 mi) southeast on RP5 to Río Gallegos.

Sernatur, the national tourism agency, has offices in Punta Arenas and in Puerto Natales. The Punta Arenas office is open daily 8–5, and the small Puerto Natales office is open Monday–Thursday 8:15–6 and Friday 8:15–5. The Punta Arenas City Tourism Office, in an attractive kiosk in the main square, is quite helpful. It's open December–March, Monday–Saturday 8–8 and Sunday 9–3; April–November, Monday–Thursday 8–5 and Friday 8–4. They offer a free Internet connection.

⌗ Contacts in Chile Punta Arenas City Tourism ✉ Plaza Muñoz Gamero, Punta Arenas ☎ 61/200–610 ⊕ www.puntaarenas.cl. **Sernatur Punta Arenas** ✉ Av. Magallanes 960, Punta Arenas ☎ 61/248–790. **Sernatur Puerto Natales** ✉ Av. Pedro Montt 19, Puerto Natales ☎ 61/412–125.

⌗ Contacts in Argentina El Calafate Tourist Office ✉ Terminal de Omnibus, Julio A. Roca 1004 ☎☎ +54 2902/491–090 ⊕ www.elcalafate.gov.ar. **Tierra del Fuego Tourism Institute** ✉ Maipú 505, Ushuaia ☎ +54 2901/421–423. **Ushuaia Tourist Office** ✉ Av. San Martín 674 ☎ +54 2901/432–000 ⊕ www.e-ushuaia.com.

Easter Island

WORD OF MOUTH

"The giant *moai* statues really let you know you're in Polynesia now, not Latin America. I felt that somehow these ancient gods were always watching me. But my favorite part of Easter Island was snorkeling and scuba diving in the amazing, clear water. All the colorful species made me feel like I was in my own extra-large fish tank."

—Brian K.

Updated by
Brian Kluepfel

BELCHING OUT GREAT COLUMNS OF SMOKE, the volcano pushed its way out of the Pacific Ocean about 2.5 million years ago. Poike's anger had barely subsided when it was joined by two fiery siblings, Rano Kau and Terevaka. The triangular landmass that formed between the trio is what is known today as Easter Island.

The most isolated island in the world—2,985 km (1,850 mi) from its nearest populated neighbor, and 3,700 km (2,295 mi) off the Chilean coast—was uninhabited until around 1,500 years ago. That's when, according to local legend, King Hotu Matu'a and his extended family landed on a beach on the northern shore. Exactly where they came from is still a mystery. Norwegian archaeologist Thor Heyerdahl, asserting that the fine masonry found on the island resembles that of the Incas, believed they came from South America. To prove the journey was possible, Heyerdahl set sail in 1947 from Peru in a balsa-wood boat called the *Kon-Tiki*. Most archaeologists, however, believe the original inhabitants were of Polynesian descent, citing similarities in language and culture.

Its earliest inhabitants called the island Te Pito O Te Henua—the navel of the world. They cleared vast forests for cultivation and fished the surrounding waters for tuna and swordfish. As the population grew, they moved from the caves along the shore into tight-knit communities of *hare paengas,* or boat-shape houses. To communicate they created *rongo-rongo,* a beautiful script and the only written language in all of Polynesia. But their greatest achievement was the hundreds of sad-eyed stone statues called *moais* they erected to honor their ancestors.

Dutch explorer Jacob Roggeveen, the first European to encounter the island, gave it the name most people recognize when he landed here on Easter Sunday in 1722. Here he found a thriving community of thousands. But when British Captain James Cook anchored here in 1774, he found only several hundred people so impoverished they could barely afford to part with a few sweet potatoes. What's more, many of the moais had been toppled from their foundations. What happened during those 50 years? Archaeologists believe overpopulation and overdevelopment devastated the island. Warfare broke out between clans, who knocked down the moais belonging to their opponents.

This period pales in comparison to the devastation the island suffered in 1862, when slave traders from Peru captured more than 1,000 islanders. Forced to work in guano mines on the mainland, most of them died of hunger or disease. Religious leaders interceded, and the few that remained alive were returned to their island. They spread smallpox to the rest of the population, killing all but 110 people. Everyone who could read the rongo-rongo script died, and to this day no one has been able to decipher the language.

With the collapse of Spanish influence in South America, several countries began to covet Easter Island. In 1888 a Chilean ship raced westward and claimed the island before France or Britain could do so. Chile leased the entire island to a British sheep company, which restricted the islanders from venturing outside the little town of Hanga Roa. The sheep company left in 1953, but life didn't really begin to improve for islanders

In a few days, you can visit the island's major sights. Spend one day in **Hanga Roa,** stopping by the Iglesia Hanga Roa, the Cementerio, and the Museo Antropológico Sebastián Englert. Finish the day with sunset at Tahai. On your second day visit the volcano of **Rano Kau,** where you'll find the ceremonial village of **Orongo.** In the afternoon head inland to the small quarry of **Puna Pau** and the seven moais of **Ahu Akivi.** Tour the coastal road on your last day, visiting the hundreds of moais in the quarry at **Ranu Raraku** and the 15-moai lineup at **Ahu Tongariki.**

10

If you have more time, go for a swim at **Playa Ovahe** and **Playa Anakena,** home to some of the island's most striking moais.

until an airport was constructed in 1967. The promise of large-scale tourism encouraged the Chilean government to make much-needed improvements on the island.

Tourism is now the biggest industry on Rapa Nui—the name locals give the island (known as Isla de Pascua by mainland Chileans). Most of the 3,500 residents are involved in this endeavor in some way. The residents, most of whom are descended from the original inhabitants, are extremely proud of the island's past. Ask anyone here about Poike, the volcano that poked its head out of the Pacific so long ago, and they'll probably tell you the whole tale.

EXPLORING EASTER ISLAND

An adventurous spirit is a prerequisite for visiting Easter Island. It's possible to sign up for a package tour, but you'd visit only a handful of the sights. To fully experience the island, hire a private guide. Even better, rent a four-wheel-drive vehicle or a mountain bike and head out on your own. Tour buses often bypass fascinating destinations that are off the beaten path. Even in the height of the high season you can find secluded spots.

It's nearly impossible to get lost on Easter Island, which is just 22 km (14 mi) from end to end. Two major thoroughfares—a gravel road that winds its way around the coastline past most of the major archaeological sites, and a paved road that leads across the island to the beaches—traverse the island; both meet near Playa Anakena.

Almost all of Easter Island's businesses, including those catering to tourists, close for a few hours in the afternoon. Most are open 9–1 and 4–8, but a few stay open late into the evening. Many are closed Sunday. Few restaurants or shops accept credit cards.

About the Restaurants
If you spot an unassuming place filled with Rapa Nui residents, chances are you'll find delicious and inexpensive food. Barbecue of all types, especially lamb, is extremely popular. As this is an island, seafood appears

CloseUp

EASTER ISLAND FESTIVALS & SEASONAL EVENTS

The annual Tapati Rapa Nui festival, a two-week celebration of the island's heritage, takes place every year from late January through early February. The normally laid-back Hanga Roa bursts to life in a colorful festival that includes much singing and dancing. The Dia de la Lengua (Language Day), which usually takes place toward the end of November, celebrates the Rapa Nui language.

on nearly every menu. Don't hesitate to ask which type is the freshest—the tuna may have been caught that morning. Meals are often accompanied by fresh fruit, especially bananas, papayas, and intensely sweet pineapples, or *camote* (sweet potato).

Hotels on the island include breakfast in the room rate and sometimes lunch and dinner. However, if you plan to spend your days exploring the island, ask your hotel to prepare a picnic for you or drop by a *supermercado* (supermarket) for provisions.

About the Hotels

Easter Island has two types of accommodations: *hoteles* and *residenciales*. A hotel is built specifically to house many tourists, whereas a residencial is often a private home with a few rooms added to accommodate guests. If you can't get by without amenities such as a swimming pool, opt for a hotel. You'll miss out, however, on the chance to stay with a local family at a residencial—the best way to learn about life on Rapa Nui.

All accommodations on the island will arrange for someone to welcome you at the airport with a garland of flowers. It's a good thing, as most places would be hard to find because Hanga Roa doesn't post the street names. Breakfast and airport transfer are included almost everywhere. Most places accept credit cards, but many add a surcharge (around 4%) because it often takes months for them to be reimbursed. It's best to settle on a rate beforehand and bring cash or traveler's checks. It's often possible to negotiate significant discounts off-season, including the shoulder months of November, December, and March.

Although it's possible to show up on the island without a reservation—owners of residenciales with spare rooms crowd the airport—it's best to reserve in advance, especially in January and February. Many flights arrive late in the evening, and the last thing you'll want to do is search for a place to stay.

Astounding Archaeology
With petroglyphs, cave paintings, and *ahus* (ceremonial sites where the giant *moai* stand), Easter Island is a treasure trove for the amateur archaeologist. Even if Easter Island held not a single moai, there would still be plenty to see. Hundreds of well-preserved petroglyphs stand on the cliffs near the ancient village of Orongo, and a few are near the ceremonial sights of Ahu Tongariki and Ahu Te Pito Kura. Cave paintings can be viewed at Ana Kai Tangata. More than 300 of the stone platforms called ahus line the coast, and many are worth exploring.

10

Souvenir Shopping
The locals have carved out a living out of the stone and driftwood of Rapa Nui. Local handicrafts such as miniature moais, elaborate bowls, and eerie masks are sold on Easter Island. Your first opportunity to shop comes the minute you step into the airport, where dozens of vendors hawk miniature moais in the form of paperweights or earrings.

Extraordinary Diving
Diving into the cobalt-blue waters is one of the most popular pastimes on Easter Island. Visibility is up to 120 feet, meaning that you won't miss the bright tropical fish—a quarter of which aren't found anywhere else in the world. Coral formations like the Cavern of the Three Windows make for an unforgettable underwater experience.

WHAT IT COSTS In pesos (in thousands)					
	$$$$	**$$$**	**$$**	**$**	**¢**
RESTAURANTS	over 11	8–11	5–8	3–5	under 3
HOTELS	over 105	75–105	45–75	15–45	under 15

Restaurant prices are for a main course at dinner. Hotel prices are for a double room in high season, excluding tax.

When to Go
Most people visit in summer, between December and March. Many time their visit to coincide with Tapati Rapa Nui, a two-week celebration with music and dancing that starts at the end of January. Temperatures can soar above 27°C (81°F) in summer. In winter, temperatures reach an average of 22°C (72°F), although brisk winds can often make it feel much cooler. Be sure to bring a light jacket. The wettest months are June and July.

Hanga Roa
Hugging the coast on the southwest side of the island is the village of Hanga Roa. About 3,500 people, many of Polynesian descent, make this tangle of streets their home. Few live outside the village because the bulk of the island forms the Rapa Nui National Park. The population is be-

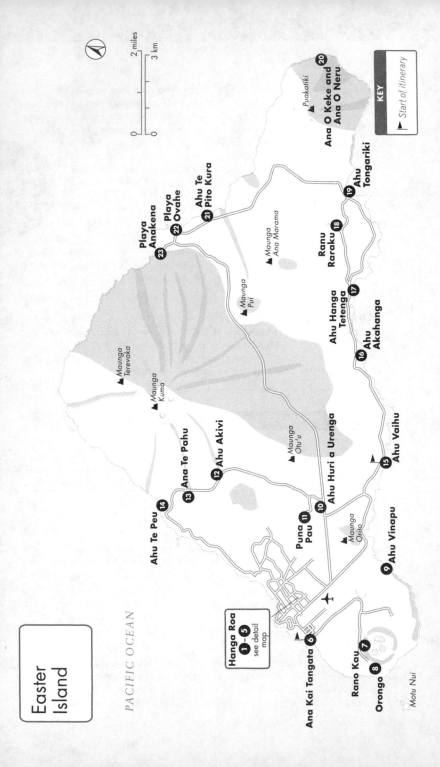

Easter Island

PACIFIC OCEAN

Ahu Te Peu
Ana Te Pahu
Ahu Akivi
Maunga Terevaka
Maunga Kuma
Maunga Ohu'u
Ahu Huri a Urenga
Puna Pau
Maunga Orito
Ahu Vinapu
Ana Kai Tangata
Hanga Roa
see detail map
Rano Kau
Orongo
Motu Nui
Ahu Vaihu
Ahu Akahanga
Ahu Hanga Tetenga
Rano Raraku
Ahu Tongariki
Maunga Ana Marama
Maunga Pui
Playa Anakena
Playa Ovahe
Ahu Te Pito Kura
Puakatiki
Ana O Keke and Ana O Neru

2 miles
3 km

KEY
Start of itinerary

ginning to spread out, however, as the Chilean government cedes more land to the locals.

The two main roads in Hanga Roa intersect a block from the ocean at a small plaza. Avenida Atamu Tekena, which runs the length of the village, is where you'll find most of the tourist-oriented businesses. Avenida Te Pito O Te Henua begins near the fishing pier and extends two blocks uphill to the church. These two roads are paved, but most others in town are gravel.

Buildings are not numbered and signs are nonexistent (street names are sometimes painted on curbstones), so finding a particular building can be frustrating at first. Locals will give directions from landmarks, so it's not a bad idea to take a walk around town as soon as you arrive so you can get your bearings.

a good tour

Start at the **Iglesia Hanga Roa** ❶ ⌐, the squat colonial church near the center of Hanga Roa. Peek inside to see the carved wooden statues that put a Polynesian spin on traditional Christian iconography. Walk two blocks downhill on Avenida Te Pito O Te Henua to reach the **Caleta Hanga Roa** ❷, the town's little fishing pier. To the north along the coast is the colorful **Cementerio** ❸. Head east on Petero Atamu for a block, then turn left and walk north on Avenida Atamu Tekena. On your left is the **Museo Antropológico Sebastián Englert** ❹, a museum that takes a fascinating look at the island's history. From here it's a short walk to **Tahai** ❺, a ceremonial site where impressive moais stand with their backs to the sea.

TIMING   If you decide to walk, this tour will take a good part of the day. If you drive, you can take in all these sights in two or three hours. Either way, try to plan your tour so you arrive at Tahai in time to watch the sunset.

What to See

❷ **Caleta Hanga Roa.** Colorful fishing boats bob up and down in the water at Hanga Roa's tiny pier. Here you may see fisherfolk hauling in the day's catch of tuna, or a boatload of divers returning from a trip to the neighboring islets. Nearby is **Ahu Tautira**, a ceremonial platform with two restored moais. ⊠ *Av. Policarpo Toro at Av. Te Pito O Te Henua.*

❸ **Cementerio.** Hanga Roa's colorful walled cemetery occupies a prime position overlooking the Pacific and is unlike any other in the world. Its overgrown beds of flowers and brightly painted tombstones lend the cemetery a cheerful feeling. The central cross is erected on a *pukao*, the reddish headdress that once adorned a moai. ⊠ *Av. Policarpo Toro at Petero Atamu.*

⌐ ❶ **Iglesia Hanga Roa.** Missionaries brought Christianity to Rapa Nui, but the Rapa Nui people brought their own beliefs to Christianity. In this colonial church you'll find the two religions intertwined. The figure on the cross above the altar is obviously Christ, but it looks surprisingly similar to many ancient carvings found on the island. A bird in the hand of the statue of St. Francis of Assisi strongly resembles the god Make-Make. Try to visit on Sunday morning, as the hymns have a distinctly Polynesian flavor. ⊠ *Av. Te Pito O Te Henua.*

Caleta
Hanga Roa 2

Cementerio 3

Iglesia
Hanga Roa 1

Museo
Antropológico
Sebastián
Englert 4

Tahai 5

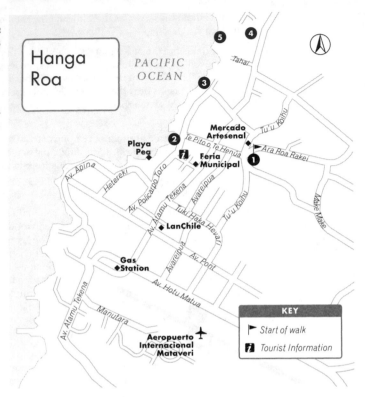

❹ Museo Antropológico Sebastián Englert. The museum, named for a German priest who dedicated his life to improving conditions on Rapa Nui, focuses on daily life on the island. Explanations on how the islanders caught fish and cultivated the land accompany exhibits of ancient tools. Displays describe the various theories about how the moais were transported and set upright. Here, too, is the only female moai on the island, as well as a coral eye found during the reconstruction of an ahu at Playa Anakena. Most of the text is in Spanish, but a guide will be happy to explain the displays. ✉ *Tahai s/n* ☎ *32/551–020* ⊕ *www.museorapanui. cl* 🎫 *1,000 pesos* ☉ *Weekdays 9:30–12:30 and 2–5:30, weekends 9:30–12:30.*

❺ Tahai. The ancient ceremonial center of Tahai, where much of the annual Tapati Rapa Nui festival takes place, was restored in 1968 by archaeologist William Mulloy, who is buried nearby. Tahai consists of three separate ahus facing a wide plaza that once served as a community meeting place. You can still find the foundations of the boat-shape dwellings where religious and social leaders once lived. In the center is Ahu Tahai, which holds a single weathered moai. To the left is Ahu Vai Uri, where five moais, one little more than a stump, cast their stony gaze over the island. Also here is Ahu Kote Riku, holding a splendid moai with its red topknot intact; this is the only moai on the island to have had its gleaming white eyes restored. These are the only moais standing on the western coast, so this is an especially good place to come to see the blazing yellow sunsets. ⊠ *On the coast near Museo Antropológico Sebastián Englert.*

The Western Circuit

On the western tip of the island are the cave paintings of Ana Kai Tangata and the petroglyphs near the ceremonial village of Orongo. You'll also be treated to a spectacular view of the crater lake inside the long-dormant volcano of Rano Kau.

a good tour

Heading south from Hanga Roa you'll soon reach **Ana Kai Tangata** ❻ ▶, a shallow cave in a protected cove on the coast. Look up to the cave ceiling to see the remains of reddish paintings of birds. Continue south and the road suddenly winds uphill to the crater of **Rano Kau** ❼. On its rim is the partially restored ceremonial village of **Orongo** ❽, where islanders worshipped the god Make-Make and where you'll see petroglyphs of birdlike creatures carved into the rock. Take Avenida Hotu Matu'a southeast to **Ahu Vinapu** ❾, which has some of the best stonework on the island. Head back toward town, then turn northeast on the paved road leading across the island. You'll soon pass **Ahu Huri a Urenga** ❿, a solitary moai noted for its four hands. A sign on the left marks the turnoff to **Puna Pau** ⓫, the small quarry where the rust-color topknots for the moais were carved. Several miles farther north is **Ahu Akivi** ⓬, where seven moais stare toward the sea. Continuing down the same road you'll have to look hard for the entrance to the cave dwellings of **Ana Te Pahu** ⓭. Finally, as you reach the coast, you'll come to the ruins of the boat-shape houses at **Ahu Te Peu** ⓮.

TIMING   Because much of this tour is over rough gravel roads, it will take most of the day. Consider stopping for lunch in Hanga Roa after visiting Ahu Vinapu, or pack a lunch and picnic on the rim of Ranu Rao and take in its unmatched views of the crater.

What to See

⓬ **Ahu Akivi.** These seven stoic moais—believed to represent explorers sent on a reconnaissance mission by King Hotu Matu'a—are among the few that gaze out to sea. Researchers say they actually face a ceremonial site. Archaeologists William Mulloy and Gonzalo Figueroa restored the moais in 1960. ⊠ *Past Puna Pau on a gravel road branching north from the paved road to Playa Anakena.*

❿ **Ahu Huri a Urenga.** One of the few ahus to be erected inland, Ahu Huri a Urenga appears to be oriented toward the winter solstice. Its lonely moai is exceptional because it has two sets of hands, the second carved above the first. Researchers believe this is because the lower set was damaged during transport to the ahu. ⊠ *3 km (2 mi) from Av. Hotu Matu'a on the paved road to Playa Anakena.*

⓮ **Ahu Te Peu.** As at Ahu Vinapu, the tightly fitting stones at the unrestored Ahu Te Peu recall the best work of the Incas. The foundations for several boat-shape houses, including one that measures 131 feet from end

CloseUp
MYSTERIES OF THE MOAIS

WHEN EUROPEAN EXPLORERS FIRST SPOTTED Easter Island in 1722, they were bewildered by the dozens of massive stone heads that lined the coast. Just how the small band of islanders he encountered could have constructed these monoliths mystified Dutch explorer Jacob Roggeveen. "The stone images at first caused us to be struck with astonishment," Roggeveen wrote in his log, "because we could not comprehend how it was possible that these people, who are devoid of heavy thick timber for making any machines, as well as strong ropes, nevertheless had been able to erect such images."

When British captain James Cook anchored here in 1774, he was also impressed by the "stupendous figures" that had been "erected in so masterly a manner." But he noted in his journal of the expedition that many had been knocked from their pedestals. By the time French admiral Abel Dupetit-Thouars visited in 1838, almost all had been toppled. Now the question was not only how and why the massive carvings had been erected, but also how and why they had been destroyed.

After hundreds of years of study, we still know very little about these stone statues called moais. Archaeological evidence suggests that most of these statues, apparently memorials to ancestors, were constructed during a period of fevered activity between 1400 and 1600. Most were erected on ahus, or stone platforms, along the coast. All but a few come from Ranu Raraku, the quarry where 397 moais can still be seen today. By studying those left behind, archaeologists know that most were carved in a horizontal position, and that once finished they were moved to a nearby trench where they stood until moved to their ahus.

But how were they transported? The more than 90 moais that were abandoned en route provide few clues. Many are broken, but most are intact. Most are facedown, but a few gaze up at the sky. Although theories abound, most archaeologists believe they were either dragged on wooden platforms or rolled along on top of tree trunks. It's not clear, though, how they could have been moved several miles without damaging the delicate features that were carved at the quarry.

Once they arrived at their ahus, how were the moais lifted into place? In 1955, Norwegian archaeologist Thor Heyerdahl and a team of a dozen men were able to raise the single moai on Ahu Ature Huki in 18 days. In 1960 archaeologists William Mulloy and Gonzalo Figueroa and their men raised the seven moais at Ahu Akivi. They struggled for a month to lift the first, but the last took only a week. Both teams used the same method—lifting them with a stone ramp and wooden poles. This technique would be unwieldy for lifting the larger moais, however. It also fails to explain how the pukaos, or topknots, were placed on many of the heads.

And why were the moais destroyed? The reason, ironically enough, may have been that creating the moais required a tremendous amount of natural resources. Most of the palm trees that had once covered the island were felled to move the moais. This had a devastating effect on the island—there soon was little wood for constructing dwellings or boats. Fuel for fires was increasingly hard to find. Crops were ruined as erosion washed away the soil. Archaeological evidence suggests internecine battles developed between clans that had once worked together peacefully. Bloody battles ensued, during which members of one clan toppled the moais belonging to another. In a period of about 100 years, the islanders themselves laid waste to their greatest artistic achievement. The battles eventually ended, but no more moais were ever erected.

— Mark Sullivan

to end, are clearly visible. From here you can begin the six-hour hike around the island's northern coast to Playa Anakena. ⊠ *Past Ana Te Pahu on a gravel road branching north from the paved road to Playa Anakena.*

⑨ Ahu Vinapu. The appeal of this crumbled ahu isn't apparent until you notice the fine masonry on the rear wall. Anyone who has seen the ancient Inca city of Machu Picchu in Peru will note the similar stonework. This led Norwegian archaeologist Thor Heyerdahl to theorize that Rapa Nui's original inhabitants may have sailed here from South America. Most others disagree, believing that the first settlers were Polynesian. The moais here still lie where they were toppled, one staring sadly up at the sky. ⊠ *Southeast of Hanga Roa on Av. Hotu Matu'a.*

▶ **⑥ Ana Kai Tangata.** A small sign just past the entrance of Hotel Iorana points toward Ana Kai Tangata, a seldom-visited cavern on the coast that holds the island's only cave paintings. Directly over your head are images of red and white birds in flight. Dramatic cliffs shelter the cave from the crashing surf. ⊠ *South of Hanga Roa.*

⑬ Ana Te Pahu. A grove of banana trees marks the entrance to these underground caverns that once served as dwellings. Partly shielded from the blazing sun, a secret garden of tropical plants thrives in the fissure where the caves begin. Below ground is a passage leading to a second cave where the sunlight streams through a huge hole. ⊠ *Past Ahu Akivi on a gravel road branching north from the paved road to Playa Anakena.*

★ **⑧ Orongo.** The 48 oval huts of this ceremonial village, constructed in 1600 and used by locals until 1866, were occupied only during the ceremony honoring the god Make-Make. The high point of the annual event was a competition in which prominent villagers designated servants to paddle small rafts to Motu Nui, the largest of three islets just off the coast. The first servant to find an egg of the sooty tern, a bird nesting on the islets, would swim back with the prize tucked in a special headdress. His master would become the *tangata manu,* or birdman, for the next year. He was honored by being confined to a cave until the following year's ceremony. Dozens of petroglyphs depicting birdlike creatures cover nearby boulders along the rim of Rano Kau. There's a ranger station at the entrance to Orongo, where you pay admission to the Rapa Nui National Park. ⊠ *South of Hanga Roa on Rano Kau* 🎫 *750 pesos.*

⑪ Puna Pau. Scoria, the reddish stone used to make the topknots for the moais, was once excavated at this quarry. About two dozen finished topknots can still be found here. The views of the island from the top of the hill are well worth the climb. ⊠ *Off a gravel road branching north from the paved road to Playa Anakena.*

⑦ Rano Kau. This huge volcano on the southern tip of the island affords wonderful views of Hanga Roa. The crater, which measures a mile across, holds a lake nearly covered over by bright green reeds. The opposite side of the crater has crumbled a bit, revealing a crescent of the deep blue ocean beyond. ⊠ *South of Hanga Roa.*

The Southeastern Circuit

Most of the archaeological sites on the island line the southeastern coast. Driving along the coast you'll pass many ahus, all of them completely untouched. Busloads of tourists hurry past most of these on their way to Ranu Raraku, the quarry where 397 moais wait in stony silence, and Ahu Tongariki, where 15 moais stand in line.

a good tour

The coastal road starts out paved but soon disintegrates into dusty gravel, so make sure you rent a four-wheel-drive vehicle. Heading east on the road you'll soon encounter a string of unrestored ahus—including **Ahu Vaihu** 15 , **Ahu Akahanga** 16, and **Ahu Hanga Tetenga** 17—all worth exploring. From miles away the dome-shape volcano of **Ranu Raraku** 18 is visible. As you approach, look for scores of unfinished moais covering its upper reaches. From Ranu Raraku you can see the 15 stern-faced moais of **Ahu Tongariki** 19. The coastal road veers north, soon passing the bare slopes of the volcano Poike. A dirt path meandering over the hill leads to **Ana O Keke and Ana O Neru** 20, the Caves of the Virgins. The largest moai ever erected on an ahu lies shattered at **Ahu Te Pito Kura** 21, on the northern coast. At the end of the road you reach the island's two beaches, **Playa Ovahe** 22 and **Playa Anakena** 23.

TIMING Depending on how many sights you visit, this tour will take at least a day. If you have time you might want to break it into two separate tours, visiting the sights on the southern coast on one day and those on the northern coast the next. If you want to spend more time at the beach, consider starting the tour at Playa Anakena and working your way backward.

What to See

16 **Ahu Akahanga.** Tradition holds that this is the burial site of Hotu Matu'a, the first of the island's rulers. The 12 moais lying facedown on the ground once stood on the four long stone platforms. ✉ *2 km (1 mi) east of Ahu Viahu on the coastal road.*

17 **Ahu Hanga Tetenga.** Lying here in pieces is the largest moai ever transported to a platform, measuring nearly 10 meters (33 feet). The finishing touches were never made to its eye sockets, so researchers believe it fell while being erected. ✉ *3 km (2 mi) east of Ahu Akahanga on the coastal road.*

21 **Ahu Te Pito Kura.** The largest moai ever successfully erected—a fraction of an inch shorter than the one at Ahu Hanga Tetenga—stands at Ahu Te Pito Kura. Also here is the perfectly round stone (believed to represent the navel of the world) that Hotu Matu'a is said to have brought with him when he arrived on the island. ✉ *9 km (5½ mi) north of Ahu Tongariki on the coastal road.*

★ 19 **Ahu Tongariki.** One of the island's most breathtaking sights is Ahu Tongariki, where 15 moais stand side by side on a 200-foot-long ahu, the longest ever made. Tongariki was painstakingly restored after being destroyed by a massive tidal wave in 1960. The moais here, some whitened with a layer of sea salt, have holes in their extended earlobes that might have once been filled with chunks of obsidian. They face an expansive ceremonial area where you can find petroglyphs of turtles and fish. ⊠ *2 km (1 mi) east of Ranu Raraku on the coastal road.*

🚩 ⓯ **Ahu Vaihu.** Eight fallen moai lie facedown in front of this ahu, the first you'll encounter on the southern coastal road. Three reddish topknots are strewn around them. Even after the ahu was destroyed, this continued to be a burial chamber, evidenced by the rocks piled on the toppled moais. ⊠ *11 km (7 mi) southeast of Hanga Roa on the coastal road.*

⓴ **Ana O Keke and Ana O Neru.** Legend has it that young women awaiting marriage were kept here in the Caves of the Virgins so that their skin would remain as pale as possible. You need an experienced guide to find the caverns, which are hidden in the cliffs along the coast. Take a flashlight to see the haunting petroglyphs of flowers and fish thought to have been carved by these girls. ⊠ *Reached via a dirt road through a ranch on Poike.*

★ ㉓ **Playa Anakena.** Here, beside the swaying palm trees, stand the island's best-preserved moais on **Ahu Nau Nau.** Buried for centuries in the sand, these five statues were protected from the elements. The minute details of the carving—delicate lips, flared nostrils, gracefully curved ears—are still visible. On their backs, fine lines represent belts. It was here during the 1978 restoration that a white coral eye was found, leading researchers to speculate that all moais once had them; the eye is now on display at the Museo Antropológico Sebastián Englert.

Staring at Ahu Nau Nau is a solitary moai on nearby **Ahu Ature Huki.** This statue was the first moai to be replaced on his ahu. Thor Heyerdahl conducted this experiment in 1955 to see if the techniques islanders said were used to erect the moais could work. It took 12 islanders nearly three weeks to lift the moai into position using rocks and wooden poles. ⊠ *1 km (½ mi) west of Playa Ovahe.*

㉒ **Playa Ovahe.** This beautiful stretch of pinkish sand is the island's best-kept secret, passed over by most tourists in favor of nearby Playa Anakena. The pile of volcanic rocks jutting out into the water is actually a ruined ahu. ⊠ *10 km (6 mi) north of Ahu Tongariki on the coastal road.*

⓲ **Ranu Raraku.** When it comes to moais, this is the mother lode. Some 397 **Fodor's**Choice moais have been counted at the quarry of this long-extinct volcano, both ★ on the outer rim and clustered inside the crater. More than 150 are unfinished, some little more than faces in the rock. Among these is El Gigante, a monster measuring 22 meters (72 feet). It's twice the height of the second tallest, which crumbled while being erected at Ahu Hanga Tetenga. Also here is Moai Tukuturi, the only moai in a kneeling position; it's thought to predate most others. ⊠ *5 km (3 mi) east of Ahu Hanga Tetenga on the coastal road.*

WHERE TO EAT

$$$–$$$$ ✕ **La Taverne du Pêcheur.** The dishes at this charming little eatery occupying a prime position on the corner of Caleta Hanga Roa are undoubtedly some of the most innovative on the island—and the most expensive. Try the tuna with morel mushrooms, one of the many dishes that uses local ingredients combined with French recipes. Catch the French owner in a good mood and he'll be more than happy to discuss his wine list. ⊠ *Caleta de Hanga Roa* ☎ *32/100–619* ▭ *AE, DC, MC, V.*

$–$$$$ ✕ **Cuerito Regalon.** The staff will happily tell you about the dishes made from the day's fresh catches—perhaps a tasty grilled tuna steak or *rape rape* (a small lobster). Just across the street from the Feria Municipal, this plant-filled restaurant fronts a supermarket; neatly laid out tables afford great views of Hanga Roa's busiest street. ⊠ *Av. Atamu Tekena s/n* ☎ *32/551–232* ▭ *No credit cards.*

$$–$$$ ✕ **Orongo.** When the owner Raúl Teave is around, this small seafood restaurant, alongside the hotel of the same name and set back from the island's main thoroughfare, is exceedingly popular (when he's out of town, the restaurant closes, so you may want to call ahead). He whips up all the local fresh catches of the day—toremo and kana kana (both are meaty white fish), and tuna—and serves them with fragrant sauces of his own invention. The sauce you order might include caramel, cassava, or white wine, among other ingredients. ⊠ *Av. Atamu Tekena s/n* ☎ *32/100–294* ▭ *No credit cards.*

$$–$$$ ✕ **Playa Pea.** With its dazzling view of the bay, this seafood restaurant is a great place to catch the sunset. Much of the fish is bought at the nearby *caleta* (cove), so it couldn't be fresher. The standout on the menu is the lemony *atún con salsa alcaparras* (tuna with caper sauce). ⊠ *Av. Policarpo Toro s/n* ☎ *32/100–382* ▭ *No credit cards* ☯ *Closed Sun.*

$$ ✕ **Iorana.** A large carved wooden fish adorns the entrance to this simple restaurant; you can't miss it. The service is a little slow but the seafood dishes are wholesome, tasty, and large—so a good appetite is essential. Ask for the special of the day, and you can't go too far wrong. ⊠ *Av. Atamu Tekena s/n* ☎ *32/100–265* ▭ *No credit cards.*

$$ ✕ **KopaKavana.** Twice a week (usually Tuesday and Friday) this large, airy restaurant hosts the group Polinesia, so while you enjoy a tasty fish steak, you can marvel at the flexible limbs of these local dancers. (Note that there's a cover charge of $20—10,000 pesos—to see the performance.) The menu, written in Japanese, Spanish, and English, includes seafood dishes, fried bananas, and sweet potatoes. Ornate shell lamp shades hang from the ceiling, adding a Polynesian touch. ⊠ *Av. Te Pito O Te Henua s/n* ☎ *32/100–447 or 32/551–176* ▭ *No credit cards.*

$$ ✕ **La Tinita.** Little more than a handful of tables on a shady front porch, this restaurant near Plaza Policarpo Toro is a pleasant place to stop for lunch. The dishes are simple but good. Try the atún *a la plancha* (grilled tuna) or *pollo asado* (roast chicken). ⊠ *Av. Te Pito O Te Henua s/n* ☎ *32/ 100–813* ▭ *No credit cards.*

WHERE TO STAY

$$$$ ✕▨ **Casas Rapa Nui.** This luxury property, opened in 2005 by Explora,
Fodor'sChoice   offers the only truly high-end accommodations on Easter Island. Currently,
★   the lodge (two converted native Rapa Nui homes) has nine airy rooms fitted with traditional rattan furnishings (the "Motu" rooms have bathtubs while the "Rani" rooms have only showers). There's also an expansive terrace, a restaurant that serves fresh-caught seafood, and an indoor bar

where you can choose from a list of Chilean wines (or just enjoy a fabulous pisco sour). By 2007, however, the property will have achieved full-blown resort status; there are plans to add another 30-room lodge, along with a swimming pool, a second restaurant, and a wellness center. Current accommodation packages offered by Explora range from three to seven nights, depending on the season. Each package includes a series of hikes (ranging from easy to difficult) to Moai sites, volcanoes, and beaches around the island. ⊠ *Av. Hotu Matu'a s/n, across from the airport,* ☎ *02/206–6060* ⊕ *www.explora.com* ↝ *9 rooms* ⚊ *Dining room, bar, outdoor hot tub, Internet room, laundry service, airport transfers* ▤ *AE, DC, MC, V.*

$$$$ 🏨 **Hotel Taha Tai.** Open and airy, this hotel seems to have sunlight streaming in from everywhere. The intimate bar has a view of the ocean, as does the expansive dining room, which has a tropical feeling lent by its soaring arched ceiling and lazily spinning fans. Guests gather here or in the garden to share the sunset. Rooms in the newer building are larger than the older ones in the bungalows, but all are clean and comfortable, and decorated with Polynesian-style paintings. The outdoor pool is flanked by billowy palm trees. ⊠ *Av. Apina Nui s/n* ☎☎ *32/551–192, 32/551–193, or 32/551–194* ⊕ *www.hotel-tahatai.co.cl* ↝ *40 rooms* ⚊ *Restaurant, room service, some in-room safes, pool, bar, laundry service, Internet, airport shuttle, car rental, travel services; no TV in some rooms* ▤ *AE, DC, MC, V* ⋈ *BP.*

$$$–$$$$ 🏨 **Hotel Hanga Roa.** This hotel—one of the oldest on the island—attracts lots of tour groups. The common areas, from the spacious lobby to the more intimate bar, are comfortable. Ask for one of the newer bungalows, with private terraces overlooking the ocean. Make sure you ask for a room with a sea view. ⊠ *Av. Pont s/n* ☎☎ *32/100–299* ↝ *90 rooms, 1 suite* ⚊ *Restaurant, fans, some in-room safes, some minibars, pool, bar, laundry service, airport shuttle, car rental; no a/c* ▤ *AE, DC, MC, V* ⋈ *BP.*

$$$–$$$$ 🏨 **Hotel Iorana.** Perched high on a cliff that juts into the ocean, this hotel entices its visitors with unmatched views. From your private terrace you can hear the sound of the waves crashing on the rocks. The rooms are simply furnished and have generously proportioned baths. Masses of ruby-red hibiscus flowers grow at one end of the small triangular pool, making this the perfect place to relax with a fruity cocktail. The hotel, which is popular with tour groups, is some 2 km (1 mi) south of town, so you may feel a little isolated. ⊠ *Av. Ana Magaro s/n* ☎ *32/100–608* ☎☎ *32/100–312* ⊕ *www.hotelirona.cl* ↝ *50 rooms, 2 suites* ⚊ *Restaurant, some fans, in-room safes, some minibars, tennis court, pool, bar, laundry service, meeting room, airport shuttle, car rental, travel services; no a/c in some rooms, no TV in some rooms* ▤ *AE, DC, MC, V* ⋈ *BP.*

$$–$$$$ 🏨 **Hotel Hotu Matua.** Set well back from the coast is this secluded accommodation that played host to former Chilean president Eduardo Frei. A small sitting area in each guest room, furnished with comfortable lounge chairs, overlooks the pool and surrounding tropical vegetation. The owner's collection of artifacts rivals that of the island's museum. ⊠ *Av. Pont s/n* ☎ *32/100–242* 🖷 *32/100–445* ⊕ *www.hotumatua.cl* ↝ *55 rooms, 5 suites* ⚊ *Dining room, minibars, pool, bar, recreation room, shops, laundry service, airport shuttle, car rental, travel services; no a/c, no room TVs* ▤ *AE, DC, MC, V* ⋈ *BP.*

★ **$$** ⊞ **Aloha Nui.** One of the most charming accommodations on Easter Island, Aloha Nui begins to feel like home even before you can unpack. The genial owner, Maria Reina Pacomio Paoa, makes you feel very welcome, and though you'll start out in the dining room, it probably won't be long before you're in the kitchen having breakfast with the family. The generously proportioned rooms, in a separate building behind the main house, look out on the palm-shaded gardens. You can book excellent ecotours through the hotel. ⊠ *Av. Atamu Tekena s/n* ☎ *32/100–274* ⊕ *www.haumakatours.com* ⇥ *6 rooms* ⌂ *Dining room, bar, airport shuttle, car rental, travel services; no a/c, no room phones, no room TVs* ⊟ *MC, V* �[◯] *CP.*

$$ ⊞ **Chez Maria Gorretti.** The beautiful garden and lovely airy, plant-filled dining room are the main attractions of this guesthouse on the northern edge of town. All the rooms have sliding doors that open onto clumps of banana trees and lush vines that wrap around the trunks of papaya trees. Pretty tile floors keep the rooms cool, which is a plus on summer afternoons. ⊠ *Av. Atamu Tekena s/n* ☎☎ *32/100–459* ⊕ *www.rapanuiweb.com/chezmariagoretti* ⇥ *18 rooms* ⌂ *Dining room, horseback riding, bar, laundry service, Internet, airport shuttle, car rental, travel services; no a/c, no room phones, no room TVs* ⊟ *DC, MC, V* �[◯] *BP.*

★ **$$** ⊞ **Hotel Gomero.** A long drive lined by palm and papaya trees leads to this charming small hotel. Guests gather in the comfortable dining room, which has rattan furniture and beautifully carved wooden columns. The guest rooms, some with handcrafted furnishings, have private terraces overlooking a beautifully attended garden. The owners, a multilingual Austrian–Rapa Nui couple, run a tight ship, so everything is spotless. ⊠ *Av. Tu'u Koihu s/n* ☎ *32/100–313* ☎☎ *32/100–591* ⊕ *www.hotelgomero.com* ⇥ *13 rooms* ⌂ *Dining room, fans, minibars, pool, bar, laundry service, Internet, airport shuttle, car rental, travel services; no a/c, no room TVs* ⊟ *DC, MC, V* �[◯] *BP.*

$$ ⊞ **Hotel Manavai.** This friendly lodging's spacious rooms, constructed from native woods, are rustic and cozy. Rooms open out onto a garden of flourishing vegetation and a small pool. Four suites have televisions, hot tubs, and terraces hung with hammocks. Hotel Manavai sits on one of Hanga Roa's main thoroughfares. ⊠ *Av. Te Pito O Te Henua* ☎ *32/100–670* ⊟ *32/100–658* ⇥ *30 rooms, 4 suites* ⌂ *Dining room, fans, pool, bar, shop, airport shuttle, car rental, travel services; no a/c, no room phones, no room TVs* ⊟ *AE, DC, MC, V* �[◯] *CP.*

$$ ⊞ **Hotel Manutara.** Palm trees tower over this low-slung resort on the southern edge of Hanga Roa. The hotel invites you to relax, whether reclining in a lounge chair by the bean-shape pool or reading in one of the overstuffed sofas in the sunny lobby. Especially nice is the shaded dining room, which has rattan tables covered with tropical-print tablecloths. The homey rooms overlook the lush gardens overflowing with red and orange hibiscus. ⊠ *Av. Hotu Matu'a s/n* ☎ *32/100–297* ⊟ *32/100–768* ⇥ *26 rooms* ⌂ *Dining room, room service, fans, pool, bar, lounge, shop, laundry service, car rental, travel services; no a/c* ⊟ *DC, MC, V* �[◯] *BP.*

★ **$$** ⊞ **Hotel Otai.** Although the hotel is right in the center of town, its beautiful gardens make you feel like you're miles from anywhere. From the flower-scented deck surrounding the pool you can catch a glimpse of the sea. Pretty wicker furniture fills the spacious rooms, which open out onto shady wooden verandas. The wood-ceilinged dining room is cool and quiet. ⊠ *Av. Te Pito O Te Henua s/n* ☎ *32/100–250* 🖷 *32/100–482* ⤺ *35 rooms* ⚭ *Restaurant, fans, pool, bar, airport shuttle, car rental, travel services; no a/c in some rooms, no room TVs* ⊟ *AE, DC, MC, V* ⏄ *BP.*

$$ 🏨 **Hotel Victoria.** Fabulous views of the Pacific are what make this hotel special. The rooms in the low-slung main building are furnished with little more than beds and dressers, but that hardly matters when you can just sit on the covered terrace or in the leafy garden and enjoy the sliver of blue on the horizon. Shops and restaurants are a short walk away. ⊠ *Av. Pont s/n* ☎ *32/100–272* ⤺ *7 rooms* ⚭ *Dining room, airport shuttle, car rental, travel services; no a/c, no room phones, no room TVs* ⊟ *V* ⏄ *CP.*

$$ 🏨 **Martín and Anita.** Papaya and banana trees surround this little hostelry with clean, spacious rooms that open onto plant-lined terra-cotta pathways. Enthusiastic owner Martín Hereveri also runs several different tours of the island that cover most of the ancient ceremonial sites. ⊠ *Av. Simon Paoa s/n* ☎🖷 *32/100–593* ⊕ *www.hostal.co.cl* ⤺ *13 rooms* ⚭ *Dining room, bar, laundry service, Internet, airport shuttle, car rental, travel services, no-smoking rooms; no a/c, no room phones, no room TVs* ⊟ *AE, DC, MC, V* ⏄ *BP.*

$$ 🏨 **Vai Moana.** The name of this lovely lodging means "blue sea," and you'll soon discover why. A long stretch of azure can be seen from just about everywhere, from the glass-enclosed dining room to the umbrella-shaded veranda. Little white cabanas strewn around the grounds are simply furnished, with wood-beamed ceilings and wide windows. The effusive staff speaks English and French. ⊠ *Av. Atamu Tekena s/n* ☎🖷 *32/100–626* ⊕ *www.vai-moana.cl* ⤺ *14 rooms* ⚭ *Dining room, fans, minibars, bar, lounge, laundry service, Internet, car rental, travel services, no-smoking rooms; no a/c, no room phones, no room TVs* ⊟ *AE, MC, V* ⏄ *BP.*

★ $ 🏨 **Tadeo and Lili.** Individual bungalows fronted in black volcanic rock form part of this lovely guesthouse on the coast with unspoiled views of Hanga Roa and the rolling surf of the Pacific. Lili is French and Tadeo Rapa Nui. Together they created these attractive cabins, each with a stamp of individuality. Lili is also a renowned guide. ⊠ *Av. Policarpo Toro s/ n* ☎🖷 *32/100–422* ⊘ *tadeolili@entelchile.net* ⤺ *6 bungalows* ⚭ *Dining room, Internet, airport shuttle, travel services; no a/c, no room phones, no room TVs* ⊟ *MC, V* ⏄ *CP.*

NIGHTLIFE & THE ARTS

The Arts

For a taste of the excitement of the annual Tapati Rapa Nui festival, take in a performance by the folk troupe Kari Kari or Polinesia. In a dance called the *sau sau*, the men and women spin wildly as the music gets faster and faster. The exuberant movements of the dancers are punctuated by shouts of joy. Another dance called the *hoko* incorporates birdlike movements. Shows start at around 11,500 pesos each. **Kari Kari** (☎ 32/100–595) performs at various hotels. The dance group **Polinesia** (☎ 32/100–447) performs at the restaurant Kopa Kavana on Avenida Te Pito O Te Henua.

Nightlife

You're in for a late night if you want to sample the scene in Hanga Roa. Locals don't hit the bars until around midnight. The most popular place to stop for a beer is the **Banana Pub** (⊠ Av. Atamu Tekena s/n ☎ No phone), a laid-back bar on the main road. **Aloha** (⊠ Av. Atamu Tekena s/n ☎ No phone), a bar-restaurant with a palm tree growing through its front porch, plays both Rapu Nui and international music. **Tavake** (⊠ Av. Atamu Tekena s/n ☎ No phone) is a small, popular bar with a front porch and plastic tables along the main thoroughfare.

On weekends, the younger set heads to **Toroko** (⊠ Av. Policarpo Toro s/n ☎ No phone), a dance club a stone's throw from the beach. You won't need directions—just follow the thumping disco beat. **Piditi** (⊠ Av. Hotu Matu'a s/n ☎ No phone), a dance club close to the airport, blares music into the wee hours of the morning.

SPORTS & THE OUTDOORS

Haka pei, or sliding down hillsides on banana trunks, is one of the more popular activities during the Tapati Rapa Nui festival. Another is racing across the reed-choked lake that's hidden inside the crater of Ranu Raraku. Visitors who take to the water usually prefer swimming at one of the sandy beaches or snorkeling near one of the offshore islets. Another option is to hike out to isolated spots on the northern coast.

Beaches

Easter Island's earliest settlers are believed to have landed on idyllic **Playa Anakena.** Legend has it that the caves in the cliffs overlooking the beach are where Hotu Matu'a, the island's first ruler, dwelled while constructing his home. It's easy to see why Hotu Matu'a might have selected this spot: on an island ringed by rough volcanic rock, Playa Anakena is the widest swath of sand. Ignoring the sun-worshipping tourists are the five beautifully carved moais standing on nearby Ahu Nau Nau. On the northern coast of the island, Playa Anakena is reachable by a paved road that runs across the island, or by the more circuitous coastal road.

A lovely strip of pink sand, **Playa Ovahe** isn't as crowded as neighboring Playa Anakena. But the fact that most tourists pass it by is what makes this secluded beach so appealing. Families head here on weekends for afternoon cookouts. The cliffs that tower above the beach were once home to many of the island's residents. Locals proudly point out caves where relatives were born.

The only beach in Hanga Roa is **Playa Pea,** a tiny stretch of sand near the caleta. It's a popular spot among local families with small children.

Diving

The crystal-clear waters of the South Pacific afford great visibility for snorkelers and divers. Dozens of types of colorful fish flourish in the warm waters surrounding the island's craggy volcanic rocks. Some of the most spectacular underwater scenery is at Motu Nui and Motu Iti, two adjoining islets just off the coast. **Orca Diving Center** (⊠ Caleta de Hanga Roa ☎ 32/550–877 or 32/550–375 🖷 32/550–448 ⊕ www. seemorca.cl) provides a boat, a guide, and all your diving gear for about 27,000 pesos per person. You can rent a snorkeling mask and fins. **Mike Rapu Dive Center** (⊠ Caleta de Hanga Roa ☎ 32/551–055 ⊕ www. mikerapudiving.cl) arranges night dives for 45,500 pesos and various excursions for around 75,000 pesos.

Hiking

The breezes that cool the island even in the middle of summer make this a perfect place for hikers. Be careful, though, as the sun is much stronger than it feels. Slather yourself with sunblock and bring along plenty of water.

You can take numerous hikes from Hanga Roa. A short walk takes you to Ahu Tahai. More strenuous is a hike on a gravel road to the seven moais of Ahu Akivi, about 10 km (6 mi) north of town. One of the most rewarding treks is along a rough dirt path on the northern coast that leads from Ahu Te Peu to Playa Anakena. The six-hour journey around Terevaka takes you past many undisturbed archaeological sites that few tourists ever see. If you're planning on heading out without a guide, pick up a copy of the *Easter Island Trekking Map* at any local shop.

Horseback Riding

One popular way to see the island is on horseback, which typically costs up to 210,000 pesos per day. Many locals rent out their horses, and you can also often rent horses and guides from tour operators and car-rental agencies. Also try asking your hotel to arrange this for you.

Mountain Biking

Mountain biking is a great way to get around and see the sights of Easter Island. Most car-rental agencies also rent mountain bikes for up to 14,000 pesos per day.

SHOPPING

Souvenir shops line Hanga Roa's two main streets, Avenida Atamu Tekena and Avenida Te Pito O Te Henua. **Feria Municipal** (⊠ Av. Atamu Tekena s/n ☎ No phone), an open-air market, has good buys on hand-made jewelry. **Hotu Matu'a's Favorite Shop** (⊠ Av. Atamu Tekena s/n ☎ No phone) sells the widest selection of T-shirts on the island. Next to the church is the **Mercado Artesenal** (⊠ Av. Ara Roa Rakei s/n ☎ No phone), a large building filled with crafts stands. Here, local artisans whittle wooden moais and string together seashell necklaces. It's open Monday–Saturday 9 AM–8 PM and Sunday 9 AM–12:30 PM.

EASTER ISLAND ESSENTIALS

Transportation

BY AIR

Easter Island's shoe-box-size Aeropuerto Internacional Mataveri is on the southern edge of Hanga Roa.

Lan operates all flights from Santiago to the east and Tahiti to the west. Three or four flights a week arrive from Santiago during the high season between December and March, two the rest of the year; two flights a week arrive from Tahiti. The planes are often full in January and February, so it's best to book far ahead and reconfirm your flights.

Tickets to Easter Island are expensive—up to $1,000 for a round-trip flight from Santiago. However, you'll get a better deal if you combine it with a flight to Santiago.

🛈 Airline **Lan** ⊠ Av. Atamu Tekena s/n ☎ 32/100-279 or 32/100-920 ⊕ www.lan.com.
🛈 Airport **Aeropuerto Internacional Mataveri** ⊠ Av. Hotu Matu'a s/n ☎ 32/100-277 or 32/100-278.

BY CAR

To see many of Easter Island's less traveled areas, a four-wheel-drive vehicle is a necessity. Except for the well-maintained roads leading to Rano Kau and Playa Anakena, the best you can hope for are gravel roads. The most isolated spots are reached by dusty dirt roads or no roads at all.

None of the international car-rental chains have offices on Easter Island, but you have many reputable local agencies from which to choose. Most charge about 30,000 pesos for eight hours, or 35,000 pesos per day for a four-wheel-drive vehicle. If you plan on visiting during January and February, call a few days ahead to reserve a car.

You can also rent cars at many restaurants, souvenir shops, and possibly the guesthouse where you're staying. If you ask around, you may find a significantly cheaper rate than what the rental companies charge.

🛈 Rental Agencies **Aku Aku** ⊠ Av. Tu'u Koihu s/n ☎ 32/100-770 ⊕ www.akuakuturismo. cl. **Insular** ⊠ Av. Atamu Tekena s/n ☎ 32/100-480 or 32/551-276. **Kia Koe** ⊠ Av. Atamu Tekena s/n ☎ 32/100-282 ⊕ www.kiakoetour.co.cl. **Oceanic Rapa Nui** ⊠ Av. Atamu Tekena s/n ☎ 32/100-985 or 32/551-392. **Toki** ⊠ Av. Atamu Tekena s/n ☎ 32/551-157.

BY TAXI

Taxis have become extremely popular among residents, so it's never difficult to find one during the day. Most trips to destinations in Hanga Roa should cost less than 1,000 pesos. After 8 or 9 PM, the price doubles.

Contacts & Resources

BANKS & EXCHANGE SERVICES

The official currency is Chilean pesos, but U.S. dollars are accepted just about everywhere, and most restaurants and hotels will present your bill in U.S. dollars.

The only bank on the island is the Banco del Estado de Chile, on Avenida Tuumaheke. It's open weekdays 8–noon. You can exchange U.S. dollars and traveler's checks, or get a cash advance on your Visa card.

There is one ATM on the island, where you can withdraw cash with MasterCard, Visa, and Cirrus cards. It's near the Sernatur office on Avenida Tuumaheke, but it's still a good idea to bring cash before you arrive just in case the ATM breaks down.

MAIL & SHIPPING

Correos de Chile, the island's tiny post office, is on Avenida Te Pito O Te Henua across from Hotel Otai. Postage is the same as in the rest of Chile. Bear in mind that mail is sent via Lan Airlines flights, so you're likely to travel back to the mainland on the same plane as the letter you posted. If you want an Easter Island postmark, you might want to bring your own stamps. The post office here sometimes runs out.

TOURS

Rapa Nui is filled with companies selling tours of the island. Most run similar half-day and full-day excursions to major archaeological sites, although a few offer "adventure" tours to lesser-known areas. Make sure to settle on the itinerary before booking a tour. If you know exactly where you want to visit, consider a private tour guide. Haumaka Tours' Josefina Nahoe Mulloy and Ramón Edmunds Pacomio, both English speakers, can show you sights not on any tour-bus itinerary.

Aku Aku, Kia Koe, Mahinatur, and Manu Iti are all reputable tour agencies. Kia Koe attracts a lot of street traffic, so its tours are often crowded. Mahinatur generally books tours in advance, so the groups are often smaller. Both have friendly, knowledgeable guides.

🚹 Tour Agencies **Aku Aku** ✉ Av. Tu'u Koihu s/n ☏ 32/100-770 ⊕ www.akuakuturismo. cl. **Haumaka Tours** ✉ Av. Hotu Matu'u s/n ☏☏ 32/100-274 or 32/100-411 ⊕ www. haumakatours.com. **Kia Koe** ✉ Av. Atamu Tekena s/n ☏ 32/100-282 ⊕ www.kiakoetour. co.cl. **Mahinatur** ✉ Av. Atamu Tekena at Av. Hotu Matu'a ☏ 32/551-513 ⊕ www. mahinatur.cl. **Manu Iti** ✉ Av. Tuukoihu s/n ☏ 32/100-313 ⊕ www.manuiti.de.

VISITOR INFORMATION

The staff at the local Sernatur office can provide you with maps and lists of local businesses. It's open weekdays 8:30–1 and 2:30–6, and Saturday 8:30–1.

🚹 Sernatur **Oficina de Tourismo** ✉ Av. Tuumaheke s/n ☏ 32/100-255.

Adventure & Learning Vacations

11

With terrain ranging from towering Andean peaks to deserts, wetlands, and glaciers, the topographical diversity of Chile (and neighboring Argentina) provides ideal settings for many types of active or ecotourism adventure. The country also contains some fascinating indigenous and archaeological sites, and an array of wildlife.

Updated by
Joyce Dalton

CHOOSING A TOUR PACKAGE CAREFULLY IS ALWAYS IMPORTANT, but it becomes even more critical when the focus is adventure or sports. You can rough it or opt for comfortable, sometimes even luxurious, accommodations. You can select easy hiking and canoeing adventures or trekking, rafting, and climbing expeditions that require high degrees of physical endurance and technical skill. Study multiple itineraries to find the trip that's right for you. This chapter describes selected trip offerings from some of the best adventure tour operators in today's travel world. Wisely chosen, special-interest vacations lead to distinctive, memorable experiences—just pack flexibility and curiosity along with the bug spray.

For additional information, contact Chile's tourist office or the **South American Explorers Club** (⌨ 126 Indian Creek Rd., Ithaca, NY 14850 ☎ 607/277–0488 or 800/274–0568 🖷 607/277–6122 ⊕ www. saexplorers.org).

Choosing a Trip

With dozens of choices for special-interest trips to Chile, there are a number of factors to keep in mind when deciding which company and package will be right for you.

- **How strenuous a trip do you want?** Adventure vacations commonly are split into "soft" and "hard" adventures. Hard adventures, such as strenuous treks (often at high altitudes), Class IV or V rafting, or ascents of some of the world's most challenging mountains, generally require excellent physical condition and previous experience. Most hiking, biking, canoeing/kayaking, and similar soft adventures can be enjoyed by people of all ages who are in good health and are accustomed to a reasonable amount of exercise. A little honesty goes a long way—recognize your own level of physical fitness and discuss it with the tour operator before signing on.

- **How far off the beaten path do you want to go?** Although many trips described in this chapter might seem to be headed into uncharted territory, tour operators carefully check each detail before an itinerary goes into a brochure. While you won't be vying with busloads of tourists for photo ops, you'll probably run into small groups of like-minded travelers. Journeys into truly remote regions typically involve camping or the simplest of accommodations, but they reward with more abundant wildlife and locals who are less accustomed to the clicking of cameras. Ask yourself if it's the *reality* or the *image* of roughing it that appeals to you. Stick with the reality.

- **Is sensitivity to the environment important to you?** If so, then determine if it is equally important to the tour operator. Does the company protect the fragile environments you'll be visiting? Are some of the company's profits designated for conservation efforts or put back into the communities visited? Many of the companies included in this chapter are actively involved in environmental organizations and projects with indigenous communities visited on their trips. On ecotourism programs, check out the naturalist's credentials. A string of degrees can be less important than familiarity with the area.

- **What sort of group is best for you?** At its best, group travel offers curious, like-minded people with whom to share the day's experiences. Do you enjoy a mix of companions or would you prefer similar demographics—for example, age-specific, singles, same sex? Inquire about the group size; many companies have a maximum of 10 to 16 members, but 30 or more is not unknown. With large groups, expect little flexibility in the published itinerary and more time spent (or wasted) at rest stops, meals, and various arrivals and departures.

  If groups aren't your thing, many companies will customize a trip just for you. In fact, this has become a major part of many tour operators' business. The itinerary can be as loose or as complete as you choose. Such travel offers all the conveniences of a package tour, but the "group" is composed of only you or you and those you've chosen as travel companions. Responding to a renewed interest in multigenerational travel, many tour operators also offer designated family departures, with itineraries carefully crafted to appeal both to children and adults.

- **The client consideration factor—strong or absent?** Gorgeous photos and well-written tour descriptions go a long way in selling a company's trips. But the "client consideration factor" is important, too. Does the operator provide useful information about health (suggested or required inoculations, tips for dealing with high altitudes)? A list of frequently asked questions and their answers? Recommended readings? Equipment needed for sports trips? Packing tips when baggage is restricted? Climate info? Visa requirements? A list of client referrals? The option of using your credit card? What is the refund policy if you must cancel? (No refund at all for cancellations 60 days or less before departure date and only a partial refund for cancellations earlier than 60 days are not unusual.) If you're traveling alone and want to avoid the sometimes exorbitant single supplement, will the company match you up with a like-minded traveler? Does the company have a local office in Chile or Argentina? While not vital in most situations, this can lead to a speedier resolution of problems should they arise.

- **Are there hidden costs?** Make sure you know what is and isn't included in basic trip costs when comparing companies. International airfare is usually extra. Sometimes, domestic flights are additional. Is trip insurance required, and if so, is it included? How much does it cost and what situations are covered? Are airport transfers included? Visa fees? Departure taxes? Gratuities? Equipment? Meals? Bottled water? All excursions? While some travelers prefer the option of an excursion or free time, many, especially those visiting a destination for the first time, want to see as much as possible. Paying extra for a number of excursions can significantly increase the total cost of the trip. Many factors affect the price, and the trip that looks cheapest in the brochure could well turn out to be the most expensive. Don't assume that roughing it will save you money, as prices rise when limited access and a lack of essential supplies on-site require costly special arrangements.

Tour Operators

Below you'll find contact information for all tour operators mentioned in this chapter. For international tour operators, we list both the tour operator and its North American representative, so you can contact whichever company is easier for you. For example, Exodus is represented in North America by Adventure Center. While the list below hardly exhausts the number of reputable companies, these were chosen because they are established firms that offer a good selection of itineraries. Such operators are usually the first to introduce great new destinations, forging ahead before luxury hotels and air-conditioned coaches tempt less hardy visitors.

Abercrombie & Kent ⊠ *1520 Kensington Rd., Oak Brook, IL 60523* ☎ *630/954–2944 or 800/323–7308* ⊕ *www.abercrombiekent.com.*

Adventure Life ⊠ *1655 S. 3rd St. W, Suite 1, Missoula, MT 59801* ☎ *406/541–2677 or 800/344–6118* ⊕ *www.adventure-life.com.*

Alpine Ascents International ⊠ *121 Mercer St., Seattle, WA 98109* ☎ *206/378–1927* ⊕ *www.AlpineAscents.com.*

American Alpine Institute ⊠ *1515 12th St., Bellingham, WA 98225* ☎ *360/671–1505* ⊕ *www.aai.cc.*

Andes Adventures ⊠ *1323 12th St., Suite F, Santa Monica, CA 90401* ☎ *310/395–5265 or 800/289–9470* ⊕ *www.andesadventures.com.*

Arun Treks & Expeditions ⊠ *301 E. 33rd St., Suite 3, Austin, TX 78705* ☎ *512/407–8314 or 888/495–8735* ⊕ *www.aruntreks.com.*

Austin-Lehman Adventures ⊕ *PO Box 81025, Billings, MT 59108* ☎ *406/655–4591 or 800/575—1540* ⊕ *www.austinlehman.com.*

Australian & Amazonian Adventures ⊠ *2711 Market Garden, Austin, TX 78745* ☎ *512/443–5393 or 800/232—5658* 🖶 *512/442—8515* ⊕ *www.amazonadventures.com.*

Big Five Tours & Expeditions ⊠ *1551 SE Palm Ct., Stuart, FL 34994* ☎ *772/287–7995 or 800/244–3483* ⊕ *www.bigfive.com.*

BikeHike Adventures ⊠ *316 W. 5th Ave., Suite 13, Vancouver, BC V5Y 1J5 Canada* ☎ *604/731–2442 or 888/805–0061* ⊕ *www.bikehike.com.*

Butterfield & Robinson ⊠ *70 Bond St., Toronto, Ontario M5B 1X3 Canada* ☎ *416/864–1354 or 800/678–1147* ⊕ *www.butterfield.com.*

Clipper Cruise Line ⊠ *11969 Westline Industrial Dr., St. Louis, MO 63146* ☎ *314/655–6700or 800/325–0010* ⊕ *www.clippercruise.com.*

Colorado Mountain School ⊠ *341 Moraine Ave., Estes Park, CO 80517* ☎ *970/586–5758 or 888/267–7783* ⊕ *www.cmschool.com.*

Country Walkers ⊕ *Box 180, Waterbury, VT 05676* ☎ *802/244–1387 or 800/464–9255* ⊕ *www.countrywalkers.com.*

Cruceros Australis ⊠ *4014 Chase Ave., Suite 202 Miami Beach, FL 33140* ☎ *305/695–9618 or 877/678–3772* ⊕ *www.australis.com.*

Earth River Expeditions ⊠ *180 Towpath Rd., Accord, NY 12404* ☎ *845/626–2665 or 800/643–2784* ⊕ *www.earthriver.com.*

Earthwatch ⊠ *3 Clocktower Pl., Suite 100, Maynard, MA 01754* ☎ *978/461–0801 or 800/776–0188* ⊕ *www.earthwatch.org.*

ElderTreks ⊠ *597 Markham St., Toronto, Ontario M6G 2L7, Canada* ☎ *416/588–5000 or 800/741–7956* ⊕ *www.eldertreks.com.*

Equitours ✆ *Box 807, Dubois, WY 82513* ☎ *307/455–3363 or 800/545–0019* ⊕ *www.equitours.com.*

Experience Plus! ✉ *415 Mason Ct., #1, Fort Collins, CO 80524* ☎ *970/484–8489 or 800/685–4565* ⊕ *www.ExperiencePlus.com.*

Explore! Worldwide ✉ *1 Frederick St., Aldershot, Hampshire GU11 1LQ UK* ⊕ *www.explore.co.uk.*

Far Horizons ✆ *Box 2546, San Anselmo, CA 94979* ☎ *415/482–8400 or 800/552–4575* ⊕ *www.farhorizons.com.*

Fishing International ✉ *5510 Skylane Blvd., Suite 200, Santa Rosa, CA 95405* ☎ *707/542–4242 or 800/950–4242* ⊕ *www.fishinginternational.com.*

FishQuest ✉ *3375B Hwy. 76 West, Hiawassee GA 30546* ☎ *706/896–1403 or 888/891–3474* ⊕ *www.fishquest.com.*

Fly Fishing And ✆ *Box 1719, Red Lodge, MT 59068* ☎ *406/446–9087* ⊕ *www.flyfishingand.com.*

Focus Tours ✉ *111 Malaga Rd., Santa Fe, NM 87505* ☎ *505/989–7193* ⊕ *www.focustours.com.*

Frontiers ✆ *Box 959, Wexford, PA 15090* ☎ *724/935–1577 or 800/245–1950* ⊕ *www. frontierstravel.com.*

G.A.P. Adventures ✉ *19 Charlotte St., Toronto, Ontario M5V 2H5 Canada* ☎ *416/260–0999 or 800/465–5600* ⊕ *www.gapadventures.com.*

Geographic Expeditions ✉ *1008 General Kennedy Ave., San Francisco, CA 94129* ☎ *415/922–0448 or 800/777–8183* ⊕ *www.geoex.com.*

Global Adventure Guide ✉ *14 Kennaway Rd., Unit 3, Christchurch, 8002 New Zealand* ☎ *800/732–0861 in North America* ⊕ *www.globaladventureguide.com.*

Hidden Trails ✉ *202–380 West 1st Ave., Vancouver, BC V5Y 3T7 Canada* ☎ *604/323–1141 or 888/987–2457* ⊕ *www.hiddentrails.com.*

Inca ✉ *1311 63rd St., Emeryville, CA 94608* ☎ *510/420–1550* ⊕ *www.inca1.com.*

International Expeditions ✉ *One Environs Park, Helena, AL 35080* ☎ *205/428–1700 or 800/633–4734* ⊕ *www.ietravel.com.*

Joseph Van Os Photo Safaris ✆ *Box 655, Vashon Island, WA 98070* ☎ *206/463–5383* ⊕ *www.photosafaris.com.*

Journeys International ✉ *107 Aprill Dr., Suite 3, Ann Arbor, MI 48103* ☎ *734/665–4407 or 800/255–8735* ⊕ *www.journeys-intl.com.*

KE Adventure Travel ✉ *1131 Grand Ave., Glenwood Springs, CO 81601* ☎ *970/384–0001 or 800/497–9675* ⊕ *www.keadventure.com.*

Ladatco Tours ✉ *2200 S. Dixie Hwy., Suite 704, Coconut Grove, FL 33133* ☎ *305/854–8422 or 800/327–6162* ⊕ *www.ladatco.com.*

Lindblad Expeditions ✉ *96 Morton St., New York, NY 10014* ☎ *212/765–7740 or 800/397–3348* ⊕ *www.expeditions.com.*

Mountain Madness ✉ *4218 SW Alaska, Suite 206, Seattle, WA 98116* ☎ *206/937–8389 or 800/328–5925* ⊕ *www.mountainmadness.com.*

Mountain Travel-Sobek ✉ *1266 66th St., Suite 4, Emeryville, CA 94608* ☎ *510/594–6000 or 888/687–6235* ⊕ *www.mtsobek.com.*

Myths and Mountains ✉ *976 Tee Ct., Incline Village, NV 89451* ☎ *775/832–5454 or 800/670–6984* ⊕ *www.mythsandmountains.com.*

Nature Expeditions International ✉ *7860 Peters Rd., Suite F-103, Plantation, FL 33324* ☎ *954/693–8852 or 800/869–0639* ⊕ *www.naturexp.com.*

Off the Beaten Path ✉ *7 E. Beall, Bozeman, MT 59715* ☎ *406/586–1311 or 800/445–2995* ⊕ *www.offthebeatenpath.com.*

OutWest Global Adventures ✆ *PO Box 2050, Red Lodge, MT 59068* ☎ *406/446–1533 or 800/743–0458* 🖷 *406/446–1338* ⊕ *www.outwestadventures.com.* This company operates gay- and lesbian-oriented tours.

PanAmerican Travel Services ✉ *320 E. 900 S, Salt Lake City, UT 84111* ☎ *801/364–4300 or 800/364–4359* ⊕ *www.panamtours.com.*

PowderQuest Tours ✉ *7108 Pinetree Rd., Richmond, VA 23229* ☎ *206/203–6065 or 888/565–7158* ⊕ *www.powderquest.com.*

Rod & Reel Adventures ✉ *32617 Skyhawk Way, Eugene, OR 97405* ☎ *541/349–0777 or 800/356–6982* 🖷 *541/338–0367* ⊕ *www.rodreeladventures.com.*

Snoventures ✉ *Cedar Ave., Huddersfield HD1 5QH UK* ☎ *775/586–9133 in North America* ⊕ *www.snoventures.com.*

South American Journeys ✉ *9921 Cabanas Ave., Tujunga, CA 91042* ☎ *818/951–8986* ⊕ *www.southamericanjourneys.com or www.gosouthamerica.org.*

Southwind Adventures ✆ *Box 621057, Littleton, CO 80162* ☎ *303/972–0701 or 800/377–9463* 🖷 *303/972–0708* ⊕ *www.southwindadventures.com.*

The World Outdoors ✉ *2840 Wilderness Pl., Suite D, Boulder, CO 80301* ☎ *303/413–0938 or 800/488–8483* 🖷 *303/413–0926* ⊕ *www.theworldoutdoors.com.*

Tours International ✉ *12750 Briar Forest Dr., Suite 603, Houston, TX 77077* ☎ *281/293–0809 or 800/247–7965* 🖷 *281/293–0409* ⊕ *www.toursinternational.com.*

Wilderness Travel ✉ *1102 9th St., Berkeley, CA 94710* ☎ *510/558–2488 or 800/368–2794* 🖷 *510/558–2489* ⊕ *www.wildernesstravel.com.*

Wildland Adventures ✉ *3516 N.E. 155th St., Seattle, WA 98155* ☎ *206/365–0686 or 800/345–4453* 🖷 *206/363–6615* ⊕ *www.wildland.com.*

WINGS ✉ *1643 N. Alvernon, Suite 109, Tucson, AZ 85712* ☎ *520/320—9868 or 888/293–6443* ⊕ *www.wingsbirds.com.*

World Expeditions ✉ *580 Market St., Suite 225, San Francisco, CA 94104* ☎ *415/989–2212 or 888/464–8735* ⊕ *www.worldexpeditions.com.*

CRUISES

Antarctic Cruises

Founded to promote environmentally responsible travel to Antarctica, the **International Association of Antarctica Tour Operators** (☎ 970/704–1047 ⊕ www.iaato.org) is a good source of information, including suggested readings. Most companies operating Antarctica trips are members of this organization and display its logo in their brochures.

Season: November–March.
Location: Most cruises depart from Ushuaia, in Argentine Patagonia.
Cost: From $2,995 (triple-occupancy cabin) for 12 days from Ushuaia.

Tour Operators: Abercrombie & Kent; Adventure Center; Big Five Tours & Expeditions; Clipper Cruise Line; ElderTreks; G.A.P. Adventures; Lindblad Expeditions; Mountain Travel-Sobek; Quark Expeditions; Travcoa; Wilderness Travel; Zegrahm Expeditions.

Ever since Lars-Eric Lindblad operated the first cruise to the "White Continent" in 1966, Antarctica has exerted an almost magnetic pull for serious travelers. From Ushuaia, the world's southernmost city, you'll sail for two (sometimes rough) days through the Drake Passage and then on to the spectacular landscapes of Antarctica. Most visits are to the Antarctic Peninsula, the continent's most accessible region. Accompanied by naturalists, you'll travel ashore in motorized rubber crafts called Zodiacs to view penguins and nesting seabirds. Some cruises visit research stations, and many call at the Falkland, South Orkney, South Shetland, or South Georgia Islands. Adventure Center and Big Five Tours & Expeditions offer sea kayaking and, at an extra cost, the chance to camp for a night on the ice.

Expedition vessels have been fitted with ice-strengthened hulls; many originally were built as polar-research vessels. On certain Quark Expeditions itineraries you can travel aboard an icebreaker, the *Kapitan Khlebnikov,* which rides up onto the ice, crushing it with its weight. This vessel carries helicopters for aerial viewing. Quark has made two circumnavigations of Antarctica, a 21,000-km (13,000-mi) journey lasting almost three months, and may offer this trip again.

When choosing an expedition cruise, it's wise to inquire about the qualifications of the on-board naturalists and historians; the maximum number of passengers carried; the ice-readiness of the vessel; on-board medical facilities; whether there is an open bridge policy, and the number of landings attempted per day.

Argentine & Chilean Patagonia Cruises

Cruising the southern tip of South America and along Chile's western coast north to the lake district reveals some of Earth's most spectacular scenery: fjords, glaciers, lagoons, lakes, narrow channels, waterfalls, forested shorelines, fishing villages, and wildlife. While many tour operators include a one- or two-day boating excursion as part of their Patagonia itineraries, the companies listed below offer from four to 12 nights aboard ship.

Season: October–April.
Locations: Chilean fjords; Puerto Montt and Punta Arenas, Chile; Tierra del Fuego and Ushuaia, Argentina.
Cost: From $1,078 for a 4-day, 3-night cruise between Punta Arenas and Ushuaia.
Tour Operators: Abercrombie & Kent; Adventure Life; Big Five Tours & Expeditions; Clipper Cruise Line; Cruceros Australis; Explore! Worldwide; International Expeditions; Lindblad Expeditions; Mountain Travel-Sobek; Off the Beaten Path; Wilderness Travel; Wildland Adventures.

Boarding your comfortable vessel in Punta Arenas, Chile or Ushuaia, Argentina, you'll cruise the Strait of Magellan and the Beagle Channel, visiting glaciers, penguin rookeries, and seal colonies before heading north along the fjords of Chile's western coast. Adventure Life and Lindblad Expeditions include the Chiloé Archipelago, a region rich in folklore about ghost ships, magical sea creatures, and troll-like beings known as the Trauco. With Abercrombie & Kent, Clipper Cruise Line, and Wildland Adventures, you'll savor the mountain scenery of Torres del Paine National Park for several days before or following the cruise, while Lindblad Expeditions, Mountain Travel-Sobek, and International Expeditions visit Tierra del Fuego National Park. Cruceros Australis, and some other companies, also include Cape Horn National Park. Wilderness Travel allows time for hiking at Volcano Osorno and in Alerce Andino National Park; the latter protects the second largest temperate rain-forest ecosystem in the world. Following a five-day cruise, Off the Beaten Path travelers fly to Puerto Montt for a three-night stay at nearby Lake Llanquihue with opportunities for hiking in the mountains. Most itineraries begin or end with days in Santiago, Chile or Buenos Aires, Argentina.

LEARNING VACATIONS

Cultural Tours

Among the many types of travel, some find the most rewarding to be an in-depth focus on one aspect of a country's culture. This could mean exploring the archaeological remains of great civilizations, learning about the lives and customs of indigenous peoples, or trying to master a foreign language or culinary skills.

Season: Year-round.
Locations: Atacama Desert; Easter Island; Santa Cruz.
Cost: From $1,795 for seven days from Santiago.
Tour Operators: Abercrombie & Kent; Big Five Tours & Expeditions; Far Horizons; G.A.P. Adventures; Ladatco Tours; Myths and Mountains; Nature Expeditions International; Off the Beaten Path; PanAmerican Travel; South American Journeys; Tours International; World Expeditions.

In the Pacific Ocean 3,680 km (2,300 mi) west of the Chilean mainland, remote Easter Island is famed for its *moais,* nearly 1,000 stone statues whose brooding eyes gaze over the windswept landscape. Abercrombie & Kent, Far Horizons, Myths and Mountains, and Nature Expeditions are among the tour operators who will take you there. Far Horizons' departure is timed for the annual Tapati festival. Vying with Easter Island as a cultural experience, the Atacama, generally considered the world's driest desert, is a region of bizarre landscapes, ancient petroglyphs (designs scratched or cut into rock), and geoglyphs (designs formed by arranging stones or earth). G.A.P., Ladatco, Myths and Mountains, Tours International, World Expeditions, and South American Journeys all have Atacama programs. The latter's itinerary revolves around astronomy with visits to the Atacama Large Millimeter Array Site (ALMA) and the Very Large Telescope Observatory (VLT). For a cultural experience of another sort, join PanAmerican Travel's nine-day round of Chilean vineyards where you'll enjoy tours, tastings, and even the occasional vineyard lunch. Off the Beaten Path offers a unique trip to Parque Pumalín (a Yosemite-size nature reserve), the Yelcho Glacier, and six days at a historic 360,000-acre working ranch for horseback riding, fly fishing, birding, and a gaucho festival.

THE OUTDOORS

Bird-Watching Tours

When selecting a bird-watching tour, ask questions. What species might be seen? What are the guide's qualifications? Does the operator work to protect natural habitats? What equipment is used? (In addition to binoculars, this should include a high-powered telescope, a tape recorder to record and play back bird calls (a way of attracting birds), and a spotlight for night viewing.)

Seasons: October–November.
Locations: Atacama Desert; Lake District; Patagonia.
Cost: From $3,999 for 16 days from Santiago.
Tour Operators: Focus Tours; WINGS.

Chile spans a number of distinctive vegetational and altitudinal zones, ensuring a varied and abundant avian population. On a 16-day journey to the northern and central regions, Focus Tours participants visit the ski areas of Farellones and Valle Nevado to spot the rare crag chilia, an earthcreeper-like bird; Los Cipreses Reserve, stronghold of the burrowing parrot; La Campana National Park, which holds five of Chile's eight endemic species; the Andes for the rare and threatened white-tailed shrike-tyrant; plus the arid Atacama and Lauca National Park. WINGS's itinerary covers the country from Patagonia in the south to the Atacama Desert in the north, also spending time in the lake district around Puerto Montt.

Natural History

Many operators have created programs that provide insight into the importance and fragility of South America's ecological treasures. The itineraries mentioned below take in the deserts, glaciers, rain forests, mountains, and rivers of this continent, as well as the impressive variety of its wildlife.

Season: October–April.
Locations: Atacama Desert; Buenos Aires; Lake District; Patagonia; Santiago.
Cost: From $1,860 for nine days from Buenos Aires.
Tour Operators: Abercrombie & Kent; Adventure Life; Big Five Tours & Expeditions; ElderTreks; G.A.P. Adventures; Geographic Expeditions; Inca; Journeys International; Myths and Mountains; Nature Expeditions International; Off the Beaten Path; OutWest Global Adventures; PanAmerican Travel; South American Journeys; Southwind Adventures; Wilderness Travel; Wildland Adventures; World Expeditions.

The southern tip of Argentina and Chile, commonly referred to as Patagonia, has long been a prime ecotourism destination, and nature lovers will find no lack of tour offerings for this region. You'll view the glaciers of Los Glaciares National Park where the Moreno Glacier towers 20 stories high, the soaring peaks of Torres del Paine, the fjords of the Chilean coast, and a Magellanic penguin colony. Most itineraries spend some days in the Lake District, and a few visit Alerce Andino National Park and Osorno volcano. Many programs include day walks and, often, a one- to three-day cruise. Several operators feature a stay at a historic ranch, *Estancia Helsingfors,* on Lago Viedma. The Atacama Desert of northern Chile is nature of another sort. Abercrombie & Kent has a "Fire and Ice" itinerary, combining the deep south with this arid zone.

Antarctic Photo Safaris

A benefit of photo tours is the amount of time spent at each place visited. Whether the subject is a rarely spotted animal, a breathtaking waterfall, or villagers in traditional dress, you get a chance to focus both your camera and your mind on the scene before you. The tours listed below are led by professional photographers who offer instruction and hands-on tips. Only consider these trips if you're serious about improving your photographic skills; otherwise, you might find the pace maddeningly slow.

Season: October; February.
Locations: Antarctic Peninsula; Falkland, South Georgia, and South Orkney Islands.
Cost: From $8,495 for 16 days from Ushuaia, Argentina.
Tour Operator: Joseph Van Os Photo Safaris; Lindblad Expeditions.

Photograph seabirds, Adélie and gentoo penguin colonies, albatross nesting areas, elephant and fur seals, plus the spectacular landscapes of the Antarctic. With Joseph Van Os, you'll travel aboard the helicopter-carrying icebreaker, *Kapitan Khlebnikov.* A high point of this trip is the chance to cruise the Weddell Sea and visit the Snow Hill colony of Emperor Penguins where some 4,000 breeding pairs are found. Lindblad Expeditions has one departure designated as a photo expedition where you can learn in the field with nature photographer Tom Mangelsen. This 25-day program calls at the islands listed above, as well as the Antarctic Peninsula.

Patagonia & Easter Island Photo Safaris

Season: March–April.
Locations: Central Patagonia; Easter Island; Los Glaciares & Torres del Paine National Parks.
Cost: From $3,495 for 12 days from Santiago.
Tour Operators: Joseph Van Os Photo Safaris; Myths and Mountains.

Timed for vibrant fall colors among ice fields, snow-capped mountains, glaciers, and rushing streams, Joseph Van Os has 12- and 13-day departures during Patagonian fall (the Northern Hemisphere's spring). While one trip visits the famed sites of Torres del Paine and Los Glaciares National Parks, the second concentrates on lesser known regions, such as the Cavernas de Mármol, or Marble Caves. Led by photographer Bill Chapman, Myths and Mountains offers a 15-day program combining Torres del Paine National Park with the desolation and *moais* (giant stone statues) of Easter Island.

SPORTS

A sports-focused trip offers a great way to see the country and interact with local people. A dozen bicyclists entering a village, for instance, would arouse more interest and be more approachable than a group of 30 stepping out of a tour bus. While some programs are designed for those with a high level of experience, others don't require a high level of skill; however, in either case, your interest in the particular sport should be more than casual. Weather can be changeable, dictating choices of hiking or climbing routes. Companies that operate mountaineering programs usually build an extra day or two into their itineraries to allow for weather conditions. If you're not a particularly strong hiker or cyclist, ask if support vehicles accompany the group or if alternate activities or turn-around points are available on more challenging days.

Bicycling

Season: October–March.
Locations: Atacama Desert; Lake District; Mendoza, Argentina; Patagonia.
Cost: From $1,225 for eight days from Puerto Montt.
Tour Operators: Australian & Amazonian Adventures; Butterfield & Robinson; Experience Plus!; Global Adventure Guide; Southwind Adventures.

Global Adventure's 15-day journey, graded moderate with some uphill challenges and occasional single-track riding, criss-crosses the Lower Andes as you ride along paved and dirt roads through forests and past volcanoes. The itinerary encompasses both the Lake District and Patagonia with occasional options for rafting, canyoning, or volcano climbing. Another tour combines biking in Chile and neighboring Bolivia. With Southwind, bike and hike the Lake District's gently rolling terrain, visiting Osorno Volcano, Puyehue and Huerquehue National Parks, and the resort town of Pucón. Nicknamed "a two-wheeled tango," Butterfield & Robinson's 9-day trip travels from Santiago, Chile to Buenos Aires, Argentina (not entirely by bike!), stopping in Chile's Atacama Desert and the Argentine wine country along the way. Starting in Bariloche, Experience Plus! cycles up to 93 km (58 mi) a day around Lake Llanquihue for views of Osorno and Calbuco volcanoes with the opportunity for Class III rafting on Río Petrohué. You can opt for a four-day extension on Chiloé Island. Choose from two biking journeys with Australian & Amazonian Adventures, one to Chile's lake district, the other visiting a number of national parks, including Isluga, Surire, Vicuña, and Lauca. Most nights are spent camping.

Canoeing, Kayaking & White-Water Rafting

White-water rafting and kayaking can be exhilarating experiences. You don't have to be an expert paddler to enjoy many of these adventures, but you should be a strong swimmer. Rivers are rated from Class I to Class V according to difficulty of navigation. Generally speaking, Class I to III rapids are suitable for beginners, while Class IV and V rapids are strictly for the experienced. Canoeing is a gentler river experience.

Season: November–March.
Locations: Chiloé Archipelago; Northern Patagonia; Río Futaleufú.
Cost: From $680 for four days from Castro, Chiloé.
Tour Operators: Adventure Life; Australian & Amazonian Expeditions; Earth River Expeditions; Hidden Trails; PanAmerican Travel.

Chile has both scenic fjords for sea kayaking and challenging rivers for white-water rafting. With PanAmerican Travel, sea kayakers can spend nine days exploring the fjords, waterfalls, hot springs, and wildlife of the country's rugged coast, camping at night in splendid scenery. Australian & Amazonian Adventures offers three- to nine-day kayaking adventures. On the four-day itinerary, you'll discover the islands of the Chiloé Archipelago, a region rich in folklore, while the six-day program explores the fjords of northern Patagonia.

For the experienced rafter, the Class IV and V rapids of Río Futaleufú offer many challenges. Its sheer-walled canyons boast such well-named rapids as Infierno and Purgatorio. Earth River's 10-day program here includes a rock climb up 98-meter (320-foot) Torre de los Vientos and a Tyrolean traverse where, wearing a climbing harness attached to a pulley, you pull yourself across a rope strung above the rapids. With treehouses and riverside hot tubs formed from natural potholes carved from the stone, overnight camping becomes an exotic experience. Earth River also offers a kayaking journey over a chain of three lakes, surrounded by snow-capped mountains. Access is by float plane. Hidden Trails and Adventure Life have Futaleufú rafting trips; the latter's program, in addition to shooting the rapids, offers kayaking, fishing, and horseback riding in the mountains.

Fishing

Season: September–March.
Locations: Chiloé Island; Lake District; Patagonia.
Cost: From $2,975 for seven days from Balmaceda.
Tour Operators: Fishing International; FishQuest; Fly Fishing And; Frontiers; PanAmerican Travel; Rod & Reel Adventures.

For anglers, Chile is the Southern Hemisphere's Alaska, offering world-class trout fishing in clear streams. An added bonus is the availability of landlocked salmon and golden dorado, known as the "river tiger." Bilingual fishing guides accompany groups, and guests stay in comfortable lodges with private baths. While November is the usual opening date for freshwater fishing, the season begins two months earlier at Lago Llanquihue due to the large resident fish population. Rod & Reel takes advantage of this, basing participants at a lodge near Osorno volcano. With Fly Fishing And, your 10 days will be divided between two lodges, meaning you can fish several rivers and creeks. PanAmerican's seven-day program breaks up lodge stays with a night of riverside camping. Fishing International offers a trip based at an *estancia* (ranch) where you can fish two rivers for brown trout weighing up to 15 pounds. FishQuest has four offerings, fishing a variety of rivers for brown and rainbow trout, dorado, giant catfish, and salmon. With Frontiers, you can choose from a great variety of lodges and rivers in Chile.

Hiking, Running & Trekking

South America's magnificent scenery and varied terrain make it a terrific place for trekkers and hikers. The southern part of Argentina and Chile, known as Patagonia, and Peru's Inca Trail are especially popular and numerous tour operators offer hiking and trekking trips to these regions. The trips outlined below are organized tours led by qualified guides. Camping is often part of the experience, although on some trips you stay at inns and small hotels. Itineraries range from relatively easy hikes to serious trekking and even running.

Season: October–April.
Locations: Atacama Desert; Lake District; Patagonia.
Cost: From $1,065 for 12 days from Salta, Argentina.
Tour Operators: Adventure Life; American Alpine Institute; Andes Adventures; Australian & Amazonian Adventures; BikeHike Adventures; Butterfield & Robinson; Country Walkers; Geographic Expeditions; KE Adventure Travel; Mountain Travel-Sobek; Southwind Adventures; The World Outdoors; Wilderness Travel; Wildland Adventures; World Expeditions.

Patagonia may be the most trekked region in South America. All of the above companies have programs here, ranging from relatively easy hikes (Butterfield & Robinson, Country Walkers) to serious treks involving daily elevation gains up to 800 meters (2,625 feet) and ice and snow traverses using crampons (American Alpine Institute). Highlights include Torres del Paine, Los Glaciares, and/or Tierra del Fuego National Parks and crossing the Patagonian Ice Cap. Adventure Life's program lets you overnight in igloo-shape tents at EcoCamp in Torres del Paine. In addition to its hiking trip, Andes Adventures offers an 18-day running itinerary with runs covering as much as 31 km (19 mi) per day. Other options include an Atacama Desert trek and volcano ascent with KE Adventure Travel, or a Futaleufú Canyon trek with Wilderness Travel.

Horseback Riding

Season: October–April; year-round, Atacama.
Locations: Atacama Desert; Patagonia; Río Hurtado Valley.
Cost: From $1,450 for seven days from Calama.
Tour Operators: Equitours; Hidden Trails.

On Equitours' 12-day "Patagonia Glacier Ride" you cross the pampas to Torres del Paine National Park, a region of mountains, lakes, and glaciers. Nights are spent camping or in lodges. Hidden Trails has six itineraries: you can opt for a ride in southern Chile through lonely valleys, along historic mule trails created by gold diggers, and into the Andes; join an Atacama Desert adventure riding over the crusted salt of the Salar de Atacama and across expanses of sand, visiting ancient ruins and petroglyphs, or choose from four Patagonia programs, camping or staying at *estancias,* depending on the itinerary selected. If getting off the beaten path appeals to you, consider the company's "Glacier Camping Ride" which ventures into remote areas accessible only by foot or horse.

Antarctic Mountaineering

Only the most towering peaks of Asia vie with the Andes in the challenges and rewards awaiting mountaineers. This is no casual sport, so choose your tour operator carefully, ask questions, and be honest about your level of fitness and experience. Safety should be the company's, and your, first priority. Are the guides certified by professional organizations, such as the American Mountain Guides Association? Are they certified as Wilderness First Responders and trained in technical mountain rescue? What is the company's safety record? What is the climber-to-guide ratio? Are extra days built into the schedule to allow for adverse weather? Is there serious adherence to "leave no trace" environmental ethics? Several of the tour operators mentioned below have their own schools in the U.S. and/or other countries which offer multi-level courses in mountaineering, ice climbing, rock climbing, and avalanche education.

Season: November–January.
Location: Mount Vinson.
Cost: $26,500 for 22 days from Punta Arenas.
Tour Operator: Alpine Ascents International; Mountain Madness.

If you have a solid mountaineering background and are accustomed to cold weather camping, this could be the ultimate mountaineering adventure. A short flight from Patriot Hills brings you to the base camp. With loaded sleds, you'll move up the mountain, establishing two or three camps before attempting the 4,897-meter (16,077-foot) summit of Mt. Vinson. Although the climb itself is considered technically moderate, strong winds and extreme temperatures, as low as -40°F, make this a serious challenge. The two companies above will help you achieve this mountaineering goal. Additionally, Alpine Ascents offers the chance to ski from the 89th parallel to the 90th. Aircraft will bring you within 70 miles of the South Pole; then, ski the rest of the way. This unique adventure can be made independently or as an extension of the Vinson climb.

Argentine & Chilean Patagonia Mountaineering

Season: November–February.
Locations: Mount Aconcagua; Cerro Marconi Sur; Gorra Blanca; Patagonian Ice Cap.
Cost: From $2,980 for 11 days from Calafate, Argentina.
Tour Operators: Alpine Ascents International; American Alpine Institute; Arun Treks & Expeditions; Colorado Mountain School; KE Adventure Travel; Mountain Madness; World Expeditions.

At 6,960 meters (22,835 feet), Argentina's Mount Aconcagua is the world's highest peak outside of Asia. Though some routes are not technically difficult, Aconcagua is quite demanding physically and requires the use of ice axes, crampons, and ropes. All of the above operators offer climbs of Aconcagua, some via the more difficult Polish glacier route. Frequent high winds and ice make this route very challenging and only for those with extensive mountaineering experience at high altitudes. American Alpine Institute has a second expedition with ascents of Cerro Marconi Sur and Gorra Blanca in southern Patagonia. On this program, you'll also traverse part of the Patagonian Ice Cap.

Multisport

Only a few years ago, multisport offerings were so few that the topic didn't merit inclusion in this chapter. However, such trips have grown in popularity every year and now form an important part of many adventure tour operators' programs. Innovative itineraries combine two or more sports, such as biking, fishing, canoeing, hiking, horseback riding, kayaking, rafting, and trekking.

Season: November–April.
Locations: Lake District; Patagonia; Río Futaleufú.
Cost: From $765 for five days from Puerto Montt.
Tour Operators: American Alpine Institute; Austin-Lehman Adventures; Australian & Amazonian Adventures; BikeHike Adventures; Earth River Expeditions; Fishing International; Hidden Trails; Mountain Madness; Mountain Travel-Sobek; Nature Expeditions International; The World Outdoors; Wilderness Travel; World Expeditions.

Whether you choose the Lake District or Patagonia, the scene for your active vacation will be one of great beauty. Both regions offer superb trekking, kayaking, horseback riding, and biking. Hidden Trails combines horseback riding with sea kayaking in Patagonia, while Mountain Madness offers hut-to-hut trekking in the Torres del Paine area along with kayaking on the Río Serrano and an optional ice climb. With Nature Expeditions, you'll have soft adventure options most days, such as hiking, rafting (Class II and III rapids), and horseback riding. BikeHike has two multisport trips in Argentina and Chile; you can hike, raft, sea kayak, bike, and ride horses in the Lake District or hike, ride horses, and sand board in northern Chile. On Austin-Lehman's Pagatonia and lake district itinerary, rest at night in five-star hotels and upscale lodges after horseback riding, biking, rafting, kayaking, and hiking during the day. If you want to try serious rafting, consider a trip down Río Futaleufú, such as those run by Earth River Expeditions and The World Outdoors; these programs also include hiking and horseback riding.

Skiing and Snowboarding

When ski season's over in the Northern Hemisphere, it's time to pack the gear and head for resorts in Argentina or Chile. Advanced and expert skiers will find seemingly endless terrain, and powder hounds will discover the ultimate ski. If your present level leans more toward beginner or intermediate, not to worry. Adventures aplenty await you, too. Snowboarders, also, will find the southern mountains much to their liking. In addition to marked trails, there's off-piste terrain, often with steep chutes and deep powder bowls, plus backcountry areas to try. Those with strong skills could opt for heli-skiing on peaks reaching 4,200 meters (13,600 feet) as condors soar above. As hard as it might be to break away from the slopes, a day of hiking or snowshoeing would be well-spent. Many of the resorts exude a European ambience with a lively nightlife scene. Everywhere, you'll be surrounded by some of Earth's grandest natural beauty. The tour operators mentioned below have created all-inclusive ski packages covering airport/hotel and hotel/ski mountain transfers, accommodations, two meals daily, and lift tickets for a number of mountains and resorts in both Argentina and Chile; many packages combine the two countries. Costs vary with the accommodations selected. Prices quoted are per person double; costs are even lower if four people share a room. Be aware that less expensive packages, while providing the services mentioned, generally are not guided tours. Eight-day guided packages start around $1,795.

Season: June–October.
Locations: El Colorado; La Parva; Portillo; Pucón; Termas de Chillán; Valle Nevado.
Cost: From $730 for a seven-day nonguided inclusive package from Santiago.
Tour Operators:; Ladatco Tours; Myths and Mountains; PowderQuest; Snoventures.

A short drive from Santiago, Valle Nevado has more than 300 acres of groomed runs and a 792-meter (2,600-foot) vertical drop. Famous for powder, it's also home to the Andes Express, a chair lift so super-fast, you can get in extra runs each day. From Valle Nevado you can interconnect with the slopes of nearby El Colorado and La Parva, making for a vast amount of skiable terrain. First-rate heliskiing, heliboarding, and even hang gliding can be taken out of Valle Nevado; the off-piste is excellent, as well. A snowboard camp is based here coached by North American AASI level-three certified instructors. Participation in the seven-day program, divided into first-time and advanced groups, can be arranged by PowderQuest. Near the base of Mount Aconcagua, the highest mountain in the Western Hemisphere, Portillo, serviced by 12 lifts, ranks as one of the top 10 ski resorts in the world on numerous lists. Several national ski teams have their off-season training here. While there's terrain for all ability levels, 43% is designated expert. The heliskiing is enviable, and Portillo's lively après-ski life comes as an added bonus. Yet another world-class resort, Termas de Chillán, has what one tour operator terms "killer slopes," plus a network of forest tracks for cross-country skiers. Its 28 runs along 35 km (22 mi) of groomed trails include South America's longest at 13 km (6 mi). Boasting one of Chile's deepest snow packs, the resort offers varied terrain on two volcanoes for skiing or snowboarding, plus a thermal area consisting of nine pools for end-of-the-day relaxation. The trails are fairly evenly divided among skill levels. Termas de Chillán presents some of the best off-piste adventures on the continent plus fine hiking opportunities. At the small resort of Pucón, situated on the edge of Lago Villarrica, ski on the side of Chile's most active volcano. You can hike to the crater to gaze at molten magma, then ski or snowboard back down. Bordering two national parks plus a national reserve, Pucón offers great snowshoeing as well as such sports as rafting and caving. PowderQuest and Snoventures offer inclusive packages to all resorts mentioned. Ski weeks without guides run in the $730 to $800 range. PowderQuest's main focus is guided tours of eight to 16 days with time spent at as many as seven resorts in both Argentina and Chile. Myths and Mountains has an 11-day trip to Portillo led by Rusty Crook, a former World Cup skier, while Ladatco offers packages to Valle Nevado, Portillo, and Chillán.

UNDERSTANDING CHILE

TRAVELING IN A THIN COUNTRY

SPANISH VOCABULARY

TRAVELING IN A THIN COUNTRY

WHEN CHILEANS JOKE THAT THEIR NATION was crafted from the universe's leftovers, they are only partly jesting. Chile's thin ribbon of territory comprises some of nature's most spectacular anomalies: the looming Andes impose the country's eastern boundaries, stretching from the desolate Atacama Desert to the archipelagos and fjords of forbidding Patagonia, where the concept of the final frontier is still fresh in the hearts of its inhabitants. Just above Puerto Montt lies a land of alpine lakes, with its distinctively German and Swiss cultural enclaves. The central Maipo Valley, fertile home of Chile's famous vineyards and fruit fields, also houses the frenzy of cosmopolitan Santiago.

All of this fits into one sliver of land squeezed between the Andes and the Pacific Ocean. In some places the 320-km (200-mi) territorial limit is actually wider than the country itself, making Chile as much water as earth.

As might be expected in a country with a coastline stretching for more than 4,000 km (2,500 mi), many parts of Chile are inaccessible by land. Because of the unusual topography, highways simply end when they reach fjords or ice fields. You'll need to take a ship to see the mammoth glacier in the heart of Parque Nacional Laguna San Rafael. A ferry ride is necessary to visit Chiloé, an archipelago where you'll find charming wooden churches built by missionaries. Distant Easter Island, in the middle of the Pacific Ocean, is reachable only by a five-hour flight from the mainland.

The region known today as Chile has been inhabited for millennia. One of the oldest known people were the Chinchorros, who lived along the coast of El Norte Grande beginning about 6000 BC. This nomadic people learned the process of mummifying their dead 5,000 years ago—thousands of years before the Egyptians. Nearby in the antiplano lived the Aymara, who herded llamas and alpacas and cultivated barley and potatoes. In El Norte Chico were the Diaguitas, whose finely detailed bowls and pitchers are among the most beautiful of pre-Columbian ceramics, and the Molles, who carved the intricate petroglyphs in the Valle del Encanto.

The first invaders did not come from Europe, but from elsewhere in South America. The Mapuches crossed the Andes from what is today Argentina and established a stronghold in the Lake District. In the process they gradually absorbed the peoples already living in the region. The Incas, who arrived in the 15th century, were much more brutal. Pushing southward from their empire in Peru, the Incas dismantled existing cultures, forcing indigenous peoples to give up their language and their rituals. Only the fierce resistance of the Mapuches halted the expansion of the Inca empire.

The first European to reach Chile barely gave it a glance: Spanish conquistador Hernando de Magallanes left his name and little else behind when he journeyed up the Southern Coast in 1520. Diego de Almagro was the first Spaniard actually to explore the region. Setting out from Peru in 1535, Almagro and a ragged crew of 500 adventurers marched south in search of fame and fortune. When the band reached the Aconcagua Valley, they fled after an extended battle with the Mapuches. Pedro de Valdivia, who led another gang of adventurers south along the roads constructed by the Incas, broke ground for Santiago in 1541. He founded several other towns, including Concepción and Villarrica, before he died during a skirmish with the Mapuches.

Spain had its hands full with the rest of its empire in South America, so Chile was pretty much ignored. The residents, even those who had profited under colonial rule, eventually grew tired of having others govern their land. After Chile won its independence from Spain in a war that lasted from 1810 to 1818, the new nation sought to establish firm control of its entire territory. In 1843, it sent a frigate carrying a ragtag contingent of 19 men to the Strait of Magellan. There the men built a wooden fort called Fuerte Bulnes, thus establishing the country's first permanent settlement in the southernmost reaches of Patagonia. Chile also began to dream about expansion northward. The 1879 War of the Pacific pitted Chile against its two neighbors to the north, Bolivia and Peru. Chile gained much of the nitrate-rich land of the Atacama Desert, and Bolivia lost its only outlet to the sea.

For more than 300 years, the Mapuches successfully defended much of the Lake District against the encroachment of the Spanish. But the proud people could not hold out against the Chileans. The last great rebellion of the Mapuche people failed in 1881, and soon afterward the Chilean government started shipping in German, Swiss, and other European colonists to fill the "empty" lands.

Chile's government was hampered for almost a century by an 1830 constitution that granted enormous powers to the president, thus encouraging autocratic rule. After a civil war in 1891, Congress seized control, diminishing the president to a mere figurehead. This unstable system, which caused constant clashes between the presidential and legislative branches, was replaced in 1925 with a new constitution that sought to find a delicate balance.

By the 1950s, left-wing political parties representing working-class people began to gain considerable strength. In 1970, the push for governmental reform led to the election of Salvador Allende, Chile's first socialist president. Although widely popular at first, Allende lost favor when he failed to find a way to shore up the country's sagging economy. Strikes by labor unions and protests by farmworkers made it clear that his administration was ailing.

From 1973 to 1990, Chile was virtually synonymous with the name of General Augusto Pinochet. With support from the United States, the military leader led a bloody coup in September 1973. He dissolved the legislature, banned political organizations, and exiled opponents. Tens of thousands are said to have been murdered during his years in power.

Pinochet's regime discouraged many visitors, but in the decades since his fall from power tourism has steadily increased. Chile's beaches draw sun worshippers from all over South America, and its towering volcanoes and roaring rivers attract adventure travelers from around the world. Fishing aficionados, skiers, hikers, and other outdoors enthusiasts head south to the Lake District, and armchair archaeologists are attracted to the 5,000-year-old mummies of the Atacama. Today Chile is one of the most popular destinations in South America. It doesn't hurt that the country also has one of the continent's most stable economies.

SPANISH VOCABULARY

Words and Phrases

English	Spanish	Pronunciation
Basics		
Yes/no	Sí/no	see/no
Please	Por favor	pore fah-**vore**
May I?	¿Me permite?	may pair-**mee**-tay
Thank you (very much)	(Muchas) gracias	(**moo**-chas) **grah**-see-as
You're welcome	De nada	day **nah**-dah
Excuse me	Con permiso	con pair-**mee**-so
Pardon me	¿Perdón?	pair-**dohn**
Could you tell me?	¿Podría decirme?	po-dree-ah deh-**seer**-meh
I'm sorry	Lo siento	lo see-**en**-to
Good morning!	¡Buenos días!	**bway**-nohs **dee**-ahs
Good afternoon!	¡Buenas tardes!	**bway**-nahs **tar**-dess
Good evening!	¡Buenas noches!	**bway**-nahs **no**-chess
Goodbye!	¡Adiós!/¡Hasta luego!	ah-dee-**ohss**/**ah**-stah-**lwe**-go
Mr./Mrs.	Señor/Señora	sen-**yor**/sen-**yohr**-ah
Miss	Señorita	sen-yo-**ree**-tah
Pleased to meet you	Mucho gusto	**moo**-cho **goose**-to
How are you?	¿Cómo está usted?	**ko**-mo es-**tah** oo-**sted**
Very well, thank you.	Muy bien, gracias.	**moo**-ee bee-**en**, **grah**-see-as
And you?	¿Y usted?	ee oos-**ted**
Hello (on the telephone)	Diga	**dee**-gah

Numbers

1	un, uno	oon, **oo**-no
2	dos	dos
3	tres	tress
4	cuatro	**kwah**-tro
5	cinco	**sink**-oh
6	seis	saice
7	siete	see-**et**-eh

8	ocho	**o**-cho
9	nueve	new-**eh**-vey
10	diez	dee-**es**
11	once	**ohn**-seh
12	doce	**doh**-seh
13	trece	**treh**-seh
14	catorce	ka-**tohr**-seh
15	quince	**keen**-seh
16	dieciséis	dee-es-ee-**saice**
17	diecisiete	dee-es-ee-see-**et**-eh
18	dieciocho	dee-es-ee-**o**-cho
19	diecinueve	**dee-es**-ee-new-**ev**-ah
20	veinte	**vain**-teh
21	veinte y uno/veintiuno	**vain**-te-**oo**-noh
30	treinta	**train**-tah
32	treinta y dos	train-tay-**dohs**
40	cuarenta	kwah-**ren**-tah
43	cuarenta y tres	kwah-**ren**-tay-**tress**
50	cincuenta	seen-**kwen**-tah
54	cincuenta y cuatro	seen-**kwen**-tay **kwah**-tro
60	sesenta	sess-**en**-tah
65	sesenta y cinco	sess-**en**-tay **seen**-ko
70	setenta	set-**en**-tah
76	setenta y seis	set-**en**-tay **saice**
80	ochenta	oh-**chen**-tah
87	ochenta y siete	oh-**chen**-tay see-**yet**-eh
90	noventa	no-**ven**-tah
98	noventa y ocho	no-**ven**-tah-**o**-choh
100	cien	see-**en**
101	ciento uno	see-**en**-toh **oo**-noh
200	doscientos	doh-see-**en**-tohss
500	quinientos	keen-**yen**-tohss
700	setecientos	set-eh-see-**en**-tohss
900	novecientos	no-veh-see-**en**-tohss
1,000	mil	meel
2,000	dos mil	dohs meel
1,000,000	un millón	oon meel-**yohn**

Colors

black	negro	**neh**-groh
blue	azul	ah-**sool**
brown	café	kah-**feh**
green	verde	**ver**-deh
pink	rosa	**ro**-sah

purple	morado	mo-**rah**-doh
orange	naranja	na-**rahn**-hah
red	rojo	**roh**-hoh
white	blanco	**blahn**-koh
yellow	amarillo	ah-mah-**ree**-yoh

Days of the Week

Sunday	domingo	doe-**meen**-goh
Monday	lunes	**loo**-ness
Tuesday	martes	**mahr**-tess
Wednesday	miércoles	me-**air**-koh-less
Thursday	jueves	hoo-**ev**-ess
Friday	viernes	vee-**air**-ness
Saturday	sábado	**sah**-bah-doh

Months

January	enero	eh-**neh**-roh
February	febrero	feh-**breh**-roh
March	marzo	**mahr**-soh
April	abril	ah-**breel**
May	mayo	**my**-oh
June	junio	**hoo**-nee-oh
July	julio	**hoo**-lee-yoh
August	agosto	ah-**ghost**-toh
September	septiembre	sep-tee-**em**-breh
October	octubre	oak-**too**-breh
November	noviembre	no-vee-**em**-breh
December	diciembre	dee-see-**em**-breh

Useful Phrases

Do you speak English?	¿Habla usted inglés?	**ah**-blah oos-**ted** in-**glehs**
I don't speak Spanish	No hablo español	no **ah**-bloh es-pahn-**yol**
I don't understand (you)	No entiendo	no en-tee-**en**-doh
I understand (you)	Entiendo	en-tee-**en**-doh
I don't know	No sé	no seh
I am American/ British	Soy americano (americana)/ inglés(a)	soy ah-meh-ree-**kah**-no (ah-meh-ree-**kah**-nah)/ in-**glehs** (ah)
What's your name?	¿Cómo se llama usted?	koh-mo seh **yah**-mah oos-**ted**
My name is . . .	Me llamo . . .	may **yah**-moh
What time is it?	¿Qué hora es?	keh **o**-rah es

It is one, two, three . . . o'clock.	Es la una. . . . Son las dos, tres	es la **oo**-nah/sohn lahs dohs, tress
Yes, please/No, thank you	Sí, por favor/No, gracias	**see** pohr fah-**vor**/no **grah**-see-us
How?	¿Cómo?	**koh**-mo
When?	¿Cuándo?	**kwahn**-doh
This/Next week	Esta semana/ la semana que entra	**es**-teh seh-**mah**-nah/lah seh-**mah**-nah keh **en**-trah
This/Next month	Este mes/el próximo mes	**es**-teh mehs/el **proke**-see-mo mehs
This/Next year	Este año/el año que viene	**es**-teh **ahn**-yo/el **ahn**-yo keh vee-**yen**-ay
Yesterday/today/ tomorrow	Ayer/hoy/mañana	ah-**yehr**/oy/mahn-**yah**-nah
This morning/ afternoon	Esta mañana/ tarde	**es**-tah mahn-**yah**-nah/**tar**-deh
Tonight	Esta noche	**es**-tah **no**-cheh
What?	¿Qué?	keh
What is it?	¿Qué es esto?	keh es **es**-toh
Why?	¿Por qué?	pore **keh**
Who?	¿Quién?	kee-**yen**
Where is . . . ?	¿Dónde está . . . ?	**dohn**-deh es-**tah**
the train station?	la estación del tren?	la es-tah-see-**on** del **train**
the subway station?	la estación del Tren subterráneo?	la es-ta-see-**on** del trehn soob-tair-**ron**-a-o
the bus stop?	la parada del autobus?	la pah-**rah**-dah del oh-toh-**boos**
the post office?	la oficina de correos?	la oh-fee-**see**-nah deh koh-**reh**-os
the bank?	el banco?	el **bahn**-koh
the hotel?	el hotel?	el oh-**tel**
the store?	la tienda?	la tee-**en**-dah
the cashier?	la caja?	la **kah**-hah
the museum?	el museo?	el moo-**seh**-oh
the hospital?	el hospital?	el ohss-pee-**tal**
the elevator?	el ascensor?	el ah-**sen**-sohr
the bathroom?	el baño?	el **bahn**-yoh
Here/there	Aquí/allá	ah-**key**/ah-**yah**
Open/closed	Abierto/cerrado	ah-bee-**er**-toh/ser-**ah**-doh
Left/right	Izquierda/derecha	iss-key-**er**-dah/dare-**eh**-chah

Straight ahead	Derecho	dare-**eh**-choh
Is it near/far?	¿Está cerca/lejos?	es-**tah sehr**-kah/ **leh**-hoss
I'd like . . .	Quisiera . . .	kee-see-ehr-ah
a room	un cuarto/una habitación	oon **kwahr**-toh/ **oo**-nah ah-bee-tah-see-**on**
the key	la llave	lah **yah**-veh
a newspaper	un periódico	oon pehr-ee-**oh**-dee-koh
a stamp	un sello de correo	oon **seh**-yo deh koh-**reh**-oh
I'd like to buy . . .	Quisiera comprar . . .	kee-see-**ehr**-ah kohm-**prahr**
cigarettes	cigarrillos	ce-ga-**ree**-yohs
matches	cerillos	ser-**ee**-ohs
a dictionary	un diccionario	oon deek-see-oh-**nah**-ree-oh
soap	jabón	hah-**bohn**
sunglasses	gafas de sol	**ga**-fahs deh sohl
suntan lotion	loción bronceadora	loh-see-**ohn** brohn-seh-ah-**do**-rah
a map	un mapa	oon **mah**-pah
a magazine	una revista	**oon**-ah reh-**veess**-tah
paper	papel	pah-**pel**
envelopes	sobres	**so**-brehs
a postcard	una tarjeta postal	**oon**-ah tar-**het**-ah post-**ahl**
How much is it?	¿Cuánto cuesta?	**kwahn**-toh **kwes**-tah
It's expensive/ cheap	Está caro/barato	es-**tah kah**-roh/ bah-**rah**-toh
A little/a lot	Un poquito/ mucho	oon poh-**kee**-toh/ **moo**-choh
More/less	Más/menos	mahss/**men**-ohss
Enough/too much/too little	Suficiente/ demasiado/ muy poco	soo-fee-see-**en**-teh/ deh-mah-see-**ah**-doh/**moo**-ee **poh**-koh
Telephone	Teléfono	tel-**ef**-oh-no
Telegram	Telegrama	teh-leh-**grah**-mah
I am ill	Estoy enfermo(a)	es-**toy** en-**fehr**-moh(mah)
Please call a doctor	Por favor llame a un medico	pohr fah-**vor ya**-meh ah oon **med**-ee-koh
Help!	¡Auxilio! ¡Ayuda!	owk-**see**-lee-oh/ ah-**yoo**-dah/

	¡Socorro!	soh-**kohr**-roh
Fire!	¡Incendio!	en-**sen**-dee-oo
Caution!/Look out!	¡Cuidado!	kwee-**dah**-doh

On the Road

Avenue	Avenida	ah-ven-**ee**-dah
Broad, tree-lined boulevard	Bulevar	boo-leh-**var**
Fertile plain	Vega	**veh**-gah
Highway	Carretera	car-reh-**ter**-ah
Mountain pass, Street	Puerto Calle	poo-**ehr**-toh **cah**-yeh
Waterfront promenade	Rambla	**rahm**-blah
Wharf	Embarcadero	em-bar-cah-**deh**-ro

In Town

Cathedral	Catedral	cah-teh-**dral**
Church	Templo/Iglesia	**tem**-plo/ee-**glehs**-see-ah
City hall	Casa de gobierno	kah-sah deh go-bee-**ehr**-no
Door, gate	Puerta portón	poo-**ehr**-tah por-**ton**
Entrance/exit	Entrada/salida	en-**trah**-dah/sah-**lee**-dah
Inn, rustic bar, or restaurant	Taverna	tah-**vehr**-nah
Main square	Plaza principal	plah-thah prin-see-**pahl**
Market	Mercado	mer-**kah**-doh
Neighborhood	Barrio	**bahr**-ree-o
Traffic circle	Glorieta	glor-ee-**eh**-tah
Wine cellar, wine bar, or wine shop	Bodega	boh-**deh**-gah

Dining Out

A bottle of . . .	Una botella de . . .	**oo**-nah bo-**teh**-yah deh
A cup of . . .	Una taza de . . .	**oo**-nah **tah**-thah deh
A glass of . . .	Un vaso de . . .	oon **vah**-so deh
Ashtray	Un cenicero	oon sen-ee-**seh**-roh
Bill/check	La cuenta	lah **kwen**-tah

Bread	El pan	el pahn
Breakfast	El desayuno	el deh-sah-**yoon**-oh
Butter	La mantequilla	lah man-teh-**key**-yah
Cheers!	¡Salud!	sah-**lood**
Cocktail	Un aperitivo	oon ah-pehr-ee-**tee**-voh
Dinner	La cena	lah **seh**-nah
Dish	Un plato	oon **plah**-toh
Menu of the day	Menú del día	meh-**noo** del **dee**-ah
Enjoy!	¡Buen provecho!	bwehn pro-**veh**-cho
Fixed-price menu	Menú fijo o turistico	meh-**noo** **fee**-hoh oh too-**ree**-stee-coh
Fork	El tenedor	el ten-eh-**dor**
Is the tip included?	¿Está incluida la propina?	es-**tah** in-cloo-**ee**-dah lah pro-**pee**-nah
Knife	El cuchillo	el koo-**chee**-yo
Large portion of savory snacks	Raciónes	rah-see-**oh**-nehs
Lunch	La comida	lah koh-**mee**-dah
Menu	La carta, el menú	lah **cart**-ah, el meh-**noo**
Napkin	La servilleta	lah sehr-vee-**yet**-ah
Pepper	La pimienta	lah pee-me-**en**-tah
Please give me	Por favor déme	pore fah-**vor** **deh**-meh
Salt	La sal	lah sahl
Savory snacks	Tapas	**tah**-pahs
Spoon	Una cuchara	**oo**-nah koo-**chah**-rah
Sugar	El azúcar	el ah-**thu**-kar
Waiter!/Waitress!	¡Por favor Señor/Señorita!	pohr fah-**vor** sen-**yor**/sen-yor-**ee**-tah

INDEX

A

Addresses, F25
Aduana de Arica, 155–156
Ahu Akahanga, 328
Ahu Akivi, 325
Ahu Hanga Tetenga, 328
Ahu Huria Urengu, 325
Ahu Tautira, 323
Ahu Tongariki, 328–329
Ahu Te Peu, 325, 327
Ahu Te Pito Kura, 328
Ahu Vaihu, 328, 329
Ahu Vinapu, 325, 327
Air travel, F25–F27
  Central Coast, 104
  Central Valley, 185
  Chiloé, 253
  Easter Island, 335–336
  El Norte Chico, 127–128
  El Norte Grande, 161
  Lake District, 210–231
  Patagonia & Tierra del Fuego,
    310, 311–312
  Santiago, 61–62
  Southern Coast, 270
Airports, F27
Algarrobo, 92–94
Aloha Nui 🏨, 331–332
Altamar Aparthotel
  (Maitencillo) 🏨, 100
Alto del Carmen, 121
Ana Kai Tangata, 325, 327
Ana O Keke and Ana O Neru,
  328, 329
Ana Te Pahu, 325, 327
Anakena (Las Condes) 🏨, 32
Ancud, 239, 241–242
Andacollo, 118–119
Antiqua Casa Beben, 304
Antiques, shopping for, 49
Antofagasta, 134–135, 137
Aqui Está Coco (Providencia)
  ✕, 34
Aqui Jaime (Concón) ✕, 98
Archaeological sites
  Easter Island, 321, 326
  El Norte Grande, 142–143
Arica, 155–159
Arica area, 155–161
Art galleries. ⇨ See Museums
Arts. ⇨ See Nightlife and the
  arts
Asador Patagónico (Puerto
  Natales) ✕, 291
Ascensors. ⇨ SeeFuniculars
Astrid y Gaston (Providencia)
  ✕, 33

Atacama Desert, F15, 141
Athletic clubs & spas, 47
ATMs, F42
Auto Museum Moncopulli,
  218
Avenida Bernardo O'Higgins,
  176
Azul Profundo (Santiago) ✕,
  25

B

Bahía Bonita (Concón) 🏨, 98
Bahía Inglesa, 124–125
Banks. ⇨ SeeMoney matters
Baños de Colina, 55
Baños Ipla, 151
Baquedano, 138
Barrio Paris-Londres, 11–12
Barros El Chino, 151
Bars and clubs
  Central Coast, 82–83, 90
  Central Valley, 184
  Easter Island, 334
  El Norte Chico, 114, 116, 121,
    124, 125, 126
  El Norte Grande, 149–150,
    158
  Patagonia & Tierra del Fuego,
    288, 309–310
  Santiago, 45–46
  Southern Coast, 269
Basilica (Andacollo),
  118–119
Beaches
  Central Coast, 73, 83, 90–104
  Chiloé, 251
  Easter Island, 328, 329, 334
  El Norte Chico, 111, 114, 125,
    126
  El Norte Grande, 135,
    137–138, 150, 158–159
  Lake District, 210, 216, 222
Bellavista & Parque
  Metropolitano, 18, 20–21,
  24–25, 28, 45
Biblioteca Nacional, 11, 12
Bice (Las Condes) ✕, 31
Bicycling, F27, 348Easter
  Island, 335
  El Norte Grande, 144
  Lake District, 207
  Santiago, 47
Bird watching, 346
  Central Valley, 175
  Chiloé, 251
  El Norte Chico, 126
  El Norte Grande, 146, 161

Patagonia & Tierra del Fuego,
  283, 289, 293
Blowholes, 103–104
Boat & ferry travel, F27, 231,
  253, 270–271, 279,
  312–313
Boating, 83
Bolsa de Comercio, 11, 12
Books, shopping for, 49
Breweries, 212
Brighton B&B (Valparaíso)
  🏨, 81–82
Bristol (Santiago) ✕, 28
Bus travel, F27–F28
  Central Coast, 104
  Central Valley, 185
  Chiloé, 253–254
  El Norte Chico, 128
  El Norte Grande, 161–162
  Lake District, 231–232
  Patagonia & Tierra del Fuego,
    313
  Santiago, 62–63
  Southern Coast, 271
Business hours, F28

C

Cabañas Caleta Gonzalo 🏨,
  261, 263
Cabo de Hornos, 311
Café Adobe ✕, 143
Café Capuccini ✕, 221
Café Turri (Valparaíso) ✕, 79
Cajón del Maipo, 53–55
Calama, 139–140
Caldera, 125–126
Caleta Angelmó, 227
Caleta Hanga Roa, 323
Caleta de Zapallar, 101
Caleuche, 244
Calle Baquedano, 147
Cameras & photography,
  F28–F29
Camping, 209, 215, 229, 307
Canal Beagle, 305
Canoeing, 349
Canto de Luna ✕, 183
Car travel & rentals, F29–F31
  Central Coast, 105
  Central Valley, 185
  Chiloé, 254
  Easter Island, 336
  El Norte Chico, 128
  El Norte Grande, 162
  Lake District, 232
  Patagonia & Tierra del Fuego,
    313–314

Santiago, 63–64
Southern Coast, 271
Carretera Austral, *264*
Casa Colorado, *5, 9*
Casa de los Madariaga
   (Vicuña), *115*
Casa de Pilar de Esquina,
   169
Casa del Arte, *182*
Casa Escuela (Monte Grande)
   116
Casa-Museo Isla Negra,
   95–96
Casa Thomas Somerscales 🖭 ,
   81
Cascada de las Animas (San
   Alfonso) 🖭 , *54*
Casino Español (Iquique) ✕,
   148
Casinos
Central Coast, 90
Casona (Coyhaique) ✕, *268*
Castillo San Sebastián de la
   Cruz, *216*
Castro, *246–249*
Catedral (Puerto Montt), *227*
Catedral (Santiago), *4, 9*
Catedral de Chillán, *180*
Catedral de Concepción, *182*
Catedral de Nuestra Señora
   del Rosario, *211*
Catedral de San Mateo
   Apostol, *217*
Catedral de Temuco, *191–192*
Catedral San Juan Bautista,
   139
Caves
Central Coast, 93
Chiloé, 243
Easter Island, 327, 329
El Norte Chico, 119
El Norte Grande, 152
Patagonia & Tierra del Fuego,
   291
Cementerio (Hanga Roa),
   323
Cementerio General
   (Santiago), *22*
Cementerio Municipal (Punta
   Arenas), *282*
Cemetery (Quemchi), *243*
Central Coast, *F7, 68–106*
beaches, 73, 83, 90–104
children, attractions for, 78,
   101
essential information, 104–106
exploring, 69, 71, 73, 76–79,
   84, 86–87, 92–93, 94–98,
   99–100, 101, 102–104

hotels, 70, 81–82, 88–90, 93,
   94, 96, 97, 98, 99, 100, 102,
   103, 104
itineraries, 71
nightlife and the arts, 82–83,
   90, 97
Northern Beaches, 96–104
price categories, 70
restaurants, 70, 79–81, 87–89,
   92, 93, 94, 96, 97, 98, 99,
   100, 102, 103
shopping, 73, 84, 91
Southern Beaches, 91–96
sports & the outdoors, 73,
   83–84, 90–91, 92, 93–94, 98,
   101, 102, 104
timing the visit, 70–71
Valparaíso & Viña del Mar &,
   71, 73–91
Central Valley, *F8, 164–187*
essential information, 185–187
exploring, 165, 166–167,
   169–170, 171–173, 174–175,
   176–177, 178–181, 182, 184
hotels, 165–166, 171, 173–174,
   175–176, 177–178, 179, 180,
   181–182, 183–184
itineraries, 167
nightlife, 178, 184
price categories, 166
restaurants, 165, 166, 171, 173,
   175, 177, 180, 182–183
Río Bío Bío, 179–184
shopping, 174, 178, 184
sports & the outdoors, 169,
   171, 174, 178
timing the visit, 166
Wine Country, 166–167,
   167–169
Centro, *28–29, 36–39, 45*
Centro Cultural El Austral,
   212
Cerro Concepcíon (Valparaíso),
   76
Cerro Caracol, *182*
Cerro de la Virgen
Talca, 176
Vicuña, 115
Cerro San Cristóbal, *18, 20*
Cerro Santa Lucía, *11, 12*
Cerros Pintados, *154*
Cerveceria Kunstmann
   (brewery), *212*
Chacabuco, *138–139*
Chaitén, *259–260*
Chez Manu ✕, *308*
Children, attractions for, *F31*
Central Coast, 78, 101
El Norte Chico, 126–127

Lake District, 212
Santiago, 20, 21, 23
Children, traveling with, *F31*
Chillán, *179–180*
Chiloé, *F12, 236–255*
beaches, 251
essential information,
   253–255
exploring, 237, 239, 241,
   243–244, 245, 246–248,
   249–252
folklore, 241
hotels, 238–239, 242, 245, 246,
   248–249, 250, 252
itineraries, 239
price categories, 239
restaurants, 238, 239, 242,
   245–246, 248, 250, 252
shopping, 241, 245, 249, 252
sports & the outdoors, 241
timing the visit, 239
Chiu Chiu, *140–141*
Chol Chol, *198–199*
Chonchi, *249–250*
Chuquicamata (copper mine),
   139
Churches
Central Coast, 103
Central Valley, 167, 171, 174,
   180, 182
Chiloé, 241, 243, 244, 245,
   246, 247, 249–250
Easter Island, 323
El Norte Chico, 111, 115,
   118–119, 120, 122, 125
El Norte Grande, 139,
   140–141, 151, 155, 159,
   160
Lake District, 191–192, 211,
   217, 227
Patagonia & Tierra del Fuego,
   291
Santiago, 9, 12
Southern Coast, 266
City Hotel (Centro) 🖭 , *37*
Climate, *F21*
Clothing, shopping for, *50*
Cloud forests, *120*
Club de la Unión, *11, 12*
Club de Yates Algarrobo, *93*
Club Hotel La Fayette 🖭 , *97*
Club Viña del Mar, *86*
Cocha Resbaladero, *152*
Cofradía Náutica
   (Algarrobo), *93*
Colbún, *179*
Colleges and universities, *14*
Como Agua Para Chocolate
   (Bellavista) ✕, *25*

Computers, F32

Concepción, 182–184

Concepto Indigo (Puerto Natales) ✕, 291–292

Concepto Indigo (Puerto Natales) 🖾, 293

Concón, 97–98

Condominio Nuevo Parva (LaParva) 🖾, 57

Confiltería Torres (Centro) ✕, 28

Conozca Castro Caminando, 248

Consumer protection, F32

Copiapó, 122–124

Copiapó Valley, 122–127

Copper mines
Central Valley, 170
El Norte Grande, 139
Santiago (San Alfonso), 54

Correo Central, 4, 9

Coyhaique, 266–269

Credit cards, F6, F43

Cruises, F17, F32, 343–345

Curicó, 174–175

Currency exchange, F43.
  ⇨ *Also* Money matters

Customs & duties, F32–F34

D

Dalcahue, 244–245

Dance
Easter Island, 333
Santiago, 43

Dance clubs
Central Coast, 82–83, 90
El Norte Grande, 150

De Tapas y Copas (Santiago) ✕, 25

Delicias del Mar (Viña del Mar and Renaca) ✕, 88, 97

Der Münchner Hof (El Quisco) ✕🖾, 94

Dining, F36–F37. ⇨ *Also* Restaurants
Central Coast, 70, 79–81, 87–89, 92, 93, 94, 96, 97, 98, 99, 100, 102, 103
Central Valley, 165, 166, 171, 173, 175, 177, 180, 182–183
Chiloé, 238, 239, 242, 245–246, 248, 250, 252
Easter Island, 319–320, 321, 329–330
El Norte Chico, 108–109, 113, 115–116, 118, 119, 121, 123, 124, 125

El Norte Grande, 132, 133, 134–135, 137, 139–140, 143, 148–149, 151, 152, 155, 157–158, 159
Lake District, 189, 190, 193, 195, 197, 200–201, 204–205, 209, 213–214, 217, 220, 221–222, 223, 225, 228
Patagonia & Tierra del Fuego, 276, 277, 285–286, 291–292, 295, 298, 300, 308
price categories, 24, 70, 109, 133, 166, 190, 239, 258, 276, 277, 321
Santiago, 3, 24–36
Santiago side trips, 53–54, 56, 61
Southern Coast, 258, 260, 263, 265, 268, 269

Disabilities & accessibility, F34–F35

Discounts & deals, F35–F36

Distilleries, 115, 116, 117, 121

Diving
Central Coast, 92, 94, 104
Easter Island, 321, 334–335
El Norte Chico, 125

Domaine Oriental (winery), 176–177

Donde Augusto (Centro) ✕, 29

Donde el Guatón (La Serena) ✕, 113

Duty-free shopping, 150

E

Easter Island, F10, 317–337
archaeology, 321, 326
beaches, 328, 329, 334
essential information, 335–337
exploring, 319, 321, 323–325, 327–329
Hanga Roa, 321, 323–325
hotels, 320, 321, 330–333
itineraries, 319
nightlife & the arts, 333–334
price categories, 321
restaurants, 319–320, 321, 329–330
shopping, 321, 335
Southeastern Circuit, 328–329
sports & the outdoors, 321, 334–335
timing the visit, 321
Western Circuit, 325, 327

Eiffel, Alexandre Gustave, 156

El Calafate, Argentina, 297–298, 300–302

El Chiringuito (Zapallar) ✕, 102

El Cid (Providencia) ✕, 33

El Fraile, 267

El Morro de Arica, 156

El Norte Chico, F7, 107–129
beaches, 111, 114, 125, 126
children, attractions for, 126–127
Copiapó Valley, 122–127
Elqui Valley, 110–111, 113–116, 118–120
essential information, 127–129
exploring, 108–109, 110–111, 113, 114–115, 116, 118–119, 120–121, 122–123, 124–125, 126, 127
Huasco Valley, 120–122
itineraries, 109
hotels, 109, 113–114, 115–116, 118, 119–120, 121, 123–125, 126, 127
nightlife & the arts, 114, 116, 118, 121, 124, 125, 126
price categories, 109
restaurants, 108–109, 113, 115–116, 118, 119, 121, 123, 124, 125
shopping, 111, 114, 116, 118, 124
sports & the outdoors, 111, 125, 126
timing the visit, 109

El Norte Grande, F8, 130–163
Arica area, 155–161
beaches, 135, 137–138, 150, 158–159
essential information, 161–163
exploring, 131–132, 134, 135, 137, 138–139, 140–143, 145–148, 150–152, 154–157, 159–161
hotels, 133, 135, 137, 140, 143–144, 149, 151, 152, 157–158, 159–160
Iquique area, 146–152, 154–155
itineraries, 133
nightlife and the arts, 137, 140, 144, 149–150, 158
Nitrate Pampa, 133–135, 137–141
price categories, 133
restaurants, 132, 133, 134–135, 137, 139–140, 143, 148–149, 151, 152, 155, 157–158, 159

shopping, 135, 137, 140, 145, 150, 159
sports & the outdoors, 135, 137–138, 144–145, 150, 158–159
timing the visit, 133
El Plateao (Bahía Inglesa) ✕, 124
El Quisco, 94
El Rincón del Tata (Puerto Natales) ✕, 292
El Tesoro de Elqui (Pisco Elqui) ✕⛺, 118
El Volcán, 54
Electricity, F37
Elqui Valley, 110–111, 113–116, 118–120
Embassies, F37
Emergencies, F37
Chiloé, 254
Lake District, 233
Santiago, 65–66
English-language media, F37
Santiago, 66
Ensenada, 225–226
Escuela México, 180
Escuela San Pedro de Quintay, 92
Esperanza, 298
Estación Central (Santiago), 21, 22
Estación Ferrocarril
Arica, 156
Caldera, 125
Estación Mapocho, 14, 16
Ex Congreso Nacional, 5, 9
Exploring
Central Coast, 69, 71, 73, 76–79, 84, 86–87, 92–93, 94–98, 99–100, 101, 102–104
Central Valley, 165, 166–167, 169–170, 171–173, 174–175, 176–177, 178–181, 182, 184
Chiloé, 237, 239, 241, 243–244, 245, 246–248, 249–252
Easter Island, 319, 321, 323–325, 327–329
El Norte Chico, 108–109, 110–111, 113, 114–115, 116, 118–119, 120–121, 122–123, 124–125, 126, 127
El Norte Grande, 131–132, 134, 135, 137, 138–139, 140–143, 145–148, 150–152, 154–157, 159–161

Lake District, 189, 190–193, 198–200, 202, 204, 208–209, 210–212, 216, 217, 218–221, 222, 223, 225, 226, 227–228, 230
Patagonia & Tierra del Fuego, 275, 279–280, 282–285, 288–291, 293–295, 297–298, 299, 302–307, 310–311
Santiago, 2–23
Southern Coast, 257–258, 259–261, 263, 265–267, 269, 270

F

Farellones & El Colorado (ski area), 57
Feria de Chillán, 179–180
Festivals and seasonal events, F22–F24
Central Coast, 70
Central Valley, 166
Chiloé, 238
Easter Island, 333
El Norte Chico, 110
El Norte Grande, 132
Lake District, 192
Film
Central Coast, 83, 90
Lake District, 229–230
Santiago, 44
Fishing. 349–350
Central Valley, 179
El Norte Chico, 125
Lake District, 215, 224
Southern Coast, 261, 265
Fjord cruises, F17
Flamingos, 146, 161
Folklore, 241
Forts
Chiloé, 241
El Norte Grande, 142, 156
Lake District, 212, 216
Patagonia & Tierra del Fuego, 289
Frutillar, 220–222
Fuerte Bulnes, 289
Fuerte de Niebla, 216
Fuerte de San Antonio, 241
Funiculars
Central Coast, 73, 76, 78
Santiago, 20
Futaleufú, 263

G

Galería de Arte, 191
Galería de la Historia de Concepción, 182

Galería Municipal de Arte (Valparaíso), 76–77
Galleries. ⇨ *See* Museums
Gardens
Central Coast, 87
Chiloé, 252
El Norte Chico, 113
Lake District, 212
Santiago, 20–21
Gay & lesbian clubs (Santiago), 46
Gay & lesbian travel, F37–F38
Geoglyphs, 153, 154
Geysers de Tatio, 145
Ghost towns, 244
Gigante de Atacama, 154
Glacier Grey, 294
Glacier Martial, 306
Glaciers, 261, 265–266, 270, 279, 290, 299
Golf, 91, 101
Gorinda (Puerto Varas) ✕, 223
Gran Hotel Termas de Chillán ⛺, 181
Gran Hotel Termas de Puyehue ⛺, 219
Guest House, The, (Puerto Varas) ⛺, 224

H

Hacienda Los Lingues (outside Rancagua) ✕⛺, 171
Haka pei, 334
Handicrafts, shopping for, 50–51, 84, 193, 261
Hang gliding, 101
Hanga Roa, 321, 323–325
Health issues, F38–F39
Hiking, 350
Central Valley, 179, 182
Easter Island, 335
El Norte Grande, 144
Lake District, 198, 208
Patagonia & Tierra del Fuego, 305–306, 311
Southern Coast, 198
Holidays, F39
Horse racing
Central Coast, 91
Santiago, 47
Horseback riding, 350–351
Central Coast, 98, 101
Central Valley, 171, 174, 178
Easter Island, 335
El Norte Grande, 145
Lake District, 202, 226

Hostal Belisario Jara
(Coyhaique) 🖭, 268
Hostal Oro Fueguino 🖭,
287–288
Hostería Ancud 🖭, 242
Hostería de la Colina
(Villarrica) 🖭, 201–202
Hosteria los Notros ✕🖭,
300
Hostería Patagonia Jarké 🖭,
309
Hot springs
Central Valley, 169–170
El Norte Chico, 119, 127
El Norte Grande, 152
Lake District, 193
Santiago side trips, 55
Southern Coast, 260
Hotel Antofagasta 🖭, 135
Hotel Antumalal (Pucón) 🖭,
205
Hotel Arica 🖭, 157–158
Hotel Atenas 🖭, 149
Hotel Centinela (Puerto
Octay) 🖭, 220
Hotel Continental (Temuco)
✕🖭, 195, 197
Hotel del Cid (La Serena) 🖭,
114
Hotel Del Mar (Viña del Mar)
🖭, 89
Hotel El Mirador 🖭, 140
Hotel Elun (Frutillar) 🖭, 222
Hotel Explora
Parque Nacional Torres del
Paine, 296
San Pedro de Atacama, 143
Hotel Halley (Vicuña) 🖭,
116
Hotel Huincahue 🖭, 206
Hotel Jose Nagueira (Punta
Arenas) 🖭, 287
Hotel La Casona (Copiapó)
🖭, 123
Hotel los Cardenales 🖭, 151
Hotel los Emelios 🖭, 152
Hotel Malalhue 🖭, 206
Hotel Naguilán 🖭, 214
Hotel Oceanic (Viña del Mar)
✕🖭, 88
Hotel Orly (Providencia) 🖭,
42
Hotel Otai 🖭, 332–333
Hotel Plaza San Francisco
(Centro) 🖭, 37
Hotel Rocas de Bahia (Bahia
Inglesa) 🖭, 124–125
Hotel Santa Cruz Plaza 🖭,
173–174

Hotel Unicornio Azul 🖭,
248–249
Hotel y Resort Las Hayas 🖭,
309
Hotels, F41
Central Coast, 70, 81–82,
88–90, 93, 94, 96, 97, 98,
99, 100, 102, 103, 104
Central Valley, 165–166, 171,
173–174, 175–176, 177–178,
179, 180, 181–182, 183–184
Chiloé, 238–239, 242, 245,
246, 248–249, 250, 252
Easter Island, 320, 321,
330–333
El Norte Chico, 109, 113–114,
115–116, 118, 119–120, 121,
123–125, 126, 127
El Norte Grande, 133, 135,
137, 140, 143–144, 149,
151, 152, 157–158, 159–160
Lake District, 189–190, 195,
197–198, 200, 201–202,
204–207, 208, 209–210, 214,
216, 217–218, 219, 220,
221–222, 223–224, 225, 226,
228–229
Patagonia & Tierra del Fuego,
276, 277, 286–288, 292–293,
295–297, 300–301, 307,
308–309, 311
price categories, 36, 70, 109,
133, 166, 190, 239, 258,
276, 277, 321
Santiago, 4, 36–42, 43
Santiago side trips, 53–54, 55,
57, 58–59
Southern Coast, 258, 260, 261,
263, 265, 266, 268–269
Houses, historical
Central Coast, 78–79, 86, 87,
95–96
Central Valley, 169
El Norte Chico, 115, 116
Lake District, 212, 217
Patagonia & Tierra del Fuego,
304
Santiago, 5, 9, 20
Huasco Valley, 120–122
Humberstone, 150
Hyatt Regency Santiago(Las
Condes) 🖭, 39–40

I

Ice-trekking, 302
Iglesia Catedral, 111
Iglesia Catedral Nuestra
Señora del Rosario
(Copiapó), 122

Iglesia de la Immaculada
Concepción (Vicuña), 115
Iglesia de la Merced, 167
Iglesia de Nuestra Señora de
Gracia, 245
Iglesia de Nuestra Señora de
los Dolores, 244
Iglesia de Putre, 159
Iglesia de San Antonio de
Padua, 243
Iglesia de San Carlos,
249–250
Iglesia de San Francisco
(Castro), 247
Iglesia de San Francisco (Chiu
Chiu), 140–141
Iglesia de San Marcos, 155,
156
Iglesia de San Pedro, 243
Iglesia de San Vincente de
Paul, 125
Iglesia de Santa María de
Loreto, 245
Iglesia de Tenaún, 243
Iglesia Hanga Roa, 323
Iglesia Nuestra Señora del
Rosario, 151
Iglesia Parinacota, 160
Iglesia Parroquial
Patagonia & Tierra del Fuego,
291
Santa Cruz, 171
Vallenar, 120
Iglesia Porroquial de Papudo,
103
Iglesia San Francisco
Copiapó, 122
Curicó, 174
La Serena, 111
Santiago, 11, 12
Iglesia San Pedro, 141
Iglesia San Vincente Ferrer
(Ovalle), 119
Iglesia Santo Domingo, 111
Insurance, F39–F40
Internet access, F40
Central Coast, 105–106
Central Valley, 186
Chiloé, 255
El Norte Grande, 162–163
Lake District, 234
Patagonia & Tierra del Fuego,
314–315
Santiago, 66
Southern Coast, 272
Iquique, 147–150
Iquique area, 146–152,
154–155
Isla de Aucar, 243

Isla de Lobos, 97
Isla de los Lobos Marinos (Los Molles), 103
Isla de los Pájaros Niños (Algarrobo), 93
Isla Huapi, 216
Isla Lemuy, 250
Isla Magdalena, 282
Isla Negra, 94–96
Isla Puduguapi, 259
Isla Quinchao, 245–246
Isla Seca (Zapallar) 🍴, 102
Itineraries, F19–F21
Central Coast, 71
Central Valley, 167
Chiloé, 239
Easter Island, 319
El Norte Chico, 109
El Norte Grande, 133
Lake District, 191
Patagonia & Tierra del Fuego, 277
Santiago, 3
Southern Coast, 259

J

Jardin Botánico (Valdivia), 212
Jardin Botánico Mapulemu, 18, 20–21
Jardin Japonés, 18, 21
Jardin Zoológico, 18, 21
Jewelry, shopping for (Santiago), 51
Juan López, 137–138

K

Kayaking, 349
El Norte Chico, 125
Lake District, 226

L

La Alameda, 11–14
La Araucanía, 190–193, 195, 197–202, 204–210
La Casa de Doña Paula (Valle de Maipo) ✕, 61
La Chascona, 18, 20
La Cornisa (Farellones & El Colorado) ✕, 57
La Parva (ski area), 57
La Portada, 137
La Sebastiana (Valparaíso), 76, 78–79
La Serena, 110–111, 113–114
La Tablita ✕, 300

La Tirana, 151–152
Lago Chungará, 160
Lago Escondido, 305
Lago General Carrera, 267
Lago Yelcho, 259–260
Laguna Miñeques, 146
Laguna Miscanti, 146
Lagunas Cotacotani, 160
Lake District, F8, 188–235
beaches, 210, 216, 222
camping, 209, 215, 229
children, attractions for, 212
essential information, 230–235
exploring, 189, 190–193, 198–200, 202, 204, 208–209, 210–212, 216, 217, 218–221, 222–223, 225, 226, 227–228, 230
German origins, 215
hotels, 189–190, 195, 197–198, 200, 201–202, 204–207, 208, 209–210, 214, 216, 217–218, 219, 220, 221–222, 223–224, 225, 226, 228–229
itineraries, 191
La Araucanía, 190–193, 195, 197–202, 204–210
Los Lagos, 210–230
nightlife & the arts, 207, 224, 229–230
price categories, 190
restaurants, 189, 190, 193, 195, 197, 200–201, 204–205, 209, 213–214, 217, 220, 221–222, 223, 225, 228
shopping, 193, 198, 215–216, 218, 230
sports & the outdoors, 193, 198, 199, 202, 207–208, 209, 210, 215, 216, 222, 224–225, 226, 227
timing the visit, 190
Language, F40
Las Condes, 31–32, 39–41, 45
Las Terrazas (Los Molles), 104
Libraries, 12
Lican Ray, 209–210
Lo Valdés, 54–55
Lodge Andino Terrantai (San Pedro de Atacama) 🍴, 143
Lodging, F40–F42. ⇨ Also Hotels
Lomit's (Providencia) ✕, 33
Los Ganaderos (Punta Arenas) ✕, 285
Los Lagos, 210–230

Los Molles, 103–104
Los Naranjos (Pomaire) ✕, 56
Los Varietales ✕, 173

M

Majestic (Centro) ✕, 29
Mail & shipping, F42
Central Coast, 105–106
Central Valley, 186
Chiloé, 255
Easter Island, 337
El Norte Chico, 129
El Norte Grande, 162–163
Lake District, 234
Patagonia & Tierra del Fuego, 314–415
Santiago, 66
Southern Coast, 272
Maitencillo, 99–101
Malls (Santiago), 49
Mamiña, 150–151
Mapuche, 196
María Elena, 138–139
Markets. ⇨ Also Shopping
Central Coast, 73, 77
El Norte Grande, 135
Lake District, 211
Santiago, 14, 16, 48–49
Meal plans, F6
Mercado Central (Santiago), 14, 16
Mercado Central (Valparaíso), 73, 77
Mercado Fluvial, 211
Mercado Municipal, 211
Merlin (Puerto Varas) ✕, 223
Mina El Teniente, 170
Mirador (Queilón), 251
Mirador Cerro la Cruz, 280, 282
Mirador Las Torres, 294
Moais, 324–325, 326, 327, 328–329
Money matters, F42–F43
Central Coast, 105
Central Valley, 186
Chiloé, 254
Easter Island, 336
Lake District, 233
Patagonia & Tierra del Fuego, 314
Santiago, 65
Southern Coast, 271
Monolith, 289
Monte Grande, 116
Monumento al Ovejero, 267

Monumento Nacional Isla Cachagua, *99–101*
Monumento Natural Cerro Ñielol, *193*
Monumento Natural Cueva de Milodón, *291*
Monumento Natural El Morado, *55*
Monumento Natural Pichasca (Ovalle), *119*
Mud baths, *151*
Muelle Asimar (Quintero), *99*
Muelle Prat (Valparaíso), *76, 77*
Municipalidad de Santiago, *4, 9*
Museo a Cielo Abierto (Valparaíso), *76, 77*
Museo Antropológico Sebastián Englert, *323, 324*
Museo Arqueológico
La Serena, *113*
María Elena, *139*
Santiago, *14, 16*
Museo Arqueológico de San Miguel de Azapa, *156–157*
Museo Arqueológico Gustavo Le Paige, *141*
Museo Artequín, *21, 23*
Museo Chileno de Arte Precolombino, *5, 9–10*
Museo Colonial Alemán (Frutillar), *221*
Museo Colonial de San Francisco, *11, 12–13*
Museo Colonial de Vichuquén, *175*
Museo de Arqueólogio a Historia Francisco Fonck (Viña del Mar), *86*
Museo de Arte Contemporáneo (Santiago), *14, 16*
Museo de Arte Contemporáneo (Valdivia), *212*
Museo de Arte Moderne de Chiloé, *248*
Museo de Artes Visuales, *14, 17*
Museo de Bellas Artes (Valparaíso), *76, 77, 87*
Museo de Chol Chol, *198–199*
Museo de Ciencia y Tecnologia, *21, 23*
Museo de Colchagua, *172*
Museo de Historia Natural de Valparaíso, *76, 77*
Museo de Huasco, *121*
Museo de las Tradiciones Chonchinas, *250*

Museo de Puerto Montt, *227*
Museo del Fin del Mundo, *304–305*
Museo del Mar Lord Cochrane, *73, 78*
Museo del Recuerdo, *282, 284*
Museo del Salitre, *152*
Museo El Colono, *219–220*
Museo Ferroviario
El Norte Grande, *138*
Santiago, *21, 23*
Museo Gabriela Mistral (Vicuña), *115*
Museo Histórico de Dalcahue, *244*
Museo Histórico Gabriel González Videla, *113*
Museo Histórico Municipal (Puerto Natales), *291*
Museo Histórico Nacional (Santiago), *4, 10*
Museo Histórico Regional (Copiapó), *123*
Museo Histórico y Antropológico Maurice van de Maele, *211*
Museo Histórico y Arqueológico de Villarrica, *200*
Museo Inchin Cuivi Ant, *252*
Museo Maritimo, *304*
Museo Mineralógico (Copiapó), *122–123*
Museo Mineralógico (La Serena), *113*
Museo Municipal Osorno, *217*
Museo Nacional de Bellas Artes, *14, 17*
Museo Nacional de Historia Natural, *21, 23*
Museo Nacional Ferroviario, *192–193*
Museo Naval (Iquique), *148*
Museo Naval y Maritimo (Punta Arenas), *280, 282*
Museo Naval y Maritimo de Valparaíso, *73, 78*
Museo O'Higginiano, *176*
Museo Philippi, *212*
Museo Provincial Fernando Cordero Rusque, *303*
Museo Regional (Iquique), *147–148*
Museo Regional de Ancud, *241*
Museo Regional de Antofagasta, *134*
Museo Regional de Castro, *247*

Museo Regional de la Araucanía, *192*
Museo Regional de Magallanes, *280, 284*
Museo Regional de la Patagonia, *267*
Museo Regional de Rancagua, *169*
Museo Salesiano de Maggiorino Borgatello, *282, 284*
Museo San José del Carmen de El Huique, *172*
Museums and galleries
Central Coast, *76–77, 78, 86, 87, 92, 95–96*
Central Valley, *169, 172, 175, 176, 182*
Chiloé, *241, 244, 247, 248, 250, 252*
Easter Island, *324*
El Norte Chico, *113, 115, 116, 121, 122–123*
El Norte Grande, *134, 138, 139, 141, 147–148, 152, 156–157*
Lake District, *191, 192–193, 198–199, 200, 211, 212, 217, 218, 219–220, 221, 227*
Patagonia & Tierra del Fuego, *282, 284, 291, 303, 304–305*
Santiago, *9–10, 12–13, 16, 17, 23, 50*
Southern Coast, *267*

N

Navimag cruise, *290*
Neruda, Pablo, *94, 95–96*
Niebla, *216*
Nightlife & the arts
Central Coast, *82–83, 90, 97*
Central Valley, *178, 184*
Easter Island, *333–334*
El Norte Chico, *114, 116, 118, 121, 124, 125, 126*
El Norte Grande, *137, 140, 144, 149–150, 158*
Lake District, *207, 224, 229–230*
Patagonia & Tierra del Fuego, *288, 309–310, 311*
Santiago, *43–46*
Southern Coast, *269*
19th-century houses (Osorno), *217*
Nitrate Pampa, *133–135, 137–141*
Northern Beaches, *96–104*

O

Observatorio Cerro Mamalluca (Vicuña), *115*
Octavio (Castro) ✖, *248*
Oficina de Turismo, *298*
Orongo, *325, 327*
Osorno, *217–218*
Outdoor activities. ⇨ *See* sports & the outdoors; specific activity
Ovalle, *119–120*

P

Palaces
Central Coast, 87
El Norte Grande, 147
Patagonia & Tierra del Fuego, 284
Santiago, 13
Palacio Astoreca, *147*
Palacio Carrasco, *86*
Palacio Cousiño, *13*
Palacio de la Moneda, *11, 13*
Palacio de los Tribunales de Justicia, *5, 10*
Palacio Recart (Papudo), *103*
Palacio Rioja (Viña del Mar), *86, 87*
Palacio Sara Braun, *280, 284*
Palacio Vergara (Viña del Mar), *86, 87*
Pan-American Highway, *264*
Pao Pao (Algarrobo) 🖭, *93*
Papudo, *102–103*
Parador Jamón, Pan y Vino 🖭, *181–182*
Pargua, *230*
Parinacota, *160*
Parks and reserves
Central Coast, 73, 78, 101
Central Valley, 169, 175, 179, 184
Chiloé, 250–251
Easter Island, 321
El Norte Chico, 113, 120, 122, 126–127
El Norte Grande, 145–146, 152, 154, 160–161
Lake District, 199–200, 208–209, 218–219, 226–228
Patagonia & Tierra del Fuego, 289, 293–302, 306–307
Santiago, 10, 12, 14, 16–18
Southern Coast, 260–261, 263, 265–266, 267, 270
Parque Bernardo O'Higgins, *10*

Parque de las Esculturas, *17*
Parque Forestal, *14, 16–18*
Parque Japones, *113*
Parque Metropolitano. ⇨ *See* Bellavista & Parque Metropolitano
Parque Nacional Alerce Andino, *227–228*
Parque Nacional Bernardo O'Higgins, *302*
Parque Nacional Chiloé, *250–251*
Parque Nacional Conguillio, *199–200*
Parque Nacional Fray Jorge (cloud forest), *120*
Parque Nacional Huerquehue, *208*
Parque Nacional Laguna del Laja, *184*
Parque Nacional Laguna San Rafael, *270*
Parque Nacional Lauca, *160*
Parque Nacional Llanos de Challe, *122*
Parque Nacional los Glaciares, *297–298, 299, 301–302*
Parque Nacional Nevado Tres Cruces, *127*
Parque Nacional Pan de Azúcar, *126–127*
Parque Nacional Puyehue, *218–219*
Parque Nacional Queulat, *265–266*
Parque Nacional Tierra del Fuego, *306–307*
Parque Nacional Torres del Paine, *293–297*
Parque Nacional Vicente Pérez Rosales, *226–227*
Parque Nacional Villarrica, *208–209*
Parque Pumalin, *260–261, 263*
Parque Quinta Normal area, *21–21*
Parques Nacionales, *298*
Parrilladas, *F16–F17*
Passeo 21 de Mayo (Valparaíso), *73, 78*
Passports, *F44–F45*
Pasta y Vino (Valparaíso) ✖, *80*
Patagonia & Tierra del Fuego, *274–316*
cruises, 279, 290
essential information, 311–316

exploring, 275, 279–280, 282–285, 288–291, 293–295, 297–298, 299, 302–307, 310–311
hotels, 276, 277, 286–288, 292–293, 295–297, 300–301, 307, 308–309, 311
itineraries, 277
nightlife and the arts, 288, 309–301, 311
price categories, 276, 277
restaurants, 276, 277, 285–286, 291–292, 295, 298, 300, 308
shopping, 279, 288
sports & the outdoors, 279, 301–302, 310, 311
timing the visit, 277
Penguins, *127, 251, 282, 283, 289*
Pérgola de las Flores, *14, 17*
Perito Moreno Glacier, *290*
Petroglyphs
Easter Island, 327, 329
El Norte Chico, 119
El Norte Grande, 151
Pica, *152*
Pingüinera de Seno Otway, *289*
Pisagua, *154*
Pisco distilleries, *116, 117, 121*
Pisco Elqui, *116, 118*
Planetario, *21, 23*
Planta Pisquera Alto del Carmen, The, *121*
Planto Capel (Vicuña), *115*
Playa Anakena, *328, 329*
Playa de Queilén, *251*
Playa Lelbun, *251*
Playa Ovahe, *328, 329*
Playa Zapallar, *101*
Plaza Anibal Pinto, *191*
Plaza de Armas
Chillán, 180
Coyhaique, 266
Curicó, 174
Ovalle, 119
Puerto Natales, 290
Santa Cruz, 171
Plaza de Armas (Santiago), *4, 10–11*
Plaza de la Constitución, *11, 13*
Plaza de la Independencia, *182*
Plaza de los Héroes, *167*
Plaza del Mar Bravo (Zapallar), *101*

Plaza José Francisco Vergara, 86, 87
Plaza O'Higgins (Vallenar), 120
Plaza Muñoz Gamero, 280, 284–285
Plaza Prat (Copiapó), 122
Plaza Prat (Iquique), 147
Plaza Simon Bolívar, 78
Plaza Sotomayor, 76, 78
Plaza Teodoro Schmidt, 192
Plaza Tupahue, 18, 21
Plaza Victoria (Valparaíso), 76, 78
Plazuela del Tren, 247
Pomaire, 55–56
Portillo (ski resort), 59
Porvenir, 303
Price categories
Central Coast, 70
Central Valley, 166
Chiloé, 239
Easter Island, 321
El Norte Chico, 109
El Norte Grande, 33
Lake District, 190
Patagonia & Tierra del Fuego, 276, 277
Santiago, 24, 36
Southern Coast, 258
Providencia, 33–35, 41–42, 46
Pucón, 202–208
Puerto Aisén, 269
Puerto Chacabuco, 269
Puerto Hambre, 288–289
Puerto Montt, 227–230
Puerto Natales, 290–293
Puerto Octay, 219–220
Puerto Puyuhuapi, 263, 265
Puerto Varas, 222–225
Puerto Williams, 310–311
Pukara de Quitor, 142
Pukara del Cerro Inca, 151
Puma Verde ⌂, 260
Puna Pau, 325, 327
Punta Arenas, 280–282, 284–288
Puquén (blowhole), 103–104
Pura (shop), 50–51
Putre, 159–160
Puyuhuapi Lodge & Spa (Puerto Puyuhuapi) ✕⌂, 263, 265

Q
Queilén, 251
Quellón, 251–252
Quemchi, 243
Quicaví, 243
Quinta Vergara, 86, 87
Quintay, 92
Quintero, 99

R
Rafting, 349
Rain forests, 260–261
Ramal Talca–Constitución, 177
Rancagua, 167, 169–171
Rano Kau, 325, 327
Ranu Raraku (Easter Island) 328, 329
Refugio de Navegantes, 251
Reñaca, 96–97
Reserva Nacional Alto de Lircay, 179
Reserva Nacional Coyhaique, 267
Reserva Nacional Laguna Parillar, 289
Reserva Nacional Las Vicuñas, 160–161
Reserva Nacional los Flamencos, 145–146
Reserva Nacional Pampa del Tamarugal, 152, 154
Reserva Nacional Radal Siete Tazas, 175
Reserva Nacional Río de los Cipreses, 169
Reserva Nacional Río Simpson, 267
Reserves. ⇨ See Parks and reserves
Residencia 555 (Viña del Mar) ⌂, 89
Residencial Londres (Centro) ⌂, 38
Restaurant Arriero ✕, 134
Restaurant La Picada de Don Gato ⌂, 155
Restaurants, F14. ⇨ Also Dining
Río Bío Bío, 179–184
Roca Oceánico, 97–98
Rodeos, F16, 169
Rubén Tapío (Talca) ✕, 177
Ruta del Vino, 172, 174

S
Safety, F45
Salar de Atacama, 146
Salar de Surire, 161
Salar de Uyuni, 146
Salsa clubs
El Norte Chico, 121, 125
El Norte Grande, 150
Santiago, 46
Salt flats, (El Norte Grande), 146, 161
San Alfonso, 54
San Clemente, 177
San Felix (Vallenar), 121
San Javier, 178–179
San José de Maipo, 53–54
San Pedro de Atacama, 141–145
Santa Cruz, 171–174
Santiago, F7, 1–67
Bellavista & Parque Metropolitano, 18, 20–21, 24–25, 28, 45
Centro, 28–29, 36–39, 45
children, attractions for, 20, 21, 23
essential information, 61–67
exploring, 2–23
hotels, 4, 36–42, 43, 53–54, 55, 57, 58–59
itineraries, 3
La Alameda, 11–14
Las Condes, 31–32, 39–41, 45
nightlife & the arts, 43–46
Parque Forestal, 14, 16–18
Parque Quinta Normal area, 21–23
price categories, 24, 36
Providencia, 33–35, 41–42, 46
restaurants, 3, 24–36, 53–54, 56, 61
Santiago Centro, 4–5, 9–11
shopping, 5, 48–51
side trips, 51
ski resorts, 56–59
sports & the outdoors, 5, 47–48
timing the visit, 4
Vitacura, 35–36, 42
wineries, 5, 59–61
Santiago Centro, 4–5, 9–11
Santuario de la Tirana, 152
Scuba diving. ⇨ See Diving
Semanas Musicales de Frutillar, 220–221
Senior-citizen travel, F45–F46
Sheraton Santiago and San Cristóbal Tower (Providencia) ⌂, 41
Shopping, F46. ⇨ Also Markets
Central Coast, 73, 84, 91
Central Valley, 174, 178, 184
Chiloé, 241, 245, 249, 252
duty-free, 150
Easter Island, 321, 335

El Norte Chico, 111, 114, 116, 118, 124
El Norte Grande, 135, 137, 140, 145, 150, 159
Lake District, 193, 198, 215–216, 218, 230
Patagonia & Tierra del Fuego, 279, 288
Santiago, 5, 48–51
Southern Coast, 261, 265, 269
Sightseeing. ⇨ *See* Exploring
Skiing, *352–354*
Central Valley, 169
Lake district, 209, 226
Patagonia & Tierra del Fuego, 310
Santiago, 5, 47, 56–59
Southern Coast, 267
Soccer
Central Coast, 84, 91
Santiago, 47–48
Solar de Pisco Eliqui (distillery) *116*
Sotito's ✕, *285*
Southeastern Circuit, *328–329*
Southern Beaches, *91–96*
Southern Coast, *F12, 256–273*
essential information, 270–273
exploring, 257–258, 259–261, 263, 265–267, 269, 270
hotels, 258, 260, 261, 263, 265, 266, 268–269
itineraries, 259
nightlife and the arts, 269
price categories, 258
restaurants, 258, 260, 263, 265, 268, 269
shopping, 261, 265, 269
sports & the outdoors, 261, 265
timing the visit, 258–259
Sports & the outdoors, *F14, 348–354.* ⇨ *Also* specific activities
Central Coast, 73, 83–84, 90–91, 92, 93–94, 102, 104
Central Valley, 169, 171, 174, 178
Chiloé, 241
Easter Island, 321, 334–335
El Norte Chico, 111, 125, 126
El Norte Grande, 135, 144–145, 150, 158–159
Lake District, 193, 198, 199, 202, 207–208, 209, 210, 215, 216, 222, 224–225, 226, 227

Patagonia & Tierra del Fuego, 279, 301–302, 310, 311
Santiago, 5, 47–48
Southern Coast, 261, 265
Student travel, *F46*
Subway travel, *64*
Symbols, *F6*

T

Taberna Club de la Unión (Punta Arenas) ✕, *286*
Tadeo and Lili 🏨, *333*
Tahai, *323, 324–325*
Talca, *176–178*
Taxes, *F46*
Taxis
Central Coast, 105
Chiloé, 254
Easter Island, 336
El Norte Chico, 128–129
El Norte Grande, 162
Lake District, 233
Patagonia & Tierra del Fuego, 314
Santiago, 65
Teatro del Lago, *221*
Teatro Municipal
Iquique, 147
Pisagua, 155
Santiago, 11, 13–14
Vicuña, 115
Telephones, *F47–F48*
Templo Antiguo (Andacollo), *118*
Temuco, *191–193, 195, 197–198*
Tenaún, *243*
Tennis, *102*
Termas de Amarillo, *260*
Termas de Cauquenes, *169–170*
Termas de Chillán, *180–181*
Termas de Socos (Ovalle), *119*
Theater
Central Coast, 83, 90
Santiago, 13–14, 44–45
Tierra del Fuego. ⇨ *See* Patagonia & Tierra del Fuego
Time, *F48*
Tipping, *F48*
Torre Bauer (Vicuña), *115*
Torre Reloj
Antofagasta, 134
Iquique, 147
Pisagua, 154
Torreón Los Canelos, *212*

Torres del Paine, *290*
Tour operators & packages, *F48, 338–354*
Central Coast, 106
Central Valley, 186–187
Chiloé, 255
Easter Island, 337
El Norte Chico, 129
El Norte Grande, 163
Lake District, 234
Patagonia & Tierra del Fuego, 305, 306–307, 311, 315–316
Santiago, 66–67
Southern Coast, 272–273
Tourist office (Osorno), *217*
Tourist office (Ushuaia, Argentina), *304*
Train travel, *F48–F49*
Central Coast, 105
Central Valley, 169, 172–173, 177, 185–186
Lake District, 233
Patagonia & Tierra del Fuego, 305
Santiago, 65
Transportation around Chile, *F49*
Travel agencies, *F49*
Tren del Fin del Mundo, *305*
Tren del Vino, *172–173*
Tulor, *142–143*

U

Universidad de Chile, *11, 14*
Ushuaia, Argentina, *303–310*

V

Valdivia, *210–216*
Valle de la Luna, *146*
Valle de la Muerte, *146*
Valle del Encanto (Ovalle), *119*
Valle del Maule Ruta del Vino, *176*
Valle Nevado (ski region), *57–59*
Vallenar, *120–121*
Valparaíso, *71, 73–84*
Vega Chica and Vega Central (Parque Forestal), *14, 17*
Vertiente del Radium, *151*
Vichuquén, *175–176*
Vicuña, *114–116*
Villarrica, *200–202*
Viña Balduzzi, *178–179*
Viña Bisquertt, *173*
Viña Concha y Toro, *60–61*
Viña Cousiño-Macul, *181*

Viña del Mar, *84–91*
Viña Laura Hartwig, *173*
Viña Miguel Torres, *175*
Viña San Pedro, *174*
Viña Santa Rita, *61*
Viña Undurraga, *59–60*
Vineyards. ⇨ *See* Wine and
  liquor
Visas, *F44–F45*
Visitor information, *F49*
Central Coast, 106
Central Valley, 187
Chiloé, 255
Easter Island, 337
El Norte Chico, 129
El Norte Grande, 163
Lake District, 234–235
Patagonia & Tierra del Fuego,
  316

Santiago, 67
Southern Coast, 273
Vocabulary, *358–364*
Volcanos
Easter Island, 329
El Norte Grande, 141,
  145–146, 160
Lake District, 193, 199, 204,
  226
Volver ✕, *308*

W

"W" Route, *294*
Water sports, *125, 193*
Waterfalls
Central Valley, 175
Lake Districts, 218
Southern Coast, 261, 266, 267,
  269

Weather, *F21*
Web sites, *F50*
Western Circuit, *325, 327*
Whaling factory, *92*
Wine and liquor, *F15*
Central Valley, 170, 172–173,
  174, 175, 176–177, 178–179
El Norte Chico, 116, 117
Santiago, 5, 18, 51, 59–61
Wine Country, *166–167,*
  169–179

Z

Zapallar, *101–102*
Zapato Amarillo (Puerto
  Octay) , *220*
Zoos, *21*
Zully (Centro) ✕, *28*

PHOTO CREDITS

Cover Photo (Torres del Paine National Park): *Art Wolfe.* F7, *Walter Bibikow/viestiphoto.com.* F8, *Juan Carlos Muñoz/age fotostock.* F9 (left), *Alan Kearney/viestiphoto.com.* F9 (right), *Gonzalo Azumendi/age fotostock.* F10, *Ken Welsh/age fotostock.* F14, *Bill Murray/viestiphoto.com.* F15 (left), *Craig Lovell/ viestiphoto.com.* F15 (right), *Peter Adams/Agency Jon Arnold Images/age fotostock.* F16, Alan Kearney/ viestiphoto.com. F17, *Robert Harding Picture Library/Alamy.* F22, *Wojtek Buss/age fotostock.* F23 (left), *Wojtek Buss/age fotostock.* F23 (right), *Joe Viesti/viestiphoto.com.* F24, *Walter Bibikow/viestiphoto.com.*

NOTES

NOTES

NOTES

NOTES

NOTES

NOTES

ABOUT OUR WRITERS

Robin Goldstein's familiarity with Chile goes back as far as the birth of his adopted Chilean sister, but his current beat is the wilder region of Patagonia, where he enjoys downing cocktails with egg whites after a day of glacier-trekking. Robin's other credits for Fodor's include guides to Italy, Argentina, Mexico, Cancún, Rome, and Venice. He has also been food critic for *Metro New York* and the *New Haven Advocate*, and has published several books of restaurant reviews, including *The Menu: New Haven Restaurant Guide* and *The Fearless Critic Austin Restaurant Guide*. He updated the Patagonia & Tierra del Fuego chapter of this book.

Brian Kluepfel has lived in the Bronx, Berkeley, and Bolivia. He has updated several Fodor's books including Alaska, Guatemala, and Peru. He now lives within spitting distance of New York City and is an avid beer drinker, soccer fan, bird watcher, and folk guitarist. He has also reported on the World Cup of soccer from Japan, and the World Championship Chili Cook-off in Reno, Nevada. He updated many of the chapters of this book: El Norte Grande, El Norte Chico, the Central Valley, the Southern Coast, and Easter Island.

Former Fodor's editor **Mark Sullivan** has traveled extensively through South America, seeing everything from the glaciers of Tierra del Fuego to the mysterious monoliths of Easter Island. One of his favorite places is the port city of Valparaíso, where more than a dozen funiculars rumble up the steep hills to give you stunning views of the Pacific. He wrote about Valparaíso, Viña del Mar, and other seaside towns in the Central Coast chapter, and also updated the Santiago chapter. He has contributed to editions of Fodor's South America, Fodor's Central America, and Fodor's Mexico, as well as many other Fodor's titles.

Costa Rica–based freelance writer and pharmacist **Jeffrey Van Fleet** divides his time between Central America and Wisconsin, but looks for any opportunity to visit South America's more cosmopolitan southern cone. After several trips to Chile, he is still intrigued that the noonday sun sits in the northern sky. (He hasn't yet figured out that business about which way water goes down the drain in the Southern Hemisphere.) Jeff has contributed to Fodor's guides to Costa Rica, Peru, Argentina, and Central and South America. He updated the Lake District and Chiloé chapters, as well as the introductory front pages of this book.